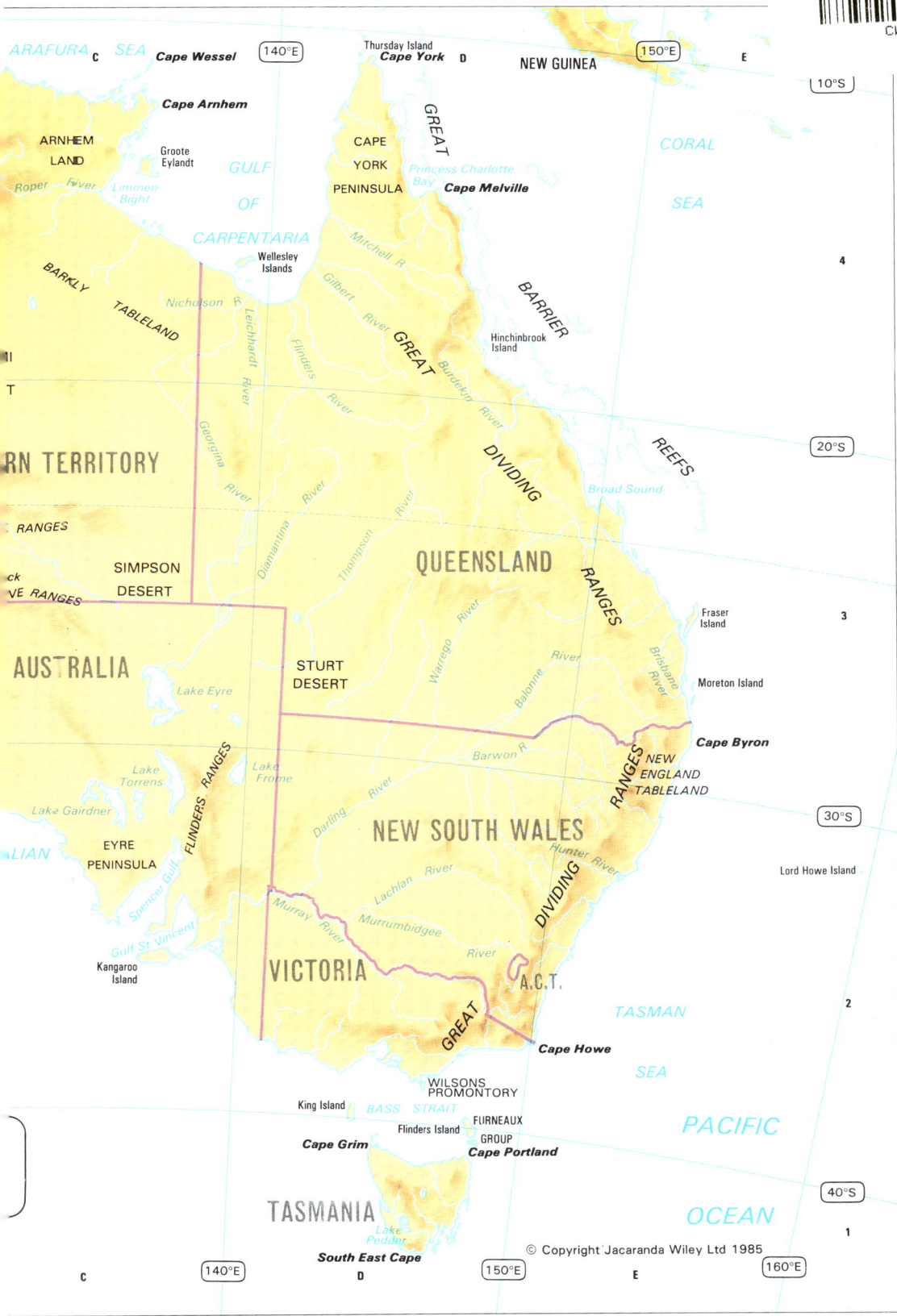

ARAFURA C SEA Cape Wessel 140°E Thursday Island Cape York D NEW GUINEA 150°E E

Cape Arnhem

ARNHEM LAND Groote Eylandt GULF CAPE YORK PENINSULA GREAT CORAL

Roper River Limmen Bight OF Princess Charlotte Bay Cape Melville SEA

BARKLY TABLELAND Nicholson CARPENTARIA Wellesley Islands Mitchell R. BARRIER

Leichhardt River Gilbert River GREAT Burdekin River Hinchinbrook Island

T Georgina River Flinders River DIVIDING REEFS 20°S

RN TERRITORY Broad Sound

RANGES Diamantina River Thompson River QUEENSLAND RANGES Fraser Island 3

ck SIMPSON DESERT Warrego River River Brisbane River Moreton Island

VE RANGES AUSTRALIA Lake Eyre STURT DESERT Balonne River

Lake Torrens Lake Frome Barwon R. Cape Byron

FLINDERS RANGES Darling River NEW ENGLAND TABLELAND 30°S

Lake Gairdner EYRE PENINSULA NEW SOUTH WALES RANGES Lord Howe Island

LIAN Spencer Gulf Lachlan River Hunter River

Gulf St Vincent Murray River Murrumbidgee River DIVIDING

Kangaroo Island VICTORIA A.C.T. TASMAN 2

GREAT Cape Howe

SEA

WILSONS PROMONTORY PACIFIC

King Island BASS STRAIT FURNEAUX GROUP

Flinders Island Cape Portland

Cape Grim 40°S

TASMANIA OCEAN 1

Lake Pedder

South East Cape C 140°E D 150°E E 160°E

Australia's Reptiles

Australia's Reptiles

A Photographic Reference to the Terrestrial Reptiles of Australia

Stephen K. Wilson & David G. Knowles

COLLINS
PUBLISHERS
AUSTRALIA

COLLINS PUBLISHERS AUSTRALIA

First published in 1988 by William Collins Pty Ltd,
55 Clarence Street, Sydney NSW 2000

National Library of Australia
Cataloguing-in-Publication data:

Wilson, Stephen K., 1958–
Australia's reptiles.

Bibliography.
Includes index.
ISBN 0 7322 0011 3.

1. Reptiles – Australia – Pictorial works.
2. Lizards – Australia – Pictorial works.
3. Snakes – Australia – Pictorial works.
4. Reptiles – Australia. 5. Lizards –
Australia. 6. Snakes – Australia. I. Knowles,
David G., 1959–   . II. Title.
597.9'0994

Typeset in Bembo by Graphicraft Typesetters Ltd, Hong Kong
Printed by Mandarin Offset, Hong Kong

For
Peter Rankin

Foreword

Scientific work on Australia's reptiles began with Cook's voyage, but the first study of them that could lay claim to being at all comprehensive was that of John White, Surgeon-General to the First Fleet. That work began soon after his arrival in Sydney. His account, which includes descriptions and illustrations of the reptiles he encountered, as well as observations of their natural history, was published in 1790, just two years later.

It is fitting that *Australia's Reptiles* should be published almost exactly 200 years later in this Bicentennial Year, for White was a self-taught naturalist, and David Knowles and Stephen Wilson are also outstanding self-taught naturalists. Their subject — Australia's reptiles in their natural environment — is a demanding one. To have created a volume which is both complete and aesthetically superior demands meticulous attention to detail and great patience. This is more than a good book. It is an excellent one, comprehensive, well researched, well illustrated and beautifully presented.

The production of any book of quality requires knowledge, talent, imagination, courage, discipline, and determination. Wilson and Knowles have applied all those qualities, and others, to this work in an extraordinary way, at times in the face of seemingly insurmountable difficulty. What special tasks are required by anyone who embarks on a project of this ambition? They must work, slave almost, for two to three years full-time, virtually to the exclusion of everything else in their lives.

They must wade through a voluminous taxonomic literature; travel to far-flung and often inaccessible places in search of reptile 'specials'; and wait apprehensively for the return of precious never-again-obtainable photographs. They must file, write, rewrite, check, argue, worry, and strive, strive, strive.

This book is the fruit of such efforts. Every Australian lizard and land, freshwater or mangrove snake known to December 1987 is included. Here are the restricted, possibly rare species, never before photographed, and known only to taxonomists. Here, too, are the bizarre, the striking, the beautiful, the elegant . . . and the coy, the elusive, and the quizzical. They have been captured in superb shots by photographic perfectionists. Even the many colour forms of species which play identification tricks on newcomers to herpetology have been covered.

Australia's reptiles command attention. They are the envy of the herpetological world. So many species — over 700 — are found here. Their forms, colours, and patterns are enormously varied. Many species are new to science, the result of very recent work; others are known to taxonomists, but not yet described; and there are still, no doubt, many undiscovered ones to tantalise us. Australia is also home to the world's most venomous and, arguably, most dangerous snakes. After 200 years, we still know very little about the origins of our reptiles.

The achievement of Stephen Wilson and David Knowles in producing this book is very great. The publication of their superlative tome assures their place among others who have contributed substantially to knowledge of our unique plants and animals. There are fewer than a dozen volumes which could be judged classics of Australian herpetology. This volume joins that select library whose hallmarks combine all that is highest in both science and art.

Jeanette Covacevich
SENIOR CURATOR (REPTILES)
Queensland Museum

Contents

ILLUSTRATIONS

PLATES

Preface

Modern colour photography is playing an increasingly significant role in promoting awareness and interest in our natural heritage.

The popularity of the photographic references currently available, such as *The Readers Digest Complete Book of Australian Birds*, *The Australian Museum Complete Book of Australian Mammals* and Merrick and Schmida's *Australian Freshwater Fishes*, provides ample evidence for this.

Through this book we hope to augment these excellent publications by way of a comprehensive photographic documentation of the largest and most diverse group of Australian vertebrates, the lizards and non-marine snakes. We hope to stimulate the interest both Australian and international readers are already displaying in our reptile fauna. In particular we wish to promote the enthusiasm of young people, in whose hands the future conservation of our environment lies.

The book is designed to have the broadest possible appeal. It includes sufficient detail to be of use to the serious herpetologist, and considerable effort has been made to provide information in a clear and concise style suitable for the casual naturalist and layperson.

Acknowledgements

In order to compile a publication of this magnitude the authors have had to draw heavily on information from numerous sources, including works published in journals, books and newsletters and the valuable data freely given by many fellow herpetologists through correspondence, conversations and extracts from their personal field notes. To augment this the authors have incorporated many of their own personal observations.

We are extremely grateful to the following persons for generously providing photography. It has been an honour, and an education in itself, collating such a large collection of high-quality photographs. We sincerely hope that our representation of what must amount to thousands of hours in the field and hundreds of thousands of kilometres of travel will do them justice.

Greg Harold, Phil Griffin, Glen Shea, Mark Hanlon, John Weigal, John Wombey, Gunther Schmida, Paul Horner, Hal Cogger, the late Peter Rankin, Mike Swan, Grant Husband, Tim Helder, Hank Jenkins, Ron Johnstone, Harry Ehmann, the Queensland Museum, Brian Miller, Allen Greer, Steve Swanson, John Bevan, Christine Vye, Steve Crane, Mike Gillam, Peter Mirtschin, Mike Powell, Mark Stewart-Jones, Greg Barron, Andrew Burbidge, Peter Canty, Mark Golding, Tim Low, Derek Mead-Hunter, Steve Donnellan, and the Western Australian Museum.

The following people made valuable contributions in many ways, assisting with information, critically reviewing the manuscript, providing subjects for photography, congenial company in the field, transport, strategic accommodation and much more. To them we owe our deepest thanks.

Jeanette Covacevich, Greg Czechura, Glen Ingram, Neil Charles, Glen Storr, Laurie Smith, Anthony and Kate Hiller, Ross Sadlier, Geoff Witten, Liz Cameron, Max King, John Coventry, Terry Schwaner, Chris Harvey, Brian Hancock, Marc and Trish Harvey, Patrick Johnson, Marie Brady, Mark Dixon, Pete de Boer, Anne Kreger, Magnus Peterson, Meryl Knowles, Tony Drake, Rob Lachowicz, Ken and Joy Wilson, David Rounsevell, Keith and Janice Martin, Wayne Longmore, the late Ramon Straatman, Frank Isenbert and Ian and Maggie Goudie (Comalco Australia), Paul Phelan (Air Queensland), and many members of the Queensland Museum staff.

Special thanks are further extended to the late Carmel Reid, Christine Vye, Greg Czechura, Greg Harold, Jeanette Covacevich, Neil Charles and Glen Shea, for the numerous ways in which they have assisted us throughout the preparation of the manuscript.

We are also indebted to Gill Luxton for her diligence and patience in typing the manuscript.

Finally we offer apologies and thanks to those who, through our oversight, have been omitted from these acknowledgements.

Introduction

HOW TO USE THIS BOOK

The area covered by this book includes the Australian continent, Tasmania and offshore islands. Species from Australia's oceanic territories and those restricted to marine environments are excluded. A total of 650 described species of lizards and snakes are discussed alphabetically in order of family, genus and species.

In order to identify an animal we recommend the following approach.

- Look carefully through the photographs and locate that which most clearly matches your animal.

- Refer to the maps and determine whether your animal's range coincides with the shaded area. It must be remembered that distributional limits are rarely precisely known, though extensions of over 500 km are unlikely.

- Read the description carefully and see how closely it applies to your animal. Differences between it and similar species may be slight, and if they are likely to occur together a brief diagnosis is provided.

- Read the notes on preferred habitat and microhabitat. Each species usually favours a particular habitat or suite of habitats and each is normally associated with various basking, foraging and shelter sites. This information is often helpful in making an identification.

- To avoid excessive text, features and habits shared by all members of a family, and characteristics common to all members of a genus, are discussed under those headings and are not repeated in the individual accounts. The reader is advised to refer back to the appropriate section for further information.

- If an identification cannot be made, the reader is referred to the more detailed publications listed in the bibliography at the back of this book. Alternatively consult the experienced herpetologists at your local museum for a positive identification.

GUIDE TO THE TEXT

Names Where common names have been generally accepted, these are provided. Unfortunately common names are available for only a minority of species. They may also be misleading, as in many cases one name applies to a number of species, or several names may be used for a single species. For example, 'spinifex snake' generally applies to any limbless reptile, be it a snake or legless lizard, which inhabits hummock grasslands. For this reason, all species are arranged alphabetically by scientific names.

Scientific names may sound unusual or foreign to the layperson, consequently many people are reluctant to familiarise themselves with them. A scientific name is generally derived from Greek or Latin in accordance with stringent rules laid down in the International Code of Zoological Nomenclature. The rules ensure that scientific names receive not only international recognition, but also independence of any particular language group.

A complete scientific name is composed of several parts, arranged as follows.

Genus species   Author, date

Both generic and specific names always appear in italics.

A genus, loosely defined, is a group of species which share a number of distinct (usually morphological) characteristics, suggesting both a close relationship and common origin. This first part of a scientific name, the generic name, always begins with a capital letter.

Each genus comprises one or more species: natural populations which freely interbreed to produce normal fertile offspring. This second part of a scientific name, the specific name, is never capitalised.

A third name, the subspecific name, is added to some species which display extensive geographic variation. This category allows for recognition of geographically defined local populations which differ from other subgroups of the same species. Subspecific names are also italicised.

The final part of a scientific name consists of the author who first named and described the genus or species, accompanied by the date of its publication. It is not necessary to include this additional information each time the name is used.

As we gain insights into animal relationships it sometimes becomes necessary to remove a species from one genus to another more closely reflecting its true affinities. If such a change has occurred it is indicated by placing the original author and date in brackets. The following example illustrates how scientific names may change, and how brackets are used to denote these changes.

Lygosoma colletti Boulenger, 1896, is now known as *Ctenotus colletti* (Boulenger, 1896). Subsequent descriptions of subspecies have resulted in recognition of the following:

Ctenotus colletti colletti (Boulenger, 1896)
C.   c.   nasutus Storr, 1969
C.   c.   rufescens Storr, 1979

Species groups In some cases it has proven useful to divide large diverse genera into species groups: clusters of species which display a closer similarity to each other than to other members of their genus.

Generally species groups represent natural assemblages (indeed, some may constitute distinct genera) though a few are arranged tentatively and/or for convenience. Nevertheless it is felt that collective morphological and behavioural traits are most easily discussed as a species group rather than repetitively throughout the accounts of individual species.

Photography Photographs are provided for over 95 per cent of described species, many of which are pictured for the first time. Several presently undescribed taxa have been included, and published descriptions of some of these will probably be available by the time this book is in the readers' hands.

We have made every effort to obtain colour pictures of live animals in their natural habitats, particularly where diagnostic features are clearly depicted. In several instances only black and white photographs of animals on neutral backgrounds are available. Some elusive or restricted species have never been photographed alive, in which case we have included photographs of preserved material, if these aid in identification.

Descriptions These are based on the most easily visible external characters which enable an identification to be made. They are largely concerned with such aspects as size, arrangement and variation of colour and pattern, and any morphological peculiarities. Descriptions are designed to augment the photography, drawing the reader's attention to the most salient features.

Sizes given represent those of typical adults. When reliable records exist for abnormally large individuals, these are included.

Lizard measurements are taken from the tip of the snout to the vent (SVL). Tails of lizards are generally long and easily broken, hence measurements including tail-length may lead to inaccurate and misleading information. Snakes with damaged tails are not normally encountered, so these are measured from the snout to the tail-tip (TL).

When two or more genera or species are very similar in appearance and have overlapping distributions, a brief diagnosis indicating one or two major distinguishing features is included. In these instances it may be necessary to refer to such characters as number and arrangement of scales, relative proportions and minor pattern differences.

Preferred habitat Distributional limits are summarised to augment the maps, and remarks are made on the most important features which comprise each species' preferred habitat. For the most part these include climatic zone, substrate-type and vegetation. Where applicable, comments are made on other aspects such as altitude. The major regions, climatic zones and habitats referred to in the text are explained in greater detail in 'The Australian Habitats', below, and the reader is advised to refer to that section.

Microhabitat Within its preferred habitat, each species occupies a limited range of basking, foraging and shelter sites. Many are adaptable and may be encountered in a variety of situations, while others are extremely specialised. Microhabitats are often characteristic of a species, hence may provide useful clues to its identity. In addition, a knowledge of where to look is invaluable if one wishes to observe reptiles in their natural environments.

Comments This section deals with the known aspects of life history. It includes diet, breeding season, mode of reproduction, clutch or litter size, foraging time, defensive strategy, distinctive behavioural traits, and (if applicable) whether a snake is dangerously venomous. Unfortunately extensive data are unavailable for the majority of species, though some or all of the above items are included in most accounts. Features common to all members of a species group, genus or family are summarised under those headings and the reader is referred back to them.

Maps These are marked with State boundaries and the Tropic of Capricorn. The shaded area indicates approximate distributional limits for each species. Question marks denote areas where, on the basis of known localities and habitat preferences, species are likely to occur but have not yet been recorded. Significant or isolated localities are marked with a dot and arrow. Although these maps provide a valuable guide to an animal's distribution, the following limitations must be borne in mind.

- Precise distributional data are unavailable for the majority of species, hence an animal may occur outside the area indicated.
- Few reptiles extend continuously throughout their ranges, each favouring a particular habitat or suite of habitats.
- The small scale maps necessary in a publication of this nature preclude the portrayal of important factors such as topography and vegetation which affect reptile distributions.

THE AUSTRALIAN HABITATS

The environment where a given animal or plant lives or grows is known as its habitat. It is not surprising that such a vast area as Australia contains a wide variety of habitats, ranging from rainforests and sclerophyll forests to heathlands and deserts.

With the exception of a few greatly disturbed regions, such as areas under intensive industrial and urban development, reptiles are found throughout the continent. Diversity is higher in the warm tropical areas of the north than in the cool temperate regions of the south—a trend which is mirrored worldwide. However, Australia contains extensive, well-vegetated dry regions in which reptiles have undergone extensive radiation, so much so that these semi-arid and arid habitats contain the most diverse assemblage of arid-adapted reptiles known on earth. On the other hand, humid habitats occupy only a small proportion of our dry continent and this is reflected in their low herpetological diversity; Australian rainforests are relatively depauperate in comparison to those occurring in nearby New Guinea and South-East Asia.

In addition to the climatic factors of temperature and rainfall, the habitat requirements of reptiles are governed by soil and rock type and, to a large extent, by the nature of the vegetation. Topographical features, particularly mountain ranges, may also affect reptile distribution patterns, acting as inhospitable barriers to some species and corridors of dispersal for others.

Alpine and subalpine zones   These are restricted to the southern highlands of eastern Australia, from the Central Plateau of Tas. to the Snowy Mountains of NSW. Alpine and subalpine conditions occur in areas above approximately 1370–1520 m on the mainland and above approximately 900 m in Tas. Frosts may occur at any time of year and snow falls are common from June to early October. Areas too cold to support trees (mean temperature of the warmest month less than 10°C) are considered alpine. Both areas support a ground cover of herbfields, *Sphagnum* bogs, heathlands and tussock grasslands. Subalpine zones include woodlands of smooth-barked eucalypts. See p. 18 .

Humid zones   Isolated humid pockets occur throughout northern and eastern Australia, the south-east (including Tas.) and the deep south-west. These areas receive over 800 mm of rain per annum in the south, to over 1200 mm per annum in the north. Northern areas receive most of their rain during summer (between October and March), while in the south most rain falls during winter (roughly between May and September). Local topography has a marked effect on weather patterns and many areas within the humid zones are considerably drier. The wettest area is Tully, between Cairns and Cardwell in north-eastern Qld, which receives up to 4400 mm per annum.

Vegetation of the humid zones is characterised by various rainforest types, wet sclerophyll forests and, in some areas, heathlands.

Rainforests   These occupy less than 1 per cent of the Australian surface area. They are largely restricted to well-watered slopes, gullies and watercourses of eastern and northern Australia.

Approximately 20 distinct structural types have been identified. Rainforests typically include a closed canopy comprising a diverse assemblage of tree species. Many of the trees occurring in rainforests have buttressed bases which provide added support on shallow soils.

Tropical and subtropical rainforests occur disjunctly from mideastern NSW to northern Qld. The largest tracts occur between Cooktown and Ingham in north-eastern Qld, and in the McPherson Range on the Qld–NSW border. The trees (including palms) are predominantly evergreen and arranged in tiered canopies; the uppermost are often over 30 m tall. Vines and epiphytes are usually present, often abundant. Distinctive elements of other vegetation types (e.g. *Eucalyptus*, *Casuarina*, *Melaleuca* and *Acacia*) are usually absent. Beneath the canopies vegetation becomes more open, comprising slender shade-tolerant trees. Ground cover includes dense layers of leaf-litter, rotting logs, fungi and mosses. Tropical and subtropical rainforests often merge into wet sclerophyll forests, indicated by a gradual increase in emergent eucalypts. In some areas the two associations may be sharply delineated. See pp. 18,19.

Monsoon forests   Small isolated pockets of monsoon forests occur across northern Australia. They are often associated with ranges, dissected plateaux and drainage systems. Dominant trees include a significant proportion of large-leaved deciduous species. Vines are abundant, while epiphytes are scarce. See p.19.

Wet sclerophyll forests   These forests occur on the coast and ranges of south-western and south-eastern Australia, including Tas. They are best represented in well-watered mountainous terrain and areas protected by deep gullies. Several species of large eucalypts are dominant, each with a shaft-like branchless trunk and an open crown. The canopy is usually 30–70 m high. Shrubs, saplings and tree ferns usually form a dense understorey. See p. 19 .

Mangrove communities   Comprising the outer limit of the land-based vegetation and forming a distinctive buffer zone between the land and the sea are mangrove communities. They occur in a narrow belt along the coastlines and estuaries of north-western, northern and eastern Australia. The most extensive stands occur in the north. Mangroves grow in areas periodically inundated by tides, a condition few other terrestrial plants can tolerate. Though numerous structural types of mangrove communities are recognised, they typically include a dense canopy up to 5 m high, and trunks are often supported by buttresses. See p. 20.

Subhumid zones   These extend in a broad band through northern, eastern and south-western Australia. Northern areas receive approximately 650–1200 mm of summer rain per annum, while southern regions receive 500–800 mm of winter rainfall. Vegetation is characterised by a variety of woodlands, dry sclerophyll forests and heathlands.

Woodlands   Trees 2–30 m tall, the canopy of each not contacting its neighbour, characterise woodlands. Most subhumid woodlands are dominated by eucalypts over a ground cover of shrubs, herbs and grasses (southern Australia), or tall grasses interspersed with termitaria (northern tropical regions). In some areas trees such as *Acacia, Callitris, Casuarina* or *Melaleuca* predominate. Woodlands merge into shrublands or grasslands at one extreme and dry sclerophyll forests at the other, and hence may contain elements of each. See p. 20.

Dry sclerophyll forest This type of forest is widespread through south-western and eastern Australia. It is usually dominated by at least two species of eucalypts, up to 30 m tall with an open canopy cover of 30–70 per cent. Ground cover may be dominated by herbs, shrubs or grasses. Communities of brigalow (*Acacia harpophylla*) between 5 and 10 m tall may also be referred to as dry sclerophyll forest. At one extreme, dry sclerophyll forest merges into wet sclerophyll forest and at the other into woodland, hence it may contain elements of either. See p. 21.

Heathlands These are widespread, though patchily distributed, along the coast and hinterland of southern Australia. Isolated pockets occur on Cape York Peninsula in Qld, northern NT, and the Kimberley region of WA. They comprise a community of hard-leaved shrubs, normally less than 2 m tall. Dominant plant families include Epacridaceae (e.g., *Leucopogon* and *Lissanthe*), Myrtaceae (e.g., *Leptospermum* and *Baeckea*), Proteaceae (e.g., *Banksia, Grevillea* and *Hakea*) and Mimosaceae (e.g., *Acacia*). See p. 21.

Semi-arid zones Extensive throughout northern, eastern and southern Australia. Northern areas receive 350–600 mm of summer rain and southern regions receive 250–500 mm of winter rainfall. Semi-arid zones are characterised by various open vegetation types, including low woodlands, hummock grasslands, heathlands, shrublands and tussock grasslands. See pp. 21, 22.

Mallee woodlands These comprise a distinctive habitat occurring disjunctly through semi-arid southern Australia, from the interior of NSW to the midwest coast of WA. Mallee eucalypts are usually less than 9 m tall and each bears several slender trunks arising from a single swollen base (lignotuber). Ground cover is relatively open, typically including hummock grasses, heath plants or chenopodiaceous shrubs. Mallees favour sandy soils, particularly sand plains or interdunes. See p. 22.

Chenopod shrublands Distributed throughout semi-arid to arid southern Australia; usually on flat to undulating alkaline or saline soils. Chenopod shrubs, such as bluebush (*Maireana* spp.) and saltbush (*Atriplex* spp.), are characterised by their succulent leaves. They are usually well spaced with little or no vegetation between them. Extensive tracts occur in western NSW, much of SA and the Nullarbor Plain. To the north and west they are less continuous, becoming closely associated with margins of intermittent saltlakes and claypans. See p. 22.

Arid zones These occupy vast tracts of the interior, reaching the north-west coast and the Great Australian Bight. Rainfall is sporadic (up to 350 mm during northern summers and 250 mm during southern winters) and extended droughts are common.

Daytime temperatures are high for much of the year but central and southern areas may experience winter frosts. Vegetation is usually low and sparse, and most areas are dominated by hummock grasslands. Low *Acacia*-dominated woodlands and shrublands, tussock grasslands and chenopod shrublands are also widespread.

Hummock grasslands Extensive throughout the arid and semi-arid regions, occupying approximately 23 per cent of the continent. Ground cover is dominated by *Triodia* or *Plectrachne*, commonly known as 'spinifex' or 'porcupine grass'. These may occur in pure stands or in association with woodlands, shrublands, and occasionally heathlands. In northern areas hummock grasses may be present on virtually all soil and rock types, including plateaux, stony slopes, sandy and loamy plains and sand ridges. South of the tropic hummock grasses become increasingly restricted to sandy soils. Each plant comprises a matrix of hard, slender, spiny leaves forming a hummock up to 1.5 m across. Some species die off in the centre, growing outwards to form a ring over 2 m across. Spaces between hummocks are usually devoid of vegetation, though ephemeral herbs and grasses may appear in profusion following rain. Hummock grasslands comprise an arid-adapted floral component unique to Australia and support the richest assemblage of reptile species. The dense foliage offers a secure retreat from predators and temperature extremes, while the sheltered, relatively moist soil beneath hummock grasses provides ideal burrowing sites. See pp. 22, 23.

Shrublands These comprise the major woody vegetation of Australia's semi-arid to arid regions. Shrubland may be loosely defined as a community of sclerophyllous shrubs with an open canopy up to 3 m tall. The most widespread shrubland species is mulga (*Acacia aneura*), which in tree or shrub form now occupies approximately 20 per cent of Australia's surface area. See p. 23.

Tussock grasslands A number of distinctive types of tussock grasslands occur sporadically throughout northern and eastern Australia. The most extensive are on the black-soil plains: featureless landscapes of heavy, deeply cracking clays vegetated with Mitchell grasses (*Astrebla* spp.). This distinctive habitat extends from the arid eastern interior to eastern NT. Disjunct outliers occur in the western NT and the adjacent eastern Kimberley region, WA. See p. 23.

Sand ridge deserts These occupy over a million

square kilometres of the Australian continent. Sand ridges are usually parallel, approximately 90–120 m apart, and aligned in the direction of prevailing winds. Each ridge is generally between 10 and 30 m high, comprising a relatively loose bare crest and semiconsolidated slopes. These are vegetated with hummock grasses (*Triodia* and *Plectrachne*) or cane-grass (*Zygochloa*), often in association with sparse low shrubs. Interdunes are usually well vegetated with hummock grasses and trees or shrubs, such as

Acacia and desert oaks (*Casuarina decaisneana*). See p. 24.

Gibber deserts Featureless stony plains, sparsely vegetated with shrubs, grass hummocks or tussocks, and occasionally low trees. Extensive tracts of gibber occur disjunctly from western Queensland and New South Wales to the western interior of Western Australia. See p. 24.

Approximate boundaries of the climatic zones

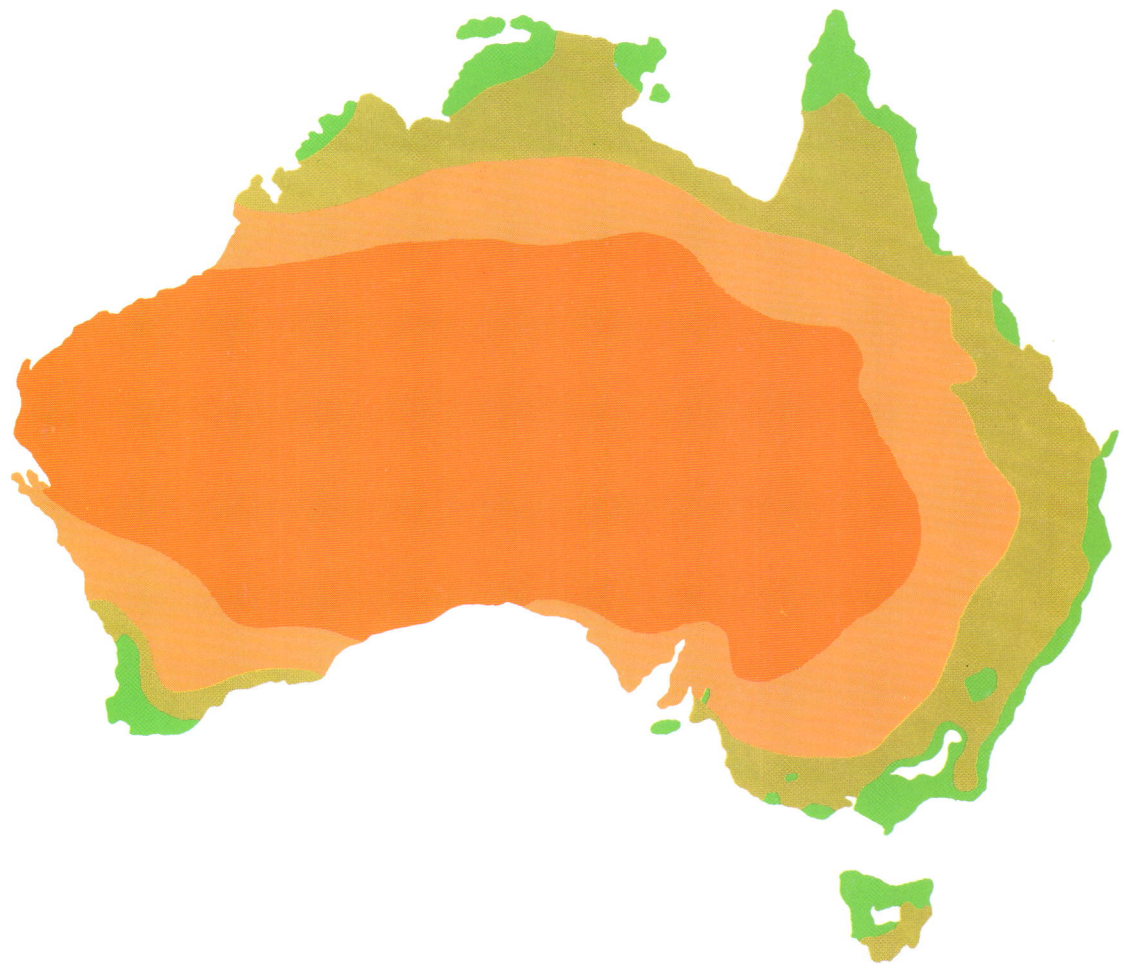

HUMID

ALPINE AND SUBALPINE

SUBHUMID

SEMIARID

ARID

Alpine heathland. Mt Hartz National Park, Tas. (S. Wilson)

Subalpine woodland/heathland association. Mt Kosciusko
National Park, NSW (D. Knowles)

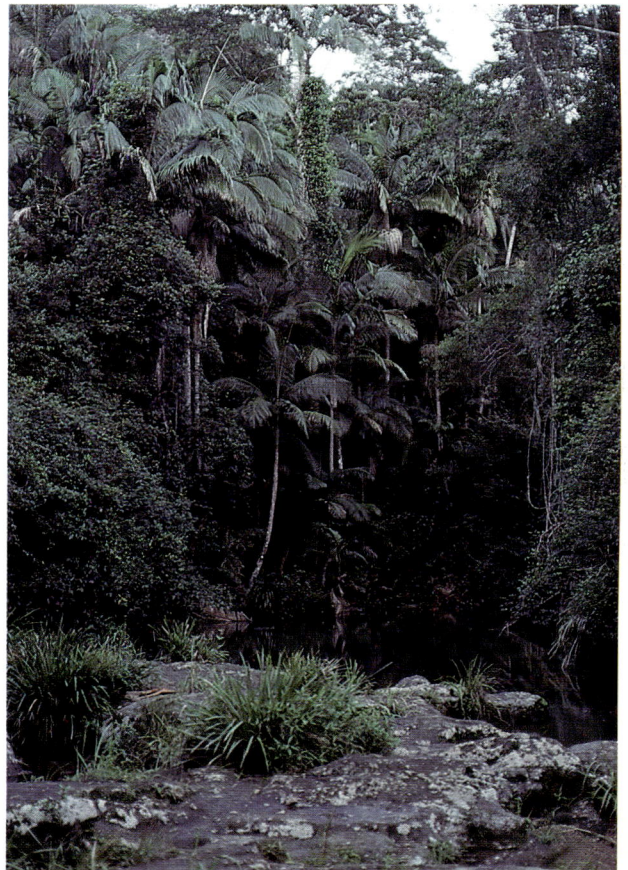

Rainforest. Terania Creek, NSW. (D. Knowles)

Rainforest. Lamington Plateau, Qld. (S. Wilson)

Monsoon forest. Lockerbie Scrub, Cape York Peninsula,
Qld. (S. Wilson)

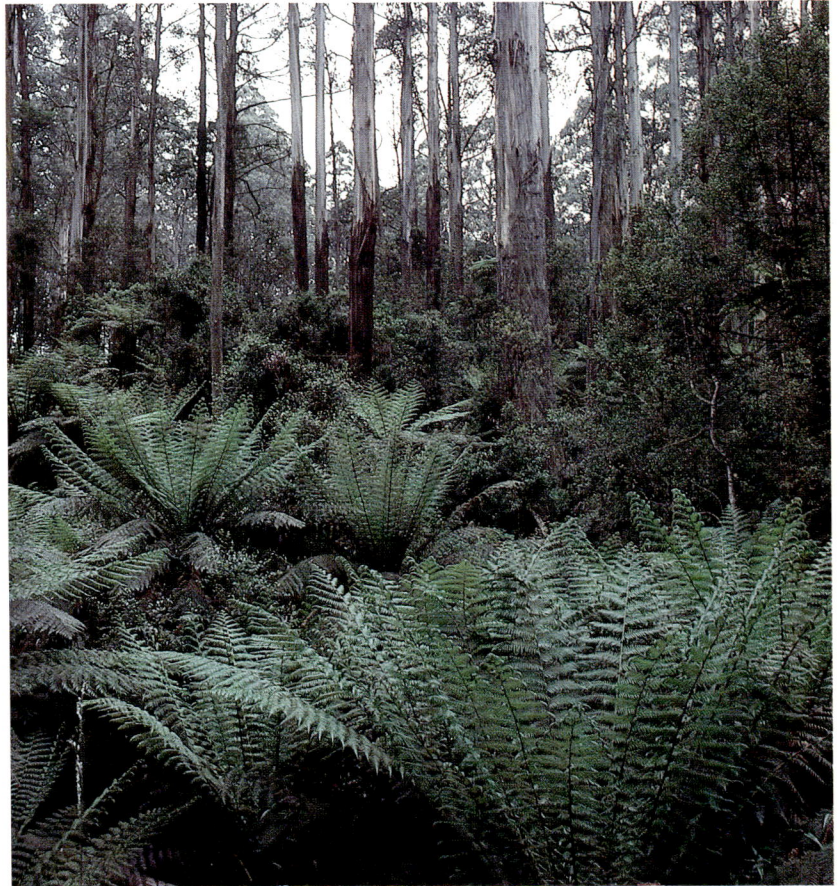

Wet sclerophyll forest. Sherbrooke Forest, Vic. (S. Wilson)

Mangrove communities. North-west Kimberley region, WA. (M. Hanlon)

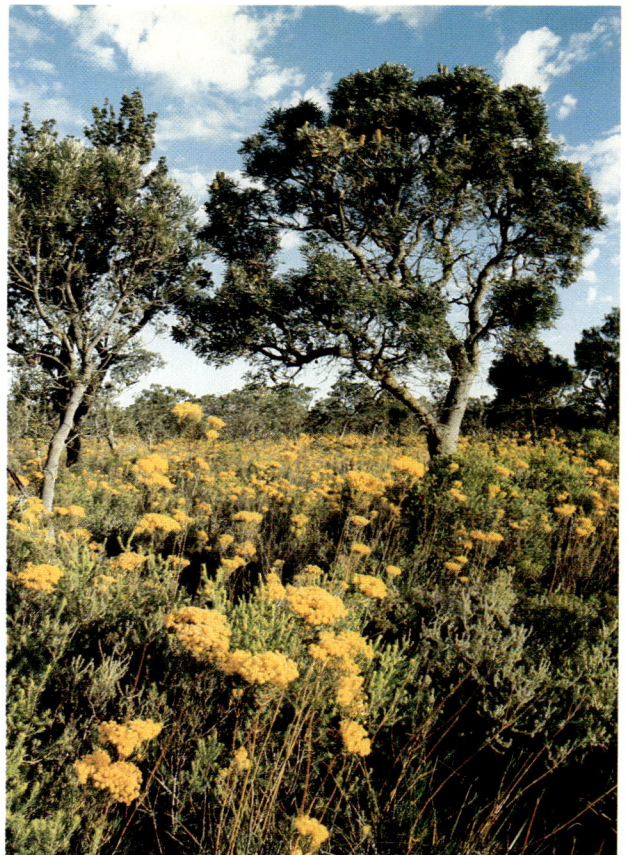

Woodland communities on the sandy coastal plain of WA typically comprise *Banksia*/eucalypt associations over a ground cover of heath plants. Wanneroo, WA. (S. Wilson)

Woodland with a grassy understorey. Peak Ranges, mideastern Qld. (S. Wilson)

Dry sclerophyll forest. Warrumbungle National Park, NSW. (S. Wilson)

The finest examples of heathland occur on the sandplains and lateritic soils of south-western WA, a region which supports some of the most complex assemblages of flowering plants in the world. Green Head area, WA. (D. Knowles)

Right: Semi-arid heathland. Lake Cronin area, south-western interior of WA. (S. Wilson)

Heathland. Much of Australia's coastline is dominated by pale dunes. These are usually vegetated with shrubs, or grasses such as beach spinifex (*Spinifex* spp.). Behind the coastal dunes, soils are consolidated by heathlands, shrublands and woodlands. Rottnest Island, WA. (S. Wilson)

Mallee/hummock grass association. Dedari area, south-western interior of WA. (M. Powell)

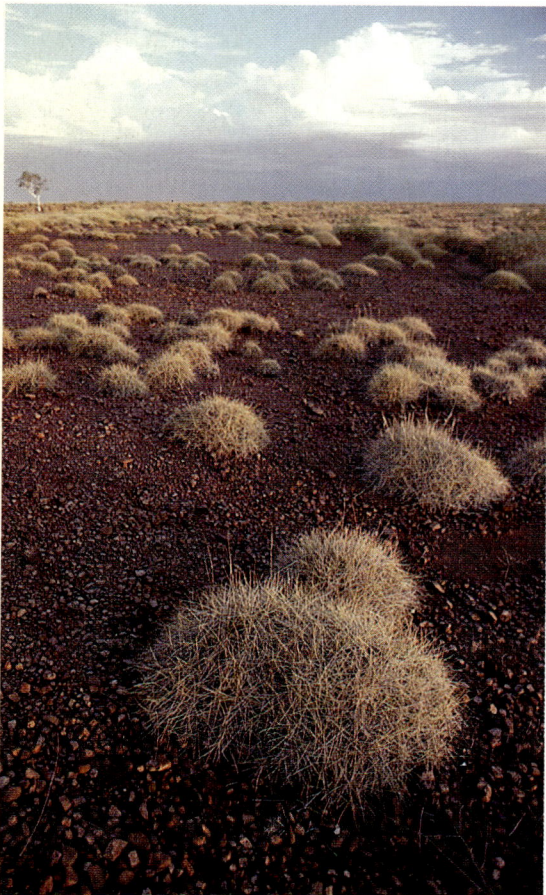

Hummock grassland. Mt Isa district, Qld. (M. Hanlon)

Chenopod shrublands. Madura area, WA. (M. Powell)

Hummock grasses and stony mesas typify the Pilbara and Mt Isa regions of WA and Qld. Panawonnica area, WA. (S. Wilson)

Acacia shrubland subject to grazing by sheep. Winning Station, Exmouth Gulf area, WA. (M. Hanlon)

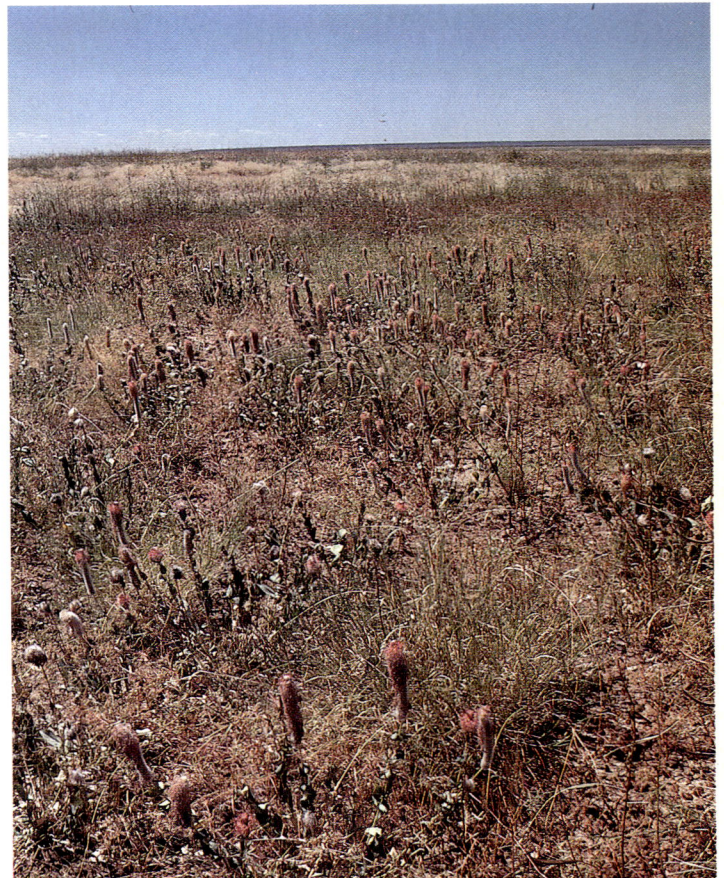

Tussock grassland. Julia Creek/Richmond area, Qld, following good rains. (D. Knowles)

Sand ridge desert. Over most of Australia, sand ridge vegetation is dominated by hummock grasses. Exmouth Gulf, WA. (S. Wilson)

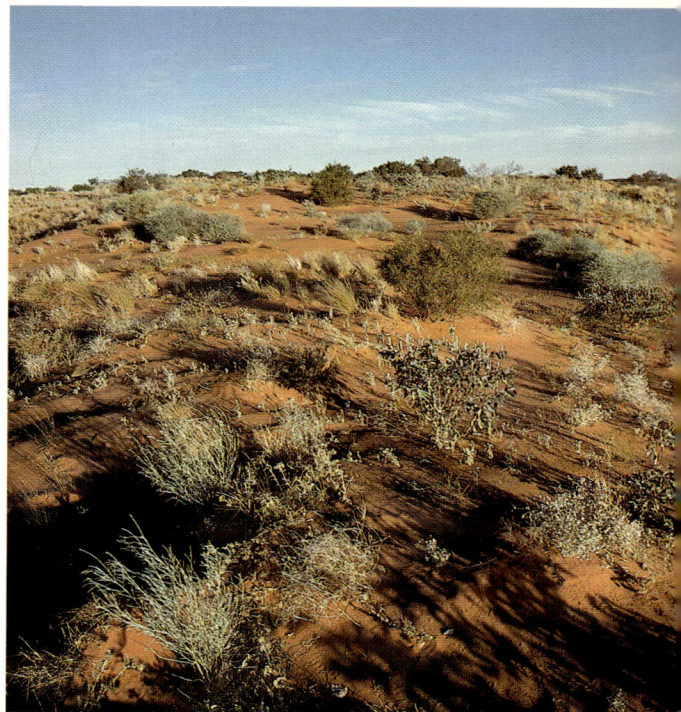

Sand ridge desert. In deserts of eastern Australia cane grass (*Zygochloa*) forms a significant component of sand ridge vegetation. Diamantina Lakes Station area, Qld. (D. Knowles)

Gibber desert. Waldburg Station, Gascoyne area, WA. (S. Wilson)

Left: Isolated humid habitats occur throughout many of Australia's arid areas. The most conspicuous of these are riverine gorges. Dale Gorge, Hamersley Ranges, WA. (S. Wilson)

LIZARDS

(Order Squamata, Suborder Sauria)

Lizards comprise the most speciose group of terrestrial vertebrates in Australia. Five families occur on the continent, encompassing 61 genera and 514 described species.

Agamidae (dragon lizards): 12 genera and 64 species.

Gekkonidae (geckos): 16 genera and 91 species.

Pygopodidae (flap-footed lizards): 8 genera and 32 species.

Scincidae (skinks): 24 genera and 303 species.

Varanidae (goannas or monitor lizards): 1 genus and 24 species.

Lizards are distinguished from snakes in bearing some (usually all) of the following characters:
- limbs
- ear-openings
- fleshy tongues
- movable lower eyelids (able to blink)
- long tails, usually considerably greater than SVL, and
- small ventral scales, approximately equal in size to adjacent body scales

Naturally in a group as diverse as lizards there are numerous exceptions to these trends.
- Several fossorial skinks have completely lost all external trace of limbs. Others may retain some evidence of limbs, their presence indicated by a groove, dimple or clawless style. Flap-footed lizards bear no trace of forelimbs, and the hindlimbs are reduced to scaly flaps.
- Ear-openings are absent on some dragon lizards, and reduced to absent on several cryptozoic skinks. Their position is usually indicated by a scaly depression.
- Tongues of monitor lizards or goannas are long, slender and deeply forked like those of snakes. It is interesting to note that the remaining fleshy-tongued lizards display a hint of bifurcation of the tongue, in the form of a noticeable notch at the tip.
- Flap-footed lizards, geckos and some skinks have immovable lower eyelids, which have fused to form transparent spectacles.
- Although the tails of most lizards are significantly longer than the SVL, this is only a reliable distinguishing character if the original tail is intact. Many lizards have fragile tails which may be completely or partially lost in instances such as attempted predation, rough handling or fighting. A regenerated tail is rarely as long as the original and is usually more simple in pattern, shape and ornamentation. The vertebrae of the original are replaced by a cartilaginous rod, so any further breakages must occur between the previous point of injury and the body.
- Ventral scales of most flap-footed lizards differ from those of other lizards in being significantly larger than adjacent body scales. However, these are arranged in a paired series, unlike the broad transverse plates of most snakes.

DRAGON LIZARDS
Family AGAMIDAE

Moderately large family comprising approximately 230 species in 36 genera, distributed from southern Europe, through Africa and Asia to New Guinea, Australia and islands of the western Pacific. Represented in Australia by 64 species in 12 genera. Seven genera are endemic. Diversity is greatest in arid areas, particularly in western half of continent. Alpine regions, wet sclerophyll forests and rainforests support few species. Only one extends into Tas.

Australian dragons vary in snout–vent length (SVL) from 42 to 260 mm. Limbs are well developed (the hindlimbs usually significantly longer), each bearing 5 strongly clawed digits. Tail usually slender, tapering, and longer than head and body; shorter than SVL on only 2 monotypic genera (*Moloch* and *Cryptagama*). Tail is non-fragile, though limited regeneration may occur if broken. Eyelid movable and scaly. Ear opening usually distinct, bearing exposed tympanum; covered by scaly skin on most *Tympanocryptis* and the Lake Eyre dragon (*Ctenophorus maculosus*). Tongue short and fleshy; notched at tip. Males (and sometimes females) of most species bear one or more pores along under surfaces of thighs (femoral pores), and/or in front of vent (preanal pores). These are openings of ducts which excrete a waxy substance. Skin is loose fitting, usually forming distinct folds beneath throat and occasionally on sides of neck, forebody or flanks. Scales are small, rough, non-glossy and imbricate; occasionally juxtaposed. These may be mixed with enlarged, scattered to longitudinally aligned spines or strongly keeled scales. Those on nape are often compressed to form a crest, set on an erectable fleshy ridge. Crests may attain impressive proportions on some species, particularly the rainforest dragons (*Hypsilurus* spp.). Head scales are usually granular; never enlarged to form shields.

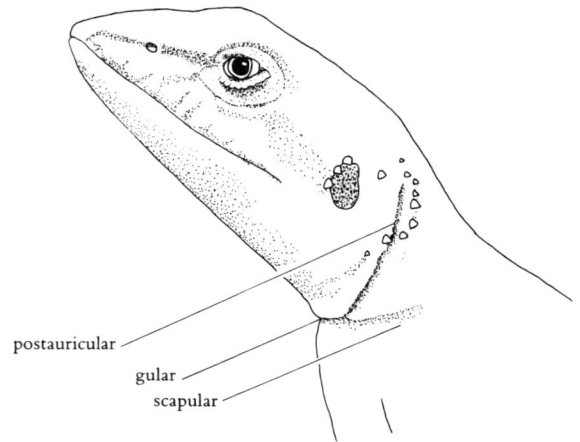

postauricular

gular

scapular

Arrangement of skin-folds on a typical dragon (*Diporiphora bennettii*)

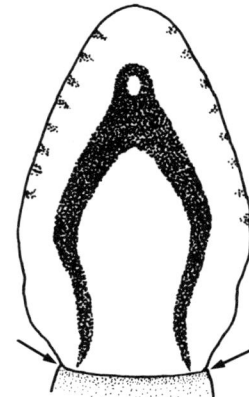

Throat of *Ctenophorus maculatus griseus* showing the location of gular fold. Black ventral pigments are common to many dragons and tend to be most intense on mature males, particularly those of *Ctenophorus* spp.

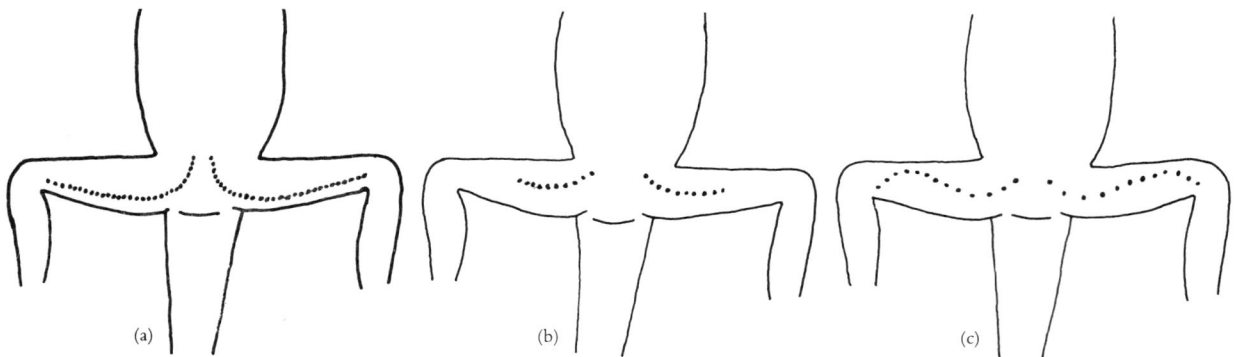

(a)   (b)   (c)

Location and alignment of femoral and preanal pores
(a) extending full length of thigh, and curving sharply forward towards midline (*Ctenophorus isolepis*)

(b) restricted to inner portion of thigh, and curving weakly forward towards midline (*Ctenophorus femoralis*)
(c) curving forward towards front of thigh (*Ctenophorus nuchalis*)

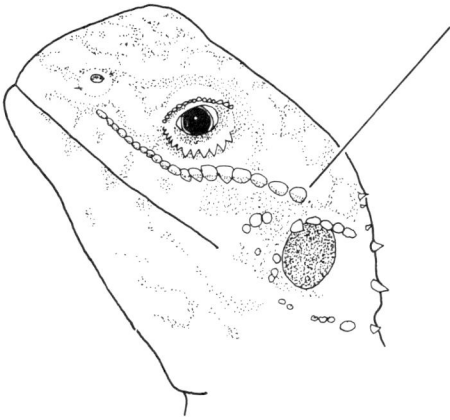

Series of enlarged scales curving from below eye to above ear; shared by all *Ctenophorus* spp. (*C. nuchalis*)

The family contains some of Australia's most familiar and spectacular lizards, such as the frilled lizard (*Chlamydosaurus kingii*).

Most dragons are swift, diurnal lizards. In very hot weather some may be crepuscular. They comprise a diverse group, largely adapted to a terrestrial existence. One species (*Diporiphora superba*) appears to be strictly arboreal, and many others spend considerable time in trees. The water dragon (*Physignathus lesueurii*) is semi-aquatic. All lay parchment-shelled eggs.

Dragons feed on arthropods or any other creatures small enough to be swallowed. Prey is rarely pursued unless it attracts attention by moving. Diets may be augmented with variable quantities of vegetable matter, particularly flowers. The proportion of vegetation consumed tends to increase with the size of the species.

Dragons tend to favour elevated perching sites such as rocks, shrubs, stumps and fallen timber, from which they survey their surroundings with a keen eye. They possess high visual acuity, consistent with their active, diurnal way of life. Consequently, their behaviour patterns, which include some of the most complex social interactions known for Australian lizards, are strongly visually oriented. Many species are territorial, with dominant males displaying the brightest colours and patterns. Courtship and territorial behaviour involves a series of ritualised display sequences: head-bobbing, arm-waving, push-ups, and occasionally fighting. Individuals of both sexes and all age groups may perform some form of display (particularly head-bobbing and arm-waving) during social interactions. The significance of these display sequences when performed by solitary animals is not understood.

The majority of dragons show a marked ability to change colour according to mood or temperature. During early morning when body temperatures are low, dark hues enable rapid absorption of heat. As the body temperature rises, the ground colour lightens and pattern intensifies. Radical fluctuations of colour (individuals may change from dull grey to brick red in minutes) renders comprehensive colour descriptions difficult. For this reason our discussions of colour and pattern are based (where possible) on hues and patterns of active individuals.

Diurnal activity in hot climates has necessitated some behavioural adaptations for thermoregulation. Some species avoid excessive heat gain by posturing. Overheating is avoided if the body is angled directly into the sun, reducing the amount of exposed surface area. When the substrate is hot the body is raised high, supported only by heels of hindlimbs and claws of forelimbs. As temperature rises, lizards may be forced to shuttle between sun and shade, or even retire to cover until later in the day.

As yet, no universally accepted suggestion has been put forward regarding the function of femoral and preanal pores. They may be associated with the equally unexplained habit of 'substrate licking': dabbing the tongue against the surface on which the lizard is resting. Pores could possibly serve to lay a marking, identifiable by taste.

Agamidae is an Old World family, replaced in the New World by the superficially similar iguanas (Iguanidae). The distributions of the families are mutually exclusive. In the few areas where iguanas extend out of the Americas (Fiji Islands and Madagascar), dragons are absent. Many striking examples of convergent evolution occur. Members of each family share upright postures, keen vision and complex display sequences. The arboreal rainforest dragons (*Hypsilurus*) are mirrored by some members of the genus *Iguana*, both possessing prominent spinose nuchal crests and deep gular pouches. Similarly, the terrestrial dragons *Cryptagama* and most *Tympanocryptis* spp., share with the horned toads (*Phrynosoma*) of North America, rotund cryptic forms, ant-dominated diets and a preference for arid habitats.

Genus *CAIMANOPS* Storr, 1974

Endemic monotypic genus restricted to arid central and western interior of WA.

Moderately small slender dragon with short limbs, short blunt-tipped tail, and upturned wedge-shaped snout. Dorsum bears 5 low ridges of enlarged keeled scales (continuous vertebral, broken dorsals and dorsolaterals) from neck to level of hindlimbs. Nuchal crest well developed and erectable. Tympanum exposed. Scales small, juxtaposed and weakly keeled on body; larger and more strongly keeled on tail. Femoral pores absent. Preanal pores present.

Terrestrial to semi-arboreal. Arthropod feeder.

Caimanops amphiboluroides
(Lucas and Frost, 1902)
Photo 2

Description Dorsal ground colour pale or dark grey to greyish brown, usually bearing obscure darker streaks. Paravertebral series of 3–5 elongate dark blotches usually extend from base of head to hips. Upper lateral zone darker shade of ground colour (usually dark-edged), often enclosing irregular darker streaks. This extends from snout or eye, becoming broader at level of forelimb, and tapering back to hindlimb. Obscure broad dark-edged pale grey midlateral and ventrolateral stripes usually extend from forelimb to hindlimb. Remaining lower lateral surfaces pale grey to white, longitudinally streaked with darker pigment. Top of head bears narrow dark median streak on posterior half of snout, irregular dark transverse bar between eyes, and an angular dark streak extending from above eye towards nape. Broad white to pale grey stripe extends from upper and lower lips to side of neck. Limbs irregularly streaked with darker pigment. Tail barred with white and pale grey to brown. Ventral surfaces white, bearing numerous irregular dark streaks and lines. SVL 90 mm.

Preferred habitat Arid central and western interior of WA; reaching coast near Carnarvon. Occurs in woodlands and shrublands dominated by mulga (*Acacia aneura*), with sparse ground cover on heavy (often stony) soils.

Microhabitat Most often encountered among accumulations of twigs and fallen timber at bases of trees or shrubs.

Comments Relatively slow moving. Predominantly terrestrial, though occasionally ascends fallen timber and low trees, where it is difficult to locate due to disruptive 'bark-like' colouration and cryptic behaviour. When at rest on timber, the longitudinally oriented pattern is aligned with the woodgrain or bark. Slowly slides from direct view (rather than fleeing) if approached. When foraging on ground, tail is held in an upward curve. If harassed, turns side to aggressor and raises spinose nuchal crest.

Genus *CHELOSANIA* Gray, 1845

Endemic monotypic genus restricted to western half of northern Australia.

Moderately large dragon with large deep head, short limbs, strongly laterally compressed body and short blunt-tipped tail. Unique series of oblique parallel skin-folds are present behind exposed (distinctly wedge-shaped) tympanum. Low spinose erectable nuchal crest present, set above a fleshy ridge, which is continuous with vertebral ridge from nape to tail. Gular pouch deep and erectable. Body scales large, mostly keeled and homogeneous. Femoral and preanal pores absent.

Predominantly arboreal. Arthropod feeder.

Swell-headed or Chameleon Dragon
Chelosania brunnea Gray, 1845
Photo 3

Description Ground colour pale reddish brown, yellowish brown to shades of grey. Pattern prominent to virtually absent. Dark variegations, streaks and mottling extend from top of head to base of tail. Side of head ground colour to paler, usually bearing a series of darker streaks radiating from eye. Most prominent pair extend to upper temple, and through ear to side of neck. Dark patch usually present on rear margin of tympanum. Tail marked with 4–7 obscure to very prominent dark bands; equal to or narrower than pale interspaces. Gular pouch white, orange-yellow to brown, marked with oblique dark lines or rows of spots. These tend to converge on chest. Remainder of ventral surfaces whitish, obscurely flecked to streaked with brown, particularly around vent. SVL 115 mm.

Preferred habitat Subhumid woodlands, usually with understorey of tall grasses. Extends from Coulomb Point in western Kimberley region, WA, to northern NT, south to Daly Waters. Apparently absent from far north-west of NT.

Microhabitat Though most individuals are encountered on ground, considerable time is spent perched cryptically on trunks and limbs of standing trees.

Comments Alternative common name alludes to laterally compressed form, slow deliberate chameleon-like gait, and cryptic habits. Seldom attempts to flee when observed, sliding slowly from view behind perch. Clutches of 2–9 eggs are recorded; laid in shallow burrows. If harassed, individuals present broadest lateral aspect of body, raise nuchal crest, and distend deep gular pouch.

Genus *CHLAMYDOSAURUS* Gray, 1825

Monotypic genus containing one of Australia's most distinctive and familiar lizards. Widespread across northern Australia, extending to south-eastern Qld. Extralimital in southern New Guinea.

Extremely large, moderately robust dragon with long limbs and moderately long tail. Head relatively large with pointed snout, and acutely angular ridge from snout to above eye. Large erectable frill is comprised of thin loose scaly skin (edged by enlarged tooth-like scales creating serrated margin), and almost completely surrounds neck. When at rest this is folded over chest and anterior body to just beyond forelimbs, overlapping on top of neck. Erected, it stands at right angles to body, encircling head. Interior of mouth pink to pale yellow. Prominent enlarged pair of teeth present at front of upper and lower jaw. Nuchal and vertebral crests absent. Tympanum exposed. Dorsal scales heterogeneous (a row of slightly enlarged scales on nape) and mostly keeled. Femoral and preanal pores present.

Predominantly arboreal. Arthropod feeder.

Frilled Lizard
Chlamydosaurus kingii Gray, 1825
Photos 4, 5

Description Ground colour pale or dark grey, brownish grey to dull reddish brown. Juveniles and populations from eastern half of range tend to have less red pigment. Pattern usually obscure to absent, particularly on adults. When present, paravertebral series of large elongate pale blotches (enclosed by dark zone) extend from nape to hips. Similar lateral series may also be present. Remainder of dorsal and lateral surfaces bears obscure dark mottling and/or variegations. These sometimes coalesce to form vague reticulum. Obscure narrow broken vertical bars (composed of pale scales) are occasionally present on flanks of boldly marked animals. Head ground colour or darker; patternless on adults. Juveniles bear dark bars radiating from eye. Tail obscurely barred, and tipped with dark grey. Frill extremely variable. On some eastern populations the upper half is dark grey (with or without pale yellow flecks), in contrast to pale yellow lower half. In WA and NT, ground colour is flushed to densely flecked with bright orange to red or yellow, and usually marked with large pale grey and black patches. Ventral surfaces cream, dull yellow to brown. Belly of mature males black. This usually extends onto lower flanks. SVL 250 mm.

Preferred habitat Subhumid to semi-arid grassy woodlands and dry sclerophyll forests from Kimberley region, WA, across northern NT to northern and eastern Qld, extending as far south as Brisbane.

Microhabitat Most of time is spent on trunks and limbs of standing trees. Frequently descends to ground after rain.

Comments This familiar lizard is portrayed on the Australian 2 cent coin. In recent years (since the 1960s) south-east Qld populations have undergone a dramatic decline in numbers. When disturbed, frilled lizards usually dash to the nearest tree, running on powerful hindlimbs with body erect and tail held back as a counterbalance. Alternatively they may hide beneath low vegetation, assuming an immobile cryptic posture. Cornered individuals turn to face aggressor, enacting the spectacular display for which they are most famous. The frill (measuring up to 30 cm across) is erected by opening bright-coloured mouth. This sudden apparent increase in size and display of colour may be accompanied by loud hissing, raising body on hindlimbs, swaying from side to side and leaping at, or chasing, the antagonist. At rest the frill aids in camouflage by disrupting the body outline. As a result, frilled lizards may resemble a broken branch or the coarse bark on which they frequently rest. In addition to these display and camouflage functions the frill is also thought to act as a heat dispersal mechanism. In western Arnhem Land, Aborigines use the name 'bemmung' (blanket lizard), associating the frill with the prepuce of the human penis. Like most cryptic arboreal agamids, frilled lizards slide slowly from view when approached. Feeds largely on invertebrates, though small vertebrates are also taken. Individuals have been recorded with the heads of soldier termites still attached to the face and lips. Clutch of 13 eggs recorded.

Genus CRYPTAGAMA Witten, 1974

Endemic monotypic genus restricted to arid north-eastern interior of WA and adjacent NT.

Very small robust dragon with short limbs and short blunt-tipped tail. Tail shorter than SVL; a characteristic shared by only one other Australian agamid genus (*Moloch*). Head bulbous with blunt snout. Tympanum exposed. Scales along upper lip form unique serrated fringe. Dorsal scales heterogeneous; very small, and mixed with enlarged tubercles. Femoral and preanal pores present.

Terrestrial.

Distinguished from *Tympanocryptis* by tail length (shorter than SVL vs longer). Differs further from sympatric species of *Tympanocryptis* in possessing an exposed (vs covered) tympanum.

Cryptagama aurita (Storr, 1981)
Photo 6

Description Ground colour pale reddish brown to brick red, suffused on head and back with pale brownish grey. Irregular paravertebral series of small dark brown blotches may extend from nape to hips. Tail obscurely marked with irregular dark brown to brownish grey bands; approximately equal in width to pale interspaces. Ventral surfaces whitish. SVL 45 mm.

Preferred habitat Lateritic soils supporting *Triodia* in the vicinity of Halls Creek and Wolf Creek Meteorite Crater in arid north-eastern interior of WA, east to Wave Hill, NT.

Microhabitat Holotype and paratype were collected beneath *Triodia* hummocks.

Comments *Cryptagama aurita* shows a remarkable similarity in form to *Tympanocryptis cephalus*. This resemblance suggests convergence in morphology and habits, resulting from similar lifestyles.

Genus CTENOPHORUS Fitzinger, 1843

Large endemic genus containing 22 species. This figure represents approximately one-third of the Australian Agamidae. Widespread throughout continent, particularly in semi-arid to arid areas. Absent from Cape York Peninsula, Qld, east coast and ranges, south-east (including Tas.) and lower south-west.

Small to moderately large dragons with weakly laterally compressed to strongly dorsally depressed bodies, moderately short to very long limbs and long to moderately short tails. Head bulbous to depressed, bearing weak to strongly angular brow. Tympanum exposed (hidden on *C. maculosus*). Nuchal crest and vertebral ridge of enlarged scales are well developed (often erectable) to absent. Lower (and sometimes upper) eyelid usually bears serrated scaly fringe. Dorsal body scales homogeneous or heterogeneous (small, mixed with enlarged blunt tubercles; never scattered spines), their keels usually directed back towards midline. Distinctive row of enlarged ridged scales curves from below eye to above ear. Clusters of enlarged spines or tubercles are often present on side of neck and rear of lower jaw. Preanal and femoral pores present, often reduced on females.

Most exhibit sexual colour and pattern differences. Adult males develop brighter hues, stronger pattern, and varying amounts and arrangement of black ventral pigment. These may be seasonal, or retained after maturity.

Tentatively divided into 8 species groups.

C. ornatus **group** Contains 2 moderately large *Ctenophorus*. Each has a strongly depressed head and body, long limbs and moderately long tail. Nuchal crest very low to absent. Dorsal scales homogeneous. Female and juvenile colouration similar: shades of brown with variable darker marbling. Mature males bear prominent rings around tail. Rock-inhabiting. One species occurs on open expanses of granite, the other on low fragmented outcrops. Extremely swift, running on all 4 limbs with body and tail held high off substrate. Narrow rock crevices (occasionally burrows) are used for shelter. Able to inflate body by gulping air, making extraction from cover difficult. Suitable basking or shelter sites may be shared by several individuals. Restricted to WA. Group comprises *C. ornatus* and *C. yinnietharra*.

Ring-tailed Dragons

C. caudicinctus **group** Comprises 6 taxa, all referred to one species. Moderate to large *Ctenophorus* with slightly laterally compressed to weakly depressed heads and bodies, long limbs and relatively long tails. Nuchal crest weak to moderately well developed; erectable and continuous with a low vertebral ridge of enlarged scales. Dorsal scales homogeneous. Males of some races develop swollen jowls and laterally compressed bodies. Pattern variable, typically including reddish to grey ground colour and longitudinal to transversely aligned dark spots, alternating with pale transverse lines. Body pattern may become diffuse, and tail strongly banded, on males of some subspecies. Predominantly rock-inhabiting, though some populations inhabit gibber-strewn or loamy plains. Elevated perches are favoured for basking and display. Extremely swift, running on hindlimbs or all 4 limbs to shelter of crevices when disturbed. Widely distributed through rocky ranges and outcrops of subhumid to arid northern and central Australia. Group comprises *C. caudicinctus caudicinctus*, *C. caudicinctus graafi*, *C. caudicinctus infans*, *C. caudicinctus macropus*, *C. caudicinctus mensarum* and *C. caudicinctus slateri*.

C. pictus **group** Contains 2 species of medium-sized *Ctenophorus*, each with a deep blunt head, robust body, and moderately short limbs and tail. Nuchal crest and vertebral ridge weak and erectable to absent. Dorsal body scales homogeneous or heterogeneous; one species (*C. salinarum*) bears en-

larged smooth scales, arranged in transverse rows among smaller keeled scales. Pattern extremely variable, typically including transversely aligned pale spots (often contracted to vertebral region) mixed with irregular dark variegations over yellowish, brown to reddish ground colour. Breeding males of one species (*C. pictus*) develop prominent blue flush over throat and lower flanks. Terrestrial, rarely selecting elevated perches. Moderately swift, running on all 4 limbs to nearby shallow burrow. This is usually an oblique U shape (with escape exit terminating close to surface), situated at the base of low vegetation. Restricted to semi-arid and arid southern Australia, favouring shrublands (particularly chenopod communities), hummock grasslands or margins of saltflats. Both species feed predominantly on ants. Group comprises *C. pictus* and *C. salinarum*.

C. decresii **group** Contains 4 species of medium-sized *Ctenophorus*, each with a depressed head and body, moderately long limbs and moderately short to long tail. Nuchal crest low and erectable. Vertebral ridge absent or weak, represented by an erectable fold of skin. Dorsal scales homogeneous or heterogeneous. Female and juvenile colouration similar: shades of brown to reddish brown with variable darker marbling. With exception of *C. rufescens*, adult males are prominently marked with varying combinations of deep red, orange, blue, yellow and black.

These species exhibit some of the most complex and spectacular territorial displays of any Australian lizards. Brightly coloured gular region is lowered, and nuchal crest and vertebral ridge raised. Body is laterally compressed and turned to present broadest aspect to opponent. Tail is coiled vertically, or horizontally to obliquely away from opponent (position varying according to species), while hindquarters are rhythmically raised and lowered, and forelimb rotated. Display is terminated with a series of head-bobs and head-dips. If intruder persists, fighting may ensue, and display sequence may be repeated.

Rock-inhabiting. Elevated perches are favoured as basking sites, while crevices or exfoliations are used for shelter. Each species or population appears closely associated with distinctive rock types and substrate colours. Largely restricted to rocky ranges and outcrops of SA, extending into adjacent WA and NSW. Group comprises *C. decresii*, *C. fionni*, *C. rufescens* and *C. vadnappa*.

C. reticulatus **group** Contains 5 small to moderately large *Ctenophorus*, each with a deep blunt head, robust body, and short limbs and tail. Tympanum exposed (except on *C. maculosus*). Nuchal crest weak to absent. Dorsal scales homogeneous or heterogeneous; mixed with larger flat transversely aligned scales. Pattern variable, usually including a dark reticulum. Some species are sexually dichromatic: breeding males may develop a red to orange flush over head and throat; occasionally on body, including ventral surfaces. Terrestrial, perching on stones, fallen timber, stumps or termitaria. Not particularly swift, running on all 4 limbs to shelter of shallow burrow, usually situated close to perch. Most are opportunistic feeders, preying on a broad range of arthropods, occasionally augmented with small quantities of vegetable matter. One species (*C. maculosus*) appears to specialise on ants. Widespread throughout most of generic range. Diversity is greatest in arid parts of SA. Group comprises *C. clayi, C. gibba, C. maculosus, C. nuchalis* and *C. reticulatus*.

Military Dragons

C. maculatus group Contains 10 taxa. Small to medium-sized *Ctenophorus*, each with a weakly depressed head and body, long limbs, and very long slender tail. Nuchal crest absent; barely discernible on one species. Body scales homogeneous. Pattern typically includes reddish to yellow or grey ground colour (differing according to substrate), marked with pale dorsolateral stripes or equivalent series of spots or blotches. Adult males bear varying amounts of black pigment on ventral (occasionally lateral) surfaces. Dark pigment usually present on females, though greatly reduced in extent. Entirely terrestrial, rarely or never perching on elevated sites. Members favour open (usually sandy) heathlands or hummock grasslands, foraging around margins of low ground cover. Extremely swift, dashing on all 4 limbs from one open space to another if pursued. Most do not retreat to cover of vegetation unless hard pressed. Diets consist almost entirely of ants, though other small arthropods are taken opportunistically. At least 2 species (probably applicable to most members) are known to be short lived, following a yearly or biennial lifecycle. Restricted to deserts and adjacent semi-arid habitats. Diversity is greatest in WA. Group comprises *C. femoralis, C. fordi, C. isolepis citrinus, C. isolepis gularis, C. isolepis isolepis, C. maculatus badius, C. maculatus dualis, C. maculatus griseus, C. maculatus maculatus* and *C. rubens.*

C. scutulatus group Contains 2 species. Medium-sized to large *Ctenophorus*, each with a deep head and body, very long limbs, and moderate to long tail. Nuchal crest weak to well developed; composed of compressed spinose scales. Vertebral ridge of enlarged scales weakly to very strongly developed. Body scales homogeneous. Pattern usually includes dorsolateral series of oblong pale blotches. Terrestrial. Extremely swift, running on hindlimbs to cover of low vegetation when disturbed. Restricted to arid and semi-arid woodlands or shrublands from western interior of WA to south-western SA. Members are *C. mckenziei* and *C. scutulatus.*

C. cristatus group Contains one large *Ctenophorus* with a deep head and body, very long limbs and long tail. Nuchal crest very well developed, composed of compressed spines, and continuous with vertebral ridge of enlarged scales. Distinctive spi-

nose dorsolateral fold present. Body scales heterogeneous; mixed with enlarged scales, and aligned transversely. Pattern includes prominent dark reticulum over anterior body, and strongly banded tail. Mature males are significantly brighter. Terrestrial, utilising elevated perching sites such as fallen timber. Extremely swift, dashing on hindlimbs for cover of burrow or hollow log when disturbed. Restricted to semi-arid woodlands from southern SA to southern WA.

Ctenophorus is distinguished from *Pogona* and *Tympanocryptis* in lacking scattered spines over body. When present, these are restricted to nuchal crest, sides of neck and dorsolateral fold. Differs further from these, and from *Diporiphora* and *Gemmatophora* in possessing an enlarged series of ridged scales curving from below eye to top of ear.

Ring-tailed Dragon
Ctenophorus caudicinctus (Günther, 1875)
Photos 7–12

Description Sole member of *C. caudicinctus* group, comprising 6 described subspecies. Some of these may warrant recognition as distinct species while others may be clinal variants. Only mature males are separable with relative certainty.

C. c. caudicinctus Juveniles have reddish brown to reddish orange ground colour. Pattern usually prominent. Paravertebral (and sometimes dorsolateral) series of large dark spots extend from nape onto base of tail. These alternate with narrow pale grey transverse lines or series of spots. Remainder of body and limbs irregularly flecked with blackish brown. Prominent dark lines radiate from eye to snout, chin and base of head. Tail ground colour, overlaid with alternating dark spots and pale bands. Ventral surfaces white, reticulated with grey on throat.

Females tend to lose pale transverse lines and dark spots, and dark interspaces between pale bands on tail contract to form bands. SVL 75 mm.

Adult male develops laterally compressed body and tail, deeper head, more prominent nuchal crest and swollen jowls. Head and back become dull blood red. Dorsal and lateral pattern becomes dominated by wavy longitudinal reddish streaks. Tail brown to yellowish brown, almost completely encircled by prominent blackish brown rings. Ventral surfaces whitish, bearing dark reticulum on throat, black patch on chest, and orange flush on inner surfaces of limbs. SVL 90 mm.

C. c. mensarum (Storr, 1967) Females and juveniles tend to have larger, darker, and more numerous dorsal spots. Paravertebral series are more narrowly separated. Adjacent dorsal spots frequently coalesce to form short transverse bars. SVL 80 mm.

Adult males are not laterally compressed, except on distal portion of tail. Jowls are not noticeably swollen. Ground colour pale reddish brown (vs blood red) with brown (vs blackish brown) caudal bands, tending to form less complete rings. SVL 90 mm.

C. c. infans (Storr, 1967) Females and juveniles are brick red to orange-brown, dotted with black and dark brown. Small elongate dark brown paravertebral spots present, forming a single series on tail. SVL 60 mm.

Adult males do not develop lateral compression or swelling of jowls. Nuchal crest very weak. Ground colour reddish brown with obscure pale vertebral stripe. Paravertebral spots are retained, alternating with transverse rows of small pale pinkish brown to pinkish white spots. Blackish and dark brown variegations extend over body. Tail bears broad obscure dark greyish brown bars. Ventrolateral surfaces brownish yellow. Ventral surfaces whitish, dappled with grey on throat. Narrow black patch extends from chest to abdomen, continuing to vent as grey streak. SVL 65 mm.

C. c. graafi (Storr, 1967) Females and juveniles are reddish brown flecked with blackish brown. Paravertebral, and occasionally dorsolateral, spots present; inner 2 rows narrowly separated. Transverse rows of pale spots are reduced to absent. SVL 70 mm.

Adult males do not develop lateral compression. Dark paravertebral spots tend to disappear. Dorsolateral surfaces and flanks dark grey. An indistinct pale dorsolateral stripe present on some individuals. Caudal bands obscure, restricted to distal three-quarters of tail. Large black patch present on chest, extending to anterior abdomen and inner surfaces of forelimbs. Pale grey variegation may be present on throat. Vicinity of gular fold often suffused with salmon pink. SVL 80 mm.

C. c. slateri (Storr, 1967) Females and juveniles are dull pale reddish brown. Paravertebral spots prominent; the 2 series broadly separated. White dorsal spots usually present; scattered to transversely aligned, and most dense on dorsolateral zone. Faint dark lines radiate from eye. Throat dappled with dark grey. SVL 70 mm.

Adult males have poorly developed lateral compression and swelling of jowls. Ground colour darker, and pattern duller. Paravertebral spots sometimes retained. Head and flanks obscurely variegated with dark grey, and usually sparsely dotted with pale yellowish brown. Tail marked with obscure dark brown bars; often absent anteriorly. Throat dappled with grey. Dark grey triangular patch present on chest, margined posteriorly with pale reddish flush. Limbs and tail shorter than those of nominate race. SVL 85 mm.

C. c. macropus (Storr, 1967) Females and juveniles are similar to those of nominate form.

Males have lateral compression restricted to distal part of tail. Swelling of jowls poorly developed to absent. Ground colour dull reddish brown to grey.

Widely separated series of paravertebral spots may be retained, and mixed with irregular dark variegations. Tail prominently to obscurely banded. Black patch covers entire chest, from gular fold to anterior part of abdomen, including inner surfaces of forelimbs. Somewhat divergent population from western edge of Great Sandy Desert differs in bearing bluish grey ground colour, and pattern dominated by pale transverse bands (at least on the few specimens available). Largest subspecies with longest appendages. SVL 100 mm.

Preferred habitat Widespread through rocky ranges and outcrops of subhumid to arid northern and central Australia. *C. c. caudicinctus* occurs in Pilbara region, WA (including several offshore islands), extending north to Great Sandy Desert, and south to Gascoyne area. *C. c. mensarum* merges with *C. c. caudicinctus* in Gascoyne area, extending southeast through low rocky hills and breakaways to Murchison area, WA. *C. c. infans* occurs on low granite outcrops in southern interior of WA, from Laverton south-west to Kookynie. *C. c. graafi* inhabits outcrops and ranges on northern edge of Great Victoria Desert, in eastern interior of WA. *C. c. slateri* occupies rocky highlands of southern NT. *C. c. macropus* extends across northern Australia from Kimberley region, WA, to western Qld.

Microhabitat See species group.

Comments Feeds almost entirely on arthropods. Breeding season of *C. c. caudicinctus* appears to last for at least 5 months. Gravid females are present from about November to March, and eggs hatch between January and May. Young males begin to develop sexual characteristics between June and September, and are fully mature by the following March. Adults die at about 20 months of age. Otherwise as for species group.

Ctenophorus clayi (Storr, 1966)
Photo 13

Description Smallest member of *C. reticulatus* group. Ground colour brownish white to pale yellowish brown, overlaid (on adults) with prominent dark red to blackish brown reticulum over head and body. Narrow vertebral stripe of ground colour extends from nape onto base of tail, margined on either side by large (often obscure) transversely elongate blotches. These may alternate with a series of narrow pale transverse or longitudinal bars. Prominent black patch present on side of neck, sometimes extending around gular fold to form a broad collar. Tail uniform, or marked with obscure dark lateral blotches. Ventral surfaces white. Mature males bear prominent yellow patch on either side of gular fold. SVL 50 mm.

Distinguished from *C. nuchalis* and *C. reticulatus* in possessing a large black patch on side of neck, and in attaining much smaller size (SVL 50 mm vs 115 and 105 mm, respectively).

Preferred habitat Arid red sand ridges and adjacent habitats, usually vegetated with hummock grass associations. Extends from south-western NT and north-western SA to eastern interior of WA. Isolated population occurs on North West Cape and lower Exmouth Gulf region, WA.

Microhabitat Excavates shallow burrow beneath grass hummock.

Comments See species group.

Crested Dragon or Bicycle Lizard
Ctenophorus cristatus (Gray, 1841)
Photo 14

Description Sole member of *C. cristatus* group. Pattern brightest on males, duller on females, and invariably drab on juveniles. Head, forelimbs and anterior body cream, yellow, orange to reddish orange, prominently variegated to mottled with black. Broad broken black dorsolateral stripe commences as streak behind eye, fading at midbody or hips. Posterior body, hindlimbs and base of tail, grey to greyish brown; uniform, sparsely flecked with black, or obscurely barred with pale grey. Forelimbs uniform, to banded or variegated with black. Distal three-quarters of tail prominently ringed with blackish brown, and cream to pale orange. Ventral surfaces white to pale yellow, marked with black (males) or grey (females and juveniles) as follows: a broad strip on throat (margined laterally with wavy dark streaks), and a dark patch on chest and forelimbs, extending narrowly over abdomen to vent. Hindlimbs (and sometimes forelimbs) of mature males, black. SVL 110 mm.

Distinguished from *C. mckenziei*, in lacking a pale vertebral stripe. Differs from *C. scutulatus*, and further from *C. mckenziei*, by nature of nuchal crest (well developed vs weak), and in bearing a dorsolateral ridge of enlarged scales, greater amount of dark ventral pigment, and broad contrasting bands on tail.

Preferred habitat Semi-arid woodlands in southern Australia, from Spencer Gulf in SA to southern interior of WA.

Microhabitat See species group.

Comments Feeds on a variety of arthropods, particularly ants and grasshoppers. Occasionally small lizards are taken. Colour changing ability (common to many dragons) is especially marked. An individual may change from brilliant orange to dull grey within minutes of handling. Colloquial name 'Bicycle Lizard' results from its bipedal gait when running at high speed. Otherwise as for species group.

Tawny Dragon
Ctenophorus decresii
(Duméril and Bibron, 1837)
Photo 15

Description Member of *C. decresii* group.
Females and juveniles: Ground colour brown, greyish brown to grey, dotted with dark brown to black over head, body, limbs and tail. Dark pigment tends to concentrate on flanks, forming broad wavy-edged stripe or series of blotches. Upper lips paler shade of ground colour. Ventral surfaces white to grey, mottled with dark grey on chin and throat.

Males: Dorsal ground colour grey, bluish grey to brown. Broad dark grey to black lateral zone (margined irregularly above, and usually below, with white, yellow, orange to red stripes or elongate blotches) extends from ear or side of neck to midbody or hindlimb. Lower flanks blue to bluish grey. Males of southern populations (Kangaroo Island and southern Mt Lofty Ranges) bear prominent blue flush over lips, chin and gular area. Those from further north (northern Mt Lofty Ranges, Flinders Ranges, Olary Spur and western NSW) bear yellow, pink to red flush. Remaining ventral surfaces white, with yellow to orange flush over anterior chest and gular fold. Throat marbled with grey or (in NSW) marked with a blackish longitudinal streak. SVL 80 mm.

Distinguished from *C. fionni* and *C. vadnappa* in possessing tiny scattered pale tubercles on flanks (vs body scales homogeneous).

Preferred habitat Subhumid to arid rocky ranges and outcrops of eastern SA, from Kangaroo Island, through Mt Lofty and Flinders Ranges and Olary Spur to Noonthorangee Range, NSW. Though adults are restricted to rocky substrates, juveniles are often encountered foraging on surrounding soils.

Microhabitat As for species group.

Comments Little or no gene flow occurs between populations and differences between them may be sufficient to warrant elevation to subspecific level. Complex territorial display of males includes coiling of tail horizontally away from opponent. This is discussed more fully under species group.

Ctenophorus femoralis (Storr, 1965)
Photo 16

Description Small slender member of *C. maculatus* group. Ground colour brick red to dull orange, marked over head, body and limbs with small pale spots and smaller dark flecks. Obscure pale broken dorsolateral stripe may extend from nape to hips, continuing onto tail as a line of pale blotches. These coalesce distally to form narrow pale bands. Pale midlateral stripe extends from forelimb to middle of tail; bordered above on base of tail by a narrow dark stripe. Ventral surfaces white. This often extends far enough onto flanks to obscure the pale lateral stripe. Black patch on chest of males extends onto forearms. SVL 55 mm.

Distinguished from *C. isolepis* and *C. rubens* by arrangement of preanal pores—curving slightly (vs sharply) forward towards midline—and in attaining smaller maximum size (SVL 55 vs 70 and 80 mm, respectively). Differs from *C. maculatus badius*, and further from *C. isolepis*, by nature of pattern (weak vs strong).

Preferred habitat Restricted to arid midwest coast and hinterland of WA, from North West Cape and Cane River, south to Kennedy Range. Inhabits sand ridges and sand plains vegetated with hummock grasses.

Microhabitat As for species group.

Comments Occurs in sympatry with other members of *C. maculatus* group, and this influences habitat preferences. When *C. rubens* is present (e.g., at Giralia Station in Exmouth Gulf), *C. femoralis* occurs on sparsely vegetated dune crests. Elsewhere it occurs with *C. isolepis isolepis* and *C. maculatus badius* in a variety of open habitats vegetated with shrubs and/or hummock grasses. Otherwise as for species group.

Peninsula Dragon
Ctenophorus fionni (Procter, 1923)
Photos 17–20

Description Member of *C. decresii* group. Males are subject to extensive geographic variation in colour, pattern, and to a lesser extent, size. Females do not vary markedly.

Females and juveniles: Ground colour brown, brownish grey to grey (reddish brown in Gawler Ranges), fading to paler shade of ground colour or cream on lower flanks. Pattern prominent to obscure, including sparse grey to black speckling or heavy mottling over head, body, limbs and tail. This may concentrate on upper flanks, leaving irregular wavy transverse streaks of ground colour. Ventral surfaces whitish; chin and throat streaked, striped or mottled with grey.

Neptune and Wedge Island males: Dorsal ground colour brown, darkening to black on neck, shoulders and flanks. Prominent dark-edged transversely aligned white spots extend between nape and base of tail. Largest race. SVL 95 mm.

Southern males: Dorsal ground colour pale grey; darker on neck and anterior flanks. Pale markings are usually reduced to pale yellow spots along skinfolds on side of neck, and white spots on body; particularly along dorsolateral area. Obscure pale spots may extend across back. SVL 75 mm.

Western males: Similar to southern males, differing in bearing an intense black zone (edged with pale spots) along flanks and sides of neck. SVL 85 mm.

Port Lincoln males: Dorsal ground colour brown, heavily speckled with black. Back and flanks marked with numerous scattered white spots; some edged in black. SVL 75 mm.

Central males: Ground colour black, prominently marked with scattered white spots. These change into orange blotches and spots on shoulders, nape and sides of neck. Head brown, often flushed with orange around eye and ear. Limbs and tail grey. SVL 75 mm.

Northern males: Ground colour brown, merging to blackish brown on neck, shoulders and flanks. Pattern includes irregular spots and blotches. Those on flanks are reddish, and aligned vertically; remainder white or yellow. SVL 90 mm.

Distinguished from *C. decresii* in possessing homogeneous body scales (vs heterogeneous: small pale tubercles on flanks). Differs from *C. vadnappa* in lacking enlarged keeled vertebral scales. Mature males differ further from those of *C. decresii* and *C. vadnappa* in lacking blue pigment.

Preferred habitat Subhumid to arid rocky ranges and outcrops of Eyre Peninsula, adjacent interior of SA, and offshore islands. Neptune and Wedge Island form is restricted to these islands, situated south-east of Eyre Peninsula. Southern form occurs on lower western Eyre Peninsula. Western form extends along north-western Eyre Peninsula (including Isles of St Francis and the Investigator Group). Port Lincoln form occurs on the southern tip of Eyre Peninsula. Central form extends from northeast coast of Eyre Peninsula, north-west to Kokatha Station area on western edge of Lake Gairdner. Northern form occurs in Andamooka ranges, in an area bordered by south-western shoreline of Lake Torrens in east, and Island Lagoon in west.

Microhabitat As for species group.

Comments Striking differences between populations are almost certainly a result of their restriction to rocky areas. Each population is isolated from its neighbour by unsuitable habitat, and little or no gene flow occurs between them. The rock substrates inhabited vary in colour, each type supporting its own distinctive form. Complex territorial displays of males include coiling of tail horizontally or obliquely away from opponent. This is described more fully under species group.

Mallee Dragon
Ctenophorus fordi (Storr, 1965)
Photo 21

Description Member of *C. maculatus* group. Dorsal and upper lateral ground colour reddish brown, yellowish brown, greyish brown to grey, often finely spotted with black and/or white. Laterodorsal series of small black blotches usually extend from nape to hips. Cream to grey dorsolateral stripe extends from nape to hips; usually continuing as an entire or broken line on tail. Upper lateral series of black blotches (aligned with laterodorsal series) extends onto tail, coalescing beyond hips to form dark stripe. Broad pale midlateral stripe (margined below by narrow black stripe) extends from forelimb, through both sides of thigh to tail. Ventral surfaces white. Throats of males marked with black spots or bars. On many populations, some of these spots may coalesce to form V shape. Black transverse bar present on chest, extending onto inner edges of forelimbs. SVL 55 mm.

Distinguished from *C. isolepis* by arrangement of

preanal pores: curving slightly (vs sharply) forward towards midline. Mature males differ further from those of *C. isolepis* by extent of black ventral pigment: largely restricted to throat and chest (vs extending well onto abdomen). Differs from *C. maculatus* by extent of femoral pores; restricted to inner three-quarters of thigh (vs extending full length of thigh), and in bearing spots (vs chevron) on throat.

Preferred habitat Semi-arid to arid regions of southern Australia, extending disjunctly from interior of NSW, through north-western Vic. to Eyre Peninsula of SA, then more or less continuously to southern interior of WA. Favours reddish sand plains and sand ridges vegetated with hummock grasses, usually in association with mallee. In some areas of SA it occurs on dunes supporting canegrass (*Zygochloa*).

Comments Eastern population has been studied in some detail, and aspects of its ecology may apply to other members of species group. Feeds almost exclusively on ants, though other small insects such as flies are also taken. Inactive during winter; males emerging in August, 4–5 weeks prior to females. During reproductive season (from October to January) females display to any males in visual range. Hindquarters and tail are arched off ground exposing cloacal region. Purposes of this are unclear, as it does not appear a prelude to copulation. When mating occurs it is not preceded by ritualised courtship displays. Up to 3 clutches of 2 or 3 eggs are laid per season. These are deposited in burrows situated in open sites clear of shade, and hatch after 7–9 weeks. Lizards appear to live for 1 year, 2 at most. Otherwise as for species group.

Gibber Dragon
Ctenophorus gibba (Houston, 1974)
Photo 22

Description Small member of *C. reticulatus* group with low nuchal crest. Ground colour yellowish brown, pinkish brown, reddish brown to grey. Pattern usually obscure. Series of 6–9 dark grey to black paravertebral spots extend from nape to hips. Similar series may be present on flanks. Remainder of body and basal portions of limbs bear fine dark reticulum or flecking. Side of head bears 3 or 4 prominent to obscure dark oblique lines, radiating from eye to lower lip. Sides of tail bear 20–30 dark squarish blotches from base to tip. Lower flanks, sides of neck and ventral surfaces white. Elongate black blotch present on chin, followed by a larger round blotch on throat, and a large patch on chest. Pale yellow suffusion may be present on anterior chest and shoulders. SVL 80 mm.

Preferred habitat Arid north-eastern interior of SA. Restricted to sparsely vegetated gibber plains.

Microhabitat Shelters in oblique 20–50 cm long burrows in soft soil between stones.

Comments In hot weather activity appears restricted to late afternoon and early evenings. Diet of arthropods (particularly ants) is augmented by small quantities of vegetable material. When alarmed, these dragons inflate their bodies by gulping air. Otherwise as for species group.

Military Dragon
Ctenophorus isolepis (Fischer, 1881)
Photos 23–26

Description Member of *C. maculatus* group comprising 3 subspecies.

C. i. isolepis Ground colour reddish brown, irregularly marked on dorsum with blackish brown dots and dark-edged whitish spots. Laterodorsal series of widely spaced blackish brown spots extends from nape to hips. Dark-edged yellow dorsolateral stripe extends from eye or side of neck onto tail, becoming increasingly obscure and broken beyond hips. Upper flanks enclose a series of large dark brown spots. On males these coalesce to form a broad stripe. Dark-edged pale midlateral stripe extends from snout (males) or shoulder (females) to hindlimbs; breaking on side of tail. Lower flanks ground colour or darker. Limbs bear dark flecks and dark-edged pale spots. Ventral surfaces white. Males bear broad black stripe from chin to middle of abdomen, constricting on throat, and extending on anterior edges of forelimbs. Anterior edges of hindlimbs black. SVL 70 mm.

C. i. gularis (Sternfeld, 1924) Ground colour orange-brown to brick red. Dorsolateral stripe breaks into a series of dark-edged pale spots or elongate blotches at anterior or midbody. Flanks to side of head of adult males are extensively flushed with black. Lips white to yellow. Black throat pigment extends to edge of lower jaw. Remaining ventrolateral surfaces white, sharply contrasting with black lateral flush. SVL 60 mm (males), 65 mm (females).

C. i. citrinus (Storr, 1965) Ground colour dull to bright yellow. Dorsum densely marked with black (males) or dark brown (females) spots and dark-edged pale spots. Dorsolateral stripe breaks into a series of blotches at anterior or midbody. Flanks and side of head extensively flushed with black on breeding males; occasionally extending across snout. Lips yellow. Ventral surfaces similar to nominate race. SVL 50 mm (males), 55 mm (females).

Mature males of *C. i. isolepis* are distinguished from those of *C. rubens* and *C. femoralis* in possessing dark upper lateral zone. Differs further from *C. rubens* in attaining smaller maximum size (SVL 70 vs 80 mm). Mature males differ from *C. maculatus*, *C. fordi*, and further from *C. femoralis* by extent of black ventral pigment—extending well onto abdomen (vs largely restricted to throat and chest)—and by arrangement of preanal pores: curving sharply (vs weakly) forward towards midline.

Preferred habitat Arid western two-thirds of Australia, from north-west coast of WA, through southern half of NT and northern half of SA to far western Qld. *C. i. isolepis* favours reddish sand plains (occasionally stony clay-based soils) supporting low vegetation, particularly hummock grasses. Extends from North West Cape to southern ·and eastern Kimberley region, WA, and through northern interior of NT to western interior of Qld. *C. i. citrinus* is restricted to yellow sand plains supporting heathland/*Triodia* associations in semi-arid southern interior of WA. *C. i. gularis* occupies remainder of range: interior of WA, northern SA and southern NT. Occurs on sand plains and interdunes (occasionally stony slopes) supporting hummock grasses. Also recorded among dead roly-poly bush (*Salsola* sp.).

Comments Aspects of the ecology of *C. i. gularis* have been studied. Though ants comprise bulk of diet, small quantities of vegetable matter and occasional small lizards (one record of a juvenile skink, *Ctenotus pantherinus ocellifer*) are also taken. Lizards are active all year round; during morning and afternoon in summer, and midday in winter. Clutches of 1–6 eggs are recorded, deposited between September and February. Two (possibly 3) clutches may be laid during this period. Hatchlings appear between January and May, growing rapidly to reach sexual maturity at 6–9 months of age. Otherwise as for species group.

Ctenophorus maculatus (Gray, 1831)
Photos 27–31

Description Small member of *C. maculatus* group comprising 4 subspecies.

C. m. maculatus Dorsal and upper lateral ground colour brown, occasionally finely flecked with black. Cream to yellow, dark-edged dorsolateral stripe extends from side of neck well onto tail; becoming paler beyond hips. Short blackish brown bars may break dorsolateral stripe, or contract to form a series of blotches above and below it. Upper blotches extend to hips, and lower series coalesce on tail to form a dark lateral stripe. These alternate with a series of small pale spots. Broad pale grey midlateral stripe extends from neck, through hindlimb onto tail. Black ventrolateral stripe (often broken) extends from forelimb or anterior body, along hindlimb onto base of tail. Ventral surfaces white. Males bear small black patch on chin, spots on lower lips, chevron on throat, and kite-shape on chest. SVL 60 mm.

C. m. griseus (Storr, 1965) Differs from nominate form by larger size, grey colouration and broad (usually broken) dorsolateral stripe, flushed anteriorly with red to orange. Flanks may be blackish brown, obscuring dark upper lateral blotches. Ventral surfaces of males similar to nominate form, though chevron on throat is more angular, and chest patch is anchor-shaped. SVL 65 mm.

C. m. badius (Storr, 1965) Differs from nominate form by smaller size and reddish brown to brick red colouration. Dorsolateral stripe yellow. Black ventrolateral stripe usually continuous. Males bear black chevron on throat and bar (broken or constricted at midline) across chest. SVL 55 mm.

C. m. dualis (Storr, 1965) Differs from all forms by marked sexual dichromatism. Males are similar to *C. m. griseus*. Flanks almost invariably blackish brown, obscuring upper lateral blotches. Ventral surfaces bear narrow (often broken) black stripe along line of jaw, broad chevron on anterior half of throat (often continuous with black stripe extending back to side of neck and arm) and rhomboid-shaped patch on chest.

Females are drab reddish brown with more obscure pattern. SVL 60 mm.

Mature males of all subspecies are distinguished from those of *C. isolepis* and *C. rubens* by extent of black ventral pigment—largely restricted to throat and chest (vs extending well onto abdomen)—and by arrangement of preanal pores: directed slightly (vs sharply) forward towards midline. Differs from *C. fordi* and *C. femoralis* by extent of femoral pores—extending full length of thigh (vs restricted to inner three-quarters of thigh)—and by nature of black pigment on throat: a chevron (vs spots, bars or no pigment).

Preferred habitat Semi-arid to arid southern and midwest coasts and adjacent interior of WA. *C. m. maculatus* occurs on pale coastal dunes and sand plains supporting heathland associations, from Hill River north to Shark Bay. *C. m. badius* occurs further north, on pale coastal sands supporting heathland associations, red dunes vegetated with proteaceous shrubs, and heavy loams vegetated with hummock grasses. Extends from Ningaloo Station, south to Carnarvon, and inland to Doorawarrah and Narryer Stations. *C. m. griseus* inhabits loams and pale sand plains supporting heathlands and woodlands, from Coorow south-east to Hopetoun area. *C. m. dualis* occupies a narrow band of mallee/*Triodia* association on shallow reddish loam over limestone on southern edge of Nullarbor Plain. One record from chenopod shrubland in far south-western SA.

Microhabitat As for species group.

Comments Clutch of 4 eggs recorded for *C. m. griseus*. Otherwise as for species group.

Lake Eyre Dragon
Ctenophorus maculosus (Mitchell, 1948)
Photo 32

Description Small divergent member of *C. reticulatus* group with tympanum completely covered by scales. Ground colour white, very pale grey to pale brown, flecked or finely blotched with black or reddish brown. Prominent dorsolateral series of large roughly circular black blotches extend from nape to hips, fading on base of tail. Lower lips, ventrolateral and ventral surfaces white, bearing a black median streak from chin to gular fold. Mature dominant males develop bright orange-yellow ventrolateral flush, grading to reddish orange toward belly. This extends onto thighs and base of tail, leaving a white midventral area. Submissive males develop pale yellow ventral colouration. Fertilised females develop bright orange-red ventrolateral flush, orange edges to lower jaws, 2 orange patches between forelimbs, and 2 elongate orange patches on flanks. These fade after egg laying. SVL 60 mm (females), 70 mm (males).

Preferred habitat Featureless salt lakes in arid mideastern interior of SA. Occurs on southern shoreline of Lake Eyre North, northern and south-eastern edges of Lake Eyre South, southern end of Lake Callabonna, south through salt channels to northern tip of Lake Frome, and along northern and north-western shorelines of Lake Torrens.

Microhabitat Lizards dwell near margins of salt lakes, burrowing into fine wind-blown sand beneath the buckled salt crust. Elevated rims of ant nests provide shade and perching sites. During periodic flooding, burrows are excavated in sandy shorelines.

Comments Australia's most salt-adapted terrestrial vertebrate. Behaviour has been studied in some detail. Feeds almost exclusively on harvester ants (*Melophorus* sp.), augmented by insects blown onto lake surface. These are also utilised by the ants. During breeding season (September to December) males develop a complex hierarchical system of dominance. Dominant males develop the prominent ventral colours described above. These hold territories of approximately 30 m diameter, centred around an elevated site such as an ant nest or piece of embedded driftwood. Boundaries are recognised to within a metre or so. Encroachment over borders invariably initiates a challenge, in which the intruder almost always loses. Threat displays involve push-ups, frog-like leaps, distension of gular area, opening mouth, and lateral compression of body to increase apparent size and expose bright ventrolateral colours. Physical contact involves tail-lashing, and biting of head or hindlimbs and tail. Subdominant males also develop prominent ventral colours. These males will retreat instantly from a dominant male, establishing a 'pecking order' among themselves. Territories of subdominant males tend to overlap. They usually adjust their emergence so only one is above ground at any given time. Subservient males develop only faint ventral colours and avoid conflicts with all other males, emerging when others are inactive (usually during heat of day). If approached by another male, subservients flatten themselves to the ground in an attempt to hide. If challenged they roll onto their backs in a submissive 'belly-up' posture. Male approach to female commences with series of head-bobs and 'frog-leaps'. Female may indicate unwillingness to mate by waving forelimb, or failing this, rolling onto back. If receptive, she turns away and waits to be mounted. Following fertilisation, prominent ventral colours appear. Clutches of 2–4 eggs are laid in a steeply angled burrow up to 25 cm deep. These hatch after about 70 days, first young appearing in January. Adults live approximately 3–5 years.

Ctenophorus mckenziei (Storr, 1981)
Photo 33

Description Small member of *C. scutulatus* group with low nuchal crest. Ground colour blackish brown; browner on head. Narrow irregular greyish white vertebral stripe extends from nape to base of tail. Broad irregular greyish white to orange-brown dorsolateral stripe extends from eye to base of tail. These stripes are connected by irregular greyish white transverse lines. Upper flanks irregularly spotted with greyish white, or suffused with orange-brown. Irregular greyish white midlateral stripe present. Limbs and tail greyish brown, irregularly marked with fine transverse greyish white lines. Ventral surfaces white, striped with dark grey on female. Male bears dark grey triangular patch on throat and kite-shaped patch on chest. SVL 65 mm.

Distinguished from *C. cristatus* and *C. scutulatus* in possessing a pale vertebral stripe.

Preferred habitat Known from 2 widely spaced localities: near Ponier Rock in semi-arid south-eastern interior of WA, and in the vicinity of Colona Station, south-western SA. Favours chenopod shrublands. In WA these are associated with woodlands.

Microhabitat SA population forages in open spaces between shrubs, sheltering in burrows at their bases.

Comments Little known, though aspects of ecology may be similar to those of *C. scutulatus*.

Central Netted Dragon
Ctenophorus nuchalis (De Vis, 1884)
Photo 34

Description Largest member of *C. reticulatus* group, bearing low nuchal crest. Ground colour pale yellowish brown (often flushed with pale orange on head), marked over head and body with brown, reddish brown to grey reticulum. Narrow vertebral stripe of ground colour extends from nape to hips or base of tail. Ventral surfaces whitish, usually bearing coarse grey reticulum on throat. Breeding males develop bright orange-red flush over head and throat. SVL 115 mm.

Distinguished from *C. reticulatus* by colour of claws (pale vs dark), and number and alignment of femoral and preanal pores: 6–17 arranged in a curve, sweeping forward to anterior thigh (vs 15–28 arranged in a straight line along rear of thigh). Differs from *C. clayi* in attaining much greater size (SVL 115 vs 50 mm) and in lacking a large black patch on side of neck.

Preferred habitat Widespread through semi-arid to arid areas of all mainland States except Vic. Occurs in most open habitats, favouring heavy (occasionally stony) reddish sandy soils.

Microhabitat Excavates shallow burrows in sloping ground, usually at bases of shrubs, hummocks or stumps. These are situated close to favoured basking perches. Several burrows may be situated within home range. Burrows occupied during winter inactivity are plugged with soil.

Comments Extremely heat tolerant. Regulates temperature in hot weather by shuttling between open and shaded perches. A conspicuous element of Australia's desert lizard fauna, due to its abundance, moderately large size, and preference for elevated perching sites. Otherwise as for species group.

Ornate Dragon
Ctenophorus ornatus (Gray, 1845)
Photos 35–39

Description Strongly depressed member of *C. ornatus* group. Adult males are subject to geographic variation in colour and pattern.

Females and juveniles: Ground colour shades of brown, olive-brown to grey, marked with coarse dark marbling over dorsum. This sometimes coalesces to form broad dark vertebral region, and tends to break into blotches on flanks. Vertebral series of large pale brown, pale grey to cream blotches or ocelli usually extend from nape to hips. Approximately 6 or 7 transverse series of small pale dots extend between nape and hips. Lower flanks paler shade of ground colour (in moderate to sharp contrast to upper flanks), enclosing a series of large dark blotches. Dark streak extends from eye to ear. Lips pale grey to whitish, with or without dark bars. Tail obscurely banded with ground colour and pale brown. Ventral surfaces grey to white; streaked with dark grey on throat.

Adult males of southern and western population: Ground colour black, marked with a prominent vertebral series of irregular white, cream to pale grey blotches or clusters of spots from nape to hips. Remainder of dorsal and lateral surfaces bears transverse series of prominent white, pale yellow to pale grey spots. Top of head white, cream to pale grey, sparsely to densely marbled or mottled with black. Limbs prominently spotted and/or banded. Tail marked with prominent black, and white to cream rings. Ventral surfaces greyish white, bearing longitudinally aligned dark spots on throat, a black patch from chest to anterior abdomen, and bright reddish orange ventrolateral flush.

Adult males of wheat-belt form: Ground colour dull to rich reddish brown. Vertebral zone black to dark grey, enclosing small cream to white blotches. Dark pigment may be reduced to broad margins of pale blotches. Remaining dorsal and upper lateral surfaces bear obscure dark streaks or blotches, and

diffuse pale spots. Lower flanks cream to grey, sharply contrasting (and clouded with dark pigment) along junction with ground colour. Head and tail similar to preceding form. Limbs dorsal colour, bearing obscure dark bands or variegations.

Adult males of northern form: Ground colour rich reddish brown, marked with broad dark-edged white to cream vertebral stripe from nape to hips. Remaining dorsal and upper lateral surfaces bear a few diffuse pale dots. Junction of ground colour and pale lower flanks, suffused with blackish brown. Head and tail similar to preceding forms. Limbs grey to pale brown, bearing diffuse pale spots and obscure bands.

Adult males of Hospital Rocks form: Superficially similar to southern and western form. Vertebral blotches extend to outer dorsum as irregular bands; often displaced on either side of vertebral line. Pale pigment on head, limbs and tail is suffused with reddish brown. SVL 90 mm.

Preferred habitat Subhumid to semi-arid south-western interior of WA. Restricted to granite, favouring expanses of bare rock strewn with exfoliations and boulders. Southern and western form occurs in moister parts of range; on dark granites of Darling Range and on south coast (including Gull, Mondrain and Middle Islands, and Archipelago of Recherche). Wheat-belt form occurs on brown to reddish orange outcrops and open granite 'sheets', north to Jibberding Well and Beacon areas. Northern form extends from Paynes Find to Meka, Cue and Sandstone. Melanistic Hospital Rocks form appears restricted to those and adjacent outcrops, situated near Menzies in north-east of range.

Microhabitat See species group.

Comments Granite outcrops are conspicuous features of south-western landscapes. Because of their location and characteristics they act as islands, supporting distinctive floral and faunal components on and around them. Populations of *C. ornatus* are restricted to these outcrops, and little or no gene flow occurs between them. As a result, different colour forms have evolved. The situation is paralleled by most members of the *C. decresii* group, which have been subject to even greater fragmentation. Curiously, females of all species undergo little change.

Males defend prime elevated territories against other males, though movements of females are unimpeded. Juveniles are actively chased, resulting in the formation of 'juvenile areas' situated at bases of, or near, outcrops. Courting behaviour begins in November, followed by egglaying in December. Clutches of 2 or 3 eggs are probably deposited in deep burrows beneath boulders around edges of outcrop. Juveniles hatch between January and late March. They fall into 2 categories: fast-growers (which tend to be cold resistant, drought sensitive and short-lived) and slow-growers (cold sensitive, drought resistant and long-lived). At about 2 years of age these sexually mature adults take up residence on the open granites, displacing new juveniles to the peripheral habitats they have just vacated. Predation during transition periods is high, particularly from birds of prey. As a result individuals keep a sharp watch above them. Lizards feed on a broad range of arthropods, particularly ants (*Iridomyrmex* spp.). In spring, diet may be augmented by small quantities of flowers from *Borya nitida*, a low prickly granite-adapted plant.

Painted Dragon
Ctenophorus pictus (Peters, 1866)
Photos 40, 41

Description Highly variable member of *C. pictus* group, with low nuchal crest and erectable vertebral ridge of enlarged scales. Sexually dichromatic.

Males: Ground colour grey, brown, yellowish brown to reddish brown or orange; fading on lower flanks. Broad bluish grey vertebral stripe (broken by alternating black, and dark-edged white or yellow bars, blotches or spots) extends from nape to hips. On some individuals this may be black, broken with white. Remainder of body usually bears irregular transverse series of dark-edged pale spots (often coalesced to form bars), alternating with broken black bars, spots or variegations. Head ground colour or paler, often flushed with pale orange to yellow. Ventral surfaces white, bearing narrow black triangle on throat, and kite-shaped patch on chest. Breeding males develop striking blue vertebral stripe, and blue flush over lower lips, chin, throat, limbs, ventrolateral surfaces and tail. Anterior chest and shoulders flushed with bright yellow to orange.

Females and juveniles are duller, lacking blue and bright yellow pigment. Ventral surfaces whitish, mottled with grey on throat and chest. SVL 65 mm.

Distinguished from *C. salinarum* by nature of dorsal scales (homogeneous, vs heterogeneous: mixed with transverse rows of large smooth scales), and presence of prominent blue and yellow male breeding colouration.

Preferred habitat Semi–arid to arid southern Australia, from north-western NSW, to central Qld and southern NT, through SA (excepting far south-east and Kangaroo Island) to south-eastern WA. Most abundant in chenopod-dominated shrublands and margins of salt lakes, though also common in open mallee/*Triodia* associations, and sand ridges supporting shrubs and hummock grasses or cane-grass (*Zygochloa* sp.)

Microhabitat Excavates a shallow burrow at the base of a shrub or grass hummock, favouring soil-bound root systems from which adjacent substrate has been eroded. In some areas, large burrows excavated by monitor lizards, rabbits or wombats are utilised.

Comments Strongly patterned breeding males are

among Australia's most colourful lizards. Males have been observed to engage in combat during March. Nuchal crest and vertebral ridge are erected, throat is distended, and body is held high off ground; presenting broadest lateral aspect to opponent. This may be accompanied by tail-lashing. If biting occurs it is centred on the head. Head-bobbing (a significant component in most dragons' social behaviour) was barely discernible during an observed confrontation. Otherwise as for species group.

Western Netted Dragon
Ctenophorus reticulatus (Gray, 1845)
Photos 42, 43

Description Large member of *C. reticulatus* group with low nuchal crest. Subject to sexual and ontogenetic variation in pattern.

Juveniles: Ground colour olive-grey, yellowish to reddish brown. A series of blackish paravertebral spots alternate with transverse rows of small whitish spots between nape and hips. Remainder of head, body and limbs is variegated to flecked with blackish brown. Tail barred with dark brown.

Females and subadults: Similar in colour to juveniles. Whitish transverse rows of spots usually disappear. Dorsolateral series of elongate dark-edged grey blotches extend from nape to hips. Upper lateral series of small dark blotches may be present. Remainder of dorsum irregularly variegated with blackish brown. Bands on base of tail become obscure as pale interspaces darken. Ventral surfaces whitish, bearing coarse dark reticulum on throat.

Males: Ground colour tends to become redder. Narrow pale vertebral stripe often extends from nape to hips. Remainder of head and body prominently marked with black reticulum. Head paler shade of ground colour to yellow or white. Limbs suffused with dark grey. Distal portion of tail banded; remainder grey. Throat yellowish. Breeding males develop deep red ground colour, and reddish flush on chin and throat. SVL 105 mm.

Distinguished from *C. nuchalis* by colour of claws (dark vs pale), and number and alignment of femoral pores (15–28 aligned along rear edge of thigh vs 6 or 7 arranged in a curve, sweeping forward to anterior thigh). Differs from *C. clayi* in attaining much greater maximum size (SVL 105 vs 50 mm), and in lacking a large black patch on side of neck.

Preferred habitat Arid and semi-arid regions from midwest coast, through central and southern interior of WA to western interior of SA. Favours heavy reddish (often stony) soils supporting *Acacia*-dominated woodlands or shrublands over sparse low ground cover.

Microhabitat Excavates shallow burrow or depression beneath rocks or logs, and at bases of shrubs. Occasionally encountered beneath exfoliations of granite, on or adjacent to outcrops. See species group.

Comments Similar in most respects to *C. nuchalis*. See species group.

Ctenophorus rubens (Storr, 1965)
Photo 44

Description Largest member of *C. maculatus* group, subject to sexual variation in pattern.

Females: Ground colour dark reddish brown, sparsely dotted with brown over dorsal (and sometimes lateral) surfaces. These are mixed with dark-edged white spots or transversely elongate bars. Narrow broken white to pale yellowish brown dorsolateral and midlateral stripes commence on nape and forebody respectively, and extend onto tail. Limbs spotted with white and dotted with brown.

Males: Pinkish brown, flushed with brown on head, and reddish brown on tail. Pattern obscure to virtually absent. Indications of dark and pale spots, and pale dorsolateral stripe are usually discernible. Sides of head and neck flushed with yellow to red. Ventral surfaces white, extensively marked with black (more so than on other members of *C. maculatus* group) over throat, chest, undersurfaces of limbs, abdomen, and sometimes vent. SVL 80 mm.

Mature males are distinguished from those of *C. maculatus badius* and *C. femoralis* by extent of black ventral pigment (covering most of ventral surfaces vs largely restricted to throat and chest), and by alignment of preanal pores (curving sharply forward towards midline vs curving weakly forward). Differs from *C. isolepis*, and further from *C. m. badius*, in bearing weak (vs strong) adult pattern. Differs further from all in attaining greater maximum size. (SVL 80 vs 70 mm or less).

Preferred habitat Arid Exmouth Gulf and adjacent interior of WA. Extends from Onslow south to Mardathuna, Yalobia and Gnaraloo Stations, and inland to Gascoyne Junction. Isolated population occurs south of Hamelin Pool. At Giralia Station, interdunes vegetated with hummock grasses are inhabited, while *C. femoralis* occupies adjacent sparsely vegetated dune crests. Gascoyne Junction population occurs in sympatry with *C. m. badius* on red dunes vegetated with proteaceous shrubs. Population south of Hamelin Pool inhabits reddish sand plains supporting mallee/*Triodia* associations.

Microhabitat As for species group.

Comments As for species group.

Rusty Dragon
Ctenophorus rufescens
(Stirling and Zeitz, 1893)
Photo 45

Description Strongly depressed, somewhat divergent member of *C. decresii* group.

Females and juveniles: Ground colour reddish brown, blotched with blackish brown. Irregular paravertebral blotches tend to coalesce, forming transverse bars. Irregular upper lateral series tends to align longitudinally, and a lower lateral series aligns vertically. Head and remainder of dorsal and lateral surfaces are sparsely marked with dark speckling and mottling. Lips may bear dark bars. Limbs and tail banded or marbled with dark pigment. Ventral surfaces white, bearing a grey reticulum on throat.

Males are suffused with pinkish brown. Pattern virtually absent. Obscure blotches may be present on flanks. Bands are usually present on limbs and sides of tail. Ventral surfaces white, marked with a dark reticulum on throat. Diffuse grey patch may be present on chest. SVL 90 mm.

Preferred habitat Granite outcrops and ranges in arid interior of north-western SA, south-western NT and adjacent WA.

Microhabitat As for species group.

Comments Poorly known. Closely resembles *C. ornatus* in form, and in its preference for open expanses of granite. Differs markedly from members of *C. ornatus* group in lacking prominent caudal rings on mature males. Divergent from other members of *C. decresii* group, lacking the vivid contrasting colours on mature males. Absence of strong pattern may indicate differences in social structure. See species group.

Salt Lake Dragon
Ctenophorus salinarum (Storr, 1966)
Photo 46

Description Member of *C. pictus* group with ground colour of greyish to reddish brown. Transverse series of dark-edged pale spots (usually coalesced to form bars across vertebral region) extend between nape and hips. These alternate with dark blotches (usually including a paravertebral series), mottling or variegations. Limbs marked with pale spots and dark variegations. Tail bears obscure pale bands. Ventral surfaces white to pale yellow. Breeding males develop pale orange flush on side of head, yellow wash on forelimbs and lower flanks, dark grey median strip on throat, and a dark patch on chest, extending narrowly back to anterior abdomen. SVL 70 mm.

Distinguished from *C. pictus* by nature of body scales (heterogeneous—mixed with enlarged smooth scales aligned transversely—vs homogeneous), and absence of blue or bright yellow pigment on breeding males.

Preferred habitat Arid to semi-arid southwestern interior of WA. Largely associated with chenopod shrublands margining salt lakes in north and west of range. Southwards and eastwards this vegetation type is more continuous (often associated with woodlands) and it occurs throughout it, extending into adjacent sandy heathlands.

Microhabitat Shelters in burrows at bases of low shrubs.

Comments Females containing well–developed eggs recorded in September. Otherwise as for species group.

Lozenge-marked Dragon
Ctenophorus scutulatus
(Stirling and Zeitz, 1893)
Photo 47

Description Member of *C. scutulatus* group with well-developed nuchal crest. Ground colour pale reddish brown to greyish brown. Pattern variable; most prominent anteriorly, and usually overlaid with dark vermiculations. Series of short dark brown to black transverse bars extend across nape and forebody, tending to fade and break into paravertebral blotches posteriorly. These may alternate with narrow pale transverse lines, particularly on juveniles. Broad pale-edged orange to grey dorsolateral stripe (usually constricted to form a series of dark-centred lozenge-shaped blotches on adults) extends from nape to base of tail. Broad dark-edged pale midlateral stripe may be present. Limbs and tail marked with narrow pale bands. Ventral surfaces pale orange-brown. Breeding males bear a broad black stripe on throat and a black patch on chest, extending narrowly onto forelimbs and abdomen. SVL 115 mm.

Distinguished from *C. mckenziei* in lacking a pale vertebral stripe. Differs from *C. cristatus* by nature of nuchal crest (weak vs strong), and in absence of dorsolateral ridge of enlarged scales. Differs further in bearing less black pigment on ventral surfaces of breeding males, and in absence of broad contrasting bands on tail.

Preferred habitat Arid to semi-arid central and southern interior of WA, extending to north-western SA. Favours hard to stony soils supporting *Acacia*-dominated woodlands, and shrublands including chenopods.

Microhabitat Forages in open areas and among debris accumulated at bases of shrubs, occasionally ascending fallen timber or bases of tree trunks to bask.

Comments Feeds largely on termites and ants, though a variety of other arthropods are taken. Clutches of 5–10 eggs are probably laid during February. One of Australia's swiftest dragons. See species group.

Red-barred Dragon
Ctenophorus vadnappa (Houston, 1974)
Photo 48

Description Member of *C. decresii* group bearing enlarged series of keeled scales along vertebral line; reduced on females.

Females and juveniles: Ground colour reddish brown to greyish brown, flecked and mottled with dark grey to black over head, body, limbs and tail. Dark pigment tends to concentrate on flanks, forming irregular vertical bars. Upper lip paler shade of ground colour. Ventral surfaces greyish white, marked with grey stripes on chin and throat.

Males: Ground colour black, bearing broad bluish grey to blue vertebral stripe from nape to hips. Remainder of dorsal and lateral surfaces prominently marked with red to reddish orange blotches and spots, aligned to form vertical bars. Lower flanks may bear a series of bright yellow blotches. Head bluish grey to brown. Limbs and tail bluish grey to blue. Hindlimbs and base of tail may be obscurely banded. Ventral surfaces greyish white, marked with bluish grey on chest and beneath limbs, bright yellow on anterior chest and gular region, and bluish grey stripes on throat. SVL 85 mm.

Distinguished from *C. decresii* and *C. fionni* in possessing an enlarged series of keeled vertebral scales. Differs further from *C. decresii* by nature of body scales (homogeneous, vs heterogeneous: mixed with minute pale tubercles on flanks).

Preferred habitat Rocky outcrops and ranges, particularly sparsely vegetated scree slopes, in semi-arid to arid northern Flinders Ranges, hills north of Lake Torrens, and Peak-Denison Ranges west of Lake Eyre, SA. Slightly divergent isolated population occurs on gibber-strewn hills north-east of Oodnadatta, SA.

Microhabitat As for species group.

Comments Breeding males are among Australia's most strikingly coloured lizards. Complex display sequence by rival males includes coiling of tail vertically. This is described more fully under species group.

Yinnietharra Rock Dragon
Ctenophorus yinnietharra (Storr, 1981)
Photo 49

Description Member of *C. ornatus* group.

Adult males: Ground colour reddish brown, suffused (and largely obscured) over all but vertebral region with bluish grey to greyish olive. Obscure dark grey marbling usually extends over head, neck, back and upper flanks. Dark streak extends from eye to ear, and a dark patch is usually present on side of neck. Basal third of tail ground colour, bearing obscure narrow greyish bands. Remainder orange-brown, pinkish to cream, prominently marked with 3 or 4 broad black rings. Ventral surfaces pale yellowish brown to pale orange-brown, often marked with brownish grey stippling on chest.

Females and juveniles: dull reddish to greyish brown, obscurely blotched with dark grey. Obscure indication of narrow irregular pale vertebral line and transverse dorsal lines may also be discernible. Limbs and proximal third of tail obscurely marked with dark bands. SVL 85 mm.

Preferred habitat Known only from low fragmented granite outcrops surrounded by coarse gibbers and sparse *Acacia* shrublands on Yinnietharra Station, in arid central-western interior of WA.

Microhabitat Basks on low rocks and *Acacia* limbs. Shelters in crevices, burrows, or hollow timber.

Comments Extremely wary. When approached dashes for cover; sometimes for considerable distances over open gibber. Males have been recorded to lash their conspicuous tails when females or other males are present. Otherwise as for species group.

Genus *DIPORIPHORA* Gray, 1842

Large genus containing 14 described species. Greatest diversity occurs in subhumid to semi-arid northern Australia; a few species extend into arid southern interior. One species is extralimital in southern New Guinea.

Small to medium-sized, moderate to extremely slender dragons with relatively narrow heads, moderate to very long limbs, and long slender tails. Nuchal and dorsal series of enlarged scales weak to absent. Tympanum exposed. A pair of prominent sharp teeth present at front of upper and lower jaws. Body scales usually homogeneous, most bearing strong to weak keels. Femoral pores usually absent (occasionally 1 on each side; rarely 2). Preanal pores usually present (up to 3 on each side).

Pattern often includes grey vertebral and cream dorsolateral stripes; usually bisecting dark transverse dorsal bars. Large dark patch may be present on anterior flanks, above forelimb. Males of some species (e.g., *D. magna*) display seasonal breeding colouration. Many or all aspects of pattern may disappear with age, hence this does not always provide a reliable clue to identification. Many species require close examination to determine the presence and strength of gular, scapular and postauricular folds. When weak, these may be indicated by a sharp change in scale-size.

Predominantly terrestrial (one species is entirely arboreal) though most ascend rocks, low vegetation or fallen timber to bask. Body stripes are often aligned with foliage, providing effective camouflage. Most are not particularly swift (relative to other dragons), scuttling on all 4 limbs to cover of shrubs or grasses when disturbed. Arthropod feeders.

Distinguished from *Gemmatophora* by nature of nuchal ridge (weak to absent vs prominent; usually forming a crest), and in usually lacking a vertebral ridge (vs vertebral scales enlarged, forming a ridge or low crest). Differs further in attaining smaller maximum size (SVL 90 mm or less vs usually 90 mm or greater). Differs from *Ctenophorus* in lacking a series of enlarged scales curving from below eye to above ear. Differs further (excepting *Diporiphora convergens*) by alignment of keels on dorsal scales:

parallel with (vs converging towards) midline.

Diporiphora albilabris Storr, 1974
Photos 50, 51

Description Robust short-limbed *Diporiphora* with moderately strong gular fold and very strong postauricular fold. Scapular fold weak to absent. Dorsal scales heterogeneous; an enlarged strongly keeled series just outside paravertebral row, and an enlarged, strongly keeled, and slightly raised dorsolateral series. Two subspecies recognised. These may constitute distinct species.

D. a. albilabris Dorsal ground colour brown to reddish brown. Obscure narrow grey vertebral stripe usually extends from nape to base of tail. Pale dorsolateral stripe (boldest and whitest anteriorly) extends from above ear to hips, breaking on base of tail. Body marked with 5 or 6 broad dark brown bars (interrupted by dorsolateral and vertebral stripes) between nape and hips. Flanks blackish brown, sometimes marked with white and pale brown dots. White stripe extends from upper and lower lips to side of neck; margined above by a blackish streak. Limbs and tail barred with brown. Ventral surfaces (from chest to beneath limbs and tail) orange. This is possibly a seasonal breeding character. Throat white, marked with 2 or 3 grey chevrons. SVL 55 mm.

D. a. sobria Storr, 1974 Differs from nominate form in virtually lacking pattern. Ground colour reddish brown. Dorsolateral stripe and dark bars weak to absent. White labial stripe absent.

Distinguished from all sympatric *Diporiphora* by build (robust vs relatively more slender), and (excepting *D. bilineata*) by nature of scales (an enlarged, slightly raised series along dorsolateral line). Differs further from *D. bilineata* in possessing a gular fold.

Preferred habitat *D. a. albilabris* occurs in grassy woodlands and rocky areas of subhumid north-western Kimberley region, WA. *D. a. sobria* occurs on rocky hills in subhumid north-western interior of NT.

Microhabitat Shelters beneath rocks or logs. See genus.

Comments As for genus.

Diporiphora arnhemica Storr, 1974
Photo 52

Description Moderately slender *Diporiphora* with weak gular and scapular folds, and strong postauricular fold. Ground colour brown, dark greyish brown to pale grey. Narrow grey vertebral stripe sometimes present. Narrow pale grey to white dorsolateral stripe extends from nape onto tail; sometimes breaking into dashes beyond hips. Series of approximately 8 or 9, prominent to obscure dark reddish brown to dark brown bands (broken by dorsolateral and vertebral stripes) may extend between nape and hips; fading and breaking on flanks. Pale midlateral stripe may extend between forelimb and hindlimb. Lower flanks pale grey, pale brown to white; uniform or bearing obscure dark markings. Top of head may bear dark speckling. Pale streak usually extends from eye to top of ear. Lips pale grey to white. Limbs and tail uniform or obscurely marked with dark grey bands. Ventral surfaces pale grey to white. Throat often longitudinally streaked with grey. SVL 60 mm.

Distinguished from *D. bennettii* and *D. lalliae* in possessing a femoral pore. Differs further from *D. bennettii* by alignment of posterior lateral scales (parallel with midline vs curving upwards and backwards). Differs from *D. albilabris* by nature of dorsal scales (homogeneous, vs heterogeneous: those along dorsolateral line enlarged and slightly raised), and build (relatively slender vs robust). Differs from *D. magna* and *D. bilineata* in possessing a gular fold. Differs further from *D. bilineata* in possessing a postauricular fold, and further from *D. lalliae* by nature of gular fold (weak vs strong).

Preferred habitat Subhumid to semi-arid western half of far northern Australia, from Mt Percy in south-western Kimberley region, WA, to Arnhem Land Plateau, NT. Favours woodlands over ground cover of spear grass or hummock grasses. Usually occurs in association with sandstone outcrops.

Microhabitat As for genus.

Comments As for genus.

Tommy Roundhead
Diporiphora australis (Steindachner, 1867)
Photo 53

Description Moderately robust *Diporiphora* with gular, scapular, and spiny postauricular folds. Vertebral (and occasionally dorsolateral) ridge of enlarged scales present.

Ground colour grey, greyish brown, yellowish brown to reddish brown. Grey to pale brown vertebral stripe usually extends from nape to hips. Cream, yellow, brown to grey dorsolateral stripe extends from nape to base, or well onto tail; often converging with its opposite posteriorly. Series of brown to dark brown or grey bars extend between nape and hips; broken by vertebral stripe. These are subject to considerable variation: broad, prominent and rectangular, to narrow and triangular (broadest face abutting vertebral stripe). Upper flanks patternless, marked with obscure extensions of dorsal bands, or lightly to heavily flecked with paler pigment. Dark patch often present on shoulder, below dorsolateral stripe. Pale midlateral stripe dark-edged and prominent, to weak or absent. This extends forward from hindlimb, rarely reaching forelimb. Lower flanks ground colour to white. Head ground colour or paler; often bearing a broad pale to dark bar from eye to corner of mouth. Limbs and tail marked with obscure dark bands. Ventral surfaces

pale yellow to white, often sparsely to densely flecked with dark brown to grey. SVL 50 mm.

Distinguished from *D. bilineata* by nature of gular, scapular and postauricular folds (strong vs weak to absent). Differs from *D. magna* in possessing a gular fold. Differs from *D. lalliae* by build (relatively more robust), and nature of dorsal scales (heterogeneous—an enlarged dorsolateral series— vs homogeneous).

Preferred habitat Dry sclerophyll forests, woodlands, shrublands and margins of vine thickets, on coast (including many offshore islands) and eastern interior of Qld. Extends from Brisbane area, north to Cape York Peninsula, and west to Gulf of Carpentaria.

Microhabitat As for genus.

Comments As for genus.

Diporiphora bennettii (Gray, 1845)
Photo 54

Description Large, moderately robust *Diporiphora* with weak gular fold, strong spiny postauricular fold, and weak to absent scapular fold. Low nuchal crest present. Ground colour reddish brown, brown to greyish brown. Pattern usually present on juveniles and subadults; obscure to absent on adults. Narrow to moderately broad grey to greyish brown vertebral stripe usually extends from nape to hips. Cream, yellow, grey to brown dorsolateral stripe (most prominent anteriorly) extends from nape or eye onto base of tail; breaking into dashes beyond hips. Obscure dark brown to dark grey bars (broken by vertebral stripe) extend between nape and hips. Upper flanks ground colour, sometimes bearing obscure extensions of dorsal bars. Indication of pale midlateral stripe may be present. Lower flanks ground colour, often spotted to flecked with yellow to white. Top of head uniform, or bears obscure dark markings. Pale streak may extend from eye to ear. Adults usually bear a large black patch above forelimb. Breeding males develop an orange flush over head, chest, hips, hindlimbs and base of tail, and a greenish yellow flush on flanks. Ventral surfaces white, streaked with grey on throat. SVL 80 mm.

Distinguished from *D. convergens* by alignment of keels on dorsal scales (parallel to midline vs sharply converging on midline). Differs from *D. albilabris* by nature of dorsal scales (homogeneous, vs heterogeneous: an enlarged, slightly raised dorsolateral series). Differs from *D. bilineata* and sympatric populations of *D. lalliae* by nature of postauricular fold (strong and spiny vs absent to weak). Differs from *D. arnhemica* by alignment of posterior lateral scales (converging toward midline vs parallel with midline). Differs from *D. pindan* and *D. magna* in possessing a weak gular fold (vs absent).

Preferred habitat Extends from subhumid northern Kimberley region, WA, to adjacent NT. Largely

associated with rocky areas, particularly sandstones.
Microhabitat As for genus.
Comments As for genus.

Two-lined Dragon
Diporiphora bilineata Gray, 1842
Photo 55

Description Gular fold absent to very weak. Scapular and postauricular folds absent. Low nuchal ridge may be present. Ground colour shades of grey, yellowish brown, brown to reddish brown. Pattern prominent to virtually absent. Narrow pale grey vertebral stripe may extend from nape to hips. Narrow white to yellow dorsolateral stripes extend from nape well onto tail, often breaking and/or converging beyond hips. Series of 6–9 dark brown, grey to black bars (often with pale margins) usually extend across back; broken by vertebral stripe (if present). These are usually broadest at contact with vertebral stripe. Upper lateral zone ground colour or paler, sometimes bearing prominent to obscure (often fragmented) extensions of dorsal bars. Dark blotch often present on shoulder, below dorsolateral stripe. Narrow (often dark-edged) white, pale grey to yellow midlateral stripe often present, extending forward from hindlimb, nearly to forelimb. Lower flanks paler to darker shade of ground colour, usually bearing pale flecks. Top of head uniform or speckled with pale pigment. Pale-edged dark band often extends between eyes. One or more pale-edged dark streaks may extend from eye, to ear or corner of mouth. Tail uniform, banded, or marked with broken extensions of dorsolateral stripes (each segment dark-edged).

Weakly patterned individuals tend to retain some indication of dorsolateral stripes. Some may be marked only with small and sparse, dark-edged pale spots. Ventral surfaces white to pale yellow, often bearing narrow dark lines from throat to vent. Mature males of some Qld populations develop a black flush on throat. SVL 60 mm.

Distinguished from *D. albilabris*, *D. australis*, *D. bennettii*, *D. arnhemica* and *D. lalliae* in lacking a gular fold; occasionally very weak (vs present). Differs from *D. magna*, and further from *D. australis*, *D. bennettii* and *D. arnhemica*, in lacking a postauricular fold (vs present and strong).
Preferred habitat Extends across subhumid northern Australia, from western NT, to Gin Gin area, Qld. Occurs in a wide variety of vegetation types, favouring woodlands and sandy coastlines.
Microhabitat Frequently shelters in short shallow burrows. Otherwise as for genus.
Comments As for genus.

Diporiphora convergens Storr, 1974

Description Small, slender long-limbed *Diporiphora* with strong gular and scapular folds. Postau-

ricular fold absent. Ground colour brown. Pattern obscure, comprising a series of faint narrow dark bars; widely broken at midline. Edges of eyelids white. SVL 34 mm.

Distinguished from all other *Diporiphora* by nature of keels on dorsal scales: converging back toward (vs parallel with) midline.
Preferred habitat Known only from Crystal Creek on Admiralty Gulf in north-western Kimberley region, WA.

Microhabitat No data available.
Comments Known only from one specimen. See genus.

Diporiphora lalliae Storr, 1974
Photo 56

Description Moderately large slender *Diporiphora* with strong gular fold and weak to moderately strong scapular fold. Postauricular fold moderately strong and spinose throughout most of range; becoming weak in Kimberley region. Low nuchal ridge present in south and west of range. Dorsal ground colour pale brown to reddish brown, with or without prominent pattern. Broad grey vertebral stripe extends from nape to hips. Narrow white to cream dorsolateral stripe extends from eye or ear onto tail, becoming broken beyond hips. Series of short rectangular dark brown bars (interrupted by vertebral stripe) extends between nape and base of tail. Upper flanks bear obscure extensions of dorsal bars, and occasionally a dark anterior patch. Obscure pale midlateral stripe may be present; most prominent posteriorly. Lower flanks grey, sometimes bearing paler and darker flecks. Top of head uniform or marked with sparse dark flecks. Anterior half of tail marked with obscure dark blotches on either side of dorsolateral stripe; remainder uniform. Weakly patterned individuals bear only a few scattered dark and pale flecks over dorsal and lateral surfaces. Breeding males tend to develop a pink flush on lateral surfaces of tail. Ventral surfaces whitish; often streaked with grey, particularly beneath throat. SVL 75 mm.

Distinguished from *D. bennettii*, *D. arnhemica*, *D. bilineata*, *D. magna*, *D. pindan* and *D. winneckei* by nature of gular fold (strong vs weak to absent). Differs further from *D. pindan* and *D. winneckei* in possessing a postauricular fold. Differs further from *D. bennettii* by pattern (when present): vertebral stripe is broader, and dorsal bars sharper. Differs from *D. australis* by nature of dorsal scales (homogeneous, vs heterogeneous: an enlarged dorsolateral series).

Preferred habitat Subhumid to arid north-western interior of Australia, from Derby area, WA through southern NT to Mt Isa district, Qld. Favours woodlands with ground cover dominated by hummock grasses on heavy to stony soils.

Microhabitat Shelters beneath grass hummocks. See genus.

Comments As for genus.

Diporiphora linga Houston, 1977
Photo 57

Description Moderately slender *Diporiphora* with well-developed gular and scapular folds. Postauri-cular fold absent. Low nuchal ridge occasionally present. Sexually dichromatic.

Males: Ground colour pale yellowish brown to greyish brown. Narrow white to yellow dorsolater-al stripes extend from nape, well onto tail; converg-ing on base. Series of 6–9 obscure and irregular dark brown blotches or short bars may be present; broken by dorsolateral stripe. Remainder of dorsum usually immaculate, occasionally marked with small dark flecks. Irregular pale midlateral stripe may be present; most prominent posteriorly. Remaining lateral surfaces may be speckled with dark brown, and obscurely blotched with paler pigment. Dark-edged pale streak extends from eye to top of ear. Narrow dark brown line extends from eye to snout. Lips whitish. Breeding males develop bright pink flush over flanks, sides of tail, vent and inner thighs. Dorsolateral stripes become bright yellow. Ventral surfaces white to grey (almost invariably white on throat) marked with dark-edged ocelli. SVL 50 mm.

Females: Similar to males though larger, and bearing more dark pigment. Dorsolateral blotches invariably present; prominent. Body and limbs more heavily flecked with dark pigment. Midlateral stripe dark-edged. SVL 60 mm.

Distinguished from *D. winneckei* in lacking a vertebral stripe, and bearing ocellated (vs striped) ventral surfaces. Breeding males differ further in bearing pinkish lateral flush. Differs further by build: moderately (vs very) slender.

Preferred habitat Sand ridges vegetated with mallee/*Triodia* associations in semi-arid to arid southern-central interior of SA; from near Mara-linga to Wirrulla and Gawler Ranges.

Microhabitat Usually encountered basking on *Triodia* hummocks, taking shelter in them if dis-turbed.

Comments Males develop breeding colouration during spring. Captive individuals observed buried in loose sand when torpid. Otherwise as for genus.

Diporiphora magna Storr, 1974
Photo 58

Description Large *Diporiphora* with weak to moderately strong scapular fold, spiny postauricular fold, and no gular fold. Low nuchal ridge present. Ground colour yellowish brown, brown, brownish grey to olive-green. Pattern usually prominent on juveniles and subadults; obscure to absent on adults. Narrow to moderately broad pale grey vertebral, and narrow white dorsolateral stripes, extend from nape to base of tail. Series of narrow rectangular dark brown bars (broken by vertebral stripe) extend between nape and hips. Pale dots and indication of pale midlateral stripe may be present; most promin-ent posteriorly. Top of head may be speckled, and lips obscurely barred, with darker pigment. Limbs and tail uniform or marked with obscure dark bands. Adults bear prominent dark patch on ante-rior flanks, and occasionally some indication of dorsolateral stripe; often restricted to anterior body. Ventral surfaces white to bright yellow. SVL 85 mm.

Distinguished from *D. convergens* by alignment of dorsal keels (parallel to midline vs converging on midline). Differs from *D. albilabris* by nature of dorsal scales (homogeneous, vs heterogeneous: dorsolateral series enlarged and slightly raised). Dif-fers further from both, and from *D. australis*, *D. bennettii*, *D. arnhemica* and *D. lalliae*, in lacking a gular fold (vs present). Differs from *D. pindan* and *D. bilineata* in bearing a spiny postauricular fold (vs absent). Differs further from all in attaining greater size (SVL 85 vs 80 mm or less).

Preferred habitat Favours grassy woodlands on heavy soils in subhumid northern Australia; from Kimberley region, WA, through northern NT to far north-western Qld.

Microhabitat As for genus.

Comments As for genus.

Diporiphora pindan Storr, 1979
Photo 59

Description Moderately slender *Diporiphora* with very weak scapular fold. Gular and postauricular folds absent. Ground colour pale to moderately dark reddish brown. Pattern usually prominent, though patternless individuals of all ages occur. Moderately broad grey vertebral stripe extends from nape to hips. Narrow grey to white dorsolateral stripe ex-tends from nape onto base of tail, tending to break into dashes beyond hips. Approximately 8 irregular blackish brown bars extend between nape and hips; broken (and often slightly displaced) by vertebral stripe. Upper lateral zone may be marked with obscure (often broader) extensions of dorsal bars. Indication of pale midlateral stripe usually present, extending forward from hindlimb to anterior flanks or forelimb. Lower flanks white to dark grey, spot-ted with white. Pale streak extends from eye to top of ear. Lips grey to white, often margined above by a dark streak from eye to snout. Base of tail bears obscure continuation of dorsal pattern; remainder obscurely banded. Ventral surfaces white, occasionally bearing 5 or 6 grey stripes on throat. SVL 60 mm.

Distinguished from *D. bennettii* and *D. lalliae* in lacking a gular fold (vs present). Differs further from *D. bennettii* by build (moderately slender vs robust). Differs from *D. magna* in lacking a postauricular fold (vs present and spiny). Differs from *D. winneckei* by nature of gular scales (keeled vs smooth), pattern (vertebral stripe narrower), and build (moderately slender vs very slender).

Preferred habitat Subhumid to semi-arid southwestern Kimberley region, WA, east to Fitzroy Crossing. Favours low grassy woodlands supporting *Acacia*-dominated thickets on reddish sandy soils (this habitat is known as 'Pindan'), extending into sparsely vegetated interdunes. In contrast *D. winneckei* (sympatric in south-east of range) favours sand ridge habitats.

Microhabitat As for genus.

Comments As for genus.

Diporiphora reginae Glauert, 1959
Photo 60

Description Moderately robust *Diporiphora*. Gular fold present. Scapular fold weak to absent. Postauricular fold absent. Ground colour brown to reddish brown, lacking dorsal pattern. White to yellow dorsolateral stripe usually extends from nape, well onto tail. Flanks may be flecked with brownish white. Head ground colour or paler. Eyelids and lips whitish. Breeding males develop bright orange-red flush on sides of tail-base. Ventral surfaces white. SVL 70 mm.

Distinguished from *D. winneckei* in lacking grey vertebral and ventral stripes, and by build (moderately robust vs very slender).

Preferred habitat Restricted to sandy *Triodia*/heathland associations in arid central-southern interior of WA; from Goddard Creek south-west to Fraser Range.

Microhabitat Basks on *Triodia* hummocks, sheltering in them when disturbed.

Comments As for genus.

Diporiphora superba Storr, 1974
Photo 61

Description Large extremely slender *Diporiphora* with very long slender limbs, digits and tail. Gular, scapular and postauricular folds absent. Ground colour pale lime green to greenish yellow. Broad pale reddish brown vertebral zone may extend from nape to hips. Prominent lemon yellow blotch present on anterior flanks. Remainder of lateral surfaces uniform, or with obscure vertically aligned dark variegations. Ventral surfaces yellow. SVL 90 mm.

Preferred habitat Sandstone plateaux of humid to subhumid north-western Kimberley region, WA.

Microhabitat Dwells almost exclusively in foliage of slender-leaved *Acacia* spp.

Comments This spectacular lizard is possibly one of the world's most slender dragons, and Australia's most consistently arboreal. The gracile form is reminiscent of foliage-inhabiting stick insects (Phasmatodea).

Diporiphora valens Storr, 1979
Photo 62

Description Gular and scapular folds strong. Postauricular fold weak, sometimes bearing spines. Ground colour pale yellowish brown, reddish brown to greyish brown. Pale grey to brownish grey vertebral stripe usually extends from nape to hips or base of tail. Narrow pale grey to white dorsolateral stripes extend from nape onto tail, converging well beyond base. Series of 8 or more irregular narrow dark brown bars extend between nape and hips, interrupted by vertebral and dorsolateral stripes. Whitish midlateral stripe usually extends from base of tail, forward nearly to forelimb. Lower flanks paler shade of ground colour. White streak occasionally extends between eye and top of ear. Lips white. Tail uniform or marked with obscure continuation of dorsal pattern. Ventral surfaces whitish, occasionally bearing 3 obscure grey stripes. SVL 65 mm.

Preferred habitat Arid interior of Pilbara region, WA. Favours shrublands and low woodlands over ground cover of hummock grasses.

Microhabitat As for genus.

Comments As for genus.

Diporiphora winneckei Lucas and Frost, 1896
Photo 63

Description Very slender *Diporiphora* with long limbs and tail. Gular and scapular folds weak to absent. Postauricular fold absent. Ground colour brown, pale yellowish brown, reddish brown, brownish grey to bluish grey. Pattern usually prominent. Broad grey to brownish grey vertebral stripe (sometimes enclosing narrow dark median line) extends from nape to base of tail. White, cream to yellow dorsolateral stripe extends from behind ear to base, or onto tail. Dark dorsal bars absent, or reduced to blotches between dorsolateral and vertebral stripes. Upper lateral zone uniform, or bears obscure dark blotches. White, cream to yellow midlateral stripe often present, extending from forelimb, to hindlimb or onto tail. Top of head uniform, or bears dark longitudinal markings which coalesce on snout. White to yellow streak usually extends from eye to ear; continuous with dorsolateral stripe. Lips white. Limbs and tail uniform, or obscurely striped and/or banded. Ventral surfaces silky white, striped with silver-grey on males; grey and yellow on females. SVL 65 mm.

Distinguished from *D. pindan* by pattern (vertebral stripe broader), nature of gular scales (smooth vs keeled), and build (very slender vs moderately slender). Differs from *D. lalliae* in lacking a postauricular fold and bearing smooth (vs keeled) gular scales. *D. winneckei* differs ecologically from these species in favouring sand ridge habitats (vs heavier to stony soils). Differs from *D. linga* and *D. reginae* in bearing grey vertebral and ventral stripes, and by much more slender build.

Preferred habitat Arid western interior of Australia, from eastern edge of Simpson Desert in south-western Qld, through northern half of SA and southern NT, to north-west coast of WA. An apparently isolated population occurs in Onslow and North West Cape areas of WA. Favours sand ridge habitats; supporting canegrass (*Zygochloa*) in eastern parts of range, hummock grasses throughout most of western portion of range, and beach spinifex (*Spinifex longifolius*) along north-west coastal dunes.

Microhabitat Basks on grass hummocks, taking refuge in them when disturbed.

Comments In addition to arthropods, one record shows a significant amount of vegetable matter (particularly petals). This may have been taken accidentally with flower-visiting insects. Individuals active in hot weather have been observed to rest on their heels, with body and digits raised off ground. Each limb is then lifted alternately. This thermo-regulatory posture has been observed in other agamids, and in lacertids and iguanids from deserts of Africa and North America. Clutches of 1–3 eggs have been recorded, laid in shallow burrows on crests of dunes. Otherwise as for genus.

See photos 64 and 65 for further (undescribed) species of *Diporiphora*.

Genus *GEMMATOPHORA* Kaup, 1827

Small genus containing 6 species. Widespread throughout Australia, excepting Tas. Extralimital from southern New Guinea to Timor.

Medium to moderately large dragons with slender to moderately robust bodies, long limbs and tails. Spinose nuchal crest and vertebral ridge present, usually set atop a fold of erectable skin. This is weak on juveniles, and often strongly developed on adult males. Dorsal and dorsolateral series of enlarged scales present or absent. Tympanum exposed. Body scales weakly to strongly keeled; heterogeneous (mixed with enlarged spinose scales) to homogeneous. Femoral and preanal pores present (sometimes reduced to absent on females); few in number. Mature males tend to develop swollen jowls. Pattern variable, including pale dorsolateral stripes or equivalent series of blotches.

Terrestrial to semi-arboreal. Arthropod feeders. Swift dragons which usually run on hindlimbs when alarmed. Most favour woodlands or margins of waterways.

Distinguished from *Pogona*, in lacking a transverse series of spines across base of head, and a longitudinal series along flanks. Differs from *Diporiphora*, and further from *Pogona*, in possessing a moderate to well-developed nuchal crest (vs reduced to absent). Differs from *Ctenophorus* in lacking a series of enlarged scales curving from below eye to above ear.

Gilbert's Dragon, Ta-Ta or Bye-Bye Lizard
Gemmatophora gilberti (Gray, 1842)
Photos 66, 67

Description Large, relatively robust *Gemmatophora*, with or without a spinose dorsolateral skinfold. Two subspecies recognised. These intergrade in several areas.

G. g. gilberti Nuchal crest and vertebral ridge moderately well developed and erectable. Dorsolateral fold absent. Dorsal scales homogeneous; their keels parallel to midline. Ground colour shades of grey, yellowish brown, reddish brown to almost black. Series of short narrow dark dorsal bars may be present; sometimes broken to form paravertebral blotches. These usually fade to absence with age, particularly on males. Broad (usually dark-edged) white to cream dorsolateral stripe extends from side of neck to hips. Inner edge may be interrupted by dark dorsal markings (when present). Narrower midlateral stripe may be discernible, rarely extending as far forward as forelimb. Remaining dorsal and lateral surfaces indistinctly marked with darker and paler flecks and mottling. Narrow white to pale grey streak extends from eye to top of ear. Broad white to cream stripe extends from snout, through lips to corner of jaw. Limbs, digits and tail usually marked with indistinct bands. Ventral surfaces white to pale grey, usually bearing darker flecks on throat.

Mature males develop swollen jowls, stronger crest, more robust body, and black flush over head, forelimbs, anterior body, throat and chest; in sharp contrast to vivid white labial stripe. SVL 125 mm.

G. g. centralis (Loveridge, 1933) Differs from nominate form by more robust body, stronger nuchal crest, and presence of dorsal and dorsolateral series of enlarged spinose scales. Keels of innermost dorsal scales parallel to midline; remainder converge on midline. White labial stripe is usually restricted to, or largely centred on, lower lip. Pale streak from eye to top of ear rarely present.

Distinguished from *G. longirostris* and *G. temporalis* by alignment of keels on all or some dorsal scales; parallel to (vs all scales converging on) midline. *G. g. centralis* differs from *G. muricata* and *G. nobbi* by nature of nuchal crest (strong vs weak). Differs further from *G. muricata* by colour of mouth-lining (pink vs yellow), and further from *G. nobbi* in lacking arc of spinose scales enclosing area behind ear.

Preferred habitat Widespread in subhumid to arid areas. *G. g. gilberti* occurs across northern Australia, from North West Cape, WA, through northern NT to northern Qld. Inhabits woodlands, edges of vine thickets, river margins, mangroves and sandy coastlines. *G. g. centralis* occupies remainder of range: south and interior of NT (north to about Larrimah), northern SA, northern interior of NSW and southern interior of Qld. *G. g. gilberti* occurs largely in woodland habitats. In arid areas it follows eucalypt-lined drainage systems.

Microhabitat Usually encountered perched on timber, termitaria or among foliage. Shelters in hollows or among dense vegetation. In warm weather individuals may be found sleeping on exposed limbs.

Comments Colloquial name 'ta-ta lizard' refers to the habit of arm-waving; well known in Agamidae, and particularly noticeable in this species. Dorsal ridge is not obvious when relaxed, though when erected with spinose nuchal crest the appearance of the lizard is radically enlarged. Though possibly serving as a territorial or mating display, its erection at other times appears random. Clutch of 6 eggs recorded for south-eastern *G. g. centralis*; well developed in oviducts during November. Otherwise as for genus.

Gemmatophora longirostris (Boulenger, 1883)
Photo 68

Description Slender long-limbed *Gemmatophora* with long snout and very long tail. Nuchal crest and vertebral ridge moderately well developed, and erectable. Dorsal scales homogeneous, their keels converging on midline. Ground colour pale greyish brown, yellowish brown, reddish brown to almost black. Series of short dark reddish brown dorsal bars (sometimes broken to form paravertebral blotches) may be present. Prominent white to yellow dorsolateral stripe (sometimes dark-edged) extends from behind ear to middle of back or base of tail. Flanks uniform or marked with obscure dark mottling or spots; often enclosing narrow pale midlateral stripe from hindlimb to anterior flanks. Sides of head often flushed with reddish brown. Dark patch (enclosing sharp white spot) usually present behind ear. White stripe extends from lower jaw to behind ear. Limbs and tail uniform, or bear obscure dark bands. Ventral surfaces white. Chin and throat clouded with dark brown, and occasionally flecked with white. Mature adults bear prominent row of 3 orange spots on each side of belly. SVL 110 mm.

Distinguished from *C. gilberti* by alignment of keels on dorsal scales; converging on (vs parallel to) midline, by build (slender vs robust), and in bearing longer snout. Differs from *G. temporalis* by position of white labial stripe (not, or only narrowly, continuous with dorsolateral stripe, and restricted to lower lips or barely extending onto upper jaw vs broadly continuous with dorsolateral stripe, and extending broadly onto upper jaw).

Preferred habitat Arid western interior of Australia, from midwest coast of WA, through southern NT and northern SA to south-western Qld. Most abundant along gorges and eucalypt-lined ephemeral watercourses. Some coastal populations inhabit ecotonal mangrove communities. In some areas individuals may occur on red sand ridges or stony plains supporting hummock grasses, well away from drainage systems.

Microhabitat May be encountered on the ground, or on tree trunks and limbs. Shelters in hollows during cool weather. On warm evenings individuals usually sleep on exposed limbs or foliage.

Comments As for genus.

Jacky Lizard or Tree Dragon
Gemmatophora muricata (White, 1790)
Photo 69

Description Small moderately robust *Gemmatophora* with relatively short tail. Nuchal crest moderately well developed. Dorsal and dorsolateral crests present. These do not appear erectable. Dorsal scales strongly heterogeneous. Interior of mouth bright yellow. Ground colour shades of grey, sometimes darker on vertebral region. Dorsolateral series of pale grey, elongate to angular blotches extend from nape to hips. These may coalesce to form broad, wavy to straight-edged stripes. Remainder of dorsal and lateral surfaces may be lightly to heavily flecked, mottled or variegated with dark and pale pigment. Indication of pale midlateral stripe may be present. Dark bar may extend between eyes. Dark (often pale-edged) bar usually extends from eye to ear. Tail usually prominently banded. Ventral surfaces white to pale grey, marked with darker streaks or flecks, particularly on throat. SVL 120 mm.

Distinguished from *G. nobbi* by colour of mouth-lining (yellow vs pink), and by nature and alignment of dorsal body scales (strongly heterogeneous and keels converging toward midline vs homogeneous and keels parallel to midline). Differs further from *G. nobbi*, and from *G. gilberti centralis*, by arrangement of spinose scales on dorsal surface of thigh: mixed with (vs grading into) smaller scales. Differs from *G. norrisi* by head-pattern—lacking a dark streak from nostril to eye—and by possessing dark transverse markings on top of head and snout (vs bearing dark streak and lacking transverse markings). Juveniles differ from superficially similar *Tympanocryptis diemensis* in lacking enlarged spinose scales on sides of tail-base, and by colour of mouth-lining (yellow vs blue).

Preferred habitat Largely associated with dry sclerophyll forests and woodlands. Extends from south-eastern SA to Vic. (excluding semi-arid north-west corner and humid south-east corner), and along coast and Great Dividing Range to Clermont district, Qld. Though present in eastern highlands, it does not occur in alpine areas.

Microhabitat Usually encountered perched on fallen or standing timber. Shelters in hollows, or beneath low vegetation, rocks, timber and bark.

Comments Feeds largely on invertebrates, though skinks and small amounts of vegetable matter are also taken. Each individual utilises several favoured perching sites within home range. Territorial displays include tail-waving, raising and lowering body, head-bobbing, arm-waving and darkening of colour. Opponents may circle each other with bodies raised and laterally compressed, presenting their broadest aspect. If biting occurs it is usually directed at the tail. Breeding occurs from spring to early summer. Clutches of up to 8 eggs are deposited beneath rocks or logs. Otherwise as for genus.

Nobby Dragon
Gemmatophora nobbi (Witten, 1972)
Photos 70, 71

Description Smallest *Gemmatophora*, with weakly developed nuchal crest and moderately short tail. Vertebral, dorsal and dorsolateral ridges of enlarged scales present. These do not appear erectable. Body scales homogeneous. Interior of mouth pink. Sexually dichromatic. Two subspecies recognised.

G. n. nobbi Females, non-breeding males and juveniles: Ground colour pale or dark grey, brownish grey, brown to olive-grey. Prominent to obscure paravertebral series of dark angular blotches extends from nape to base of tail. White to cream or pale yellow dorsolateral stripe (sometimes broken or interrupted by paravertebral blotches) extends from nape or level of ear to base of tail. Flanks uniform, or bear irregular dark markings. Cream to pale yellow ventrolateral stripe may extend between fore- and hindlimbs. Dark streak usually extends from eye, to ear or corner of mouth. Lips ground colour to white. Limbs and tail uniform or obscurely banded. Ventral surfaces white to pale grey, flecked with darker pigment.

Breeding males develop pink, mauve to red flush on sides of tail-base, and body stripes become bright yellow. Anterior upper flanks and throat may be flushed with black. SVL 75 mm.

G. n. coggeri (Witten, 1972) Similar in colouration to *G. n. nobbi*, differing by more robust build, stronger nuchal crest and larger size. SVL 80 mm.

Distinguished from *G. muricata* and *G. norrisi* by nature and alignment of dorsal body scales (homogeneous and keels more or less parallel to midline vs strongly heterogeneous and keels converging on midline). Differs further by arrangement of spinose scales on dorsal surface of thigh (grading into smaller scales vs mixed with smaller scales), and by colour of mouth-lining (pink vs yellow). Differs from *G. gilberti centralis* in possessing an arc

of spinose scales enclosing area behind ear, and in attaining much smaller maximum size (SVL 80 vs 125 mm).

Preferred habitat Widespread on coast, ranges, and subhumid to semi-arid hinterland of eastern Australia. *G. n. nobbi* occurs in dry sclerophyll forests, woodlands and heathlands, from New England area, NSW, along both sides of Great Dividing Range to about Cairns area, Qld. *G. n. coggeri* favours drier habitats west of Great Dividing Range, from Warrumbungle Mountains area, NSW, through interior of NSW to north-western Vic. and adjacent SA. In southern parts of range it appears most abundant in mallee/*Triodia* associations.

Microhabitat Usually encountered among rocks, fallen timber and low vegetation.

Comments Population of *G. n. nobbi* from New England Tableland, NSW, is recorded to aggregate at selected breeding sites, favouring north-facing slopes. These sites are used annually, during late spring and autumn; dispersal occurring during summer. Hatchlings appear from October to April. Otherwise as for genus.

Gemmatophora norrisi
(Witten and Coventry, 1984)
Photo 72

Description Small moderately robust *Gemmatophora* with relatively short tail. Nuchal crest weakly developed. Dorsolateral (and usually lateral) series of enlarged scales present. These do not appear erectable. Dorsal and lateral scales strongly heterogeneous. Interior of mouth pale yellow. Ground colour pale grey to reddish brown; darker on vertebral region and flanks. Obscure pale dorsal stripes extend from nape to base of tail. These are notched, or broken into lozenge-shapes, by lateral extensions of dark vertebral region. Dark median line may extend from top of snout back to level of eyes. Broader dark streak extends from snout to eye, and another from eye, through ear to side of neck. Broad pale grey to whitish streak extends through upper and lower lips to jowls; occasionally tinged posteriorly with orange. Tail marked with obscure dark blotches on base; becoming sharper and forming distinct bands posteriorly. Ventral surfaces pale grey with darker flecks. SVL 115 mm.

Distinguished from *G. muricata* by nature of head-pattern; a dark streak from snout to eye, and no transverse dark markings on top of head (vs streak absent and transverse markings present). Differs from *G. nobbi* by nature and alignment of dorsal body scales (strongly heterogeneous and keels converging toward midline vs homogeneous and keels parallel to midline). Differs further from *G. nobbi* by arrangement of spinose scales on dorsal surface of thigh—mixed with (vs grading into) smaller scales—and by colour of mouth-lining (yellow vs pink).

Preferred habitat Mallee/heathland and mallee/

Triodia associations of semi-arid north-western Vic. and eastern SA. Disjunct populations occur from Eyre Peninsula, SA, to south-eastern WA.

Microhabitat Usually encountered perched on fallen timber. Shelters in hollows, beneath leaf-litter, timber and low vegetation.

Comments Feeds on a broad range of arthropods, occasionally taking skinks opportunistically. Clutches of 3–7 eggs are laid between September and late November. These are deposited in a shallow burrow situated in a shady clearing. Hatchlings first appear in January. Otherwise as for genus.

Gemmatophora temporalis (Günther, 1867)
Photo 73

Description Slender *Gemmatophora* with moderately long snout. Nuchal crest moderately well developed, set atop an erectable ridge. Dorsal scales homogeneous, their keels converging towards midline. Ground colour pale to dark grey, greyish brown, yellowish brown to reddish brown. Irregular darker bands or blotches may be present, particularly on foreback. Broad pale grey, cream to white dorsolateral stripe (sometimes broken by dorsal bands; particularly on juveniles) extends from lips to base of tail. Remainder of dorsal and lateral surfaces uniform, or marked with irregular (often prominent) pale and dark variegations or mottling. Broad dark streak often extends from eye to ear or side of neck. Limbs, digits and tail uniform, or irregularly marked with pale bands. Ventral surfaces whitish, speckled with grey.

Mature males develop black flush over anterior flanks, throat and chest. SVL 120 mm.

Distinguished from *G. longirostris* by nature of labial stripe (extending broadly through upper and lower lips and continuous with dorsolateral stripe vs largely centred on lower lip and narrowly continuous or discontinuous with dorsolateral stripe). Differs from *G. g. gilberti* by alignment of keels on dorsal scales: converging towards (vs parallel with) midline.

Preferred habitat Humid to subhumid far northern Australia, from north-eastern Kimberley region, WA, through northern NT to western Cape York Peninsula, Qld. Extralimital in southern New Guinea. Favours *Pandanus*- and *Melaleuca*-lined rivers, creeks and billabongs. NT populations are widespread through low-lying woodlands, particularly where *Pandanus* is present.

Microhabitat Usually encountered basking on limbs, trunks and foliage of waterside vegetation.

Comments Feeds on arthropods, including green tree ants (*Oecophylla smaragdina*), a pugnacious species shunned by many other arthropod feeders. Otherwise as for genus.

Rainforest Dragons
Genus *HYPSILURUS* Peters, 1867

Widespread throughout New Guinea, Moluccas and Solomon Islands. Two endemic Australian species occur in subtropical and tropical rainforests of east coast. Represented in South-East Asia (west of Sulawesi) by superficially similar genus *Gonocephalus* Kaup, with which *Hypsilurus* has long been included.

Moderately large, strongly laterally compressed dragons, each with a large angular head (bearing strong ridge from snout to above eye), and long slender limbs and digits. Spinose nuchal crest well developed, set above an erectable fleshy ridge, and continuous or discontinuous with a prominent vertebral crest of enlarged compressed spines. Gular pouch deep and erectable. Tympanum exposed. Tail moderately long, bearing blunt tip. Body scales heterogeneous: small, mixed with enlarged tubercles. Femoral and preanal pores absent.

Predominantly arboreal. Rainforest dragons forage on trunks, limbs, buttresses and vines, regularly descending to ground or fallen timber. They are usually encountered basking in filtered sunlight after rain. In warm weather rainforest dragons sleep on exposed trunks or limbs. During cooler periods, hollows or dense thickets of vegetation are probably used. Slow moving, relying on the camouflage afforded by cryptic colouration and disruptive outline. When approached, individuals remain motionless or slowly edge out of view, keeping trunk or limb between themselves and viewer. Due to obvious difficulties in investigating the canopy it is not known whether Australian species frequent these upper levels. Arthropods probably constitute a major portion of diet, though other invertebrates and small vertebrates are also taken.

Boyd's Forest Dragon
Hypsilurus boydii (Macleay, 1884)
Photo 74

Description Largest Australian *Hypsilurus*, bearing large 'tooth-like' spines on leading edge of gular pouch, and enlarged plate-like scales on lower corner of jaw. Nuchal and vertebral crests very large; discontinuous above level of forelimbs. Ground colour variable, ranging from rich purplish brown, chocolate brown to pale grey. Many individuals are flushed with green. Irregular narrow dark vertical bars often extend from vertebral crest onto flanks. Flanks usually bear prominent to obscure cream spots, each centred on an enlarged scale. Side of neck flushed with black, and bisected by a broad horizontal cream to white bar. Nuchal crest bears 1 or 2 cream to white blotches or bars. Broad reddish brown blotch or bar extends from behind eye to ear or side of neck. Lips paler shade of ground colour. Limbs and tail patternless or marked with obscure dark bands. Gular pouch bright to dull brownish yellow. Remainder of ventral surfaces pale brown to whitish. SVL 150 mm.

Preferred habitat Highland and lowland rainforests of north-eastern Qld, from Mt Spec north to Shipton's Flat.

Microhabitat As for genus.

Comments Poorly documented. Presumably similar to *H. spinipes*. See genus.

Southern Angle-Headed or Rainforest Dragon
Hypsilurus spinipes
(Duméril and Duméril, 1851)
Photos 75, 76

Description Smallest Australian *Hypsilurus*. Nuchal and vertebral crests moderately large and continuous. Angular brow (common to both Australian *Hypsilurus*) is extremely pronounced on juveniles. Ground colour ranges through shades of brown, grey and green. Pattern (when present) comprises irregular dark brown to reddish brown, and pale brown, yellow to greenish mottling, blotches or variegations. These are often centred on anterior flanks. Obscure dark vertical bars sometimes extend from vertebral crest onto flanks. Dark brown bar usually present from eye to ear. Short dark streaks may radiate from eye to brow. Lower lips paler shade of ground colour to white, often obscurely barred with brown. Gular pouch paler shade of ground colour, occasionally bearing yellow flush near gular fold. Remainder of ventral surfaces pale brown to white, sometimes flushed with reddish on chest. SVL 110 mm.

Preferred habitat Rainforests and adjacent margins of wet sclerophyll forest on coast and ranges of mideastern Australia, from Gympie district, Qld, south to Gosford area, NSW.

Microhabitat As for genus.

Comments Angular form and uniform pattern of juveniles closely resembles the coarse leaf-litter in which they dwell. Adults appear more 'lichen-like'. Despite their cryptic nature, elaborate territorial and defensive behaviour has been observed. Individuals adopt a distinctive stance when cornered, or when rival males confront each other. Body is inflated and raised high off substrate. Mouth is opened and gular pouch and nuchal crest are erected, presenting the broadest lateral aspect to opponent; rivals then slowly circle each other. When harassed, a juvenile faces its aggressor and leaps forward in a series of short hops. Mouth is opened to display coloured interior: pink with a bluish purple spot on the corner of each jaw. Clutches of 3–6 eggs are recorded, laid in early summer. These are deposited in a burrow, usually situated in a rainforest clearing. Hatchlings appear in late summer. See genus.

Genus *MOLOCH* Gray, 1841

Endemic monotypic genus containing one of the world's most distinctive and bizarre lizards. Widespread through arid central and western interior of Australia.

Moderately small, very robust dragon bearing large thorn-like spines over head, body, limbs and tail. Head small and blunt, bearing a large curved spine over each eye. Prominent bulbous hump, bearing 2 large spines, is situated on nape. Limbs short and approximately equal in length, bearing short digits. Tail shorter than SVL, bearing blunt tip. Scales between spines small and granular. Femoral and preanal pores absent.

Terrestrial. Ant feeder.

Moloch, Thorny or Mountain Devil
Moloch horridus Gray, 1841
Photo 77

Description Ground colour yellow, rich orange-red to olive grey. Pattern prominent, including large dark-edged dark brown to reddish brown blotches; broken by narrow pale vertebral, and usually dorso-lateral stripes. Y-shaped mark present on nape, each fork extending forward to spine over eye. Limbs and ventral surfaces similarly marked. Females considerably larger than males. SVL 100 mm.

Preferred habitat Arid and adjacent semi-arid sandy regions, from far western Qld, through southern NT and western SA, to midwest coast of WA. Most abundant in areas dominated by hummock grasslands, extending into heathlands and mallee woodlands in some southern and western parts of range.

Microhabitat Shelters beneath low vegetation or in shallow burrows, possibly including those of other animals. Forages in open areas between vegetation. Often encountered on roads.

Comments Very slow-moving, maximum speed barely equals human walking pace. Adopts a distinctive posture, with tail curved over hips, and moves with a jerky gait similar to a clockwork toy. Well camouflaged and easily overlooked, despite bold colouration. Feeds exclusively on small black ants of the genus *Iridomyrmex*. Up to 6 non-stinging species are taken, according to locality. These are consumed by positioning body over ant-trails. Stray ants, or those milling randomly, are not pursued. One meal may comprise up to 5000 ants, captured at a rate of approximately 30–45 per minute. A specific defecation site may be used for several days in succession. Two activity peaks are apparent: from March to May, and from August to December. Mating probably occurs in spring, during which time individuals may travel over large areas. Males are recorded to engage in combat (butting each other) over this period. Clutches of 6–10 (usually about 7) eggs are laid in long shallow slanting burrows, hatching after approximately 10–12 weeks.

Moloch is famous for its unique method of obtaining water. Granular scales between spines enclose capillary-like channels, leading to corner of mouth. Contact with moisture by any part of body enables these channels to draw water and carry it to mouth. In addition, spines appear able to collect condensing dew, which then dribbles into capillaries.

The purpose of *Moloch*'s distinctive spinose nuchal hump is poorly known. When harassed, individuals raise body, with head tucked between forelimbs. In this posture, hump occupies the approximate position of head. Specimens with scarred humps are virtually unknown, so its use as a false head to deter predation may not be the case. The fearsome appearance of this inoffensive dragon has resulted in the common name of 'devil' and the generic name '*Moloch*' (a Canaanite god to whom children were sacrificed). Some Aboriginal tribes believe them to be harmful and regard them as totems. Others regularly include them on their diets.

Genus *PHYSIGNATHUS*   Cuvier, 1829

Small genus extending from Asia to New Guinea. Represented in eastern Australia by one species. Two subspecies recognised.

Characterised in Australia by extremely large size, robust laterally compressed body, deep head, long powerful limbs and long laterally compressed tail. Nuchal crest prominent and erectable, consisting of compressed spinose scales atop a low fleshy ridge. This is continuous with a strong vertebral ridge which extends onto tail; dividing into 2 low ridges on posterior portion. Tail capable of limited regeneration if broken. Tympanum exposed. Body scales heterogeneous: very small with widely spaced transverse series of larger spinose scales. Colour-changing ability (widespread among dragons) is reduced to absent. Preanal pores absent. Femoral pores present.

Arboreal, terrestrial and semi-aquatic. Omnivorous.

Eastern and Gippsland Water Dragons
Physignathus lesueurii (Gray, 1831)
Photos 78, 79

Description   *P. l. lesueurii* (eastern water dragon) Adults: Ground colour pale to dark yellowish brown, shades of grey to brownish grey. Up to 7 broad blackish bars extend across dorsum (most intense anteriorly), becoming narrower and fading on upper flanks. Numerous enlarged spinose transversely aligned pale scales form broken irregular lines across body, hindlimbs and tail. Prominent broad black stripe extends from eye, through ear onto side of neck. Limbs darker shade of ground colour to almost black; with or without irregular pale bands. Tail prominently to obscurely marked with dark and pale bands, becoming darker and drabber towards tip. Ventral surfaces flushed with yellowish brown to bright red; often extending onto lower flanks. Mature males are larger with stronger pattern, heavier jowls and greater development of crest.

Juveniles are darker; ground colour obscuring

black dorsal and temporal markings. Pattern dominated by transversely aligned series of pale scales. Ventral surfaces lack red pigment.

P. l. howittii McCoy, 1844 (Gippsland water dragon)   Differs from nominate form in bearing olive-green to bluish green colouration, and by absence or reduction of dark streak behind eye. Dorsal bars are reduced to one or more upper lateral blotches. Red ventral pigment absent, replaced by olive-green. Throats of mature males blackish, blotched and streaked with combinations of yellow, orange, and occasionally blue. SVL 200 mm.

Preferred habitat   Margins of creeks, rivers and lakes (including semi-polluted creeks and drains in urban areas) on coast, ranges and hinterland of eastern Australia. *P. l. lesueurii* extends from between Cairns and Cooktown, Qld, south to Kangaroo Valley, NSW. From this point southwards into eastern Vic. it is replaced by *P. l. howittii*.

Microhabitat   Usually encountered on waterside rocks, logs or overhanging branches. Juveniles favour low vegetation or accumulated flood debris. Shelters in burrows, rock crevices, hollow limbs or trunks, and beneath vegetation. Frequently sleeps on exposed surfaces during warm weather.

Comments   Extremely wary. If approached, will not hesitate to drop many metres into water from overhanging vegetation. A powerful swimmer, using lateral undulations of strongly compressed tail, with limbs held close to sides. Able to remain submerged for over one hour. Feeds on a broad range of invertebrates (including molluscs and crustaceans), small vertebrates (including fish, hatchling tortoises and small mammals) and vegetable matter. Dominant males usually occupy a choice section of riverbank, accompanied by a small harem of females. Juveniles tend to aggregate separately, possibly to avoid predation by adults. Gregarious behaviour has led to a variety of social interactions by both sexes at all ages. These include head-bobbing and licking of substrate. Combat has been recorded between rival males: biting and scratching head and neck area, and attempting to overbalance opponent. Clutches of 6–18 eggs are laid in burrows. May live for over 15 years.

Bearded Dragons
Genus *POGONA*   Storr, 1982

Endemic genus containing 5 species. Occurs virtually throughout Australia, excepting humid south-west and south-east, Tas., Cape York Peninsula, Qld, northern NT, rainforests and alpine areas.

Moderate to very large robust agamids with relatively short limbs and tails. Body weakly to strongly dorsally depressed. Head large and triangular, bearing transverse series of spines across base. Tympanum exposed. Scales heterogeneous: small, mixed with larger spines over body, limbs and tail. Additional zones of slender spines are present on ventrolateral edge at rear of lower jaw (extending across throat and erectable to form a 'beard' on some species), along scapular fold, and along dorsoventral angle of body. Preanal and femoral pores few, and aligned backward towards midline.

Terrestrial and arboreal, favouring elevated perches such as stumps, fence posts or rocks. Hollow limbs and shallow depressions beneath vegetation or surface debris are used for shelter. Omnivorous, consuming a broad range of invertebrates, small vertebrates, flowers and fruits.

Common name alludes to the defensive strategy employed by most species. Body is dorsally flattened and raised obliquely, presenting broadest aspect to aggressor. Mouth is opened to display bright pink or yellow interior, and spinose gular pouch or 'beard' is erected.

Distinguished from *Gemmatophora*, *Ctenophorus* and *Tympanocryptis* in possessing transverse series of spines across base of head; and long slender spines on ventrolateral edge at rear of jaw, and along dorsoventral angle of body.

Common or Eastern Bearded Dragon or Jew Lizard
Pogona barbata (Cuvier, 1829)
Photo 80

Description Large robust *Pogona* with well-developed 'beard' and strongly depressed body. Interior of mouth usually bright yellow. Ground colour shades of grey; occasionally yellowish brown, brown to reddish brown. Pattern prominent on juveniles, and obscure to absent on adults. Paravertebral series of pale lozenge-shaped blotches extend from nape to hips. Indications of obscure transverse lines occasionally present. Dark blotch sometimes present on side of neck. Outer dorsal area darker, sometimes bearing obscure irregular dark and pale markings. Top of head bears broad dark stripes directed obliquely backwards. These usually fade to absence with age. Pale-edged dark stripe extends from eye to rear level of jaw. Limbs and tail uniform (occasionally tinged with orange-yellow), or marked with obscure pale bands; often darker and obscure posteriorly. 'Beard' usually dorsal colour or darker. Ventral surfaces white to pale grey, marked with short longitudinal dark streaks; approximating open lateral margins of ocelli. Mature males develop dark grey to black 'beard', and obscure pale green to blue tinge on forepart of head. SVL 250 mm.

Distinguished from *P. vitticeps* by alignment of spines across rear of head (arranged in backward curving arc vs a more or less straight transverse line), and shape of erected beard (squarish vs rounded). Differs from *P. m. minor* by location of spines on rear of jaw (extending across throat vs restricted to ventrolateral edge at rear of lower jaw), and in attaining much greater maximum size (SVL 250 vs 145 mm).

Preferred habitat Woodlands and dry sclerophyll forests (extending into many urban and rural areas) in eastern Australia, from Cooktown area, Qld, to south-eastern SA. Disjunct populations occur in southern Mt Lofty Ranges and southern Eyre Peninsula, SA.

Microhabitat As for genus.

Comments One of Australia's most familiar reptiles, due to its large size, conspicuous perching behaviour, and widespread occurrence in populated areas. Frequently known as 'frillneck' or 'frilly lizard' because of superficial resemblance to the frilled lizard (*Chlamydosaurus kingii*) to which it is only distantly related. Individuals (especially dominant males) regularly engage in a variety of display sequences, particularly during courtship or defence of territory. These include head-bobbing, arm-waving, head-licking, push-ups, pawing of substrate, biting, erecting beard, expanding body and changing colour. Up to 75 separate display sequences have been observed. Clutches of 15–35 eggs are laid in shallow burrows. Occasionally 2 clutches are laid per season. When approached, individuals tend to remain motionless, relying on cryptic colouration for protection. Defensive posture (see photo) is particularly well developed, and is used as a last resort. Otherwise as for genus.

Small-scaled Bearded Dragon
Pogona microlepidota (Glauert, 1952)
Photo 81

Description Moderately large *Pogona* with narrow head and moderately poorly developed 'beard'. Ground colour dull yellowish brown, greyish brown to reddish brown. Pattern (obscure when present) includes narrow broken pale yellowish brown bands, fading on side of body. Lips and side of head may be suffused with pale grey. Tail dark greyish brown, narrowly banded with dull yellowish brown. Mature males may exhibit a more sharply contrasting pattern, and reddish brown suffusion on lips and side of head. Ventral surfaces brownish white, occasionally spotted with grey. SVL 180 mm.

Distinguished from *P. minor* in bearing more numerous series of slender spines along dorsoventral angle of body (3–8 vs 1 or occasionally 2). Differs further by build (relatively more dorsally depressed), and in attaining greater maximum size (SVL 180 vs 160 mm or less).

Preferred habitat Woodlands associated with sandstones over dominant ground cover of hummock grasses in subhumid north-western Kimberley region, WA.

Microhabitat As for genus.

Comments As for genus.

Western Bearded Dragon
Pogona minor (Sternfeld, 1919)
Photos 82–84

Description Small to moderately large, highly variable *Pogona* with poorly developed 'beard'. Three subspecies recognised.

P. m. minor Widespread, subject to greatest variation. Interior of mouth yellow in south, pale pink in north. Ground colour ranges through shades of grey to greyish brown; browner in north. Pattern most prominent on juveniles, including paravertebral series of pale to dark grey blotches from nape to hips; occasionally coalesced to form wavy broken stripes. These may be connected by obscure narrow transverse lines. Less frequently, a series of narrow pale bands may extend across dorsum, dominating pattern. Pale-edged dark stripe extends from eye to side of neck. Large dark blotch present on side of neck on juveniles; occasionally retained by adults. Limbs irregularly banded on juveniles; usually patternless on adults. Tail obscurely banded with pale greyish brown. Ventral surfaces white to pale grey, sometimes marked with large white longitudinal spots, bearing dark lateral margins. Southern breeding males develop black flush over head, neck, throat and chest (sometimes extending onto abdomen), and a pale yellow to white stripe may extend from lip to ear. Greatest size is attained in north. SVL 145 mm.

P. m. minima (Loveridge, 1933) Similar in colouration to *P. m. minor*, differing by more slender body, longer limbs and tail. SVL 115 mm.

P. m. mitchelli (Badham, 1976) Differs from *P. m. minor* in attaining greater maximum size, in bearing broader head, more robust build, usually brownish (vs greyish) colouration, and larger spines ('beard') on rear of throat. Breeding males develop reddish flush over head, and black beard. SVL 160 mm.

Preferred habitat *P. m. minor* extends through a variety of dry sclerophyll forests, woodlands, coastal dunes and heathlands from southern WA (excluding humid lower south-west) north to Pilbara region, east to south-western NT and Eyre Peninsula, SA. *P. m. minima* is restricted to limestone soils supporting heathlands and shrublands, and sandy areas vegetated with beach spinifex (*Spinifex longifolius*) on larger northern islands of Houtman Abrolhos, off midwest coast of WA. *P. m. mitchelli* occurs in woodlands (occasionally sparsely wooded areas dominated by hummock grasses) from semi-arid Kimberley region, south to the Pilbara, WA. Hybridises with *P. m. minor* in southern Pilbara.

Subspecies of *P. minor* are distinguished from *P. microlepidota*, *P. barbata*, *P. vitticeps* and *P. nullarbor* in bearing fewer series of slender spines along dorsoventral angle of body (1 or occasionally 2 vs 3 or more), and relatively narrower body (vs dorsally depressed). Further distinguished from *P. barbata*, *P. vitticeps* and *P. nullarbor* by size of 'beard' and location of spines at rear of lower jaw; small 'beard', comprising large spines on ventrolateral surface at rear of lower jaw (vs large erectable 'beard', composed of spines continuous across throat).

Microhabitat As for genus.

Comments With the exception of *P. m. mitchelli*, the 'beard' is very poorly developed, and hence is used to lesser extent in defensive bluff than in other *Pogona*. Clutch of 7 eggs is recorded for *P. m. minor*, laid in a shallow burrow in an open sandy area. Otherwise as for genus.

Nullarbor Bearded Dragon
Pogona nullarbor (Badham, 1976)
Photo 85

Description Robust *Pogona* with moderately weak 'beard' and strongly depressed body. Ground colour shades of grey, reddish brown to orange-brown, marked with 6 or 7 narrow irregular creamy white to pale grey bands between nape and hips. Paravertebral series of pale longitudinally elongate blotches (sometimes coalescing to form wavy broken stripes) present or absent. Top of head marked with obscure dark stripes, aligned obliquely backwards. Pale-edged dark streak extends from eye to rear level of jaw. Limbs and tail bear obscure pale bands. Ventral surfaces grey to white, marked with longitudinally elongate white spots; each with a dark lateral edge. Throat marked with 3 or 4 dark chevrons, the smaller inside the larger. SVL 140 mm.

Distinguished from *P. m. minor* by nature of 'beard' (relatively larger, comprising a continuous transverse series of spines across throat, vs relatively small with spines restricted to ventrolateral edge at rear of lower jaw).

Preferred habitat Restricted to arid Nullarbor Plain of south-eastern WA and south-western SA. Habitat comprises limestone-based soils supporting extensive areas of stunted vegetation, dominated by chenopod shrublands.

Microhabitat As for genus.

Comments Clutches of 14–19 eggs are recorded; hatching in December. Otherwise as for genus.

Central Bearded Dragon
Pogona vitticeps (Ahl, 1926)
Photo 86

Description Large robust *Pogona* with well-developed 'beard', strongly depressed body and broad head. Interior of mouth usually pink. Ground colour shades of grey, brown, reddish brown to bright orange. Pattern prominent on juveniles; obscure to absent on adults. Paravertebral series of pale lozenge-shaped blotches extends from nape to hips. These may coalesce to form broad wavy stripes; occasionally joined by pale transverse bars. Outer dorsal area may be darker, bearing obscure dark and pale markings. Top of head bears broad dark stripes, directed obliquely backwards. These fade to absence with age. Some individuals bear bright orange flush on side of head, particularly around eye. Pale-edged dark streak extends from eye to rear level of jaw. Tail usually marked with obscure pale bands on proximal half; remainder dull grey to black. Ventral surfaces pale to dark grey, bearing elongate white spots; each edged laterally with black. 'Beard' dorsal colour; black on mature males. SVL 250 mm.

Distinguished from *P. barbata* by alignment of spines across rear of head (arranged in a more or less straight transverse line vs a backward curving arc), and shape of erected 'beard' (rounded vs squarish). Differs from *P. minor* in attaining much greater maximum size (SVL 250 vs 160 mm or less), build (robust and dorsally depressed vs relatively slender), and nature of beard (spines extending from rear of jaw across throat vs restricted to ventrolateral edge on rear of jaw).

Preferred habitat Semi-arid to arid woodlands in eastern interior of Australia, from central Qld and NSW, through north-western Vic. to eastern half of SA (excluding south-east) and south-eastern NT.

Microhabitat As for genus.

Comments Clutches of 11–16 eggs are recorded; laid in early summer. Similar in most behavioural respects to *P. barbata*. Otherwise as for genus.

Photo 87 shows a moderately small very robust undescribed *Pogona* with poorly developed 'beard'. Apparently restricted to deeply cracking clay soils (black-soil plains) in the interior of Queensland.

Genus *TYMPANOCRYPTIS*
Peters, 1863

Endemic genus comprising 9 species. Widespread throughout Australia (including Tas.), from south-eastern highlands through deserts of interior to sandy midwest coast. Diversity is greatest in arid areas, including some of the harshest, most feature-less landscapes in Australia. Hard clay soils and gibber flats are particularly favoured.

Small, moderate to very robust dragons with blunt heads, short limbs and tails, and depressed bodies. Tympanum exposed or covered by scaly skin. Femoral and preanal pores present to absent; usually few in number. Pores are often difficult to detect; particularly on females. Nuchal and vertebral crests absent. Dorsal scales heterogeneous: small, mixed with enlarged scattered spines.

Terrestrial, often utilising elevated perching sites such as stones and fallen timber. These dragons may be active during extremely high temperatures. Diet consists of arthropods, particularly ants.

Four species groups are tentatively recognised.

T. lineata group Comprises 6 taxa. Tympanum completely hidden. Tail relatively long. Preanal pores few in number. Femoral pores few to absent. Pattern is dominated by pale longitudinal stripes, interrupting dark transverse bars. Though predominantly arid-adapted, one subspecies extends into south-eastern highlands, and basalt plains of southern Vic. Members are *T. lineata centralis*, *T. lineata houstoni*, *T. lineata lineata*, *T. lineata macra*, *T. lineata pinguicolla* and *T. tetraporophora*.

T. cephalus group Contains 3 species of extremely robust *Tympanocryptis*. Tympanum hidden. Head bulbous and rounded. Tail short; usually tapering rapidly from hips. Head scales usually smooth. Femoral pores absent. Preanal pores 2. Pattern usually obscure; dominated (when present) by broad transverse bands. Two species occur in stony deserts. The 3rd (*T. uniformis*) is poorly known and appears restricted to the Darwin area, NT. Extremely cryptic and relatively slow moving, relying on their uncanny resemblance to gibber pebbles. Members are *T. cephalus*, *T. intima* and *T. uniformis*.

T. adelaidensis group Comprises 3 taxa. Tympanum exposed. Tail relatively short to long; bearing lateral series of enlarged spinose scales on base. Femoral and preanal pores few to numerous. Pattern variable, including sharply angular dark dorsal markings. Members occur in woodland to heathland habitats in south-eastern and south-western corners of Australia. Group comprises *T. adelaidensis adelaidensis*, *T. adelaidensis chapmani* and *T. diemensis*.

T. parviceps group Contains 2 species. Tympanum hidden. Tail moderately short. Dorsal spines relatively weak. Pattern prominent to virtually absent; including broad vertebral stripe of ground colour, margined by short dark transverse bars or angular blotches. Largely restricted to pale sands supporting heathlands or beach spinifex (*Spinifex longifolius*) on midwest coast of WA. Members rarely seek elevated perches, favouring open sandy areas between vegetation. When disturbed they scuttle to shelter of low ground cover or shallow burrows. Group comprises *T. butleri* and *T. parviceps*.

Tympanocryptis is distinguished from *Pogona* in lacking a transverse series of spines across base of head, and in attaining much smaller maximum size (SVL 75 or less vs 115 mm or greater). Differs from *Ctenophorus* in bearing enlarged spinose scales scattered over dorsum (vs absent or largely restricted to vertebral line). Differs from *Cryptagama* by length of tail (longer than SVL vs shorter). Sympatric species differ further in bearing covered (vs exposed) tympanum.

Tympanocryptis adelaidensis (Gray, 1841)
Photos 88, 89

Description Member of *T. adelaidensis* group comprising 2 subspecies.

T. a. adelaidensis Ground colour pale grey, bluish grey to greyish brown. Broad vertebral stripe of ground colour (often bearing narrow reddish brown margin and broken median line) extends from nape well onto base of tail. Irregular reddish brown to black dorsolateral stripe may extend from nape onto base of tail. Series of prominent pale-edged angular dark blotches (widest at point of contact with vertebral stripe; narrowest towards dorsolateral area) extend between nape and hips. Upper flanks bear similar series of blotches; widest at point of contact with dorsolateral line. Obscure wavy-edged pale midlateral line or zone is occasionally discernible on posterior flanks. Remaining flanks uniform, or bear complex dark and pale mottling. Dark bar extends across top of head, between eyes. Dark bar usually extends from eye to corner of mouth. Another may extend from eye toward nape. Lips irregularly barred with dark pigment. Tail usually patternless above (occasionally bears an irregular narrow dark median line). Side of tail marked with large dark blotches; becoming obscure posteriorly. Ventral surfaces white, marked with black (males) or grey (females), as follows: lips reticulated, a chevron on throat, and a black patch on chest. Chest marking is continuous with a median stripe and curving ventrolateral stripes, all of which converge in front of vent. SVL 50 mm.

T. a. chapmani (Storr, 1977) Differs from nominate form in bearing a distinctive ventral pattern: coarse dark reticulum or marbling. This is sometimes sufficiently dense on throats of males to leave only small white dots. Markings are paler to virtually absent on females.

Distinguished from *T. butleri*, *T. parviceps* and *T. lineata* in bearing an exposed (vs hidden) tympanum, and in possessing prominent dark ventral markings. Differs further from *T. butleri* in lacking a yellow patch on chin and lips.

Preferred habitat *T. a. adelaidensis* occurs along subhumid to semi-arid lower-west coast and hinterland of WA, from just north of Murchison River south to Perth area, and inland to Coorow. Favours pale sands (including semi-consolidated coastal dunes) supporting heathlands, often in association with *Banksia* and eucalypt woodlands. *T. a. chapmani* occurs along semi-arid southern coast and hinterland of Australia, from Stirling Ranges, WA, east to Yorke Peninsula, SA. Favours similar habitats to *T. a. adelaidensis*, extending onto chenopod-dominated heavy soils of Nullarbor Plain.

Microhabitat Forages in open clearings between shrubs, sheltering beneath low surface vegetation.

Comments Utilises elevated perching sites to a much lesser extent than other *Tympanocryptis*. Relatively slow moving, relying on disruptive colouration and close proximity of cover. When foraging the tail is often held in a distinctive upward curve. Otherwise as for genus.

Tympanocryptis butleri (Storr, 1977)
Photo 90

Description Member of *T. parviceps* group.

Ground colour pale to dark grey. Pattern usually prominent. Broad vertebral stripe of ground colour (often enclosing narrow broken dark median line) extends from nape onto base of tail. Series of 8–10 angular pale-edged dark bars extend from nape; reduced on base of tail to lateral blotches. Upper lateral zone dark grey dotted with white, enclosing a series of large dark squarish blotches; continuous with dorsal bars. Irregular white midlateral stripe extends from hindlimb to behind forelimb, reappearing on side of neck. Lower flanks marbled or clouded with grey and white. Top of head and lips barred with darker pigment. Dark streak extends from eye to corner of jaw. Limbs and tail obscurely banded. Ventral surfaces white, bearing a yellow patch on chin and lips, and grey markings on throat; less frequently on chest. SVL 40 mm.

Distinguished from *T. adelaidensis* in lacking an exposed tympanum, and by arrangement of dark ventral pigment (largely centred on throat and chest vs prominent stripes or marbling extending well onto abdomen). Differs from *T. parviceps* by nature of dorsal pattern (strong vs weak). Differs further from both in bearing distinctive yellow patch on chin and lips.

Preferred habitat Semi-arid midwest coast of WA, from Murchison River north to Dirk Hartog Island and Edel Land, Shark Bay. Inhabits white coastal sands (including semi-consolidated littoral dunes) vegetated with open heathlands, *Plectrachne* or beach spinifex (*Spinifex longifolius*), and adjacent pinkish sand plains supporting low shrubs.

Microhabitat As for species group.

Comments As for species group.

Tympanocryptis cephalus Günther, 1867
Photos 91, 92

Description Member of *T. cephalus* group. Dorsal body scales small, mixed with raised conical tubercles. These are irregularly arranged to form short transverse or oblique ridges. Ground colour brick red, reddish brown, yellowish brown to greyish brown; with or without obscure pattern. Three narrow pale stripes (vertebral and dorsolaterals) may be present, usually fading on forebody. Remainder of dorsum may bear broad darker bands or a dark suffusion. Tail usually banded; obscurely, or with contrasting combinations of black, white and ground colour. These often form sharp V-shapes on base. Ventral surfaces white. SVL 55 mm.

Distinguished from *T. lineata* and *T. tetraporophora* by shape and texture of head (rounded and bulbous, bearing smooth scales vs angular brow and sharply keeled scales), build (very robust vs relatively more slender), and nature of tail (short and tapering rapidly from base vs moderately long and tapering gradually from base). Differs from *T. intima* by alignment of dorsal tubercles (arranged in short, oblique or transverse ridges vs longitudinal series).

Preferred habitat Arid stony areas, particularly

gibber deserts. Widespread through interior of WA, with apparently disjunct populations occurring in western interior of Qld, and in central-northern SA.
Microhabitat Basks on elevated perches such as dead wood or stones, sheltering in shallow burrows or depressions.
Comments Variation in ground colour is closely associated with that of the substrate. Torpid individuals have been recorded embedded in hardened mud, with only dorsal surfaces exposed. Otherwise as for species group.

Mountain Dragon
Tympanocryptis diemensis (Gray, 1841)
Photos 93, 94

Description Member of *T. adelaidensis* group. Largest *Tympanocryptis*. Ground colour shades of grey to reddish brown. Broad vertebral stripe of ground colour extends from nape to base of tail. This is margined by a much broader white to pale grey dorsal stripe, with straight outer edge and deeply serrated inner edge. Flanks usually bear series of obscure dark bars or variegations. Indication of a narrow pale midlateral (and occasionally lower lateral) stripe may be present. Head usually bears obscure pale bar between eyes, and a dark streak from eye to corner of mouth. Lips may be obscurely barred. Tail banded, often bearing obscure continuation of dorsal pattern on base. Ventral surfaces pale grey; uniform or with sparse to dense dark flecks. Southern populations (Tas. and Bass Strait Islands) tend to be larger and more spinose. SVL 80 mm.

Superficially similar to juvenile *Gemmatophora muricata*, differing in bearing enlarged spinose scales on sides of tail-base, and within zones of overlap by colour of mouth lining (blue vs yellow).
Preferred habitat Extends from Tamworth area in NSW, south along Great Divide and coastal ranges to eastern Vic., islands of Bass Strait and Tas. Occurs in heathlands, woodlands, dry sclerophyll forests and margins of wet sclerophyll forests. Populations living in forests favour clearings.
Microhabitat Perches on low stones or fallen timber. Shelters among low vegetation, and beneath perching site.
Comments Differs from other *Tympanocryptis* in favouring cool, well-timbered habitats, and from most other dragons by its occurrence in many areas which receive regular winter snowfall. It is the only dragon extending as far south as Tas. Feeds on a broad range of arthropods. Social interactions have been observed on captive individuals. A dominant male will approach a submissive male to within 10 cm before raising hindquarters high off ground and placing chest over submissive's body. Submissive usually retreats rapidly, though if it hesitates it may be mounted by the dominant. Wrestling and mouth-gaping have also been observed. Females

present to prospective mates by raising hindquarters and lowering forebody. Head is bobbed (quickly up, slowly down) at a rate of approximately once per second. Both sexes often 'flick' hindfeet when in the vicinity of another individual. Purposes of this are not clear. Clutches of 2–7 eggs are deposited beneath rocks, logs or in burrows excavated in open areas. These are laid from late November to December, hatching in March or April.

Tympanocryptis intima Mitchell, 1948
Photo 95

Description Member of *T. cephalus* group. Dorsal body scales small, mixed with enlarged spinose scales which tend to align in 4 longitudinal rows. Ground colour rich reddish brown to greyish brown. Pattern obscure, including a dark bar across nape, and paravertebral series of 4 dark blotches. Dark suffusion may extend over anterior flanks. Limbs and tail may be banded or blotched with darker pigment. Ventral surfaces white, occasionally finely spotted with brown on throat and chest of male. SVL 60 mm.

Distinguished from *T. lineata* and *T. tetraporophora* by shape and texture of head (bulbous and bearing smooth scales vs angular brow and sharply keeled scales), build (very robust vs relatively more slender), and dorsal pattern (dark blotches vs pale stripes). Differs from *T. cephalus* by alignment of dorsal tubercles (arranged in longitudinal series vs oblique or transverse ridges).
Preferred habitat Arid gibber flats and sparsely vegetated heavy soils of north-eastern SA, south-eastern NT, south-western Qld and north-western NSW.
Microhabitat Basks on elevated perches such as stones or dead wood, sheltering in shallow burrows or depressions.
Comments As for species group.

Tympanocryptis lineata Peters, 1863
Photos 96–99

Description Variable member of *T. lineata* group. Currently recognised as comprising 5 subspecies, though additional races are known to occur.
T. l. lineata Ground colour grey, brown, yellowish brown to reddish brown. Pattern usually prominent. Narrow pale grey to white vertebral stripe extends from nape to hips. Similar (sometimes broken) dorsolateral stripes extend to hips or onto base of tail. Approximately 5 broad dark bands (broken by stripes) extend between nape and hips; fading on upper flanks. Narrow pale midlateral stripe sometimes discernible from forelimb to hindlimb. Top of head usually prominently marked with dark and pale, transverse and oblique markings. These usually include a pale bar or blotch between eyes, and a dark-edged pale streak from eye to corner of lower jaw. Limbs and tail usually irregularly

marked with dark bands. Ventral surfaces white, bearing grey speckling on chin, and occasionally a yellow flush on lips, chin and side of neck. SVL 60 mm.

T. l. centralis Sternfeld, 1924 Differs from nominate form in usually bearing redder colouration, reduced head pattern (absent or restricted to a pale bar across head), and narrow (vs very broad) neck.

T. l. houstoni Storr, 1982 Ground colour greyish brown to grey. Vertebral stripe 2–4 times broader than dorsolateral and midlateral stripes. Head-pattern usually strongly developed. Ventral surfaces marked with irregular wavy grey streaks. SVL 65 mm.

T. l. macra Storr, 1982 Ground colour grey to greyish brown. Vertebral stripe grey and consistently narrow. Differs from other subspecies by more slender body, and longer limbs and tail. SVL 65 mm.

T. l. pinguicolla Mitchell, 1948 Ground colour shades of grey. Neck extremely thick (broader than head), and strongly spinose. Chin, lower lips and throat may be yellow, marbled with black.

Upper Eyre Peninsula form: Brown to reddish brown with consistently narrow vertebral stripe. Dorsolateral lines broad. These merge with pale interspaces, reducing dark bands to a series of roughly circular blotches. Throat sparsely speckled with dark pigment.

Distinguished from *T. tetraporophora* in lacking femoral pores (vs 1 on either side). These may be undetectable on female *T. tetraporophora*, rendering positive identification difficult. Differs from *T. cephalus* and *T. intima* by shape and texture of head (angular brow and keeled scales vs rounded and bulbous, bearing smooth scales). Differs from *T. adelaidensis* in bearing a hidden (vs exposed) tympanum.

Preferred habitat Distributional limits of subspecies are poorly defined, particularly in eastern Australia. *T. l. lineata* occurs in subhumid to arid areas, from eastern half of SA, through north-western Vic. to interior of NSW and Qld. Favours sparsely vegetated gibber plains, and chenopod or *Acacia* shrublands. *T. l. centralis* occurs in arid stony habitats from north-western SA, through NT to southern Kimberley region, WA. Favours hummock grasslands. *T. l. macra* inhabits deeply cracking black-soil plains of southern Kimberley region and adjacent NT. *T. l. houstoni* occurs among scattered limestone rocks in chenopod shrublands of Nullarbor Plain. *T. l. pinguicolla* occurs on basalt plains of southern Vic., and in woodlands of south-eastern NSW and ACT. Upper Eyre Peninsula form occurs on sandy to stony mallee-dominated areas in central-southern interior of SA.

Microhabitat Favours elevated perching sites such as low stones, fallen timber, and low ridges or mounds, taking shelter beneath any available surface cover or in soil cracks. *T. l. pinguicolla* is recorded to utilise abandoned burrows of trapdoor spiders.

Comments *T. l. pinguicolla*, once abundant on basalt plains north and west of Melbourne, has not been seen in these areas since the 1960s. *T. l. macra* has been observed to raise body on hindlimbs, using tail as support. Otherwise as for genus.

Tympanocryptis parviceps Storr, 1964
Photo 100

Description Member of *T. parviceps* group with ground colour of pale bluish grey, brownish grey to yellowish brown. Pattern obscure to virtually absent. Broad vertebral stripe or zone of ground colour extends from nape onto tail. This is margined by a broad, slightly darker dorsal zone, enclosing a series of pale, longitudinally elongate hourglass-shaped blotches. These may coalesce to form an irregular anterior stripe. Upper flanks may be dotted obscurely with white. Narrow white midlateral stripe or series of spots usually discernible. Lower flanks white, usually bearing sparse grey flecks or clouding. Obscure dark bars may extend across snout, and in front of eyes. Side of tail-base bears a series of large grey blotches; fading posteriorly. Ventral surfaces white, marbled with grey to black on throat. SVL 45 mm.

Distinguished from *T. butleri* and *T. adelaidensis* by nature of pattern (weak vs strong). Differs further from *T. adelaidensis* in lacking an exposed tympanum, and by extent of ventral pigment (largely centred on throat vs extending well onto abdomen).

Preferred habitat Arid midwest coast of WA, from Bernier Island and Carnarvon district north to North West Cape. Inhabits white coastal sands (particularly semi-consolidated littoral dunes) vegetated with open heathlands and beach spinifex (*Spinifex longifolius*), extending marginally onto adjacent *Triodia*-dominated sand plains.

Microhabitat As for species group.

Comments As for species group.

Tympanocryptis tetraporophora Lucas and Frost, 1895
Photo 101. See also photo 1.

Description Member of *T. lineata* group with ground colour of dull reddish brown to greyish brown. Pattern usually present, though obscure. Narrow pale grey to white vertebral and dorsolateral stripes extend from nape to base of tail; occasionally fading at midbody. Vertebral stripe invariably continuous. Dorsolaterals may be broken; represented only where they bisect a series of approximately 5 short dark bands between nape and hips. Flanks uniform, or bear obscure extensions of dorsal bands. Obscure broken midlateral stripe may be present. Head-pattern obscure; rarely including a pale bar between eyes. Limbs and tail marked with obscure dark bands. Ventral surfaces white, sometimes flushed with pale brown, and mottled with black on throat. SVL 70 mm.

Distinguished from *T. lineata* in possessing one femoral pore on each side (vs femoral pores absent). These may be virtually undetectable on females, rendering positive identification difficult. Differs further by duller colouration, including virtual absence of a pale bar between eyes. Differs from *T. cephalus* and *T. intima* by shape and texture of head (angular brow and keeled scales vs rounded and bulbous, bearing smooth scales), and build (relatively more slender with longer appendages).

Preferred habitat Arid gibber and black-soil plains from interior of Qld to north-western NSW and central SA; south to Port Augusta area.

Microhabitat Perches on elevated sites such as low rocks, ridges or mounds. Shelters beneath stones or in soil cracks.

Comments During periods of intense heat, individuals have been observed to stand erect on hindlimbs and base of tail, with body angled directly into sun. Other as for genus.

Tympanocryptis uniformis Mitchell, 1948
Photo 102

Description Member of *T. cephalus* group. Dorsal scales more or less homogeneous. Ground colour dull greyish brown; greyer on head. Pattern obscure to absent. Indications of broad dark bands may extend across body; broken on vertebral region. Obscure dark dorsolateral stripes may also be present. Tail-pattern slightly more distinct, comprising pale and dark grey bands. Ventral surfaces whitish, marked with darker flecks on jaws. SVL 50 mm.

Preferred habitat Only known from northern NT, from Darwin and Top Springs.

Microhabitat Probably as for species group.

Comments Poorly known. Probably as for species group.

GECKOS
Family GEKKONIDAE

Large family represented by approximately 750 species in 88 genera. Widespread through tropical, temperate and arid regions of the world.

Australia has a relatively rich gecko fauna, comprising 91 species in 16 genera. These have been placed in 2 subfamilies. Diplodactylinae, which includes approximately 70 per cent of the gecko fauna, is endemic to the Australian region (east to New Caledonia and New Zealand) while the Gekkoninae have a wide extralimital distribution. Diversity is greatest in northern and arid regions. Absent from Tas., extreme south-east mainland and alpine areas.

Small lizards (up to SVL 160 mm) with large eye bearing vertically elliptic pupil (reduced to slit or series of dots in daylight). This is covered by an immovable transparent spectacle. Tongue short, fleshy and weakly notched. Limbs well developed, each with 5 digits. Digits clawed (except on *Crenadactylus*). Claws fixed or retractile. Tail fragile (except on *Nephrurus asper*). Skin soft with small juxtaposed scales. Scales homogeneous (smooth and granular) to heterogeneous (mixed with conical to spinose tubercles). Capable of vocalisation in the form of a wheezing squeak or bark.

Geckos have adapted to suit a broad range of life-styles and climatic conditions. Greatest variation can be seen in the nature of the digits, tail and skin texture.

Digits may be slender (cylindrical to laterally compressed; sometimes angular and bird-like) to broad (flattened to form pads). Subdigital lamellae vary from minute spinose tubercles to enlarged, divided or entire transverse plates bearing thousands of microscopic hooks. These enable some geckos to forage with ease on vertical surfaces such as glass. Close examination reveals that the tip of each pad is lifted to disengage these hooks before a step is taken.

Tails range from long and slender (sometimes prehensile) to bulbous, carrot-shaped or broadly depressed, according to their function: as an aid to stability when climbing, as fat storage, as a means of camouflage or as combinations of these. Most bear numerous cleavage points along their lengths. This allows economy in tail-loss and only a small portion need be discarded if necessary. Others are constricted at the base with a single cleavage point. In these cases tails are forfeited completely.

Skin may be thin and transparent (rendering internal organs and developing eggs clearly visible), to velvety in texture, coarsely granular or spinose. Sloughed skin (similar in appearance to tissue-paper) is shed as a single piece or in fragments. Some geckos use their mouths to dislodge loose skin from their feet, in the manner a tight-fitting glove is removed.

Geckos are nocturnal though some occasionally forage or bask in weak sunlight. All are predators, feeding on a wide variety of arthropods. A few specialise in feeding on termites while others include smaller geckos on their diets. Prey is stalked in a slow cat-like manner. Geckos often wave their tails

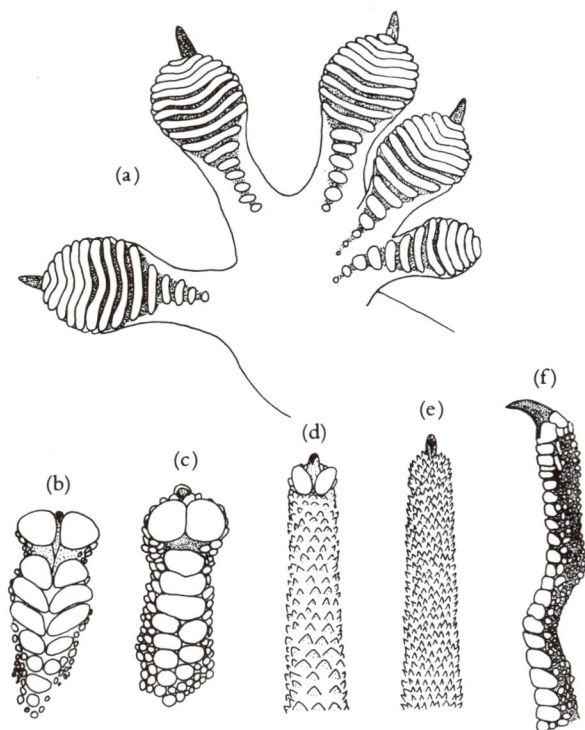

Variations in nature of digits and arrangement of subdigital lamellae in Australian geckos (not to scale)

(a) digits greatly expanded to form semicircular pads. Subdigital lamellae enlarged to form transverse plates. Ventral aspect of *Gehyra robusta*

(b) digit expanded to form a pad. Subdigital lamellae enlarged; divided distally and single proximally. Enlarged subapical plates present. Ventral aspect of *Oedura robusta*

(c) digit expanded to form a pad. Subdigital lamellae enlarged; single distally and divided proximally. Enlarged subapical plates present. Ventral aspect of *Diplodactylus ciliaris*

(d) Digit slender. Subdigital lamellae small and spinose. Subapical plates small. Ventral aspect of *Diplodactylus stenodactylus* (western form)

(e) Digit slender. Subdigital lamellae minute and spinose. Subapical plates absent. Ventral aspect of *Diplodactylus damaeus*

(f) Digit long, slender, angular, strongly clawed and bird-like; subdigital lamellae enlarged and transverse. Ventrolateral aspect of *Phyllurus cornutus*

or sway their hips prior to lunging, presumably to aid balance or assess distance. Like their close relatives, the legless lizards, geckos use the tongue to wipe dust and grit from the transparent spectacle covering the eye.

Many geckos exhibit elaborate defensive responses, usually combining vocalisations with inflation of body and abrupt mock lunges at adversary. Several species can deter predators by ejecting viscous repellent fluid from the dorsal surface of the tail.

Geckos are egglayers, producing 2 (occasionally 1) eggs per clutch. Members of the subfamily Diplodactylinae lay soft parchment-shelled eggs typical of most lizards while those of the subfamily Gekkoninae differ in producing brittle calcareous-shelled eggs. This is probably an adaptation against desiccation in dry conditions. Some arboreal geckos glue their eggs to vertical surfaces.

Australian geckos are largely nocturnal, with most activity occurring during the first few hours after sunset.

Genus *CARPHODACTYLUS* Günther, 1897

(Subfamily Diplodactylinae)

Endemic monotypic genus restricted to north-east Qld.

Large slender gecko with laterally compressed body and distinct acute vertebral ridge. Tail long, carrot-shaped and constricted at base with a single cleavage point. Limbs and digits long and slender. Digits strongly clawed; bird-like. Enlarged subapical plates absent. Subdigital lamellae swollen, arranged in a single transverse series. Body scales small, granular and homogeneous.

Terrestrial and arboreal. Lays 1 or 2 parchment-shelled eggs per clutch.

Chameleon Gecko
Carphodactylus laevis Günther, 1897
Photo 104

Description Large distinctive gecko with forward-directed eyes. Ground colour pale to rich brown, fading on lower lateral surfaces. Scattered dark and pale flecks, spots or blotches usually present. Prominent narrow cream vertebral line extends from nape to hips. Top of snout (back to about level of eyes) conspicuously paler than ground colour, usually in sharp contrast to blackish brown flush from eye to about nostril. Narrow dark sharp-edged line curves back from behind eye to about ear. Lips whitish. Original tail dark brown to blackish with 4 or 5 contrasting whitish bands. Regenerated tail brownish, blotched and streaked with pale and dark brown. Ventral surfaces pale purplish pink, finely peppered and/or speckled with darker pigment. SVL 130 mm.

Preferred habitat Highland rainforests of northeastern Qld from Kirrama, north through Atherton Tablelands to Mt Finnigan.
Microhabitat Shelters beneath leaf-litter, in hollow limbs, decaying trunks and buttresses, or among epiphytes. Usually encountered foraging on vines, tree trunks and small saplings, often descending to ground.
Comments Agitated individuals discard their tails readily. Severed regenerated tails produce a very loud distinctive squeaking noise. It is not known whether original tails behave in the same manner. This unusual phenomenon has not been recorded for any other Australian gecko and is doubtless effective in distracting a predator. Often reported resting head downwards on saplings, presumably waiting to ambush climbing invertebrate prey.

Genus *CRENADACTYLUS* Dixon and Kluge, 1964

(Subfamily Diplodactylinae)

Endemic monotypic genus containing Australia's smallest gecko. Widespread through subhumid to arid western half of continent.

Tail moderately long, slightly constricted at base and round in cross-section. Limbs and digits relatively short. Digits bear greatly enlarged pair of subapical plates, followed by moderately enlarged lamellae. Claws absent (a unique character in Australian geckos). Terminal bone of each digit forked (unique in family). Dorsal surfaces of body covered by small homogeneous conical scales; smooth, keeled, or with single sharp apex. Tail covered by large flat smooth overlapping scales arranged to form rings.

Terrestrial. Lays 1 or 2 parchment-shelled eggs per clutch.

Clawless Gecko
Crenadactylus ocellatus (Gray, 1845)
Photos 105–107

Description Four subspecies recognised.
C. o. ocellatus Ground colour pale to dark grey or brown, with or without scattered to longitudinally aligned small pale ocelli or spots on back, flanks and dorsal surfaces of limbs. Occasionally, irregular ocelli coalesce to form whitish reticulations. Pale dorsolateral stripe may extend from snout to tail-tip. Tail often flushed with yellowish brown to orange. Ventral surfaces whitish; immaculate to densely covered with greyish brown reticulations. SVL 35 mm.
C. o. horni (Lucas and Frost, 1895) Variable subspecies patterned with 4 or more simple, prominent to obscure dark stripes. Some individuals bear narrow white dorsolateral line from snout to tail-tip. Interspaces immaculate or enclose numerous fine white spots. Ventral surfaces greyish, usually striped

with darker grey. SVL 35 mm.

C. o. naso Storr, 1978 Similar in appearance to *C. o. horni*, differing by flatter head and longer snout. Dorsal and lateral surfaces pale olive with 5 dark-edged pale stripes: obscure vertebral from nape to base of tail, white dorsolateral from snout to middle of tail, and slightly wavy midlateral from eye and corner of mouth to hindlimb and onto tail. Ventral surfaces white sparsely dotted with dark brown. SVL 30 mm.

C. o. rostralis Storr, 1978 Variable in colour and pattern, approaching *C. o. naso* in north and *C. o. horni* in south. Typically, ground colour is pale olive-brown with 4 darker stripes: paravertebral from above each eye to middle of tail, and upper lateral from snout to middle of tail. Ventral surfaces pale olive with up to 5 obscure darker stripes. SVL 30 mm.

Preferred habitat *C. o. ocellatus* occupies various subhumid to semi-arid habitats, particularly woodlands, rock outcrops and limestone-based heathlands. Restricted to south-west WA, from about Twilight Cove in south-east to Houtman Abrolhos Islands in north-west. Common on offshore islands south to about Tern island. *C. o. horni* occurs in arid habitats, especially hummock grasslands. Extends from central Australia to west coast of WA, north to southern Kimberley region. *C. o. rostralis* occurs in arid and semi-arid south and east Kimberley region, on *Triodia*-dominated stony hills and gravelly plains. *C. o. naso* is restricted to subhumid north-west Kimberley region, on sandstones supporting *Triodia*.

Microhabitat *C. o. ocellatus* shelters beneath exfoliating granite, fallen timber and mats of dead vegetation. On coast and offshore islands, limestone rocks and reef debris are utilised. Other subspecies dwell predominantly in or beneath hummock grasses.

Comments Highly secretive. Nature of arthropod prey recorded suggests most activity takes place under cover. Infrequency of individuals located active at night supports this.

Genus *CYRTODACTYLUS* Gray, 1827

(Subfamily Gekkoninae)

Large cosmopolitan genus containing approximately 70 described species. Extends from southern Europe, through Africa, Asia and Indo-Malayan Archipelago to New Guinea and islands of western Pacific. The single Australian species is restricted to north-east Qld.

Head large, broad and moderately dorsally depressed. Tail long, slender and round in cross-section, bearing enlarged transverse ventral scales. Limbs long and moderately slender with angular clawed bird-like digits. Enlarged subapical plates absent. Subdigital lamellae slightly swollen, in a single transverse series. Dorsal scales heterogeneous: smooth and granular, mixed with enlarged blunt tubercles. Pattern consists of prominent bands.

Terrestrial, arboreal and rock-inhabiting. Lays 1 or 2 calcareous-shelled eggs per clutch.

Australian species differs from *Nactus* and sympatric *Heteronotia* by much greater size (SVL 160 vs 80 mm or less) and pattern (body bands sharply defined and relatively regular vs irregular to absent).

Ring-Tailed Gecko
Cyrtodactylus louisiadensis (De Vis, 1892)
Photo 108

Description One of Australia's largest geckos. Two distinctive forms occur.

Common form: Ground colour whitish, pale pinkish brown to pale brown, marked with approximately 6 dark purplish brown to dark brown bands between nape and hips. These commence with a broad curved band across base of head from eye to eye. Bands bear dark margins, and extend onto lower lateral surfaces. Tubercles enclosed by dark bands are usually paler. Top of head usually mottled with dark brown. Tail prominently marked with approximately 13 white rings and black interspaces. Lips white. Ventral surfaces pinkish to white. SVL 160 mm.

Rainforest form: Differs in possessing fewer bands: approximately 4 between nape and hips, and 7 on tail. These fade laterally, and are usually pale-edged. Top of head and limbs usually uniform. Tail prehensile, held in laterally oriented coil when at rest (vs held in upward curve). Size presumably similar to common form.

Preferred habitat Subhumid to humid areas of Cape York peninsula, south to Chillagoe district, Qld. Common form is usually associated with woodlands, rock outcrops and vine thickets. Rainforest form is poorly documented; recorded from Iron Range.

Microhabitat Common form shelters in caves, rock crevices, hollow limbs and beneath surface debris. Occasionally resides in abandoned buildings. Forages on ground, cliff and boulder faces, tree trunks, limbs and among foliage.

Comments Status uncertain. Only tentatively regarded here as *C. louisiadensis*, the type locality of which is Tagula Island, off southern coast of New Guinea. Feeds on large arthropods and possibly small vertebrates such as other geckos. Pugnacious when handled and capable of inflicting a painful bite.

Genus *DIPLODACTYLUS* Gray, 1832

(Subfamily Diplodactylinae)

Endemic. Largest Australian gecko genus, represented by 34 species which display a broad array of physical characteristics to suit varied ecological requirements. Widespread through continental Australia, excluding extreme south-east, Tas. and most humid regions of east coast. Diversity is greatest in semi-arid to arid areas.

Terrestrial to arboreal. Arthropod feeders. Two parchment-shelled eggs are laid per clutch.

The genus has recently been dismembered and now comprises 2 subgenera, *Diplodactylus (Diplodactylus)* and *Diplodactylus (Strophurus)*, based on absence or presence of specialised glands deep in tail.

Subgenus *Diplodactylus (Diplodactylus)* contains 20 species, arranged in 4 groups. Robust to very slender terrestrial geckos. Digital pads moderately well developed (enlarged transverse and/or divided subdigital lamellae with expanded subapical plates) to absent (subdigital scales minute and spinose). Tail short, swollen and depressed, to long, slender and round in cross-section. Dorsal scales usually homogeneous. Caudal glands absent.

D. vittatus group Comprises 9 species of moderately slender to robust geckos with short limbs and moderately well-developed digital pads. Tail short and swollen, to long and slender. Pattern usually includes broad pale zigzagging, ragged-edged to straight vertebral stripe, or series of equivalent blotches. Largely southern in distribution (though some occur as far north as Pilbara region, WA, and central NT), penetrating cool and humid areas more effectively than other *Diplodactylus*. Geckos shelter beneath stones or fallen timber and in disused burrows or soil cracks. Some appear capable of enacting a defensive response: raising body high on legs with mouth agape while uttering a wheezing bark. Members are *D. byrnei*, *D. galeatus*, *D. granariensis*, *D. mitchelli*, *D. ornatus*, *D. polyophthalmus*, *D. pulcher*, *D. tessellatus* and *D. vittatus*.

D. stenodactylus group Contains 8 species of swift slender geckos with long limbs and tails. Digital pads usually poorly developed to absent. Pattern usually includes pale reddish ground colour, scattered pale spots, and sometimes a narrow pale vertebral stripe or series of blotches. Best represented in central to northern Australia though also present in subhumid to arid southern areas. Most favour sand ridge or sand plain habitats with sparse ground cover, sheltering in abandoned reptile and spider burrows. Alert and quick to flee when disturbed at night. Group comprises *D. alboguttatus*, *D. damaeus*, *D. fulleri*, *D. maini*, *D. occultus*, *D. squarrosus*, *D. stenodactylus* and *D. wombeyi*.

D. conspicillatus group Contains 2 species of terrestrial geckos with elongate bodies, short limbs and short dorsally depressed tails. Digital pads are poorly to moderately well developed. All but anterior upper and lower labial scales are granular and equal in size to adjacent scales (unique in genus). Pattern normally includes pale spots on brownish to reddish ground colour. Widespread through northern and western Australia in a variety of subhumid to arid habitats. Members usually shelter beneath stones or in disused spider burrows. Comprises *D. conspicillatus* and *D. savagei*.

D. steindachneri group Represented by one species with moderately slender body, limbs and tail. Digital pads well developed. Pattern includes pale, sharply defined angular dorsal blotches on brownish to pale reddish brown ground colour. Occurs in eastern interior of Australia, usually on hard soils.

Subgenus *Diplodactylus (Strophurus)* contains 14 species arranged in 3 groups. Moderately robust to slender, arboreal and hummock-inhabiting geckos. Digital pads well developed; enlarged divided proximal subdigital lamellae, entire transverse distal lamellae and expanded subapical plates. Tail round in cross-section; moderately short and robust to long and slender. Dorsal scales usually heterogeneous. Caudal glands present. These are capable of ejecting sticky irritant fluid; similar in appearance to treacle and drying to cobweb-like filaments on contact with air. This is a unique defensive response in Gekkonidae. Some species are able to raise their tails, aiming and projecting fluid at an aggressor from a distance of up to 60 cm.

D. strophurus group Contains 11 taxa of predominantly arboreal geckos, usually with long slender bodies, tails and limbs. Iris of most species is brightly coloured and boldly patterned. Most bear scattered to longitudinally aligned tubercles and/or spines on back and tail. Widespread, covering most of distribution of genus. Shelter sites including hollow limbs, loose bark or hummock grasses are favoured. Though largely nocturnal, some species bask on sheltered branches in weak sunlight. Comprises *D. assimilis*, *D. ciliaris ciliaris*, *D. ciliaris aberrans*, *D. intermedius*, *D. rankini*, *D. spinigerus*, *D. strophurus*, *D. taenicauda*, *D. williamsi*, *D. wellingtonae* and *D. wilsoni*.

D. michaelseni group Contains 3 semi-arboreal to hummock- and tussock-inhabiting species of medium to very slender build. Pattern includes dark and pale stripes on dorsal, lateral and ventral surfaces, providing effective concealment among foliage and contrasting shadows of grasses. Extends through arid western Qld and NT to lower west coastal plain, sandy deserts, and Kimberley region of WA. Comprises *D. mcmillani*, *D. michaelseni* and *D. taeniata*.

D. elderi group Comprises one hummock grass-inhabiting species of medium build with moderately slender tail and relatively long limbs. Pattern consists of prominent pale dots on leaden grey ground colour. Widely distributed through arid and semi-arid areas of all mainland States except Vic.

Excepting *D. pulcher*, which is easily distinguishable by pattern, *Diplodactylus* differs from *Rhynchoedura* by shape of snout: rounded vs beak-like.

Diplodactylus alboguttatus Werner, 1910
Photo 109

Description Member of *D. stenodactylus* group

with relatively large subapical plates. Ground colour pale yellowish brown to pale reddish brown. Irregular series of large ragged-edged pale dorsal blotches extend from top of head to tail-tip. Though occasionally fused, these are usually separated by narrow dark-flecked interspaces of ground colour. Dorsolateral to lateral series of circular cream to white spots extend from behind eye onto tail. Regenerated tail ground colour with scattered to longitudinally aligned blackish flecks. Limbs ground colour with large cream to white spots. Ventral surfaces white. SVL 50 mm.

Distinguished from *D. maini* by size of subapical plates (considerably larger than adjacent lamellae vs very small and scarcely larger).

Preferred habitat Coast and hinterland of sub-humid to semi-arid south-western WA, from Perth north to Gnaraloo Station and inland to Marchagee. Favours sandy soils supporting heathlands, often in association with *Banksia* woodlands.

Microhabitat Shelters in vertical shafts of spider burrows; rarely beneath surface debris.

Comments Feeds on various terrestrial insects and spiders. Otherwise as for species group.

Diplodactylus assimilis Storr, 1988
Photo 110

Description Small member of *D. strophurus* group with short spines on tail, and usually up to 7 very short spines over eye. Large, high orange to orange-brown dorsal tubercles present, arranged in a wavy line along either side of vertebral region. Spines on tail usually arranged in whorls. Iris greyish white edged with black and enclosing a fine black reticulum. Mouth-lining bluish black. Ground colour shades of grey marked with 5–8 dark-edged paler lateral blotches from side of neck to base of tail. These often link with their opposites to form a chain-like pattern. Ventral surfaces whitish, usually dotted with darker pigment. SVL 75 mm.

Distinguished from *D. ciliaris* and *D. wellingtonae* in bearing much smaller spines over eye and on tail. Differs further from *D. ciliaris* by mouth colour (bluish vs orange to yellow). Differs from *D. intermedius* and *D. strophurus* by arrangement of dorsal tubercles (discontinuous and wavy vs continuous and parallel, and randomly scattered, respectively). Differs from *D. spinigerus* in bearing spines over eye and by nature of tail spines (short and broad and orange-brown vs long and very slender and black).

Preferred habitat Semi-arid to arid southern interior of WA, from Yalgoo in north-west to Zanthus in east. Occupies a variety of habitats north and south of the mulga/eucalypt line.

Microhabitat See *D. strophurus* species group.

Comments Previously regarded as a western population of *D. intermedius*. See subgenus *Diplodactylus (Strophurus)*.

Diplodactylus byrnei Lucas and Frost, 1896
Photo 111

Description Small long-tailed member of *D. vittatus* group bearing scattered reddish conical tubercles over dorsal surfaces. Ground colour pale yellowish brown, reddish brown to dark brown, usually marked with 4 broad irregularly shaped dorsal bands or transversely aligned blotches; across nape, behind shoulders, at midbody, and on hips. Top of head paler shade of ground colour with darker blotches. Flanks and upper surfaces of limbs ground colour with paler spots or marbling. Tail marked with 6–9 pale bands or blotches, becoming obscure towards tip. Ventral surfaces white. SVL 50 mm.

Preferred habitat Semi-arid to arid western NSW, north-eastern SA, south-eastern NT and south-western Qld. Favours loamy to sandy soils supporting sparse ground cover of shrubs (particularly chenopods), occasionally in association with woodlands.

Microhabitat Shelters in soil cracks and spider burrows; occasionally beneath surface debris. Forages in open spaces between shrubs.

Comments See *D. vittatus* group.

Diplodactylus ciliaris Boulenger, 1885
Photos 112, 113. See also photo 103.

Description Large member of *D. strophurus* group with long spines over eye and on tail. Two subspecies recognised.

D. c. ciliaris Up to 4 spines may margin top of eye, and 2 behind eye. Dorsal tubercles usually low and arranged irregularly. Two rows of long orange and/or black spines commence on base of tail, becoming shorter towards tip. Iris greyish white to brownish orange, margined with orange or white and enclosing a fine black reticulum. Mouth-lining brownish yellow to dull orange. Ground colour shades of grey to brownish grey. Some individuals are very pale and virtually patternless, while others are prominently marked with an upper lateral series of 4–7 pale grey blotches between side of neck and base of tail. Fine white flecks often present over all dorsal surfaces. Populations from northern NT tend to be browner, with upper lateral blotches often replaced by clusters of pale flecks, and much of dorsal surface marked with irregular areas of orange-red to reddish-brown. Ventral surfaces ground colour to white, usually dotted with dark brown. SVL 85 mm.

D. c. aberrans Glauert, 1952 Similar in most aspects to nominate form, differing by nature of non-spinose scales on tail (tubercular vs granular) and by colour of dorsal tubercles and caudal spines (mostly black vs mostly orange).

Both subspecies differ from *D. wellingtonae* and *D. intermedius* by arrangement of dorsal tubercles (randomly scattered vs aligned in 2 parallel rows).

Differs further from both, and from *D. assimilis*, by mouth colour (yellow or orange vs bluish). Differs further from *D. assimilis* and *D. intermedius* in having much longer spines above eye and on tail.

Preferred habitat *D. c. ciliaris* extends through subhumid and humid northern Australia, from north and north-eastern Kimberley region of WA, through northern NT to north-western Qld. *D. c. aberrans* occurs in semi-arid to arid regions dominated by shrublands and low woodlands on red sandy soils. Extends from south-western Kimberley region south to Lake Yeo, WA.

Microhabitat See *D. strophurus* species group.

Comments See subgenus *Diplodactylus (Strophurus)*.

Fat-Tailed Gecko
Diplodactylus conspicillatus
Lucas and Frost, 1897
Photo 114

Description Large member of *D. conspicillatus* group with plump dorsally depressed tail bearing flat plate-like scales and irregular rings of conical tubercles. Ground colour yellow, grey, brown to reddish brown patterned with fine to coarse dark reticulum. Scattered pale spots sometimes present. Pale stripe usually extends from nostril to eye, bordered below by dark stripe or flush extending through eye. Ventral surfaces whitish bearing darker pigment on throat and distal surfaces of limbs. SVL 60 mm.

Preferred habitat Wide range of subhumid to arid habitats on sandy to hard stony soils occurring through greater part of all States except Vic., Tas.

Microhabitat Shelters in vertical shafts of spider burrows or soil cracks; rarely beneath surface debris. Forages on open ground between vegetation.

Comments Distinctive tail is used to plug entrance to spider burrow. Appears to feed solely on termites. When aggravated body is inflated with air, presumably to increase apparent size.

Beaded Gecko
Diplodactylus damaeus (Lucas and Frost, 1896)
Photo 115

Description Member of *D. stenodactylus* group. Only *Diplodactylus* lacking any enlargement of subapical plates. All subdigital lamellae minute and spinose. Ground colour pale reddish brown to pink. Broad dark-edged yellowish brown to whitish vertebral stripe, or narrowly separated series of blotches, extends from nape to tail-tip. Lateral series of large circular cream spots and scattered smaller dots usually extend from neck or forebody onto tail. Top of head (enclosing upper half of each eye) ground colour or paler, variegated and/or dotted with darker pigment. Narrow dark line extends from nostril to eye. Broader dark line extends back from eye, curving to meet its opposite on base of head. Lower

flanks and ventral surfaces white. SVL 50 mm.

Preferred habitat Semi-arid to arid regions of southern Australia, from western NSW and north-western Vic., through SA and southern NT to south-eastern interior of WA. Occurs on sandy to loamy soils supporting mallee/*Triodia* associations, chenopod shrublands and hummock grasslands.

Microhabitat Shelters in abandoned reptile, spider and ant burrows. Occasionally excavates its own shallow burrow, favouring the slope of a mound supporting a grass hummock or a shrub.

Comments Feeds on a variety of arthropods. Ritualised combat recorded between males. This involves uttering a chirping call, raising and arching body, slowly waving tail, jerking head movements and biting opponent's head and body. Hatchlings are present during late February in western NSW, while gravid females have been recorded during January in WA. Otherwise as for *D. stenodactylus* group.

Jewelled Gecko
Diplodactylus elderi
Stirling and Zeitz, 1893
Photo 116

Description Sole member of *D. elderi* group. Ground colour dark brown, lead grey to blackish marked with prominent, sparsely to densely scattered or transversely aligned dark-edged pale spots; each centred on an enlarged tubercle. These are absent to very sparse on flanks and limbs. Ventral surfaces greyish white with scattered dark flecks. SVL 45 mm.

Preferred habitat Semi-arid to arid regions from south-western NSW through SA, south-western Qld and southern NT, to interior and north-west of WA. Occurs on sand plains and sand ridges (to a lesser extent stony hills) where hummock grasses occur.

Microhabitat Shelters and forages in hummock grasses, venturing into open spaces infrequently.

Comments Feeds on a variety of arthropods, though termites constitute bulk of diet. In south-eastern SA eggs are laid in late January, hatching in early March. Shares microhabitat throughout entire range with predatory lizard-feeder, Burton's legless lizard (*Lialis burtonis*), enjoying apparent immunity due to its ability to eject sticky repellent fluid from glands beneath skin on dorsal surface of tail. See subgenus *Diplodactylus (Strophurus)*.

Diplodactylus fulleri Storr, 1978
Photo 117

Description Large moderately short-tailed member of *D. stenodactylus* group with very small subapical plates. Scales on tail large, rectangular, and arranged in whorls. Ground colour pale reddish brown to pale brownish white with indistinct darker reticulum. Original tail dark reddish brown with indistinct paler bands. Ventral surfaces pinkish white. SVL 50 mm.

Preferred habitat Arid north-western interior of WA. Known only from the vicinity of Lake Disappointment.

Microhabitat Presumably as for *D. stenodactylus* group.

Comments See *D. stenodactylus* group.

Diplodactylus galeatus Kluge, 1963
Photo 118

Description Robust, thick-tailed boldly patterned member of *D. vittatus* group. Ground colour dark reddish brown to pale pinkish brown marked with 4–6 large, diamond-shaped to irregularly circular, dark-edged pale yellowish brown blotches between nape and hips. Top of head bears large pale yellowish brown blotch bordered posteriorly by dark brown line which curves forward to each eye. Smaller dark-edged pale blotch may be present on side of neck. Prominent fine white spots usually present on flanks and limbs. Original tail bears 4–6 prominent dark-edged pale dorsal blotches. Regenerated tails patternless. Lower lateral and ventral surfaces white. SVL 50 mm.

Preferred habitat Rock outcrops (particularly quartz) in McDonnell Range of southern NT and Stuart Range of northern SA.

Microhabitat Shelters in shallow depressions beneath rocks during mild weather, seeking deeper retreats in summer.

Comments As for *D. vittatus* group.

Diplodactylus granariensis Storr, 1979
Photos 119, 120

Description Moderately large slender-tailed member of *D. vittatus* group subject to considerable variation in pattern and build.

Northern form: Ground colour brown to reddish brown. Broad, straight to mildly serrated, dark-edged pale brown to grey vertebral stripe extends to tail-tip. This forks on nape, branching forward through upper half of each eye to snout. Pale lateral spots rarely present and never dark-edged. Lower lateral row of dark spots sometimes present. Lips, lower lateral and ventral surfaces whitish. SVL 60 mm.

Southern and coastal form: Tends to become more robust with shorter tail and increasing development of pale lateral blotches southwards. Ground colour reddish brown to grey. Vertebral stripe broken into series of angular, irregularly sized blotches.

West coast form: Similar in pattern to southern form, lacking pale midlateral blotches.

Northern and west coast forms differ from *D. ornatus* in lacking midlateral series of whitish spots. All forms differ from *D. polyophthalmus* by arrange-

ment of scales on lower lip: a gradual decrease in size of anterior lower labial scales vs a sharp decrease between 2nd and 3rd. Differs from *D. vittatus* by tail-shape: relatively long and slender vs short and robust.

Preferred habitat Subhumid to arid regions of southern Australia from Hutt River, WA, in north to Spencer Gulf, SA, in east. Favours hard to stony soils supporting a variety of open vegetation types. Northern limits of range appear associated with transition zone between eucalypt-dominated areas of south and *Acacia* associations of interior. One record exists from Wiluna, nearly 500 km north-east of this area. Northern form extends south to Narrogin, Kondinin, Newman Rocks and Frazer Range, and west to New Norcia, Marchagee and Darlington, WA. Southern form occupies remainder of distribution, excepting coastal areas from Hutt River south to Green Head. Northern and southern forms mix in the southern wheat belt, where striped and blotched lizards occur in about equal numbers.

Microhabitat Shelters in spider burrows, soil cracks or beneath surface debris. At night individuals often rest on small sticks or shrubs, up to 30 cm in height.

Comments Low tempratures in south of range require a marked degree of cold tolerance. Individuals may be encountered foraging in temperatures sufficiently low to render most reptiles inactive. Terrestrial spiders and insects constitute major prey items. See *D. vittatus* group.

Diplodactylus intermedius Ogilby, 1892
Photo 121

Description Small member of *D. strophurus* group bearing 2 parallel dorsal rows of well-developed enlarged orange-brown conical tubercles. These may be continuous with 2 rows of larger tubercles on tail. Low conical spines usually present over eye. Iris margined by pink to reddish orange and marked with prominent complex geometric designs. Ground colour shades of grey. Mid-dorsal area (roughly enclosed by tubercles) darker to almost black with wavy to zigzagging edges. This extends from base of head to tail-tip. Remainder of dorsal and lateral surfaces marked with a dark reticulum. Ventral surfaces pale grey densely covered with small dark spots; usually one per scale. SVL 65 mm.

Distinguished from *D. wellingtonae* and *D. ciliaris* in bearing much shorter spines above eye and on tail. Differs from *D. williamsi* in bearing 2 (vs 4) rows of enlarged tubercles on tail. Differs from *D. assimilis* by arrangement of dorsal tubercles (continuous and parallel vs discontinuous and wavy).

Preferred habitat Semi-arid to arid southern Australia, from eastern interior of NSW, through north-west Vic. and southern SA to western edge of Nullarbor Plain, WA. Occurs in a variety of habitats including *Acacia* shrublands, eucalypt woodlands (particularly mallee/hummock grass associations), chenopod communities and rock outcrops.

Microhabitat Shelters in hollow limbs and hummock grasses, and beneath loose bark or rocks. May be encountered basking in weak sunlight.

Comments See subgenus *Diplodactylus (Strophurus)* and *D. strophurus* group.

Diplodactylus maini Kluge, 1962
Photo 122

Description Small member of *D. stenodactylus* group with very poorly developed subapical plates. Ground colour pale yellow to reddish brown marked with numerous large dark-edged paler dorsal blotches from nape to tail-tip. Flanks and limbs marked with round, variably sized, pale brown to cream spots and heavy to fine dark reticulum. Top of head encloses large dark-edged pale grey to brownish blotch; continuous with dorsal blotches or separated by dark posterior margin which curves forward from base of head to each eye. Ventral surfaces white. SVL 45 mm.

Distinguished from *D. alboguttatus* by size of subapical plates (very small, scarcely larger than adjacent lamellae, vs considerably larger).

Preferred habitat Salmon gum and gimlet woodlands, shrublands, heathlands and mallee woodlands (including mallee/hummock grass associations) in semi-arid southern interior of WA.

Microhabitat Shelters in vertical shafts of spider burrows. Forages in open spaces between vegetation.

Comments On cool nights geckos rest with heads protruding from spider burrows, presumably allowing ambush of small invertebrates with minimal exposure to predation. Otherwise as for *D. stenodactylus* group.

Diplodactylus mcmillani Storr, 1978
Photo 123

Description Moderately robust relatively short-tailed member of *D. michaelseni* group, somewhat intermediate between other 2 members. Ground colour pale olive-grey with usually 4 dorsal lines of dark brown dots. These represent margins of obscure stripes. Faint dark-edged dorsolateral stripe usually discernible. Pale upper lateral stripe (edged with dark brown dots) extends from eye to tail-tip. Obscure midlateral line usually present. Greyish white dark-edged ventrolateral stripe extends from forelimb to hindlimb. Ventral surfaces whitish. SVL 50 mm.

Distinguished from *D. taeniata* by build: relatively robust vs extremely slender.

Preferred habitat Humid to subhumid north-west Kimberley region, WA, occurring on sandstone outcrops vegetated with *Triodia*.

Microhabitat Shelters in *Triodia* hummocks.

Comments See *D. michaelseni* group and subgenus *Diplodactylus (Strophurus)*.

Diplodactylus michaelseni Werner, 1910
Photo 124

Description Robust member of *D. michaelseni* group. Ground colour pale olive-brown, patterned with paler greyish stripes bearing broken dark margins. Narrow vertebral stripe (often forked anteriorly) extends from top of head to hips. Broader dorsolateral stripe extends from snout narrowly above eye onto tail, becoming wavy and less distinct beyond hips. Narrow (sometimes broken) upper lateral stripe extends from in front of forelimb, narrowly above hindlimb to base of tail. Similar midlateral stripe extends from below ear to forelimb, thence to hindlimb. Ventral surfaces greyish with scattered dark flecks. Indistinct median and ventrolateral stripes occasionally present on throat and upper chest. SVL 50 mm.

Preferred habitat Yellow to white sand plains on mid- to lower west coast and adjacent interior of WA, from Marchagee north to Shark Bay. Favours *Banksia* woodlands and heathlands where sedge tussocks or *Plectrachne* hummocks are present.

Microhabitat Shelters in foliage of sedge or *Plectrachne*, foraging among adjacent shrubs and low bushes.

Comments See *D. michaelseni* group and subgenus *Diplodactylus (Strophurus)*.

Diplodactylus mitchelli Kluge, 1963
Photo 125

Description Largest member of *D. vittatus* group with short thick tail. Two distinct populations occur.

Pilbara population: Ground colour yellowish to dark reddish brown. Broad paler yellowish brown to whitish vertebral zone (broadly expanded laterally to form deep serrations) extends from nape to base of tail. Flanks and top of head paler shade of ground colour without pattern. Dark streak may extend from eye to above ear. Regenerated tail ground colour, flecked or spotted with dark brown. Original tail not known. Ventral surfaces white. SVL 65 mm.

North West Cape population: Differs in bearing prominent dark reticulum on dorsal and lateral surfaces, including on original tail.

Preferred habitat Pilbara population occurs where ground cover is dominated by hummock grasses on rocky Hamersley Range, WA, and on adjacent hard loamy coastal flats. North West Cape population occurs on rocky slopes of Cape Range, North West Cape, WA.

Microhabitat Shelters beneath rocks and in abandoned burrows.

Comments Predominantly terrestrial, occasionally climbing into low shrubs. Clutch of 2 eggs recorded in March. Otherwise as for *D. vittatus* group.

Diplodactylus occultus
King, Braithwaite and Wombey, 1982
Photo 126

Description Small member of *D. stenodactylus* group with moderately well-developed subapical plates. Dorsal ground colour dark brown marked with usually 4 large, roughly square paler brown dorsal blotches. Flanks, limbs and sides of tail bear prominent scattered white spots. Top of head reddish brown bordered posteriorly by dark brown bar which curves forward through each eye. Side of head blotched with dark brown. Dark brown bar extends from nostril to eye. Tail and limbs mottled with reddish brown and dark brown. Lips and ventral surfaces white. SVL 40 mm.

Distinguished from sympatric population of *D. stenodactylus* by nature of subdigital lamellae (enlarged and roughly rectangular vs granular to spinose).

Preferred habitat. Known only from subhumid eucalypt woodlands in Alligator Rivers Region west of Arnhem Land, NT.

Microhabitat Only known specimens collected beneath cover of grass or thick leaf-litter.

Comments See *D. stenodactylus* group.

Diplodactylus ornatus Gray, 1845
Photo 127

Description Medium-sized long-tailed member of *D. vittatus* group. Ground colour dark grey, dark brown to pale olive-brown, marked with broad prominent pale grey to pale brown vertebral stripe (bearing shallow to deeply serrated edge) from nape to tail-tip. This forks on nape, branching forward through each eye to snout. Broad ragged-edged strip of ground colour (bearing scattered pale spots) covers dorsolateral and upper lateral surfaces from snout to tail-tip. Prominent to obscure midlateral series of large pale blotches usually present. Lower lateral surfaces greyish. Top of head ground colour to paler, usually bearing darker flecks. Ventral surfaces white. SVL 55 mm.

Distinguished from northern form of *D. granariensis* in bearing midlateral series of pale blotches. Differs from southern and coastal forms, and from *D. polyophthalmus*, in possessing pale vertebral stripe (vs dorsal series of blotches).

Preferred habitat Sandy lower west coast and hinterland of WA, from North West Cape south to Jurien Bay and inland to Marchagee. Favours low open vegetation such as heathlands.

Microhabitat Shelters beneath rocks or fallen timber and in tussocks.

Comments Feeds on a wide variety of arthropods. Otherwise as for *D. vittatus* group.

Diplodactylus polyophthalmus Günther, 1867
Photo 128

Description Small member of *D. vittatus* group with short thick tail. Ground colour dark reddish brown marked with irregularly sized pale reddish to greyish spots and blotches. These are largest on back and tail, often most prominent on flanks; occasionally sufficiently large to exclude all but reticulum of ground colour. Short obscure pale bar sometimes present from nostril to eye. Ventral surfaces whitish, each scale bearing small dark dot. SVL 50 mm.

Distinguished from *D. ornatus* and northern form of *D. granariensis* in possessing pale dorsal series of blotches (vs vertebral stripe). Differs further from all forms of *D. granariensis* by arrangement of scales on lower lip: a sharp decrease in size between 2nd and 3rd lower labial scales vs a gradual decrease.

Preferred habitat Humid to subhumid southwestern WA from Stirling Range north to Darling Range. Apparently disjunct population occurs further north at Cockleshell Gully. Favours rocky habitats in Stirling and Darling Ranges. Occurs on sandy to lateritic soils supporting heathlands and eucalypt/*Banksia* woodlands in northern suburbs of Perth and at Cockleshell Gully.

Microhabitat Shelters in shallow depressions beneath rocks or fallen timber.

Comments See *D. vittatus* group.

Diplodactylus pulcher (Steindachner, 1870)
Photos 129, 130

Description Small slender member of *D. vittatus* group. Ground colour brown to reddish brown, marked with a dorsal series of large, finely dark-edged cream to pale yellowish brown blotches from nape to tail-tip. Occasionally these coalesce to form a broad straight-edged vertebral stripe, especially in north of range. Flanks usually bear scattered smaller blotches. Top of head cream to pale yellowish brown edged posteriorly with dark brown. Ventral surfaces white, sharply defined against pigmented lower flanks. SVL 45 mm.

Preferred habitat Semi-arid to arid interior of WA and adjacent SA, particularly on hard to stony *Acacia*-dominated soils supporting sparse ground cover. Extends south-west to Darling Range, on lateritic soils and granites supporting dry sclerophyll forest.

Microhabitat Shelters in spider burrows, termitaria and shallow burrows or depressions beneath rocks or fallen timber. Forages in open spaces between shrubs.

Comments Apparently feeds almost exclusively on termites. See *D. vittatus* group.

Diplodactylus rankini Storr, 1979
Photo 131

Description Slender member of *D. strophurus* group bearing sparse irregular dorsolateral series of slightly enlarged tubercles. These become larger (though not spinose), forming 2 parallel rows on tail. Iris rimmed with yellow and marked with prominent geometric designs. Ground colour shades of grey. Broad darker serrated-edged dorsal zone extends from head onto tail. Broad dark grey mid-lateral zone (serrated or constricted to form series of lozenge shapes) extends from behind eye onto tail. Flanks and limbs streaked with dark grey. Ventral surfaces pale grey. SVL 60 mm.

Distinguished from *D. strophurus* by nature of tail (unsegmented vs segmented with bands of pale connective tissue). Differs from *D. ciliaris* and *D. spinigerus* in lacking spines on tail, and further from *D. ciliaris* in lacking spines over eye.

Preferred habitat Pale coastal dunes supporting proteaceous shrubs and beach spinifex (*Spinifex longifolius*) on arid western North West Cape, south to Carnarvon, WA.

Microhabitat Shelters in hollows, on shaded branches and among foliage of coastal shrubs.

Comments See subgenus *Diplodactylus (Strophurus)* and *D. strophurus* group.

Diplodactylus savagei Kluge, 1963
Photo 132

Description Small member of *D. conspicillatus* group with elongate body, short limbs and plump dorsally depressed tail. Ground colour deep purplish brown marked with numerous prominent yellow spots of variable size, tending to become larger on tail. Top of head tinged with yellow. Broad blackish brown bar extends from snout through each eye, curving upwards to meet its opposite on base of head. Ventral surfaces white with darker pigment beneath limbs. SVL 45 mm.

Preferred habitat Rocky slopes and mesas vegetated with *Triodia* in arid Pilbara region, WA.

Microhabitat Shelters in burrows beneath rocks, and in spider holes.

Comments Probably feeds largely on termites.

Western Spiny-tailed Gecko
Diplodactylus spinigerus Gray, 1842
Photos 133, 134

Description Member of *D. strophurus* group bearing 2 prominent rows of soft black dorsal spines which become larger on tail. Iris rimmed with yellow in south, white in coastal areas north of Kalbarri, and red in east; marked with intricate geometric designs. Ground colour grey to greyish brown. Broad dark grey to black dorsal stripe (with straight to zigzagging edge) extends from head or nape to tail-tip. This is peppered with small white spots, each centred on a scale. Remainder of body and limbs peppered with black spots; 1 per scale. Ventral surfaces pale to dark grey with darker pigmentation beneath throat; occasionally bearing dark streaks over remainder. SVL 70 mm.

Distinguished from *D. ciliaris* and *D. assimilis* in lacking enlarged spines over eye. Differs from *D.*

rankini in possessing slender spines on back and tail.

Preferred habitat Subhumid south and lower west coasts of WA, including some offshore islands. Favours sandy to limestone- or laterite-based soils supporting heathlands and woodlands. Absent from humid deep south-west.

Microhabitat Shelters in hollow limbs, beneath loose bark, on shaded branches or foliage of trees and shrubs, and among stems and leaves of grass trees (*Xanthorrhoea*) or tussocks of beach spinifex (*Spinifex longifolius*).

Comments See subgenus *Diplodactylus (Strophurus)* and *D. strophurus* group.

Diplodactylus squarrosus Kluge, 1962
Photo 135

Description Small member of *D. stenodactylus* group with relatively large subapical plates. Ground colour brick red to reddish brown, finely reticulated or flecked with dark brown to black. Dorsal series of irregularly sized and finely dark-edged pale yellowish brown blotches extend from nape to tail-tip. Flanks and limbs marked with large scattered pale spots. Top of head bears large pale blotch enclosing irregular markings of ground colour. Ventral surfaces white. SVL 45 mm.

Distinguished from *D. stenodactylus* in possessing dorsal series of pale blotches (vs vertebral stripe or scattered pale spots).

Preferred habitat Semi-arid to arid midwest coast and interior of WA, on hard to stony soils vegetated with low woodlands and shrublands.

Microhabitat Shelters in vertical shafts of spider burrows, foraging in open spaces between shrubs.

Comments See *D. stenodactylus* group.

Diplodactylus steindachneri Boulenger, 1885
Photo 136

Description Sole member of *D. steindachneri* group. Ground colour pale yellowish brown, pinkish brown to very dark brown. Pale (sometimes broken) line usually extends back from each eye, joining on nape to form broad dark-edged vertebral region, and breaking into blotches beyond hips. This encloses usually 3 large dark 'islands' of ground colour: behind shoulders, on lower back, and on base of tail. These may be sufficiently large to break dorsal region into blotches. Flanks may bear narrow pale vertical bars (connecting dorsal region with venter), a line of pale spots, or scattered pale flecks. Top of head pale yellowish brown with variable dark marbling. Ventral surfaces white. SVL 55 mm.

Preferred habitat Favours hard sandy, loamy or clay-based soils supporting woodlands and shrublands over sparse ground cover from semi-arid to arid interior of NSW north, well onto Cape York Peninsula, Qld.

Microhabitat Shelters in spider burrows or soil cracks and beneath surface debris. Forages in open spaces between shrubs.

Comments Alert and quick to flee when disturbed. Feeds on a wide variety of arthropods.

Diplodactylus stenodactylus Boulenger, 1896
Photos 137, 138

Description Large variable member of *D. stenodactylus* group comprising 2 apparently distinct populations.

Eastern form: Subapical plates large; much larger than adjacent lamellae. Ground colour pink to dark reddish brown. Broad prominent straight-edged cream vertebral stripe (margined by darker shade of ground colour) extends from shoulders or nape to tail-tip; often breaking into blotches beyond hips. This is deeply forked anteriorly, branching through top of each eye to snout. Flanks prominently spotted with cream, or bearing narrow wavy vertical lines branching from vertebral stripe. Top of head paler shade of ground colour with darker blotches. Ventral surfaces white. SVL 55 mm.

Widespread form: Differs from eastern form in bearing much smaller subapical plates. Vertebral stripe prominent to absent; usually narrow with conspicuous darker margin. Remainder of body and limbs finely variegated with blackish brown and prominently to obscurely spotted with cream. Ventral surfaces white. SVL 60 mm.

Differs from *D. squarrosus* in possessing a pale vertebral stripe or scattered spots (vs large dorsal blotches).

Preferred habitat Widespread through subhumid to arid Australia, from south-eastern interior of Qld and north-western NSW, through NT and most of SA to interior and north-west of WA. Occurs on a variety of sandy to hard stony soils with sparse shrub or *Triodia*-dominated ground cover. Eastern form is known from stony areas in northern Qld and eastern NT. Widespread form occupies remainder of range.

Microhabitat Occasionally found beneath small surface objects during mild weather. For most of the year abandoned spider and reptile burrows or soil cracks are utilised.

Comments Feeds on a variety of arthropods, particularly beetles and termites. Otherwise as for *D. stenodactylus* group.

Diplodactylus strophurus
(Duméril and Bibron, 1836)
Photo 139

Description Slender member of *D. strophurus* group with supraciliary scales enlarged to form low, blunt conical tubercles over eye. Dorsal and caudal tubercles conical; randomly scattered on back, and arranged in rings on tail. Each ring is separated by a narrow band of yellow or (rarely) white connective tissue. Iris rimmed with yellow, red or white and marked with fine black lines, forming an intricate geometric pattern. Ground colour pale to very dark grey with prominent to obscure pattern. Broad dark wavy-edged vertebral region extends from top of head onto tail. Narrow dark longitudinal lines usually present on top of head and neck. Flanks and limbs obscurely variegated to mottled with dark pigment. Ventral surfaces pale grey, sometimes bearing dark midventral stripe from throat to tail-tip. SVL 70 mm.

Distinguished from all other members of *D. strophurus* group by nature of tail (distinctively segmented by bands of pale connective tissue vs pale connective tissue absent. If tail-less, the basal-most segment of connective tissue is usually still present.

Preferred habitat Semi-arid to arid midwest coast and interior of WA. Most abundant on hard to stony soils supporting low *Acacia* shrublands.

Microhabitat Shelters in hollow limbs and among sheltered branches or foliage of trees and shrubs.

Comments See subgenus *Diplodactylus (Strophurus)* and *D. strophurus* group.

Diplodactylus taeniatus
(Lönnberg and Andersson, 1913)
Photo 140

Description Member of *D. michaelseni* group with extremely slender body, limbs and tail. Iris greyish white with fine dark lines forming intricate geometric pattern. Ground colour pale grey to brown or dull yellow. Pattern usually prominent, consisting entirely of sharp-edged stripes. Narrow dark vertebral stripe extends from top of head to tail-tip. Yellow to greyish dorsolateral stripe extends from rear of eye to tail-tip. Yellowish brown lower lateral stripe extends from corner of mouth through fore- and hindlimbs to tail-tip. Interspaces may be marked with narrow yellow median lines. Ventral surfaces ground colour or paler, bearing prominent midventral stripe extending to tail-tip, and obscure dark stripes on throat. SVL 50 mm.

Distinguished from *D. mcmillani* by build (slender vs relatively robust).

Preferred habitat Semi-arid to arid northern and central Australia, from Mt Isa/Cloncurry district, Qld, west to North West Cape, WA. Extends north to southern Kimberley region, WA, and Gulf of Carpentaria, NT. Restricted to hummock grasses growing on sandy, loamy and stony soils.

Microhabitat Shelters in hummock grasses.

Comments Unusual defensive response includes opening mouth to display bright yellow interior, and ejection of bright orange viscous fluid from pores on back and tail. Recent information suggests northern semi-arid populations are distinct from those occurring in arid zone to the south. See subgenus *Diplodactylus (Strophurus)* and *D. michaelseni* group.

Golden-tailed Gecko
Diplodactylus taenicauda De Vis, 1886
Photo 141

Description Slender strikingly patterned member of *D. strophurus* group. Dorsal tubercles absent. Caudal tubercles reduced to patches of granules. Iris bright red. Intricate eye markings characteristic of this group are intense, though reduced in extent. Ground colour grey to almost white, marked on head, body and limbs with numerous irregularly sized black spots. These tend to become larger toward vertebral region and more dense on sides of tail. Prominent ragged-edged orange to yellow vertebral stripe extends from hips to tail-tip. White to pale grey individual scales are scattered over tail, concentrating along edges of stripe. Regenerated tail bears irregular broken pattern. Ventral surfaces greyish spotted with black. SVL 70 mm.
Preferred habitat Subhumid central coast and south-eastern interior of Qld. Occurs in dry sclerophyll forests and woodlands, particularly where native pine (*Callitris*) is present.
Microhabitat Predominantly arboreal, sheltering beneath loose bark and in hollow limbs.
Comments Active at surprisingly cool temperatures. Often encountered resting head downwards on saplings or tree trunks. See subgenus *Diplodactylus (Strophurus)* and *D. strophurus* group.

Diplodactylus tessellatus (Günther, 1875)
Photos 142, 143

Description Moderately slender member of *D. vittatus* group with short tail bearing regular rings of enlarged conical scales. Ground colour pale to dark grey or brown. Pattern prominent to absent, usually consisting of dark brown to black reticulation, marbling or scattered blotches, mixed with fine dark and cream spots. Paravertebral series of pale blotches may extend from nape to tail, becoming broken and scattered beyond hips. Obscure dark line may curve back from each eye, tending to meet its opposite on base of head or on nape. Ventral surfaces whitish, distinctively marked with prominent greyish blotches. SVL 50 mm.
Preferred habitat Semi-arid to arid central and eastern interior of Australia, usually on hard cracking soils supporting sparse ground cover of shrubs (particularly chenopods) and low grasses.
Microhabitat Shelters in soil cracks or spider burrows and beneath surface debris. Forages in open spaces between shrubs.
Comments An arid-adapted member of this predominantly southern group. See *D. vittatus* group.

Stone Gecko
Diplodactylus vittatus Gray, 1832
Photo 144

Description Robust member of *D. vittatus* group with moderately short thick tail. Ground colour

shades of brown to grey. Broad to narrow, pale brown to cream, zigzagging vertebral stripe commences as large blotch on top of head, extending to hips. This breaks to form large blotches on tail. Flanks bear small to large similarly coloured spots. Ventral surfaces white. SVL 50 mm.

Distinguished from *D. granariensis* by nature of tail (short and robust vs relatively long and slender).
Preferred habitat Widespread through south-eastern Australia, from mideastern Qld, through most of NSW and northern Vic. to Spencer Gulf, SA. Occupies a variety of semi-arid to subhumid habitats, including rock outcrops, dry sclerophyll forests, woodlands and heathlands, from coast to subalpine regions.
Microhabitat Shelters beneath small stones, fallen bark, timber and surface debris. Often seen at night perching on small sticks, usually about 10–20 cm above ground.
Comments Penetrates cool moister regions to a greater extent than other *Diplodactylus*. Presence of accumulated sloughed skins suggests suitable sheltering sites may be used for extended periods. Otherwise as for *D. vittatus* group.

Diplodactylus wellingtonae Storr, 1988
Photo 145

Description Large, long-tailed member of *D. strophurus* group with long spines above eye and on tail. Up to 5 spines may margin top of eye and 3 behind eye. Dorsal tubercles orange, brown or white, almost always aligned in 2 parallel rows. Usually 2 (rarely 4 or 6) rows of long, mostly orange, spines extend along tail. Iris greyish white margined by maroon and enclosing a fine black reticulum. Ground colour shades of grey or brownish grey, usually marked with 5–8 pale grey upper lateral blotches between neck and base of tail. Ventral surfaces pale grey to white, usually dotted with dark brown. SVL 85 mm.

Distinguished from *D. ciliaris* by arrangement of dorsal tubercles (aligned in 2 parallel rows vs randomly scattered) and by mouth colour (bluish vs yellow to orange). Differs from *D. assimilis* and *D. intermedius* in having much longer spines above eye and on tail.
Preferred habitat Arid interior of WA, from Pilbara region south-east to the northern Goldfields. Favours mulga (*Acacia aneura*) shrublands and woodlands on heavy reddish soils.
Microhabitat See *D. strophurus* species group.
Comments Formerly regarded as a population of *D. ciliaris*. See subgenus *Diplodactylus (Strophurus)*.

Diplodactylus williamsi Kluge, 1963
Photo 146

Description Member of *D. strophurus* group with 4 nearly parallel rows of moderately spinose orange-brown tubercles on back and tail. Iris rimmed with reddish orange and marked with fine dark lines, forming intricate geometric pattern. Ground colour pale to dark grey. Pattern prominent to obscure, usually consisting of fine dark reticulum over dorsal and lateral surfaces, and/or broad dark wavy-edged dorsal region. Numerous black spots often present; scattered or following lines of reticulum. Ventral surfaces pale grey spotted with black. SVL 60 mm.

Distinguished from *D. intermedius* in possessing 4 (vs 2) rows of tubercles on dorsal surface of tail.

Preferred habitat Subhumid to semi-arid eastern Australia, from northern interior of NSW to southern interior and mideast coast of Qld. Apparently isolated population occurs in south-eastern SA. Favours woodlands, particularly where native pine (*Callitris*) and coarse-barked eucalypts (ironbarks) are present.

Microhabitat Shelters beneath loose bark and in hollow limbs of dead timber.

Comments Captive individuals are recorded to mate in October. Two clutches of 2 eggs have been found in disused burrows of Gould's goanna (*Varanus gouldii*) during April. These contained full-term embryos, suggesting an incubation period of approximately 6 months. Inactive during cool weather (at least in southern parts of range), hibernating on bases of trees and stumps. When agitated mouth may be opened to display bright bluish purple interior. Otherwise as for subgenus *Diplodactylus (Strophurus)* and *D. strophurus* group.

Diplodactylus wilsoni Storr, 1983
Photo 147

Description Robust short-tailed member of *D. strophurus* group. Close affinities also with *D. michaelseni* group. Dorsal tubercles brown, very small and irregular. Caudal tubercles slightly larger; conical and randomly scattered. Iris bluish grey, lacking coloured rim and bearing fine black lines, forming an intricate geometric pattern. Ground colour pale grey to pale reddish brown obscurely patterned with narrow broken dark lines. These represent margins of reduced broad pale stripes; vertebral from base of head to about midbody and more prominent dorsolateral from snout through upper half of eye, becoming fragmented and ill-defined from midbody to hips. Flanks, limbs and tail obscurely flecked with blackish brown. Ventral surfaces pale grey with indistinct dark lines. SVL 55 mm.

Distinguished from other members of *D. strophurus* group by build (robust with short tail vs relatively slender with long tail). Differs further from *D. strophurus* and *D. wellingtonae* by size (SVL 55 vs up to 70 mm or greater). Differs further from *D. strophurus* in lacking yellow or white segments of connective tissue on tail, and further from *D. wellingtonae* in lacking spines (vs present on tail and above eye).

Preferred habitat Stony plains and low outcrops vegetated with *Acacia* and *Eremophila* shrublands in arid midwestern interior of WA.

Microhabitat Individuals shelter in vertical rock crevices or under stones on gibber flats. Ascends low shrubs at night.

Comments Remnants of dorsal and ventral stripes may be relictual from a hummock-grass or tussock-inhabiting ancestor common to *D. michaelseni* group. Otherwise as for subgenus *Diplodactylus (Strophurus)* and *D. strophurus* group.

Diplodactylus wombeyi Storr, 1978
Photo 148

Description Moderately small member of *D. stenodactylus* group with moderately large subapical plates. Ground colour pale to dark reddish brown, marked with darker reticulum or irregular transverse bars. These enclose large dorsal blotches of ground colour. Body and upper surfaces of limbs sparsely marked with fine white spots. Ventral surfaces white. SVL 45 mm.

Preferred habitat Rocky hills and plains vegetated with hummock grasses in arid Pilbara region, WA.

Microhabitat Shelters beneath rocks and in soil cracks or spider burrows.

Comments As for *D. stenodactylus* group.

Photo 149 shows an undescribed member of *D. strophurus* group, allied to *D. ciliaris*, from Diamantina Lakes, Qld.

Dtellas
Genus *GEHYRA* Gray, 1834
(Subfamily Gekkoninae)

Large genus, widespread through the world's tropical to warm temperate regions, from the Pacific Islands to the Indo-Malayan Archipelago, Asia and Madagascar. Represented in Australia by 17 described species. Some of these (*G. baliola* and *G. oceanica*) have broad extralimital distributions, and their occurrence here is not confirmed. Additional taxa await description. Occurs throughout most of continent, favouring subhumid to arid areas. Diversity is greatest in north. Absent from subalpine to alpine regions, humid south-west and south-east, and Tas.

Small to moderately large, weakly to strongly dorsally depressed geckos. Tail usually slightly constricted at base. Digits (excepting inner finger and toe on each foot) clawed; greatly expanded distally to form large semicircular pads. Subdigital lamellae enlarged to form divided and/or entire transverse plates. Dorsal body scales small, smooth and homogeneous. Preanal pores present on males. Pattern extremely variable, usually including dark and pale spots and/or dark variegations. All appear to possess limited colour-changing ability, usually bearing paler hues and subdued pattern when foraging.

Gehyra are swift agile geckos, capable of making well-coordinated leaps between branches or rocks, and able to move with ease over walls and ceilings. Predominantly rock-inhabiting and arboreal; occasionally terrestrial. Rock-inhabiting species shelter beneath slabs, in crevices and caves, while arboreal geckos hide in hollow timber and beneath loose bark. Some species frequently occupy human dwellings. Often locally abundant. In many areas virtually all suitable microhabitats harbour a resident gecko. Clutches comprise 1 or 2 calcareous-shelled eggs.

Little research has been undertaken on the ecology of most *Gehyra* spp., despite their relative abundance. Extensive study has been carried out on *Gehyra variegata* in northern NSW, and aspects of this work may apply to other species.

Two species groups are apparent.

G. punctata group Contains 8 species of small to medium-sized *Gehyra*. Members are *G. catenata*, *G. minuta*, *G. montium*, *G. nana*, *G. pilbara*, *G. punctata*, *G. purpurascens*, and *G. variegata*.

G. australis group Contains 9 species of large to very large *Gehyra*. Restricted to north of continent, extending south to northern NSW. Members are *G. australis*, *G. baliola*, *G. borroloola*, *G. dubia*, *G. occidentalis*, *G. pamela*, *G. robusta* and *G. xenopus*, and tentatively *G. oceanica*.

Gehyra is distinguished from *Hemidactylus*, *Lepidodactylus* and *Phyllodactylus* by absence of claw on inner digit of each foot (vs all digits clawed).

Gehyra australis Gray, 1845
Photo 150

Description Member of *G. australis* group with little or no pattern. Ground colour pale brown, pale pink to almost white. Transversely oriented pale blotches bearing dark anterior margins, and a narrow pale vertebral line are sometimes present. Ventral surfaces pale pink to white. SVL 75 mm.

Distinguished from *G. occidentalis* in possessing much weaker pattern and paler colouration. Differs from *G. pamela* by build (relatively robust vs strongly depressed), and further from both in having fewer preanal pores (19 or fewer vs 19 or more). Differs from *G. borroloola* by nature of subdigital lamellae (undivided vs divided).

Preferred habitat Favours woodlands and rock outcrops, extending from northern NT to eastern Kimberley region, WA.

Microhabitat Arboreal and rock-inhabiting. Frequently enters human dwellings. See genus.

Comments As for genus.

Gehyra baliola (Duméril and Duméril, 1851)
Photo 151

Description Large robust member of *G. australis* group. Ground colour pale yellowish brown. Pattern usually obscure, consisting of scattered to transversely aligned paler spots, fine dark peppering and occasionally darker variegations on head, body, limbs and tail. Ventral surfaces yellow. SVL 70 mm.

Distinguished from *G. dubia* in possessing prominent skin-fold along rear edge of hindlimb.

Preferred habitat Restricted in Australia to northern islands of Great Barrier Reef and those of Torres Strait, Qld. Extralimital in New Guinea. Commonly encountered in mangrove communities.

Microhabitat Arboreal and rock-inhabiting. See genus.

Comments Australian population probably represents an undescribed taxon. Otherwise as for genus.

Gehyra borroloola King, 1983
Photo 152

Description Member of *G. australis* group. Ground colour pale pinkish brown, brown to dark brown, marked over head, body, limbs and tail with transverse rows of dark blotches. These alternate with rows of cream spots. Pattern is usually broken by a narrow vertebral line of ground colour. Dark stripe may extend from snout, through eye to ear. Another may extend from nostril to inner rim of eye. Ventral surfaces cream. SVL 65 mm.

Distinguished from *G. australis* by nature of subdigital lamellae (divided vs undivided).

Preferred habitat Rock outcrops and gorges from McArthur River to Limmen Bight River, Gulf of Carpentaria, NT.

Microhabitat Rock-inhabiting. See genus.

Comments As for genus.

Gehyra catenata Low, 1979
Photo 153

Description Member of *G. punctata* group with ground colour of pale to dark grey. Wavy dark (sometimes obscure) paravertebral stripe extends from snout through eye onto base of tail. Dark transverse bars join paravertebrals, enclosing pale dorsal blotches to form chain-like pattern. Top of head, flanks and limbs speckled to streaked with dark pigment. Ventral surfaces greyish white. SVL 55 mm.

Distinguished from *G. variegata* and *G. dubia* in possessing distinctive chain-like dorsal pattern. Differs further from *G. dubia* in attaining smaller maximum size (SVL 55 vs 65 mm).

Preferred habitat *Acacia* and *Casuarina* woodlands in subhumid interior of south-east to mideast Qld.

Microhabitat Arboreal. See genus.

Comments Individuals normally encountered singly. Otherwise as for genus.

Gehyra dubia (Macleay, 1877)
Photo 154

Description Member of G. *australis* group. Ground colour pale grey to pale brown, marked with irregular transverse series of paler grey to white spots. These may be overlaid with a dark reticulum, or each may bear a dark anterior margin. Dark pigment occasionally coalesces to form irregular longitudinal lines. Narrow dark streak extends from eye to side of neck. Y-shaped mark (forked anteriorly) may be discernible on neck and base of head. Tail marked with dark bands, each with a pale posterior margin. Ventral surfaces white to shades of pink. SVL 65 mm.

Distinguished from G. *baliola* in lacking prominent skin-fold along rear edge of hindlimb. Differs from G. *variegata* by nature of subdigital lamellae (undivided vs divided). Differs further from G. *variegata*, and from G. *catenata*, in attaining much greater maximum size (SVL 65 vs 55 mm).

Preferred habitat Woodlands, dry sclerophyll forests and rock outcrops from central northern NSW, through central Qld to Cape York Peninsula and islands of Torres Strait.

Microhabitat Arboreal and rock-inhabiting. Frequently enters human dwellings. See genus.

Comments Clutches of eggs have been recorded between October and January in northern NSW, and in August on Cape York Peninsula, Qld. Otherwise as for genus.

Gehyra minuta King, 1983
Photo 155

Description Small member of G. *punctata* group with deep head, short snout and large eyes. Ground colour pale orange-brown. Pattern prominent to virtually absent, consisting of alternating transverse series of blackish and cream spots. These often coalesce to form bands. Top of head, limbs and tail spotted with dark and pale pigment. Ventral surfaces greyish pink. SVL 45 mm.

Distinguished from sympatric Gehyra in possessing combination of very short snout, very large eyes and small maximum size (SVL 45 vs 50 mm or more).

Preferred habitat Isolated rock outcrops in narrow band of red soil on south-western margin of Barkly Tablelands, semi-arid central NT.

Microhabitat Rock-inhabiting. See genus.

Comments Locally abundant. Otherwise as for genus.

Gehyra montium Storr, 1982
Photo 156

Description Member of G. *punctata* group with ground colour of pale reddish brown. Pattern usually prominent, consisting of blackish brown streaks or spots, aligned transversely on body and tail, and obliquely on head. These alternate with obscure transversely to longitudinally aligned pale spots. Two blackish brown longitudinal streaks extend from side of head back to neck. Ventral surfaces pinkish white. SVL 50 mm.

Distinguished from G. *variegata* by ground colour (reddish vs brownish), and pattern (pale spots rarely contacting dark markings vs usually in contact with, and often partly enclosed by, dark markings). Differs from G. *purpurascens* by colouration (reddish vs greyish), microhabitat preference (rock-inhabiting vs arboreal) and in attaining a smaller size (SVL 50 vs 60 mm).

Preferred habitat Rocky hills, ranges and granite outcrops of southern NT, northern SA and adjacent interior of WA.

Microhabitat Rock-inhabiting. See genus.

Comments As for genus.

Gehyra nana Storr, 1978
Photo 157

Description Small strongly dorsally depressed member of G. *punctata* group. Ground colour pinkish grey to reddish brown. Pattern usually prominent, consisting of brown and smaller pinkish white spots oriented and aligned transversely in alternating rows. Top of head and limbs dotted with brown and pinkish white. Ventral surfaces pale pinkish brown. SVL 50 mm.

Distinguished from G. *punctata*, G. *occidentalis* and G. *pilbara* in attaining smaller maximum size (SVL 50 vs 65 mm). Differs further from G. *pilbara* by head-shape (strongly depressed vs moderately deep) and size of pale dorsal spots (smaller than dark dorsal spots vs absent or larger than dark dorsal spots). Differs from young G. *xenopus* in lacking a distinctive crocodile-like snout in profile.

Preferred habitat Rock outcrops and ranges in subhumid to arid areas from Kimberley region, WA, through northern NT to Cape York Peninsula, Qld.

Microhabitat Rock-inhabiting. See genus.

Comments As for genus.

Gehyra occidentalis King, 1984
Photo 158

Description Large moderately slender dorsally depressed member of G. *australis* group. Ground colour chocolate brown. Pattern on body and tail consists of transverse rows of black spots (coalesced to form bands) alternating with bands of brownish white spots. Two narrow parallel blackish brown stripes on side of head extend from snout or eye to level of ear. Top of head and limbs bear scattered blackish brown and brownish white spots. Ventral surfaces pinkish white. SVL 65 mm.

Distinguished from G. *australis* by stronger pattern and in bearing more preanal pores (23 or more vs 19 or fewer). Differs from *G. xenopus* in attaining smaller maximum size (SVL 65 vs 75 mm) and lacking upturned, crocodile-like snout. Differs from *G. nana* in attaining much greater maximum size (SVL 65 vs 50 mm). Differs from *G. variegata* by pattern (bands of dark and pale markings not in contact vs pale markings contacting, and partly enclosed by, dark markings).

Preferred habitat Subhumid to semi-arid western Kimberley region of WA, from Mitchell Plateau south to Napier Range. Occurs in rocky ranges and outcrops.

Microhabitat Rock-inhabiting, occasionally arboreal. See genus.

Comments As for genus.

Gehyra oceanica (Lesson, 1830)
Photo 159

Description Very large robust member of *G. australis* group. Ground colour pale grey, olive to brown; usually variegated, flecked or spotted with blackish brown on head, body and limbs. Dark pigment may coalesce to form dorsal blotches or obscure bands on tail. Ventral surfaces white. SVL 120 mm.

Distinguished from other Australian *Gehyra* by much larger average size and presence of prominent webbing between third and fourth toes.

Preferred habitat Apparently restricted in Australia to islands of Torres Strait, Qld. Widespread through lowland forests of New Guinea and Pacific Islands.

Microhabitat Arboreal; shelters among dead fronds hanging from crowns of palms, in hollows and crevices. Frequently inhabits buildings throughout most of extralimital range.

Comments As for genus.

Gehyra pamela King, 1982
Photo 160

Description Large dorsally depressed member of *G. australis* group with ground colour of reddish grey. Pattern prominent to obscure, comprising transverse series of large pale spots. These become scattered on head and limbs and usually alternate with (often accentuating) faintly darker transverse lines. Ventral surfaces cream. SVL 70 mm.

Distinguished from *G. australis* by build (strongly dorsally depressed vs relatively robust), shape of snout (nostrils raised into a pronounced mound), and (in zone of overlap) preference for rocky (vs arboreal) habitats.

Preferred habitat Massive rock faces of Arnhem Escarpment, NT. Isolated populations occur as far south-east as Roper River and west to Bullo River.

Microhabitat Rock-inhabiting. See genus.

Comments As for genus.

Gehyra pilbara Mitchell, 1965
Photo 161

Description Robust deep-headed member of *G. punctata* group. Ground colour pale brown to bright or pale orange. Pattern prominent, becoming obscure to absent on large individuals. A series of transversely aligned blackish brown markings extend from nape, occasionally coalescing to form bands, particularly on tail. These may alternate with transverse rows of circular pale spots. Dark longitudinal streak present through top of eye, another through middle. Ventral surfaces white to yellow. SVL 65 mm.

Distinguished from *G. nana* and *G. punctata* by build (relatively robust vs dorsally depressed), and in possessing dark longitudinal streaks on side of head. Differs from *G. variegata* by ground colour (reddish brown vs brownish grey).

Preferred habitat Subhumid to arid regions from Tanami Desert in western NT to southern Kimberley and Pilbara regions, WA.

Microhabitat Favours termitaria, foraging on exposed surfaces and sheltering in crevices or deep in mounds. Also reported foraging on ground and sheltering in disused nests of fairy martins (*Hirundo ariel*).

Comments Often occurs in high density: 15 or more individuals recorded from a single termite mound. Mounds inhabited by geckos are easily recognisable by accumulated droppings adhering to outer surfaces. Termites and small cavernicolous crickets recorded as prey items. Uniform temperatures inside mounds, coupled with year-round food supplies, permit a prolonged breeding season. Clutch consists of 1 or 2 eggs.

Spotted Dtella
Gehyra punctata (Fry, 1914)
Photos 162, 163

Description Moderately robust dorsally depressed member of *G. punctata* group. Ground colour pale yellowish brown, brown, reddish brown to shades of pink. Pattern usually prominent, consisting of transverse rows of dark brown spots alternating with rows of whitish to yellowish spots over head, back, limbs and tail. Individuals from south of range are usually more conspicuously marked: pale spots yellower and dark spots often pale-edged. Ventral surfaces whitish to dull yellow. SVL 65 mm.

Distinguished from *G. nana* and *G. montium* in attaining greater maximum size (SVL 65 vs 50 mm) and relatively more robust build. Differs from *G. pilbara* by head-profile (flattened vs deep).

Preferred habitat Rocky hills and outcrops of arid north-western Australia from Pilbara region south to Yalgoo, WA. Isolated population occurs in Kimberley region.

Microhabitat Rock-inhabiting. See genus.
Comments As for genus.

Gehyra purpurascens Storr, 1982
Photo 164

Description Member of *G. punctata* group. Ground colour pale purplish grey, with or without pattern. If present, pattern is irregular: sparse to moderately dense brownish grey to dark grey spots or short streaks form reticulum over body, limbs and tail. Ventral surfaces pale pinkish brown. SVL 65 mm.

Distinguished from *G. montium* by ground colour (greyish vs pale reddish brown). Differs from *G. variegata* in being larger (SVL 65 vs 55 mm), usually less prominently marked, and by shape of rostral scale when viewed from above (almost horizontal vs peaked or gabled).
Preferred habitat Arid western interior of Australia, from northern SA to central NT and interior of WA (including northern Goldfields, Pilbara, Great Victoria, Gibson and Great Sandy Deserts). One record exists from south-western Qld.
Microhabitat Arboreal, favouring *Acacia* spp., eucalypts and desert oaks (*Casuarina decaisneana*). See genus.
Comments In zones of overlap with *G. variegata*, prefers smooth white-barked eucalypts, often ascending to the highest branches. See genus.

Gehyra robusta King, 1983
Photos 165, 166

Description Robust, relatively dorsally depressed member of *G. australis* group. Ground colour pinkish brown to orange-brown, marked with transversely aligned dark blotches; often coalesced to form bars. These alternate with transverse series of obscure pale spots. Pattern tends to break on vertebral region, leaving narrow line of ground colour. Top of head spotted with black. Dark stripe extends from snout, through eye to ear opening. Ventral surfaces greyish pink. SVL 75 mm.
Preferred habitat Rocky ranges and outcrops of semi-arid north-western Qld, in the Mt Isa and Winton areas.
Microhabitat Rock-inhabiting. See genus.
Comments See genus.

Tree Dtella
Gehyra variegata (Duméril and Bibron, 1836)
Photos 167, 168

Description Member of *G. punctata* group. Composite species as currently recognised. Three distinct chromosome races occur, each of which probably constitutes a distinct taxon.

Eastern form: Ground colour pale brown, usually marked on body, limbs and tail with bands of paler dots overlaid with a blackish brown reticulum; irregular or arranged as a series of transverse bars joined by longitudinal lines. Side of head bears 2 or 3 narrow dark lines extending back to neck. Ventral surfaces pinkish white. SVL 55 mm.

Western form: Ground colour brown to grey, marked on body, limbs and tail with transverse to scattered white to pale brown spots; each margined anteriorly and partly enclosed by dark transversely oriented crescents or curved bars. Side of head bears 2 or 3 narrow dark lines extending back to neck. Ventral surfaces pinkish white.

Southern form: Similar in appearance to eastern form.

Distinguished from *G. montium* and *G. pilbara* by ground colour (brownish vs reddish). Differs further from *G. montium* and from *G. occidentalis* by pattern (pale spots usually in contact with, and often partly enclosed by, dark markings, vs pale spots rarely contacting dark markings). Differs from *G. purpurascens* by ground colour (brownish vs greyish), shape of rostral scale when viewed from above (peaked or gabled vs almost horizontal), presence of pale spots, and in attaining smaller maximum size (SVL 55 vs 65 mm). Differs from *G. dubia* by nature of subdigital lamellae (divided vs undivided) and in attaining smaller maximum size (SVL 55 vs 65 mm).
Preferred habitat Widespread through sub-humid to arid woodlands, shrublands and rock outcrops. Absent from most of east coast, south-east, Nullarbor Plain, south-west, northern NT, and Kimberley region. Eastern form extends to central Australia. Western form extends from west coast to interior of WA. Southern form occurs in SA, from about Adelaide to north-eastern Eyre Peninsula.
Microhabitat Eastern form is predominantly arboreal, particularly when sympatric with rock-inhabiting *Gehyra*. Western form is both arboreal and rock-inhabiting. All populations frequently utilise terrestrial shelter sites. See genus.
Comments Ecology of eastern form in northern NSW has been extensively studied. Shelter sites approximately 1 m from ground are favoured. Males are strongly territorial, usually dwelling singly or with up to 3 females. Individuals forage in a 10 m radius of home site. Although foraging takes place at night (particularly during first 3 hours after dark) thermoregulatory activity occurs throughout day; lizards moving to or away from bark heated by sun. Feeds on a variety of arthropods, particularly beetles, spiders, termites and grasshoppers. Most of these occur in geckos' microhabitats. In NSW 2 clutches, each comprising 1 egg, are laid about 1 month apart on ground or beneath bark close to ground.

Gehyra xenopus Storr, 1978
Photo 169

Description Very large member of *G. australis* group with flat head, large eyes and long upturned snout. Ground colour dark brown to greyish brown. Pattern consists of large (sometimes dark-edged) circular brownish white spots arranged in irregular transverse rows. These are mixed with blackish brown blotches and flecks. Ventral surfaces white. SVL 75 mm.

Distinguished from all sympatric *Gehyra* spp. in possessing a markedly upturned snout, crocodile-like in profile.

Preferred habitat Sandstones of subhumid north-west Kimberley region, WA, including off-shore islands. Extends from Prince Regent River and Champagny Island in south-west to Kalumbaru in north-east.

Microhabitat Rock-inhabiting, favouring cliff faces and larger boulders.

Comments As for genus.

See also photos 170, 171, 172 for 3 undescribed taxa of *Gehyra*.

Genus *HEMIDACTYLUS* Gray, 1825

(Subfamily Gekkoninae)

Large genus, widespread through world's tropical and temperate regions. Represented in Australia by a single introduced species, restricted to far north.

Moderately small dorsally depressed geckos. Digits clawed and expanded to form pads. Subdigital lamellae divided to form broad transverse plates; not noticeably wider distally. Dorsal scales heterogeneous: small and smooth mixed with low scattered tubercles.

Arboreal. Feeds on a broad range of arthropods. Clutch consists of 1 or 2 calcareous-shelled eggs.

Distinguished from *Gehyra* in possessing claws on all digits (vs inner digit on each foot lacking claw). Australian species differs further by presence of lateral series of enlarged tubercles on original tail. Differs from *Lepidodactylus* by position of claw (arising from upper surface of expanded pad (vs arising from anterior edge).

House Gecko
Hemidactylus frenatus
Duméril and Bibron, 1836
Photo 173

Description Small gecko bearing prominent lateral series of tubercles on original tail. Ground colour shades of grey, from almost white to almost black, marked with prominent to obscure darker and paler flecks or mottling. Dark pigment tends to align in 4 irregular stripes: dorsals and midlaterals. Pale streak usually present from snout to eye, often extending back to form obscure pale upper lateral zone. Ventral surfaces white. SVL 60 mm.

Preferred habitat Isolated populations occur in settled areas of northern Australia, from Darwin (including towns along Stuart Highway) south to

about Renner Springs, NT, and towns of northern Qld south to Cairns. Almost entirely restricted to urban areas.

Microhabitat Utilises virtually all available shelters. Encountered by day in crevices along walls, behind wallhangings and in dark cupboards, etc. Able to forage with ease over ceilings and windows.

Comments A swift agile gecko, probably introduced to Australia in cargo from South-East Asia. Now well established in tropical cities throughout the world. Predominantly nocturnal, though often forages by day during overcast weather or in shaded situations. Possesses limited colour-changing ability, bearing pale hues with reduced pattern when active. The loud 'chuck...chuck...chuck' call is a familiar sound wherever house geckos occur. At night numerous geckos aggregate on walls beneath lights to prey on attracted insects. Breeding is continuous throughout year.

Genus *HETERONOTIA* Wermuth, 1965

(Subfamily Gekkoninae)

Endemic genus comprising 2 described species, though almost certainly involving a complex of closely allied taxa. Widespread throughout continent, excepting extreme south (including Tas.) and humid areas east of Great Dividing Range.

Small, slender to moderately robust geckos with long to very long tail. Digits long, slender and clawed. Subdigital lamellae slightly enlarged in a single series, terminating in a pair of small subapical plates. Dorsal scales heterogeneous: small and granular mixed with enlarged, scattered to longitudinally aligned tubercles.

Swift, terrestrial and rock-inhabiting geckos which feed on a broad range of arthropods. Clutch consists of 2 calcareous-shelled eggs. Parthenogenetic populations are known from some areas.

Distinguished from *Nactus* and *Cyrtodactylus* by nature of digits: each claw set between 1 dorsal and 2 lateroventral plates (*Heteronotia*) vs each claw set between single dorsal and ventral plates (*Cyrtodactylus* and *Nactus*). Differs further from *Cyrtodactylus* in attaining much smaller maximum size (SVL 50 vs 160 mm).

Bynoe's Gecko
Heteronotia binoei (Gray, 1845)
Photos 174–177

Description An extremely variable *Heteronotia* almost certainly comprising a number of distinct taxa. Dorsal tubercles scattered to aligned in irregular longitudinal rows. Ground colour ranges through shades of pale yellowish brown, rich brown, reddish brown to almost black. Pattern usually prominent comprising irregular broad to narrow bands, or scattered to transversely aligned dark and pale spots (each often centred on an individual tubercle). Bands (when present) are often sharper on original tail. Regenerated tail smooth, usually without pattern. Most populations bear dark brown to black temporal streak, usually margined above and/or below with paler pigment. Ventral surfaces whitish to pale pinkish brown, finely dotted with darker brown. SVL 50 mm.

Distinguished from *H. spelea* by arrangement of dorsal tubercles (irregularly aligned to scattered vs arranged in regular longitudinal series), build (robust vs relatively slender) and pattern (bands tend to be narrow and irregular when present vs broad and sharp-edged). Readily subject to confusion with *Nactus*. See genus.

Preferred habitat Widespread through virtually all subhumid to arid habitats, extending into some highland areas of Great Dividing Range and outliers. Absent from alpine areas, rainforests, and extreme south and east of continent.

Microhabitat Shelters beneath rocks, logs, loose bark at bases of stumps, dead vegetation, in soil cracks and beneath surface debris. Locally abundant in many areas with almost all available cover harbouring resident geckos.

Comments In northern NSW foraging commences at dusk, reaching a peak 2–3 hours after sunset. Temperature is regulated during day by sheltering beneath debris heated by sun in early morning, and retreating to deeper, more shaded cover as temperature rises. Each adult occupies a home range of approximately 10 m radius. Feeds on a broad range of terrestrial arthropods. In NSW eggs are laid beneath sheltered sites from October to December or January, hatching from late February to March. Sexual maturity is attained at just over 1 year at earliest. Several parthenogenetic races are known from central to western Australia.

Desert Cave Gecko
Heteronotia spelea (Kluge, 1963)
Photo 178

Description Slender long-tailed *Heteronotia* with dorsal tubercles aligned in regular longitudinal series. Ground colour yellowish brown, brown to reddish brown, prominently marked with 4 or 5 dark-edged dark brown bands (approximately equal in width to pale interspaces) between nape and base of tail. First dark band curves forward to fuse with temporal streak, forming collar. Original tail bears approximately 8–12 blackish brown rings, contrasting sharply with whitish interspaces. Regenerated tails brown, usually without pattern. Top of head usually flushed with reddish brown, occasionally bearing an obscure dark bar between ears. Ventral surfaces whitish. SVL 50 mm.

Distinguished from banded *H. binoei* in possessing sharper broader bands, and by alignment of dorsal tubercles (arranged in regular longitudinal series vs irregularly aligned to scattered).

Preferred habitat Rocky ranges and outcrops from subhumid to arid Kimberley and Pilbara regions, WA to western NT. Disjunct populations occur in Arnhem Land and Groote Eylandt, NT.

Microhabitat Shelters in crevices and caves, or beneath rocks.

Comments See genus.

Genus *LEPIDODACTYLUS*
Fitzinger, 1843

(Subfamily Gekkoninae)

Large genus occuring through Asia, the Indo-Malayan Archipelago, New Guinea and islands of Pacific Ocean. Two species occur in Australia; restricted to far northern Qld.

Small slender moderately dorsally depressed geckos with long tails. Digits clawed and expanded distally, bearing small subapical plates and single or divided transverse lamellae. Body scales small, granular and homogeneous.

Arboreal. Clutch of 1 or 2 calcareous-shelled eggs.

Distinguished from *Gehyra* in possessing claws on all digits (vs inner digit on each foot lacking claw). Differs from *Hemidactylus* by position of claw (arising from anterior edge of expanded pad vs arising from upper surface).

Lepidodactylus lugubris
(Duméril and Bibron, 1836)
Photo 179

Description Small slender gecko with long strongly dorsally depressed tail bearing lateral fringe of fine spinose scales. Ground colour yellowish brown, pinkish brown to dark brown. Pattern prominent to obscure, consisting of fine dark flecking and a series of narrow transverse blackish brown W-shaped markings, extending from nape to tail-tip. Obscure dark streak extends from eye to side of neck or flanks. Ventral surfaces pinkish grey. SVL 50 mm.

Distinguished from *L. pumilus* by tail-shape (dorsally depressed bearing lateral fringe vs cylindrical without lateral fringe).

Preferred habitat Restricted in Australia to north-east Qld, in the vicinity of Cairns and on tip of Cape York Peninsula. Favours beach and near-coastal habitats such as woodlands, monsoon forests and mangrove communities. Frequently enters buildings.

Microhabitat Shelters in crevices and hollows in trees (particularly mangroves) or among foliage.

Comments Predominantly nocturnal though individuals are often observed foraging by day in sheltered positions, or basking in weak sunlight. Parthenogenetic: all individuals are females. Breeding appears continuous throughout the year. One egg is laid per clutch. This is sticky when laid, and usually deposited on a vertical surface to which it adheres. Probably accidently introduced to Australia, considering its disjunct distribution and close association with humans throughout most of extralimital range.

Lepidodactylus pumilus (Boulenger, 1885)
Photo 180

Description Very slender gecko with long, more or less cylindrical tail. Ground colour pale pinkish brown. Pattern variable; usually obscure. Comprises pale vertebral suffusion and narrow irregular darker transverse lines. These often fail to meet on vertebral region and are usually broadest and most prominent on tail. Ventral surface pinkish white. SVL 48 mm.

Distinguished from *L. lugubris* by tail-shape: cylindrical, vs dorsally depressed and bearing lateral fringe of fine spinose scales.

Preferred habitat Restricted in Australia to islands of Torres Strait, Qld. Extralimital in New Guinea.

Microhabitat Poorly known. Presumably similar to *L. lugubris*.

Comments See *L. lugubris*.

Genus *NACTUS* Kluge, 1983

(Subfamily Gekkoninae)

Represented in Australia by 2 species of moderately small geckos restricted to north-east Qld. Extralimital on Mascarene Islands of western Indian Ocean, New Guinea and southern central Pacific.

Slender to moderately robust geckos. Tail long and round in cross-section. Digits long, slender and clawed. Subdigital lamellae slightly enlarged, in a single series. All species bear conical dorsal body tubercles and raised ventral scales, each bearing several minute ridges.

Terrestrial and rock-inhabiting. Clutch of 1 or 2 calcareous-shelled eggs.

Nactus has only recently been separated from *Cyrtodactylus*. It differs from Australian *Cyrtodactylus* in attaining much smaller maximum size (SVL 80 vs 160 mm), and bearing weak to irregular banded pattern (vs distinct and sharp-edged). Differs from *Heteronotia* by nature of digits: each claw set between single dorsal and ventral plates (*Nactus*) vs each claw set between 1 dorsal and 2 lateroventral plates (*Heteronotia*).

Pelagic Gecko
Nactus arnouxii (Duméril, 1851)
Photo 181

Description Large robust *Nactus* bearing over 12 longitudinally aligned rows of dark and pale tubercles on dorsal and lateral surfaces. Ground colour pinkish brown to very dark brown. Pattern (when present) consists of pale (usually transversely aligned) blotches, each with broad to narrow darker anterior margin. Pattern usually weaker and more fragmented on flanks; sharper and more regular on tail. Top of head may be finely dotted with black. Dark brown to black bar usually extends from eye to about ear. Lips whitish barred with brown. Ventral surfaces whitish to shades of pink. SVL 80 mm.

Often confused with *Heteronotia binoei*. See genus.

Preferred habitat Subhumid to humid areas of Cape York Peninsula and islands of Torres Strait, Qld. Extralimital in New Guinea and islands of western Pacific. Occurs in a variety of habitats, from woodlands, rock outcrops and monsoon forests to relatively open coastal sands.

Microhabitat Shelters beneath rocks, logs, surface debris and in crevices, soil cracks, abandoned burrows and termitaria.

Comments Australian population may represent a distinct taxon. Otherwise as for genus.

Black Mountain Gecko
Nactus galgajuga (Ingram, 1978)
Photo 182

Description Very slender large-eyed *Nactus* with long limbs and tail. Dorsal and lateral surfaces bear 10 longitudinally aligned rows of blackish tubercles. Ground colour purplish brown to blackish; darker on tail. Pattern consists of broad irregular whitish bands or transversely oriented blotches. These become more regular and sharply defined on tail. Head spotted and blotched with white. Lips white barred with dark brown. Limbs blotched to banded with white. Ventral surfaces pale pinkish brown. SVL 50 mm.

Preferred habitat Known only from large piled black boulders of Trevethan Range ('Black Mountain') south of Cooktown, north-east Qld.

Microhabitat Shelters in crevices and caverns between boulders. Forages on exposed rock faces.

Comments Most restricted distribution of any Australian gecko. Extremely swift and agile, able to make well-coordinated leaps between boulders.

Knob-tailed Geckos
Genus *NEPHRURUS* Günther, 1876

(Subfamily Diplodactylinae)

Endemic genus containing 10 taxa. Widespread through subhumid to arid areas of all mainland States except Vic.

Robust deep-bodied geckos with large heads and long slender limbs. Tail short to very short, constricted at base with a single cleavage point, and tapering rapidly (when original) to terminate in a unique spherical enlargement or 'knob'. Regenerated tail bulbous, lacking attenuate tip and knob. All digits short and clawed. Enlarged subapical plates absent. Subdigital lamellae small and spinose. Body scales heterogeneous: small and granular, mixed with low to spinose tubercles.

Terrestrial geckos which forage in open spaces between low vegetation for arthropods and smaller geckos. Relatively slow moving, raising their plump bodies high on slender limbs when in motion. Clutch consists of 2 parchment-shelled eggs. Threat display consists of rhythmically raising and lowering inflated body, arching back and forth slowly waving tail, and leaping abruptly at adversary while uttering a loud wheezing bark. Function of distinctive knob on tail-tip is unclear.

Distinguished from *Underwoodisaurus* in lacking enlarged subdigital lamellae, and in possessing a knob on original tail.

Prickly Knob-tailed Gecko
Nephrurus asper Günther, 1876
Photo 183

Description Very large *Nephrurus* with extremely short tail bearing 8 or 9 transverse rows of enlarged tubercles. Back, flanks and limbs adorned with rosettes, composed of large spinose conical tubercles surrounded by smaller tubercles. Ground colour pale brown, greyish brown to reddish brown, marked with numerous (prominent to obscure) fine dark transverse lines. These alternate with rows of paler spots, each centred on a tubercle. Distinctive Cape York population bears cream and rich reddish brown bands of approximately equal width. Head of all populations bears reticulum of narrow blackish lines. Ventral surfaces pale brownish grey. SVL 105 mm.

Preferred habitat Rocky hills, outcrops and woodlands in subhumid to arid areas from Kimberley region, WA, through NT to mideastern Qld. Penetrates well-timbered habitats more effectively than other *Nephrurus*.

Microhabitat Shelters in shallow depressions beneath rocks or logs, and in burrows.

Comments Appears to be one of the few geckos unable to discard its tail. Individuals are reported to flick dust over themselves, probably as an aid to camouflage. See genus.

Nephrurus deleani Harvey, 1983
Photo 184

Description Moderately large *Nephrurus* with small slender tail bearing 9 regular longitudinal rows of enlarged white tubercles. Back and flanks bear numerous low conical tubercles. Ground colour pale brown mottled with purplish brown. Pattern variable to virtually absent, usually including 3 broad pale yellowish brown V-shaped bars. First extends across base of head, second across neck, and third back from neck to mid-dorsal line. Additional less regular (often broken) pale transverse lines may be present. Narrow white vertebral line (occasionally broken) may extend from base of head to hips on some juveniles. Flanks spotted to variegated with cream. Top of head darker shade of ground colour, with or without obscure paler variegations. Tail dark brown. Ventral surfaces white. SVL 100 mm.

Preferred habitat Restricted to arid *Acacia*-vegetated sand ridges north and west of Pernatty Lagoon, SA. Apparently isolated from all other *Nephrurus* spp. by surrounding salt lakes, gibber plains and the Gawler Ranges.

Microhabitat Shelters in burrows at bases of low vegetation.

Comments Feeds on a variety of arthropods. Adults include the small geckos *Rhynchoedura ornata*, *Diplodactylus damaeus* and *Gehyra variegata* on their diets. These are stalked and pounced on from a crouched position. Venomous spiders and scorpions (probably capable of inflicting fatal injuries) are approached more carefully from behind. Scorpions are grasped by their tails, and spiders by their abdomens. Both are consumed from the rear. Gravid females have been recorded in January, April, May and October, suggesting a prolonged, opportunistic breeding season. Aspects of these data may apply to other *Nephrurus* spp. The restricted range of *N. deleani* is subject to marked disturbance by sheep and cattle, resulting in destruction of vegetation and trampling of burrows. Previous authors have regarded the species as 'rare' and suggest its inclusion in the IUCN Red Data Book.

Nephrurus laevissimus Mertens, 1958
Photo 185

Description Small *Nephrurus* with relatively slender tail bearing approximately 6 longitudinal series of enlarged white tubercles. Back, flanks and limbs are virtually smooth; a few scattered low conical tubercles present on vertebral region. Ground colour pink to pinkish brown; immaculate or with numerous small whitish spots. Three dark brown (sometimes broken) lines present on head and forebody: the 1st curves back from each eye to base of head, the 2nd extends across neck, and the 3rd curves back from each shoulder. Short dark stripe present on either side of body above hips. Short dark bar present on vertebral region above hips; sometimes absent or reduced to dark patch. Juveniles are more boldly patterned, with an additional 4 broken dark bands across body. Top of head may bear irregular small dark blotches. Tail dark brown to grey. Ventral surfaces white. SVL 75 mm.

Distinguished from *N. levis* in possessing much more slender tail and lacking lateral tubercles.

Preferred habitat Edgar Ranges in south-west Kimberley region, WA, south through Great Sandy Desert to eastern interior of WA, south-western NT and northern SA. Occurs on crests and slopes of red to yellow desert sand ridges vegetated with hummock grasses.

Microhabitat Shelters in burrows excavated at bases of hummock grasses. Forages on open spaces between vegetation.

Comments   As for genus.

Smooth Knob-tailed Gecko
Nephrurus levis De Vis, 1886
Photos 186–188

Description   Medium-sized *Nephrurus* with moderately long tail (moderately slender to broad and depressed), bearing 8–12 dorsal series of enlarged white tubercles arranged in irregular longitudinal rows. Body and upper surfaces of limbs bear small conical tubercles. Three subspecies recognised.

N. l. levis   Ground colour pale pinkish brown to dark purplish brown, patterned with narrow transverse cream to pale grey lines. The 1st extends across base of head, the 2nd extends across neck, and the 3rd curves forward at about level of shoulder. Pale lines may be present across back. These are less regular and usually broken into series of spots, occasionally alternating with narrow darker interspaces. Head and neck darker shade of ground colour, usually without pattern. Tail moderately slender and blackish brown. Ventral surfaces white. SVL 85 mm.

N. l. occidentalis Storr, 1963   Differs from nominate form in possessing much broader, more depressed tail and usually paler colouration. SVL 90 mm.

N. l. pilbarensis Storr, 1963   Differs from both other forms in possessing stronger, more complex pattern. Pale transverse lines on forebody are intensified by prominent dark margins. Spots on back are less regular and mixed with irregular reticulum of dark lines and blotches. Differs further from *N. l. levis* in possessing much broader, more depressed tail. SVL 90 mm.

Distinguished from *N. laevissimus* by skin-texture (lateral tubercles present vs absent) and tail-width (relatively broad vs relatively slender).

Preferred habitat   Arid regions of all mainland States except Vic. Extends from north-western NSW and south-western Qld, through SA and southern NT to interior and west coast of WA. Favours sandy to loamy areas supporting open vegetation types. *N. l. occidentalis* occurs on midwest coast and hinterland of WA from about Karratha south to Geraldton. *N. l. pilbarensis* is restricted to arid Pilbara region and Great Sandy Desert, WA. *N. l. levis* occupies remainder of range.

Microhabitat   Shelters in burrows; its own or those dug by other lizards, particularly dragons.

Comments   As for genus.

Nephrurus stellatus Storr, 1968
Photos 189, 190

Description   Moderately small *Nephrurus* with small slender tail bearing approximately 13 transverse rows of enlarged tubercles. Back and flanks bear numerous enlarged low conical tubercles or

rosettes; each comprising a large tubercle surrounded by smaller tubercles. Two forms occur. These may constitute distinct taxa.

Western form: Ground colour pale yellowish brown, pinkish brown to rich reddish or purplish brown, marked with 3 narrow white transverse lines. The 1st extends across base of head, the 2nd across neck and the 3rd across level of forelimb. Remainder of dorsal and lateral surfaces covered with numerous prominent white to yellowish spots, each centred on a tubercle or rosette. Top of head ground colour or darker, with or without pale to dark variegations, or blotches and spots. Ventral surfaces white. SVL 80 mm.

Eastern form: Head darker. Anterior transverse lines dark purplish brown and broader.

Preferred habitat   Arid to semi-arid southern WA east to Eyre Peninsula, SA. Occurs on yellow to pinkish sand plains and sand ridges vegetated with mallee/*Triodia* associations and/or heathlands.

Microhabitat   Shelters in burrows at bases of shrubs or hummock grasses.

Comments   See genus.

Nephrurus vertebralis Storr, 1963
Photo 191

Description   Medium-sized *Nephrurus* with moderately slender tail bearing approximately 6 longitudinal series of enlarged pale tubercles. Back and upper surfaces of limbs bear small conical tubercles arranged in irregular longitudinal rows. Ground colour dull to bright reddish brown, marked with prominent narrow white vertebral stripe from base of head to tail-tip. Four obscure and irregular narrow pale lines extend across head and forebody. First extends across head behind eyes, 2nd across base of head, 3th across neck, and 4th from level of forelimb back to midline. Remainder of dorsum spotted with cream to white, each spot centred on a tubercle. Head and neck dark purplish brown, sometimes with paler marbling. Tail dark purplish brown. Ventral surfaces white. SVL 90 mm.

Preferred habitat   Arid interior of southern WA on heavy to stony soils dominated by *Acacia* woodlands and shrublands.

Microhabitat   Shelters in burrows, such as those of dragons.

Comments   As for genus.

Banded Knob-tailed Gecko
Nephrurus wheeleri Loveridge, 1932
Photos 192, 193

Description   Moderate to large *Nephrurus* with moderately long broad depressed tail bearing approximately 4–6 dorsal series of large rosettes. Back, flanks and limbs bear rosettes consisting of large conical tubercles surrounded by smaller tubercles. Two subspecies recognised.

N. w. wheeleri   Ground colour pinkish, yellowish

brown to rich reddish brown, prominently marked with 4 broad dark brown bands on body and tail. The 1st extends across nape and shoulders, the 2nd across lower back, the 3rd across base of tail, and the 4th across tail-tip. Front and sides of head patterned with reticulum of dark brown lines. Limbs usually patternless. Ventral surfaces pale pinkish brown to white. SVL 90 mm.

N. w. cinctus Storr, 1963 Differs from nominate form in possessing larger tubercles and greater number of bands (4 vs 5). The 1st band is divided into 2 of equal width (across nape and across shoulders) by interspace of ground colour. SVL 100 mm.

Preferred habitat Arid midwestern interior of WA. *N. w. wheeleri* inhabits hard stony soils dominated by *Acacia* woodlands and shrublands in Murchison and northern Goldfields areas of WA. *N. w. cinctus* occurs on rocky ranges and outcrops vegetated with hummock grasses in Pilbara region, WA.

Microhabitat Shelters in disused burrows and beneath rocks. Forages in open spaces between vegetation.

Comments Individuals reported to flick dust over themselves, presumably as an aid to camouflage. Otherwise as for genus.

Velvet Geckos
Genus *OEDURA* Gray, 1842
(Subfamily Diplodactylinae)

Endemic genus containing 13 species. Widespread through subhumid to arid northern two-thirds of Australia. Absent from south-east (including Vic. and Tas.).

Moderately small to large dorsally depressed geckos. Tail moderately long; slender and round in cross-section to robust and depressed; often constricted at base. Digits long and expanded to form pads; bearing small retractile claws and a pair of enlarged subapical plates. Subdigital lamellae enlarged to form transverse plates; divided distally and mostly single proximally. Dorsal scales homogeneous; small, flat and juxtaposed with a smooth velvety texture. This has resulted in the common name of 'velvet geckos'. Pattern usually prominent, consisting of pale spots, broad bands, or blotches.

Arboreal to rock-inhabiting, sheltering beneath loose bark, in hollows, crevices or caves. Velvet geckos feed on arthropods, though large adults of some species occasionally prey on smaller lizards, particularly other geckos. Plump tails probably serve as fat storages, and providing water is available, an individual may be sustained for 6 months or more. Clutch consists of 2 parchment-shelled eggs.

Distinguished from *Phyllodactylus* by nature of subdigital lamellae (excluding enlarged subapical plates). These are divided distally and single proximally (*Oedura*) vs all single (*Phyllodactylus*). Differs from *Gehyra* in possessing claws on all digits (vs inner digit on each foot lacking claw).

Northern Velvet Gecko
Oedura castelnaui (Thominot, 1889)
Photo 194

Description Large *Oedura* with plump depressed tail. Ground colour yellowish orange to yellowish brown, flecked or blotched with blackish brown. Pattern consists of 5 broad dark-edged whitish bands (almost as wide to wider than ground colour) between nape and hips. Lateral extremities tend to curve forward, particularly on nape and forebody. Broad blackish stripe extends from nostril through eye, curving to meet its opposite on base of head. This is margined below by white stripe from upper lip; continuous with first pale band. Original tail marked with approximately 5 pale bands. Regenerated tail bears irregular transversely aligned black streaks. Ventral surfaces whitish. SVL 90 mm.

Distinguished from *O. marmorata* in possessing broader pale bands (invariably present, and almost as wide to wider than interspaces of ground colour, vs often reduced or fragmented, and considerably narrower than interspaces of ground colour).

Preferred habitat Dry sclerophyll forests and woodlands of north-eastern Qld. Some populations occur on rock outcrops.

Microhabitat Predominantly arboreal. Usually shelters beneath loose bark of dead trees.

Comments Known to survive without food for 12 months, relying on fat deposits in tail. Often dwells in small communities, with records of up to 12 individuals beneath 1 sheet of bark. Eggs recorded in December, hatching after 60 days of artificial incubation.

Oedura coggeri Bustard, 1966
Photo 195

Description Moderately large robust *Oedura*. Ground colour dull yellowish grey to rich orange-brown, usually prominently marked with numerous irregular transverse rows of dark-edged yellowish grey to cream spots. These often coalesce to form bands. Dark margins may be sufficiently broad to obscure ground colour. Each spot may enclose smaller dark dot. Dark purplish brown stripe (margined above and below with cream to yellow or brown) extends from snout through eye to nape; sometimes curving to join its opposite, forming collar. Ventral surfaces white. SVL 70 mm.

Preferred habitat Rock outcrops and stony hills of subhumid south-eastern Cape York Peninsula, Qld.

Microhabitat Shelters in rock crevices and beneath loose bark of dead trees.

Comments Breeding appears continuous throughout year. When harassed body is raised high off substrate with back and tail arched in a cat-like manner. Otherwise as for genus.

Oedura filicipoda King, 1984
Photos 196, 197

Description   Largest *Oedura*, bearing unique fringe composed of laterally expanded lamellae on each digit, long limbs and a short broad tail. Ground colour dark brown, prominently spotted over head, body and limbs with yellow to yellowish brown. A series of widely spaced pale brown bands present between nape and hips. Original tail bears black and greyish white bands, the dark markings enclosing yellow spots. Regenerated tail black mottled with greenish yellow. Ventral surfaces white, finely flecked with darker pigment. SVL 105 mm.

Distinguished from all other *Oedura*, indeed all other Australian geckos, in bearing prominent fringes along edges of digits.
Preferred habitat   Known only from sandstone escarpments and outcrops of Mitchell Plateau in humid northern Kimberley region of WA.
Microhabitat   Inhabits cave walls and adjacent rock faces.
Comments   Fringed digits may facilitate climbing on coarse sandstone surfaces, especially when hanging upside-down on overhangs and cave ceilings. Agile, its long limbs enabling it to leap from one rock face to another. Cornered individuals observed to enact a defensive response, flattening body onto substrate while arching and waving tail from side to side.

Oedura gemmata King and Gow, 1983
Photo 198

Description   Large *Oedura* with broad flat tail. Ground colour pinkish brown to black. Pattern usually prominent, consisting of numerous lemon-yellow to brown spots over head, body and limbs. Original tail bears approximately 11 narrow white bands. Regenerated tail marked with irregular transversely aligned pale flecks. Ventral surfaces greyish pink. SVL 100 mm.
Preferred habitat   Arnhem Escarpment and associated outliers, NT.
Microhabitat   Shelters in rock crevices. Forages on exposed rock surfaces, among low shrubs, and occasionally on ground.
Comments   As for genus.

Oedura gracilis King, 1984
Photo 199

Description   Slender flat-headed *Oedura*. Tail long slender and round in cross-section. Ground colour pinkish brown marked with dark-edged pale yellowish brown bands. Pattern stronger on tail, ground colour being darker to almost black and bands paler to almost white. Blackish brown stripe extends from nostril through eye to ear, contrasting with whitish lips. Ventral surfaces whitish, finely flecked with darker pigment. SVL 84 mm.

Distinguished from *O. marmorata* by having a flatter head.
Preferred habitat   Known only from sandstone escarpments and outcrops in humid northern Kimberley region of WA, from Mitchell Plateau south to Mt Daglish.
Microhabitat   Shelters in rock crevices and forages on exposed rock faces.
Comments   Sympatric with *O. filicipoda*, apparently favouring more exposed sandstone areas, in contrast with the larger species which appears to prefer caves. See genus.

Lesueur's Velvet Gecko
Oedura lesueurii (Duméril and Bibron, 1836)
Photo 200

Description   Small *Oedura* with long, moderately dorsally depressed tail. Ground colour grey, pinkish brown to greyish brown. Broad ragged-edged vertebral region, broken into irregular dark-edged blotches, extends from nape to tail-tip. Regenerated tail variegated with blackish brown. Flanks and limbs marked with small, prominent to obscure pale blotches and dark variegations. Top of head paler shade of ground colour, lightly to heavily variegated with blackish brown. Ventral surfaces whitish to pale pinkish brown. SVL 55 mm.
Preferred habitat   Rocky ranges, hills and outcrops (particularly granite and sandstone) of humid to subhumid south-eastern NSW, north to Kroombit Tops, Qld. Favours cooler habitats than other *Oedura* spp., becoming increasingly dependent on high altitudes northwards.
Microhabitat   Shelters beneath rock slabs and in crevices.
Comments   Eggs are laid in summer, hatching in autumn. Otherwise as for genus.

Marbled Velvet Gecko
Oedura marmorata Gray, 1842
Photos 201, 202

Description   Large variable *Oedura*. Tail slender and round in cross-section to plump and weakly depressed. Ground colour dark purplish brown. Juveniles bear simple pattern of broad, prominent yellow to cream bands; 5 or 6 between nape and hips, and 4 or 5 on tail. Dark band extends from snout, through eye, curving to meet its opposite on base of head. This is margined by yellow to cream band from lips, curving on nape to form 1st pale band. Pattern becomes broken and more complex with age. Pale bands may develop dark centres and ragged edges, and irregular pale spotting tends to develop on ground colour. Occasionally all transverse pattern is replaced by irregular pale flecks or variegations. Ventral surfaces whitish. SVL 95 mm.

Distinguished from *O. castelnaui* in possessing narrower pale bands (often fragmented, and considerably narrower than interspaces, vs invariably present, and almost as wide as to wider than interspaces). Differs from *O. gracilis* by head-profile (relatively deep vs strongly depressed).

Preferred habitat Widely distributed through subhumid to arid areas west of Great Dividing Range. Extends from interior of NSW, north to Gulf of Carpentaria, Qld, through NT (excluding north-east) and northern SA to northern two-thirds of WA.

Microhabitat Arboreal and rock-inhabiting. See genus.

Comments Eggs are laid between September and November (in east of range). Otherwise as for genus.

Ocellated Velvet Gecko
Oedura monilis De Vis, 1888
Photo 203

Description Moderately large *Oedura*. Ground colour throughout most of range yellowish brown, heavily peppered to variegated with darker brown or grey. Northern populations are darker. Pattern consists of approximately 12 dark-edged pale greyish (bright yellow on juveniles) dorsal blotches (6 to hips and 6 on tail), commencing with crescent-shape on nape (apices directed forwards). Remaining blotches are divided into paravertebral pairs or joined to form transverse hourglass shapes. Irregular, obscure pale blotches may be present on flanks. Dark streak extends through eye to side of neck. Limbs and regenerated tail heavily to lightly flecked or variegated with blackish brown. Lips and ventral surfaces whitish. SVL 85 mm.

Preferred habitat Dry sclerophyll forests and woodlands in subhumid eastern interior of Qld and northern NSW. Most abundant in associations of coarse-barked eucalypts (ironbarks) and *Callitris* pines.

Microhabitat Arboreal. See genus.

Comments Individuals usually dwell on a home-tree from which they forage widely in search of food. Each year, 1 or possibly 2 clutches of eggs are laid from late December to early February, hatching from mid-February to end of March. Otherwise as for genus.

Oedura obscura King, 1984
Photo 204

Description Small slender *Oedura*. Tail long, slender and round in cross-section. Ground colour pale yellowish brown to pinkish brown, marked with approximately 12 irregular dark brown bands between nape and hips. Interspaces broader than bands, each enclosing a wavy transverse series of white spots. Head spotted with white. Dark stripe extends between nostril and eye. Original tail banded as on body. Regenerated tail marked with

dark stripes. Ventral surfaces whitish. SVL 60 mm.

Preferred habitat Sandstone plateaux and outcrops in humid to subhumid north-western Kimberley region of WA.

Microhabitat Shelters beneath sandstone slabs, in rock crevices and under bark of trees.

Comments See genus.

Reticulated Velvet Gecko
Oedura reticulata Bustard, 1969
Photo 205

Description Small *Oedura* with ground colour of grey to greyish brown. Pattern usually obscure. Broad straight-edged pale grey vertebral zone extends from top of head to tail-tip, becoming obscure beyond hips. This is usually incompletely broken by irregular narrow dark vertebral stripe and transverse lines. Dark grey laterodorsal zone (most prominent between eye and shoulder or midbody) commences as dark streak from nostril. Flanks and limbs grey, finely peppered with darker grey. Top of head marked with dark variegations. Regenerated tail grey, flecked with darker and paler pigment. Ventral surfaces whitish. SVL 70 mm.

Preferred habitat Eucalypt woodlands and *Acacia* thickets in subhumid south-western interior of WA, from Zanthus area west to Darling Range. Restricted in many areas to roadside verges and windbreaks due to intensive wheat cultivation.

Microhabitat Favours hollow trunks and limbs of smooth-barked eucalypts.

Comments As for genus.

Zigzag Velvet Gecko
Oedura rhombifer Gray, 1845
Photo 206

Description Small slender *Oedura* with long, nearly cylindrical tail. Ground colour pale to dark grey or brown. Broad pale serrated-edged vertebral stripe extends from nape to base of tail; often broken beyond hips to form a series of angular blotches. Anterior section forked; each branch extending through upper half of eye to enclose variably sized patch of ground colour on top of head. All aspects of pattern are margined with blackish brown, commencing with streak on snout. Flanks and limbs obscurely marked with dark flecks and pale spots. Ventral surfaces whitish. SVL 70 mm.

Preferred habitat Occurs extensively through subhumid northern half of Australia. Favours woodlands and occasionally rock outcrops. Penetrates arid areas via eucalypt-lined watercourses.

Microhabitat Arboreal and rock-inhabiting. Often resides in human dwellings. Otherwise as for genus.

Comments See genus.

Robust Velvet Gecko
Oedura robusta Boulenger, 1885
Photo 207

Description Moderately large *Oedura* with broad plump depressed tail. Ground colour brown to blackish brown. Pattern usually prominent, consisting of approximately 5 or 6 large, roughly square-shaped, pale grey to pale brown dorsal blotches from nape to hips, and approximately 7 on original tail. Regenerated tail usually broader, irregularly flecked or streaked with dark brown. Flanks and limbs obscurely marked with whitish dots and dark mottling. Top of head pale grey to pale brown, usually continuous with dorsal blotches. Ventral surfaces white. SVL 80 mm.

Preferred habitat Dry sclerophyll forests, woodlands, rocky ranges and outcrops on coast and interior of eastern Australia, from northern NSW to northern Qld.

Microhabitat Shelters in hollow trunks and limbs, particularly those of large smooth-barked eucalypts. Rock-inhabiting populations occurring in sandstone ranges of interior of south-east Qld shelter in crevices, foraging on walls and ceilings of wind-blown caves.

Comments See genus.

Tryon's Velvet Gecko
Oedura tryoni De Vis, 1884
Photo 208

Description Moderately large *Oedura* with weakly depressed tail. Ground colour brown, yellowish brown to reddish brown; dark purplish brown on juveniles. Pattern usually prominent, consisting of numerous small dark-edged pale yellow to whitish spots over body, limbs and tail. Diffuse yellowish brown streak may extend from snout through top of eye to base of head. Top of head marked with dark variegations. Ventral surfaces whitish. SVL 80 mm.

Preferred habitat Dry sclerophyll forests and woodlands, especially where rock outcrops occur, from north-eastern NSW to south-eastern Qld. Extends from sea-level to cooler high altitudes.

Microhabitat Shelters beneath rock exfoliations and in crevices. Occasionally utilises debris at ground level or loose bark of standing and fallen trees.

Comments Eggs are laid in midsummer, hatching from late summer to early autumn. Otherwise as for genus.

Photo 209 shows an undescribed *Oedura* taxon allied to *O. rhombifer*.

Genus *PHYLLODACTYLUS*
Gray, 1828
(Subfamily Gekkoninae)

Large genus, widespread through the world's tropical and temperate regions. A single Australian mainland species is restricted to south. Absent from Tas. Relationship with extralimital *Phyllodactylus* is poorly understood.

Medium-sized moderately dorsally depressed geckos with long fleshy tail. Digits clawed (each claw retractile, set in a groove) and expanded distally to form pads. Subdigital lamellae enlarged to form a single transverse series. Subapical plates moderately large and divided. Scales homogeneous; small, smooth and granular.

Arboreal and rock-inhabiting. Arthropod feeders. Clutch consists of 2 calcareous-shelled eggs.

Distinguished from *Gehyra* in possessing claws on all digits, each claw not normally extending beyond pad (vs inner digit on each foot lacking claw, each claw extending well beyond pad). Differs from *Oedura* by nature of subdigital lamellae (excluding enlarged subapical plates). These are all single (*Phyllodactylus*) vs divided distally and single proximally (*Oedura*).

Marbled Gecko
Phyllodactylus marmoratus (Gray, 1845)
Photos 210–212

Description Three distinct chromosome races have been identified, 2 of which have been named as subspecies.

P. m. marmoratus Subject to considerable variation in size and pattern, with greatest size being attained in eastern Australia. Ground colour pale to dark grey or pinkish brown, prominently to obscurely marked with blackish brown lines which form irregular marbling, reticulations or zigzagging transverse bands. Irregular ragged-edged pale grey blotches often present, alternating with dark markings and tending to be centred on vertebral region. Pattern on tail similar, though transverse lines straighter, and a series of reddish brown vertebral blotches may be present, particularly on juveniles. Regenerated tail ground colour, streaked with darker pigment. Ventral surfaces pale pinkish grey to white. SVL 70 mm.

P. m. alexanderi Storr, 1987 Differs from nominate form by dorsal pattern: dark transverse lines on back shallowly zigzagging or undulating, not followed by pale blotches or spots. SVL 60 mm.

Preferred habitat Humid to semi-arid southern Australia, including many offshore islands. Extends north in eastern Australia to Warrumbungle Mountains, NSW, and to Shark Bay in WA. *P. m. alexanderi* extends from Israelite Bay in southern WA, across the Nullarbor Plain to Yalata area in western SA. Both subspecies occur in woodlands, coastal heathlands and rock outcrops.

Microhabitat Shelters beneath loose bark and exfoliating rock. WA coast and island populations tend to be less arboreal, utilising limestones and granites.

Comments Australia's most southerly gecko,

being the only member of its family in some areas. Eggs are deposited beneath bark or debris at bases of trees and rocks. In Vic. they are laid during spring, hatching from early summer to midsummer.

Leaf-tailed Geckos
Genus *PHYLLURUS* Schinz, 1822
(Subfamily Diplodactylinae)

Endemic genus restricted to humid and subhumid eastern Australia, from northern Qld to mideastern NSW. Represented by 4 described species.

Large to very large strongly dorsally depressed geckos, with flat splayed leaf-shaped tail; narrower to cylindrical on *P. caudiannulatus*. This is constricted at base with a single cleavage point. Original tail tapers sharply; distal third to half thin and cylindrical. Regenerated tail is broader and flatter with shorter attenuate tip. Digits long, slender, angular, strongly clawed and somewhat bird-like; lacking enlarged subapical plates. Dorsal and lateral scales heterogeneous; small and granular mixed with larger conical to spinose tubercles (smooth on regenerated tails), usually most prominent on flanks. Colour and pattern variable consisting of shades of brown to olive with darker and paler mottling.

Arboreal and rock-inhabiting. Depressed form, splayed tail and cryptic colouration effectively conceal these geckos against the variegated backgrounds on which they forage. The proportion of regenerated tails is very high (almost 75 per cent on one species). This probably reflects disputes between individuals rather than actions of predators. Adults almost invariably support colonies of red mites. It is doubtful whether these ubiquitous parasites pose any harm to their hosts under normal circumstances. Diet consists mainly of large arthropods. Clutch consists of 2 parchment-shelled eggs.

Phyllurus caudiannulatus Covacevich, 1975
Photos 213, 214

Description Small leaf-tailed gecko comprising 2 distinct populations. These may constitute separate taxa.

Southern form bears narrow cylindrical tail. Ground colour dark grey to brown marked with fine dark mottling or blotches and scattered to transversely aligned pale spots. Original tail bears 5 or 6 cream to white bands. Regenerated tail mottled with blackish brown. Ventral surfaces cream to shades of grey, sometimes finely spotted with brown. SVL 85 mm.

Northern form differs in possessing broader tail; flattened to form narrow leaf-shape, with attenuate tip constituting approximately half total tail-length. Original tail bears 4–6 pale bands.

Distinguished from *P. salebrosus* by tail-shape (cylindrical or flattened to form narrow leaf-shape vs very broad and depressed) and much smaller maximum size (SVL 85 vs 140 mm).

Preferred habitat Known only from rainforest between 350 and 950 m above sea-level at Bulburin State Forest (southern form) and Eungella National Park in mideast Qld (northern form).

Microhabitat Shelters in cavities in buttresses of trees, particularly figs (*Ficus* spp.), and beneath loose bark. Forages on exposed vertical surfaces.

Comments As for genus.

Northern Leaf-tailed Gecko
Phyllurus cornutus (Ogilby, 1892)
Photos 215–217

Description Large leaf-tailed gecko with broad tail. Attenuate tip approximately half total length of original tail. Regenerated tail usually with short well-defined tip. Several forms occur. These may constitute distinct taxa. Ground colour shades of grey, brown to olive marked with prominent disruptive lichen-like mottling, blotches and variegations. Dark-edged pale reddish brown to pale grey vertebral stripe usually present, interrupted by series of large pale dorsal blotches. Base of head usually bears blackish brown W- or M-shaped mark. Original tail usually bears broad irregular pale bands. Ventral surfaces whitish to pale olive, occasionally peppered with pale brown. SVL 130 mm.

Northern population (nominate form) appears most distinctive, attaining greatest maximum size and bearing long, closely packed, backward-curving lateral spines (vs sparser, shorter spines of southern populations).

Preferred habitat Northern form occurs in north-east Qld: in McIlwraith Range, and from Cooktown area south to Mt Spec. Southern form extends from about Taree, NSW, north to Mt Tamborine, Qld. Both forms are virtually restricted to wet sclerophyll and rainforests of coastal ranges and Great Dividing Range. Isolated rock-inhabiting form occurs in boulder-strewn dry sclerophyll forests and heathlands of the Granite Belt (above 1000 m), south-eastern Qld. Most Qld localities are over 750 m though individuals frequently occur at much lower altitudes in NSW.

Microhabitat Rainforest populations shelter in hollows or crevices of buttresses and trunks, foraging on exposed vertical surfaces. Sometimes encountered behind rafters or in dark corners of disused buildings. Granite Belt population shelters in rock crevices and beneath exfoliating slabs, foraging on lichen-covered boulder faces.

Comments Often active at temperatures low enough to preclude most other reptile activity. Otherwise as for genus.

Broad-tailed Gecko or Southern Leaf-tailed Gecko
Phyllurus platurus (White, 1790)
Photo 218

Description Small *Phyllurus* with relatively narrow tail. Attenuate tip constitutes approximately half total length of original tail. Regenerated tail broader with long to very short attenuate tip. Ground colour pale brown to dark grey, marked on head, body, limbs and tail with darker mottling, spots or flecks. Original tail may bear irregular bands towards tip. Ventral surfaces pale olive. SVL 80 mm.

Preferred habitat Restricted to sandstones of mideastern NSW, extending inland to Blue Mountains.

Microhabitat Shelters in crevices and wind-blown sandstone caves. Occasionally enters human dwellings when these are adjacent to sandstone outcrops.

Comments Large numbers may share a suitable shelter site. Up to 16 individuals recorded from a single crevice. These sites may be littered with sloughed skins. When disturbed, individuals emit loud prolonged rasping bark. Mating occurs during May. Eggs are laid communally deep in crevices from October to November, hatching in January. Otherwise as for genus.

Phyllurus salebrosus Covacevich, 1975
Photo 219

Description Largest leaf-tailed gecko with very broad tail. Attenuate tip constitutes less than one-third total length of original tail. Regenerated tail broader, lacking attenuate tip. Ground colour shades of grey, usually with some indication of brownish dark-edged vertebral stripe. This is broken by 3 (usually dark-edged) pale dorsal blotches located at about shoulders, midbody and hips. Head and limbs variegated with blackish brown. Original tail bears irregular blackish brown and pale grey bars and mottling. Regenerated tail flecked to mottled with blackish brown. Ventral surfaces cream, sparsely to densely flecked with brown. Dark pigment tends to align transversely on throat. SVL 140 mm.

Distinguished from *P. caudiannulatus* by tail-shape (very broad and depressed vs cylindrical, or flattened to form narrow leaf-shape) and much greater size (SVL 140 vs 85 mm).

Preferred habitat Mideastern to southern-central Qld. Favours sandstone or granite outcrops surrounded by woodlands. Population from Bulburin State Forest occurs in rainforest.

Microhabitat Shelters in rock crevices or on ceilings and walls of wind-blown sandstone caves and in cavities in rainforest tree trunks.

Comments As for genus.

Genus *PSEUDOTHECADACTYLUS* Brongersma, 1936

(Subfamily Diplodactylinae)

Represented by 3 taxa. Restricted in Australia to far north and possibly extralimital in New Guinea.

Very large moderately robust geckos with relatively long slender tail; cylindrical and more or less prehensile. Scales beneath tail-tip modified to form unique adhesive lamellae. All digits (except innermost on each foot) bear retractile claws. Subdigital lamellae form broad divided transverse plates along length of digit. Dorsal body scales small smooth and homogeneous to moderately heterogeneous.

Arboreal and rock-inhabiting geckos which feed largely on arthropods, and occasionally smaller geckos. Clutch probably consists of 2 parchment-shelled eggs.

Giant Tree Gecko
Pseudothecadactylus australis (Günther, 1877)
Photo 220

Description Ground colour pale brown, brown to olive-grey, finely peppered and/or mottled with dark brown to black. Pattern usually obscure, comprising approximately 6 dark-edged transversely aligned paler blotches (often divided anteriorly by narrow irregular dark vertebral stripe) between nape and hips. These may be represented on tail by up to 6 obscure blotches or bars. Irregular dark streak extends from snout, above ear, fading at about shoulders. Lips and ventrolateral region of neck whitish. Ventral surfaces whitish flecked with dark brown, particularly on throat. SVL 120 mm.

Preferred habitat Subhumid to humid coast and hinterland of northern and eastern Cape York Peninsula, including islands of Torres Strait, Qld. Favours woodlands (especially those dominated by *Melaleuca*) and monsoon forests, extending into ecotonal mangrove communities.

Microhabitat Arboreal. Shelters in hollow trunks and limbs, foraging among branches, vine-stems and foliage.

Comments Individuals are often encountered after dusk with head and forelimbs protruding from hollows. Eggs are laid in January.

Giant Cave Gecko
Pseudothecadactylus lindneri Cogger, 1975
Photos 221, 222

Description Two subspecies recognised.

P. l. lindneri Ground colour medium to dark purplish brown, marked from nape to hips with irregular whitish, cream to pale orange bands. These are often disrupted on vertebral region. Top of head marked with prominent to obscure, coarse dark brown reticulum and/or paler blotches. Iris reddish brown. Eye rimmed with cream. Dark streak extends from nostril through eye to temple. Tail prominently banded with pale yellow and blackish brown. Regenerated tails uniform brown. Ventral surfaces pinkish white. SVL 100 mm.

P. l. cavaticus Cogger, 1975 Differs from nominate form in possessing more regular pale bands, each usually bearing darker centre. Dorsal and dorsolateral scales heterogeneous (vs homogeneous).

Preferred habitat Deeply dissected sandstone plateaux of subhumid western Arnhem land, NT (*P. l. lindneri*), and northern Kimberley region, WA (*P. l. cavaticus*).

Microhabitat Rock-inhabiting. Shelters in rock crevices, foraging on walls and ceilings of caves and overhangs.

Comments As for genus.

Genus *RHYNCHOEDURA*
Günther, 1867

(Subfamily Diplodactylinae)

Endemic monotypic genus widespread through semi-arid to arid areas of all mainland States except Vic.

Small elongate gecko with moderately long tail and moderately short limbs. Rostral and mental scales protrusive, forming distinctive beak-like snout. All digits clawed. Subdigital lamellae minute and conical. Subapical plates slightly enlarged. Tail slender and round in cross-section. Dorsal scales homogeneous; small and smooth.

Terrestrial. Clutch consists of 2 parchment-shelled eggs.

Distinguished from *Diplodactylus* except *D. pulcher* by shape of snout (beak-like vs round). Readily distinguished from *D. pulcher* by pattern (see photo).

Beaked Gecko
Rhynchoedura ornata Günther, 1867
Photo 223

Description Ground colour pale pinkish brown, brown to reddish brown. Pattern prominent to obscure, comprising variably sized cream to whitish spots and blotches overlaid with a fine black to dark brown reticulum on head, body, limbs and tail. Eye usually rimmed with white to cream. Ventral surfaces white. SVL 50 mm.

Preferred habitat Widespread in semi-arid to arid regions from north-west coast to eastern interior of Australia. Occurs on gibber flats, rocky hills, outcrops, sand plains or sand ridges dominated by hummock grasslands, *Acacia* woodlands or shrublands, and chenopod associations.

Microhabitat Occasionally encountered in shallow depressions beneath small stones, though favours vertical shafts of disused spider burrows; particularly those of wolf spiders (Lycosidae). Forages in open spaces between vegetation.

Comments Alert and quick to flee when disturbed at night. Though a variety of small arthropods are taken, termites constitute bulk of diet. On cool evenings geckos rest with only their heads protruding from burrows.

Genus *UNDERWOODISAURUS*
Wermuth, 1965

(Subfamily Diplodactylinae)

Endemic genus comprising 2 species restricted to southern half of Australia.

Large weakly depressed geckos with plump body and long slender limbs. Tail swollen and constricted at base with a single cleavage point. Distal third to half slender and more or less cylindrical when original; bulbous and lacking attenuate tip when regenerated. Digits long, slender and clawed. Enlarged subapical plates absent. Subdigital lamellae slightly enlarged; arranged in a single transverse series. Dorsal scales heterogeneous: minute and granular, mixed with numerous enlarged conical tubercles (scattered or tending to align transversely).

Relatively slow-moving terrestrial geckos which feed on a broad range of arthropods. Clutch consists of 2 parchment-shelled eggs. Distinctive threat display consists of rhythmically raising and lowering inflated body, arching back, slowly waving tail, and abruptly leaping toward adversary with mouth agape while emitting a loud wheezing bark.

Distinguished from *Nephrurus* by nature of subdigital lamellae (slightly enlarged vs small, irregular and spinose) and tip of original tail (attenuate vs terminating in a spherical enlargement or 'knob').

Thick-tailed Gecko or Barking Gecko
Underwoodisaurus milii
(Bory de Saint-Vincent, 1825)
Photo 224

Description Large *Underwoodisaurus* with carrot-shaped original tail. Ground colour pinkish, reddish brown, brown to dark purplish brown, prominently marked with numerous cream to yellow spots (and sometimes smaller dark dots) over body and limbs. These are centred on tubercles and tend to align transversely. Those on base of head and in front of shoulders (sometimes neck) usually join to form complete narrow bands. Original tail black with 5 or 6 broad contrasting white bands. Regenerated tail heart-shaped, usually smooth or bearing smaller tubercles, and pattern is reduced to irregular paler mottling. Ventral surfaces white. SVL 80 mm.

Preferred habitat Widespread through southern Australia from Rockhampton district, Qld, through NSW, SA and southern NT to just north of Shark Bay, WA. Absent from southern Vic. and southeastern NSW. Occupies a variety of subhumid to arid habitats including dry sclerophyll forests, woodlands, shrublands, heathlands and rock outcrops.

Microhabitat Shelters beneath rocks, fallen timber, beneath bark at bases of stumps and in burrows.

Comments Locally abundant in suitable areas.

Up to 13 individuals recorded beneath a granite slab. Eastern population is reported to share a single site for communal egglaying, and form winter aggregations. The majority of adults bear regenerated tails. Otherwise as for genus.

Underwoodisaurus sphyrurus (Ogilby, 1892)
Photo 225

Description Small *Underwoodisaurus* with bulbous rectangular-shaped original tail bearing large, roughly transverse tubercles. Ground colour pale to dark brownish grey, marked with numerous small transversely aligned pale spots, each centred on a tubercle. These are mixed with blackish variegations. Original tail blackish, bearing approximately 4 broad raggededged whitish bands. Regenerated tail marked with irregular paler mottling. Ventral surfaces greyish white, peppered with darker pigment. SVL 70 mm.

Preferred habitat Restricted to cool highland Granite Belt of New England, NSW, and adjacent Stanthorpe district, Qld.

Microhabitat Shelters beneath slabs of granite resting on soil, and in burrows.

Comments Adults with original tails are uncommon. Otherwise as for genus.

LEGLESS LIZARDS, SNAKE LIZARDS, FLAP-FOOTED LIZARDS, WORM LIZARDS
Family PYGOPODIDAE

One of 2 reptile families endemic to the Australian region. (The other, Carettochelydidae, contains a single wholly aquatic freshwater turtle.) Represented by 8 genera containing 32 Australian species. Pygopodids are widely distributed throughout Australia, excluding cool, moist south-east Vic., Tas. and alpine areas. One widespread species (*Lialis burtonis*) extends north to New Guinea. Another (*Lialis jicari*) is restricted to that region, being the only pygopodid not occurring in Australia.

Pygopodids share the following characteristics: eye well developed (covered by immovable transparent spectacle), forelimb absent without trace, hindlimb present (represented by scaly flap or single scale), ear opening usually visible, tongue fleshy (notched at tip), tail fragile (slightly shorter to approximately 4 times longer than body) and body scales (including ventrals) smooth to keeled, always overlapping in 12–25 rows.

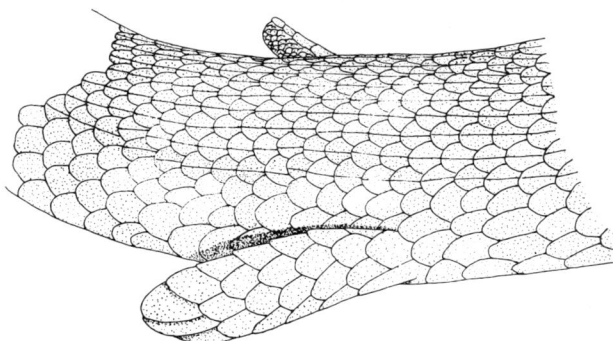

Hindlimb flaps (unique to Pygopodidae) are most strongly developed in the genus *Pygopus*

Pattern, when present, usually consists of dark bands on head and nape or longitudinally aligned dashes or stripes on body and tail. Head markings often resemble those of venomous snakes (some *Demansia* spp. and juvenile *Pseudonaja* spp.). Some pygopodids (*Pygopus* and *Paradelma*) further extend this similarity to active mimicry by raising head and body and rapidly flickering tongue. See photo 226, of *Paradelma orientalis*, for example; the obvious ear opening and thick fleshy tongue provide clues to its true identity.

Diversity at both generic and species level is greatest in southern Australia, particularly the western half of the continent. Most favour subhumid to arid habitats where dense low vegetation such as hummock grasslands or complex heathlands are present.

Pygopodids range from highly mobile terrestrial predators of small vertebrates to relatively sedentary cryptozoic and fossorial insectivores. All produce 2 parchment-shelled eggs per clutch.

Surprisingly pygopodids appear most closely related to geckos (Gekkonidae), with which they share a number of important features. Most notable are the ability to vocalise in the form of a wheezing squeak, use of tongue to wipe clean transparent spectacle covering eye and low clutch sizes (2 vs 1–2 eggs).

In evolutionary terms pygopodids may well be relatively old, considering the degree of fragmentation within the family. (Of the 8 genera, 4 are monotypic.) Most primitive species are probably those with the least number of unique morphological and behavioural characteristics; the most conventionally lizard-like. If this is the case, members of the genus *Pygopus* (bearing the largest hindlimb flaps, numerous preanal pores and high number of midbody scale rows) may be more primitive than other pygopodids.

Many species are mistakenly identified as snakes and killed. Pygopodids are readily distinguished from snakes by: fleshy tongue (vs narrow, forked); paired ventral scales (vs usually single transverse plates); fragile tail, usually much longer than body (vs non-fragile tail, considerably shorter than body); and usual presence (vs absence) of ear opening.

Genus *ACLYS* Kluge, 1974

Endemic monotypic genus restricted to lower and midwest coasts of WA. Medium-sized, slender, long-snouted, long-tailed pygopodid with well-developed hindlimb flap and conspicuous ear opening. Scales smooth in 20 rows at midbody. Ventral scales not noticeably enlarged. Diurnal. Reproduction as for family.

Distinguished from sympatric *Delma* in possessing narrow dark stripes, pointed (vs round) snout and ventral scales not noticeably (vs considerably) broader than adjacent body scales.

Aclys concinna Kluge, 1974
Photo 227

Description Very slender pygopodid with tail approximately 4 times length of body. Two subspecies recognised.

A. c. concinna Ground colour brownish grey to brown. Three narrow dark grey to black dorsal stripes (vertebral and dorsals) extend from nape to tail-tip; the area enclosed between them often a darker shade of ground colour. Narrow pale latero-dorsal and lower lateral stripes usually extend along body and tail, often edged with one or more series of dark spots. Ventral surfaces white to pale grey. Each scale on chest, belly and occasionally tail, bears a pale brown spot. SVL 100 mm.

A. c. major Storr, 1988 Differs from nominate form in being larger and having a more simple pattern. Dark dorsal stripes tend to be wider, coalescing to form a broad dark stripe. Dark ventral markings tend to be triangular in shape. SVL 110 mm.

Preferred habitat Coastal dunes and sandplains supporting heathlands, often in association with woodlands of eucalypts and/or *Banksia*, in south-western and midwestern WA. *A. c. concinna* extends from northern suburbs of Perth to Leeman. *A. c. major* occurs only on western Edel Land Peninsula in the Shark Bay area.

Microhabitat Dwells in dense matrix of low vegetation and associated leaf-litter.

Comments Probably Australia's swiftest legless lizard. Individuals of *A. c. concinna* have been observed basking in shrubs up to 2 metres above ground. Gravid females recorded during August.

Worm Lizards
Genus *APRASIA* Gray, 1839

Endemic genus containing 11 taxa occurring in subhumid, semi-arid and arid areas of southern Australia. Many have restricted distributions.

Small, slender, elongate pygopodids with moderately large eye and short blunt tail (shorter than body). Snout round to very protrusive. Ear opening absent (present but almost completely covered by notched scale on *A. aurita*). Hindlimb flap represented by single scale. Head and body scales reduced in number; never more than 14 rows at midbody.

Pattern, when present, usually consists of dorsal and lateral series of longitudinally aligned dots and/or dashes, sometimes coalesced to form stripes. Head often darker than body. Tail may be flushed with yellow or red.

Crepuscular and nocturnal. Semi-fossorial to fossorial, favouring moist substrates under rocks, debris, around embedded rotting stumps and in ant nests. Members probably feed on small arthropods, particularly eggs, larvae and pupae of ants. Elongate form facilitates access into galleries of ant nests and has resulted in the common name of 'worm lizard'. Reproduction as for family.

Aprasia aurita Kluge, 1974

Description Snout moderately protrusive. Ear opening present but almost completely covered by notched scale. Dorsal ground colour brownish fading to greyish on lateral surfaces. Pattern prominent to obscure. Each scale margined with brown. Cen-

tre of each dorsal and lateral scale bears dark bar, dash or dot arranged in longitudinal series. These tend to coalesce into lines on tail, occasionally on flanks and posterior body. Dark streak extends from tip of snout to eye. Ventral surfaces whitish. Midbody scales in 14 rows. SVL 110 mm.

Distinguished from *A. inaurita* in possessing pattern on body and lacking bright orange flush on tail.

Preferred habitat Hummock grasslands in semi-arid north-west Vic., from Ouyen to Woomelang.

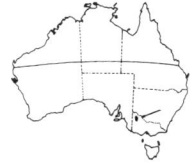

Microhabitat No data available but probably dwells in soil beneath stumps and in ant nests and *Triodia* hummocks.

Comments As for genus.

Aprasia haroldi Storr, 1978
Photo 228

Description Snout protrusive. Dorsal surfaces pale yellowish brown fading to white on lateral and ventral surfaces. Head slightly darker. Obscure brownish grey streak in centre of each dorsal scale and wavy streak from temple to snout present or absent. Tail flushed with pale pink. Midbody scales in 14 rows. SVL 106 mm.

Preferred habitat Pale coastal and near-coastal sands vegetated with low heathland and *Acacia* thickets on Edel Land (western peninsula of Shark Bay), WA.

Microhabitat Shelters beneath leaf-litter, limestone slabs, in moist sand under logs and in rotten embedded stumps.

Comments As for genus.

Aprasia inaurita Kluge, 1974
Photo 229

Description Snout weakly protrusive. Ground colour uniform pale yellowish brown, olive-brown to greyish brown, each scale with fine darker margin. Head, neck and anterior body flushed with reddish brown. Tail bright reddish orange, boldest towards tip. Lips, lower lateral and ventral surfaces white; reddish orange beneath tail. Midbody scales in 14 rows. SVL 120 mm.

Distinguished from *A. aurita* and *A. pseudopulchella* in lacking pattern on body and possessing bright reddish orange flush on tail.

Preferred habitat Sandy areas of subhumid to arid southern Australia, particularly those supporting mallee/*Triodia* associations. Restricted to pale coastal sands in far west of range. Extends disjunctly from Eyre, WA, through southern SA to north-western Vic. and south-western NSW.

Microhabitat Shelters in sand beneath stumps or surface debris and in ant nests.

Comments Reported to raise brightly coloured tail when threatened, probably diverting attention from head. Otherwise as for genus.

Aprasia parapulchella Kluge, 1974
Photo 230

Description Snout slightly protrusive. Ground colour pale grey to greyish brown merging to pink or pale reddish brown on tail. Centre of each dorsal and lateral scale bears blackish dot or dash arranged in prominent to obscure longitudinal series, often coalesced to form lines on tail. Head dark brown to blackish brown. Ventral surfaces whitish. Midbody scales in 14 rows. SVL 140 mm.

Preferred habitat Restricted to grassy woodlands in cool south-eastern interior of NSW, including ACT. Type locality is Coppins Crossing, ACT: a grassy slope with scattered native oaks (*Casuarina cunninghami*) and low weathered granite outcrops.

Microhabitat Often found beneath rocks, in tunnels of a small black ant (*Iridomyrmex* sp.).

Comments Commonly found with old sloughed skins, indicating long-term residence. Two clutches of eggs recorded in December. Possibly endangered due to loss of habitat. Otherwise as for genus.

Aprasia pseudopulchella Kluge, 1974
Photo 231

Description Snout slightly protrusive. Ground colour brown (darker on head) fading to greyish brown on posterior body and base of tail. Remainder of tail pinkish to reddish brown. Centre of each dorsal and lateral scale bears blackish dot or dash arranged in prominent to obscure longitudinal series. These often coalesce to form lines on posterior body and tail. Faint dark mottling on side of head present or absent. Ventral surfaces whitish. Midbody scales in 14 rows. SVL 140 mm.

Distinguished from *A. inaurita* in possessing pattern on body, lacking prominent reddish orange flush on tail and preference for stony (vs sandy) substrates. From eastern population of *A. striolata* by pattern reduced to lines of dashes (vs prominent blackish stripes) and more numerous midbody scale rows (14 vs 12).

Preferred habitat Favours stony soils, particularly near creeks and rivers in Flinders Ranges, SA.

Microhabitat Shelters in soil beneath stones and rotting stumps.

Comments As for genus.

Aprasia pulchella Gray, 1839
Photo 232

Description Snout slightly protrusive. Ground colour reddish brown on anterior body, merging to blackish brown on head and greyish on flanks, post-erior body and tail; becoming darker towards tip. Pattern usually obscure; a fine dark dash on centre of each dorsal and lateral scale from base of head to tail-tip. These often coalesce to form narrow lines on forebody and flanks. Ventral surfaces whitish. Midbody scales in 14 rows. SVL 110 mm.

Distinguished from *A. repens* by following characteristics: pattern (less prominent), snout (less protrusive) and more numerous midbody scale rows (14 vs usually 12). Differs from western population of *A. striolata* by greater number of midbody scale rows (14 vs 12) and darker overall colour.

Preferred habitat Occurs on pale sands supporting heathlands and eucalypt/*Banksia* woodlands and on granitic and lateritic soils supporting open dry sclerophyll forests in south-western WA.

Microhabitat Shelters in soil beneath embedded rocks, fallen timber, stumps and surface debris.

Comments As for genus.

Aprasia repens (Fry, 1914)
Photo 233

Description Snout moderately protrusive. Ground colour pale silvery brown, greyish brown to yellowish brown, darker on head. Tail flushed with pale pink to yellow. Centre of each dorsal and lateral scale bears blackish dash, aligned to form longitudinal series. These often coalesce into narrow lines on flanks and tail. Ventral surfaces whitish; yellow on chin. Midbody scales usually in 12 rows. SVL 110 mm.

Distinguished from *A. pulchella* and western population of *A. striolata* by following characters: pattern (more prominent) and snout (more protrusive). Differs further from *A. pulchella* in bearing fewer midbody scale rows (usually 12 vs 14) and in possessing a yellow chin.

Preferred habitat Widespread in dry sclerophyll forests with dominant ground cover of shrubs on granitic soils (including granite outcrops), and on pale coastal sands supporting heathlands and eucalypt/*Banksia* woodlands. Occurs on south-west coast and in wheat belt areas of south-western WA, from Eradu south-east to Oldfield River.

Microhabitat Shelters in sand or soil beneath embedded rocks, logs or stumps.

Comments As for genus.

Aprasia rostrata Parker, 1956
Photo 234

Description Snout sharp-edged; very protrusive. Two subspecies recognised.

A. r. fusca Storr, 1979 Dorsal ground colour pale brown, each scale bearing narrow blackish dash aligned to form paravertebral and laterodorsal series. Inner pair weakest, though both continue as lines on tail. Each lateral scale bears blackish edge and central streak, reducing ground colour to whitish elliptic spots. These reduce on tail to form 3 narrow lines on either side. Tail yellowish brown. Ventral surfaces of body pale brown densely flecked with dark brown. Pale yellow beneath tail. Midbody scales in 14 rows. SVL 105 mm.

A. r. rostrata Differs by paler colouration, particularly on flanks and ventral surfaces. Dorsal ground colour yellowish brown merging to pale grey on flanks. Pattern obscure consisting of 3 fine dark lines or dashes on nape, 3 narrow dark lines on flanks (coalescing anteriorly to form upper lateral stripe) and narrow dark ventrolateral stripe. Head darker brown marked with irregular blackish blotches. Tail paler shade of ground colour.

Preferred habitat *A. r. fusca* is restricted to Exmouth Gulf region, WA. Occurs on whitish coastal dunes supporting low shrubs, particularly *Banksia* and *Acacia*, or on red dunes supporting hummock grasses and scattered shrubs. *A. r. rostrata* is known only from Hermite Island, Monte Bello Group, off arid north-west coast of WA.

Microhabitat *A. r. fusca* recorded in loose upper layers of sand beneath leaf-litter at bases of shrubs and in moist soil beneath logs.

Comments Sharply protrusive snout may indicate considerable time spent deep within substrate. *A. r. fusca* leaves distinctive meandering tracks on soft sand between clumps of vegetation. Because of atomic tests carried out on the Monte Bello Islands during the 1950s the nominate form is possibly endangered. Otherwise as for genus.

Aprasia smithi Storr, 1970
Photo 235

Description Snout sharp-edged; protrusive. Ground colour reddish orange to yellowish orange contrasting sharply with glossy black head (including throat) and tail-tip. Dark brown dashes in centre of each scale form 6 longitudinal series. Lips, lower lateral and ventral surfaces white. Midbody scales in 12 rows. SVL 110 mm.

Preferred habitat Subhumid to semi-arid areas along midwest coast of WA, from Shark Bay south to Yuna. Favours reddish brown sandy loams and yellow sands vegetated predominantly with *Acacia* shrublands and low woodlands.

Microhabitat Usually associated with ant nests in soil beneath rotting *Acacia* stumps.

Comments Sharply protrusive snout indicates marked fossorial tendencies. Purposes of black head and tail-tip are unclear.

Aprasia striolata Lütken, 1863
Photos 236, 237

Description Variably patterned *Aprasia* with slightly protrusive snout. Dorsal ground colour pale brown, yellowish brown, olive-brown to grey; darker on head. Eastern mainland populations are prominently striped with black. Narrow dorsal lines or series of dashes extend from base of head to tip of tail. Broad dorsolateral stripe extends from snout or above eye to tail-tip. Broad upper lateral stripe extends from snout to tail-tip. Narrow (often obscure) lower lateral stripe extends from neck or anterior body to tail-tip. Remainder of lateral and ventral surfaces white. Pattern on western and Kangaroo Island populations reduced to absent. Dashes on each dorsal and lateral scale may align to form longitudinal series. These occasionally coalesce to form narrow lines on tail. Midbody scales in 12 rows. SVL 120 mm.

Distinguished from *A. inaurita* in lacking a bright reddish orange flush on tail and (on eastern mainland) in bearing prominent stripes. Differs from *A. pulchella* and *A. pseudopulchella* in bearing fewer scale rows at midbody (12 vs 14). Eastern population differs further from *A. pseudopulchella* in possessing sharper pattern. Western population differs from *A. repens* by weaker pattern, less protrusive snout and absence of a yellow flush on chin.

Preferred habitat Isolated populations occur in south-west WA, on coast and offshore islands of western Eyre Peninsula, on Kangaroo Island and from Mt Lofty Ranges, SA, to western Vic. One record from Mt Buring, in arid southern NT. Populations in WA and western Eyre Peninsula favour pale coastal sands. In remainder of SA and western Vic., subhumid to semi-arid woodlands (often in association with rock outcrops) are favoured.

Microhabitat Shelters in soil beneath rocks, fallen timber and rotting stumps.

Comments Predominantly nocturnal though sometimes recorded active during day.

Genus *DELMA*   Gray, 1831

Endemic genus containing 15 species distributed widely throughout Australia. Diversity is greatest in subhumid to arid areas. Absent from moist areas such as wet sclerophyll forests and rainforests. Additional taxa await description.

Small to moderately large pygopodids with long to very long tails (2–4 times length of body). Hindlimb flap well developed. Ear opening present. Scales smooth and shiny. Ventral scales paired; noticeably larger than adjacent body scales. Pattern, when present, usually consists of dark bands on head and nape, particularly on juveniles.

Many *Delma* are sufficiently distinct to be identified by combination of pattern and distribution. Others require examination of such characters as number of midbody scale rows, number of scales on top of snout between rostral and frontal scales (5 or 7) and position of 3rd or 4th upper labial scale relative to eye. These are subject to considerable variation in some species. Scale characters provided apply to most individuals. See fig.

Some are predominantly nocturnal, others diurnal. Most are both, according to temperature. *Delma*

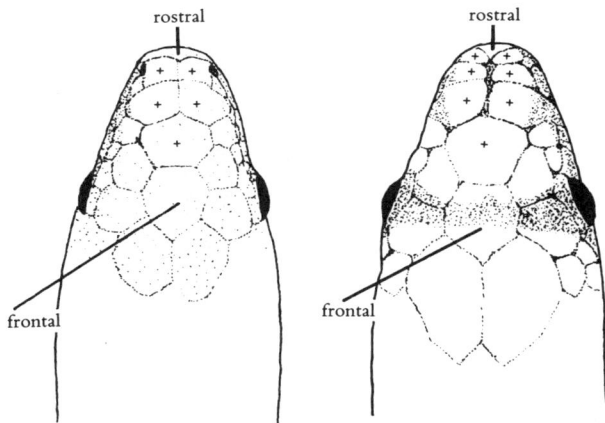

Dorsal view of 2 *Delma* showing position of rostral scale, frontal scale and the alignment of 7 (right) and 5 (left) scales between them

usually forage among low, dense vegetation such as shrubs or grasses. Locomotion appears snake-like, though on open ground lizards move in series of rapid leaps. Diets probably consist largely of small arthropods. When grasped by predators *Delma* are quite vocal, emitting a loud wheezing squeak. Tail very fragile and readily discarded. Reproduction as for family.

Distinguished from *Pygopus* and *Paradelma* by build (slender vs robust). Differs further from *Pygopus* by scale texture (glossy and smooth vs matt and usually keeled). Differs further from *Paradelma* by top of head ground colour or darker (vs significantly paler than ground colour). Differs from *Aclys* by snout (round vs pointed) and ventral scales (considerably—vs not noticeably—broader than adjacent body scales). Sympatric *Delma* differ further from *Aclys* in lacking narrow dark stripes.

Delma australis Kluge, 1974
Photo 238

Description Small moderately robust *Delma* with blunt snout. Tail relatively short: approximately twice length of body. Ground colour pale yellowish brown, rich brown to reddish brown becoming paler on lower flanks. Individuals from far south-west of range may be bluish grey. Top and sides of head occasionally blackish without pattern though usually bearing prominent to obscure variegations, reticulations or narrow bars. These extend back to nape and anterior flanks; usually continuous onto ventrolateral surfaces and occasionally throat. Lips whitish. Ventral surfaces whitish usually marked with obscure variegations or reticulations. Midbody scales in 16–20 (usually 18) rows. SVL 80 mm.

A distinctive *Delma* distinguished from sympatric species by small maximum size, robust build, blunt snout and short tail. Differs further by usual presence of dark variegations or narrow bars on head and neck (vs uniform or with broad dark bands).
Preferred habitat Subhumid to arid areas of

southern Australia, from north-west Vic. and south-west NSW, through most of SA and adjacent southern NT to southern WA. Apparently absent from Nullarbor and humid deep south-west of WA. Occurs in various vegetation types, favouring sandy substrates.
Microhabitat Shelters beneath rocks, logs, leaf-litter, mats of dead vegetation and in hummock or tussock grasses. Tends to seek slightly damper microhabitats than sympatric species.
Comments As for genus.

Delma borea Kluge, 1974
Photo 239

Description Medium-sized *Delma* with tail 2½–3 times length of body. Head pattern usually prominent; occasionally obscure on older individuals. Ground colour dull greyish brown, yellowish brown to reddish brown becoming paler on lower flanks. Three or 4 glossy dark brown to black bands present on head and nape. These are divided by the following narrow whitish to yellowish interspaces, each broadest laterally. The 1st extends across snout in front of eye (present to absent), the 2nd across head behind eye, the 3rd across base of head (level with ear opening), the 4th across nape on posterior margin of dark nuchal bar. Side of neck may bear short oblique pale bars. Ventral surfaces white. Midbody scales in 14–16 (usually 16) rows. SVL 80 mm.

Distinguished from *D. tincta* in possessing following (variable) characters: 7 scales on top of snout between rostral and frontal scales (vs 5; occasionally 7) and 16 (occasionally 14) midbody scale rows (vs 14; occasionally 12 or 16). Differs from *D. elegans* by midbody scale rows never more than 16 (vs 17–18) and more simple head pattern. From *D. nasuta* in lacking spotted or reticulated pattern and possessing prominent dark bands on head and nape (though these fade with age). Differs from *D. pax* by 4th (vs 3rd) upper labial scale beneath eye. Differs from *D. haroldi* by nature of pale markings on head and neck (straight-edged vs wavy), and in bearing fewer pale bands on side of head between eye and ear (usually 2 vs 3 or 4).
Preferred habitat Subhumid to arid areas of northern Australia from far western Qld, through NT and north-western SA to northern half of WA. Favours heavy to stony soils supporting variety of open vegetation types with grassy ground cover. Most often encountered in areas dominated by hummock grasslands.
Microhabitat Shelters beneath rocks, logs, mats of dead vegetation and hummock grasses.
Comments As for genus.

Delma butleri Storr, 1987
Photo 240

Description Relatively inornate *Delma* with tail

approximately 3 times length of head and body. Ground colour greyish brown to olive-brown; scales bearing fine dark edges. Head and neck variably marked with pale brown, blackish brown and white, the pale pigment forming spots, blotches and/or narrow vertical bars which extend from ventral surfaces onto chin. Ventral surfaces yellow to white or pale grey to pale brown. Midbody scales in 15–18 (usually 16) rows. SVL 90 mm.

Distinguished from *D. nasuta* by dorsal pattern (dorsal scales dark brown with fine darker edges vs pale brown spotted with dark brown), and in lacking dark edges to ventral and subcaudal scales. Differs further in having a shorter, more rounded snout. Differs from *D. haroldi* in lacking dark bands across head and nape.

Preferred habitat Semi-arid to arid areas of southern and central WA, extending into north-western SA. Occurs in various habitats, favouring a ground cover of hummock grasses (*Triodia* and *Plectrachne*).

Microhabitat Shelters within hummock grasses.

Comments Formerly considered a population of *D. nasuta*.

Delma elegans Kluge, 1974
Photo 241

Description Moderately large *Delma* with tail 2–4 times length of body. Ground colour olive-brown to brown, each scale with darker margin. Head and nape pattern prominent, extending onto ventrolateral surfaces of throat and neck. Approximately 5 or 6 blackish brown bands extend across head and nape; broken by yellowish to pale grey interspaces which are broadest and most prominent laterally. Side of forebody bears oblique dark-edged pale bars. Ventral surfaces whitish, each scale with dark margin. Midbody scales in 17–18 (usually 18) rows. SVL 90 mm.

Distinguished from *D. borea*, *D. pax* and *D. tincta* by more numerous midbody scale rows (17 or more vs 16 or fewer).

Preferred habitat Hamersley Range and adjacent lowlands and outcrops of arid Pilbara region, WA. Favours rocky areas dominated by hummock grasslands.

Microhabitat Shelters in hummock grasses or disused termitaria and beneath rocks or mats of dead vegetation.

Comments As for genus.

Delma fraseri Gray, 1831
Photo 242

Description Large *Delma* with relatively long snout. Tail 2–3 times length of body. Head and nape pattern prominent on juveniles becoming obscure with age. Ground colour grey, brown or reddish brown, becoming brighter on tail. Each scale may bear darker median smudge forming obscure lines.

Top of head dark brown, reddish brown, dark grey to black, separated from dark bar on nape by interspace of ground colour 1–3 scales wide. Side of head cream to white marked with 3 dark vertical bars, each extending onto ventrolateral region of throat; the 1st between nostril and eye, the 2nd through eye, the 3rd between eye and ear opening. Side of neck bears one to several dark vertical bars. Ventral surfaces whitish. Midbody scales in 16 (occasionally 15 or 17) rows. SVL 120 mm.

Preferred habitat Subhumid to semi-arid areas of south-west WA, from Shark Bay in north, south-east to Israelite Bay. Absent from humid deep south-west. Apparently isolated population occurs in vicinity of Eyre Peninsula, SA. Occupies variety of habitats from pale coastal sands supporting heathlands and eucalypt and/or *Banksia* woodlands to lateritic soils supporting mallee communities with open shrub or hummock grass understorey.

Microhabitat Shelters beneath mats of dead vegetation, rocks or logs and in grass tussocks or hummocks.

Comments See genus.

Delma grayii Smith, 1849
Photo 243

Description Large long-snouted *Delma* with tail 3–4 times length of body. Ground colour pale grey to pale greyish brown. Each dorsal and lateral scale usually marked with prominent to obscure dark spot, forming longitudinal series from nape well onto tail. Dorsolateral and upper lateral surfaces tinged with orange-brown to brown forming broad stripe from nape onto base of tail. Lateral surfaces bear obscure white bars, sometimes with irregular dark and pale margins. These are longest on side of neck, becoming indistinct at midbody. Head ground colour. Lips white, usually with dark patch under eye. Ventral surfaces white flushed with yellow from throat well onto belly. Scales usually in 16 (occasionally 15–18) rows at midbody. SVL 110 mm.

Preferred habitat Subhumid to semi-arid lower west coast and adjacent inland areas of WA, from Murchison River district in north to Perth area in south, east to Koorda. Largely restricted to heathlands; in pure stands or in association with *Banksia* and/or eucalypt woodlands on sandy to lateritic soils.

Microhabitat Shelters beneath mats of dead vegetation, fallen timber or surface debris and in dense matrix of heath plants or (in Marchagee district) hummock grasses.

Comments Diurnal. As for genus.

Delma haroldi Storr, 1987
Photo 244

Description Small *Delma* with tail approximately 3–5 times length of body. Ground colour pale brown to dull reddish brown, paler on flanks. Each scale narrowly dark-edged. Nape and top of head darker shade of ground colour, usually marked with narrow wavy pale bands which tend to become broader and whiter laterally. These include 3 or 4 vertical bars on side of head between eye and temple and a band around posterior edge of darker head and nape colouration. Series of obscure, dark-edged pale bands usually discernible on sides of forebody, fading posteriorly. Ventral surfaces white. Midbody scales in 16–18 (usually 16) rows. SVL 75 mm.

Distinguished from weakly patterned individuals of *D. borea* by nature of pale markings on head and neck (wavy vs straight-edged) and in having more pale bands on side of head. Differs from *D. tincta* by the following variable characteristics: more scales on top of snout between rostral and frontal scales (7 vs 5, occasionally 7), and more midbody scales (16–18 vs 14, occasionally 12 or 16). Differs from *D. elegans* in having weaker and simpler pattern on head and nape. Differs from *D. nasuta* and *D. butleri* in bearing dark bands on head and nape, and further from *D. nasuta* in lacking prominent ventral markings. Differs from *D. pax* in having 4th (vs 3rd) upper labial scale set beneath eye.

Preferred habitat Arid Great Sandy Desert and Pilbara region, WA.

Microhabitat Shelters in hummocks of *Triodia* grass.

Comments Formerly regarded as a population of *D. borea*. See genus.

Delma impar (Fischer, 1882)
Photo 245

Description Medium-sized robust *Delma* with tail 2½–3 times length of body and distinctive prominent linear pattern. Dorsal ground colour yellowish brown. Broad vertebral stripe of ground colour extends from nape to tail-tip. Blackish to brownish dorsal stripe, often broken into series of spots (1 per scale), extends from nape to base of tail. Narrow white dorsolateral line or stripe of ground colour extends from nape to base of tail. Broad blackish brown upper lateral stripe, usually broken into spots or enclosing prominent spots of ground colour, extends from nape to base of tail. Narrow white midlateral line or stripe of ground colour extends from neck to base of tail. This is margined below by broad to narrow blackish brown stripe or series of spots; with or without narrow white lower edge. Lower lateral surfaces whitish, sometimes enclosing narrow dark line or series of spots. Tail usually marked with oblique dark and narrow pale bars encompassing dorsolateral and ventrolateral regions. Top of head dark olive. Ventral surfaces whitish. SVL 80 mm.

Preferred habitat Far south-east SA, through central and western Vic. (excluding semi-arid northwest) to basalt plains west of Melbourne; north to ACT and adjacent NSW. Favours grassy plains and dry sclerophyll forests and woodlands.

Microhabitat Shelters beneath chunks of rock, fallen bark, logs, mats of dead vegetation and in grass tussocks.

Comments Most southerly pygopodid. Much of its habitat on fertile volcanic plains of southern Vic. has been dramatically altered by agricultural development. Little known of habits, despite occurrence adjacent to highly populated regions. Considerably more vocal than other *Delma*, emitting loud wheezing squeak when handled.

Delma inornata Kluge, 1974
Photo 246

Description Large *Delma* with long tail (up to 4 times length of body). Pattern obscure to virtually absent. Ground colour olive brown, greyish brown to brown; paler on lower lateral surfaces. Scales bear dark margins, sometimes sufficiently prominent to form obscure reticulum. Head darker shade of ground colour without pattern. Lips and ventral surfaces whitish. Midbody scales in 15–18 (usually 16) rows. SVL 125 mm.

Distinguished from *D. tincta* and *D. plebeia* by completely lacking head pattern. Differs further from *D. tincta* in possessing 7 (vs 5) scales on top of snout between rostral and frontal scales and usually 16 (vs usually 14) midbody scale rows.

Preferred habitat Subhumid to semi-arid areas west of Great Dividing Range, from south-east Qld and interior of NSW to north-western two-thirds of Vic. and south-eastern SA. Occupies wide variety of habitats from reddish sands supporting mallee/*Triodia* associations to rock outcrops and heavy soils supporting chenopod communities and/or woodlands. Also present in dry sclerophyll forests on western slopes of Great Dividing Range.

Microhabitat Shelters beneath rocks, logs, mats of dead vegetation, surface debris and in grasses, particularly *Triodia* hummocks.

Comments Clutches of eggs recorded in January. See genus.

Delma molleri Lütken, 1863
Photo 247

Description Large moderately robust *Delma* with tail 1½–2 times length of body. Head and nape pattern prominent on juveniles, becoming obscure with age. Ground colour pale brown, brown to greyish brown. Dorsal and lateral scales usually bear prominent to obscure dark median streak or smudge, aligned to form indistinct stripes. Top and sides of head and neck darker shade of ground colour to black, usually with pale yellowish brown to reddish brown interspace (2–3 scales wide) from ear to ear. Dark band on nape (3–5 scales wide) may be prominently to obscurely margined posteriorly by paler shade of ground colour. Sides of head and neck variably marked with dark vertical bars extending onto ventrolateral region; the 1st between eye and nostril (sometimes absent), the 2nd through eye, 1 or 2 between eye and ear, 2–5 on side of neck. Lips to ear dull yellow. Ventral surfaces white, each scale with dark margin. Midbody scales usually in 18 (occasionally 16) rows. SVL 100 mm.

Distinguished from *D. inornata* and *D. nasuta* in possessing dark pattern on head (reduced on aged individuals). Differs further by more numerous midbody scale rows (usually 18 vs usually 16) and fewer scales on top of snout between rostral and frontal scales (usually 5 vs usually 7).

Preferred habitat Subhumid to semi-arid chenopod shrublands, often associated with woodlands on sandy to stony soils. Restricted to Mt Lofty and southern Flinders Ranges and Yorke Peninsula, south-east SA.

Microhabitat Shelters beneath dead vegetation, rocks, logs and surface debris.

Comments As for genus.

Delma nasuta Kluge, 1974
Photo 248

Description Large *Delma* with relatively long snout and long tail; approximately 4 times length of body. Ground colour dull olive, olive-brown to brown. Each scale bears dark spot or margin forming a reticulated to spotted pattern, particularly on lateral surfaces. Head slightly darker shade of ground colour, paler on snout. Sides of head may bear obscure narrow paler brown vertical bars. Ventral surfaces whitish, each scale with dark margin or spot. Scales at midbody in 14–20 (usually 16) rows. SVL 110 mm.

Distinguished from *D. borea*, *D. butleri*, *D. haroldi*, *D. inornata*, *D. molleri*, *D. pax* and *D. tincta* in usually possessing distinctive spotted or reticulated pattern (including on ventral surfaces) and by sharper, longer snout. Differs further from all except *D. butleri*, *D. inornata* and *D. haroldi* in never possessing dark bars on head (vs present on all except old individuals). Differs further from *D. tincta* and *D. pax* by position of upper labial scale (4th beneath eye vs 3rd), and further from *D. tincta* in possessing more numerous scales on top of snout between frontal and rostral scales (7 vs 5).

Preferred habitat Semi-arid to arid western two-thirds of Australia, excluding far north and south-west. Occurs in association with hummock grasslands growing on sands, sandy loams or stony soils.

Microhabitat Shelters in hummock grasses.

Comments See genus.

Delma pax Kluge, 1974
Photo 249

Description Medium-sized *Delma* with moderately long snout. Ground colour brown to reddish brown merging with pale grey lower lateral surfaces. Each scale usually bears an obscure dark central smudge forming indistinct longitudinal lines. Head and nape pattern consists of 3 prominent broad black bands, tending to fade with age; the 1st extends across head through each eye to lower lip (often obscure dorsally, though usually retained beneath eye), the 2nd extends across base of head to corner of mouth, the 3rd extends across nape to about level of ear. Pale interspaces yellowish to reddish brown, most prominent between head and nape. Ventral surfaces whitish. Scales at midbody in 16 (rarely 15) rows. SVL 90 mm.

Distinguished from *D. tincta* in possessing more numerous midbody scale rows (usually 16 vs 14; occasionally 12–16) and greater number of scales on top of snout between frontal and rostral scales (7; occasionally 5, vs 5; occasionally 7). Differs from *D. nasuta* and *D. butleri* in possessing dark bands on head and nape and further from *D. nasuta* in lacking spotted or reticulated pattern. From *D. elegans* by fewer midbody scale rows (16 or less vs 17 or more). From *D. borea*, *D. haroldi* by position of upper labial scales (3rd beneath eye vs 4th).

Preferred habitat Hummock grasslands on heavy to stony soils of Hamersley Plateau in arid Pilbara region of WA.

Microhabitat Recorded beneath accumulated leaf-litter and mats of dead vegetation along dry water-courses and near semi-permanent pools.

Comments As for genus.

Delma plebeia De Vis, 1888
Photo 250

Description Large *Delma* with tail approximately 2½ times length of body. Ground colour grey, olive-grey to brownish grey. Lateral scales of forebody sometimes dark-edged, rarely with dark median streak. Top of head bears blackish hood or dark bands on juveniles, becoming obscure to absent with age. Blackish hood retained on southern adults. Usually restricted to side of neck, face and lips on northern adults. Lower lips to ear and side of neck whitish, sometimes flushed with reddish brown posteriorly. Lips bear 1–3 short black vertical bars (most prominent under eye); often present on lower lips only. Indication of black bar usually present between eye and ear. Variable number of vertically aligned black bars or blotches sometimes present behind ear, occasionally extending well onto side of neck. Ventral surfaces whitish, usually unmarked. Midbody scales usually in 16 (occasionally 14) rows. SVL 110 mm.

Distinguished from *D. inornata* in possessing at least some indication of dark lateral head-pattern. Differs from *D. tincta* by position of upper labial scales; 3rd (vs 4th) beneath eye, and by more numerous midbody scale rows (usually 16, occasionally 14, vs 14, occasionally 16). Differs further by more numerous scales on top of snout between rostral and frontal scales (7, occasionally 8 or 5, vs 5, rarely 7).

Preferred habitat Dry sclerophyll forests and woodlands, usually with grassy understorey on variety of soil-types in north-eastern NSW and south-eastern Qld.

Microhabitat Shelters beneath fallen timber, rocks, mats of dead vegetation and surface debris.

Comments Northern and southern populations may constitute distinct taxa. Otherwise as for genus.

Delma tincta De Vis, 1888
Photos 251, 252

Description Medium-sized *Delma* with tail 2–2½ times length of body. Head and nape markings prominent to virtually absent. Ground colour greyish brown, brown to reddish brown, fading to grey on lower flanks. Scales occasionally dark-edged, forming an obscure reticulum. Head and nape glossy black to a darker shade of ground colour, broken into broad bands by 2–3 narrow white to cream interspaces, each broadest laterally. Interspaces arranged as follows: first extends across snout between eye and nostril (sometimes absent), second extends across head behind each eye, third extends across rear of head, from ear to ear. Narrower obscure band sometimes present across neck. Narrow dark vertical bars may be present on side of neck. Ventral surfaces whitish. Midbody scales usually in 14 (occasionally 12–16) rows. SVL 80 mm.

Distinguished from *D. borea, D. haroldi, D. elegans, D. fraseri, D. inornata, D. nasuta, D. pax* and *D. plebeia* in possessing almost invariably 5 (vs usually 7) scales on top of snout between rostral and frontal scales. Differs further from *D. inornata, D. butleri* and *D. nasuta* in possessing dark head pattern (except on old individuals) and from *D. pax* by position of upper labial scales: 3rd (vs 4th) beneath eye.

Preferred habitat Wide variety of subhumid to arid regions across northern Australia. Favours open areas with grassy understorey, particularly where hummock grasslands occur.

Microhabitat Shelters beneath rocks, logs, mats of dead vegetation, in soil cracks, abandoned termitaria, ant nests and hummock grasses.

Comments Captive individuals recorded to exhibit burrowing behaviour, using sideways movement of snout. Once submerged, head only remains, broken pattern merging well with surface debris. Otherwise as for genus.

Delma torquata Kluge, 1974
Photo 253

Description Smallest *Delma* with relatively short tail (1–1½ times length of body) and blunt snout. Head and nape pattern prominent on individuals of all ages, extending onto throat and beneath neck. Ground colour reddish brown to brown, becoming grey to bluish grey on tail and pale grey on lower flanks. Head and neck glossy black broken by prominent narrow pale interspaces (yellowish to orange dorsally, whitish laterally). Interspaces are arranged as follows: the 1st, a short white vertical bar between eye and nostril, the 2nd across head behind level of eye, the 3rd across base of head through ear and 4th across nape. This is bordered posteriorly by narrow black band, broadest laterally. Ventral surfaces whitish. Scales beneath tail greyish, each with white posterior margin. Throat and neck boldly reticulated with white and grey to black. Scales in 16 rows at midbody. SVL 60 mm.

Distinguished from all other *Delma* by presence of prominent dark reticulation on throat and small maximum size.

Preferred habitat Recorded from dry lateritic ridges supporting open eucalypt/*Acacia* associations over sparse understorey of shrubs and tussock grasses. Also reported to occur in eucalypt woodland above semi-evergreen vine thicket. Restricted to south-eastern Qld, from western suburbs of Brisbane, north to Gladstone district and inland to Bunya Mountains.

Microhabitat Usually shelters beneath rocks and logs. Mats of leaf-litter probably utilised to lesser extent.

Comments Though previously regarded as a burrower our field observations show no significant difference between *D. torquata* and other *Delma* spp. Potentially endangered due to land-use in restricted range.

Genus *LIALIS* Gray, 1835

Contains 2 species. One occurs extensively in Australia, extending northwards to New Guinea. The other is restricted to New Guinea and associated islands. Absent from Tas.

Very large robust pygopodids with extremely long, sharp, wedge-shaped snout, relatively short tail, small hindlimb flap, prominent ear opening and small eye with vertically elliptic pupil. Scales smooth in 18 rows at midbody. Head scales small, fragmented. Colour and pattern extremely variable. Diurnal, crepuscular and nocturnal. Reproduction as for family.

Distinguished from all pygopodids by combination of robust build, large size, fragmented head scales and distinctive long sharp snout.

Burton's Snake Lizard
Lialis burtonis Gray, 1835
Photos 254–257

Description Largest pygopodid. Tail 1–1½ times length of body. Colour and pattern extremely variable. Most colour forms may occur in any given part of range though some local trends are apparent. Ground colour ranges from pale grey or almost white through shades of red, yellow, brown, dark grey to almost black. Pattern prominent to absent, usually including stripes or longitudinal series of spots or dashes. Obscurely marked individuals (common throughout range) frequently bear small widely spaced longitudinally aligned blackish flecks and occasionally dark bars on upper and lower lips. Dashes may coalesce to varying degrees, reaching extreme in prominent sharp-edged dark and pale stripes or combinations of stripes and spots (present throughout range, though most prevalent in semi-arid to arid areas supporting hummock grasses). Many individuals (particularly in north of range) bear broad, usually pale-edged, dark lateral stripe from snout through eye to forebody. This condition may be present on both striped and plain forms. Ventral surfaces similarly variable; paler to darker shade of ground colour with or without prominent to obscure stripes or series of spots. SVL 290 mm.

Preferred habitat Occurs throughout Australia excluding cool, high altitudes of Great Dividing Range, southern Vic., Tas., Yorke Peninsula in SA, Nullarbor and humid deep south-west of WA. Present in virtually all habitats from desert sand ridges and gibber flats to woodlands, dry sclerophyll forests and margins of wet sclerophyll and rainforests.

Microhabitat Shelters beneath rocks, logs or leaf-litter and in hummock grasses and abandoned burrows. Occasionally ascends into dense low vegetation.

Comments An alert active predator feeding upon small lizards, particularly skinks. In addition geckos, agamids, small snakes and other pygopodids are taken. Prey is usually gripped at about chest area, held fast until suffocated, then swallowed head first. When at rest distinctive posture is adopted with head and neck held at approximately 45° to substrate. Australia's most well-known and widely distributed legless lizard.

Genus OPHIDIOCEPHALUS
Lucas and Frost, 1897

Endemic monotypic genus restricted to small area of south-eastern NT and adjacent far northern SA.

Moderately slender pygopodid with relatively short tail (approximately 1½ times length of body), moderately protrusive wedge-shaped snout, hidden ear opening and small hindlimb flaps. Scales smooth in 16 rows at midbody. Ventral scales not noticeably larger than adjacent scales. Head scales large. Crepuscular and nocturnal. Fossorial. Reproduction as for family.

Bronzeback
Ophidiocephalus taeniatus
Lucas and Frost, 1897
Photo 258

Description Dorsal ground colour bronze-brown to very pale yellowish brown; paler on head and tail. Dorsal pattern absent or restricted to sparse dark peppering on tail. Narrow dark upper lateral line usually present from side of head to tail-tip. Lateral surfaces densely peppered with greyish brown, contrasting sharply with dorsal colour. Ventral surfaces whitish prominently spotted with black. SVL 100 mm.

Preferred habitat Arid open shrublands with scattered eucalypts and sparse ground cover over deeply cracking sandy loams. Known only from near Charlotte Waters, southern NT, and Abminga, northern SA.

Microhabitat A sandswimmer, sheltering in loose upper layers of soil beneath leaf-litter and plant debris at bases of trees. Retreats down deep cracks if disturbed.

Comments Rediscovered in 1978, 81 years after description of holotype. Potentially endangered due to widespread effects of cattle on apparently narrow microhabitat requirements. Recent authors suggest *Ophidiocephalus* may prove widespread through Finke and Lake Eyre drainage basins.

Genus PARADELMA   Kinghorn, 1926

Endemic monotypic genus closely allied to *Pygopus*. Restricted to lower mideastern interior of Qld.

Medium-sized, robust, blunt-snouted pygopodid with conspicuous ear opening, moderately well-developed hindlimb flap and tail approximately twice length of body. Scales smooth, glossy in 18 (occasionally 20) rows at midbody. Head scales enlarged. Crepuscular and nocturnal. Reproduction as for family.

Distinguished from *Pygopus* in possessing fewer midbody scale rows (18–20 vs 21 or more) and much smaller hindlimb flap. Differs from *Delma* by robust (vs slender) build and distinctive head colouration (significantly paler than ground colour vs ground colour or darker).

Paradelma orientalis (Günther, 1876)
Photos 226, 259

Description Ground colour glossy lead grey to greyish brown. Scales bear longitudinally aligned pale flecks; most prominent on flanks. Base of head cream, yellowish to pale brown, becoming gradually darker towards snout. This contrasts sharply with black bar 3–6 scales wide on nape. Dark streak or flush present around eye. Another may be present near ear. Lower lateral and ventral surfaces whitish. SVL 160 mm.

Preferred habitat Restricted to lower mideastern interior of Qld. Favours sandstone ridges, woodlands and vine thickets, including stands of brigalow (*Acacia harpophylla*), few of which remain undisturbed.

Microhabitat Shelters beneath sandstone slabs, logs, surface debris and in hummock grasses such as *Plectrachne*.

Comments Though generally regarded as rare our systematic investigation of habitats reveals *P. orientalis* to be moderately abundant, particularly on sandstone ridges. When alarmed, individuals rear head and forebody, flickering notched tongue, presumably mimicking venomous snakes.

Genus *PLETHOLAX* Cope, 1864

Endemic monotypic genus restricted to mid and lower west coasts of WA.

Medium-sized, extremely slender, long-snouted, long-tailed pygopodid with small hindlimb flap and minute ear opening. Dorsal, lateral and ventral scales bear multiple keels (unique condition in Pygopodidae). Scales in 16 rows at midbody. Ventral scales not noticeably wider than adjacent body scales. Diurnal. Reproduction as for family.

Pletholax gracilis Cope, 1864
Photo 260

Description Very slender pygopodid with tail approximately 4 times length of body. All scales (including ventrals) bear 2 prominent keels. Two subspecies recognised.

P. g. gracilis Dorsal ground colour pale grey to greyish brown flushed anteriorly with reddish brown. Occasionally a darker vertebral suffusion enclosing longitudinally aligned blackish streaks extends to tail-tip. Prominent dorsolateral series of oblique blackish dashes form ragged line from nape to tail-tip. Blackish stripe extends from snout, beneath eye to forebody. Flanks pale grey flushed with reddish brown on side of tail. Lips, throat and anterior ventral surfaces bright yellow. Remainder of ventral surfaces whitish. SVL 75 mm.

P. g. edelensis Storr, 1978 Similar in most respects to nominate form, attaining greater size. Dark grey upper lateral streak is bordered above and below by series of angular blackish spots. SVL 90 mm.

Preferred habitat *P. g. gracilis* occurs on pale coastal dunes and sand plains (occasionally lateritic soils) supporting heathlands; in pure stands or in association with eucalypt and/or *Banksia* woodlands. Extends from Mandurah north to Eneabba. *P. g. edelensis* appears restricted to Edel Land Peninsula, Shark Bay, on midwest coast of WA. Occurs on white coastal dunes vegetated with beach spinifex (*Spinifex longifolius*) and on pale brown loam supporting dense hummocks of *Triodia*.

Microhabitat *P. g. gracilis* shelters in dense matrix of low vegetation, in soil beneath leaf-litter, and in embedded rotten stumps. *P. g. edelensis* shelters in *Triodia* and *Spinifex*.

Comments Usually regarded as a burrower, based on observations of captive individuals. Slender build, keeled scales and long tail contrast markedly with robust builds, smooth scales and relatively short tails of most fossorial reptiles. Further investigation may reveal this body form to be an adaptation to life in dense vegetation.

Genus *PYGOPUS* Merrem, 1820

Endemic genus containing 3 taxa. One species (*nigriceps* and its races) is adapted to arid conditions throughout Australia; the other (*lepidopodus*) is adapted to cooler climates across southern Australia. Absent from Tas.

Large, robust, blunt-snouted pygopodids with conspicuous ear opening, large hindlimb flap and tail approximately twice length of body. Dorsal scales strongly to weakly keeled (occasionally smooth), matt to glossy in 21 or more rows at midbody. Head scales moderately enlarged. Diurnal, crepuscular and nocturnal. Reproduction as for family.

Distinguished from *Paradelma* and *Delma* in possessing more numerous midbody scale rows (21 or more vs 20 or fewer) and much larger hindlimb flap.

Common Scaly-foot
Pygopus lepidopodus (Lacépède, 1804)
Photos 261, 262

Description Large, variably patterned *Pygopus* with strongly keeled non-glossy dorsal scales. Pattern very prominent to virtually absent. Ground colour of boldly marked individuals grey. Prominent vertebral, dorsolateral and usually midlateral series of large elongate black blotches with sharp white lateral margins and reddish brown interspaces extend to tail-tip; often coalescing to form irregular stripes posteriorly. White margins occasionally coalesce to form lines. Lateral surfaces diffuse, combining mixture of grey, white and black scales. Top of head bears prominent broad black wavy-edged stripe; continuous with vertebral blotches. Conspicuous broad pale-edged black streak extends from eye to above ear, aligning with dorsolateral blotches. Narrow vertical black bar extends from eye, through lip to ventrolateral portion of throat. Ventral surfaces greyish white boldly variegated with black. Pattern sparser on neck and throat, consisting of narrow oblique dark lines.

Obscurely patterned individuals are reddish brown becoming grey on head, neck and posterior tail. Blotches absent or reduced to dark brown to blackish dashes, with or without pale margins. These are boldest on (occasionally restricted to) dorsolateral portion of tail. Top of head lacks pattern. Temporal and facial streaks usually retained, even on obscurely marked individuals. Ventral surfaces pinkish brown with or without darker variegations. SVL 230 mm. TL to 800 mm.

Distinguished from *P. nigriceps* in possessing strongly keeled (vs weakly keeled to smooth) dorsal scales, absence of dark head and nape bands (vs usually present) and usual presence of dark variegations on ventral surfaces.

Preferred habitat Variety of soil types supporting heathlands, woodlands, dry sclerophyll forests and margins of wet sclerophyll forests in subhumid to semi-arid southern Australia. Extends north to Shark Bay, WA, in west and Cooktown district, Qld, in east. Southern populations usually associated with sandy soils. Boldly patterned individuals predominate in heathlands and open habitats from WA to southern NSW. Those with pattern reduced to absent are widespread throughout range.

Microhabitat Shelters beneath low vegetation, leaf-litter or surface debris and in dense grasses and shrubs.

Comments Predominantly diurnal, nocturnal in hot weather. Often encountered foraging in open clearings or low vegetation on warm sunny mornings. Feeds on variety of small arthropods. Record of 6 eggs beneath log may indicate communal egglaying behaviour or regular use of site over consecutive seasons. When threatened raises head and forebody high off ground, flickering fleshy tongue, apparently mimicking a venomous snake. When grasped, struggles violently, rotating body rapidly, often emitting loud wheezing squeak.

Hooded or Black-headed Scaly-foot
Pygopus nigriceps (Fischer, 1882)
Photos 263, 264

Description Medium-sized, variable *Pygopus* with smooth to moderately keeled dorsal scales. Two subspecies recognised. A 3rd tentatively regarded as undescribed.

P. n. nigriceps Ground colour pale orange-brown to reddish brown. Pattern prominent to absent. Dark brown to blackish margins may be present on each scale, forming reticulum or variegations. Darker and paler scales may be irregularly scattered over body, tending to align transversely or obliquely on tail. Black to dark brown head markings usually prominent, becoming obscure with age. Bar extends across head through each eye to lips. Broad-

er bar extends across base of head and nape; separated by strip of ground colour. Snout usually darker shade of ground colour, occasionally with small dark blotch on rostral scale and on each side of snout. Lips and side of head paler shade of ground colour. Ventral surfaces pinkish to whitish. SVL 180 mm.

P. n. schraderi Boulenger, 1913 Differs from nominate form in usually bearing stronger pattern. Ground colour includes grey to brownish grey. Dark markings may extend over top of head, often enclosing prominent grey mottling. This tends to align longitudinally and may be more sharply defined posteriorly.

Intermediate form from northern WA may constitute undescribed subspecies.

Distinguished from *P. lepidopodus* in possessing moderately keeled to smooth (vs strongly keeled) dorsal scales, presence of dark bands on head and nape and absence (vs usual presence) of dark variegations on ventral surfaces.

Preferred habitat Subhumid to arid regions through much of Australia, excluding cool moist south-east, south-west, Nullarbor Plain and most areas east of Great Dividing Range. Occupies variety of habitats from red sand ridges supporting hummock grasses to black-soil plains vegetated with Mitchell grass (*Astrebla* spp.) and woodlands. *P. n. nigriceps* occupies western portion of range, east to about 135°E (a line drawn from Gulf of Carpentaria roughly to western coast of SA). Intermediate form occurs in northern NT and Kimberley region, WA. *P. n. schraderi* occupies remaining eastern portion of range.

Microhabitat Shelters beneath rocks, fallen timber, mats of dead vegetation and in abandoned burrows, termitaria, grass tussocks, hummocks and soil cracks.

Comments Similar in most respects to *P. lepidopodus*, though more crepuscular to nocturnal due to higher daytime temperatures experienced throughout most of range. Otherwise as for genus.

SKINKS
Family SCINCIDAE

Large worldwide family with representatives occupying virtually all terrestrial habitats, from wave-swept coastlines to alps, deserts and rainforests. Very well represented in Australia, comprising the most speciose family of terrestrial vertebrates (303 species in 24 genera; approximately 50 per cent of the described lizard fauna). Numerous taxa await description.

Australian skinks are characterised by a number of features, though diversity is so great that few easily visible external traits are shared by all taxa.

Very small to large lizards (SVL 25–320 mm) with slender to robust bodies and (excepting *Tiliqua* and some *Egernia*) tapering fragile tails. Tongue broad and fleshy; usually notched at tip. Limbs are usually well developed, each bearing 5 digits. Progressive limb and digit reduction (accompanied by elongation of body) has evolved in many cryptozoic to fossorial skinks. Some genera (e.g. *Lerista* and *Anomalopus*) lack all external trace. Eye usually well developed with round pupil (vertically elliptic on the nocturnal desert skink *Egernia striata*). Eye may be greatly reduced on some burrowing groups. Lower eyelid usually movable and scaly (able to blink), often bearing a transparent disc. On many species this disc has enlarged and fused to form an immovable spectacle. Ear opening usually visible (ranging through varying degrees of reduction to absence on some burrowing skinks), sometimes bearing enlarged lobules. Body scales usually smooth and shiny (occasionally weakly to strongly keeled or spinose); always overlapping. Head scales almost invariably enlarged to form shields.

A significant number of Australian skinks are burrowers, and have undergone varying degrees of limb and digit reduction to accommodate this lifestyle. The process is currently under investigation. Reduction of forelimbs and fingers tends to exceed that of hindlimbs and toes. Forelimbs of many *Lerista* have been lost or reduced to vestigal stumps. These skinks push themselves through loose sand using hindlimbs and lateral undulations of the body. The snout is often shovel-shaped and protrudes well beyond mouth, aiding the sand-swimming mode of locomotion. In contrast, some *Anomalopus* have tended to retain forelimbs in favour of hindlimbs, pulling themselves through soil and leaf-litter. Other groups, such as *Hemiergis, Calyptotis* and some *Sphenomorphus* have reached a somewhat intermediate level, retaining 4 short limbs which allow relatively unhindered mobility through the damp substrates they favour. Rock and tree trunk-inhabiting skinks, such as *Cryptoblepharus*, and some *Carlia* and *Leiolopisma*, have reached the opposite

extreme. Limbs and digits are long, slender and well clawed (accompanied by dorsal compression of body), ensuring a firm grip on exposed vertical surfaces.

The majority of skinks (including all the larger species) bear movable scaly lower eyelids, and examples (e.g., *Tiliqua, Egernia, Ctenotus* and *Spheno-*

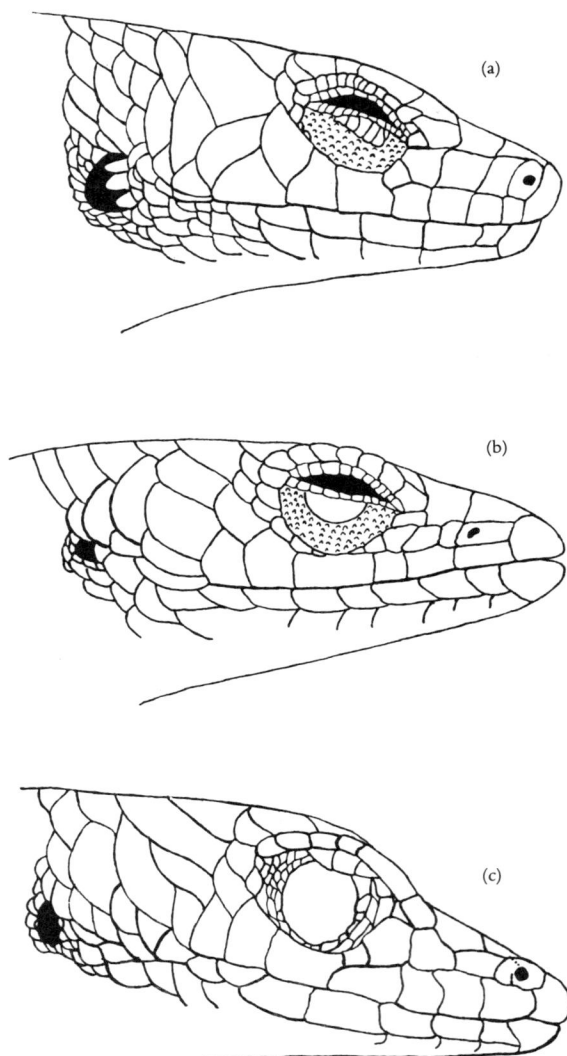

(a)

(b)

(c)

Variation in the nature of the lower eyelid in Australian skinks
(a) movable and scaly (*Ctenotus robustus*)
(b) movable, enclosing a transparent disc (*Lampropholis czechurai*)
(c) immovable, fused to form a transparent spectacle (*Cryptoblepharus litoralis*)

morphus) occur throughout the continent. A transparent disc set in a movable scaly lower eyelid has tended to develop on small skinks of humid to subhumid areas (e.g., *Leiolopisma, Lampropholis* and most *Carlia*) and on some arid-adapted skinks which dwell in well-sheltered sites (e.g., some *Lerista*). On many small species from subhumid to arid areas (e.g., *Menetia, Morethia, Cryptoblepharus* and some *Lerista*) the disc is larger, and the lower eyelid has fused with the upper to form a transparent spectacle. This is believed to aid in reducing moisture loss from the surface of the eye. Most areas support a suite of species which occupy a variety of micro-habitats, and include all eyelid types.

Most skinks thermoregulate by shuttling between direct sunlight and shade. Many others are more cryptic, obtaining their body heat by direct contact with the cover or substrate.

Small skinks feed largely on invertebrates, particularly arthropods. Large species tend to consume significantly greater proportions of vegetable material (particularly flowers and fruits), and occasionally carrion.

Ritualised territorial and courtship displays are generally poorly developed in skinks. For this reason, visual cues, such as breeding colours, are uncommon. Elaborate displays, particularly tail-waving and head-bobbing, are best developed in the genus *Carlia*, males of which are well known for the bright hues they acquire at sexual maturity.

Mating tends to be brief, with little formality. The male grasps the female by the neck, turning his body sideways to bring the cloacae into contact. Copulation usually lasts only a few seconds, after which both individuals quickly go their separate ways.

Most skinks lay parchment-shelled eggs. In cool regions where incubation is inhibited by low temperatures, the egg-carrying period may be ex-

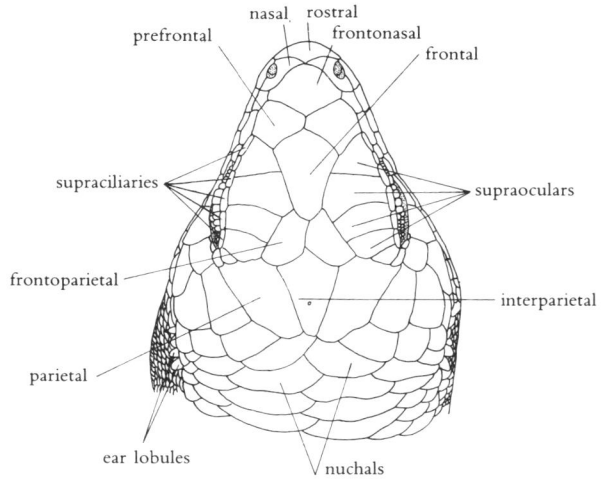

(a) *Egernia striolata* (dorsal)

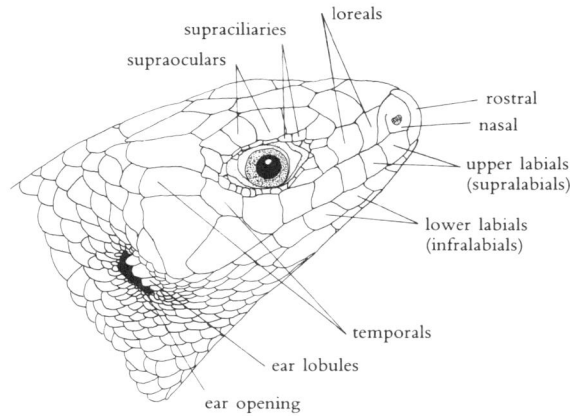

(b) *Egernia frerei* (lateral)

Arrangement of head shields on Australian skinks. Considerable variation exists as some scales may be lost due to fusion

Names and arrangement of stripes (*Ctenotus taeniolatus*)

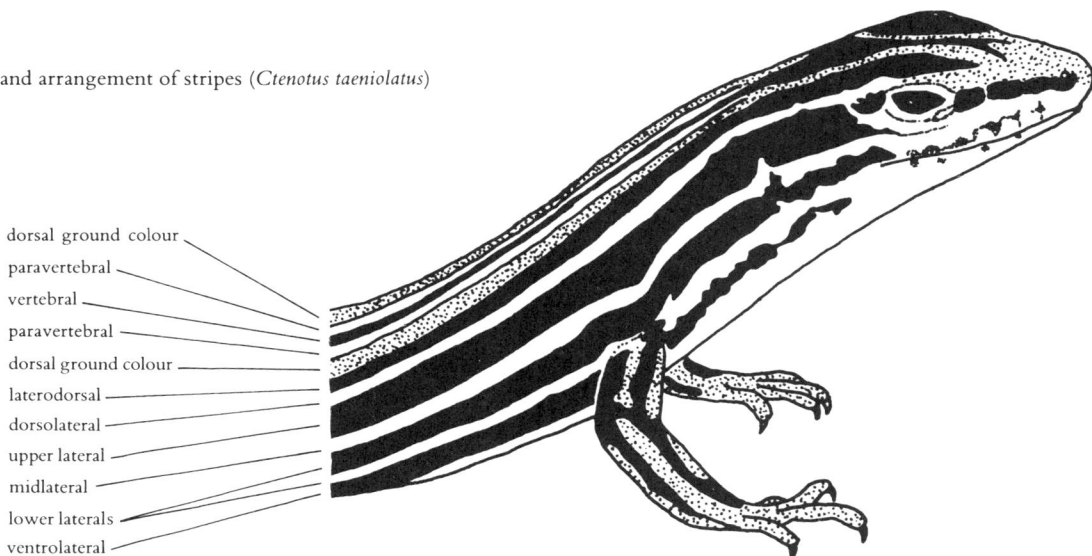

tended, and the young are free-born. A few groups have developed a placenta, providing nourishment direct from mother to offspring. In some cases sperm may be stored over winter, until ovulation the following spring. Females with missing or re-generating tails rarely breed, apparently unable to do so without this valuable fat storage.

Many genera contain large numbers of superficially similar skinks, and this has presented herpetologists and naturalists with problems of easy identification. Pattern differences are not always consistent and close examination of scale characters may be necessary. These difficulties are exacerbated by the presence of numerous undescribed forms.

Genus *ANOMALOPUS*
Duméril and Duméril, 1851

Endemic genus containing 7 species. Restricted to coast, ranges and adjacent interior of eastern Australia, from mid-eastern NSW to Cape York Peninsula. Largely confined to woodlands, sclerophyll forests and heathlands.

Small to moderately large skinks with elongate cylindrical bodies. Limbs absent or greatly reduced, bearing 0–3 short digits. Lower eyelid movable, scaly. Ear-aperture absent, represented by a depression. Scales smooth and glossy.

Two subgenera recognised: *Anomalopus (Anomalopus)* contains the largest species (SVL 135–185 mm), all of which bear 4 short limbs. Comprises *A. leuckartii*, *A. mackayi* and *A. verreauxii*. *Anomalopus (Vermiceps)* Greer and Cogger, 1985 has been erected to include the smaller (SVL 80–105 mm) limbless species, *A. brevicollis*, *A. gowi*, *A. pluto* and *A. swansoni*.

Fossorial skinks which shelter in and under logs or loose soil, beneath rocks and leaf-litter, wherever slightly moist conditions prevail. Limbed species are unique among Australian skinks in having more fingers than toes, thus retaining greater development of forelimbs than hindlimbs. When disturbed, limbed species tend to retreat horizontally into adjacent surface litter while limbless species generally burrow deeper into soft substrates. Invertebrate feeders. Excepting *A. swansoni* all are egglayers. *A. swansoni*, the most southerly occurring member of the genus, thus follows a common trend: an increasing incidence of a livebearing mode of reproduction for skinks dwelling in higher (cooler) latitudes.

Distinguished from *Hemiergis* and *Lerista* in possessing a movable scaly lower eyelid (vs bearing a transparent disc, or fused to form a spectacle). Differs from *Ophioscincus* in having more upper labial scales (6 vs 5). Differs from *Saiphos* and limbed *Coeranoscincus* in lacking a digital formula of 3 fingers and 3 toes. Limbless *Anomalopus* differ from limbless *Coeranoscincus* by much smaller size (SVL 105 vs 290 mm).

Anomalopus brevicollis
Greer and Cogger, 1985
Photo 265

Description Small limbless *Anomalopus* with ground colour of pale to dark brown or yellowish brown. Head greyish brown. Tail greyish brown to black. Base of each scale usually tinged with darker pigment, tending to align into obscure longitudinal series of spots. Ventral surfaces translucent, suffused with pink. Dark spots usually present on chin, throat and ventrolateral surfaces. SVL 80 mm.

Distinguished from *A. gowi* in bearing weaker pattern and more supraocular scales (usually 3 vs 2).
Preferred habitat Mid-eastern Qld, from Cracow district north to Finch Hatton and inland to Clermont area. Occurs in broad range of habitats, including open sclerophyll forests and rainforests on sandy soils, cracking clay-based soils and rock outcrops.
Microhabitat As for genus.
Comments Egglayer. Clutches of 1–2 recorded. See genus.

Anomalopus gowi Greer and Cogger, 1985
Photo 266

Description Small limbless *Anomalopus* with ground colour of pale to dark brown or yellowish brown, marked above and below with prominent longitudinal series of dark brown dashes, one per scale. Head and tail-tip black. SVL 105 mm.

Distinguished from *A. brevicollis* in bearing stronger pattern and fewer supraocular scales (2 vs usually 3).
Preferred habitat Woodlands and evergreen vine thickets in north-eastern Qld, from west of Townsville north to Mt Mulligan.
Microhabitat As for genus.
Comments Egglayer. Clutches of 1–3 recorded. See genus.

Anomalopus leuckartii (Weinland, 1862)
Photo 267

Description Moderately large *Anomalopus* bearing 2 digits on forelimb, and a stylar hindlimb. Snout rounded with waxy tip. Eye moderately well developed. Tail moderately long and tapering at tip. Ground colour brown, greyish brown to purplish brown. Paler edges to scales tend to form obscure longitudinal lines. Pale grey to yellowish bar may be present on nape. Ventral surfaces cream, dull yellow to pale pink; darker beneath tail. SVL 100 mm.

Distinguished from *A. verreauxii* and *A. mackayi* in bearing fewer digits on forelimb (2 vs 3).
Preferred habitat Woodlands and dry sclerophyll forests in subhumid north-eastern NSW and south-eastern Qld.
Microhabitat Usually encountered in soft soil beneath rocks, logs or leaf-litter.
Comments As for genus.

Anomalopus mackayi Greer and Cogger, 1985
Photo 268

Description Medium-sized limbed *Anomalopus* bearing 3 fingers and 2 toes. Ground colour greyish brown, paler below. Southern population unpatterned. Northern population bears longitudinal rows of dark spots, one per scale, over dorsal and lateral surfaces. Ventral surfaces occasionally marked with rows of dark spots in north of range. SVL 110 mm.

Differs from all other *Anomalopus* by digital formula of 3 and 2.

Preferred habitat Subhumid regions west of the Great Dividing Range, in a small area of northeastern NSW and south-eastern Qld.

Microhabitat As for genus.

Comments As for genus.

Anomalopus pluto Ingram, 1977
Photo 269

Description Moderately small completely limbless *Anomalopus* with rounded snout, bearing waxy tip. Eye greatly reduced. Ground colour brown; darker on tail. Pattern virtually absent, excepting paler edges to scales. Ventral surfaces pale brown. SVL 75 mm.

Preferred habitat Monsoon forests, heathlands and woodlands of far northern Cape York Peninsula, Qld.

Microhabitat Shelters beneath rocks, logs, leaf-litter and surface debris.

Comments As for genus.

Anomalopus swansoni Greer and Cogger, 1985
Photo 270

Description Small limbless *Anomalopus* with ground colour of pale to dark brown above, paler below. Pattern obscure; individual scales usually with paler edges. Tail-tip black. SVL 105 mm.

Preferred habitat Open forest on well-drained sandy soils in mid-eastern NSW, from just north of Sydney to the Hunter River Valley and inland 130 km to Sandy Hollow.

Microhabitat As for genus.

Comments Livebearing, litters of 2–3 recorded. See genus.

Anomalopus verreauxii
Duméril and Duméril, 1851
Photo 271

Description Large *Anomalopus* with 4 limbs. Forelimb bears 3 short fingers. Hindlimb stylar. Snout moderately pointed and wedge-shaped, lacking waxy tip. Eye well developed. Tail very long, tapering at tip. Ground colour brown, yellowish brown, greyish brown to grey; paler on flanks. Juveniles marked with broad prominent yellow bar across base of head. This is usually discernible (though darker and more obscure) on adults. Lower lateral and ventral surfaces pale pink, cream to dull yellow. SVL 160 mm.

Distinguished from *A. leuckartii* in bearing more digits on forelimb (3 vs 2).

Preferred habitat Dry sclerophyll forests, woodlands and margins of wet sclerophyll forests in humid to subhumid eastern Australia, from the Proserpine area of mideastern Qld, south to Red Rocks, NSW.

Microhabitat Usually encountered in soft soil beneath rocks, logs or leaf-litter.

Comments As for genus.

Genus CALYPTOTIS De Vis, 1886

Endemic genus containing 5 species. Restricted to humid and subhumid habitats from mideastern to north-eastern Australia, never extending inland further than 170 km (Bunya Mountains, Qld).

Small short-limbed skinks bearing 5 fingers and 5 toes. Lower eyelid movable and scaly. Ear opening small (reduced to a depression on *C. scutirostrum* and *C. lepidorostrum*). Scales smooth, glossy and iridescent. Pattern usually includes 4 lines of dark spots on dorsum and a poorly to well-defined dark dorsolateral stripe. Ventral colouration is a significant generic character. Adults usually bear a yellow chest and belly, and coral pink beneath tail.

Crepuscular to nocturnal. Terrestrial and cryptozoic. *Calyptotis* occur in wet and dry sclerophyll forests, woodlands, vine thickets and rainforests. They favour damp conditions beneath rocks, leaf-litter and rotting logs. Small invertebrates such as arthropods and gastropods are favoured prey items. Egglaying, producing small clutches.

Distinguished from *Saiphos* in bearing more digits on each foot (5 vs 3). Differs from small short-limbed *Sphenomorphus* in usually bearing a combination of yellow and pink ventral pigments (vs cream to yellow). Differs from *Hemiergis* by nature of movable lower eyelid (scaly vs enclosing a transparent disc).

Calyptotis lepidorostrum Greer, 1983
Photo 272

Description Dorsal ground colour pale to dark brown, marked with 4 dorsal rows of dark brown longitudinally aligned spots. These are strongest and most continuous anteriorly; fading and breaking posteriorly. Broader dark brown dorsolateral stripe extends from in front of eye onto tail. This is boldest on nape and anterior body, becoming diffuse posteriorly. Flanks pale grey to pale brown, often bearing scattered darker brown blotches and spots. Throat white. Chest and belly pale to bright yellow, merging to coral pink beneath tail. Yellow and pink pigments absent on juveniles. SVL 55 mm.

Distinguished from *C. scutirostrum* in possessing prefrontal scales, and (in narrow zone of overlap) by restriction to rainforests (vs adjacent wet and dry sclerophyll forests). Differs from *C. temporalis* by nature of ear (reduced to a depression vs a distinct tympanum), and in attaining greater maximum size (SVL 55 vs 35 mm).

Preferred habitat Restricted to rainforests in south of range, extending into wet sclerophyll forests, vine thickets and woodlands northwards. Occurs on ranges and coastal plain of south-eastern to mideastern Qld, from Fraser Island and Conondale Ranges north to Mackay district.

Microhabitat As for genus.

Comments Clutches of 2–4 eggs are recorded. Otherwise as for genus.

Calyptotis ruficauda Greer, 1983
Photo 273

Description Dorsal ground colour pale yellowish brown to dark brown. Dorsal pattern (when present) usually comprises 4 rows of dark brown longitudinally aligned spots. These are strongest (and sometimes coalesced to form continuous lines) anteriorly. Irregular dark brown dorsolateral streak (most prominent anteriorly) extends from in front of eye, fading at hindlimb. Lateral surfaces grey to pale brown, marked with scattered dark brown spots and/or small blotches. Throat whitish. Chest and belly yellow, merging to a pink flush (brightest and most extensive on males) beneath tail; occasionally posterior vent and undersides of thighs. Dark spotting often extends over chin, throat and chest. SVL 55 mm.

Distinguished from *C. scutirostrum* by nature of ear (a distinct tympanum vs reduced to a depression).

Preferred habitat Wet and dry sclerophyll forests, coastal vine thickets and edges of rainforests. Occurs on ranges and coastal plain of northeastern NSW, from Hunter Valley north to between Brinerville and Moonee Beach. Dorrigo Plateau acts as a barrier, isolating *C. ruficauda* from *C. scutirostrum*.

Microhabitat As for genus.

Comments Recorded clutches of 2–6 eggs are probably laid from late November to late January. Otherwise as for genus.

Calyptotis scutirostrum (Peters, 1873)
Photo 274

Description Large robust *Calyptotis* with dorsal ground colour of pale brown, yellowish brown to dark brown, marked with 4 dorsal rows of dark brown longitudinally aligned spots or streaks. These are boldest and tend to coalesce into lines anteriorly, breaking up and becoming diffuse posteriorly. Broad dark ragged-edged dorsolateral stripe (boldest anteriorly) extends from in front of eye onto tail. Flanks pale grey to pale brown, often bearing

scattered darker brown spots and blotches. Throat whitish. Chest and belly cream to bright yellow, merging with dull to bright coral pink flush from vent onto tail and inner surfaces of thighs. This is usually brightest and most extensive on mature males. Chin, throat, side of chest and tail may be finely spotted with dark pigment, particularly on females. SVL 55 mm through most of range; up to 59 mm in Bunya Mountains, Qld.

Distinguished from *C. lepidorostrum* in lacking prefrontal scales. Differs further in favouring wet or dry sclerophyll forests (vs rainforests within zone of overlap). Differs from *C. ruficauda* by nature of ear (reduced to a depression vs a distinct tympanum).

Preferred habitat Wet and dry sclerophyll forests and woodlands (occasionally rainforests) on coast and ranges of northern NSW and south-eastern Qld. Extends from northern Dorrigo Plateau, NSW, north to Gympie district and inland to Bunya Mountains, Qld.

Microhabitat Frequently encountered in well-watered situations in suburban gardens. Otherwise as for genus.

Comments Clutches of 2–5 eggs are laid during summer months, hatching in autumn.

Calyptotis temporalis Greer, 1983
Photo 275

Description Small moderately robust *Calyptotis* with dorsal ground colour of brown to dark brown. Four dorsal rows of dark brown to blackish, longitudinally aligned spots or streaks extend from nape onto base of tail. These coalesce anteriorly to form broken lines, becoming indistinct posteriorly. Ragged-edged dark dorsolateral stripe extends from eye, becoming diffuse at base of tail. Lateral surfaces pale brown, flecked with dark brown. Ventral colour reduced; cream to dull yellow on belly and chest. Mature males exhibit a pink flush from vent to beneath tail. Chin, throat and neck marked with scattered brown spots. SVL 35 mm.

Distinguished from *C. lepidorostrum* by nature of ear (a distinct tympanum vs reduced to a depression), and in attaining smaller maximum size (SVL 35 vs 55 mm).

Preferred habitat Rainforests, wet and dry sclerophyll forests and vine thickets on coast and ranges of mideastern Qld, from Rockhampton area north to Proserpine district.

Microhabitat As for genus.

Comments Clutch of 2 eggs recorded. Otherwise as for genus.

Calyptotis thorntonensis Greer, 1983
Photo 276

Description Small sharp-snouted, relatively dorsally depressed *Calyptotis*. Dorsal ground colour brown to dark brown, mottled with dark brown to black. Obscure dark brown dorsolateral stripe (boldest anteriorly) extends from in front of eye onto body. Lateral surfaces pale brown, bearing darker mottling. Ventral surfaces whitish, with dark spotting on side of chin, throat and tail. SVL 35 mm.

Preferred habitat Only known from rainforest on steep rocky slopes between 600 and 700 m elevation, on southern base of Thornton Peak, north-eastern Qld.

Microhabitat As for genus.

Comments Extremely heat sensitive, succumbing to the temperature of a human hand. Otherwise as for genus.

Four-fingered or Rainbow Skinks
Genus *CARLIA* Gray, 1845

Large genus comprising 24 described Australian species. Largely confined to subhumid northern Australia, extending south to central Australia and northern Vic. Extralimital in New Guinea and eastern Indonesia. Species diversity is greatest in north-eastern Qld, where several undescribed taxa occur.

Small to medium-sized (up to SVL 70 mm) skinks with well-developed limbs, bearing 4 fingers and 5 toes. Eyelid usually movable, enclosing a transparent disc (except *C. foliorum* which bears an immovable, partially fused lower eyelid, forming a fixed spectacle). Ear opening present, bearing enlarged lobules. Dorsal scales smooth, or with strong to weak longitudinal keels or striations.

Most *Carlia* are sexually dichromatic. Breeding males of many species develop dark pigment on throat, and/or a reddish to orange flush or broad stripes on flanks. Breeding males are usually sufficiently distinct to be identified by colour and pattern. Juveniles, females and non-breeding males may require examination of such characters as number and strength of keels on dorsal scales, shape of dorsal scales (4-sided with rounded posterior edge or 6-sided with angular posterior edge), alignment of ear opening (horizontal, circular or vertically elongate) and shape, size and arrangement of ear lobules.

Active sun-loving skinks that feed on arthropods. Most are terrestrial, foraging among accumulated leaf-litter. Egglayers, producing small clutches. The majority of species rely on visual stimuli such as breeding colours and display sequences (including head-bobbing and tail-waving), rivalling those of some dragons in their complexity. The common name 'rainbow skink' is derived from the bright colours on breeding males of some species.

Though the concept of species groups has not been widely applied in this genus, 3 groups appear sufficiently distinct from their congeners to warrant separate discussion.

(1) Long-limbed dorsally depressed species which forage on rock faces. Dorsal scales keeled, each keel usually composed of a series of small points. Males do not develop breeding colours. Members are agile; capable of making well-coordinated leaps between boulders. Restricted to mideastern and northern Qld. Group comprises *C. coensis*, *C. mundivensis*, *C. rimula* and *C. scirtetis*.

(2) Very large robust leaf-litter inhabiting *Carlia* with smooth to weakly carinate dorsal scales. Males develop prominent reddish orange lateral flush, sometimes in combination with a black throat. Restricted in Australia to north-eastern NT and northern Qld. Extralimital in New Guinea and eastern Indonesia. Sometimes referred to as *C. fusca* group. Represented in Australia by *C. longipes* and *C. rostralis*.

(3) Very small secretive leaf-litter inhabiting *Carlia* with smooth to weakly carinate dorsal scales. Males develop a reddish flush on posterior body, hind-limbs, tail and occasionally throat. Extends from mideastern NSW to islands of Torres Strait, Qld. Extralimital in New Guinea. This group, which may constitute a distinct genus, comprises *C. aerata*, *C. foliorum*, *C. laevis* and *C. macfarlani*. Several north Qld species await description.

Carlia is distinguished from *Morethia*, *Notoscincus*, *Cryptoblepharus*, *Leiolopisma* and *Lampropholis* (excluding *L. tetradactyla*) in bearing fewer fingers (4 vs 5). Differs from *L. tetradactyla* in lacking a row of scales between eye and upper labial scales. With the exception of *Carlia foliorum*, *Carlia* differs further from *Morethia*, *Notoscincus* and *Cryptoblepharus* by nature of lower eyelid (movable, bearing a transparent disc vs fused to form a spectacle). *C. foliorum* differs from superficially similar *Menetia* in bearing ear lobules.

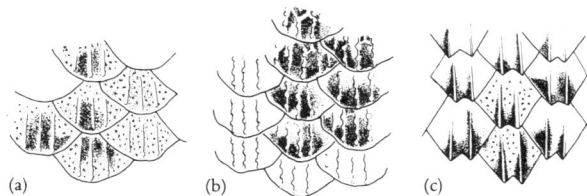

Variation in the nature of dorsal scales in *Carlia*
(a) 4-sided (posterior edge rounded) bearing 3 weak keels or striations (*C. munda*)
(b) 4-sided bearing longitudinal series of tubercles (*C. coensis*)
(c) 6-sided (posterior edge angular) bearing 2 strong keels (*C. vivax*)

Carlia aerata (Garman, 1901)
Photo 277

Description Small *Carlia* with 4-sided dorsal scales; smooth bearing 3 or 4 striations. Ear opening usually horizontally elongate, margined with large and small sharp lobules. Sexually dichromatic.

Breeding males: Dorsal ground colour olive-brown. Flanks brown, often speckled with white. Top of head copper. Side of head cream with dark bars on labial scales. Tail and hindlimbs reddish.

Ventral surfaces cream, sometimes bearing longitudinal series of brown spots from neck to tail.

Females, juveniles and non-breeding males lack reddish flush on hindlimbs and tail. SVL 35 mm.

Distinguished from *C. macfarlani* by shape of ear opening (horizontally elongate vs circular) and in lacking a pale dorsolateral stripe. Differs from *C. laevis* in bearing fewer upper labial scales (6 vs 7), and in favouring subhumid habitats (vs rainforests and their margins). Differs from *C. foliorum* by nature of lower eyelid (movable vs fused).

Preferred habitat Dry sclerophyll forests, woodlands, grasslands and rock outcrops of subhumid north-eastern Australia, from Torres Strait Islands south to Ingham area, Qld.

Microhabitat Secretive. Shelters and forages among leaf-litter and on adjacent low rock faces.

Comments As for genus.

Carlia amax Storr, 1974
Photo 278

Description Moderately small robust *Carlia* with 6-sided dorsal scales, each bearing 2 strong keels. Ear opening horizontally elongate, usually bearing one anterior lobule. Ground colour pale to dark brown. Pattern prominent to absent (usually obscure), consisting of small, pale and/or dark spots. Pale spots (when present) usually adjoin posterior margins of dark spots. Fine whitish line may extend from upper lip, through ear to forelimb. Blackish blotches may be present on flanks. Top of head copper, particularly on breeding males. Ventral surfaces white. SVL 40 mm.

Distinguished from *C. munda*, *C. gracilis*, *C. rufilatus* and *C. triacantha* by number of keels on each dorsal scale (2 vs 3). Breeding males differ further in lacking a red lateral stripe or flush. Differs from *C. johnstonei* in bearing a weaker pattern, and by nature of ear lobules: one small anterior lobule, occasionally 1 or 2 additional minute lobules on remaining margins (vs a long sharp anterior lobule and smaller pointed lobules on remaining margins).

Preferred habitat Rock outcrops and scree slopes from subhumid to semi-arid Kimberley region, WA, through northern NT to north-western Qld.

Microhabitat Forages among leaf-litter accumulations at bases of trees and rocks.

Comments As for genus.

Carlia bicarinata (Macleay, 1877)
Photo 279

Description Long-tailed *Carlia* with 6-sided dorsal scales, each bearing 2 strong keels. Ear opening circular, margined by short to long, pointed lobules. Sexually dichromatic.

Breeding males: Ground colour pale brown without pattern. Limbs and tail reddish brown.

Females, juveniles and non-breeding males: Ground colour pale brown. Pale yellowish brown vertebral stripe extends from nape to hips. Narrow yellowish brown dorsolateral stripe extends from eye or above ear onto tail, becoming diffuse beyond hips. Narrow white to cream midlateral stripe extends from ear to hindlimb. SVL 45 mm.

Distinguished from *C. vivax* and *C. schmeltzii prava* by nature of ear opening (circular, margined with lobules, vs vertically elongate, usually bearing 1 or 2, and 2 anterior lobules, respectively). Breeding males differ from those of *C. vivax* in lacking a reddish orange lateral flush or stripe.

Preferred habitat Dry sclerophyll forests and woodlands over grassy ground cover in subhumid north-eastern Australia, from about Townsville to tip of Cape York Peninsula, including Dunk, Hinchinbrook and the Torres Strait Islands, Qld. Extralimital in south-west New Guinea.

Microhabitat Associated with leaf-litter and low vegetation.

Comments Nominate *C. bicarinata* may be restricted to New Guinea. The Australian population described and pictured here probably represents an undescribed taxon.

Carlia coensis (Mitchell, 1953)
Photo 280

Description Distinctive large long-limbed *Carlia* with 4-sided dorsal scales, each bearing 3–5 longitudinal series of tubercles. Ear opening circular to vertically elongate, margined by small rounded lobules. Ground colour blackish brown. Pattern prominent, becoming obscure on very large individuals. Broad wavy, rich golden brown to silver grey vertebral stripe extends from nape to base of tail. Rich golden brown to silver grey dorsolateral stripe, commencing above and behind eye and breaking into a series of circular blotches to hips, continues as a ragged line to tail-tip. Midlateral series of roughly circular blotches extends from ear to hindlimb. Head coppery brown. Limbs blackish brown, prominently blotched with grey. Ventral surfaces greenish white. SVL 65 mm.

Preferred habitat Western edges of the McIlwraith and Table Ranges, from Coen area north to Pascoe River, in north-eastern Cape York Peninsula, Qld.

Microhabitat Forages on rock faces and strewn boulders, particularly those occurring in vine thickets along creeks.

Comments Rock-inhabiting. See genus.

Carlia dogare Covacevich and Ingram, 1975
Photos 281, 282

Description Moderately large robust *Carlia* with 6-sided dorsal scales, each bearing 2 moderately strong keels. Ear opening vertically elongate bearing 2 (rarely 1 or 3) anterior lobules. Sexually dichromatic.

Breeding males: Ground colour pale brown

marked with 6 broad pale reddish orange stripes: dorsals from about shoulder to hips, upper laterals from above forelimb to hindlimb, and lower laterals from forelimb to just in front of hindlimb. Top of head dark greyish brown. Side of head and neck dark greyish brown, prominently spotted with white. Ear opening broadly margined with black. Ventral surfaces white, boldly flecked with black on throat and ventrolateral region.

Females, juveniles and non-breeding males: Ground colour brown, with prominent to obscure pattern. Pale vertebral stripe extends from nape to hips. Broad brown dorsal zone from neck to base of tail encloses pale dashes, each usually bearing a darker anterior margin. Pale greyish brown dorsolateral stripe extends from nape onto base of tail. Greyish brown upper lateral stripe extends from snout, eye or side of neck, to hindlimb. Greyish white midlateral stripe extends from upper lip to hindlimb; represented anteriorly by a white line curving under eye to ear. Ragged-edged greyish brown lower lateral stripe extends from about ear to hindlimb. Narrow greyish brown ventrolateral stripe may extend from forelimb to hindlimb. Broad black margin to ear opening usually present. Ventral surfaces white. SVL 50 mm.

Breeding males differ from all other *Carlia* in bearing 6 reddish orange stripes. Females, juveniles and non-breeding males differ from those of *C. vivax* by nature of midlateral stripe (broad and greyish white vs sharp, narrow and white). Distinguished from *C. munda* in lacking a sharp white line from below eye onto body, disjunct at ear opening; differs further by nature of dorsal scales (bearing 2 moderately strong keels vs smooth to weakly tricarinate).

Preferred habitat Known only from heathlands on white coastal sands of mideastern Cape York Peninsula and Lizard Island, Qld.

Microhabitat Shelters and forages among low vegetation and littoral debris.

Comments Males bear strongest breeding colours during May, though indications of colour are apparent on individuals collected during October and November.

Carlia foliorum (De Vis, 1884)
Photo 283

Description Very small slender *Carlia* with 4-sided dorsal scales; smooth or bearing weak striations. Ear opening circular to horizontal, bearing one anterior lobule (in south) or margined by pointed lobules (in north). Lower eyelid immovable, forming a transparent spectacle. Populations from north of range tend to have a larger eye and attain a slightly greater size.

Ground colour pale or dark brown to greyish brown, sometimes bearing obscure darker flecks on dorsum, and fine white peppering on flanks and limbs. Head usually obscurely mottled with blackish

brown. Lips flecked, mottled or barred with dark brown. Breeding males bear a rich reddish brown flush on tail and hindlimbs. Ventral surfaces white. SVL 35 mm.

Distinguished from all other *Carlia* by nature of lower eyelid (fused to form a spectacle vs movable, enclosing a transparent disc). Differs from *Menetia* spp. by nature of ear opening (relatively larger, bearing one or more lobules, vs very small, lacking lobules). Differs further from *M. greyii* in lacking dark and pale lateral stripes.

Preferred habitat Dry sclerophyll forests and woodlands, often with grassy ground cover. Restricted to subhumid eastern Australia, from Townsville area, Qld, to about Sydney, NSW.

Microhabitat Secretive; closely associated with leaf-litter, grass and fallen bark at bases of trees.

Comments Previously known as *C. burnetti*, though *'foliorum'* (formerly applied to *C. munda*) appears to have nomenclatural priority for this species. See genus.

Carlia gracilis Storr, 1974
Photo 284

Description Small slender *Carlia* with 6-sided dorsal scales, each bearing 3 moderately strong keels. Ear opening horizontally elongate with 0–3 small anterior lobules. Sexually dichromatic.

Breeding males: Ground colour brown, coppery brown to grey, flushed with copper on forelimb and anterior flanks. Broad dull red lateral stripe extends from ear to hindlimb. Throat and lips iridescent greenish blue. Ventral surfaces white.

Females, juveniles and non-breeding males lack anterior copper flush, reddish lateral stripe and greenish blue throat and lips. SVL 40 mm.

Distinguished from *C. amax*, by number of keels on each dorsal scale (3 vs 2). Differs from *C. munda* and *C. rufilatus* in bearing stronger keels, and in lacking a sharp white stripe; disrupted at ear. This may be weak on *C. rufilatus*. Differs from *C. triacantha* by nature of ear opening (horizontally elongate, sometimes bearing a small anterior lobule, vs circular, bearing a larger anterior lobule). Breeding males differ further in bearing a dull red lateral stripe.

Preferred habitat Usually associated with well-watered habitats, such as vine thickets and monsoon forests along creek and river margins in far northern WA and NT.

Microhabitat Shelters and forages among leaf-litter.

Comments As for genus.

Carlia jarnoldae Covacevich and Ingram, 1975
Photos 285, 286

Description Dorsal scales 6-sided, each bearing 3 moderately strong keels. Ear opening horizontally elongate, bearing a small pointed anterior lobule and smaller lobules on remaining margin. Markedly sexually dichromatic.

Mature males: Ground colour brown, marked with 5–7 narrow blackish brown lines from nape onto base of tail. Interspaces usually bear cream flecks. Upper lateral zone from snout to in front of hindlimb black, enclosing 2 or 3 series of small blue spots. Mid to lower flanks and forelimbs bright orange. Top of head coppery brown. Lips, side of neck and ventral surfaces pale green. Scales on side of throat bear dark edges.

Females, juveniles and non-breeding males: Ground colour brown, usually marked with scattered dark spots and pale flecks. An obscure whitish dorsolateral stripe may extend from side of neck to base of tail. Upper lateral surfaces, from snout to base of tail, blackish. Broad white midlateral stripe extends from upper lips to base or middle of tail. Lower lateral surfaces blackish, marked with scattered pale flecks. Top of head coppery brown. Ventral surfaces white. SVL 40 mm.

Mature males are readily distinguished from all other *Carlia* by nature of colour and pattern. Females and juveniles differ from *C. munda* by nature of white midlateral stripe (extending continuously through ear opening to base of tail, vs disjunct at ear, and often fading on anterior or midbody). Differs from *C. pectoralis* by shape of ear opening (horizontally elongate vs vertically elongate).

Preferred habitat Dry sclerophyll forests and woodlands; often associated with stony soils or rock outcrops. Occurs in subhumid north-eastern Qld, from just south of Townsville, north to Nichol Creek, Cape York Peninsula.

Microhabitat Forages among leaf- and grass-litter, occasionally sheltering beneath rocks.

Comments Breeding colours are apparent on males throughout most of year, at least from July to April. Hatchlings are recorded during May.

Carlia johnstonei Storr, 1974
Photo 287

Description Moderately robust *Carlia* with 6-sided dorsal scales, each bearing 2 strong keels. Ear opening circular to horizontally or vertically elongate, bearing one large anterior lobule and numerous smaller pointed lobules around margin. Sexually dichromatic.

Breeding males: Ground colour blackish brown to dark reddish brown, marked with numerous scattered white flecks, each usually edged anteriorly with black. Flanks rich reddish brown; boldest anteriorly. Top of head blackish. Sides of head, neck and foreback suffused with blackish pigment, and prominently spotted with white. Tail and limbs blackish brown to reddish brown, flecked with black and white. Ventral surfaces pinkish white; bluish beneath throat. Chin and throat scales broadly margined with black.

Females, juveniles and non-breeding males lack black suffusion on head, neck and forebody. White spots or flecks are less prominent. Flanks greyish. Ventral surfaces whitish. SVL 50 mm.

Distinguished from all sympatric *Carlia* (except *C. amax*) in bearing 2 keels on each dorsal scale (vs 3 keels or smooth). Differs from *C. amax* in bearing stronger pattern, and by nature of ear lobules (a long sharp anterior lobule and smaller pointed lobules around margin vs a small anterior lobule and occasionally 1 or 2 minute lobules on remaining margins).

Preferred habitat Subhumid and humid northwest Kimberley region, WA. Most abundant along well-vegetated rocky creek banks and in vine thickets.

Microhabitat Forages and shelters among leaf-litter, tree roots, and rocks.

Comments Males observed in breeding condition during late September and October.

Carlia laevis (Oudemans, 1894)
Photo 288

Description Very small robust *Carlia* with 4-sided dorsal scales; smooth bearing 3 or 4 weak striations. Ear opening usually horizontally elongate, margined by sharp lobules. Sexually dichromatic.

Breeding males: Dorsal ground colour reddish brown (iridescent green and purple when viewed obliquely), each scale bearing fine blackish dashes. These sometimes align to form obscure narrow lines. Flanks greyish brown to black, often bearing pale flecks. Lips, throat and tail flushed with reddish orange. Ventral surfaces cream; reddish beneath tail.

Females, juveniles and non-breeding males lack reddish flush on throat and tail. SVL 35 mm.

Distinguished from *C. macfarlani* by shape of ear opening (horizontally elongate vs circular) and in lacking a pale dorsolateral stripe. Differs from *C. aerata* in bearing more numerous upper labial scales (7 vs 6). Differs further in favouring rainforest habitats (vs dry sclerophyll forests and woodlands).

Preferred habitat Rainforests and their margins in north-eastern Qld, from Cooktown south to Gordonvale district.

Microhabitat Secretive. Forages among leaf-litter in forest clearings.

Comments Males bearing breeding colours have been observed during August and October.

Carlia longipes (Macleay, 1877)
Photo 289

Description Large *Carlia* with 4-sided dorsal scales; smooth or bearing 3 weak carinations. Ear opening circular to vertically elongate, with 1 to numerous long pointed anterior lobules. Occasionally smaller lobules are present on remaining margins. Sexually dichromatic.

Breeding males: Dorsal ground colour brown,

usually lacking pattern. Flanks (from above forelimb to hindlimb) reddish orange. Side of neck blackish brown to grey. Dorsal surface of tail bears obscure transversely oriented blackish dashes, each bearing a paler posterior margin. Ventral surfaces whitish; suffused with pink beneath tail.

Females and non-breeding males: Dorsal ground colour brown, flecked with dark and pale pigment. Obscure narrow cream to pale brown dorsolateral stripe may extend from eye to anterior body, mid-body or hips. Blackish brown upper lateral zone extends from snout to anterior body, midbody or hips. This is often flushed posteriorly with red, and occasionally encloses a few pale spots, especially anteriorly. Obscure, wavy or broken cream to greyish midlateral stripe extends from under eye, to about midbody or hips. Lower flanks greyish brown, sometimes bearing pale greyish flecks.

Juveniles: Similar to females and non-breeding males but with more prominent pale flecking and sharper dorsolateral and midlateral stripes. SVL 65 mm.

Distinguished from *C. rostralis* in bearing obscure pale dorsolateral stripes (vs prominent). Breeding males differ further from those of *C. rostralis* in lacking a black flush on throat. Females and juveniles differ further in usually bearing a longer pale midlateral stripe (extending from under eye to midbody or hips vs from lips to forelimb).

Preferred habitat Wide variety of habitats including woodlands, grasslands, monsoon forests and vine thickets of far north Qld. Extends from Mt Spec north to Torres Strait Islands. A disjunct population occurs in north-eastern NT. Extralimital in south-western New Guinea.

Microhabitat Forages and shelters among leaf-litter, often ascending bases of trees, fallen logs and low termitaria.

Comments Breeding colours are apparent on males throughout most of year.

Carlia macfarlani Günther, 1877
Photos 290, 291

Description Very small slender *Carlia* with smooth 4-sided dorsal scales. Ear opening circular, usually bearing one large blunt anterior lobule, and several blunt lobules on remaining margins. Sexually dichromatic.

Breeding males: Ground colour pale or rich brown to olive-grey. Pattern reduced to absent. Limbs, tail, chin and throat flushed with reddish brown.

Females, juveniles and non-breeding males: A pale brown dorsolateral stripe usually extends from nape onto tail, becoming diffuse beyond hips. Upper lateral zone (from snout onto sides of tail) dark brown. Narrow obscure pale brown to cream midlateral line extends from ear to hindlimb. Lower lateral zone pale brown. Head dark brown to dark greyish brown. Lips pale brown barred with

dark brown. Limbs, tail, chin and throat lack reddish brown flush. Ventral surfaces greyish white. SVL 35 mm.

Distinguished from *C. aerata* and *C. laevis* by nature of ear opening (circular, bearing blunt lobules vs horizontally elongate, bearing sharp lobules).

Preferred habitat Grassy woodlands, vine thickets, rainforest margins and low coastal vegetation from Princess Charlotte Bay, through wetter parts of eastern Cape York Peninsula to islands of Torres Strait, Qld. Extralimital in south-western New Guinea.

Microhabitat Secretive. Shelters and forages among leaf-litter and low vegetation.

Comments Previously regarded as *C. novae-guineae* (Meyer, 1874), a species now regarded as restricted to New Guinea.

Carlia munda (De Vis, 1885)
Photo 292

Description Dorsal scales 4-sided; smooth, tristriate or weakly tricarinate. Ear opening horizontally elongate, bearing a few small lobules on upper edge, and occasionally smaller lobules on remaining edges. Sexually dichromatic.

Breeding males: Ground colour pale or dark brown to greyish brown, spotted with black, and usually flecked with pale brown, cream to white. Upper lateral zone, from snout to about forelimb, black. Reddish orange lateral flush extends from forelimb to hindlimb; boldest anteriorly. Narrow sharp-edged white midlateral stripe extends from upper lip to top of ear opening, continuing from bottom of ear opening to neck, anterior body or hindlimb. Top of head coppery brown to coppery green. Scales on side of neck and throat white to bluish, broadly margined with black. Remainder of ventral surfaces white, often bearing narrow black lateral edges to ventrolateral scales.

Females, juveniles and non-breeding males lack reddish lateral flush and dark margins to scales of throat, side of neck and ventrolateral region. SVL 40 mm.

Distinguished from *C. rufilatus* in bearing weaker keels on dorsal scales, and usually a longer white midlateral stripe. Breeding males differ further in developing a reddish orange lateral flush (vs broad red midlateral stripe).

Differs from other sympatric *Carlia* by alignment of white midlateral stripe (disjunct at ear, reaching aperture at top and continuing back from bottom, vs absent or continuous through ear).

Preferred habitat Wide variety of arid to sub-humid areas supporting dry sclerophyll forests, woodlands, shrublands or hummock grass associations. Favours heavy to stony soils. Extends from eastern and northern Qld, through northern and central NT to Kimberley region, WA. Populations from Pilbara and North West Cape are apparently isolated by the Great Sandy Desert.

Microhabitat Shelters and forages in leaf-litter at bases of trees or shrubs. Pilbara and North West Cape population is usually associated with *Triodia* and coarse leaf-litter beneath figs (*Ficus platypoda*) growing along gorges or rocky river margins.

Comments Strong breeding colours are most apparent from October to May. Gravid females are recorded in northern NT and WA from September to April. Very young juveniles are recorded in mideast Qld during October. Previously known as *C. foliorum*, though 'munda' appears to have nomenclatural priority.

Carlia mundivensis (Broom, 1898)
Photo 293

Description Large robust, moderately long-limbed *Carlia* with 4- or 6-sided dorsal scales, each bearing 2 or 3 moderately strong keels. Ear opening round, margined with short to long, pointed lobules.

Ground colour dark olive-brown. Broad vertebral stripe of ground colour extends from nape to tail-tip, or becomes diffuse beyond hips. Remainder of dorsal and lateral surfaces bear variably sized blackish blotches, often aligning into paravertebral series and coalescing into lateral variegations. Scattered pale flecks may be present, sometimes coalesced to form obscure dorsolateral and midlateral stripes. These are prominent on juveniles. Top of head coppery brown. Ventral surfaces white. SVL 55 mm.

Preferred habitat Rock outcrops surrounded by dry sclerophyll forests, woodlands or vine thickets in subhumid north-eastern to mideastern Qld. Extends from Chillagoe and Mareeba areas, south to inland from Gladstone.

Microhabitat Forages on exposed rock faces, occasionally on tree roots. Shelters in cavities or crevices between boulders, and in hollow trunks or limbs. In many localities fig trees (*Ficus* spp.) grow on boulder-strewn slopes and the margins of these are particularly favoured.

Comments See genus.

Carlia pectoralis (De Vis, 1885)
Photos 294, 295

Description Moderately large *Carlia* with 6-sided dorsal scales, each usually bearing 3 moderately strong keels. Ear opening vertically elongate with 1 or 2 anterior lobules. Sexually dichromatic.

Breeding males: Ground colour greyish brown to brown; uniform or bearing obscure longitudinally aligned pale grey dashes (each with a dark anterior margin) from shoulders to base of tail. Broad reddish orange upper and lower lateral stripes extend from forelimb to hindlimb. Midlateral zone greyish brown. Top of head coppery brown. Lips, throat and side of neck bluish, each scale broadly margined with black. Ventral surfaces cream, flushed with orange on chest, undersurfaces of limbs and ventro-

lateral area.

Females and juveniles bear more prominent pale flecking. A white midlateral stripe extends from upper lips to hindlimb. Ventral surfaces (including chin and throat) white. SVL 50 mm.

Distinguished from *C. tetradactyla* in bearing keeled dorsal scales (vs smooth to weakly striate). Differs from *C. jarnoldae* by shape of ear opening (vertically elongate vs horizontal). Differs from *C. vivax* and *C. schmeltzii prava* by number of keels on dorsal scales (3 vs 2). Differs from *C. s. schmeltzii* in attaining smaller maximum size (SVL 50 vs 65 mm). Breeding males differ further from those of *C. vivax* and *C. s. schmeltzii* by arrangement of reddish orange lateral pigment (2 stripes vs a flush). Females and juveniles differ from both subspecies of *C. schmeltzii* in bearing a white midlateral stripe, and from *C. munda* by alignment of midlateral stripe (continuous through ear opening vs disjunct at ear opening).

Preferred habitat Occurs in eastern Qld north to between Cairns and Cooktown, inland to Capella and Carnarvon Ranges, and south to NSW border. Favours dry sclerophyll forests and woodlands (usually with a grassy understorey) on heavy to stony soils.

Microhabitat Shelters and forages among leaf-litter at bases of trees and beneath low vegetation.

Comments Males may bear breeding colours through most of year, at least from March through till December in north; commencing later in south.

Carlia rhomboidalis (Peters, 1869)
Photos 296, 297

Description Large *Carlia* with 4-sided dorsal scales; smooth or bearing 3 weak carinations. Ear opening circular; with 1–3 large pointed anterior lobules, and smaller lobules on remaining margins. Two disjunct populations occur. These probably constitute distinct taxa.

Northern form: Dorsal ground colour rich brown flecked with black. Flecks may be scattered, or concentrated on paravertebral region to form broad dark stripes; often enclosing paler flecks. Narrow gold to pale brown dorsolateral stripe usually extends from above eye to tail-tip. Upper lateral surfaces blackish brown to black, often bearing yellow, cream or copper flecks. Pale midlateral stripe (often broken on body) may extend from below eye or side of neck to hindlimb. Lower flanks greyish brown. Top of head rich copper. Chin and throat of adults (often juveniles) red. Remaining ventral surfaces white.

Southern form: Differs in bearing bright blue flush on chin and lips, extending to about ear. Throat red. Remainder of ventral surfaces white. SVL 65 mm.

Both forms differ from all other *Carlia* by nature of interparietal scale (fused to frontoparietal scales vs distinct).

Preferred habitat Rainforests, wet sclerophyll forests and their margins in mideastern and north-eastern Qld. Northern population extends from Cooktown district south to Paluma Range. Southern population extends from Magnetic Island south to Mackay.

Microhabitat Forages among leaf-litter, on fallen logs and tree buttresses in rainforest clearings and margins.

Comments A distinctive *Carlia* for 2 reasons: its restriction to rainforest habitats, and a potential for bright chin and throat colouration to occur on both sexes at all ages. Aspects of ecology of the northern population have been studied. In addition to consuming arthropods, *C. rhomboidalis* preys upon smaller skinks, including those of its own kind. Mating has been observed during September, though dissection of specimens suggests males are in a reproductive condition throughout the year. Females are more seasonal, rarely containing eggs between April and August. One or 2 eggs are laid per clutch, and several sites containing 6 eggs indicate communal egglaying.

Carlia rimula Ingram and Covacevich, 1980
Photo 298

Description Small dorsally depressed *Carlia* with 4-sided dorsal scales, each bearing 4 or 5 weak carinations comprising series of 2–5 small points. Ear opening vertically elongate, margined by pointed lobules.

Dorsal ground colour coppery brown. Broad ragged-edged black laterodorsal stripe extends from nape or forebody to base of tail. This usually encloses, or is notched by, a series of obscure pale grey dashes. Broad to narrow silvery dorsolateral stripe extends from above eye onto base of tail. Upper lateral zone black, from behind ear onto side of tail, occasionally enclosing a few pale flecks. Narrow broken silvery midlateral stripe extends from behind forelimb to hindlimb. This is obscure and more broken on large males. Lower flanks blackish brown, bearing obscure pale flecks. Ventral surfaces greyish white. SVL 40 mm.

Distinguished from superficially similar *Cryptoblepharus* spp. in bearing 4 (vs 5) fingers and a movable lower eyelid (vs a large fixed spectacle).

Preferred habitat Shelters and forages among rocks and leaf-litter, usually along creeks margined with vine thickets in the vicinity of Coen, Qld.

Microhabitat Forages on rock faces and in adjacent leaf-litter, sheltering in crevices and cavities.

Comments Rock-inhabiting. Similar to sympatric *Cryptoblepharus virgatus* in size, behaviour and colour pattern. First discovered among a jar of *Cryptoblepharus* specimens in the Australian Museum.

Carlia rostralis (De Vis, 1885)
Photo 299

Description Very large robust *Carlia* with 4-sided

dorsal scales; smooth or bearing 3 weak carinations. Ear opening circular to vertically elongate, with one to numerous long pointed anterior lobules, and occasionally smaller lobules on remaining margins. Sexually dichromatic.

Breeding males: Dorsal ground colour greyish brown, each scale bearing prominent blackish speckling or a streak. Prominent cream dorsolateral stripe extends from above eye, fading at midbody. Upper lateral zone, from snout through eye nearly to hindlimb, black. This usually fades to dark brown at mid or posterior body. Broad prominent cream to yellow midlateral stripe extends from lips to forelimb. Lower lateral zone, from forelimb to hindlimb, bright reddish orange; boldest anteriorly. Forelimbs reddish brown and hindlimbs brown. Chin and throat immaculate black. Remainder of ventral surfaces white.

Females, juveniles and non-breeding males: Black upper lateral zone fades to brown on anterior body. Lower lateral zone brown, sometimes bearing a reddish tinge. Cream stripe from lips to forelimb is narrower; often broken or wavy. Ventral surfaces, including throat, white. SVL 70 mm.

Distinguished from *C. longipes* in bearing more prominent dorsolateral stripes. Breeding males differ further by throat colour (black vs white), and in bearing a dark upper lateral zone (vs a reddish lateral flush). Females and juveniles differ in bearing a shorter pale midlateral stripe (extending back to forelimb vs to midbody or hips).

Preferred habitat Variety of subhumid habitats, including dry sclerophyll forests, vine thickets and rock outcrops. Restricted to north-eastern Qld, from Paluma north to Kowanyama and Cooktown.

Microhabitat Shelters and forages among leaf-litter and low vegetation.

Comments Breeding colours are apparent on males through most of year, at least from August till May.

Carlia rufilatus Storr, 1974
Photo 300

Description Dorsal scales 6-sided, each bearing 3 weak keels or striations. Ear opening horizontally elongate, with or without one small anterior lobule. Sexually dichromatic.

Breeding males: Dorsal ground colour dark olive to dark brown, dotted with black. Each dot bears a pale greyish posterior margin. Broad red midlateral stripe extends from above forelimb to front of hindlimb. Lower flanks pale olive to brown. White stripe (broadly margined above with black) may extend from upper lip to top of ear opening. This usually continues from bottom of ear opening to forelimb or onto body. Top of head coppery brown. Ventral surfaces white, obscurely spotted with black on throat. A few chin shields bear narrow black margins.

Females, juveniles and non-breeding males lack a

red lateral stripe and black markings beneath chin and throat. SVL 40 mm.

Distinguished from *C. munda* in bearing stronger keels on dorsal scales, and usually a shorter white lateral stripe. Breeding males differ further in bearing a red midlateral stripe (vs a lateral flush). Differs from *C. amax* and *C. johnstonei* in bearing more keels on each dorsal scale (3 vs 2). Differs from *C. gracilis* and *C. triacantha* in bearing weaker dorsal keels, and in bearing a white stripe, disrupted at ear.

Preferred habitat Woodlands and riverine forests of north-western NT and northern Kimberley region, WA. Abundant in well-watered gardens of suburban Darwin, NT.

Microhabitat Shelters and forages among leaf-litter.

Comments Males recorded with breeding colours in September and October.

Carlia schmeltzii (Peters, 1867)
Photos 301, 302

Description Medium to large robust *Carlia*, comprising 2 subspecies.

C. s. schmeltzii Dorsal scales 6-sided, each with 3 strong keels. Ear opening vertically elongate, usually bearing 2 large squarish lobules on anterior margin. Sexually dichromatic.

Breeding males: Dorsal ground colour coppery brown, sometimes marked with obscure sparse black flecks. Broad yellowish brown dorsolateral stripe extends from snout or side of neck to mid-body, or well onto tail. Flanks flushed with bright reddish orange, from forelimb to mid or posterior body. Sides of head and neck (back to forelimb) greyish white, with a prominent black margin on each scale. Ventral surfaces whitish. Scales on chin and throat bluish, conspicuously margined with black.

Females, juveniles and non-breeding males lack reddish lateral flush and dark margins to scales of neck, chin and throat. Dorsal and lateral surfaces may be flecked with pale grey to white on very young individuals. SVL 65 mm.

C. s. prava Covacevich and Ingram, 1975 Differs from nominate form in bearing fewer keels on each dorsal scale (2 vs 3) and in attaining smaller maximum size. Ground colour dark grey to greyish brown. Pattern obscure (when present), comprising sparse darker flecks. Lateral edges of scales on throat may be dark-edged. Ventral surfaces whitish. SVL 55 mm.

C. s. schmeltzii is distinguished from *C. pectoralis* in attaining greater maximum size (SVL 65 vs 50 mm). Breeding males differ from those of *C. pectoralis* in bearing a reddish lateral flush (vs upper and lower lateral stripes). *C. s. prava* differs from *C. pectoralis* in bearing fewer keels on dorsal scales (2 vs 3). Differs from *C. bicarinata* by nature of ear opening (vertically elongate with squarish anterior lobules vs

circular, surrounded by sharp lobules).

Preferred habitat *C. s. schmeltzii* favours subhumid rocky ranges, ridges and scree slopes. Extends from NSW–Qld border north to Townsville area, Qld. *C. s. prava* apears to intergrade at about Townsville, extending north to about Weipa on western Cape York Peninsula. Favours grassy woodlands and river margins.

Microhabitat Shelters and forages among rocks, leaf-litter and surface debris.

Comments Breeding colours are present on *C. s. schmeltzii* males from about August to late March or early April. A record from south-east Qld suggests that *C. s. schmeltzii* may lay one large egg in mid-summer. Hatchlings are recorded during March and April. Taxonomic work is necessary in the intergradation zone to determine the true status of the subspecies.

Black Mountain Skink
Carlia scirtetis Ingram and Covacevich, 1980
Photo 303

Description Large long-limbed *Carlia* with protrusive eyes and upturned snout. Dorsal scales 4-sided, bearing 3 (occasionally 4) weak keels, each comprising 2–4 small points. Ear opening vertically elongate, margined by long pointed lobules.

Ground colour blackish brown, obscurely marked with scattered pale greenish to brownish flecks. These are most prominent on juveniles, and tend to concentrate on vertebral and dorsolateral region to form indistinct stripes. Ventral surfaces greyish, each scale bearing a dark margin. Throat, chin, under-surfaces of limbs and tail flecked with brown. SVL 60 mm.

Preferred habitat Restricted to piled black granite boulders of Trevethan Range (Black Mountain) south of Cooktown in north-east Qld.

Microhabitat Forages on exposed surfaces of boulders and shelters in cavities between them. Often utilises shade and shelter provided by roots and leaf-litter associated with the few fig trees (*Ficus* sp.) present on outcrops.

Comments Activity reaches a peak in midmorning and late afternoon, avoiding high midday temperatures. See genus.

Carlia tetradactyla (O'Shaughnessy, 1879)
Photo 304

Description Large robust *Carlia* with 4-sided dorsal scales; smooth or bearing 3 or 4 weak striations. Ear opening circular to vertically elongate with one enlarged rounded lobule on anterior margin. Markedly sexually dichromatic.

Breeding males: Ground colour blackish brown, marked with longitudinally aligned greyish spots or dashes; usually spaced 1–3 scales apart on each scale row. These are often margined anteriorly with black. Broad greyish brown dorsolateral stripe extends from side of neck, well onto tail. Broad rich reddish orange upper and lower lateral stripes extend from neck or forelimb to hindlimb. Broad pale blue to bluish green midlateral stripe extends from above forelimb to hindlimb. Lips, side of neck and ventral surfaces pale blue to bluish green.

Females, juveniles and non-breeding males bear brownish grey flanks and white ventral surfaces. SVL 65 mm.

Breeding males differ from all *Carlia* in bearing a combination of bluish green and reddish orange lateral stripes. Females and juveniles differ from *C. munda* in lacking a sharp white stripe from lips (disjunct at ear) to forelimb or anterior body. Distinguished from *C. pectoralis* and *C. vivax* by nature of dorsal scales (smooth or with 3 or 4 weak carinations vs 3 and 2 moderately strong keels, respectively).

Preferred habitat Dry sclerophyll forests and woodlands, particularly those with a tussock-dominated ground cover. Extends from Benalla in northern Vic., along western slopes of Great Dividing Range to Darling Downs, south-eastern Qld.

Microhabitat Shelters beneath rocks and logs, foraging among low vegetation, leaf-litter and surface debris.

Comments The most cool-adapted *Carlia*, penetrating well into the south-eastern highlands; the domain of largely allopatric cool temperate genera such as *Leiolopisma*. Strong breeding colours are apparent on males from about October to May. Females containing full-term eggs are recorded in February.

Carlia triacantha (Mitchell, 1953)
Photo 305

Description Moderately large *Carlia* with 6-sided dorsal scales, each bearing 3 strong keels. Ear opening circular, with one large anterior lobule, and often numerous smaller pointed lobules on remaining margins. Sexually dichromatic.

Breeding males: Dorsal ground colour greyish brown, marked with numerous dark (and sometimes pale) grey flecks or dots. Flanks flushed anteriorly with yellowish brown to reddish brown. Head and neck shining coppery green. Ventral surfaces whitish.

Females, juveniles and non-breeding males lack coppery green flush on head and neck, and reddish to yellowish flush on anterior flanks. Occasionally an obscure pale brown line extends from below eye to ear. SVL 50 mm.

Distinguished from *C. munda* and *C. rufilatus* by nature of dorsal scales (bearing 3 strong keels vs smooth to weakly tricarinate), and in lacking a white stripe from below eye onto neck or body; disrupted at ear. Differs from *C. gracilis* by nature of ear opening (circular, bearing a large anterior lobule, vs horizontally elongate, bearing 0–3 small anterior lobules). Differs from *C. amax* in bearing more keels on each dorsal scale (3 vs 2). Differs further from all in attaining greater maximum size (SVL 50 vs 40 mm).

Preferred habitat Favours hummock grassland associations growing on sandy, stony to loamy soils, and sandstone outcrops. Extends from northern WA to northern NT, and western half of southern NT.

Microhabitat Shelters and forages among leaf-litter and margins of hummock grasses.

Comments An arid-adapted *Carlia*. Males observed in breeding condition during October in central Australia, and from February to April in northern NT.

Carlia vivax (De Vis, 1884)
Photos 306, 307

Description Moderately small slender long-tailed *Carlia* with 6-sided dorsal scales, each usually bearing 2 strong keels. Ear opening vertically elongate with 1 or 2 anterior lobules. Sexually dichromatic.

Breeding males: Ground colour brown, marked with prominent reddish orange to pinkish brown lateral flush or broad midlateral stripe from forelimb to hindlimb. Top of head dark greyish brown, merging to bluish grey on sides of head and neck. Chin and throat pale blue, speckled with dark brown. Remainder of ventral surfaces white.

Females, juveniles and non-breeding males: Ground colour brown to greyish brown. Two series of dark and/or pale dashes (often enclosed within broad dark dorsal zones) extend from nape onto tail. These may be absent on northern individuals. Pale grey to yellowish brown dorsolateral stripe usually extends from neck to base or tip of tail on southern individuals. This may also be absent in north. Upper flanks greyish brown to yellowish brown. Prominent narrow sharp-edged white midlateral stripe extends from upper lips, through ear to hindlimb. Lower flanks pale greyish brown to yellowish brown. Top of head copper. Ventral surfaces white. SVL 40 mm.

Distinguished from *C. bicarinata* by nature of ear opening (vertically elongate, with one or 2 large rounded anterior lobules, vs circular, surrounded by numerous sharp lobules). Differs from *C. pectoralis* in bearing more keels on each dorsal scale (usually 2 vs 3). Differs from *C. munda* and *C. tetradactyla* by nature of keels on each dorsal scale (2 strong keels vs tricarinate to smooth). Breeding males differ from those of *C. dogare* by arrangement of reddish orange lateral pigment (a stripe or flush vs 2 stripes). Females, juveniles and non-breeding males differ from those of *C. dogare* by nature of pale midlateral stripe (sharp, narrow and white vs broad and greyish white).

Preferred habitat Mideastern NSW to northeastern Qld, from about Singleton north to Prince of Wales and Horn Islands, Torres Strait. Occurs in a variety of subhumid lowland habitats, from dry sclerophyll forests and woodlands on hard or stony soils, to heathlands on pale sands of coast and off-shore islands.

Microhabitat Shelters and forages among low vegetation and leaf-litter.

Comments Strongest breeding colours are apparent during late summer in south; earlier in north.

Photos 308–310 show 3 undescribed taxa in the genus *Carlia*.

Genus *COERANOSCINCUS*
Wells and Wellington, 1984

Endemic genus containing 2 species. Restricted to widely separated blocks of rainforest; in north-eastern Qld, and from north-eastern NSW to south-eastern Qld.

Moderately large (up to SVL 290 mm) elongate skinks with limbs reduced or absent. Lower eyelid movable, scaly. Ear-aperture absent, represented by a depression. Teeth conical and recurved. Scales smooth, glossy. Adults sombrely marked but juveniles vividly patterned with bands or stripes.

Fossorial skinks which dwell in rotting logs, beneath leaf-litter and in loose soil. The distinctive teeth, similar to those of a monitor lizard, may be associated with a diet composed largely of earthworms. At least one species is an egglayer.

Distinguished from *Ophioscincus* in bearing more upper labial scales (6 vs 5). Southern species (*C. reticulatus*) differs from *Anomalopus* and further from *Ophioscincus* in bearing 3 digits on each limb.

Coeranoscincus frontalis (De Vis, 1888)
Photos 311, 312

Description Large, completely limbless *Coeranoscincus*. Tail moderately short and blunt. Pattern prominent on juveniles, fading to virtual absence on adults. Dorsal ground colour of juveniles dark greyish brown. Pale lateral edges to dorsal scales form narrow lines from nape to tail-tip. White upper lateral stripe (broadest anteriorly) extends from neck to base of tail. Black lower lateral stripe extends from neck to tail-tip, sometimes breaking into vertical bars beyond hips. Top of head white, blotched with brown. Side of head and edges of throat grey; continuous with lower lateral stripe. Neck white, bearing a dark blotch or vertical bar, centred on ear-depression. Ventral surfaces white. Adults are yellowish brown to brown, sometimes retaining some indication of a pale flush on head and neck, a dark blotch on ear depression, and a dark lateral stripe. Flanks and ventral surfaces orange-yellow. SVL 290 mm.

Preferred habitat Rainforests on coastal ranges and lowlands of north-eastern Qld, from about Thornton Peak south to Mt Spec.

Microhabitat See genus.

Comments See genus.

Coeranoscincus reticulatus (Günther, 1873)
Photo 313

Description Limbs present, each bearing 3 digits. Tail moderately long; tapering at tip. Pattern prominent on juveniles; fading to virtual absence on adults. Juveniles are cream, pale orange to brownish grey, marked with irregular blackish brown transverse bars; most conspicuous anteriorly and often absent posteriorly. Dark blotch on top of head is often continuous with a patch encircling eye. Snout cream. Dark bar on nape is usually continuous with a blotch centred on ear depression. Scales on flanks bear darker lateral margins, forming irregular longitudinal streaks. Adults are brown, yellowish brown to grey (immaculate bluish grey on lowland populations from Cooloola and Fraser Island, Qld), sometimes retaining vague indications of bands. Dark eye patch, ear marking and pale snout are usually retained. Ventral surfaces greyish, each scale dark-edged, forming fine reticulum. SVL 195 mm.

Preferred habitat Rainforests and wet sclerophyll forests from about Grafton, north-eastern NSW, north to Fraser Island, Qld. Most localities are high altitudes on rich dark soils but those from lowlands (Cooloola and Fraser Island) occur on pale sandy soils.

Microhabitat Shelters beneath and in rotting logs, and under deep mats of leaf-litter.

Comments Clutches of 2–6 eggs recorded. See genus.

Snake-eyed Skinks, Fence or Wall Lizards
Genus *CRYPTOBLEPHARUS*
Wiegmann, 1834

Large widespread genus extending from east coast of Africa to eastern Indonesia, New Guinea, Micronesia, Melanesia and Polynesia. This broad distribution, including many isolated oceanic islands, indicates the likely ability of *Cryptoblepharus* to disperse by rafting. Represented in Australia by 6 species, occupying between them virtually the entire continent. Absent only from cool wet south-east, deep south-west and parts of the eastern highlands.

Small dorsally depressed skinks with long limbs, each bearing 5 digits. Eye large, bearing immovable lower eyelid fused to form a spectacle. Scales smooth and glossy.

Cryptoblepharus are swift, agile sun-loving skinks which favour exposed vertical surfaces of tree trunks and rock faces. Crevices and exfoliations are used for shelter. Construction of towns and cities has probably proven advantageous to some species, particularly *C. plagiocephalus* and *C. virgatus*, by providing additional suitable habitats such as fences and walls of buildings. Arthropod feeders. Egglayers, producing small clutches.

Distinguished from *Carlia* in bearing more fingers

(5 vs 4). Differs from *Leiolopisma*, *Lampropholis*, and further from all *Carlia* except *C. foliorum* by nature of lower eyelid (fused to form a spectacle, vs movable, bearing a transparent disc). Differs from *Morethia* by build (strongly dorsally depressed vs relatively deep bodied).

Cryptoblepharus carnabyi Storr, 1976
Photo 314

Description Dorsal ground colour coppery brown, brown, olive-brown to greyish brown, lightly to heavily flecked with black and spotted with pale brown. Laterodorsal series of blackish brown spots (sometimes coalescing anteriorly to form irregular stripe) extend from above eye onto tail. Broad to narrow ragged-edged pale brown to cream dorsolateral stripe extends from eye to tail-tip. Narrow ragged-edged blackish brown upper lateral zone extends from snout or eye to hips, usually becoming broken on tail. This frequently encloses a few pale brown spots or flecks. Lower lateral zone paler shade of ground colour, finely peppered with blackish brown and greyish white. Top of head coppery brown, lightly to heavily flecked with blackish brown. Ventral surfaces white, lightly peppered with brown on tail. SVL 40 mm.

Distinguished from all Australian *Cryptoblepharus* by nature of subdigital lamellae (finely keeled vs smooth). Differs further from *C. plagiocephalus* in usually bearing more supraciliary scales (5 vs 6; rarely 5). Differs further from *C. megastictus* in bearing a pale dorsolateral stripe (vs small dark blotches scattered over dorsum). Differs further from *C. virgatus* by nature of dorsolateral stripe (often obscure and fragmented and usually ragged-edged vs prominent and straight-edged).

Preferred habitat Subhumid to arid areas from western interior and coast of WA, through southern Kimberley region, northern NT and northern Qld, south through eastern interior of NSW (west of Great Dividing Range) to north-western Vic. Usually associated with woodlands and dry sclerophyll forests through most of range. In WA, occurs in highest density on limestone-based offshore islands and similar areas on adjacent mainland, where competition with *C. plagiocephalus* is reduced. Many Qld populations extend onto rock outcrops.

Microhabitat Predominantly arboreal and rock-inhabiting. Populations from some islands off WA are wholly terrestrial, foraging and sheltering among limestone crevices and reef debris. Otherwise as for genus.

Comments See genus.

Cryptoblepharus fuhni
Covacevich and Ingram, 1978
Photo 315

Description Moderately large relatively long-limbed *Cryptoblepharus* with ground colour of black to blackish brown. Paravertebral series of brownish dashes extend from nape to hips. Prominent dorsolateral series of white dots and dashes extend from nape to tail-tip. On juveniles these join to form lines on body. Flanks prominently marked with several series of longitudinally oriented pale dashes. Top of head coppery brown, heavily to lightly blotched with black. Ventral surfaces white. Soles of feet black. SVL 45 mm.

Preferred habitat Apparently restricted to large black boulders of Melville Range, Cape Melville, on subhumid eastern Cape York Peninsula, Qld.

Microhabitat Rock-inhabiting.

Comments Apparently most active during morning and late afternoon, retiring to shade during heat of day.

Cryptoblepharus litoralis (Mertens, 1958)
Photo 316

Description Large slender relatively long-limbed *Cryptoblepharus* with dorsal ground colour of coppery brown to dark greyish brown. Mid-dorsal area heavily flecked with black, and sparsely to heavily flecked with yellowish brown. Broad to narrow, ragged-edged dorsolateral stripe extends from above eye onto base of tail, often broken, and sometimes black-edged anteriorly. Flanks blackish brown from eye to hips, usually flecked with copper to yellowish brown. Head flushed with copper. Ventral surfaces white to grey; shining black on soles of feet. SVL 55 mm.

Distinguished from *C. virgatus* by pattern (pale dorsolateral stripe ragged-edged, often broken and poorly defined, vs prominent and straight-edged). Differs further in bearing much longer limbs and digits, and in attaining greater maximum size (SVL 55 vs 40 mm). Differs from *C. plagiocephalus* by colour of skin visible between scales on soles of feet (dark vs pale).

Preferred habitat Rocky coastlines of northeastern Qld from Gladstone district north on east coast of Cape York Peninsula to Torres Strait Islands. Disjunct populations occur on Oxley, New Year and Cape Wessel Islands off northern NT. Extralimital in New Guinea.

Microhabitat Forages on exposed coastal rocks, including those in splash zone. Shelters in crevices.

Comments Recorded to feed on small marine invertebrates, such as amphipods and polychaete worms.

Cryptoblepharus megastictus Storr, 1976
Photo 317

Description Very strongly dorsally depressed, long-limbed *Cryptoblepharus* with ground colour of pale to rich coppery brown. Pattern (when present) consists of large to small blackish brown spots, sometimes mixed with paler flecks. These may become larger, more prominent and less regular on lower lateral surfaces, and transversely aligned on dorsal surface of tail. Ventral surfaces white. SVL 40 mm.

Distinguished from *C. carnabyi* by pattern (pale dorsolateral stripes absent vs present), build (more strongly dorsally depressed with longer limbs), and nature of subdigital lamellae (smooth vs finely keeled).

Preferred habitat Subhumid to semi-arid rock outcrops, gorges and escarpments from northern Kimberley region, WA, across northern NT to north-western Qld.

Microhabitat Forages on exposed rock faces, extending onto splash zone on some islands off coast of Kimberley region, WA.

Comments As for genus.

Cryptoblepharus plagiocephalus
(Cocteau, 1836)
Photos 318, 319

Description Variable *Cryptoblepharus* with dorsal ground colour of grey, greyish brown to pale coppery brown. Pattern prominent to virtually absent. Populations from Kimberley region, WA, are simply dotted with brown and black. In remainder of range, mid-dorsal region is heavily to lightly flecked with black and pale grey. Broken black laterodorsal stripe or series of blotches and ragged-edged pale grey dorsolateral stripe usually extend from above eye to base of tail. Ragged-edged black upper lateral zone extends from snout onto side of tail, usually enclosing irregular pale flecks. Lower lateral zone grey, flecked with black and pale grey. Top of head grey to coppery brown, usually flecked with black. Head scales may be narrowly edged with black. Ventral surfaces white. SVL 45 mm.

Distinguished from *C. carnabyi* in usually bearing more supraciliary scales (6, rarely 5 vs 5), and by nature of subdigital lamellae (smooth or bluntly keeled vs finely keeled). Differs from *C. virgatus* by pattern (pale dorsolateral stripe ragged-edged or absent vs straight-edged and prominent). Differs from *C. litoralis* by colour of skin visible between scales on soles of feet (pale vs dark).

Preferred habitat Occurs throughout northern and western Australia, extending south on east coast to the vicinity of Rockhampton, Qld. Absent from eastern interior, and cool moist areas of south and deep south-west. Favours woodlands, dry sclerophyll forests, rock outcrops and man-made structures such as fences and walls of buildings.

Microhabitat Arboreal and rock-inhabiting. See genus.

Comments See genus.

Cryptoblepharus virgatus (Garman, 1901)
Photos 320, 321

Description Comprises 2 subspecies.
C. v. virgatus Dorsal ground colour coppery brown, reddish brown, greyish brown to grey. Broad black laterodorsal stripes extend from above eye to hips or onto tail. In far north Qld these tend to be widely spaced leaving a broad strip of ground colour at least 2 scales wide. Throughout remainder of range ground colour is usually restricted to a narrow vertebral zone; occasionally obscured completely. Prominent cream to silvery white dorsolateral stripe (often tinged with copper anteriorly) extends from above eye (occasionally snout) to hips or tail-tip. Upper lateral zone black, from snout to tail-tip. Lower lateral zone grey, flecked with white. Top of head coppery brown, flecked with black. Ventral surfaces white. SVL 40 mm.

C. v. clarus (Storr, 1961) Differs from dark south-eastern populations of nominate form by paler overall colouration.

Distinguished from *C. litoralis*, *C. plagiocephalus* and *C. carnabyi* by nature of pattern (prominent straight-edged dark laterodorsal and pale dorsolateral stripes vs stripes ragged-edged to broken; sometimes absent on *C. plagiocephalus*). Differs further from *C. litoralis* in attaining smaller maximum size (SVL 40 vs 55 mm), and further from *C. carnabyi* by nature of subdigital lamellae (smooth vs finely keeled).

Preferred habitat Wide variety of semi-arid to subhumid lowland habitats including woodlands, dry sclerophyll forests, mangroves, rock outcrops and urban areas. *C. v. virgatus* extends from south-eastern NSW north to Cape York Peninsula and Torres Strait Islands, Qld. Extralimital in southern New Guinea. It penetrates well into central areas of cities such as Sydney and Brisbane. *C. v. clarus* occurs in near-coastal and coastal woodlands, heathlands and rock outcrops from southern WA to western SA.

Microhabitat Arboreal and rock-inhabiting. See genus.

Comments In some areas *C. virgatus* occurs beside *C. plagiocephalus* with no apparent ecological separation. For example both dwell together on coastal trees at Townsville, Qld. In southern WA however, *C. plagiocephalus* occurs on Wonberna Rock, and *C. v. clarus* is present 18 km to the north-east, on Balladonia Rock. Probably active throughout year, mating during spring and summer in south.

Genus *CTENOTUS* Storr, 1964

Australia's largest reptile genus, containing 81 described species, and numerous subspecies. Future work will no doubt alter this already substantial number. Extends virtually throughout continent, excepting Tas., south-eastern Vic. and alpine areas. At least one species is extralimital in southern New Guinea. Greatest diversity occurs in arid to semi-arid regions, particularly where hummock grasses (*Triodia* and *Plectrachne*) occur. Absent from rainforests, and rarely occurring in wet sclerophyll forests.

Small to moderately large, slender to robust skinks with long tapering tails. Limbs well developed, each bearing 5 digits. Eye large, with movable scaly lower eyelid. Ear opening prominent, bearing distinct anterior lobules. Lobules may be absent on *C. essingtonii brevipes*. Scales smooth and shiny. Pattern usually consists of either stripes, or stripes in combination with longitudinally aligned series of spots (often subject to considerable variation within species). A few species display little or no pattern.

Not surprisingly, this large genus of similarly patterned skinks has proven confusing to naturalists. Some species can be readily identified by colour, alignment of pattern, size, build, habitats exploited, and distribution. Others can only be identified (with relative certainty) using scale characters. Individual variation in some species may hinder positive identification.

Swift, diurnal sun-loving skinks. Terrestrial. Egglaying.

Very little work has been undertaken on the ecology of any *Ctenotus*. E. R. Pianka studied sympatric species in southern deserts of WA. He found competition is minimised by differing daily and seasonal activity periods, prey item sizes, and foraging patterns. Some favour open areas while others seek food largely in the cover of grasses and shrubs. Open foraging species tend to have proportionally longer limbs.

Pianka's studies took place in areas where the greatest number of species in a genus occur together anywhere in Australia. Activity cycles of those with ranges extending beyond his study area will no doubt be influenced by other climatic factors, and competition from different taxa. Further ecological work is greatly needed, considering *Ctenotus* comprises approximately one-sixth of Australia's lizard fauna. The high proportion of very closely related species and large numbers of subspecies suggests *Ctenotus* may still be undergoing radiation.

Twelve species groups are tentatively recognised.

C. leonhardii group Contains 18 taxa of small to moderately large *Ctenotus* (SVL 45–90 mm). Pattern usually complex, comprising dorsal stripes, and one or more rows of pale lateral spots. Widely distributed over semi-arid to arid Australia, particularly on hard or stony soils (rarely outcrops or ranges) supporting sparse low ground cover. Most are relatively long-limbed open foragers, seeking shelter in soil cracks, beneath rocks or in shallow burrows concealed under low vegetation. Group comprises *C. alleni, C. gagudju, C. greeri, C. hebetior hebetior, C. hebetior schuettleri, C. joanae, C. kurnbudj, C. leonhardii, C. militaris, C. mimetes, C. pulchellus, C. regius, C. rutilans, C. serventyi, C. tanamiensis, C. uber johnstonei, C. uber orientalis* and *C. uber uber*.
C. lesueurii group Contains 23 taxa of medium-sized to very large *Ctenotus* (SVL 50–120 mm).

Pattern usually prominent, typically including pale-edged dark vertebral stripe, broad brownish dorsal region, and dark upper lateral zone enclosing pale spots or blotches; occasionally coalesced to form a pale upper lateral stripe. A few bear simple striped patterns. Others may lack pattern completely, particularly on large adults. Widespread throughout Australia, though most successful in temperate to subhumid tropical areas. One species extends north to southern New Guinea. Most are relatively long-limbed open foragers, sheltering in shallow burrows, beneath rocks, logs and other surface debris. Contains *C. arcanus, C. arnhemensis, C. borealis, C. brachyonyx, C. coggeri, C. eurydice, C. eutaenius, C. fallens, C. helenae, C. ingrami, C. inornatus, C. lateralis, C. lesueurii, C. rawlinsoni, C. robustus, C. saxatilis, C. severus, C. spaldingi, C. taeniolatus* and *C. vertebralis*. *C. capricorni, C. mastigura* and *C. monticola* are tentatively included.

C. colletti group Contains 8 taxa of small to medium-sized slender long-snouted *Ctenotus* (SVL 40–60 mm) with simple patterns of dark and pale stripes. Occurs largely in sandy or stony regions with dominant ground cover of hummock grasslands over much of arid Australia, extending into subhumid north-eastern Qld and north-western Kimberley region, WA. Most prefer to forage along margins of low vegetation, though some frequently utilise open spaces. Group contains *C. calurus, C. colletti colletti, C. colletti nasutus, C. colletti rufescens, C. ehmanni, C. leae, C. striaticeps* and *C. zebrilla*.
C. schevilli group Contains 3 species marked with numerous pale spots over olive ground colour. Members occur on arid stony soils or deeply cracked dark clays (black soil) of central and south-western Qld, sheltering in deep soil cracks. Group contains *C. astarte, C. schevilli* and *C. serotinus*.
C. quinkan group Tentatively recognised, containing one very large species bearing a simple pattern: pale dorsolateral stripes, and black flanks enclosing a pale midlateral stripe. Restricted to sandstone escarpments of lower eastern Cape York Peninsula, Qld.
C. rubicundus group Contains one large robust virtually patternless species with reddish brown ground colour. Restricted to Pilbara region, WA.
C. atlas group Comprises 14 species of small to medium-sized *Ctenotus* (SVL 40–65 mm), usually bearing a simple pattern of pale stripes on dark ground colour. Row of pale spots on upper lateral surfaces may also be present. Widely distributed throughout northern and arid Australia, especially in areas dominated by hummock grasslands. Sand ridges, sand plains, rocky outcrops and ranges are favoured. Most prefer to forage close to protective cover of vegetation, sheltering beneath hummock grasses or in shallow burrows. Group contains *C. alacer, C. ariadnae, C. atlas, C. decaneurus, C. duricola, C. dux, C. iapetus, C. impar, C. piankai, C. quattuordecimlineatus, C. storri, C. yampiensis, C.*

xenopleura and *C. zastictus*.

C. labillardieri group Comprises 6 species of medium-sized to moderately large *Ctenotus* (SVL 55–80 mm). Patterns are simple to complex, never consisting solely of dark and pale stripes. Dark vertebral stripe usually absent (irregular, without pale edge when present). Restricted to south-western Australia. Habitat preferences range from wet sclerophyll forest (unusual in genus) to rock outcrops and coastal dunes. Tolerance of some members to cool damp conditions, coupled with restricted south-westerly occurrence, may be evidence of the primitive nature of this group. Most do not forage widely on open ground, preferring at least partial cover. Contains *C. catenifer, C. delli, C. gemmula, C. labillardieri, C. lancelini* and *C. youngsoni*.

C. pantherinus group Contains 1 large robust species comprising 4 subspecies. Pattern consists mainly or wholly of dark-edged pale ocelli. An arid-adapted inhabitant of open areas dominated by hummock grasses. Members are *C. pantherinus pantherinus, C. pantherinus acripes, C. pantherinus calx* and *C. pantherinus ocellifer*.

C. grandis group Contains 3 taxa of moderately large to very large *Ctenotus* (SVL 70–120 mm) with dorsal pattern consisting of 5 dark stripes, and lateral pattern of pale flecks. Occurs in hummock grassland associations in arid zone of WA and adjacent NT. Contains *C. grandis grandis, C. grandis titan* and *C. hanloni*.

C. essingtonii group Contains 4 taxa of small to medium-sized (SVL 45–60 mm) slender *Ctenotus* with brown to olive dorsal ground colour, vertebral stripe reduced to absent, and dark upper lateral zone (with or without series of pale spots). Restricted to subhumid far northern Australia. Contains *C. burbidgei, C. essingtonii brevipes, C. essingtonii essingtonii* and *C. hilli*.

C. schomburgkii group Contains 11 taxa of small slender long-snouted *Ctenotus* (SVL 45–55 mm) with simple to complex patterns of spots, or stripes and spots. Upper lateral zone dark enclosing pale spots, or represented by rectangular vertical bars. Occurs throughout semi-arid to arid regions. Most prefer low sparse vegetation on sand plains, sand ridges or open stony soils, usually seeking shelter in shallow burrows at bases of tussocks, grass hummocks or shrubs. While some seldom venture far from cover, others forage widely into open spaces between plants. Contains *C. allotropis, C. brooksi aranda, C. brooksi brooksi, C. brooksi euclae, C. brooksi iridis, C. brooksi taeniata, C. pallescens, C. schomburgkii, C. strauchii strauchii, C. strauchii varius* and *C. tantillus*.

Ctenotus is distinguished from *Sphenomorphus* and *Eremiascincus* in bearing ear lobules, though these may be absent on *C. essingtonii brevipes*. Differs further from *Eremiascincus* by alignment of pattern (predominantly longitudinal vs transverse). Differs

from *Egernia* by arrangement of parietal scales (in contact behind interparietal scale vs separated by interparietal). Differs further by build (usually more slender, with longer tail), and in usually attaining smaller size. Superficially similar to striped members of the genera *Morethia, Notoscincus* and *Proablepharus*, differing by nature of lower eyelid (movable and scaly vs fused to form a transparent spectacle).

Ctenotus alacer Storr, 1970
Photo 322

Description Member of *C. atlas* group with 10 pale stripes and prominently spotted flanks. Dorsal ground colour black, marked with 6 brown to reddish brown and white stripes. Populations living on reddish substrates bear correspondingly darker stripes. White to reddish brown paravertebral and brownish dorsal stripes extend from above eye onto base of tail. White dorsolateral stripe extends from above eye onto base of tail, becoming broader beyond hips. Broad black upper lateral zone from eye to middle of tail encloses 1 series of oblong white spots, usually coalescing behind eye to form a vague stripe. White midlateral stripe (sometimes broken anteriorly) extends from upper lip well onto base of tail. White ventrolateral stripe extends from behind ear to base of tail. Limbs reddish brown striped with blackish brown. Ventral surfaces white. SVL 60 mm.

Preferred habitat Subhumid to arid areas from western Qld to southern NT and adjacent WA. Isolated population occurs in east Kimberley region, WA, and adjacent NT. Favours rocky hills and ranges.
Microhabitat Excavates a shallow depression under rocks embedded in soil, or shelters in burrows beneath hummock grasses.
Comments As for species group.

Ctenotus alleni Storr, 1974
Photo 323

Description Large member of *C. leonhardii* group with olive-brown dorsal ground colour. Vertebral stripe absent or reduced to a line on nape. Black laterodorsal stripe extends from above eye to base of tail. White dorsolateral stripe extends from eye to base of tail, becoming suffused with brown posteriorly. Upper lateral zone blackish, enclosing 1 or 2 series of pale dots or short dashes. Pale midlateral stripe extends from forelimb nearly to end of tail. Lower lateral zone blackish brown enclosing 1 or 2 irregular series of short dashes. Limbs brown, streaked with black. Tail paler shade of ground colour. Ventral surfaces white. SVL 90 mm.

Distinguished from *C. mimetes* by dark upper lateral zone enclosing small whitish spots (vs large, reddish rectangular blotches) and by pale midlateral stripe not extending forward beyond forelimb (vs extending to lips). Differs from *C. severus* by pale dorsolateral stripe contacting dark upper lateral zone (vs separated by a narrow strip of ground colour). Differs from *C. uber* in lacking pale spots within dark laterodorsal stripe.

Preferred habitat Semi-arid interior of lower midwest coast, from the vicinity of lower Murchison River drainage south to Yuna district, WA. Favours woodland/heathland associations on yellowish sandy soils.

Microhabitat Probably as for species group.

Comments See species group.

Ctenotus allotropis Storr, 1981
Photo 324

Description Sharply patterned member of *C. schomburgkii* group. Dorsal ground colour brown, becoming paler and more reddish or yellowish on tail. Black laterodorsal stripe extends from eye onto base of tail, enclosing a series of reddish brown to brownish white spots or dashes. Narrow white dorsolateral stripe extends from eye to hips, becoming wider and pale reddish to yellowish brown from base, nearly to tip of tail. Upper lateral zone black. This encloses 2 or 3 series of pinkish to pale reddish brown vertically aligned spots from eye to hips or well onto tail, and continues to tip as a broken to continuous, ragged- or sharp-edged black line. Prominent white midlateral stripe extends from upper lip (broken or wavy to midbody) to base of tail. Lower flanks blackish brown, obscurely dotted with white. Limbs pale brown, striped with blackish brown. Ventral surfaces white. SVL 50 mm.

Distinguished from *C. schomburgkii* and *C. strauchii* in lacking a dark vertebral stripe (present on both within zone of overlap).

Preferred habitat Eucalypt and/or *Acacia* woodlands in association with hummock grasses or chenopod shrubs on heavy loams, gravels or sandy soils. Extends from semi-arid central NSW to subhumid south-eastern interior of Qld.

Microhabitat Readily seeks shelter in abandoned spider burrows and ant nests, or beneath low prickly vegetation.

Comments See species group.

Ctenotus arcanus Czechura and Wombey, 1982
Photos 325, 326

Description Member of *C. lesueurii* group. Dorsal ground colour olive-brown to coppery brown. Pale-edged dark vertebral stripe extends from nape onto base of tail; most prominent on juveniles and often absent on large adults. Narrow whitish dorsolateral stripe (bordered on body by broader black laterodorsal stripe) extends from above eye to end of tail. Black upper lateral zone extends from in front of eye to hips; represented on tail by a dark stripe, sometimes faded to leave upper and lower margins only. This encloses a series of well-spaced sharp white dots on body. White midlateral stripe extends

from upper lip, curving over ear to base of tail. Lower lateral surfaces brownish black, obscurely spotted with white. Limbs reddish brown to olive, striped with black. On Stradbroke and Moreton Islands pattern is greatly reduced. Pale lateral spots smaller and fragmented into several series. Ventral surfaces whitish; pale yellowish brown beneath tail. SVL 85 mm.

Distinguished from *C. taeniolatus* and *C. eurydice* in bearing fewer pale stripes (pale lower lateral stripe usually absent vs present). Differs further in attaining larger maximum size (SVL 85 vs 65 and 75 mm, respectively). Differs from *C. robustus* by upper lateral pattern (black enclosing sharply defined pale spots vs olive-brown bearing diffuse pale spots).

Preferred habitat Stradbroke and Moreton Islands in Moreton Bay, eastern slopes of Great Dividing Range, coastal ranges and lowlands in south-eastern Qld. Extends from Kroombit Tops south to about Qld–NSW border. Occurs in heathlands or woodlands; occasionally margins of wet sclerophyll forest. On mainland, rock outcrops are favoured, particularly by northern and western populations. Island populations occur on white sands supporting woodlands, especially when these margin swamps or freshwater lakes.

Microhabitat Often excavates short tunnels in soil beneath stones or rock slabs. Forages among low vegetation, stones and fallen timbers.

Comments One of the few *Ctenotus* to occur on wet sclerophyll forest margins. Limited clearing (including road construction) has created corridors into areas which were previously too densely vegetated. Otherwise as for species group.

Ctenotus ariadnae Storr, 1969
Photo 327

Description Member of *C. atlas* group with 18–20 pale stripes. Ground colour dark brown to blackish on adults; black on juveniles. All dorsal stripes well defined, becoming increasingly ill defined on flanks, especially anteriorly. Pale brown paravertebral line extends from nape to middle of tail. Pale brown dorsal line extends from nape to base of tail. Whitish dorsolateral line extends from temple or ear well onto tail, becoming wider and browner beyond hips. Three to 4 brown upper lateral lines present; upper 1 or 2 extending forward irregularly, nearly to ear; lower pair to, or just past, forelimb. White midlateral stripe usually narrow and indistinct; not extending forward beyond forelimb. Indistinct pale lower lateral and ventrolateral lines sometimes present. Head olive-grey to brown. Limbs and tail pale reddish brown. Ventral surfaces white, bearing greyish lateral margins to ventral, and occasionally throat, scales. SVL 60 mm.

Distinguished from *C. dux* and *C. quattuordecimlineatus* by nature of lateral pattern (obscure and fragmented between ear and forelimb vs continuous and relatively more prominent). Differs further from *C. quattuordecimlineatus*, and from *C. atlas*, in bearing greater number of pale stripes (18 or 20 vs 14 or 16, and 8 or 10, respectively).

Preferred habitat Sand ridges and sand plains vegetated with hummock grass associations from arid central interior of WA to south-western Qld. These two populations may be disjunct, though the intervening area has been poorly collected.

Microhabitat As for species group.

Comments Feeds largely on termites, though insects such as small grasshoppers are also taken. In WA breeding occurs from September till October, with a recorded clutch of 4 eggs.

Ctenotus arnhemensis Storr, 1981
Photo 328

Description Small strongly patterned member of *C. lesueurii* group. Dorsal ground colour brown, fading to pale brown on tail. Moderately broad white-edged black vertebral stripe extends from nape to base of tail. Narrow black laterodorsal stripe extends from eye, fading to brown on tail. White dorsolateral stripe (sometimes broken to a series of dashes on body) extends well onto tail. Black upper lateral zone (fading to brown on tail) encloses a line of white spots from eye to hindlimb. In far east of range these may coalesce to form an additional pale stripe. White midlateral stripe (sometimes broken between ear and forelimb) extends onto tail. This is represented anteriorly by 2 white spots on temple, and a lunate marking or pale dashes under eye. Lower lateral zone brownish, obscurely dotted with white. Limbs pale brown striped with blackish brown. Ventral surfaces white. SVL 55 mm.

Distinguished from *C. robustus* and *C. inornatus* in attaining much smaller average maximum size (SVL 50 vs 115 and 95 mm, respectively). Differs further from *C. inornatus*, and from *C. essingtonii* and *C. hilli* by nature of vertebral stripe (broad, strong and pale-edged vs absent or weak, lacking pale edge).

Preferred habitat Open grasslands and woodlands on coastal lowlands west of Arnhem Escarpment, NT. Disjunct population occurs on Gulf of Carpentaria.

Microhabitat Shelters in shallow burrows beneath rocks and dead vegetation.

Comments As for species group.

Ctenotus astarte Czechura, 1986
Photo 329

Description Medium-sized member of *C. schevilli* group with ground colour of greyish brown to yellowish brown. Dark vertebral stripe usually absent; narrow, ill-defined and ragged-edged when present. Dorsal pattern complex, comprising irregular small dark blotches, pale spots and dashes. Dark markings tend to concentrate mainly on mid-dorsal region. Pale markings may align to form irregular broken paravertebral and dorsolateral stripes, particularly on juveniles. Short dark-edged pale line extends from above eye to above ear. Upper lateral zone marked with several series of small white spots, tending to align vertically. Lower flanks grey, obscurely spotted with white. Limbs obscurely striped with dark brown. Ventral surfaces white. SVL 80 mm.

Distinguished from *C. serotinus* by greater size (SVL 80 vs 49 mm), and weaker, less regular pattern.

Preferred habitat Restricted to arid south-western Qld, from Durrie and Caddapan Stations, north to Boulia and Diamantina Lakes area. Occurs on heavy, often stony soils.

Microhabitat As for *C. schevilli* group.

Comments See genus and *C. schevilli* group.

Ctenotus atlas Storr, 1969
Photo 330

Description Moderately large member of *C. atlas* group with 8 or 10 pale stripes on black ground colour. Brownish white paravertebral stripe extends from nape to tail. White dorsolateral stripe extending from eye becomes browner and wider on base of tail. Brownish white upper lateral stripe extends from above and behind ear to base of tail. White midlateral stripe extends from ear to middle of tail, becoming browner and wider posteriorly. White ventrolateral stripe present or absent. Head and tail brown. Limbs brown, striped with blackish brown. Lower lips and ventral surfaces white. SVL 65 mm.

Distinguished from *C. impar* in lacking a pale vertebral stripe. Differs from *C. piankai* in bearing more pale stripes (upper lateral present vs absent). Differs from *C. dux*, *C. ariadnae* and *C. quattuordecimlineatus* in bearing fewer pale stripes (no more than 1 fully developed line between white dorsolateral and midlateral stripes vs 2 or more).

Preferred habitat Arid to semi-arid southern Australia, from upper Ashburton River, WA, to southern SA. Disjunct population extends from east of the Flinders Ranges, SA, into central NSW. Favours mallee/*Triodia* associations on sands or loams, occasionally stony soils.

Microhabitat As for species group.

Comments Feeds largely on termites, though other insects such as grasshoppers are also taken. Active throughout year, except during cooler periods from May till September. Normally forages during early part of day. Breeds from September to October, producing 1 or 2 eggs per clutch.

Ctenotus borealis Horner and King, 1985
Photo 331

Description Large member of *C. lesueurii* group with dorsal ground colour of brown. Pattern usually weak; more intense on juveniles. Black vertebral stripe usually present, sometimes absent or reduced to a series of spots and seldom pale-edged. Cream dorsolateral stripe usually absent; obscure and broken into spots when present. Flanks and sides of tail densely mottled with greyish brown. On juveniles lateral pattern is darker enclosing large cream blotches which tend to form vertical bars. Obscure broken pale midlateral stripe commences as a streak beneath eye, extending onto body and tail where it may become indiscernible on large individuals. Limbs brown, hindlimbs speckled with black. Ventral surfaces white. SVL 120 mm.

Distinguished from *C. robustus* by weaker pattern, in particular the absence of a prominent pale-edged black vertebral stripe, black laterodorsal stripe and continuous pale dorsolateral stripes. Differs further by hindlimb pattern (speckled vs striped).
Preferred habitat North-western NT, north of 15° south, and west from El Sharana along Arnhem Escarpment to Cobourg Peninsula. Occupies a variety of habitats, from woodlands to rock outcrops and consolidated sand dunes.
Microhabitat Recorded to shelter in deep burrows. See species group.
Comments As for genus.

Ctenotus brachyonyx Storr, 1971
Photo 332

Description Member of *C. lesueurii* group with reduced pattern. Dorsal ground colour pale or dark brown to grey. Moderately broad black vertebral stripe (usually without pale edge) extends from nape, terminating abruptly at base of tail. Broad to narrow black laterodorsal stripe extends from nape or shoulder to hips or onto tail. Whitish or pale to dark brown dorsolateral stripe extends from nape or shoulders onto tail. Upper lateral zone darker than dorsal colour, sometimes bearing blackish dots or white flecks. Indistinct pale midlateral stripe extends from forelimb or below eye to base of tail. Lower lateral zone paler than dorsal colour. Limbs patternless. Ventral surfaces whitish. SVL 80 mm.
Preferred habitat Favours mallee/*Triodia* associations in Murray River Valley of semi-arid north-western Vic., south-western NSW, and adjacent SA.
Microhabitat Usually shelters beneath *Triodia* hummocks.
Comments As for species group.

Ctenotus brooksi (Loveridge, 1933)
Photos 333–335

Description Highly variable member of *C. schomburgkii* group comprising 5 recognised subspecies.
C. b. brooksi Dorsal ground colour rich reddish brown, yellowish brown to coral red, fading to yellowish brown on tail and limbs. Narrow dark vertebral stripe from nape to base or middle of tail is distinct on juveniles, becoming obscure with age. Remainder of dorsum bears small dark spots which tend to align longitudinally, occasionally forming 4 broken wavy lines. Upper lateral zone bears a series

of dark squarish dots; represented on tail by a dark lateral stripe to tip. Eyre Peninsula population is unique in bearing an almost entirely black upper lateral zone. Limbs striped with brown to dark brown. Ventral surfaces white. SVL 50 mm.
C. b. aranda Storr, 1970 Differs from *C. b. brooksi* in bearing bolder pattern, including a pale-edged dark vertebral stripe, dark dorsal and laterodorsal stripes or variegations, and indications of pale dorsolateral and midlateral stripes. SVL 55 mm.
C. b. taeniatus (Mitchell, 1949) Similar to *C. b. aranda* but with brown (vs red) dorsal ground colour. SVL 50 mm.
C. b. euclae Storr, 1971 Ground colour silvery white to pinkish, bearing a narrow white-edged black vertebral stripe from nape onto base of tail. Four blackish dorsal stripes present; wavy and usually broken into variegations. Upper lateral zone blackish, enclosing a series of irregularly sized and shaped white dots. This zone extends anteriorly to snout as a narrow dark streak, and onto tail as a black lateral stripe to tip. Limbs ground colour boldly striped with black. SVL 50 mm.
C. b. iridis Storr, 1981 Ground colour pinkish brown, bearing a black vertebral stripe from nape to anterior half of tail. Black dorsal and laterodorsal stripes extend from above eye to hips, where they coalesce and terminate. Narrow pale dorsolateral stripe extends from above eye to base of tail. Upper lateral zone black, enclosing a series of whitish spots. This zone extends forward to snout as a narrow dark streak, and onto tail as a blackish brown stripe to tip. White midlateral stripe (broadest on body) extends from upper lip to base of tail. Narrow greyish brown lower lateral zone usually encloses small white spots. Limbs striped with black. SVL 50 mm.

With exception of the distinctively patterned *C. b. iridis*, subspecies of *C. brooksi* differ from *C. schomburgkii* by nature of pale dorsolateral stripe (poorly defined to absent vs prominent). Differs further by limb pattern (usually striped vs usually marbled).
Preferred habitat *C. b. brooksi* occurs on red sand ridges vegetated with hummock grasses, from interior of WA to south-western NT and north-western SA. *C. b. aranda* dwells on paler dunes vegetated with canegrass *(Zygochloa)* of Simpson Desert in south-eastern NT, north-eastern SA and south-western Qld. In contrast, sympatric *C. strauchii varius* favours hard to stony soils. *C. b. taeniatus* is only recorded from Lake Torrens Basin, SA. *C. b. euclae* occurs on white coastal dunes and sand plains on Great Australian Bight of SA and WA. *C. b. iridis* occurs on pale sand plains and ridges supporting mallee/heathland and *Triodia* associations in eastern SA and north-western Vic.
Microhabitat As for species group.
Comments For *C. b. brooksi* in interior of WA: Feeds on a variety of arthropods such as beetles, bugs, spiders and ants. Most active during cooler

times of year, normally emerging to forage during morning and late afternoon. Breeding usually occurs from September to October.

Ctenotus burbidgei Storr, 1975
Photo 336

Description Member of *C. essingtonii* group. Dorsal ground colour yellowish brown to greyish brown, rarely bearing a faint indication of a dark vertebral stripe from above eye onto base of tail. Upper lateral zone blackish, sometimes bearing a series of pale, circular to squarish spots. These may be sufficiently large to break upper lateral zone into irregular dark vertical bars. Obscure pale grey midlateral stripe, margined below by darker mottling, extends from behind ear to base of tail. Limbs streaked with blackish brown. Ventral surfaces white. SVL 55 mm.

Formerly treated as a subspecies of *C. mastigura*; differing by absence (or only faint indication) of a pale-edged dark vertebral stripe. Adults differ further by belly colour (white vs yellow).
Preferred habitat Associated with sandstone outcrops and escarpments of subhumid north-west Kimberley region, WA.
Microhabitat Shelters in shallow burrows beneath rocks.
Comments No data available.

Ctenotus calurus Storr, 1969
Photo 337

Description Member of *C. colletti* group with 8 narrow white stripes over a black ground colour. Paravertebral stripes extend from nape well onto tail. Dorsal stripes terminate at hips. Dorsolateral stripes extend from snout, over eye and well onto tail. Broader white midlateral stripe extends from snout onto base of tail. Head reddish brown, blotched and/or variegated with black. Forelimbs reddish brown streaked with black. Hindlimbs boldly striped with white and black. Tail bluish grey to blue. Ventral surfaces white, excepting black spots beneath toes, and black edges to scales under base of tail. SVL 50 mm.

Distinguished from *C. leae* and *C. colletti* by colour of tail (bluish vs reddish and brown, respectively).
Preferred habitat Hummock grassland associations in sandy deserts of central and southern interior of WA, and adjacent corners of NT and SA. One record from Exmouth Gulf region of WA.
Microhabitat Shelters among hummock grasses. Forages among litter and in open spaces between hummocks.
Comments When foraging, *C. calurus* may wave its conspicuous bluish tail in the same manner as many members of the genus *Carlia*. Feeds largely on termites, though other insect prey is also taken. Active throughout year; at least in interior of WA.

Usually forages from early morning till late afternoon.

Breeding occurs from September till October. Clutches of 2 and 4 eggs are recorded.

Ctenotus capricorni Storr, 1981
Photo 338

Description Tentatively included in *C. lesueurii* group. Dorsal ground colour olive-brown. Narrow to broad black vertebral stripe (margined by pale yellowish brown paravertebral stripes) extends from nape, fading on base of tail. Narrow indistinct pale brown dorsal stripe sometimes present. Obscure narrow blackish laterodorsal stripe extends from nape to base of tail. Narrow whitish dorsolateral stripe extends from above eye well onto tail, becoming broader and yellower beyond hips. Upper lateral zone pale greyish brown, enclosing a series of obscure white dots or dashes; 2 series sometimes present in front of forelimb. Greyish white midlateral stripe (boldest on posterior body) extends from ear or forelimb, narrowly above hindlimb, and well onto tail. Lower lateral zone pale greyish brown. Top of head olive-brown. Tail yellowish brown. Limbs olive-brown, obscurely streaked with greyish white. Ventral surfaces white. SVL 65 mm.

Distinguished from *C. robustus* in usually bearing a pale dorsal stripe, and in attaining smaller average maximum size (SVL 65 vs 115 mm).
Preferred habitat Sandy areas supporting *Triodia*, often in association with shrub and woodland communities in semi-arid mideastern interior of Qld.
Microhabitat Shelters in shallow burrows located beneath *Triodia* hummocks. Forages widely in open spaces between vegetation.
Comments As for species group.

Ctenotus catenifer Storr, 1974
Photo 339

Description Member of *C. labillardieri* group with dorsal ground colour of brown to olive-grey, flecked with black. Narrow irregular black vertebral stripe occasionally present. Broad black ragged-edged laterodorsal stripe (enclosing a series of white dashes) borders broken white dorsolateral stripe. Upper lateral zone black, enclosing white dots. Lower lateral zone pale grey, obscurely marbled and/ or blotched with darker pigment. Limbs brown, peppered with black. Tail pale olive, speckled laterally with black. Ventral surfaces white. SVL 55 mm.

Distinguished from *C. labillardieri* by limb pattern (finely spotted vs blotched). Differs from *C. delli* and *C. gemmula* in bearing black laterodorsal stripe enclosing white spots (vs laterodorsal stripe barely present, never enclosing white markings).
Preferred habitat Heathlands on coastal sands in lower south-western WA. Apparently disjunct

populations occur near Ravensthorpe and Badgin-garra.

Microhabitat Shelters in shallow burrows at bases of dense low ground cover.

Comments As for species group.

Ctenotus coggeri Sadlier, 1985
Photo 340

Description Member of *C. lesueurii* group with dorsal ground colour of immaculate brown. Black laterodorsal stripe extends from above eye to level with hindlimb. This is bordered by white dorso-lateral stripe which extends onto tail, becoming dif-fuse beyond hips. Upper lateral zone black, immaculate except for several diffuse pale spots in vicinity of forelimb. White midlateral stripe, wavy and diffuse from ear-aperture to midbody, extends through hindlimb onto tail. Lower flanks suffused with grey; mottled grey and black anteriorly. Limbs brown, hindlimbs marked with prominent lighter stripes. Ventral surfaces yellow from throat to base of tail. SVL 80 mm.

Distinguished from *C. inornatus* by position of pale midlateral stripe (extending continuously through hindlimb vs passing above hindlimb). Dif-fers further (at least within zone of overlap) in lack-ing any indication of a pale-edged black vertebral stripe.

Preferred habitat Known only from sandstone outcroppings in Arnhem Land, NT: on outliers of Djwamba massif and Mt Brockman east to Mann River. Associated with woodlands on boulder slopes and on rocky areas of sandstone plateaux.

Microhabitat See genus and *C. lesueurii* group.

Comments As for genus.

Ctenotus colletti (Boulenger, 1896)
Photos 341, 342

Description Sharp-snouted member of *C. colletti* group with pattern consisting of 8 or 12 pale stripes. Three subspecies recognised.

C. c. colletti Ground colour dark brown with 12 brownish white stripes. Narrow paravertebral stripes extend from nape onto tail, and 4 narrow dorsal stripes extend to hips or base of tail. These are separated by dark interspaces of approximately equal width. White dorsolateral stripe extends from above eye, well onto tail. Upper lateral zone black-ish brown, from snout nearly to tail-tip. Moderately broad midlateral stripe extends from upper lip to groin. Moderately broad ventrolateral stripe extends from forelimb to hindlimb. Limbs pale brown striped with dark brown. Ventral surfaces white. SVL 45 mm.

C. c. rufescens Storr, 1979 Bears 12 pale stripes. Differs from nominate form in bearing a reddish suffusion on foreback, and by dark upper lateral zone splitting into 2 on temple.

C. c. nasutus Storr, 1969 Bears 8 pale stripes (pa-

ravertebrals, dorsals, dorsolaterals and midlaterals). Broad black vertebral stripe extends from nape well onto tail.

Distinguished from *C. calurus* and *C. leae* by colour of tail (brown vs bluish and reddish, respectively). Differs further from *C. leae* in bearing fewer ear lobules (2, rarely 3; the uppermost largest; vs 2–5; approximately equal in size).

Preferred habitat *C. c. colletti* occurs in semi-arid south-west Kimberley region, WA, from La Grange north to Beagle Bay. One specimen was collected on red sandy soils of a creek bed. *C. c. nasutus* occurs in hummock grass associations on sand ridges and interdunes in eastern deserts of WA and adjacent NT. *C. c. rufescens* favours similar habitats in North West Cape area, WA.

Microhabitat *C. c. nasutus* and *C. c. rufescens* shel-ter beneath hummock grasses. No data available for *C. c. colletti*; represented in museum collections by only a small number of specimens.

Comments Spiders constitute the bulk of prey identified from stomachs of *C. c. nasutus*. Native silverfish, insect larvae and other small invertebrates are also recorded. In interior of WA, *C. c. nasutus* appears to be most active from late autumn to mid-summer, usually during late morning and early afternoon. Clutch of 2 eggs recorded.

Ctenotus decaneurus Storr, 1970
Photo 343

Description Small member of *C. atlas* group, usually marked with 10 pale stripes (8 when ventro-laterals are missing; 12 when 2 dorsals are present). Ground colour dark coppery brown to black. Para-vertebral stripes extend from base of head onto tail. Dorsal stripes extend from base of head, terminating at hips. Dorsolateral stripe extends from above eye, well onto tail. Midlateral stripe extends from be-neath eye, over ear to hindlimb and well onto tail. Lower lateral stripe extends from about ear to hind-limb or well onto tail. Top of head (and usually tail) flushed with brown. Limbs striped with black, and white to reddish brown. Ventral surfaces white. SVL 45 mm.

Distinguished from *C. piankai* in bearing greater number of pale stripes (8–12 vs 6 or occasionally 8). Differs further in favouring stony (vs sandy) soils. Differs from *C. storri* in bearing distinct paravertebral stripes (vs coalesced; at least on nape and hips, and occasionally throughout their length). Differs from *C. yampiensis* in bearing fewer midbody scale rows (24–26 vs 30–32).

Preferred habitat Rocky hills from subhumid north-western NT and north-eastern Kimberley region, WA, to arid western Qld. Favours ground cover of grasses, particularly hummock grasses in drier parts of range.

Microhabitat Shelters in shallow burrows be-neath rocks or low vegetation.

Comments As for species group.

Ctenotus delli Storr, 1974
Photo 344

Description Member of *C. labillardieri* group. Dorsal ground colour uniform dark coppery brown. Narrow black laterodorsal stripe and white dorso-lateral stripe (broken to form a series of white dashes) extend from above eye to base of tail. Upper lateral zone black, marked with scattered white dots. White midlateral stripe is represented by a series of dashes. Limbs brown, finely peppered with black. Tail brown, speckled laterally with black. Ventral surfaces white. SVL 60 mm.

Distinguished from *C. labillardieri* and *C. gemmula* by pattern on limbs (peppered vs marbled). Differs further from *C. labillardieri* by nature of dorsolateral stripe (broken vs continuous). Differs from *C. catenifer* in lacking white spots within black laterodorsal stripe.

Preferred habitat Jarrah/marri eucalypt associations over a sparse to dense, shrub-dominated understorey on lateritic, sandy and clay soils of Darling Range, south-western WA.

Microhabitat Shelters beneath small rocks and low vegetation, or in abandoned ant nests and shallow burrows.

Comments As for species group.

Ctenotus duricola Storr, 1975
Photo 345

Description Member of *C. atlas* group with 6–8 white to brownish white stripes on black to dark reddish brown ground colour. Brownish white paravertebral stripe from nape, and dorsolateral stripe from behind eye, extend well onto tail. Broad dark upper lateral zone usually encloses one series of small brownish white spots, becoming indistinct posteriorly; sometimes only vaguely represented anteriorly. Broad white midlateral stripe (often broken anteriorly) extends from under eye onto tail. White ventrolateral stripe usually present (sometimes broken anteriorly), extending from below ear well onto base of tail. Head and tail brown. Limbs pale reddish brown. Forelimbs streaked, and hindlimbs striped, with dark brown. Ventral surfaces white. SVL 60 mm.

Distinguished from closely allied *C. piankai* in usually bearing white spots in upper lateral zone, and usually more numerous midbody scale rows (26–32 vs 24–26). Differs from *C. iapetus* in bearing fewer pale stripes (6–8 vs 12).

Preferred habitat Hard clay or stony soils vegetated with *Triodia* on north-west coast and adjacent interior of WA, including Barrow Island. In contrast, *C. piankai* favours sandy soils.

Microhabitat Shelters under rock slabs, in shallow burrows and among *Triodia* hummocks.

Comments As for species group.

Ctenotus dux Storr, 1969
Photo 346

Description Member of *C. atlas* group, usually marked with 20 pale stripes. Dorsal colour brown, tinged with reddish brown to olive. Prominent pale-edged black vertebral stripe extends from nape to base of tail. Black laterodorsal stripe (margined narrowly above with pale brown) extends from behind eye onto base of tail. Prominent narrow white dorsolateral stripe extends from behind eye almost to end of tail. Upper and lower lateral zones black, marked with 7 white and brown lines or stripes; midlateral and ventrolateral stripes broadest and whitest. Midlateral extends from below and in front of eye to middle of tail; ventrolateral from below and behind ear to hindlimb. Remainder narrow and wavy, especially between ear and forelimb. Head olive-brown, variegated with blackish brown. Tail pale yellowish brown. Limbs brown streaked with dark brown. Ventral surfaces white. SVL 60 mm.

Distinguished from *C. quattuordecimlineatus*, *C. piankai* and *C. atlas* in bearing more numerous pale stripes (usually 20 vs 16 or less). Differs further from *C. quattuordecimlineatus* by nature of dorsal zone (broad and brown vs black, enclosing narrow pale stripes). Differs from *C. ariadnae* by nature of anterior lateral stripes (relatively prominent and continuous between forelimb and eye vs obscure and fragmented).

Preferred habitat Sandy deserts dominated by hummock grasslands, from central interior of WA to adjacent NT and SA.

Microhabitat Shelters and forages in and around *Triodia* hummocks on crests of desert dunes.

Comments Grasshoppers, beetles, moths and bugs are recorded as prey items. Appears to be most active through winter and spring, breeding from September till October. Forages throughout morning, and to a lesser extent in late afternoon.

Ctenotus ehmanni Storr, 1985

Description Small member of *C. colletti* group with blackish brown ground colour and 6 cream dorsal stripes, darkening to pale brown on tail. Paravertebrals commence on tip of snout, dorsals commence on top of head and dorsolaterals commence above eye. Broad blackish brown upper lateral stripe extends from nostril well onto tail, enclosing a single series of prominent white spots between neck and hindlimb. White midlateral stripe extends from upper lip through top of ear-aperture, continuing well onto tail. This is margined below by black lower lateral and white ventrolateral stripes. Limbs prominently striped. Ventral surfaces white. SVL 40 mm.

Preferred habitat Known only from Mt Elizabeth Station in subhumid north-western interior of Kimberley region, WA. Recorded from eucalypt woodland with sparse ground cover on sandy soil.

The area also featured outcrops and embedded sandstone and quartzite boulders.

Microhabitat   No data available.
Comments   As for species group.

Ctenotus essingtonii (Gray, 1842)
Photos 347, 348

Description   Member of *C. essingtonii* group comprising 2 subspecies.
C. e. essingtonii   Dorsal ground colour brown, usually unmarked; occasionally bearing a narrow dark vertebral line. Broad blackish brown laterodorsal stripe begins near eye, extending to hips or onto tail. This is bordered by a white dorsolateral stripe. Upper lateral zone blackish; represented on tail as a distinct dark lateral stripe. Upper lateral series of small white spots may be present. These are most prominent on (or restricted to) anterior body. White midlateral stripe commences as obscure pale stripe above upper lip (often broken from side of neck to forelimb or a little behind), continuing to hindlimb. Lower lateral zone brown; uniform, or marked with obscure white spots. Tail and limbs reddish. Limbs irregularly spotted with dark brown. Ventral surfaces white. SVL 60 mm.
C. e. brevipes Storr, 1981   Differs from nominate form in having little or no indication of ear lobules, attaining smaller size, bearing shorter limbs, lacking pale lateral spots, and in bearing a broader, more prominent pale midlateral stripe. SVL 50 mm.
C. e. essingtonii differs from *C. hilli* in attaining larger maximum size (SVL 60 vs 45 mm), and in bearing less prominent upper lateral spots and fewer midbody scale rows (24–28 vs 30–34). Differs from *C. arnhemensis* in lacking a prominent pale-edged black vertebral stripe. *C. e. brevipes* differs from all other *Ctenotus* in bearing little or no indication of ear lobules.
Preferred habitat   *C. e. essingtonii* occurs on river margins and woodlands in subhumid northern NT. *C. e. brevipes* occurs in semi-arid to subhumid woodlands and margins of rock outcrops from Gulf of Carpentaria as far south as Mt Isa, extending north-east to Coen, Qld.
Microhabitat   *C. e. essingtonii* excavates shallow burrows at bases of shrubs and tussocks, or shelters beneath logs, dense grasses or surface litter.
Comments   *C. e. brevipes* tends to skulk in semi-shaded margins of ground cover, while *C. e. essingtonii* more readily forages in open areas. The two probably represent distinct species.

Ctenotus eurydice
Czechura and Wombey, 1982
Photo 349

Description   Moderately small member of *C. lesueurii* group. Dorsal ground colour olive-brown. Pattern includes 8 pale stripes: a paravertebral, dorsolateral, midlateral and lower lateral on each side. Moderately broad black vertebral stripe (margined by pale paravertebrals) extends from nape to base or middle of tail. Narrow whitish dorsolateral stripe borders broader dark laterodorsal stripe from above eye, well onto tail. Upper lateral zone black; represented on tail by a dark stripe, sometimes faded to leave upper and lower margins only. This may enclose a few small white anterior spots, or a row of widely spaced spots on body. White midlateral stripe extends from behind nostril to ear opening, continuing from posterior midportion of ear onto tail. Whitish lower lateral stripe extends from below and behind ear as a wavy line to forelimb or anterior body, thence to hindlimb. This is bordered by a narrow brownish ventrolateral line. Limbs brown striped with black. Ventral surfaces white. SVL 75 mm.
Distinguished from *C. taeniolatus* in attaining greater maximum size (SVL 75 vs 65 mm), and by shape of snout (round in profile vs relatively more pointed). Differs from *C. arcanus* in bearing a greater number of pale stripes (pale lower lateral stripe present vs usually absent). Differs from *C. robustus* by upper lateral pattern (black sometimes enclosing sharp whitish spots vs olive-brown, bearing diffuse pale spots).
Preferred habitat   Recorded among rocks in low woodland with dense heath understorey and in semi-evergreen vine thickets. Extends from Monto in Qld, south to cooler highlands of Armidale region, NSW.
Microhabitat   Excavates short tunnels beneath rock slabs, or shelters in shallow burrows at bases of low vegetation.
Comments   As for species group.

Ctenotus eutaenius Storr, 1981
Photo 350

Description   Moderately large member of *C. lesueurii* group, though arrangement of pattern is similar to members of *C. atlas* group. Ground colour blackish brown, marked with 10 narrow pale stripes. Whitish paravertebral stripe extends from nape, becoming broader and browner on tail. Pale olive dorsal stripe extends from base of head to hips. White dorsolateral stripe extends from eye to tail, darkening to pale brown or olive beyond hips. White upper lateral stripe (often broken anteriorly) extends from temple, becoming broader and browner on tail. Broad midlateral stripe extends from below eye, darkening to pale brown or olive on tail. Usually some indication of a broad white lower lateral stripe on anterior body. Ventral surfaces white; yellowish beneath tail. SVL 90 mm.

Preferred habitat Known only from a small area of subhumid north-eastern Qld, from Magnetic Island west to the Great Basalt Wall. Associated with granite and basalt outcrops in woodlands. Magnetic Island population also occurs in hummock grass associations.

Microhabitat Forages around edges of low vegetation, sheltering in it when disturbed.

Comments As for species group.

Ctenotus fallens Storr, 1974
Photo 351

Description Large member of *C. lesueurii* group. Dorsal ground colour dark to pale greyish brown or yellowish brown; darker on juveniles. Pattern includes 6 pale stripes and spotted upper flanks. Broad black vertebral stripe extends from nape to base of tail or a little beyond; bordered by pale paravertebral stripes which may be narrowly dark-edged. White dorsolateral stripe extends from eye onto tail, becoming suffused with brown or yellow beyond hips. This is broadly to narrowly edged above with black. Upper lateral zone dark brown, enclosing a series of pale spots or diffuse blotches. Pale midlateral stripe (sometimes obscure) extends from behind eye to tail; interrupted by, or narrowly passing above, hindlimb. Lower lateral zone pale grey, containing indistinct pale spots. Limbs brown striped with darker brown or black. Tip of snout often suffused with yellow to pink. Ventral surfaces yellowish. SVL 95 mm.

Distinguished from *C. lesueurii* in lacking oblique dark lines on anterior flanks, and in lacking a white inner margin to dark laterodorsal stripe. Adults differ further in possessing a yellowish (vs white) belly.

Preferred habitat West coastal dunes, sand plains and offshore islands of WA, from Ningaloo Station south to Pinjarra, extending inland to granites and laterites of Darling Range. Favours low coastal vegetation on pale sandy soils.

Microhabitat As for species group.

Comments See genus and species group.

Ctenotus gagudju
Sadlier, Wombey and Braithwaite, 1985
Photo 352

Description Member of *C. leonhardii* group with brown dorsal ground colour. Black vertebral stripe present or absent; narrow, without pale edge and terminating at hindlimbs when present. Narrow black laterodorsal and pale yellow dorsolateral stripes extend from vicinity of eye well onto tail. Upper lateral zone black (brown anterior to ear-aperture) enclosing a prominent series of white spots from behind eye to hindlimb. Prominent pale mid-

lateral stripe, flushed with yellow posteriorly, extends forward from hindlimb, breaking into dashes from midbody to neck or occasionally broken throughout its length. Lower lateral zone reddish brown with scattered pale blotches. Sides of head flushed with reddish brown. Limbs brown with paler stripes. Ventral surfaces cream. SVL 54 mm.

Distinguished from all other *Ctenotus* in having frontoparietals fused to form a single scale.

Preferred habitat Known only from lowland woodlands in vicinity of Magela Creek and Nourlangie Creek, tributaries of the East Alligator and South Alligator Rivers respectively, in Arnhem Land, northern NT. Appears to favour reddish lateritic soils.

Microhabitat See genus and *C. leonhardii* species group.

Comments A female collected in March (Wet Season) contained 3 developing eggs. Otherwise as for genus.

Ctenotus gemmula Storr, 1974
Photo 353

Description Member of *C. labillardieri* group. Dorsal ground colour uniform pale yellowish brown to silvery brown. Black laterodorsal and broken white dorsolateral stripes extend from nape to hips. Upper flanks black, usually enclosing a series of prominent white spots. White midlateral stripe (wavy or broken into series of dashes) extends from upper lip to base of tail. Lower flanks dark grey, variably marked with white. Limbs yellowish brown, boldly marbled with black and white. Tail brownish grey to bluish grey. Ventral surfaces white. SVL 55 mm.

Distinguished from *C. catenifer* and *C. delli* by pattern on limbs (marbled vs peppered). Differs further from *C. catenifer* in lacking a white spotted dark laterodorsal stripe. Differs from *C. labillardieri* by nature of dorsolateral stripe (broken vs continuous).

Preferred habitat Apparently disjunct populations occur in south-western WA, north to Perth area. Inhabits pale sand plains supporting heathlands, in association with *Banksia* or mallee woodlands.

Microhabitat Shelters in burrows at bases of tussocks or shrubs, beneath leaf-litter and in abandoned stick-ant nests (*Iridomyrmex conifer*).

Comments As for species group.

Ctenotus grandis Storr, 1969
Photos 354, 355

Description Large robust member of *C. grandis* group. Two subspecies recognised.

C. g. grandis Dorsal ground colour rich reddish brown; paler on head, neck and tail. Pattern includes 5 narrow dark dorsal stripes. Blackish brown vertebral stripe extends from nape onto tail. Narrower dark brown dorsal and laterodorsal stripes extend from nape or shoulders onto tail. Lateral surfaces of body and tail grey, bearing vertically aligned whitish flecks. Limbs dark brown, usually spotted with white to pale yellowish brown. Ventral surfaces whitish. SVL 100 mm.

C. g. titan Storr, 1980 Differs from nominate form by paler dorsal colour, larger size, and greater tendency for lateral spots to align vertically. SVL 120 mm.

Both subspecies differ from *C. hanloni* in attaining larger maximum size (SVL 100 or more vs 70 mm), and by alignment of white lateral spotting (vertical vs longitudinal).

Preferred habitat Occupies a variety of arid habitats on sands and loams, usually with ground cover of hummock grasses; occasionally chenopodiaceous shrubs. *C. g. titan* occurs on Barrow Island, Pilbara region and North West Cape, WA. *C. g. grandis* extends from interior of WA to central NT.

Microhabitat Normally shelters and forages in and around hummock grasses.

Comments *C. g. grandis*: Bulk of diet consists of termites, though smaller lizards, insect larvae, cockroaches and grasshoppers are also taken. Most active during late summer, from morning through to late afternoon. Breeding usually occurs from September to October. Some of these comments may be applicable to *C. hanloni*, recognised as distinct from *C. grandis* after information had been collected by Pianka in 1968.

Ctenotus greeri Storr, 1979
Photo 356

Description Member of *C. leonhardii* group. Ground colour dark brown, becoming paler and more reddish on forebody. Blackish brown vertebral stripe extends from nape to base of tail. Brownish white to white paravertebral stripes extend from nape, becoming browner, broader, and merging on anterior tail. Dorsal series of white dots or dashes present on body. White dorsolateral stripe extends from behind eye to tail, becoming broader and browner beyond hips. This is margined above by a black laterodorsal stripe. Upper lateral zone encloses a series of white dots. Narrow white midlateral stripe is well developed posteriorly and wavy or broken into short dashes between forelimb and ear. Limbs striped with dark brown. Tail pale brown. Ventral surfaces white. SVL 65 mm.

Distinguished from *C. leonhardii* in bearing a dorsal series of white dots or short dashes. Differs from *C. uber uber* by nature of vertebral stripe (well developed vs weak to absent).

Preferred habitat Arid south-eastern interior of WA. Apparently disjunct population occurs in NT, north to Elliot. Recorded from reddish sandy loams supporting mulga (*Acacia aneura*) woodlands or shrublands, and mallee/hummock grass associa-

tions. Favours the slightly lusher vegetation of washes or alluvial flats.

Microhabitat As for species group.

Comments As for species group.

Ctenotus hanloni Storr, 1980
Photo 357

Description Small member of *C. grandis* group. Dorsal ground colour of adults rich reddish brown to orange-brown; olive on juveniles. Five dark stripes extend from nape onto base of tail: prominent dark brown vertebral stripe (widest at hips), obscure narrow dorsals, and moderately distinct to obscure laterodorsals. White dorsolateral stripe extends from behind eye or ear, well onto tail. Flanks olive to reddish brown, densely marked with longitudinally oriented whitish flecks. Ventral surfaces white. SVL 70 mm.

Distinguished from *C. grandis* in attaining smaller maximum size (SVL 70 vs 100 mm or greater), and by alignment of lateral flecks (horizontal vs vertical).

Preferred habitat Arid sandy to loamy flats supporting hummock grass associations, from Exmouth Gulf region and Barrow Island, WA, through Great Sandy, Great Victoria and Tanami Deserts of WA, NT and SA.

Microhabitat Shelters in shallow burrows, usually situated beneath grass hummocks.

Comments Forages for insects, especially small grasshoppers, among and between grass hummocks. Readily retreats to burrow if disturbed.

Ctenotus hebetior Storr, 1978
Photos 358, 359

Description Moderately small member of *C. leonhardii* group comprising 2 recognised subspecies.
C. h. hebetior Dorsal ground colour brown. Five narrow, indistinct dark stripes (vertebral, dorsals and laterodorsals) extend from nape to base of tail. Narrow white dorsolateral stripe extends from above eye onto base of tail. Upper lateral zone dark reddish brown, enclosing 2 series of pale spots or dashes. Narrow white midlateral stripe may be present; broken anteriorly. Lower lateral zone pale reddish brown, sometimes marked with darker flecks or longitudinal streaks. Limbs pale brown, streaked with darker brown. Ventral surfaces white. SVL 60 mm.

C. h. schuettleri Börner, 1981 Dorsal ground colour brown to reddish brown. Pattern more prominent. Vertebral stripe often extends onto tail. Upper lateral zone dark reddish brown to black, bearing 2 or 3 series of sharp white spots. Midlateral stripe invariably present, sometimes broken (especially anteriorly). Lower lateral zone dark reddish brown to black, spotted with white.

Distinguished from *C. leonhardii* and *C. regius* in bearing more dark dorsal stripes (5 vs 3). Differs from *C. pulchellus* by nature of dark vertebral stripe (not normally wider than dorsals and laterodorsals vs considerably wider, at least anteriorly). Differs further in bearing a pale midlateral stripe, and by nature of upper lateral zone (not markedly different in colour from lower lateral zone vs considerably darker).

Preferred habitat *C. h. hebetior* occurs in central Qld on sandy to heavy dark soils supporting low woodlands and grasslands. *C. h. schuettleri* extends from arid north-western Qld to adjacent NT. Recorded in eucalypt/*Triodia* associations on stony soils, and on sandy flats supporting tussock grasses.

Microhabitat As for species group.

Comments Subspecific status doubtful. The two forms may constitute distinct species.

Ctenotus helenae Storr, 1969
Photo 360

Description Moderately large member of *C. lesueurii* group displaying little pattern. Dorsal surfaces olive-brown. Dark vertebral stripe (rarely pale-edged) present or absent. Occasionally faint indications of dark laterodorsal and pale dorsolateral and midlateral stripes are present. Flanks, side of head, neck and tail, pale greyish brown. Hindlimbs dark olive-brown. Lower flanks and side of tail may be speckled with black. Ventral surfaces white. SVL 90 mm.

Distinguished from *C. robustus* and *C. saxatilis* in bearing weaker pattern; particularly lack of pale edges to dark vertebral stripe. Differs from *C. spaldingi* in lacking pale spots on flanks, and possessing more supraocular scales (4 vs 3). Differs from *C. inornatus* in usually lacking pale dorsolateral stripes.

Preferred habitat Occurs in a variety of semi-arid to arid habitats, including sandy alluvial flats and sand ridge deserts (occasionally scree slopes) vegetated with woodlands or shrublands, usually in association with hummock grasses. Extends from coast and interior of north-western WA, through deserts of NT and SA to south-western Qld.

Microhabitat Shelters beneath grass hummocks, or in thick leaf-litter and loose sand at bases of trees or shrubs. Debris accumulated among roots of trees lining watercourses is also favoured. Usually forages in or at the edges of low ground cover.

Comments Feeds on small insects, particularly termites, though insect larvae, cockroaches and grasshoppers are also recorded. In interior of WA *C. helenae* is most active in late summer. Individuals are normally encountered during late morning and early afternoon. Breeding usually occurs between September and October. Clutches of 1–6 eggs (normally 3) are recorded. Populations in Pilbara region of WA are strongly patterned and closely approach *C. saxatilis* in appearance. Taxonomic work is required to clarify their relationship.

Ctenotus hilli Storr, 1970
Photo 361

Description Small member of *C. essingtonii* group, usually displaying little or no dorsal pattern. Dorsal ground colour brown, occasionally marked with a dark vertebral line or narrow stripe. White dorsolateral stripe (broadly margined above with blackish brown) extends from behind eye onto tail. Upper lateral zone blackish brown, bearing a series of small white oblong spots or dashes; continuous on tail as a prominent black stripe extending nearly to tip. White midlateral stripe commences obscurely below eye, extending back as a series of spots or dashes to forelimb, thence continuously to hindlimb. Lower lateral zone reddish brown; uniform, or marked with a series of white spots. Limbs pale brown striped with dark brown. Ventral surfaces white. SVL 45 mm.

Differs from *C. e. essingtonii* in attaining smaller maximum size (SVL 45 vs 60 mm), bearing prominent upper lateral spots (vs obscure to absent), and more midbody scale rows (30–34 vs 24–28). Differs from *C. arnhemensis* by nature of vertebral stripe (poorly developed to absent, without pale edge, vs prominent and pale-edged).

Preferred habitat Pale coastal sands and clay- or laterite-based soils supporting woodlands and sparse low ground cover in far north-western NT.

Microhabitat Shelters beneath scattered rocks, and in burrows under coarse surface litter such as dead *Pandanus* foliage.

Comments An open forager. Otherwise as for species group.

Ctenotus iapetus Storr, 1975
Photo 362

Description Moderately small member of *C. atlas* group with 12 cream to pale yellowish brown stripes on black ground colour. Paravertebral stripe extends from nape well onto base of tail, becoming browner posteriorly. Dorsal stripe extends from nape to hips. Dorsolateral and upper lateral stripes extend from eye well onto tail. Broad midlateral stripe extends from below and in front of eye well onto tail. Broad ventrolateral stripe from below ear onto base of tail. Head brown, bearing a white angular marking above each eye. Tail brown. Limbs white to brown, streaked with black. Ventral surfaces white. SVL 55 mm.

Distinguished from *C. duricola* in bearing more pale stripes (12 vs 6–8). Formerly treated as a subspecies of *C. quattuordecimlineatus*, differing in bearing fewer pale upper lateral stripes (1 vs 2).

Preferred habitat Sandy plains and dunes with dominant ground cover of hummock grasses. Occurs in coastal areas of arid north-western WA.

Microhabitat As for species group.

Comments As for species group.

Ctenotus impar Storr, 1969
Photo 363

Description Moderately large member of *C. atlas* group with 11 pale stripes on black ground colour. Greyish brown to brownish white vertebral stripe extends from level of eye to base of tail; occasionally split by prominent to obscure black median line. Dorsal stripe of similar colour extends from above eye, coalescing with its opposite on tail to form one broad stripe. Brownish white to white dorsolateral stripe extends from above eye well onto tail, becoming broader beyond hips. Upper lateral stripe of similar colour extends from behind eye to hips. Prominent white midlateral stripe (disjunct; forking upward behind ear) extends forward to upper lip, and backward to base of tail. White ventrolateral stripe extends from below ear to base of tail. Head brown, variably marked with black. Tail pale brown. Limbs brown streaked with black. Ventral surfaces white. SVL 65 mm.

Distinguished from *C. atlas* in bearing a pale vertebral stripe.

Preferred habitat Sand plains supporting heathlands, often in association with mallee or *Banksia* woodlands from subhumid south-west coast to semi-arid southern interior of WA. Also occurs in scattered eucalypt/heathland associations of Darling Range.

Microhabitat Shelters in shallow burrows among low vegetation or surface debris, occasionally in abandoned stick-ant nests *(Iridomyrmex conifer)*.

Comments As for species group.

Ctenotus ingrami Czechura and Wombey, 1982
Photo 364

Description Member of *C. lesueurii* group. Dorsal ground colour olive-brown to yellowish brown. Pattern includes 8 pale stripes: a paravertebral, dorsolateral, midlateral and lower lateral on each side. Broad black vertebral stripe (edged by narrow pale paravertebrals) extends from nape to base of tail. Prominent narrow white dorsolateral stripe (bordered by a black laterodorsal stripe) extends from behind eye to base of tail. Upper lateral zone usually black; occasionally brown dorsal colour may invade almost as far as midlateral stripe. Broad white midlateral stripe (widest on forebody) extends from below nostril, through ear opening to hindlimb and onto base of tail. White lower lateral stripe extends from below ear (interrupted by forelimb) to hindlimb. Limbs brown striped with black. Ventral surfaces white; vent and tail tinged with yellow. SVL 80 mm.

Distinguished from *C. taeniolatus* by nature of dorsal pattern (a broad strip of ground colour, vs narrow, often reduced to form dorsal stripes).

Preferred habitat Occurs in subhumid areas west of Great Dividing Range, from northern interior of NSW to eastern interior of Qld, north to about

Croydon. Occurs on a variety of soil types supporting woodland associations over sparse understorey of chenopod shrubs or tussock grasses.

Microhabitat Shelters in shallow burrows at bases of low shrubs or tussocks.

Comments As for species group.

Ctenotus inornatus (Gray, 1845)
Photo 365

Description Large member of *C. lesueurii* group. Ground colour shades of brown to brownish grey, with variably reduced pattern. Black vertebral stripe may be absent, reduced to a line on nape and forebody, or extending to base of tail. Pale paravertebral stripe may be prominent on juveniles; usually obscure to absent on adults. Broad to narrow black laterodorsal stripe borders prominent narrow, white to cream dorsolateral stripe from behind eye, usually well onto tail. Upper lateral zone, from behind ear to base of tail, darker shade of ground colour mottled or flecked with cream, dark reddish brown, and black. Pale midlateral stripe (usually obscure, and most prominent posteriorly) extends from upper lip or forelimb, above hindlimb, nearly to end of tail. Lower lateral zone pale greyish brown. Limbs pale brown to reddish brown, streaked with blackish brown. Ventral surfaces white to pale yellow. SVL 75 mm.

Distinguished from *C. arnhemensis*, *C. saxatilis*, *C. serventyi* and *C. robustus* in bearing a narrow, indistinct vertebral stripe (vs broad, prominent and pale-edged). Differs further in usually lacking pale upper lateral blotches or spots. Differs from *C. spaldingi* in bearing more supraocular scales (4 vs 3). Differs from *C. vertebralis* in bearing a weaker vertebral stripe, and in attaining a greater maximum size (SVL 95 vs 55 mm). Differs from *C. helenae* in possessing pale dorsolateral stripes (vs usually absent; obscure when present). Differs from *C. lateralis* in lacking a lower lateral stripe. Differs from *C. coggeri* by position of pale midlateral stripe (passing above hindlimb vs continuously through hindlimb).

Preferred habitat Occurs in a wide variety of habitats, including rock outcrops, river margins and sandy loam flats supporting woodlands, hummock grasses and spear grass. Extends across subhumid to semi-arid northern Australia, from Broome, WA, to eastern Cape York Peninsula, Qld.

Microhabitat As for species group.

Comments As for species group.

Ctenotus joanae Storr, 1970
Photo 366

Description Small member of *C. leonhardii* group with olive-brown ground colour. Prominent broad black vertebral stripe, bordered by narrow (often obscure) pale paravertebrals, extends from nape to base of tail. Narrow white dorsolateral and broad black laterodorsal stripes extend from above eye well onto tail. Upper lateral zone pale to dark olive-brown, sometimes enclosing a series of indistinct pale spots. Whitish midlateral stripe extends from snout, narrowly over hindlimb onto tail. Pale olive-brown lower lateral stripe begins below and behind ear, continuing well onto tail. Pale ventrolateral stripe faintly visible. Limbs brown, streaked with darker brown. Ventral surfaces whitish. SVL 50 mm.

Distinguished from *C. leonhardii* by extent of pale midlateral stripe (continuous onto side of head vs broken to absent anteriorly).

Preferred habitat Black-soil plains sparsely vegetated with grasses (*Astrebla* spp.), low shrubs and scattered small trees, from semi-arid central and eastern NT to far north-western Qld.

Microhabitat Shelters in deep soil cracks.

Comments As for species group.

Ctenotus kurnbudj
Sadlier, Wombey and Braithwaite, 1985
Photo 367

Description Member of *C. leonhardii* group with brown dorsal ground colour. Black vertebral stripe absent. Broad black laterodorsal stripe encloses cream spots. On body this may break into alternating series of black and cream blotches; invariably so on tail. Very narrow pale dorsolateral stripe extends from above eye onto tail. Upper lateral zone, from ear-aperture to hindlimb, black enclosing several series of longitudinally aligned white flecks. Narrow broken white midlateral stripe extends from forelimb to hindlimb. Lower lateral zone dark brown to black on body; light brown to grey (occasionally spotted with white) anterior to forelimb. Side of head brown to reddish brown with scattered pale spots. Hindlimbs brown with prominent black stripes or elongate blotches. Ventral surfaces white. SVL 54 mm.

Distinguished from all sympatric *Ctenotus* in bearing black laterodorsal stripe enclosing pale spots or broken into series of blotches.

Preferred habitat Woodlands, usually on heavy soils, in vicinity of West Alligator and Wildman Rivers in Arnhem Land, northern NT.

Microhabitat See genus and *C. leonhardii* species group.

Comments As for genus.

Ctenotus labillardieri
(Duméril and Bibron, 1839)
Photo 368

Description Moderately large member of *C. labillardieri* group. Variable, undergoing a clinal change in pattern from north to south.

Northern population: Dorsal ground colour rich brown to olive, without pattern. Narrow black laterodorsal and prominent sharp-edged white dorsolateral stripes extend from above eye to hips, becoming broader and diffuse on tail. Upper lateral zone immaculate black (occasionally bearing a few obscure pale spots) from snout well onto tail. Sharp white midlateral stripe extends from upper lip to hindlimb, and onto side of tail. Lower lateral zone black, enclosing ragged-edged white lower lateral stripe. Limbs reddish, boldly marbled with black. Ventral surfaces yellow. SVL 65 mm.

Southern population: Dorsum is invaded by numerous black flecks, often concentrating to form an obscure vertebral stripe. Black laterodorsal stripe broader. White dorsolateral stripe ragged-edged. Black upper lateral zone encloses scattered pale spots. SVL 75 mm.

Distinguished from *C. catenifer*, *C. delli* and *C. gemmula* by nature of pale dorsolateral stripe (continuous vs broken). Differs further from *C. catenifer* and *C. delli* by pattern on limbs (marbled vs peppered).

Preferred habitat Heathlands, forests and rock outcrops of humid south coast and islands of south-western WA, extending north on Darling Range to Mt Helena. Penetrates wet sclerophyll forests, a habitat other *Ctenotus* are rarely able to exploit.

Microhabitat Excavates shallow tunnels beneath slabs of rock and logs.

Comments Ventures into open spaces to a greater extent than other members of *C. labillardieri* group. May be locally abundant, several individuals often found sheltering beheath one rock. In high altitudes of Stirling Range, lizards are easily approachable and relatively unafraid of humans. This contrasts sharply with all other *Ctenotus*, which are quick to flee when approached.

Lancelin Island Skink
Ctenotus lancelini Ford, 1969
Photo 369

Description Large member of *C. labillardieri* group. Ground colour reddish brown to greyish brown, fading to grey on tail. Dorsal pattern consists of numerous longitudinally aligned dark streaks. Dark-edged white dorsolateral stripe extends from behind eye, fading on base of tail. Broad black upper lateral zone encloses a row of white spots. White midlateral stripe (broken and indistinct anteriorly) extends to groin; bordered below by a prominent to obscure blackish ventrolateral stripe. Limbs pale yellowish brown, irregularly marbled with black. Ventral surfaces yellowish. SVL 80 mm.

Preferred habitat Restricted to Lancelin Island (approximately 9 hectares in area) off lower west coast of WA. Occurs on limestone outcrops on northern and southern extremities. This is one of the most restricted ranges of any Australian reptile.

Microhabitat Shelters beneath limestone slabs or chunks. May dive for cover beneath loose sand in the same manner as banded sand-swimming skinks of the genus *Eremiascincus*.

Comments As for species group.

Ctenotus lateralis Storr, 1978
Photo 370

Description Member of *C. lesueurii* group. Dorsal ground colour reddish brown, greyish brown to olive-brown. Narrow pale-edged black vertebral stripe extends from nape to tail; pale margins tending to disappear with age. Prominent white to cream dorsolateral stripe extends from eye well onto tail; edged by a narrow black laterodorsal stripe. Upper lateral zone brown, bisected by a broad brownish white to greyish (often broken) stripe. On juveniles, this stripe may be black. Narrow to moderately broad greyish white midlateral stripe extends forward to eye (breaking up on side of head), and back nearly to end of tail. Lower lateral zone greyish, bisected by a narrow stripe; pale on adults, black on juveniles. Tail yellowish brown. Limbs obscurely streaked with dark brown. Ventral surfaces white, flushed with yellow beneath tail. SVL 85 mm.

Distinguished from *C. robustus*, *C. saxatilis* and *C. inornatus* by nature of pattern on flanks (a lower lateral stripe vs diffuse clouding or spotting). Differs further from *C. robustus* by nature of dark upper lateral zone (enclosing a narrow stripe vs pale blotches). Differs further from all in attaining smaller maximum size (SVL 85 vs 115, 100 and 95 mm, respectively).

Preferred habitat Alluvial plains, creek margins and stony ridges or flats dominated by hummock grass/woodland associations through arid regions of north-west and interior of Qld.

Microhabitat Shelters beneath stones or hummock grasses, and in shallow burrows.

Comments As for species group.

Ctenotus leae (Boulenger, 1887)
Photo 371

Description Large member of *C. colletti* group with 6–8 whitish stripes on black ground colour. All colour and markings flushed with reddish brown from hips onto tail. Broad black vertebral stripe (margined by pale paravertebrals) extends from nape onto base of tail. Narrow pale dorsal stripe may extend from nape to hips. Broader white dorsolateral stripe extends from above eye to middle of tail. Black upper lateral zone (split into 2 on temple) extends from behind eye well onto tail. Broad white midlateral stripe extends from snout to thigh. Brownish black ventrolateral stripe extends from forelimb to groin, forking above and below forelimb. Upper fork extends anteriorly nearly to ear; lower discontinuously to below ear or a little beyond. Top of head olive-grey; browner on snout. Limbs pinkish brown, marked with obscure darker stripes. Ventral surfaces white, suffused with pink under tail. SVL 60 mm.

Distinguished from *C. calurus* and *C. colletti* in attaining greater size (SVL 60 vs 50 and 45 mm, respectively) and by colour of tail (reddish vs bluish and brown, respectively). Differs further from *C. colletti* in bearing more ear lobules (2–5, approximately equal in size, vs 2 or rarely 3, the uppermost largest).

Preferred habitat Sand ridge deserts dominated by hummock grasses. Extends from Great Victoria Desert, WA, through northern SA and southern NT, to south-western Qld.

Microhabitat Shelters in shallow burrows, usually situated under grass hummocks on sand dunes. Forages in open spaces between vegetation.

Comments Bulk of stomach contents recorded consists of vegetable material; probably ingested with arthropod prey. Bugs and spiders constitute major prey items. In interior of WA *C. leae* is most active during autumn and spring, normally foraging from late morning till early afternoon. Breeds from September till October. Clutches of 3 and 4 eggs are recorded.

Ctenotus leonhardii (Sternfeld, 1919)
Photos 372, 373

Description Member of *C. leonhardii* group. Dorsal ground colour pale or dark brown to reddish brown. Dark brown to black vertebral stripe, bordered by pale brown paravertebral stripes, extends from nape to base of tail. Occasionally dark pigmentation on dorsal surface renders vertebral and paravertebral stripes obscure. Whitish dorsolateral stripe, bordered by narrow to broad dark laterodorsal stripe, extends from above eye to middle of tail. Upper lateral zone dark brown, enclosing 1–3 series of whitish dots. Whitish midlateral stripe (well developed posteriorly and breaking into a series of dashes anteriorly) extends back onto tail. Lower lateral zone brownish, marked with obscure pale spots. Limbs brown, bearing darker stripes. Ventral surfaces white. SVL 75 mm.

Distinguished from *C. greeri* and *C. uber* in lacking a laterodorsal series of pale spots or dashes. Differs from *C. pulchellus* in bearing a pale midlateral stripe. Differs from *C. regius*, *C. serventyi* and *C. joanae* by extent of midlateral stripe (weak and broken anteriorly vs continuous onto side of head). Differs from *C. hebetior*, and further from *C. pulchellus*, in usually bearing 3 dark dorsal stripes: vertebral and laterodorsals (vs 5 dark dorsal stripes).

Preferred habitat Arid stony, sandy, to heavy loam soils vegetated predominantly with *Acacia* woodlands and shrublands. Extends from hinterland of central-west coast, through interior of WA to southern NT, northern SA, western NSW and south-western Qld.

Microhabitat Shelters in burrows, normally excavated beneath low vegetation or objects such as rocks, logs or stumps.

Comments Forages widely in open spaces between vegetation. Feeds on insects, particularly termites. Most active in summer, often during middle of day. Breeding usually occurs between September and October. Clutches of 1–7 eggs are recorded.

Ctenotus lesueurii (Duméril and Bibron, 1839)
Photo 374

Description Large member of *C. lesueurii* group with prominent pattern. Dorsal ground colour olive-brown, pale brown to brownish grey. Narrow to moderately broad black vertebral stripe extends from nape to base or middle of tail. White to brownish white paravertebral stripe extends from top of head to base of tail. Black laterodorsal stripe (margined with white on inner edge) extends well onto tail. White dorsolateral stripe extends from behind eye to middle of tail. Black upper lateral zone encloses a series of white dots or dashes, often coalescing anteriorly with white midlateral stripe. Midlateral stripe usually present; broken between upper lip and behind forelimb to form obliquely vertical dark-edged bars. This is continuous or broken on body, becoming broader behind hips, and extends well onto tail. Lower lateral zone black to blackish brown, marked with white spots which tend to form pale vertical bars. Head brownish, marked with black. Limbs pale brown to white, streaked with black. Tail brown to brownish yellow. Juveniles tend to be darker and more heavily spotted with white. Ventral surfaces white. Northern populations tend to attain greater size and have bolder pattern. SVL 100 mm.

Distinguished from sympatric *Ctenotus* in being larger, and bearing a bolder, more complex pattern; particularly the presence of obliquely vertical bars on anterior flanks. Differs further from *C. fallens* in possessing a pale inner margin to dark laterodorsal stripe.

Preferred habitat Coastal dunes, sand plains, and limestones supporting heathlands, usually in association with eucalypt/*Banksia* woodlands. Occurs on south-west coast of WA, from just south of Perth, north to Shark Bay.

Microhabitat As for species group.

Comments Constructs deeper burrows than most other *Ctenotus*, and as a consequence emerges later in the season than other sympatric species. Otherwise as for species group.

Ctenotus mastigura Storr, 1975
Photo 375

Description Member of *C. lesueurii* group. Dorsal ground colour dark iridescent olive-brown, bearing a narrow, pale-edged dark vertebral stripe. Prominent narrow whitish dorsolateral stripe, bordered above and below with black, extends onto base of tail. Upper lateral zone brownish grey. White midlateral stripe narrowly edged with brownish grey. Ventral surfaces white. SVL 85 mm.

Distinguished from *C. burbidgei* in bearing a pale-edged dark vertebral stripe.

Preferred habitat Subhumid hinterland of Admiralty Gulf, in far northern Kimberley region of WA. Occurs in open grassy woodlands with outcropping basalt boulders on red soils.

Microhabitat No data available.

Comments Nothing known of habits.

Ctenotus militaris Storr, 1975
Photo 376

Description Member of *C. leonhardii* group with 5 dark dorsal stripes. Dorsal ground colour pale brown. Blackish to dark brown vertebral and dorsal stripes extend from nape to base of tail. Laterodorsal stripe extends from nape well onto tail. White to pale brown dorsolateral stripe extends from eye well onto tail. Upper lateral zone reddish brown (becoming darker posteriorly), bearing 1–3 series of pale spots. White midlateral stripe extends forward from hindlimb, breaks into dots or dashes toward forelimb, and sometimes reaches ear. Lower lateral zone reddish brown, enclosing one or more series of pale spots. Head greyish brown. Limbs reddish brown striped with blackish brown. Ventral surfaces white. SVL 65 mm.

Preferred habitat Woodland with grassy understorey (often including hummock grasses) on sandy soils of subhumid to semi-arid Kimberley region, WA, and adjacent NT, east to Wave Hill. Also recorded on black soil plains in west Kimberley.

Microhabitat As for species group.

Comments As for species group.

Ctenotus mimetes Storr, 1969
Photo 377

Description Moderately large member of *C. leonhardii* group, usually lacking vertebral stripe. Ground colour brown; duller on foreparts of body, brighter and redder posteriorly. Broad to narrow black laterodorsal stripe extends from above eye onto base of tail. White dorsolateral stripe extends from above eye to middle of tail, where it may be suffused with pink. Broad black upper lateral zone from eye to tail encloses 2 or 3 series of pale spots of varying colour; usually whitish suffused with reddish brown. These tend to align, forming narrowly separated, vertically elongate rectangular blotches. White midlateral stripe (often irregular anteriorly) extends from side of head to base of tail. Lower lateral zone similar in pattern to upper, but narrower and less regular. Limbs reddish brown, marbled with blackish brown. Tail paler brown. Ventral surfaces white. SVL 80 mm.

Distinguished from *C. u. uber* in lacking pale dorsal spots. Differs from *C. alleni* by nature of upper lateral spots (usually large, pinkish and rectangular vs small and whitish), and further by extent of pale midlateral stripe (extending forward to lips vs not extending forward beyond forelimb). Differs from *C. severus* by position of pale dorsolateral stripe (contacting dark upper lateral zone vs separated by a narrow strip of ground colour).

Preferred habitat Semi-arid to arid south-western interior of WA, on sandy to stony red loams supporting woodlands and shrublands. Extends south along transition zone between *Acacia*-dominated interior and eucalypt woodlands of south-west.

Microhabitat As for species group.

Comments As for species group.

Ctenotus monticola Storr, 1981
Photo 378

Description Moderately small *Ctenotus*, tentatively assigned to *C. lesueurii* group. Dorsal ground colour pale brown. Narrow black vertebral stripe extends from nape onto base of tail. This is narrowly and indistinctly edged with white. Occasionally a narrow dark dorsal stripe may be present. Narrow white dorsolateral stripe extends from eye to hindlimb or onto tail; bordered above by a black laterodorsal stripe. Blackish brown upper lateral zone encloses 1–3 series of brownish white dots, which tend to align vertically. Narrow white midlateral stripe extends from below eye to hindlimb. Lower lateral zone dark brown, irregularly spotted with brownish white. Ventral surfaces white. SVL 65 mm.

Preferred habitat Granite outcrops surrounded by eucalypt woodlands over a grassy understorey in subhumid areas of Atherton Tablelands, north-east Qld.

Microhabitat No data available.

Comments No data available.

Ctenotus pallescens Storr, 1970

Description Member of *C. schomburgkii* group with pale greyish brown ground colour; often suffused with reddish brown on back, tail and limbs. Dorsal pattern virtually absent on adults. Juveniles and subadults bear an indistinct blackish vertebral stripe from nape to base or tip of tail. Dark laterodorsal stripe from nape to base of tail encloses a series of transversely elongate pale spots. Pale dorsolateral stripe extends from above eye to base of tail. Dark upper lateral zone extends forward to side of snout, and back on tail as a dark dorsolateral line. This encloses a series of reddish brown to greyish white vertical bars. White midlateral stripe extends from upper lip (curving sharply over ear opening) to hindlimb. Ventrolateral series of alternating greyish white spots or squarish blotches extends from ear to groin. Limbs reticulated with dark brown. Ventral surfaces white. SVL 45 mm.

Distinguished from adjacent populations of *C. schomburgkii* by nature of dorsal pattern (almost patternless on adults vs marked with 5 dark stripes).

Preferred habitat Hard to stony soils vegetated with low woodlands and hummock grasses in semi-arid to arid central NT.

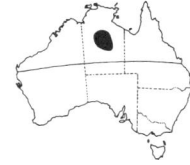

Microhabitat As for species group.

Comments As for species group.

Ctenotus pantherinus (Peters, 1866)
Photos 379–381

Description Large robust deep-headed *Ctenotus*. Sole member of *C. pantherinus* group. Four subspecies recognised.

C. p. pantherinus Ground colour coppery brown to olive. Narrow black vertebral stripe usually present, extending from nape to midbody or base of tail. Remaining dorsal and lateral pattern consists of black and white ocelli (whitish dashes margined laterally by short black bars) in 10 (occasionally 8 or 12) longitudinal series. Dark margins of ocelli occasionally coalesce to form stripes. Ocelli on flanks are broader and less elongate. White centres may coalesce on tail to form stripes. Head may be mottled with dark brown. Limbs brown. Forelimbs striped with darker brown. Hindlimbs marked with ocelli or dark stripes. Ventral surfaces white. SVL 90 mm.

C. p. acripes Storr, 1975 Similar in size to nominate form, differing in possessing more numerous midbody scale rows (36–40 vs 30–36), and in lacking a dark vertebral stripe. Scales on soles of feet spinose.

C. p. calx Storr, 1970 Largest subspecies; lacking a vertebral stripe. Scales beneath toes flat and callose. SVL 110 mm.

C. p. ocellifer (Boulenger, 1896) Medium-sized subspecies, lacking a vertebral stripe. Scales beneath toes finely keeled. SVL 100 mm.

Preferred habitat Occupies a variety of arid and semi-arid sandy, loamy, or stony regions, vegetated with low ground cover, particularly hummock grasses. *C. p. pantherinus* occurs in subhumid to semi-arid woodlands, hummock grassland and heathland habitats, from lower Murchison district southwards to Mogumber, and inland to between Southern Cross and Coolgardie, WA. It is separated from more widespread *C. p. ocellifer* by *Acacia*-dominated hard soils supporting few perennial shrubs or grasses. *C. p. ocellifer* occupies hummock grasslands in deserts of WA, northern SA and southern NT. *C. p. acripes* has a somewhat anomalous distribution, occurring on Barrow Island, WA, and in eastern NT and interior of Qld. *C. p. calx* occurs in east Kimberley, WA, and northern NT.

Microhabitat Shelters beneath low vegetation such as grass hummocks or heath plants, and occasionally under rocks. Forages in open spaces between vegetation.

Comments Carries body high off ground in a distinctive monitor-like gait when moving in open. Although *C. p. pantherinus* and *C. p. ocellifer* take a variety of arthropod prey, termites constitute the major food source. Active throughout year, foraging during most times of day. Breeding normally occurs from September to October. From 3 to 9 eggs (usually 7) are recorded per clutch.

Ctenotus piankai Storr, 1969
Photo 382

Description Member of *C. atlas* group. Dorsal ground colour brown to brownish black. Pattern consists of 6 (occasionally 8) whitish stripes; often tinged dorsally with yellow to brown. Pale paravertebral stripes extend from nape to middle of tail; flushed with brown beyond hips. Pale dorsolateral and midlateral stripes extend from behind eye, well onto tail. Pale ventrolateral stripe (if present) extends from ear to base of tail; wavy or broken between ear and forelimb. Head reddish to olive-brown. Tail pale brown. Limbs reddish brown, streaked with blackish brown. Ventral surfaces white. SVL 55 mm.

Distinguished from *C. duricola* in lacking pale spots in upper lateral zone, and bearing fewer midbody scale rows (24–26 vs 26–32). Differs from *C. decaneurus, C. quattuordecimlineatus, C. atlas, C. yampiensis* and *C. dux* in bearing fewer pale stripes (6, occasionally 8, vs 8 or more).

Preferred habitat Sandy soils vegetated with hummock grass associations from arid north-western coast to southern Kimberley region, extending through interior of WA to western NT. Isolated population occurs in the vicinity of Exmouth Gulf, WA.

Microhabitat Shelters in shallow burrows beneath grass hummocks. Forages in and around hummocks, and in open spaces between them.

Comments Feeds largely on termites. Other arthropods such as bugs and spiders are also taken. Active throughout year (at least in WA deserts), foraging during middle of day. Breeds in WA from September to October. Otherwise as for species group.

Ctenotus pulchellus Storr, 1978
Photo 383

Description Member of *C. leonhardii* group. Dorsal ground colour orange-brown to reddish brown with 5 prominent blackish brown stripes. Broad vertebral and narrow dorsal stripes extend from nape to base of tail. Dark laterodorsal stripe extends from above eye to base of tail. White dorsolateral

stripe extends from above eye onto tail. Blackish brown upper lateral zone usually encloses 1–3 irregular series of white dots; represented on tail by dark brown stripe. Side of head and mid to lower lateral zone orange-red, bearing 3–5 irregular series of prominent white dots. Limbs reddish brown, striped with blackish brown. Ventral surfaces white. SVL 65 mm.

Distinguished from *C. hebetior* by nature of upper lateral zone (considerably darker than lower lateral zone vs not noticeably darker), and by width of vertebral stripe (noticeably broader than dorsal stripes, at least anteriorly, vs more or less equal in width). Differs from *C. leonhardii* in bearing 5 (vs 3) dark dorsal stripes, and in lacking a pale midlateral stripe.

Preferred habitat Loamy to stony ridges and flats vegetated with hummock grasslands, in association with eucalypt/*Acacia* woodlands or low *Acacia* shrublands. Occurs in arid north-western interior of Qld and adjacent NT west to Brunette Downs Station.

Microhabitat As for species group.

Comments As for species group.

Ctenotus quattuordecimlineatus (Sternfeld, 1919)
Photo 384

Description Member of *C. atlas* group with ground colour of black, flushed with red on tail and lower back. Pattern consists of 14 (occasionally 16) pale stripes: paravertebrals, dorsals, dorsolaterals, 2 upper laterals, midlaterals and ventrolaterals. These are usually narrower than dark interspaces, and arranged as follows. Pale brown paravertebral stripes extend from nape to middle of tail. Pale brown dorsal stripes extend from nape to base of tail. Pale brown dorsolateral stripes extend from above and behind eye onto tail. Two whitish to pale brown upper lateral stripes (sometimes broken or irregular anteriorly) extend from above and behind ear to hips, joining to form one stripe on tail. Broad white midlateral stripe extends from behind ear onto tail. White ventrolateral stripe extends from below and behind ear (interrupted by forelimb) to groin. Tip of snout pale brown. Limbs pale brown striped with darker brown. Ventral surfaces white. SVL 65 mm.

Distinguished from *C. ariadnae* and *C. dux* in bearing fewer pale stripes (14, occasionally 16, vs 18 or more). Differs from *C. atlas, C. piankai* and *C. iapetus* in bearing a greater number of pale stripes (14, occasionally 16, vs 12 or less).

Preferred habitat Arid reddish sand ridges and sand plains vegetated with hummock grasslands; in pure stands, or in association with woodlands and shrublands. Extends from north-west and interior of WA to adjacent deserts of southern NT and north-western SA.

Microhabitat As for species group.
Comments Feeds on a variety of insects; bugs, termites and moths are most frequently recorded. Most active during late summer; individuals usually encountered during late morning to early afternoon. Usually breeds from September to October.

Ctenotus quinkan Ingram, 1979
Photo 385
Description Large robust *Ctenotus*; sole member of *C. quinkan* group. Dorsal ground colour olive-brown without pattern. Pale dorsolateral stripe extends from above eye to base of tail. Upper lateral zone, from nostril well onto tail, immaculate black. White to pale pinkish red midlateral stripe extends from ear to hindlimb; bordered below by a black line from forelimb. Limbs brown, striped with black. Ventral surfaces white. SVL 80 mm.
Preferred habitat Sandstone escarpments vegetated with low open eucalypt woodlands, with a sparse understorey of *Acacia* shrubs and hummock grasses. Occurs in subhumid areas of eastern Cape York Peninsula, between Laura and coast north of Cooktown, Qld.
Microhabitat Shelters beneath sandstone slabs.
Comments Though the largest museum specimen measures SVL 80 mm, field observations suggest *C. quinkan* greatly exceeds this size, and may well be Australia's largest *Ctenotus*.

Ctenotus rawlinsoni Ingram, 1979
Photo 386
Description Member of *C. lesueurii* group. Ground colour black, marked with 6 prominent pale stripes. White, pale grey to olive paravertebral stripes extend from nape to about middle of tail, becoming diffuse beyond hips. White dorsolateral stripe extends from above eye to middle of tail. Broad black upper lateral zone extends from about ear to middle of tail, fading beyond hips to leave dark upper and lower margins only. Broad white midlateral stripe (wavy or broken from ear to forelimb) extends to about middle of tail. Narrow dark lower lateral stripe (broken into variegations on neck and anterior body) extends onto base of tail. Tail flushed with pale yellowish brown and finely dotted with black. Limbs pale reddish brown to cream, striped with black. Ventral surfaces white. SVL 80 mm.
Preferred habitat Only known from a small area of heathlands growing on white coastal sands (excluding first coastal dunes) on subhumid eastern Cape York Peninsula, Qld.
Microhabitat Shelters in burrows beneath low vegetation.
Comments As for species group.

Ctenotus regius Storr, 1971
Photo 387
Description Brightly patterned member of *C. leonhardii* group with dorsal ground colour of pale to rich brown. Blackish vertebral, and cream to white paravertebral stripes extend from nape to base of tail. Broad to narrow black laterodorsal stripe extends from above eye to base, or well onto tail. Whitish dorsolateral stripe extends from above eye well onto tail. Upper lateral zone dark reddish brown to blackish, enclosing 1 or 2 series of pale spots or dashes. White midlateral stripe extends from upper lip, through ear to tail. Dark lower lateral stripe extends from behind ear (wavy and irregular to forelimb or a little behind) to hindlimb. This is represented on side of tail as an obscure narrow dark line. Limbs brown, streaked with black to dark brown. Ventral surfaces whitish. SVL 70 mm.

Distinguished from *C. leonhardii* and *C. hebetior* by nature of pale midlateral stripe (extending continuously forward to side of head vs indistinct and broken anteriorly). Differs further from *C. hebetior* in bearing fewer dark dorsal stripes (3 vs 5). Differs from *C. uber* in lacking pale laterodorsal spots.
Preferred habitat Semi-arid to arid interior of south-eastern Australia, from south-eastern Qld, through western NSW and north-western Vic. to midwestern SA and south-eastern NT. Favours heavy to sandy reddish soils supporting open woodlands and shrublands, often in association with hummock grasslands.
Microhabitat As for species group.
Comments As for species group.

Ctenotus robustus Storr, 1970
Photos 388–390
Description Very large to moderately large member of *C. lesueurii* group; attaining greatest size in Kimberley region, WA. Dorsal ground colour pale to dark brown or olive-brown. Broad black vertebral and prominent cream to white paravertebral stripes extend from nape to base, or beyond middle of tail. Broad to narrow black laterodorsal, and prominent narrow cream to white dorsolateral stripes extend from above eye well onto tail. Upper lateral zone, from snout to hips, dark olive-brown to dark brown; represented on tail as a stripe to tip. This encloses 1 or 2 series of diffuse pale spots or dashes on body. Pale midlateral stripe extends from nostril, narrowly over hindlimb to tail-tip. This may be obscure in eastern parts of range. Lower flanks variegated with grey and obscurely spotted with white. Limbs ground colour, streaked, striped or marbled with blackish brown. Some populations from mideast coastal lowlands and adjacent sandy offshore islands lack all pattern. Ventral surfaces white. SVL 115 mm through most of range; up to 120 mm in Kimberley region, WA.

Distinguished from *C. arcanus* and *C. eurydice* by nature of upper lateral pattern (dark olive bearing large diffuse pale spots, vs black, sometimes enclosing small, sharp white spots). Differs from *C. helen-*

ae and *C. borealis* in bearing stronger pattern, particularly a pale-edged dark vertebral stripe. Northern populations differ from *C. inornatus, C. saxatilis* and *C. spaldingi* by nature of dark vertebral and laterodorsal stripes (usually broader). Differs further from *C. inornatus* and *C. saxatilis* by extent of pale midlateral stripe (reaching forward well beyond forelimb vs absent or fading at forelimb) and in usually bearing fewer upper labial scales (usually 7 vs usually 8). Differs further from *C. spaldingi* in bearing more supraocular scales (4 vs 3). Differs from *C. arnhemensis* in attaining much greater size (SVL 115–120 vs 50 mm). Differs from *C. capricorni* in lacking a pale dorsal stripe (vs usually present). Differs from *C. lateralis* in bearing upper lateral blotches (vs a narrow stripe).

Preferred habitat Wide variety of habitats from south-eastern SA, through most of Vic. (excluding semi-arid sandy north-west and cool wet south-east), north along coast and eastern interior to Cape York Peninsula, Qld, thence through northern NT to northern Kimberley region, WA. Particularly abundant in granites through southern half of range. Equally successful in coastal dunes, black-soil plains of interior, and woodlands of north. Usually less abundant on sand plain habitats. Occasionally penetrates wet sclerophyll forests via open corridors such as rock outcrops or roads.

Microhabitat In rocky areas, short shallow tunnels are excavated in soil under slabs. Elsewhere, burrows are situated beneath debris, at bases of low vegetation, or beneath fallen timber.

Comments Status uncertain. Though differences exist between northern and south-eastern populations, these appear to merge into one another. *C. robustus* is tentatively treated here as one widespread species. Usually the dominant large *Ctenotus* within its range. Other large *Ctenotus* are usually scarce or absent in areas where *C. robustus* is present. See species group.

Ctenotus rubicundus Storr, 1978
Photo 391

Description Large robust *Ctenotus*; sole member of *C. rubicundus* group. Back, top of head and forelimbs rich reddish brown; paler on flanks. Side of head brown. Hips, hindlimbs and tail greyish brown. Each scale faintly dark-edged, otherwise pattern absent. Ventral surfaces pinkish white. SVL 95 mm.

Preferred habitat Rocky hills and escarpments vegetated with hummock grasses in interior of Pilbara region, WA.

Microhabitat Shelters beneath rock slabs and fragments, or under dense grass hummocks.

Comments No data available.

Ctenotus rutilans Storr, 1980
Photo 392

Description Small member of *C. leonhardii*

group. Anterior body, neck, base of head, and forelimbs coppery red. Posterior dorsal surface brown. Narrow pale-edged black vertebral stripe may extend from lower nape to base of tail. Broad black laterodorsal stripe extends from level of forelimb to base of tail, enclosing a series of pale spots or short dashes. Narrow pale dorsolateral stripe extends from nape to base of tail. Upper flanks blackish brown; continuing on tail as a broad dark stripe, and enclosing approximately 3 series of pale reddish brown dots on body. Prominent pale midlateral stripe extends from in front of hindlimb onto base of tail. Lower flanks reddish brown, bearing 2 or 3 series of pinkish dots. Foreparts of head greyish brown. Limbs boldly striped with black. Ventral surfaces white. SVL 50 mm.

Distinguished from *C. uber* in bearing a strong coppery red flush over head and neck, and in attaining smaller maximum size (SVL 50 vs 70 mm).

Preferred habitat Low eucalypt/*Acacia* woodlands in association with *Triodia*-dominated ground cover on heavy stony soils of arid Pilbara plateau, north-western WA, extending south into Gascoyne region as far as Byro Station, where it occurs on loams and sands vegetated with *Acacia* shrublands.

Microhabitat Shelters in *Triodia* hummocks or beneath stones and logs.

Comments As for species group.

Ctenotus saxatilis Storr, 1970
Photo 393

Description Member of *C. lesueurii* group. Dorsal ground colour pale or dark olive-brown, brown, to reddish brown. Narrow to moderately broad, pale-edged dark vertebral stripe (broadest at hips) extends from nape; usually fading to brown between base and middle of tail. Narrow white dorsolateral, and broad to narrow black laterodorsal stripes extend from nape or behind eye well onto tail; becoming broader and suffused with brown beyond hips. Upper lateral zone blackish brown; represented on side of tail by a dark-edged pale stripe, extending nearly to tip. This zone is variably mottled with pale grey or brownish white. Pale markings often cluster to form an indistinct series of large spots, particularly on juveniles. Whitish midlateral stripe extends forward from hindlimb, fading and breaking at about forelimb. Lower posterior margin usually dark-edged. Head and tail usually paler shade of ground colour. Limbs ground colour, streaked to striped with dark brown. Ventral surfaces white. SVL 100 mm.

Distinguished from *C. helenae* and *C. inornatus* in bearing a stronger pattern, particularly the presence of a prominent pale-edged dark vertebral stripe. Differs from sympatric populations of *C. robustus* by nature of dark laterodorsal and vertebral stripes (usually narrower). Differs further from *C. robustus*, and from *C. serventyi* and *C. spaldingi*, by extent of pale midlateral stripe (becoming diffuse and breaking on anterior body vs extending forward beyond forelimb). Differs further from *C. spaldingi* in bearing more supraocular scales (4 vs 3). Differs from *C. lateralis* by nature of lower lateral pattern (obscure pale mottling vs a narrow lower lateral stripe).

Preferred habitat Occurs in a wide variety of habitats in subhumid to arid areas from north-west coast of WA, through southern Kimberley region and NT (excluding far north) to northern SA and western Qld. Populations from southern NT are most abundant on river floodplains.

Microhabitat Shelters beneath rocks or low vegetation, seldom venturing far into open spaces.

Comments As for species group.

Ctenotus schevilli (Loveridge, 1933)
Photo 394

Description Largest member of *C. schevilli* group. Ground colour olive-brown, often flushed with pale reddish brown on lateral surfaces. Blackish dorsal spots may coalesce to form an irregular vertebral stripe or series of variegations from midbody to hips or proximal third of tail. Remaining pattern consists of small pale spots; scattered on dorsum, and tending to align vertically on flanks. Top of head patternless. Temples bear pale spots. Limbs pale reddish brown; forelimbs usually patternless, and hindlimbs marked with obscure darker streaks. Ventral surfaces white. SVL 85 mm.

Preferred habitat Deeply cracking black-soil plains vegetated with Mitchell grasses (*Astrebla* spp.) in arid central Qld from Richmond area south to Muttaburra and Aramac districts. Occasionally occurs in ecotonal zones of adjacent habitat types.

Microhabitat As for *C. schevilli* group.

Comments See genus and *C. schevilli* group.

Ctenotus schomburgkii (Peters, 1863)
Photos 395–397

Description Member of *C. schomburgkii* group subject to considerable geographic variation, particularly in western half of range. Three forms occur.

Western form: Dorsal ground colour olive, grey to brown. Black vertebral line extends from nape well onto tail. White dorsolateral stripe extends from above eye well onto base of tail; margined above by a black (often broken or obscure) laterodorsal stripe. Remainder of dorsum bears conspicuous black variegations. Upper lateral zone bears alternating black and reddish vertical bars. White midlateral stripe (disjunct at ear) extends from upper lip to base of tail. Irregular lower lateral series of dark bars usually present.

South-western form: Pattern considerably less complex. Dorsum olive-brown; unmarked except for narrow black vertebral stripe. This may be absent, or reduced to a dark line on nape. White dorsolateral stripe, bordered by distinct dark laterodorsal stripe, extends from above eye onto tail.

Black upper lateral zone commences as a streak on snout, and encloses a series of whitish to reddish spots or blotches. Whitish midlateral stripe (disjunct at ear) extends from upper lip onto tail. Black ventrolateral stripe (wavy or broken anteriorly) extends from side of neck to behind hindlimb. Ground colour of limbs whitish.

Widespread form, occupying eastern portion of range: Dorsal ground colour pale reddish to olive-brown. Five dark dorsal stripes extend from nape onto base of tail: vertebral, dorsals and laterodorsals. Cream dorsolateral stripe extends from above eye onto tail. Upper lateral zone black, bearing a series of prominent, irregularly shaped reddish brown blotches from behind eye onto tail. White midlateral stripe broken at ear. Limbs reddish.

Limbs of all forms marbled with black. Ventral surfaces white. SVL 50 mm.

Distinguished from *C. brooksi* (excepting the distinctively patterned *C. b. iridis*) in bearing prominent pale dorsolateral stripes (vs broken or absent). Eastern form differs further from *C. b. aranda*, and from *C. strauchii*, *C. tantillus* and *C. pallescens*, in bearing 5 prominent dark dorsal stripes.

Preferred habitat Occurs in semi-arid to arid regions, in a variety of soil and vegetation types. Favours a sparse low ground cover of shrubs, tussocks or hummock grasses. Western form occurs in western interior of WA, from the Pilbara region south to Bindoon. South-western form occurs in the south-western interior of WA. Eastern form occupies remainder of range: eastern interior of WA, through SA and southern NT to southern NSW. Disjunct population of eastern form occurs in southern Kimberley region, WA.

Microhabitat As for species group.

Comments Feeds on a variety of arthropods, particularly termites. Active throughout year, reaching a peak in summer. Pianka notes that 2 activity periods are apparent for the eastern form in WA: early morning and late afternoon. He found that breeding takes place from September to October, with 2–4 eggs laid per clutch.

Ctenotus serotinus Czechura, 1986
Photo 398

Description Small member of *C. schevilli* group. Dorsal ground colour olive-brown irregularly marked with sparse paler spots. Ragged-edged black vertebral stripe extends from nape onto base of tail, narrowly margined with diffuse pale paravertebral stripes. Diffuse pale dorsolateral stripe extends from above eye onto tail, becoming broader and more diffuse beyond hips. Upper flanks dark olive-brown enclosing several series of small white spots, tending to align vertically. Diffuse pale grey midlateral stripe (broken anteriorly) extends from behind eye onto tail. Lower flanks pale grey with darker clouding. Upper labial scales cream, each with a dark posterior edge. Limbs obscurely striped with dark and pale brown. Juveniles are more strongly marked: vertebral and paravertebral stripes sharp-edged, midlateral stripe bolder. Ventral surfaces white. SVL 49 mm.

Distinguished from *C. astarte* by smaller size (SVL 49 vs 80 mm) and stronger development of vertebral and paravertebral stripes.

Preferred habitat Known only from Diamantina Lakes area in arid south-western Qld, on a dune and on stony soil adjacent to a dune.

Microhabitat As for *C. schevilli* group.

Comments See genus and *C. schevilli* group.

Ctenotus serventyi Storr, 1975
Photo 399

Description Small member of *C. leonhardii* group. Ground colour pale yellowish brown to brown. Narrow black vertebral, and brownish white paravertebral stripes extend from nape to base of tail. Narrow dark dorsal stripe present on immature specimens. Narrow dark (often pale-edged) laterodorsal stripe extends from nape to base of tail. White dorsolateral stripe extends from above and behind eye to middle of tail or beyond. Upper lateral zone, from behind eye to hindlimb, dark brown; represented on tail as a dark stripe extending nearly to tip. This encloses 1 or 2 series of brownish white dots and/or short dashes on body. White midlateral stripe extends from upper lips (disjunct at ear) well onto tail. Lower lateral zone brown, bearing irregular white markings anteriorly. Tail pale yellowish to reddish brown. Limbs pale brown striped with darker brown. Ventral surfaces white, often suffused with pink beneath tail. SVL 55 mm.

Distinguished from *C. saxatilis*, *C. inornatus* and *C. leonhardii* by extent of pale midlateral stripe (reaching upper lip, vs obscure and broken, at least beyond forelimb). Differs further from *C. inornatus* in bearing a more prominent pattern; particularly a pale-edged dark vertebral stripe, and a prominent dark upper lateral zone enclosing sharp white spots or dashes (vs vertebral stripe often indistinct to absent, and upper lateral pattern diffuse). Differs further from *C. saxatilis* and *C. inornatus* in attaining much smaller maximum size (SVL 55 vs 100 and 95 mm, respectively).

Preferred habitat Shrublands and woodlands on sandy loams in southern Kimberley region and north-western coastal plains and offshore islands, extending east to Fitzroy Crossing and south-west to Pannawonica, WA. Pilbara populations are restricted to alluvial sands and loams.

Microhabitat As for species group.

Comments As for species group.

Ctenotus severus Storr, 1969
Photo 400

Description Member of *C. lesueurii* group. Dorsal ground colour varies through shades of brown to reddish brown. Narrow dark vertebral line (seldom pale-edged) may extend from nape to hips; often absent, or reduced to a fine line on nape. Broad dark laterodorsal stripe (narrower in north), bordered by conspicuous whitish dorsolateral stripe, extends from above eye to proximal quarter of tail. This is usually margined below by a narrow strip of ground colour. Dark brown upper lateral zone (obscure between eye and ear) extends to groin. This becomes diffuse on base of tail, and encloses pale spots of varying shape and arrangement on body. Pale midlateral stripe (indistinct to broken anteriorly) extends from ear to groin, thence onto side of tail. Limbs brown with darker streaks. Ventral surfaces white. SVL 85 mm.

Distinguished from *C. alleni* and *C. mimetes* in bearing a narrow upper lateral strip of ground colour between pale dorsolateral stripe and dark upper lateral zone.

Preferred habitat Arid midwest and interior of WA. Occurs on heavy to sandy soils (especially rocky areas) dominated by *Acacia* woodlands and shrublands. Particularly successful on river floodplains and granite outcrops.

Microhabitat As for species group.

Comments As for species group.

Spalding's Skink
Ctenotus spaldingi (Macleay, 1877)
Photos 401–403

Description Large variable member of *C. lesueurii* group. Dorsal ground colour pale greyish brown, sometimes flushed with reddish brown posteriorly. Narrow to moderately broad black vertebral stripe (with or without pale edge) usually extends from nape to base of tail in south and west of range. This may be completely absent, or reduced to foreback in north-east. Narrow dark brown to black laterodorsal stripe (sometimes broken into series of triangular spots) usually present. Narrow white dorsolateral stripe extends from above eye to base of tail. Dark brown to black upper lateral zone encloses a series of white to pale brown squarish blotches; sometimes indistinct anteriorly. White midlateral stripe extends from forebody or below eye to base of tail. Pale ventrolateral stripe present or absent. Head and tail pale brown. Limbs pale greyish brown, striped or indistinctly streaked with brownish black. Ventral surfaces white. SVL 100 mm.

Distinguished from all other members of *C. lesueurii* group in bearing fewer supraocular scales (3 vs usually 4).

Preferred habitat Woodlands, rock outcrops and grassy coastal dunes from northern NT to northern interior of Qld, Cape York Peninsula and Torres Strait Islands. Extralimital in southern New Guinea.

Microhabitat As for species group.

Comments Three apparently distinct forms occur, at least in Qld. These may constitute distinct taxa. Otherwise as for species group.

Ctenotus storri Rankin, 1978
Photo 404

Description Small member of *C. atlas* group. Dorsal ground colour dark brown, yellowish brown to bright yellow. Pattern consists of usually 8 pale stripes: paravertebrals, dorsals, dorsolaterals and midlaterals. Pale yellowish brown paravertebral stripes commence as one on nape, separating to enclose a dark vertebral stripe (occasionally fused to form a broad pale vertebral line), rejoining at about level of hindlimb, and extending well onto tail. Pale brown to yellow dorsal stripe extends from base of head to base of tail. Broad black laterodorsal, and narrow whitish dorsolateral stripes extend from above eye well onto tail. Broad black upper lateral zone extends from eye well onto tail. Moderately broad white midlateral stripe extends from upper lip and over ear, well onto tail. This is bordered below by a dark stripe from behind ear, fading behind hindlimb. Traces of a dark ventrolateral stripe may be present on anterior body. Limbs yellowish brown striped with black. Ventral surfaces white; pink beneath limbs. SVL 40 mm.

Distinguished from *C. decaneurus* by nature of paravertebral stripes (coalescing, at least on nape and hips, vs separated by a black vertebral stripe).
Preferred habitat Woodland/grassland associations on sandy or clay-based alluvial flats of subhumid coastal north-western NT.
Microhabitat Excavates narrow, steeply descending burrows into vertical surfaces of shallow depressions. Occasionally spider burrows are utilised. Forages widely in open spaces between vegetation.
Comments As for species group.

Ctenotus strauchii (Boulenger, 1887)
Photos 405, 406

Description Variable member of *C. schomburgkii* group, comprising 2 recognised subspecies.
C. s. strauchii Dorsal ground colour brown, sometimes bearing a pale-edged black vertebral stripe from nape to base of tail. Black laterodorsal stripe of variable width extends from above eye to base of tail. This encloses a series of pale spots or short dashes. White dorsolateral stripe extends from above eye to tail, becoming wider and suffused with brown posteriorly. Black upper lateral zone commences on side of head as a brown streak, and extends onto tail as a brownish (sometimes raggededged) stripe. This encloses 1–3 series of whitish to pinkish (usually vertically aligned) dots. White midlateral stripe extends from upper lip (disjunct at ear, and often wavy or broken to forelimb) to base of tail. Narrow greyish brown to black lower lateral zone sometimes encloses small irregular white spots. Limbs pale brown, streaked or mottled with black. Ventral surfaces white. SVL 55 mm.
C. s. varius Storr, 1981 Dorsal ground colour olive-grey, pale reddish brown to pale yellowish

brown. Narrow dark vertebral and dorsal stripes present or absent. Usually a laterodorsal series of short dark transverse bars or irregular spots present, sometimes coalescing to form variegations. Pale (usually narrow and poorly defined) dorsolateral stripe extends from eye to base of tail. Black upper lateral zone may enclose 1–3 series of small pale spots, or break into vertical bars or rectangular blotches alternating with similarly sized bars of ground colour. This zone extends onto side of head as a narrow black streak, and on tail as a series of squarish brown spots. Narrow whitish midlateral stripe extends from upper lip to base of tail. Narrow grey lower lateral zone usually present. Tail pale yellowish brown to reddish brown. Ventral surfaces white. SVL 50 mm.

Distinguished from sympatric eastern form of *C. schomburgkii* in lacking 5 dark dorsal stripes. Differs from *C. allotropis* in bearing a dark vertebral stripe; present on *C. s. strauchii* within zone of overlap.
Preferred habitat Favours stony soils with sparse low ground cover, usually in association with woodlands or shrublands. *C. s. strauchii* occurs in subhumid to arid areas from eastern and midwestern Qld to adjacent northern interior of NSW, where it begins to intergrade with *C. s. varius*. *C. s. varius* extends through south-western Qld, south-eastern NT, north-eastern SA and far north-western NSW. Range overlaps with *C. brooksi aranda*, but favours harder soils.
Microhabitat As for species group.
Comments As for species group.

Ctenotus striaticeps Storr, 1978
Photo 407

Description Member of *C. colletti* group with 8 prominent pale stripes (suffused on top of head with orange) over black ground colour. Paravertebral stripes converge on top of snout, and extend well back onto tail. Dorsolateral stripe extends from in front of eye, well onto tail. Black upper lateral zone extends forward to snout, and back nearly to tail-tip. Broad white midlateral stripe extends from upper lip well onto tail. Moderately narrow black lower lateral stripe extends from lower margin of upper labial scales, through ear and insertion of hindlimb onto base of tail. Narrow white ventrolateral and narrow black lateroventral stripes extend from forelimb to hindlimb. Limbs blackish brown, boldly striped with pale orange. Distal half of tail greyish. Ventral surfaces white. SVL 50 mm.

Distinguished from all other sympatric *Ctenotus* by extent of paravertebral stripes: reaching forward to, and coalescing on, snout.
Preferred habitat Undulating stony hills supporting a dominant ground cover of hummock grasses, associated with scattered eucalypts and shrubs. Occurs in subhumid to arid north-western Qld and adjacent NT.

Microhabitat Shelters in shallow burrows excavated beneath stones or grass hummocks.
Comments See species group.

Copper-tailed Skink
Ctenotus taeniolatus (White, 1790)
Photos 408, 409

Description Moderately small member of *C. lesueurii* group with simple pattern consisting of alternating dark and pale stripes. Dorsal ground colour brown to rich brown, often reduced in width to form narrow dorsal stripes. Broad black vertebral stripe extends from head to base of or well onto tail. White to cream paravertebral stripes (broadly to narrowly margined with black on body) extend from between eyes to about middle of tail, darkening to yellowish or brownish beyond hips. Black laterodorsal stripe extends from top of head, usually terminating at hips or base of tail. White to yellowish dorsolateral stripe extends from above eye, becoming broader and darker on tail. Upper lateral zone black, sometimes bearing a white spot and a short pale streak on side of head of northern populations. This is represented on tail as a black line to tip. White midlateral stripe extends from above upper lip, curving sharply over ear to tail. Black lower lateral stripe extends from upper lip, through or below ear to hindlimb. Narrow black ventrolateral stripe extends from below ear onto base of tail. Limbs reddish, striped or streaked with black. Tail rich coppery brown in south, pale olive on coastal sands, brown elsewhere. Ventral surfaces white. SVL 65 mm.

Distinguished from *C. arcanus* and *C. eurydice* in attaining a smaller maximum size (SVL 65 vs 85 and 75 mm, respectively), and by nature of snout (relatively sharp in profile vs rounded). Differs further in invariably lacking white lateral spots (vs present to absent). Differs further from *C. arcanus*, and from *C. ingrami*, by extent of dorsal ground colour (constricted by black margins to form brown dorsal stripes, vs broad, interrupted only by a black vertebral stripe with narrow pale edges).
Preferred habitat Inhabits a variety of woodland and heathland associations on stony to sandy soils. Rock outcrops such as sandstones or granites are particularly favoured. Extends along coast and ranges from north-eastern Vic. to south-eastern Cape York, Qld.
Microhabitat Excavates shallow burrows beneath rocks or logs. Populations living on coastal sands construct burrows at bases of low shrubs.
Comments Occasionally occurs in large numbers, several individuals often found beneath a single rock. Otherwise as for species group.

Ctenotus tanamiensis Storr, 1970
Photo 410

Description Large member of *C. leonhardii* group with pattern dominated by longitudinal series of white dots and dashes. Dorsal and upper lateral ground colour dark reddish brown. Broad pale-edged dark vertebral stripe extends from nape to base of tail. Dark laterodorsal zone, enclosing a series of relatively large brownish white dots, extends onto base or middle of tail as a dark brown stripe. Dorsolateral series of smaller white dashes present. Upper lateral zone bears 2 or 3 series of very small vertically aligned dots; represented on tail as a dark brown stripe extending almost to tip. Mid and lower lateral zones pinkish brown, bearing larger, increasingly irregular pale spots. Head and tail suffused with reddish brown. Lips vertically barred with white and brown. Limbs pale reddish brown, bearing darker stripes. Ventral surfaces whitish, suffused with yellowish brown beneath tail. SVL 90 mm.
Preferred habitat Recorded from reddish sand plains supporting hummock grasslands in Tanami Desert of central western NT and adjacent WA.
Microhabitat Presumably as for species group.
Comments See species group.

Ctenotus tantillus Storr, 1975
Photo 411

Description Member of *C. schomburgkii* group with olive-brown dorsal ground colour. Pale-edged dark vertebral line usually present. Dark dorsal and laterodorsal stripes present or absent. White dorsolateral stripe (sometimes broken into a series of dashes) extends from eye to base of tail. Black upper lateral zone encloses an irregular series of small white spots. Whitish midlateral stripe well developed, broken or absent. Lower lateral zone brown, bearing obscure white spots or blotches. Limbs pale brown striped with dark brown. Ventral surfaces white. SVL 45 mm.

Distinguished from sympatric eastern form of *C. schomburgkii* in bearing weaker dorsal pattern.
Preferred habitat Woodlands on sandy (occasionally heavy) soils with a ground cover of shrubs or grasses in east Kimberley region, WA, and adjacent NT.
Microhabitat As for species group.
Comments As for species group.

Ctenotus uber Storr, 1969
Photos 412–414

Description Member of *C. leonhardii* group comprising 3 recognised subspecies.
C. u. uber Dorsal ground colour reddish brown, brown, olive to yellowish brown. Narrow black vertebral line (sometimes pale-edged) present or absent. If present, this extends from nape to foreback, occasionally to base of tail. Moderately broad reddish brown, blackish brown to black laterodorsal stripe, enclosing a series of brown or white spots (sharpest posteriorly), extends from behind eye to base of tail. White to yellowish brown dorsolateral

stripe (sometimes broken into a series of spots or short dashes) extends from behind eye onto base of tail. Broad reddish brown to black upper lateral zone extends from behind eye to groin; represented on tail as a dark stripe almost to tip. This encloses 2 or 3 series of brownish white to white dots or short dashes on body. Broken white midlateral stripe barely discernible to absent; sometimes represented by small white dots or oblique dashes from snout onto base of tail. Lower lateral zone greyish brown, reddish brown to brown, spotted and/or variegated with white. Head brown to olive. Tail pale brown, reddish brown, yellowish brown to olive. Limbs pale reddish brown to brown, striped or streaked with blackish brown. Ventral surfaces white. SVL 70 mm.

C. u. orientalis Storr 1971   Differs from nominate form in bearing a well-developed vertebral stripe from nape to base of tail. Upper lateral zone represented on tail by dark stippling (vs stripe). SVL 80 mm.

C. u. johnstonei Storr, 1980   Differs from nominate form in bearing a well-developed vertebral stripe, and by arrangement of nasal scales (in contact vs rarely in contact).

All subspecies are distinguished from *C. alleni*, *C. leonhardii*, *C. mimetes* and *C. regius* in bearing a laterodorsal series of pale dots or dashes. *C. u. uber* differs from *C. rutilans* in lacking a coppery red flush from head to forebody, and in attaining larger maximum size (SVL 70 vs 50 mm). *C. u. uber* differs from *C. greeri* by nature of dark vertebral and pale midlateral stripes (poorly developed to absent vs relatively more prominent).

Preferred habitat   *C. u. uber* occupies a variety of habitats throughout semi-arid to arid central and southern interior of WA, adjacent SA and far southwest corner of NT. Where it occurs in sympatry with *C. leonhardii*, *C. u. uber* tends to favour lusher habitats: along washes and minor watercourses. *C. u. orientalis* occurs in subhumid to arid eastern portion of species range, with isolated populations in central Vic. and cooler rocky areas from northeastern Vic. to ACT. *C. u. johnstonei* is known only from an area of chenopod shrubland at the base of a sandstone hill in vicinity of Balgo, north-eastern interior of WA.

Microhabitat   *C. u. orientalis* is recorded to excavate multi-chambered burrow systems beneath rock slabs on sandy soils in Mt Lofty Ranges of SA, and in the vicinity of Canberra, ACT. Otherwise as for species group.

Comments   Populations occurring in eastern highlands may constitute an undescribed taxon. See species group.

Ctenotus vertebralis Rankin and Gillam, 1979
Photo 415

Description   Small slender member of *C. lesueurii* group. Dorsal ground colour pale coppery brown,

olive-brown to greyish brown, suffused anteriorly with copper to dark grey. Broad to narrow pale-edged black vertebral stripe (when present) extends from nape well onto tail. Prominent to obscure, continuous or broken pale dorsolateral stripe or line (boldest anteriorly) extends from ear or eye to body or base of tail. This is sometimes bordered anteriorly by an obscure black laterodorsal stripe. Narrow blackish upper lateral zone extends from behind ear to hindlimb. Narrow obscure (sometimes broken) whitish midlateral stripe extends from behind ear to hindlimb. Lower lateral zone pale to dark brown or grey. Head pale to dark silvery grey, sometimes spotted or peppered with black. Limbs pale yellowish brown, sometimes bearing scattered darker spots. Ventral surfaces whitish. Pattern of juveniles bolder than that of adults. SVL 55 mm.

Distinguished from *C. inornatus* in attaining smaller maximum size (SVL 55 vs 75 mm), and in usually bearing a more prominent vertebral stripe.

Preferred habitat   Favours woodlands, with understorey of soft spinifex *(Plectrachne)* or tall annual grasses, on lateritic to sandy soils adjacent to rock outcrops in subhumid northern NT.

Microhabitat   As for species group.

Comments   A female containing 3 or 4 well-developed eggs, and males with enlarged testes were collected in July. Very young juveniles (less than 30 mm SVL) have been observed during February. Otherwise as for species group.

Ctenotus xenopleura Storr, 1981
Photo 416

Description   Small member of *C. atlas* group with pattern consisting of 10 pale stripes on black ground colour. Narrow coppery white to pale yellowish brown paravertebral, dorsal and dorsolateral stripes extend from nape to base of tail. Broad black upper lateral zone extending from eye to hindlimb encloses 1 or 2 series of elongate whitish spots; occasionally coalescing to form irregular streaks. Broad white midlateral stripe extends from upper lip, through ear to hindlimb. This is separated from a broad white lower lateral stripe by a narrow black line from in front of ear to hindlimb. Head pale yellowish brown to pale olive, finely marked with blackish brown. Tail and limbs pale yellowish brown, sometimes with a coppery tinge. Tail usually bears indications of dark stripes. Limbs striped with black. Ventral surfaces white. SVL 45 mm.

Preferred habitat   Isolated patches of *Triodia* and heathland associated with low *Casuarina* and mallee woodlands, on yellowish sandy soils in semi-arid southern interior of WA.

Microhabitat   Closely associated with *Triodia*.

Comments   As for species group.

Ctenotus yampiensis Storr, 1975
Photo 417

Description   Member of *C. atlas* group. Dorsal

ground colour black, merging to reddish brown on head. Normally bears 10 pale olive to white stripes: paravertebrals, dorsals, dorsolaterals, midlaterals and ventrolaterals; occasionally 8 when ventrolaterals are absent, or 12 when a broken upper lateral is present. Ventral surfaces white. SVL 50 mm.

Distinguished from *C. decaneurus* in bearing more midbody scale rows (30–32 vs 24–26) and larger ear lobules. Differs from *C. piankai* in usually bearing a greater number of pale stripes (10, occasionally 8 or 12; vs 6, occasionally 8).

Preferred habitat Known only from Wotjulum Mission on Yampi Peninsula, and from Mt Elizabeth Station, in west Kimberley, WA.

Microhabitat As for species group.

Comments As for species group.

Ctenotus youngsoni Storr, 1975
Photo 418

Description Largest member of *C. labillardieri* group with robust build and thick tail. Dorsal ground colour olive-grey to pale greyish brown. Broad vertebral zone of ground colour extends to base of tail. This is margined by broad black laterodorsal stripes, each partially enclosing a series of large blotches of ground colour. Whitish dorsolateral stripe extends from above ear to base of tail. Upper lateral zone olive, flecked with black and/or grey. Pale midlateral stripe indistinct to absent. Lower flanks pale grey with obscure dark flecks. Head, limbs and tail speckled with black. Tip of snout yellow. Ventral surfaces white. SVL 85 mm.

Preferred habitat Pale coastal dunes vegetated with heathlands along western peninsula of Shark Bay, and on adjacent Dirk Hartog Island, WA.

Microhabitat Shelters beneath loose sand and leaf-litter, or under accumulated debris of dead shrubs. In this aspect it is similar to banded sand-swimming skinks (*Eremiascincus* spp.).

Comments As for species group.

Ctenotus zastictus Storr, 1984
Photo 419

Description Slender member of *C. atlas* group with long snout and tail. Pattern consists of 8 pale stripes, and laterodorsal and upper lateral spots. Ground colour blackish. Narrow white paravertebrals extend from base of head well onto tail. Prominent to obscure laterodorsal series of white to yellowish dashes (probably remnants of obsolete stripes) present on body. Narrow white dorsolateral stripe extends from base of head well onto tail. Prominent upper lateral series of white dots and dashes extend from about ear to hindlimb. Narrow white midlateral stripe commences as an obscure pale streak on upper lip, extending well onto tail. White ventrolateral stripe extends from behind ear to hindlimb. Head and tail olive-brown. Limbs blackish brown, striped with white. Ventral surfaces

white. SVL 60 mm.

Preferred habitat Restricted to isolated reddish sands supporting mallee/*Triodia* associations immediately south of Shark Bay, on midwest coast of WA.

Microhabitat As for species group.

Comments As for species group.

Ctenotus zebrilla Storr, 1981
Photo 420

Description Small member of *C. colletti* group with 8 pale stripes on black to blackish brown ground colour. Narrow pale brown paravertebral and dorsal stripes extend from nape, joining at hips to form 2 broader stripes on tail. Broader paler dorsolateral stripe extends from above eye, well onto tail. Broad white midlateral stripe extends from upper lip, through upper half of ear to hips. Wavy dark lower lateral stripe extends from upper lip to hindlimb. Top of head and tail pale brown. Limbs striped with pale brown and blackish brown. Ventral surfaces white. SVL 40 mm.

Preferred habitat Rocky hills supporting woodlands and low grasses in subhumid southern interior of Cape York Peninsula, Qld.

Microhabitat Shelters beneath rocks and low vegetation.

Comments No data available.

Photos 421–7 show 7 probably undescribed taxa of *Ctenotus*.

Genus *CYCLODOMORPHUS*
Fitzinger, 1843

Endemic genus containing 5 species. Widespread throughout Australia, including Tas. Absent from subhumid northern NT and Cape York Peninsula, Qld. Additional taxa from the Nullarbor Plain, south-eastern SA and eastern edge of Simpson Desert await description.

Moderately small to moderately large skinks with elongate bodies and short limbs, each bearing 5 digits of approximately equal length (4th toe not noticeably longer). Tail moderately long and fragile. Lower eyelid movable and scaly. Ear opening present, occasionally bearing one anterior lobule. Tongue broad and fleshy; blue to pink. Head usually not noticeably distinct from neck. Scales smooth.

Diurnal to nocturnal. Predominantly terrestrial. One species is semi-arboreal, another rock-inhabiting. Diets consist largely of small invertebrates. Livebearers, producing moderately small to very large litters.

Distinguished from *Tiliqua* by nature of tail (relatively long and fragile vs short and non-fragile) and (with the exception of the distinctive *C. gerrardii*) by head-shape (not noticeably distinct from neck vs triangular and distinct from neck). Excepting *C. gerrardii*, differs from *Egernia* in bearing short digits of approximately equal length (vs 4th toe considerably longer).

Cyclodomorphus branchialis (Günther, 1867)
Photo 428

Description Small *Cyclodomorphus* with moderately short tail. Ground colour pale greyish brown to almost white, marked with numerous narrow dark longitudinal streaks (one per scale). These are often aligned to form vertical bars on flanks. In Geraldton district they coalesce to form 3 broad dark bars on side of neck. Juveniles darker (particularly on head), marked with numerous pale spots. Ventral surfaces white, usually bearing obscure extension of dorsal pattern. SVL 90 mm.

Distinguished from *C. melanops* by nature of ear opening (very small, lacking lobules, vs relatively larger, bearing one anterior lobule). Differs further in usually bearing paler colouration, and (in areas where distributions adjoin) attaining smaller maximum size (SVL 90 vs 120 mm).

Preferred habitat Subhumid to semi-arid lower to midwest coast and offshore islands of WA, from Perth north to about Gnaraloo Station. Favours pale sandy soils and limestones vegetated with heathlands and woodlands, and coastal dunes supporting beach spinifex *(Spinifex longifolius)*. Occurs on sand ridges and sand plains supporting hummock grass associations in northern interior of range.

Microhabitat Shelters beneath dense low vegetation, leaf-litter and in abandoned stick-ant nests *(Iridomyrmex conifer)*. Frequently encountered partially submerged in loose upper layers of sand beneath cover.

Comments Feeds on a variety of arthropods, occasionally snails and small lizards. Litters of 2–5 (usually 3) young are born in late summer. Locally abundant. Approximately 40 individuals have been located during a half-hour search of coastal dunes at Leeman, in lower half of range.

She-oak Skink
Cyclodomorphus casuarinae
(Duméril and Bibron, 1839)
Photo 429

Description Large slender *Cyclodomorphus* with long tail. Ground colour pale or dark brown, reddish brown, yellowish brown, olive, shades of grey to almost black; paler on flanks. Pattern (when present) consists of paler individual scales bearing darker posterior and/or lateral margins. These are arranged in transverse or longitudinal series from nape to tail-tip. Broad dark vertical bar from eye to lower lips, and dark tip to snout usually present. Pattern prominent on juveniles; including a broad dark patch on nape. Ventral surfaces paler shade of ground colour, often bearing reddish to orange flush on belly, and extension of dorsal pattern. SVL 150 mm.

Preferred habitat Humid south-eastern Australia, extending disjunctly from northern Tas., through eastern Vic. to Tamworth area, NSW. Occurs in dry sclerophyll forests, woodlands, heathlands and swamplands, particularly where ground cover is dominated by tussock grasses.

Microhabitat Shelters in grass tussocks and beneath leaf-litter, logs and surface debris.

Comments Crepuscular to nocturnal. Feeds on small arthropods. Litters of 2–17 (usually about 4) young are born in summer. Aggressive towards other reptiles and members of its own species; at least in captivity. If threatened, raises forebody and flickers tongue, in apparent mimicry of snakes. When moving through dense vegetation, hindlimbs are held close to body, using only forelimbs. Name refers to the ship *Casuarina* of the Baudin expedition in 1902, rather than (as popularly believed) a reference to association with she-oaks (*Casuarina* spp.).

Pink-tongued Skink
Cyclodomorphus gerrardii (Gray, 1845)
Photo 430

Description Large *Cyclodomorphus* with long strongly clawed digits and long prehensile tail. Head large and moderately distinct from neck. Tongue pink on adults and blue on juveniles; blue pigment is retained almost to adulthood in far north of range. Ground colour pale brown, pinkish brown, shades of grey to black. Pattern prominent to virtually absent, consisting of approximately 5–7 broad blackish bands (each curving forward laterally) between nape and hips, and approximately 12 on tail. Dark mark usually present beneath eye. Bands may become progressively invaded by ground colour: reduced to margins forming pairs of narrow bands, or lost entirely. Patternless individuals usually retain dark tip to snout, and occasionally a few scattered dark flecks. All juveniles are prominently marked with sharp-edged dark and pale bands. Ventral surfaces white to dark pinkish brown, with or without darker marbling or broad bands. SVL 200 mm.

Preferred habitat Humid east coast and ranges, from Springwood, NSW, north to Cairns district, Qld. Favours wet sclerophyll forests and rainforests, extending into woodlands wherever damp conditions prevail. A common lizard in well-watered gardens of suburban Brisbane.

Microhabitat Shelters in hollow logs, beneath leaf-litter, and in crevices in trunks or rocks.

Comments The only partially arboreal member of genus. Largely crepuscular and nocturnal, though often encountered basking in sunny sheltered sites. Most active after rain, foraging for slugs and snails which virtually constitute its entire diet. Greatly enlarged rounded tooth at rear of upper and lower jaws facilitates crushing of snail shells. Litters of usually 10–20 (maximum recorded—67) young are born in summer. If threatened raises forebody and flickers tongue in apparent mimicry of snakes. When moving through dense vegetation, hindlimbs are held close to body, using only forelimbs.

Cyclodomorphus maximus (Storr, 1976)
Photo 431

Description Largest *Cyclodomorphus* with moderately robust body, long tail and slightly depressed head. Ground colour pale reddish brown, sometimes fading to dull olive-grey on anterior body and flanks. Adult pattern includes numerous yellow to white, transversely aligned spots on posterior two-thirds of body and tail, fading on flanks. Side of head and tip of snout cream to paler shade of ground colour. Eye margined laterally and below with obscure dark smudge. Juveniles are more prominently marked. Pale spots extend onto anterior body and flanks. Top of head dark greyish brown. Two broad dark bands extend across nape; separated by pale yellowish brown interspaces. Ventral surfaces pale yellowish brown, lacking pattern. SVL 230 mm.

Preferred habitat Subhumid north-west Kimberley region, WA. Restricted to escarpments or boulder-strewn habitats supporting a variety of vegetation types, from hummock grasses to dense vine thickets.

Microhabitat Shelters in rock crevices, beneath coarse leaf-litter, and in hummock grasses.

Comments Feeds on arthropods and snails. One litter of 7 young recorded; born in late February. Known from few specimens; usually collected in mammal traps. This suggests crepuscular to nocturnal activity.

Cyclodomorphus melanops (Stirling and Zietz, 1893)
Photos 432, 433

Description Medium to moderately large robust *Cyclodomorphus* with relatively short tail. Ground colour pale grey to pale or dark brown; paler on flanks. Pattern usually absent on southern and eastern populations. Those from north and west of range may be marked with black spots (1 per scale) on body, limbs and tail. Juveniles darker (particularly on head) bearing numerous whitish to yellowish spots. Ventral surfaces white, dull yellow to pale brown, sometimes bearing numerous dark spots. SVL to 120 mm.

Distinguished from *C. branchialis* by nature of ear-opening (relatively large and bearing one anterior lobule vs very small and lacking lobules). Differs further in usually bearing darker colouration and (in areas where distributions adjoin) attaining larger maximum size (SVL 120 vs 90 mm).

Preferred habitat Largely restricted to arid and semi-arid rocky hills and red sand plains. Favours areas supporting a dominant ground cover of hummock grasses. Disjunct populations occur in all mainland States except Vic.; from central-western Qld, through central Australia to north-west coast of WA. Extends south to Eyre Peninsula, SA, and north to southern Kimberley region, WA, and adjacent NT.

Microhabitat Shelters beneath and in grass hummocks.

Comments Feeds largely on arthropods, occasionally small lizards. Litters of 2–5 (usually 3) young are born in summer. Adults are usually found singly, even in areas of local abundance, suggesting the species may be territorial. This contrasts markedly with closely allied *C. branchialis*, numerous individuals of which may share a microhabitat.

See also Photo 434, which shows a common species of *Cyclodomorphus* not yet described.

Genus *EGERNIA*   Gray, 1838

Large genus containing 26 described species, including several subspecies. Widespread through most of Australia, including Tas. One species extends to New Guinea.

Medium-sized to very large robust skinks with well-developed limbs, each bearing 5 digits. Lower eyelid movable and scaly. Ear opening visible, bearing one or more lobules. Tail usually fragile, except on some members of *E. cunninghami* group. Dorsal scales smooth or weakly striate, to keeled or spinose.

Predominantly diurnal; a few species may be crepuscular to nocturnal in hot weather. Livebearers, rarely producing more than 6 young per litter. Most are omnivorous (particularly the larger species), consuming a variety of invertebrates and fruits. Smaller species feed largely on arthropods.

Seven species groups are tentatively recognised.

***E. cunninghami* group**   Comprises 7 taxa of medium to large *Egernia* with deep heads and bodies. Scales strongly keeled to spinose on dorsal and lateral surfaces, becoming more spinose on tail. Rock-inhabiting and arboreal, sheltering in crevices and hollows. At any attempt to remove them from cover these lizards inflate with air to bring their spiny scales into contact with irregularities in wood or rock, rendering them difficult to extract. Individuals tend to dwell in small home ranges, and their presence is often indicated by frequently used defecation sites. Suitable crevices or hollows may contain a number of individuals of all ages. Predominantly diurnal; crepuscular in hot weather. Omnivorous. Members extend from cool highlands of south-eastern Australia to arid northern interior of Qld, and coast and interior of WA. Group comprises *E. cunninghami cunninghami*, *E. cunninghami krefftii*, *E. depressa*, *E. hosmeri*, *E. stokesii aethiops*, *E. stokesii badia*, and *E. stokesii stokesii*. Further investigation is likely to define more taxa.

E. striolata group Comprises 8 taxa. Medium-sized, dorsally depressed skinks with smooth to weakly striate, or moderately to strongly keeled dorsal scales. Pattern variable, often including broad pale dorsolateral suffusions on anterior body. Members shelter in rock crevices, beneath loose bark, or in hollow tree trunks and limbs. Suitable cover may house a number of individuals of all ages. Diurnal. Omnivorous. They range from humid cool areas of southern and eastern Australia to arid western interior and subhumid north. Group comprises *E. douglasi*, *E. formosa*, *E. napoleonis*, *E. pilbarensis*, *E. richardi*, *E. saxatilis intermedia*, *E. saxatilis saxatilis* and *E. striolata*. At least 2 eastern Australian taxa await description.

E. kingii group Contains one large, terrestrial and rock-inhabiting *Egernia* with strong blunt keels on dorsal scales. Similar in many respects to *E. striolata* group but larger, with pattern (when present) consisting almost entirely of small pale spots. Diurnal. Omnivorous. Confined to south-western WA.

E. luctuosa group Comprises 2 medium-sized *Egernia* with smooth glossy scales. Terrestrial, sheltering beneath logs, dense low vegetation, or in abandoned burrows; usually along lake or swamp margins. Diurnal; nocturnal in hot weather. Restricted to cool humid south-east and south-west corners of continent. Group comprises *E. coventryi* and *E. luctuosa*.

E. whitii group Comprises 13 taxa. Small to very large *Egernia* with moderate to very deep heads and short limbs. Scales smooth (weakly keeled on *E. pulchra*). Terrestrial. Those occurring in heathlands and sandy deserts dig burrows with multiple entrances at bases of shrubs or hummock grasses. Burrows often contain more than one individual, sometimes a small colony. Species inhabiting woodlands and rock outcrops occasionally shelter in crevices, though they usually excavate shallow depressions or burrows beneath rocks or logs resting on soil. Diurnal to crepuscular and nocturnal. Arthropod feeders. Best represented in south, extending from south-west and south-east of Australia (including Tas.) to sandy deserts and rocky ranges of centre and north-west. Group comprises *E. inornata*, *E. kintorei*, *E. margaretae margaretae*, *E. margaretae personata*, *E. modesta*, *E. multiscutata bos*, *E. multiscutata multiscutata*, *E. pulchra longicauda*, *E. pulchra pulchra*, *E. slateri*, *E. striata*, *E. whitii moniligera* and *E. whitii whitii*.

E. major group Comprises 2 very large *Egernia*; among the world's largest skinks. Dorsal scales shiny and weakly keeled. Terrestrial. Diurnal. Omnivorous. Members occur in rainforests, woodlands and vine thickets from north-eastern NSW to eastern and northern Qld, and northern NT. Extralimital in southern New Guinea. Members are *E. major* and *E. frerei*. Population occurring in northern NT probably constitutes an undescribed taxon.

E. rugosa group Contains one very large robust species with a deep blunt head, thick tail, and 2 or 3 enlarged rugose ear lobules. Terrestrial. Diurnal to crepuscular. Omnivorous. Occurs on subhumid coast and eastern interior of Qld.

Egernia is distinguished from *Tiliqua* and *Cyclodomorphus* (excepting the distinctive *C. gerrardii*) in bearing a much longer 4th toe (vs all toes approximately equal in length). Differs from *Sphenomorphus* and *Eremiascincus* in possessing ear lobules. Differs further from all skinks except *Tiliqua* and *Cyclodomorphus* by arrangement of parietal scales (separated by interparietal scale vs contacting). Differs further from *Sphenomorphus*, *Eremiascincus* and *Ctenotus* in usually attaining a much greater size.

Egernia coventryi Storr, 1978
Photo 435

Description Member of *E. luctuosa* group with dorsal ground colour of yellowish brown to olive. Broad ragged-edged blackish brown laterodorsal stripe extending from nape to base of tail, encloses vertebral zone of ground colour, 2 scales wide. Prominent broad ragged-edged dorsolateral stripe of ground colour extends from nape to base of tail. Flanks blackish brown, spotted or blotched with yellow to pale brown. Head scales often irregularly marked with black. Upper lips usually streaked with white to pale yellow. Anterior half of tail ground colour, bearing a blackish brown base to each individual scale. Posterior half glossy black. Ventral surfaces whitish to yellow. SVL 100 mm.

Preferred habitat River, lake and swamp margins, often in association with *Melaleuca* or *Leptospermum* thickets, from south-eastern NSW, through southern Vic. to far south-eastern SA.

Microhabitat Often shelters in abandoned burrows of freshwater crayfish. Otherwise as for species group.

Comments As for species group.

Cunningham's Skink
Egernia cunninghami (Gray, 1832)
Photos 436–438

Description Large member of *E. cunninghami* group with long fragile tail; round in cross section. Each dorsal and lateral scale bears a sharp keel, terminating in a spine. These become longer and more pronounced on tail. Two subspecies recognised, though numerous forms appear sufficiently distinct to warrant further taxonomic investigation. **E. c. cunninghami** In far north of range, ground colour varies from very dark brown to almost black with little or no indication of pattern. Ventral surfaces pink to orange.

Populations from northern NSW (including Granite Belt of adjacent south-eastern Qld) are very dark brown to black, fading to pale brown on head and nape. Pattern prominent, comprising cream to white blotches; arranged in transverse series from nape to tail-tip. Ventral surfaces whitish, barred or variegated with dark brown on throat. Through southern NSW to Vic., ground colour is usually paler. Pale blotches are reduced to scattered dots or flecks, mixed with obscure dark variegations. In central-northern Vic., ground colour is dark brown to dark grey, obscurely marked with scattered pale flecks.

In SA colour and pattern approximates that of northern NSW populations. Juveniles of all forms are more prominently marked. SVL 200 mm.

E. c. krefftii Peters 1871 Differs from nominate form in attaining smaller maximum size, and in bearing weaker spinose keels. Ground colour dark orange-brown, sparsely flecked with white to cream. Pattern usually obscure, comprising narrow irregular dark bands. These tend to coalesce on anterior flanks, forming a ragged-edged broken black upper lateral zone. Pale flecks may concentrate on edges of dark pigment to form broken margins. Top of head ground colour; scales margined with darker brown. Lips and side of head usually flushed with dark brown to black, and spotted with white. Ventral surfaces orange-brown, irregularly barred with black, particularly on throat. SVL 150 mm.

Preferred habitat *E. c. cunninghami* is widespread in cool subhumid regions of south-eastern mainland, extending disjunctly from Carnarvon Ranges, Qld, along coastal and Great Dividing Ranges to southern Vic. Isolated populations occur on Pyramid Hill in central northern Vic., on western slopes of Mt Lofty Ranges, and on southern shores of Fleurieu Peninsula and adjacent West Island, SA. Most abundant on rock outcrops, particularly granites and basalts, though some populations dwell in open woodlands. Populations from West Island inhabit cliff-faces. *E. c. krefftii* inhabits sandstone outcrops and escarpments of mideastern NSW.

Microhabitat Shelters in rock crevices or beneath slabs, occasionally in hollow timber. Some populations occurring on basalt plains west of Melbourne, where habitat has been radically altered by agricultural development, are largely restricted to cavities in rock fences constructed during the convict era.

Comments Tends to dwell in small colonies. Produces litters of 3–8 young in late summer. Otherwise as for species group.

Pygmy Spiny-tailed Skink
Egernia depressa (Günther, 1875)
Photos 439, 440

Description Smallest member of *E. cunninghami* group. Tail short, depressed, strongly spinose and non-fragile. Dorsal scales bear 3–5 sharp keels, each central keel terminating in a prominent spine. Two populations occur.

Northern population: Ground colour pinkish brown to reddish brown, marked with irregular blackish spots or blotches which tend to form obscure transverse bars across body and tail.

Southern population: Ground colour brown to reddish brown anteriorly, merging to brownish grey at about midbody. Pale brownish grey blotches tend to form irregular bands from nape to midbody. Posterior body and tail bears blackish blotches, each usually pale-edged. Flanks and limbs pale brownish grey, often blotched with black. Scales of head and lips usually dark-edged. Ventral surfaces greyish white. Throat, chest and tail often flecked or spotted with dark pigment. SVL 115 mm.

Distinguished from *E. stokesii* in attaining smaller maximum size (SVL 115 vs 155 mm or greater), and by nature of dorsal scales (each bearing 1 large and 2 small spines vs 1 or 2 small spines).

Preferred habitat Northern population dwells in rocky ranges and outcrops. Southern population occurs in semi-arid to arid *Acacia*-dominated woodlands and shrublands of central-western interior of WA. Isolated populations occur in Great Sandy Desert of northern WA and far south-west corner of NT.

Microhabitat Northern populations usually shelter in rock crevices. In south, hollow trunks and limbs of dead standing *Acacias* are favoured, though rock crevices are also utilised.

Comments One litter of 3 young is recorded. See species group.

Egernia douglasi Glauert, 1956

Description Large member of *E. striolata* group. Each dorsal scale bears 3–7 striations. Ground colour olive-brown, yellowish brown, dark brown, brown to reddish brown; paler on head. Broad dark brown to black ragged-edged dorsal stripe extends from snout to anterior body, occasionally continuing as a series of obscure spots to base of tail. Dark brown to black ragged-edged upper lateral stripe extends from in front of eye to behind forelimb. Lips whitish; belly flushed with yellow. Dark brown transverse bars may be present on chin and throat. SVL 170 mm.

Preferred habitat Restricted to rocky areas (possibly extending into adjacent woodlands) in subhumid north-western Kimberley region, WA. An apparently isolated population occurs on Lissadell Station in eastern Kimberley.

Microhabitat Probably shelters in rock crevices. See species group.

Comments As for species group.

Egernia formosa Fry, 1914
Photos 441, 442

Description Small to moderately large member of *E. striolata* group with smooth to weakly striate dorsal scales. Two distinctive populations occur; these may constitute separate taxa.

Southern form: Dorsal ground colour pale brown to olive, marked with numerous oblong black spots from top of head to base of tail. These usually coalesce anteriorly to form broad paravertebral stripes from top of head to shoulders. Broad pale laterodorsal zone (lacking any dark markings) extends from head, fading at midbody. Broad ragged-edged dark brown to black upper lateral zone extends from snout or eye, fading and breaking at mid or posterior body. Mid to lower lateral zone ground colour to whitish; palest on side of neck and lips. Scales on top of head may be broadly margined with dark brown. Lips usually barred with brown. Ventral surfaces white to cream, barred with brown on chin and throat. SVL 95 mm.

Pilbara form differs in attaining larger maximum size, and bearing redder ground colour with weaker pattern. SVL 105 mm.

Distinguished from all other members of *E. striolata* group (except *E. pilbarensis*) in bearing much smoother scales. Differs from *E. pilbarensis* in possessing a prominent black upper lateral zone.

Preferred habitat Southern form occurs in semi-arid to arid woodlands in central to southern interior of WA. Pilbara form is restricted to rocky ranges and gorges of Pilbara region, north-western WA.

Microhabitat Southern population shelters beneath bark or in hollows of standing or fallen trees. Pilbara form inhabits rock crevices.

Comments Litters of 2 and 3 young are recorded. Otherwise as for species group.

Major Skink
Egernia frerei Günther, 1897
Photos 443, 444

Description Variable member of *E. major* group with pale yellowish brown to rich brown dorsal ground colour. Adults of some northern populations may be patternless. Each dorsal scale usually bears dark streaks, forming fine longitudinal lines. Broad pale dorsolateral stripe present or absent. Upper flanks usually dark brown to blackish, bearing several series of prominent to obscure pale spots. Juveniles are usually more conspicuously marked. Ear lobules, lips and rim of eye, cream to pale brown. Lips may be barred with brown. Ventral surfaces white, pale grey to shades of orange, often paler beneath throat and tail. SVL 180 mm.

Distinguished from *E. major* in bearing paler colouration and usually some indication of adult pattern (vs ground colour black, without pattern on adults). Differs further in attaining smaller max-

imum size (SVL 180 vs 300 mm). Differs from *E. rugosa* by nature of parietal shields (intact vs fragmented into several irregular scales).

Preferred habitat Rainforests, vine thickets, wet and dry sclerophyll forests, woodlands and rock outcrops from north-eastern NSW, through eastern Qld (including many offshore islands) to Cape York. Extralimital in southern New Guinea.

Microhabitat Shelters in hollow logs, cavities in soil-bound root systems of fallen trees, or in burrows beneath large rocks.

Comments Extremely wary and difficult to approach. Omnivorous; balance of diet probably varies with age, with juveniles consuming a higher proportion of insects, gastropods and other animal prey. Most adults lack several toes, though the reasons for this loss are unclear. Otherwise as for species group.

Hosmer's Skink
Egernia hosmeri Kinghorn, 1955
Photo 445

Description Member of *E. cunninghami* group with moderately spinose non-fragile tail. Dorsal scales bear 3 or 4 weak spines. Ground colour pale yellowish brown to reddish brown; blackish, flecked with cream on some northern populations. Back and flanks usually irregularly marked with whitish and blackish brown scales, the darker often forming broken transverse bars; boldest on tail. Head and nape usually a darker shade of ground colour, bearing prominent pale brown to cream blotches. Ventral surfaces cream, pale yellow to white. Brown flecks and blotches sometimes present on throat. SVL 180 mm.

Distinguished from *E. stokesii* by nature of tail (relatively long and round in cross-section vs broad, very spiny and depressed).

Preferred habitat Rocky ranges and outcrops in subhumid to arid northern interior of Qld. Dark population occurs on basalt cliffs.

Microhabitat Usually shelters in rock crevices, occasionally hollows in dead timber. See species group.

Comments As for *E. cunninghami* group.

Rosen's Skink or Desert Skink
Egernia inornata Rosén, 1905
Photo 446

Description Small member of *E. whitii* group with blunt deep head. Ground colour yellowish brown to rich coppery red, varying according to substrate colour. Posterior margins of dorsal scales often paler. Dorsum immaculate, or each scale may bear dark edges forming fine longitudinal lines. Scattered black spots often extend over back, becoming vertically aligned on flanks. These are represented on sides of tail as dark bars. Ventral surfaces white. SVL 80 mm.

Distinguished from *E. striata* by shape of pupil (round vs vertically elliptic). Differs from *E. slateri* by ground colour (reddish vs greyish), and in lacking white flecks on lateral scales.

Preferred habitat Arid to semi-arid sand ridges or sand plains supporting hummock grasses; often in association with mallee woodlands. Extends from southern interior of WA to southern NT, SA, north-western Vic., western NSW and south-western Qld.

Microhabitat Excavates burrows of varying complexity (with entrances usually facing north to north-west), situated at the bases of shrubs or grass hummocks. Normally an escape exit terminates a centimetre or so below ground, a short distance from the entrance. Often 2 burrows are excavated 10–20 m apart.

Comments Mainly crepuscular. Inactive during winter, retiring to a sealed off section of burrow (at least in WA). Feeds on a variety of arthropods, occasionally small lizards. Often rests with head protruding from burrow, possibly awaiting passing prey. Litters of 1–4 (usually 2) young are born from September to early May. Otherwise as for species group.

King's Skink
Egernia kingii (Gray, 1838)
Photo 447

Description Large variably marked *Egernia*; sole member of *E. kingii* group. Ground colour brown, greyish brown, dark grey to almost black. Juveniles are sparsely to densely marked with prominent cream to yellow dashes and dots. Many populations retain this pattern to adulthood. Drab adults often bear fine indistinct longitudinal lines, formed by darkening on sides of dorsal and lateral scales. Indistinct vertical bars may be present on flanks. Ventral surfaces cream, pale yellow to grey, marked with darker reticulations or streaks, particularly beneath throat and tail. SVL 230 mm.

Preferred habitat Humid to subhumid south-west WA mainland, from Hutt River in north to Duke of Orleans Bay in east. Most abundant on offshore islands, north to Houtman Abrolhos and east to Archipelago of the Recherche. Often associated with granite outcrops on mainland, and heathlands over sand or limestone on coast and islands.

Microhabitat In some areas rock crevices provide shelter. On coast and islands, burrows of fairy penguins and shearwaters and dense low vegetation are often utilised.

Comments Omnivorous; eggs of nesting seabirds are included on diet. Litter of 2 recorded.

Great Desert Skink
Egernia kintorei Stirling and Zietz, 1893
Photo 448

Description Very large member of *E. whitii* group with blunt deep head, reddish brown dorsal colour and grey to bluish grey flanks. Dark brown lateral edges to dorsal scales form series of narrow dark longitudinal lines from nape to base of tail. Darker scales on sides of neck, flanks and sides of tail align to form vertical bars. Pale spots are scattered through grey interspaces. Ventral surfaces white to cream. SVL 190 mm.

Preferred habitat Red sand ridges, sand flats and clay-based or loamy soils vegetated with hummock grass associations. Extends from arid central interior of WA to south-western NT and north-western SA.

Microhabitat Excavates large complex multientranced burrow systems.

Comments Little documented. Occupied burrow systems are often indicated by the presence of regular defecation sites. Otherwise as for species group.

Egernia luctuosa (Peters, 1866)
Photo 449

Description Member of *E. luctuosa* group. Dorsal ground colour yellowish brown to dark brown. Usually 6 longitudinal series of oblong to square (often pale-edged) black spots extend from nape to base or middle of tail. Obscure narrow ragged-edged black upper lateral zone extends from behind eye or ear to hindlimb, continuing on tail as a series of dashes. Mid to lower lateral zone heavily marked with lemon yellow to yellowish brown flecks. Head scales irregularly edged with black. Ventral surfaces white to yellow, often spotted with black. SVL 125 mm.

Preferred habitat Dense vegetation surrounding swamps, lakes, creeks and rivers on coast and hinterland in humid south-west corner of WA, from Perth south-east to Albany district.

Microhabitat As for species group.

Comments Little known of habits. Seldom ventures far from cover of vegetation. Readily enters water when pursued, swimming and diving well. Otherwise as for species group.

Land Mullet
Egernia major (Gray, 1845)
Photo 450

Description Very large robust member of *E. major* group. Ground colour uniform glossy black to very dark brown. Adults are unmarked, except for a conspicuous pale rim to eye. Juveniles bear bold white to cream spots on flanks. Ventral surfaces white, yellow to orange-brown. SVL 300 mm.

Distinguished from *E. frerei* by black (vs brown) colouration and absence of pattern on adults.

Preferred habitat Rainforests and wet sclerophyll forests of central-eastern NSW and south-eastern Qld, from Gosford north to Gympie.

Microhabitat Extensive burrows are excavated beneath fallen logs or thickets of introduced *Lantana*. Soil-bound root systems of large fallen trees are particularly favoured. Basks in sunny patches on forest floor or logs.

Comments Largest member of genus, and among the largest of the world's skinks. Omnivorous; plant material such as fungi and fallen fruits constitutes a significant portion of diet. The land mullet is a conspicuous element of subtropical rainforest fauna, making a noisy dash through surface litter and vegetation to burrow when disturbed. Active from spring to autumn. Most adults lack some toes, though the reasons for this loss are unclear. Otherwise as for species group.

Egernia margaretae Storr, 1968
Photos 451, 452

Description Long-tailed dorsally depressed member of *E. whitii* group. Two subspecies recognised.
E. m. margaretae Dorsal ground colour reddish brown. Pattern usually obscure to absent. If present, includes irregular or longitudinally aligned black spots on back and tail. Flanks reddish brown to greyish brown, bearing oblique rows of spots directed upwards and backwards. Ventral surfaces whitish, bearing irregular dark brownish grey spots or short wavy longitudinal lines on throat. SVL 105 mm.
E. m. personata Storr, 1968 Differs from nominate form in bearing paler colouration and stronger pattern; including a pale dorsolateral stripe, margined by remaining edges of a blackish laterodorsal stripe. May warrant recognition as a distinct species.
Preferred habitat *E. m. margaretae* occurs on arid central Australian highlands: James and George Gill Ranges of southern NT, and Mann and Musgrave Ranges of north-western SA. Favours sandstone habitats. *E. m. personata* occupies virtually all rocky areas in subhumid to arid central and northern Flinders Ranges, SA.
Microhabitat *E. m. margaretae* excavates shallow depressions beneath sandstone slabs. Sites receiving moisture from water run-off are favoured. *E. m. personata* is locally abundant, sheltering in rock crevices and depressions beneath rocks.
Comments See species group.

Egernia modesta Storr, 1968
Photo 453

Description Large, virtually patternless member of *E. whitii* group with pale brown to greyish brown ground colour. Darkened edges to each scale form narrow longitudinal lines. A few large scattered pale spots usually extend from rear of upper lips to anterior flanks; occasionally extending to hindlimbs and base of tail. Eye conspicuously rimmed with white. Tip of snout orange-brown. Head shields margined with dark brown. Ventral surfaces white. SVL 110 mm.

Distinguished from *E. whitii* in bearing weaker pattern; particularly the lack of a pale streak through

upper lips. Pale lateral spots (if present) are largely restricted to anterior body (vs prominent, extending along flanks).
Preferred habitat Dry sclerophyll forests, woodlands and rock outcrops, in subhumid areas from Hunter River Valley, NSW, to south-eastern Qld. An isolated population occurs in hilly country north of Roto, NSW.
Microhabitat Shelters beneath rocks or fallen logs.
Comments See species group.

Egernia multiscutata
Mitchell and Behrndt, 1949
Photo 454

Description Small robust deep-headed member of *E. whitii* group. Two subspecies recognised.
E. m. bos Storr, 1960 Dorsal ground colour brown to brownish grey; paler laterally. Pattern prominent to virtually absent. Broad vertebral stripe of ground colour extends from nape, fading on tail. This borders a broad dark brown to blackish dorsal stripe, which encloses one or 2 series of pale spots or short longitudinal dashes. Pale weakly defined dorsolateral stripe extends from above eye to base of tail. Flanks may be suffused or streaked with dark brown and occasionally spotted with white. Eye rimmed with white to cream. Ventral surfaces pale grey to white, occasionally flushed with orange. SVL 90 mm.
E. m. multiscutata Differs in bearing darker colouration, and in lacking a dorsolateral stripe. Ventral surfaces may be flushed with bright orange.

Distinguished from *E. pulchra* by head-shape (deep and blunt vs relatively depressed), and by nature of dorsal scales (smooth vs weakly keeled).
Preferred habitat *E. m. bos* occurs in heathlands and woodlands, particularly those on well-drained pale sands, in subhumid to semi-arid southern Australia. Extends disjunctly from Big Desert in north-western Vic. to southern SA and south-western WA; north on mainland to Green Head area. Occurs on offshore islands north to Bernier Island, Shark Bay. *E. m. multiscutata* is restricted to Greenly Island, off south-west coast of Eyre Peninsula, SA.
Microhabitat Excavates multi-entranced burrows, usually at the bases of low shrubs in clearings. In some areas flat rocks resting on sand provide shelter. Otherwise as for species group.
Comments A secretive skink, usually located by the presence of its burrow, rather than by its activity. Diurnal, foraging in early morning and late afternoon. See *E. whitii* group.

Egernia napoleonis (Gray, 1838)
Photo 455

Description Variable member of *E. striolata* group with strongly keeled dorsal scales. Dorsal ground colour pale or dark olive-brown, grey to blackish, often flushed with brown on hips, hind-limbs and base of tail. Blackish brown spots of variable size and shape are arranged in 3 longitudinal series from nape: a vertebral extends to hips, and dorsals extend well onto tail. Broad pale laterodorsal zone extends from nape to midbody, occasionally to hips. Numerous small whitish dots may be scattered over back and flanks. Prominent to obscure blackish brown to dark grey upper lateral zone extends from in front of eye, fading before hindlimb. Lower lateral zone usually pale brownish grey, irregularly marked with dark and pale scales. Head scales prominently edged with blackish brown. Ventral surfaces salmon pink to orange-brown. Scales on throat greyish, sometimes margined with black. Eastern populations tend to be larger, with bolder pattern. SVL 130 mm.

Distinguished from *E. richardi* by nature of keels on dorsal scales (strong vs weak). Differs further by arrangement of dark dorsal spots (not extending into pale laterodorsal zone vs spread evenly over dorsal surfaces).

Preferred habitat Wet and dry sclerophyll forests, woodlands, coastal heathlands and rock outcrops in humid to subhumid south-west of WA. Extends north to about Green Head area and east to Twilight Cove.

Microhabitat Arboreal and rock-inhabiting. In heathland and woodland communities, hollow stems of dead grass trees *(Xanthorrhoea)* are often used as shelter sites.

Comments Litters of 3 or 4 offspring are recorded. Otherwise as for species group.

Egernia pilbarensis Storr, 1978
Photo 456

Description Moderately large virtually patternless member of *E. striolata* group with smooth scales. Ground colour reddish brown; darkest on anterior flanks and sides of head. Obscure dark vertebral zone sometimes discernible anteriorly. Lateral surfaces may be immaculate, dotted with white, or marked with obscure pale vertically oblique lines. Upper lips pale brown to off-white, in variable contrast to darker adjacent scales. Lower lips and ventral surfaces yellowish, with or without dark edges to lower labial and chin scales. SVL 120 mm.

Distinguished from *E. formosa* in lacking a prominent black upper lateral zone.

Preferred habitat Rocky ranges and outcrops vegetated with hummock grass associations of arid Pilbara region, WA, from coast (including Rosemary Island) to Chichester Ranges.

Microhabitat Rock-inhabiting. See species group.

Comments See species group.

Egernia pulchra Werner, 1910
Photos 457, 458

Description Member of *E. whitii* group with weakly keeled dorsal scales. Two subspecies recognised.

E. p. pulchra Ground colour pale yellowish brown to reddish brown. Dorsal pattern (when present) usually includes a broad vertebral stripe of ground colour from nape to base of tail. This is bordered on either side by a broad dark dorsal stripe, enclosing a series of pale spots. Flanks may be spotted with cream and dark brown, or flecked to heavily variegated with dark brown. Eyelid conspicuously rimmed with cream. Lips and ear lobules may be marked with orange. Ventral surfaces cream to grey. SVL 100 mm.

E. p. longicauda Ford, 1963 Differs from nominate race in bearing a much longer tail (proportionally the longest in genus), and an orange suffusion on ventral surfaces.

Distinguished from all other members of *E. whitii* group in bearing keeled (vs smooth) dorsal scales. Differs further from *E. multiscutata* by head-shape (relatively depressed vs deep and blunt).

Preferred habitat *E. p. pulchra* favours forests, woodlands and heathland associations on rocky ranges and coastlines of southern WA; north along Darling Range to just north of Perth, and east to Stirling Range and Cheyne Beach. *E. p. longicauda* occurs on islands of Jurien Bay, approximately 280 km to the north.

Microhabitat Both subspecies shelter in burrows beneath rocks, or in rock crevices. *E. p. longicauda* also utilises petrel burrows.

Comments Litter of 3 young recorded for *E. p. pulchra*, containing both patterned and plain forms. Otherwise as for species group.

Egernia richardi (Peters, 1869)
Photo 459

Description Small member of *E. striolata* group bearing 2–5 low keels on each dorsal scale. Ground colour olive-brown to grey; paler on lips, neck and anterior flanks. Dorsum usually marked with up to 8 series of small dark oblong spots, often edged laterally with white. Reddish brown flush usually present over nape and foreback of WA populations. Narrow blackish upper lateral zone enclosing scattered white spots extends from eye or ear, fading at midbody. Labial scales often narrowly edged with dark brown. Ventral surfaces pale grey. SVL 105 mm.

Distinguished from *E. formosa* and *E. napoleonis* in lacking a pale dorsolateral zone on anterior body. Differs further from *E. formosa* by nature of dorsal scales (keeled vs smooth to weakly striate). Differs further from *E. napoleonis* in bearing weaker dorsal keels.

Preferred habitat Eucalypt woodlands in semi-arid southern interior of WA. Apparently disjunct population extends east along coast of SA, from about Eucla, WA, to western Eyre Peninsula (in-

cluding Flinders Island).
Microhabitat Shelters in hollow trunks and limbs or beneath loose bark; occasionally granite exfoliations.
Comments As for species group.

Yakka Skink
Egernia rugosa De Vis, 1888
Photo 460

Description Sole member of *E. rugosa* group. Very large *Egernia* with thick tail. Broad dark brown to black dorsal zone extends from nape onto tail. Individual scales may be variegated with dark and pale brown. Narrow whitish to pale brown dorsolateral stripe usually present; at least anteriorly. Flanks pale reddish brown to paler shade of dorsal colour, bearing scattered darker and paler scales; sometimes forming indistinct variegations. Upper lips whitish, cream to reddish brown, contrasting with darker adjacent scales. Ventral surfaces cream, flushed with yellowish orange on chest and belly. Throat may be flecked or spotted with dark brown, and tail tinged with reddish brown. SVL 200 mm.

Distinguished from *E. frerei* by nature of parietal scales (fragmented into several irregular scales vs intact). Differs further in bearing very large plate-like ear lobules.

Preferred habitat Woodlands in subhumid to semi-arid eastern interior of Qld, from St George area north to Cape York Peninsula.

Microhabitat Excavates burrow systems among low vegetation, or shelters in hollow logs, cavities in soil-bound root systems of fallen trees, and beneath rocks.

Comments Extremely secretive, its presence often indicated by a frequently used defecation site. Otherwise as for species group.

Black Rock Skink
Egernia saxatilis Cogger, 1960
Photos 461, 462

Description Member of *E. striolata* group, bearing 2–5 strong keels on each dorsal scale. Two subspecies recognised.

E. s. saxatilis Dorsal ground colour dark brown to almost black. Many dorsal scales bear black central dashes, tending to align into broken longitudinal lines from nape onto base of tail. Numerous small paler flecks may be present over body and limbs, particularly on juveniles. Upper flanks black, marked with scattered dark brown scales. Lower flanks paler, bearing scattered pale and dark scales. Upper lips white, variegated or barred with darker pigment. Ventral surfaces, from chest onto tail, dull to bright orange. Throat whitish, variegated with black. SVL 130 mm.

E. s. intermedia Cogger, 1960 Differs from nominate form by darker colouration (usually black to very dark grey; rarely brown), and in bearing fewer midbody scale rows (28–35 vs 36–40).

Both subspecies differ from *E. striolata* in bearing strongly keeled dorsal scales (vs striated to weakly carinated), bearing less prominent pattern (particularly the absence of a pale dorsolateral suffusion), attaining a greater maximum size (SVL 130 vs 100 mm), and by colour beneath feet (dark vs pale).

Preferred habitat *E. s. saxatilis* is restricted to volcanic outcrops and scree slopes of Warrumbungle Mountains in subhumid north-eastern interior of NSW. *E. s. intermedia* favours rock outcrops, though it penetrates into more humid habitats such as in wet and dry sclerophyll forests. Extends from the Grampians in western Vic., through southern Vic. and along eastern highlands to about Cunningham's Gap, south-eastern Qld.

Microhabitat *E. s. saxatilis* is exclusively rock-inhabiting, sheltering in crevices or beneath slabs. *E. s. intermedia* favours similar situations throughout most of range, though some populations shelter beneath loose bark or in crevices of fallen or standing timber.

Comments *E. s. intermedia* usually produces 2 young per litter. Otherwise as for species group.

Egernia slateri Storr, 1968
Photo 463

Description Robust deep-headed member of *E. whitii* group, comprising 2 recognised subspecies.

E. s. slateri Ground colour grey to greyish brown. Black or dark brown spots on many individual dorsal scales align longitudinally to form series of narrow lines from nape to base of tail. Scales on dorsolateral and lateral surfaces usually bear narrow white to pale brown posterior flecks. Tail pale brown, spotted with black and dark brown. Eyelid rimmed with white to cream. Ventral surfaces greyish. SVL 90 mm.

E. s. virgata Storr, 1968 Differs from nominate form in bearing a black vertebral stripe.

Both subspecies are distinguished from *E. inornata* by ground colour (greyish vs reddish), and in bearing white-flecked lateral scales.

Preferred habitat *E. s. slateri* occurs on heavy loamy soils of alluvial plains and valleys of major central Australian drainage systems: Todd, upper Finke and upper Palmer Rivers, NT. Favours woodlands; often in association with grasses and chenopod shrubs. *E. s. virgata* occurs in far northern SA, between Oodnadatta and the Everard Range.

Microhabitat Excavates multi-entranced burrows at the bases of shrubs or tussocks.

Comments Preference for heavy soils (vs sands) tends to separate *E. slateri* from sympatric *E. inornata*. Otherwise as for species group.

Spiny-tailed Skink, Gidgee Skink
Egernia stokesii (Gray, 1845)
Photos 464–466

Description Large member of *E. cunninghami* group. Tail short, strongly spinose, dorsally depressed and non-fragile. Dorsal scales bear 2 (rarely 3) weak keels, each terminating in a spine. Three subspecies recognised in WA. Relationship with widespread eastern form is unclear.

E. s. stokesii Ground colour pale brown to blackish brown. Pale individuals bear little pattern. Prominent whitish blotches are sometimes present on snout, sides of head and neck. Scales on top of head and back bear dark margins. Tail bears obscure irregular yellowish brown and dark brown blotches. Dark individuals bear large whitish blotches, arranged in irregular transverse rows across head, body and tail. Top of head and upper lips blotched with pale brown. Ventral surfaces pale greyish brown; darker on chin and throat. Pale grey spots occasionally present; enlarged on chin to leave coarse reticulum or bars of ventral colour. SVL 155 mm.

E. s. aethiops Storr, 1978 Differs from nominate form by shorter snout and almost total lack of pattern. Ground colour blackish brown. Small clusters of brownish white scales are sometimes present, especially on flanks. Ventral surfaces dark brownish grey, occasionally bearing paler spots. SVL 160 mm.

E. s. badia Storr 1978 Largest subspecies. Northern populations wholly black. Elsewhere, ground colour is reddish brown. Pattern bold to obscure, comprising pale blotches arranged in 4–20 irregular bands. Head scales pale brown, finely edged with dark brown. Ventral surfaces pale brown. SVL 190 mm.

Eastern form: Ground colour pale brown to dull reddish brown. Sparse to dense dark and pale scales sometimes coalesce to form small blotches, arranged in irregular transverse rows. Pattern is most prominent on central Qld populations. Ventral surfaces pale brown. SVL 180 mm.

E. stokesii is distinguished from *E. depressa* by nature of dorsal scales (each bears 1 or 2 small spines vs 1 large, and 2 small spines). *E. s. badia* differs further in attaining greater maximum size (SVL 190 vs 115 mm). Differs from *E. hosmeri* by nature of tail (broad, very spiny and depressed vs relatively longer, less spiny and round in cross-section).

Preferred habitat *E. s. stokesii* is restricted to Wallabi and Pelsart groups of Houtman Abrolhos Islands off midwest coast of WA. These are predominantly vegetated with heathlands on limestone. *E. s. aethiops* occurs in similar conditions on Baudin Island in Shark Bay, WA. *E. s. badia* occurs in semi-arid to arid zones of south-western WA, largely along transition zone between eucalypt-dominated south and *Acacia*-dominated interior.

Also occurs on Dirk Hartog Island, Shark Bay. Eastern form dwells in rocky ranges, outcrops and woodlands, extending disjunctly throughout semi-arid to arid SA, western NSW, interior of Qld and southern NT.

Microhabitat *E. s. stokesii* and *E. s. aethiops* shelter beneath limestone slabs or chunks, and in crevices. *E. s. badia* favours hollow tree trunks and limbs. Dark populations north of eucalypt/*Acacia* transition zone appear restricted to rock outcrops. Eastern form utilises rock crevices throughout most of range, sheltering in hollow timber such as gidgee (*Acacia cambagei*) in interior of Qld.

Comments See species group.

Night Skink
Egernia striata Sternfeld, 1919
Photo 467

Description Large robust member of *E. whitii* group with vertically elliptic pupil. Ground colour brown to brick red, sometimes fading to grey on flanks. Darker lateral edges to dorsal and upper lateral scales may form fine longitudinal lines or dark variegations. Head and limbs usually unmarked. Ventral surfaces white to cream. SVL 110 mm.

Distinguished from all *Egernia* by unique pupil shape (vertically elliptic vs more or less round).

Preferred habitat Sand plains and interdunes vegetated with hummock grass associations from arid central interior of WA to southern NT and north-western SA.

Microhabitat Constructs a deep multi-entranced burrow system. Excavated sand is usually piled outside a south to south-westerly entrance. This possibly provides a visual vantage point or basking site.

Comments Predominantly nocturnal and crepuscular. Inactive during winter, retiring to a sealed-off section of burrow. Feeds on a variety of arthropods, though termites constitute nearly 70 per cent of prey volume. From 1–4 (usually 2 or 3) young are born from late October to mid-January. Otherwise as for species group.

Tree Skink
Egernia striolata (Peters, 1870)
Photo 468

Description Small member of *E. striolata* group, bearing 2–5 striations or weak keels on each dorsal scale. Dorsal ground colour pale or dark olive-grey to grey; darker along vertebral zone. Each scale may bear a dark streak, forming narrow broken lines from nape to base, or onto tail. Broad paler dorso-lateral suffusion extends from nape, fading at midbody or base of tail. Small paler flecks or spots are usually scattered over body and limbs, particularly on juveniles. Black upper lateral zone (usually boldest anteriorly) extends from eye, fading at midbody or hips. Lower flanks paler shade of ground colour. Sides of throat, neck and forebody pale grey. Scales on top of head usually margined with dark brown to black. Upper lips white to pale grey, each scale narrowly margined with dark grey. Ventral surfaces pale orange to dull yellow, bearing dark bars on chin and throat. Dark brown speckling occasionally present on chest and lower flanks, sometimes forming a narrow median stripe extending from chest to lower abdomen. SVL 100 mm.

Distinguished from *E. saxatilis* in bearing more prominent pattern (particularly the presence of a pale dorsolateral suffusion), and in bearing smoother scales. Differs further by colour beneath feet (pale vs dark), and in attaining smaller maximum size (SVL 100 vs 130 mm).

Preferred habitat   Dry sclerophyll forests, woodlands and rock outcrops in subhumid eastern Australia, from interior of Qld, through NSW (excluding coast and highlands) to northern Vic. and south-eastern SA.

Microhabitat   Shelters in hollow trunks or limbs, beneath loose bark or rock slabs, and in crevices.

Comments   As for species group.

White's Skink
Egernia whitii (Lacépède, 1804)
Photos 469, 470

Description   Member of *E. whitii* group comprising 2 currently recognised, variable subspecies.

E. w. whitii   Both striped and plain-backed forms occur. Dorsal ground colour pale to rich brown or (in many alpine areas) almost black. Dorsal pattern (when present) includes a broad vertebral stripe of ground colour or paler, extending from nape to hips. This is margined by a dark brown dorsal stripe of equal width, enclosing a series of white to cream spots. Pale dorsolateral line often extends from nape to hips. Flanks usually paler and greyer than dorsum, marked with one or more series of large dark-edged pale spots. Dark vertical bar enclosing 1 or 2 pale spots usually extends from above forelimb to dorsolateral stripe. Eye prominently rimmed with cream. Pale stripe usually extends from nostril, through upper lip to ear. Tail usually patternless. Ventral surfaces pale grey. SVL 90 mm.

E. w. moniligera (Duméril and Bibron, 1839) Differs from nominate form in attaining greater size, bearing dark stippling on tail, and (when present) more ragged dorsal pattern. SVL 110 mm.

Distinguished from *E. modesta* in frequently bearing dorsal pattern (vs invariably absent on all but smallest juveniles). Differs further in bearing prominent pale lateral spots (vs usually absent, or largely restricted to anterior flanks).

Preferred habitat   Dry sclerophyll forests, woodlands and heathlands (particularly where rock outcrops are present) from alpine to lowland regions of south-eastern Australia. Extends from southern

Eyre Peninsula and far south-eastern SA, through southern Vic. and northern Tas. to Granite Belt of south-eastern Qld. *E. w. moniligera* occurs in coastal and adjacent areas south to about Nowra, NSW.

Microhabitat   Excavates shallow depressions or tunnels beneath rocks or logs. Rock crevices and abandoned burrows of larger animals are also utilised.

Comments   Predominantly terrestrial, though ascends fallen timber, stumps or low rock faces to bask. Frequently gregarious; individuals of all ages may be encountered sharing a single shelter site. Though a variety of invertebrate prey is taken, ants appear to form a significant portion of diet. Mating occurs in spring (at least in far south of range), with 2–4 young born from late January to early March. A litter may comprise both patternless and striped forms. Recorded to live up to 8 years.

See also photos 471, 472, 473, which show 3 undescribed taxa of *Egernia*.

Genus *EMOIA*   Gray, 1845

Very large genus, containing over 100 species. Widespread from southern Japan to the Indo-Malayan Archipelago, New Guinea and Pacific Islands. This broad oceanic distribution is indicative of the ability of some species to successfully disperse by rafting. Only 2 species penetrate Australia, as far as Cape York Peninsula, Qld. Both occur extralimitally, with one subspecies of *E. atrocostata* occurring as far north as the southern islands of Japan.

The Australian species are moderately large, each with a long pointed snout and long slender tail. Limbs well developed, each bearing 5 slender, strongly clawed digits. Eye moderately large. Lower eyelid movable, bearing a transparent disc. Scales smooth and glossy.

Diurnal.   Predominantly arboreal and rock-inhabiting. Egglaying, producing 2 eggs per clutch. Invertebrate feeders.

Emoia atrocostata irrorata (Macleay, 1877)
Photo 474

Description   Dorsal ground colour dark greyish brown, dark brown to blackish (often paler on head) bearing sparse white to pale yellow spots and blackish flecks. Broad ragged-edged, black to dark brown upper lateral zone (immaculate or enclosing scattered to vertically aligned pale spots) extends from behind eye to hips. This is most conspicuous on juveniles and subadults. Side of neck and lower lateral zone pale to dark grey, marked with numerous pale spots. Tail black. Ventral surfaces cream, bearing yellowish to brown edges on scales of throat and chest. SVL 100 mm.

Preferred habitat   Mangroves and rocks along intertidal zone, from tip of Cape York Peninsula and

Torres Strait islands, Qld, to New Guinea. Other subspecies are extralimital throughout most of range of genus.

Microhabitat Basks and forages on mangrove branches and rocks, sheltering in hollow limbs and rock crevices.

Comments Arboreal and rock-inhabiting. One of the few Australian lizards restricted to the littoral zone. Observed avoiding breaking waves in splash zone, quickly returning to forage after they subside. Diet probably includes small soft-bodied marine crustaceans and molluscs. Studies on Philippine Island populations (possibly applicable to Australia) reveal an average life span of 3–4 years. Reproduction occurs throughout year. Clutches of usually 2 eggs are laid in rotting parts of mangroves, or among debris accumulated in cavities and hollows above high-water mark. Rock-inhabiting populations probably deposit their eggs in sheltered crevices. A powerful swimmer, readily taking to water if pursued.

Emoia longicauda (Macleay, 1877)
Photo 475

Description Sharp-snouted long-tailed *Emoia* with ground colour of coppery brown to pale yellowish brown; immaculate or flecked with pale orange-brown to pale yellow and dark brown scales, in irregular transverse alignment. Dark streak often extends from nostril to eye, sometimes continuing back to ear. Labial scales are occasionally margined with black, or bear dark spots. Short pale, widely separated dorsal bars are usually present on tail. Lower lips, sides of throat, neck, lower lateral zone and ventral surfaces are tinged with bright yellowish green to lemon yellow. SVL 95 mm.

Preferred habitat On Australian mainland *E. longicauda* is restricted to stream and river margins in monsoon forests, from McIlwraith Range to Cape York, Qld. On islands of Torres Strait and in southern New Guinea it is common in disturbed habitats such as gardens and plantations.

Microhabitat Arboreal. Basks on trunks and logs.

Comments As for genus.

Banded Sand-swimmers
Genus *EREMIASCINCUS* Greer, 1979

Endemic genus containing 2 species. Widespread throughout arid and semi-arid areas of all mainland States except Vic.

Medium-sized skinks with short well-developed limbs, each bearing 5 digits. Lower eyelid movable and scaly. Ear lobules absent. Scales smooth and glossy, with or without a weak keel. Pattern (when present) consists of dark bands.

Crepuscular and nocturnal. Terrestrial, sheltering by day beneath leaf-litter, and in loose sand and abandoned burrows. Often encountered resting with head protruding from cover, possibly employing an ambush strategy to catch passing prey. Feeds on arthropods (particularly termites), and occasionally smaller reptiles. Like many skinks and geckos, *Eremiascincus* wave their tails in a cat-like manner prior to lunging at prey. Egglaying.

Popular name, 'sand-swimmer', reflects the usual escape behaviour of diving beneath loose sand.

Distinguished from *Ctenotus* and *Egernia* in lacking ear lobules. Differs further from *Egernia* by arrangement of parietal shields (contacting each other vs separated by interparietal). Differs from *Sphenomorphus*, and further from *Ctenotus*, in bearing low longitudinal ridges on dorsal surface of tail and (usually) body. Differs further from *Sphenomorphus* in favouring arid (vs humid) habitats, and further from all in bearing a pattern of dark bands.

Narrow-banded Sand-swimmer
Eremiascincus fasciolatus (Günther, 1867)
Photo 476

Description Ground colour flesh pink, pale yellowish brown to reddish brown, with or without an obscure dark margin to each scale. Pattern prominent to absent (usually retained on tail and flanks), consisting of numerous narrow dark bands: 10–19 between nape and hips, and 35–40 on tail. Pattern tends to be strongest on populations from hard soils, and weaker on those from sandy soils. Population from Lake Eyre, SA (known as 'ghost skinks') lacks all pigment. Ventral surfaces white, often in sharp contrast to lateral colour. SVL 90 mm.

Distinguished from *E. richardsonii* in usually bearing weaker pattern, including more numerous and narrower bands, especially on tail. Differs further in usually attaining smaller maximum size (SVL 90 vs 110 mm).

Preferred habitat Variety of subhumid to arid habitats, particularly sandy areas supporting hummock grasses. Extends from north-western WA, through most of NT (excluding north-west) to north-eastern SA, western NSW and southern Qld. Reaches east coast in the vicinity of Port Curtis, Qld.

Microhabitat As for genus.

Comments As for genus.

Broad-banded Sand-swimmer
Eremiascincus richardsonii (Gray, 1845)
Photo 477

Description Ground colour very pale brownish white to rich golden brown, with or without an obscure dark margin to each scale. Pattern prominent to obscure, comprising numerous moderately broad dark brown to pale purplish brown bands; 8–14 between nape and hips and 19–32 on tail. These are often irregular; oblique, branching and/or disjunct. Ventral surfaces white. SVL 110 mm.

Distinguished from *E. fasciolatus* in usually bearing stronger pattern, comprising broader, fewer and less regular bands, especially on tail. Differs further in usually attaining greater maximum size (SVL 110 vs 90 mm).

Preferred habitat Variety of subhumid to arid areas, particularly hard or stony substrates supporting woodlands, shrublands or hummock grasslands. Extends through most of WA (excluding far north and south), through southern NT and most of SA (excluding far south) to western NSW and southern Qld. Penetrates eastern coastal areas in the vicinities of Ipswich, Port Curtis and Rockhampton, Qld.

Microhabitat As for genus.

Comments Clutches of 3–7 eggs are recorded. See genus.

Genus *EUGONGYLUS* Fitzinger, 1843

Small genus occurring in eastern Indonesia, New Guinea, and Solomon and Santa Cruz Islands. Represented in far northern Australia (Cape York Peninsula and Torres Strait Islands) by one species.

Australian species is a large robust skink with elongate body and thick short limbs, each bearing 5 strongly clawed digits. Tail long and fragile. Lower eyelid movable and scaly. Eye bears a pale iris and round pupil. Ear opening small, bearing anterior lobules. Scales smooth to weakly keeled.

Crepuscular and nocturnal. Terrestrial and partially arboreal. Egglaying. Invertebrate feeder.

Eugongylus rufescens (Shaw, 1802)
Photo 478

Description Adults are reddish brown, brown to dark or pale grey (iridescent purple whe viewed obliquely), becoming paler on side of head and anterior flanks. Pattern (if present) consists of obscure narrow lines formed by dark lateral margins to individual scales. Juveniles are prominently marked with numerous narrow and irregular, widely spaced whitish bands. These extend from snout to tail-tip, merging with pale lower lateral and ventral surfaces. Limbs banded as on body. Pale bands usually disappear with age. Ventral surfaces pale yellowish brown to white. SVL 150 mm.

Preferred habitat Monsoon forests on tip of Cape York Peninsula and Torres Strait Islands, Qld. Extralimital in New Guinea and Moluccas.

Microhabitat Shelters in cavities in rotting logs, and beneath logs and coarse leaf-litter. Recorded living well above ground in rotten buttresses and hollow limbs.

Comments Moves in a similar manner to she-oak skinks (*Cyclodomorphus casuarinae*) and pink-tongued skinks (*C. gerrardii*), except with forelimbs (vs hindlimbs) tucked to sides. Feeds on arthropods, and possibly snails and slugs.

Genus *HEMIERGIS* Wagler, 1830

Endemic genus containing 7 species, restricted to southern Australia, north on east coast to south-east Qld. Absent from Tas. Two divergent species (*H. graciloides* and *H. maccoyi*) are tentatively included; their status as *Hemiergis* is doubtful.

Small slender elongate skinks with moderate to long, thick fragile tails. Limbs short, bearing 5, 4, 3 or 2 digits. Lower eyelid movable, bearing a transparent disc. Ear opening absent (a minute opening present on *H. graciloides* and *H. maccoyi*), represented by a depression. Scales smooth and glossy. Pattern usually includes dark dorsal lines or equivalent series of spots or dashes. Ventral surfaces are usually flushed with reddish orange to yellow.

Nocturnal; possibly foraging beneath cover during day. Terrestrial to semi-fossorial. Cryptozoic; sheltering beneath logs, leaf-litter or rocks, wherever damp conditions prevail. Livebearing or egglaying. Arthropod feeders.

Distinguished from *Sphenomorphus*, *Calyptotis* and *Saiphos* by nature of movable lower eyelid (bearing transparent disc vs scaly). Differs from *Lampropholis*, and those *Lerista* with equal numbers of fingers and toes, in bearing yellow to reddish orange ventral pigments. Differs further from *Lampropholis* by build (an elongate body and weak, widely spaced limbs vs relatively shorter body and well-developed limbs). Excluding the aberrant *H. graciloides* and *H. maccoyi*, *Hemiergis* differs further from *Sphenomorphus*, *Lerista* and *Lampropholis* in lacking an ear opening; represented by a depression.

Hemiergis decresiensis (Cuvier, 1829)
Photos 479–481

Description Comprises 4 subspecies, each bearing 3 fingers and toes. Subspecies become larger and increasingly elongate with shorter limbs from south to north. Dorsal ground colour brown to brownish grey. Black paravertebral and/or dorsal lines (often broken into series of dashes) extend for various lengths between nape and tail-tip. Broader black dorsolateral stripe (sometimes edged above with coppery brown) extends from snout or behind eye to tail-tip. Lateral surfaces greyish, finely peppered and/or streaked with dark pigment. Ventral surfaces cream to yellow. Scales of throat dark-edged, forming a reticulum. Tail heavily spotted with dark brown.

H. d. decresiensis Smallest subspecies. Limbs relatively well developed. Dark dorsolateral line broad and prominent. Paravertebral lines obscure and broken. Dorsal lines more or less continuous. Midbody scales in 24 rows. SVL 45 mm.

H. d. continentis Copland, 1946 Differs from nominate population by larger size and more robust build. Pattern similar, though paravertebral lines are often well developed. Midbody scales in 24 rows. SVL 50 mm.

H. d. talbingoensis Copland, 1946 Differs from nominate form in attaining larger size. Paravertebral, dorsal and dorsolateral lines range from prominent and continuous to broken and obscure. Midbody scales normally in 22 rows, occasionally 20; rarely 24. SVL 60 mm.

H. d. davisi Copland, 1946 Differs from nominate form in attaining larger size. Pattern variable, usually including well-developed paravertebral and dorsal lines. Midbody scales usually in 20 rows, rarely 22 or 18. SVL 60 mm.

Distinguished from *H. maccoyi* and eastern populations of *H. peronii* in bearing fewer digits on each foot (3 vs 5 and 4, respectively).

Preferred habitat Cool temperate wet and dry sclerophyll forests and woodlands of south-eastern Australia, excluding Tas. Damp slopes, gullies and depressions associated with higher altitudes are favoured in north of range. *H. d. decresiensis* is restricted to Kangaroo Island, SA. *H. d. continentis* occurs in south-eastern SA. *H. d. talbingoensis* extends through north-eastern Vic. into highlands of southern and mideastern NSW. *H. d. davisi* is restricted to New England Plateau, north-eastern NSW.

Microhabitat As for genus.

Comments Livebearing. *H. d. talbingoensis* produces litters of 2–5 young during late summer. Otherwise as for genus.

Elf Skink
Hemiergis graciloides
(Lönnberg and Andersson, 1913)
Photo 482

Description Aberrant *Hemiergis* bearing 4 fingers and 5 toes. Ear opening present. Snout pointed. Eye large. Ground colour greyish brown, reddish brown to dark brown (iridescent pinkish red and green when viewed obliquely) with or without a narrow, poorly defined blackish dorsolateral line. Dorsal and upper lateral scales each bear 2–5 (usually 3) dark striae, sometimes replaced by obscure clusters of black spots on flanks. Flanks may be marked with pale flecks. Rear of head and temples usually bear blackish variegations, aligned to form an obscure M-shaped mark. Lips obscurely barred with dark brown and pale yellowish brown. All aspects of head pattern are more strongly defined on juveniles. Tail usually bears a broad orange-brown dorsolateral zone, fading posteriorly. Ventral surfaces white and semi-translucent, with dark speckling on tail. Hindlimbs, vent and tail suffused with pinkish brown to reddish orange on breeding individuals. SVL 30 mm.

Preferred habitat Isolated populations occur in vine thickets, wet sclerophyll forests and rainforests on lowlands and coastal ranges of south-eastern Qld. Extends from Fraser Island south to Ipswich area.

Microhabitat Shelters in shaded damp situations beneath leaf-litter, logs and stones, especially near streams or creeks.

Comments Inclusion within *Hemiergis* tentative, as it more closely resembles the New Caledonian genus *Nannoscincus*. Foraging individuals rarely expose themselves to direct sunlight. May be encountered in open situations after rain, or in late afternoon during overcast weather. Group of 4 eggs recorded in January. These may have been a product of communal laying, or a clutch of one female. See genus.

Hemiergis initialis (Werner, 1910)
Photos 483, 484

Description Small short-tailed *Hemiergis* bearing 5 fingers and toes. Two subspecies recognised.

H. i. initialis Dorsal ground colour brown, dark brown to reddish brown, bearing a metallic sheen. Dorsal pattern (if present) consists of 2 or 4 prominent to obscure longitudinal rows of blackish spots or dashes (1 per scale) from nape onto tail. Narrow dark grey to black (sometimes ragged-edged) dorsolateral line extends from behind eye, breaking and/or becoming diffuse on tail. Lateral surfaces grey to dark grey, peppered with darker pigment. Ventral surfaces, from chest to base of tail, bright reddish orange. Throat to chest grey. Tail grey to bluish grey. Ventral scales occasionally dark-edged, forming an obscure reticulum. SVL 45 mm.

H. i. brookeri Storr, 1975 Differs from nominate form in having prefrontals fused to frontonasal scale, attaining much smaller maximum size, and usually bearing little indication of a dark dorsolateral line. SVL 35 mm.

Distinguished from *H. peronii* and *H. quadrilineata* in bearing a greater number of fingers and toes (5 vs 3 or 4, and 2, respectively). Differs further by ventral colouration (reddish orange vs yellow).

Preferred habitat *H. i. initialis* occurs in sub-humid to semi-arid areas from south-western WA, to the Eyre Peninsula, SA. Occurs on lateritic soils supporting dry sclerophyll forests on Darling Range in south-west of distribution; in mallee/heathland associations of southern Wheat Belt; on loams and stony soils supporting sparse *Acacia* associations in the vicinity of Mt Jackson in north of distribution, and on sandy loams supporting mallee/chenopod associations in SA. *H. i. brookeri* usually occurs in ecotonal zone between Nullarbor Plain and coast of Great Australian Bight, from Mt Ragged, WA, east to far western SA. Recorded in low eucalypt woodlands on loamy soils, and *Banksia*-dominated shrublands on sandy limestone-based soils.

Microhabitat As for genus.

Comments Livebearing. When *H. initialis* and *H. peronii* are sympatric *H. initialis* tends to seek drier conditions. Otherwise as for genus.

Hemiergis maccoyi (Lucas and Frost, 1894)
Photos 485, 486

Description Divergent *Hemiergis* bearing a pointed snout, minute ear opening, and 5 fingers and toes. Two distinctive forms occur, and their inclusion within *Hemiergis* is tentative.

Widespread form: Dorsal ground colour yellowish brown, rich brown to almost black, usually marked with scattered to longitudinally aligned dark and pale flecks. Pale vertebral zone or stripe occasionally present. Narrow dark (often broken) dorsolateral line extends from above eye, fading on tail. This is often edged above with orange-brown to yellowish brown. Flanks, side of neck and tail pale grey to pale yellowish brown, sometimes bearing light to heavy darker pigmentation. Lips usually barred with black. Tail-tip occasionally tinged with yellowish brown to reddish brown. Chest and belly cream to orange-yellow. Throat whitish, often heavily spotted with brown. SVL 50 mm.

Illawarra form may represent a distinct taxon. Differs from nominate form in possessing a sharper snout and brow, broader head, shorter body and tail, orange (vs yellow) iris, and generally paler colouration.

Distinguished from all other *Hemiergis* except *H. graciloides* in bearing an ear opening. Differs further from *H. decresiensis* and eastern population of *H. peronii* in bearing a greater number of fingers and toes (5 vs 3 and 4, respectively).

Preferred habitat Highland wet and dry sclerophyll forests and woodlands. Extends disjunctly from south-eastern NSW and ACT, to south-western Vic. Illawarra form is restricted to temperate rainforest and adjacent margins of wet sclerophyll forests on Illawarra escarpment of south-eastern NSW, from Mt Keira south to Mt Cambewarra, and west to Kangaroo Valley.

Microhabitat Shelters and forages among leaf-litter and beneath stones and logs, wherever moist conditions prevail.

Comments Egglaying; ACT population produce clutches of 2–4 in late November or December, hatching in January or February. Recorded to lay communally with *Lampropholis delicata*. Illawarra form produces 2–6 eggs per clutch. Both forms are able to tolerate low temperatures, allowing foraging and feeding to occur year round.

Hemiergis millewae Coventry, 1976
Photo 487

Description Moderately small *Hemiergis* with 5 fingers and toes. Dorsal ground colour brown to dark olive, fading on lateral surfaces to paler shade or white. Burnt orange dorsolateral stripe usually extends from above and behind ear to hindlimb. Tail prominently marked with longitudinally aligned black spots. Ventral surfaces, from chest to base of tail, pale yellow. Chin and throat whitish,

each scale bearing a darker margin. Tail whitish with darker spots. SVL 55 mm.

Preferred habitat Sandy soils supporting mallee/*Triodia* associations from semi-arid north-western Vic., through Eyre Peninsula, SA, to south-eastern interior of WA, near Zanthus. Populations are disjunct, according to presence of suitable habitat.

Microhabitat Shelters and forages in and beneath *Triodia* hummocks.

Comments Livebearing; 1 or 2 young are born in late summer or early autumn. Otherwise as for genus.

Hemiergis peronii (Gray, 1831)
Photo 488

Description Large long-tailed *Hemiergis* with 3 fingers and toes in far west of range; 4 fingers and toes throughout remainder of WA, SA and Vic. Dorsal ground colour brown, coppery brown to olive-brown. Complete or broken paravertebral (and occasionally mid-dorsal) lines (each composed of dark spots and dashes) extend for various lengths between nape and tail-tip. Paravertebral lines occasionally coalesce to form a broad dark vertebral stripe. Narrow broken black dorsolateral line (sometimes narrowly margined above with a yellowish to reddish tinge) commences as a streak between snout and eye and extends nearly to tail-tip. This marking is usually absent in far eastern WA and SA. Lateral surfaces pale grey to pale brown, bearing variable amounts of scattered to longitudinally aligned black flecks or mottling on body and tail. Ventral surfaces, from chest to base of tail, bright yellow. Chin and throat whitish, remainder of tail greyish. Ventral scales may bear dark spots and/or dark edges. Size differs between disjunct populations in WA and SA. SVL 65 mm (WA); SVL 75 mm (SA).

Distinguished from *H. initialis* and *H. quadrilineata* by number of fingers and toes (4 or 3 vs 5 and 2, respectively). Differs further from *H. initialis* in attaining much larger size (SVL 65–75 vs 35–45 mm), and in bearing yellowish (vs reddish orange) ventral colouration. Eastern population differs from *H. decresiensis* by number of fingers and toes (4 vs 3).

Preferred habitat Humid to semi-arid coast, islands and adjacent interior of southern WA; east nearly to Nullarbor Plain. Widely distributed on SA coastline and offshore islands, from west of Ceduna to south-western Vic. Occurs in a variety of habitats ranging from wet sclerophyll forests to coastal dunes.

Microhabitat As for genus.

Comments When *H. peronii* and *H. initialis* are sympatric, *H. peronii* tends to seek moister conditions. Feeds largely on small arthropods and snails (probably applicable to most *Hemiergis*). A small skink (*Menetia greyii*) is recorded from the gut of one individual. Livebearing. Males are sexually mature at 2 years, and females bear their first litter at 3 years. Mating occurs in late summer. Females store sperm over winter, fertilisation occurring between late October and late November. Litters range from 2 to 5 young (depending on size of female), born in February.

Hemiergis quadrilineata
(Duméril and Bibron, 1839)
Photo 489

Description Large long-tailed *Hemiergis* with 2 fingers and toes. Dorsal ground colour pale to dark reddish brown, yellowish brown to greyish brown. Complete or broken, narrow blackish paravertebral lines usually extend from nape well onto tail, sometimes coalescing on body to form a broad dark vertebral stripe. Distinct narrow black dorsolateral stripe extends from snout to tail-tip. Flanks, side of head, tail and limbs grey to brownish grey, lightly to heavily flecked or peppered with darker pigment. Ventral surfaces, from chest to base of tail, yellow. Chin and throat whitish, remainder of tail greyish. Ventral scales bear dark edges, forming an obscure reticulum. SVL 70 mm.

Distinguished from *H. initialis* and *H. peronii* in bearing fewer fingers and toes (2 vs 5, and 4 or 3, respectively). Differs further from *H. initialis* in bearing yellow (vs reddish orange) ventral colouration, and in attaining greater maximum size (SVL 70 vs 45 mm or less).

Preferred habitat Sandy limestone-based soils on coastal plain and islands of south-western WA, from Geraldton area south to Bunbury district.

Microhabitat As for genus.

Comments Livebearing. Otherwise as for genus.

Genus *LAMPROPHOLIS* Fitzinger, 1843

Endemic genus containing 10 species and several undescribed forms. Restricted to eastern Australia, including Tas. One species *(L. delicata)* is introduced into Hawaii and New Zealand.

Small skinks with moderate to long fragile tails. Limbs usually well developed, each bearing 5 digits (except *L. tetradactyla* with 4 fingers). Lower eyelid movable, bearing a transparent disc. Ear opening present. Scales smooth; weakly to strongly glossed.

Diurnal. Terrestrial (some species are partially arboreal, and 1 is rock-inhabiting). Most forage among leaf-litter and low ground cover. Egglaying, often sharing communal deposition sites. Arthropod feeders. The genus includes many of the common garden skinks dwelling in the major cities of eastern Australia.

Divisible into 2 species groups; possibly representing separate genera.

L. challengeri group Contains 5 described species. Most are comparatively slender skinks with long limbs and tails and weakly glossed scales; somewhat translucent in texture. Dorsal pattern usually ill-defined, usually including an orange-brown to orange dorsolateral flush on tail. Prominent white to yellow spot or patch invariably present on posterior base of hindlimb. Breeding colouration is apparent on males of many species. Most shun direct sunlight, favouring damp microhabitats associated with wet sclerophyll forests, rainforests, dry sclerophyll forests and woodlands. Widespread from southern Vic. to far north-eastern Qld. Greatest diversity occurs in highlands of northern Qld. Group comprises *L. basiliscus*, *L. challengeri*, *L. czechurai*, *L. mustelina* and *L. tetradactyla*.

L. delicata group Contains 5 species (numerous taxa undescribed). Most are comparatively short-limbed, moderately robust skinks with moderately to strongly glossed scales. Pattern variable, usually including a coppery brown to greyish brown dorsum and darker grey to black flanks, sometimes enclosing a pale midlateral stripe. Head almost always tinged with coppery brown. No distinctive breeding colouration is recorded for males. Members are sun-loving skinks which rarely penetrate closed forest, favouring margins and clearings. Extends from Tas. through south-eastern SA and eastern NSW to north-eastern Qld. Group comprises *L. amicula*, *L. caligula*, *L. delicata*, *L. guichenoti* and *L. mirabilis*.

Lampropholis differs from *Leiolopisma* by arrangement of nasal scales: usually widely (vs narrowly) separated. Differs from *Hemiergis* and *Calyptotis* by build (moderate, with well-developed limbs, vs elongate, with weak widely spaced limbs). Differs further from *Calyptotis*, and from *Sphenomorphus* and *Morethia*, by nature of lower eyelid: movable, bearing a transparent disc, vs movable and scaly (*Calyptotis* and *Sphenomorphus*), and fused to form a spectacle *(Morethia)*. Excluding *L. tetradactyla*, *Lampropholis* differs from *Carlia* in bearing more fingers (5 vs 4). *L. tetradactyla* differs from *Carlia* in bearing a row of scales between eye and upper labials.

Lampropholis amicula
Ingram and Rawlinson, 1981
Photo 490

Description Small weak-limbed member of *L. delicata* group with dorsal ground colour of dark coppery brown to greyish brown. Pattern obscure, consisting of longitudinal dorsal series of blackish dashes, or each scale variably peppered with black. Fine yellowish to greyish dorsolateral line usually extends from nape to posterior body, or onto base of tail; represented on tail as obscure pale flecks. Upper lateral zone, from snout well onto tail, dark grey to black, contrasting with dorsal colour. Lips whitish spotted with black. Ventral surfaces greyish white, usually bearing small dark spots. These tend to align longitudinally on throat and venter, and transversely on tail. SVL 30 mm.

Distinguished from sympatric *Lampropholis* spp. in bearing fewer supraciliary scales (5 vs 6 or 7). Differs further in bearing weaker limbs, and in attaining smaller maximum size (SVL 30 vs 40 mm or greater). Superficially similar to immature *L. delicata*, differing further in always lacking a pale midlateral stripe (vs often present on sympatric populations).

Preferred habitat Dry sclerophyll forests, heathlands and margins of vine thickets in south-eastern Qld, from just south of Brisbane, north to the Burnett River and inland to the Great Dividing Range.

Microhabitat Shelters and forages among leaf-litter, usually adjacent to well-watered areas.

Comments Throughout its range *L. amicula* occurs alongside *L. delicata*, differing in a number of behavioural aspects. *L. amicula* is secretive, rarely venturing far from cover. If approached, it dives beneath leaf-litter in a manner resembling the similarly sized cryptozoic skinks, *Menetia* spp. It is most active during warm cloudy weather. In contrast, *L. delicata* is a conspicuous forager which favours more open areas and brighter sunshine. Hatchlings appear during February and March. Otherwise as for species group.

Lampropholis basiliscus
Ingram and Rawlinson, 1981
Photo 491

Description Member of *L. challengeri* group. Dorsal ground colour pale brown to reddish brown, usually marked with dark and pale flecking; sometimes coalesced to form variegations. Dark-edged pale dorsolateral stripe occasionally present, at least anteriorly. Dark brown to black ragged-edged upper lateral zone usually present, commencing as a streak from nostril to eye and extending back for varying distances along body. Flanks pinkish brown anteriorly, merging to grey; sparsely to heavily marked with dark and pale spots and variegations. Ventral surfaces cream, often speckled with darker pigment; generally more pronounced on throat. Dark pigment may concentrate to form a median row of flecks extending onto tail. SVL 45 mm.

Distinguished from *L. czechurai* by build and snout-shape (relatively robust with a moderate snout vs dorsally depressed with relatively pointed snout). Differs further in attaining greater maximum size (SVL 45 vs 30 mm).

Preferred habitat Known from 2 large isolated patches of rainforest in central and north-eastern Qld. Southern population occurs in Eungella area, north-west of Mackay. Northern population extends from Paluma north to Cooktown district.

Microhabitat Shelters and forages among leaf-litter, fallen timber, stones and buttresses. Penetrates into open areas to a greater extent than most other members of species group.

Comments As for species group.

Lampropholis caligula
Ingram and Rawlinson, 1981
Photo 492

Description Drably patterned member of *L. delicata* group. Dorsal ground colour dull brownish grey, bearing a copper sheen. Dorsal markings (if present) consist of obscure longitudinally aligned dark dashes and scattered paler flecks. Narrow pale dorsolateral stripe may extend from nape to base of tail. Upper lateral zone, from about level of ear well onto tail, dark grey to black, becoming paler and flecked with grey to brown on lower flanks. Dark streak usually present between snout and eye. Top of head suffused with copper. Side of head and neck greyish, finely peppered with darker pigment. Ventral surfaces greyish white; black beneath tail. SVL 45 mm.

Distinguished from other members of *L. delicata* group in bearing fewer upper labial scales (usually 6 vs 7). Differs further from *L. guichenoti* and *L. delicata* in bearing fewer supraocular scales (3 vs 4), and attaining a greater maximum size (SVL 45 vs 40 mm). Differs further from *L. guichenoti* in lacking a dark vertebral stripe.

Preferred habitat Cool highland swamps with a dominant ground cover of tussock grasses and sedges, surrounded by dry sclerophyll forests. Only known from 2 sites on Barrington Tops, mideastern NSW.

Microhabitat Shelters in tussock grasses and sedges lining small streams running through swamps.

Comments As for species group.

Lampropholis challengeri (Boulenger, 1887)
Photos 493–495

Description Large variable member of *L. challengeri* group, probably involving a complex of taxa. Dorsal ground colour pale brown, yellowish brown, brown to grey; paler and greyer on flanks and sides of head. Pattern (when present) consists of dark and pale flecking over dorsal and lateral surfaces; sometimes fusing to form bands, blotches or variegations. Dark-edged pale dorsolateral stripe or zone sometimes present (often irregular and broken), extending for varying distances between neck and tail. Tail usually flushed with yellowish brown to bright reddish orange, tending to concentrate on dorsolateral zone. Dark streak extends from tip of snout to behind eye or onto body. Mature males may exhibit a distinct cream to yellow lateral stripe from lips well onto tail. Some develop a strong black lateral flush. Ventral surfaces white to yellow, usually speckled, spotted or flecked with dark brown. These markings usually align in longitudinal series, sometimes forming irregular stripes. Populations from subcoastal ranges of south-east Qld are known to attain a smaller maximum size than those from adjacent Great Dividing Range.

SVL up to 50 mm.

Distinguished from *L. mustelina* in lacking a dark-edged pale bar behind eye.

Preferred habitat Highland and lowland wet sclerophyll forests, rainforests, vine thickets, and occasionally montane heathlands. Occurs on coastal ranges, extending inland to Great Dividing Range, from north-eastern NSW to Gympie district, south-eastern Qld.

Microhabitat Shelters and forages among leaf-litter, stones, fallen timber, buttresses and surface debris. Penetrates exposed, well-lit areas to a greater extent than most other members of species group.

Comments Affinities between populations of *L. challengeri* are uncertain. Predominantly terrestrial, though regularly ascends low foliage to bask and to roost at night. Individuals have been encountered chasing each other or other skinks, possibly in defence of territory. In confrontations observed between adults, opponents raised their heads and waved exposed throats from side to side. Females recorded to deposit their eggs communally. See species group.

Lampropholis czechurai
Ingram and Rawlinson, 1981
Photo 496

Description Small relatively dorsally depressed member of *L. challengeri* group with long pointed snout and short tail. Dorsal ground colour brown, dark brown to dark reddish brown, paler to grey on flanks. Pattern consists of numerous small dark and pale flecks, sometimes coalescing to form wavy lines and/or variegations. These are finest on back and sides, and larger and more prominent from behind eye to about forelimb. Narrow irregular (often dark-edged) pale dorsolateral stripe exhibits strongest development on hips and tail, usually fading or breaking anteriorly. Blackish streak extends from snout to temple. Lips whitish, bearing irregular flecks. Breeding males develop a black flush enclosing contrasting white spots over sides of head and neck. Hindlimbs and tail often flushed with brownish orange. Ventral surfaces cream with scattered dark dots; most prominent on tail. SVL 30 mm.

Distinguished from *L. basiliscus* by build and snout-shape (dorsally depressed with a pointed snout vs relatively more robust with a moderate snout). Differs further in attaining smaller maximum size (SVL 30 vs 45 mm). Differs from *L. tetradactyla* in bearing more fingers (5 vs 4).

Preferred habitat Highland rainforests of north-eastern Qld from Ravenshoe district north to Rossville area.

Microhabitat Shelters and forages among large pebbles and fallen timber adjacent to well-shaded creeks and streams.

Comments As for species group.

Lampropholis delicata (De Vis, 1888)
Photo 497

Description Variable member of *L. delicata* group, probably comprising several distinct taxa as presently defined. Dorsal ground colour bronze-brown, coppery brown to brownish grey. Dorsum may be immaculate, or bear fine dark peppering or scattered dark and pale flecks, dashes and streaks, occasionally coalescing to form short transverse bars on tail. Narrow (often broken) whitish to pale copper dorsolateral line present or absent. Broad dark brown to black upper lateral stripe or zone, commencing as a streak between nostril and eye, extends onto base of tail, tending to break beyond hips. White midlateral stripe (often dark-edged below) may be prominent to absent in northern populations; usually obscure to absent in south. Top of head (sometimes nape) coppery brown. Ventral surfaces white to cream, often bearing dark brown flecks, which tend to coalesce to form striations on throat. SVL 40 mm.

Distinguished from *L. guichenoti* in lacking an irregular ragged-edged dark vertebral stripe. Southern populations tend to differ further in bearing stronger copper tinge to dorsal ground colour; lacking pale flecks or dots. Differs from *L. amicula* (within zone of overlap) in usually bearing a pale midlateral stripe, in attaining larger maximum size (SVL 40 vs 30 mm), and in possessing longer limbs. Differs from *L. caligula* in possessing more supraocular scales (4 vs 3) and more upper labial scales (7 vs usually 6). Differs further from *L. guichenoti*, *L. amicula* and *L. caligula* in usually bearing more supraciliary scales (7 vs 6, 5 and 5, respectively).

Preferred habitat Cool temperate to tropical rainforests, wet and dry sclerophyll forests, woodlands and heathlands. Common in many settled areas, including the cities of Melbourne, Sydney and Brisbane. Extends from north-eastern Tas. to western Vic. and along Great Dividing Range and coast to Cairns district, Qld. Isolated populations occur on Eyre Peninsula, south-eastern SA, and adjacent Vic. Introduced into Hawaii and New Zealand.

Microhabitat Shelters and forages among leaf-litter, fallen timber, logs, stones, grasses and surface debris. Occasionally ascends trunks and lower branches of small trees, garden fences and walls. Commonly encountered among litter, stones, wood-piles, etc., of suburban gardens.

Comments Females produce 1–4 eggs per clutch, often laid communally. Up to 110 eggs are recorded from one site. Another record of 132 eggs included those of *L. guichenoti*. Southern populations may produce 2 clutches per year. The first is laid from November to early December, hatching in late January or early February. Second clutch is laid as first hatches; the young emerging from late March to early April. Otherwise as for species group. See also *L. amicula* and *L. guichenoti*.

Garden or Grass Skink
Lampropholis guichenoti
(Duméril and Bibron, 1839)
Photo 498

Description Variable member of *L. delicata* group with dorsal ground colour of brown, olive-brown, dark brown to grey. Prominent to obscure dark ragged-edged vertebral stripe or zone usually present, extending from nape to base of tail. Remainder of dorsum usually bears scattered dark flecks and pale scales; sometimes aligning transversely on tail. Dark brown to black upper lateral stripe or zone, commencing as a streak from nostril to eye, extends to hips or well onto tail. This is often margined finely above by a pale dorsolateral line, and below by a prominent dark-edged pale midlateral stripe, extending from ear or forelimb onto base of tail. Head and nape coppery brown. Tail occasionally bears obscure pinkish grey flush. Ventral surfaces white to grey; immaculate or bearing scattered dark and pale markings. SVL 40 mm.

Distinguished from *L. delicata* in usually bearing a dark vertebral zone or stripe and fewer supraciliary scales (6 vs 7). Differs from *L. caligula* in bearing more upper labial scales (7 vs usually 6), more supraocular scales (4 vs 3), more supraciliary scales (6 vs 5), stronger pattern, and attaining smaller maximum size (SVL 40 vs 45 mm).

Preferred habitat Dry sclerophyll forests and woodlands, occasionally margins of cool temperate to subtropical rainforests or wet sclerophyll forests, particularly where tussock grasses occur. Common in many settled areas, including the cities of Melbourne and Sydney. Extends from far south-eastern SA, through southern and eastern Vic. to eastern NSW, Granite Belt of south-eastern Qld, and islands of Moreton Bay. Isolated populations occur on Kangaroo Island, in Adelaide district, and in southern Flinders Ranges, SA.

Microhabitat Shelters and forages among leaf-litter, fallen timber, stones, grasses and surface debris. Especially common in suburban gardens.

Comments Females lay 3–5 eggs; deposited in single clutches or in communal sites. These sites may be shared with *L. delicata*, and over 130 eggs of both species have been recorded together. More than one clutch may be produced per year. Young hatch in late summer or early autumn. Otherwise as for species group. See also *L. delicata*.

Lampropholis mirabilis
Ingram and Rawlinson, 1981
Photo 499

Description Large, somewhat divergent member of *L. delicata* group with long limbs and distinctive pattern. Ground colour pale olive-grey to coppery brown, marked over back, flanks and limbs with numerous dark blotches, mixed with scattered white flecks or spots. Dark blotches on flanks and side of tail tend to coalesce, forming irregular vertical bars. Top and sides of head and neck coppery brown with little or no pattern. Ventral surfaces greyish white. SVL 50 mm.

Preferred habitat Favours large granite boulders, often in association with thickets of hoop pine (*Araucaria cunninghamii*) and pockets of rainforest. Restricted to Townsville district of north-eastern Qld, extending from Magnetic Island inland to Great Basalt Wall.

Microhabitat Basks and forages on exposed granite surfaces, sheltering in cracks, crevices and beneath slabs.

Comments Only wholly rock-inhabiting species of *Lampropholis*. In common with other rock-inhabiting skinks (e.g., *Cryptoblepharus*, and some *Carlia* and *Leiolopisma*), the body is dorsally depressed and the limbs are long with strongly clawed digits. Otherwise as for species group.

Weasel Skink
Lampropholis mustelina
(O'Shaughnessy, 1874)
Photo 500

Description Moderately large long-tailed member of *L. challengeri* group. Ground colour yellow-brown, orange-brown, rich red to grey, often paler on flanks. Pattern consists of numerous obscure scattered paler and darker flecks; sometimes aligning longitudinally on flanks. Obscure pale dorsolateral stripe bearing irregular dark edges may extend between eye and hips. This is invariably present on tail; represented as an orange-brown zone or stripe which extends almost to tip. Conspicuous dark-edged white to cream bar present behind and below ear; sometimes continuous with pale lips. Lips spotted or barred with dark pigment. Tail often tinged with yellowish brown. Ventral surfaces white to yellow, bearing dark longitudinal streaks from throat onto base of tail. SVL 45 mm.

Distinguished from *L. challengeri* in bearing a dark-edged pale bar behind eye.

Preferred habitat Favours wet sclerophyll forests, temperate rainforests, woodlands and heathlands, from southern and eastern Vic. to mideastern NSW; becoming increasingly altitude dependent northwards. Isolated populations occur in Otway Ranges of southern Vic., and on New England Plateau of north-eastern NSW.

Microhabitat Shelters beneath leaf-litter, logs, stones and surface debris, where damp conditions prevail.

Comments Most southerly occurring member of *L. challengeri* group. Cryptozoic and predominantly crepuscular; rarely encountered foraging. Invertebrates such as isopods probably constitute bulk of diet. Communal egglaying recorded. Otherwise as for species group.

Lampropholis tetradactyla
Greer and Kluge, 1980
Photo 501

Description Small highly iridescent member of *L. challengeri* group. Sole member of genus bearing 4 fingers. Ground colour brown, dark brown to dark reddish brown, fading on lower lateral surfaces. Dorsal and upper lateral pattern consists of black longitudinal dashes, extending from nape and side of neck well onto base of tail. Obscure dark W-shaped mark often present on rear of head, between eyes. Lips cream, barred with dark brown. Head and neck usually finely dotted with obscure dark and pale scales. Ventral surfaces pale lemon yellow; brightest on belly, beneath hindlimbs and base of tail. SVL 30 mm.

Distinguished from all *Lampropholis* in bearing fewer fingers (4 vs 5).

Preferred habitat Lowland and highland rainforests of north-eastern Qld, from Kuranda south to Paluma.

Microhabitat Shelters beneath stones, logs and leaf-litter. Individuals may be encountered foraging in damp conditions such as creek margins and in spray zone of waterfalls.

Comments Breeding occurs during summer months (Wet Season) and clutches of 2 eggs are recorded.

See also photos 502–6, which illustrate 5 undescribed taxa of *Lampropholis*.

Genus *LEIOLOPISMA*
Duméril and Bibron, 1839

Contains 40–45 species occurring in New Zealand, New Caledonia, Vanuatu, Loyalty Islands, Mauritius (Round Island) and Lord Howe Island. Represented in Australia by 14 species, most of which are largely confined to cool temperate Tas. and southeastern mainland, and north to higher altitudes of southern Qld. Two species occur in southern WA; a third is isolated in montane north-eastern Qld.

Small, slender to moderately robust skinks with moderate to long fragile tails. Limbs well developed, each bearing 5 digits. Lower eyelid movable, bearing a transparent disc. Ear opening well developed. Scales smooth to striate, and weakly to strongly glossed. Females tend to be noticeably larger than males.

Diurnal sun-loving skinks. Predominantly terrestrial; a few are arboreal and rock-inhabiting. Arthropod feeders. Predominantly livebearing, but at least 3 species are egglayers.

Divisible into 2 species groups.

L. baudini group Contains 8 small to moderately large (SVL 50–80 mm) *Leiolopisma*, bearing relatively short limbs and 20–33 scale rows at midbody. Pattern includes narrow dark and pale dorsal and lateral stripes, or a brown dorsum and contrasting darker flanks. Breeding males (occasionally both sexes at all ages) usually bear an orange-red to pink flush on throat, or a red lateral stripe. Predominantly terrestrial. Egglaying or livebearing, producing relatively large clutches or litters. Widespread through wet and dry sclerophyll forests, woodlands, swamplands and heathlands. Group comprises *L. baudini*, *L. coventryi*, *L. duperreyi*, *L. entrecasteauxii*, *L. metallicum*, *L. platynotum*, *L. trilineatum* and *L. zia*. Photo 507, of *Leiolopisma platynotum*, shows the red throat colouration typical of many members of the *L. baudini* species group.

L. spenceri group Contains 6 moderate to large (SVL 65–95 mm) *Leiolopisma* with relatively depressed bodies, long limbs and 30–58 scale rows at midbody. Pattern usually includes pale spots over head, body, limbs and tail; occasionally in combination with irregular pale dorsolateral and dark lateral stripes. Reddish flushes are usually absent; sometimes present on the venter of *L. pretiosum*. Predominantly rock-inhabiting; 1 species (*L. spenceri*) is arboreal. Livebearing, producing relatively small litters. Greatest diversity occurs in highlands and lowlands of Tas., including adjacent islands. Members tend to favour cooler, moister habitats than *L. baudini* group. Comprises *L. greeni*, *L. jigurru*, *L. ocellatum*, *L. palfreymani*, *L. pretiosum* and *L. spenceri*.

Distinguished from *Lampropholis* by arrangement of nasal scales: usually narrowly (vs widely) separated. Differs from *Cryptoblepharus*, *Morethia* and *Sphenomorphus* by nature of lower eyelid; movable, bearing a transparent disc vs fused to form a spectacle (*Cryptoblepharus* and *Morethia*), or movable and scaly (*Sphenomorphus*).

Leiolopisma baudini Greer, 1982

Description Small member of *L. baudini* group with dorsal ground colour of olive-brown (in preservative). Dorsal scales margined laterally by dark pigment; coalescing to form obscure lines from nape to base of tail. Prominent narrow white dorsolateral stripe extends from nape, becoming diffuse on base of tail. This is margined above and below by obscure dark brown lines. Dark grey upper lateral stripe (commencing as a streak from snout to eye) extends to hindlimb, fading on base of tail. White midlateral stripe extends from lips, through ear to hindlimb, margined above and below by obscure dark lines. Lower lateral zone greyish brown, bearing numerous dark-edged scales. Head pale olive-brown, bearing obscure darker reticulations posteriorly. Ventral surfaces greyish white. SVL 50 mm.

Distinguished from *L. trilineatum* by nature of frontoparietal scales (divided vs fused to form a single shield).

166

Preferred habitat Semi-arid near-coastal areas of Great Australian Bight, WA. Known from widely separated localities of Point Culver area in west, and Madura and Eyre areas in east. Holotype was collected from a low *Acacia* shrubland association, adjacent to a whitish coastal dune.

Microhabitat No data available.
Comments No data available.

Leiolopisma coventryi Rawlinson, 1975
Photo 508

Description Small obscurely patterned member of *L. baudini* group with brown to dark brown dorsal ground colour. Individual scales bear 3 or 4 fine dark striae, which may coalesce to form blackish patches. Scattered pale olive flecks usually present, tending to align transversely on tail. Dorsolateral scale row yellowish, tinged with copper above and black below, forming an obscure dark-edged line from nape to base of tail. Dark grey to black upper lateral zone (often enclosing scattered pale brown flecks or spots) commences as a streak between snout and eye, extending to tail-tip; often broken beyond hips. Lower lateral zone and sides of head and neck grey, smudged with darker pigment. Ventral surfaces pale grey, bearing scattered dark flecks; most dense on chin. SVL 50 mm.

Distinguished from *L. metallicum* by nature of frontoparietal scales (divided vs fused to form a single shield). Differs from *L. entrecasteauxii* in bearing a more simple pattern (a brown dorsum and darker flanks vs dark and pale stripes). Differs from *L. platynotum* in lacking a reddish flush on throat. Differs further from all in attaining smaller maximum size (SVL 50 vs 65 mm or greater).
Preferred habitat Highland wet sclerophyll forests of south-eastern Australia, from Bowenfels area of Blue Mountains, NSW, extending disjunctly to the Grampians, Vic. Prefers clearings created by fire, rock outcrops and fallen trees.
Microhabitat Shelters in cracks or hollows of decaying logs, basking on their surfaces and foraging in adjacent leaf-litter.
Comments Communal hibernation occurs, with dens containing up to 8 individuals recorded. This does not necessarily imply gregarious behaviour, but rather a heavy utilisation of suitable shelter sites. Livebearing. Mating occurs in autumn; females storing sperm over winter. Fertilisation occurs in October. Litter sizes vary from 1–7 offspring. Otherwise as for species group.

Leiolopisma duperreyi
(Duméril and Bibron, 1839)
Photo 509

Description Boldly striped member of *L. baudini* group with dorsal ground colour of silvery grey to greyish brown. Narrow (sometimes broken) black vertebral stripe extends from nape onto base of tail. Narrow whitish dorsolateral stripe, margined by black laterodorsal stripe, extends from nape to base of tail. Prominent broad black upper lateral stripe (often broken or obscure on side of head) extends from snout (encompassing eye) onto base of tail. White midlateral stripe extends from upper lip, over ear onto tail; sometimes margined below by a narrow black line. Lower lateral surfaces pale silvery grey, each scale finely margined with black. Head often tinged with bronze-brown. Ventral surfaces whitish. Orange-red throat flush may be present on both sexes at all ages; boldest on breeding males. SVL 70 mm.

Distinguished from *L. platynotum* and *L. metallicum* in bearing a prominent white midlateral stripe. Differs further from *L. metallicum* by nature of upper lateral stripe (immaculate vs usually spotted). Differs from *L. entrecasteauxii* by nature of frontoparietal scales (fused to form a single shield vs divided).
Preferred habitat Occurs in cool temperate highland and lowland dry sclerophyll forests, woodlands, shrublands and heathlands, favouring a low ground cover of tussock grasses. Extends from north and east coasts of Tas., through Bass Strait islands to south-eastern SA (including Kangaroo Island), southern Vic., and eastern NSW, north to New England area.
Microhabitat Shelters among tussocks or beneath rocks and logs, ascending low vegetation and rocks to bask and forage.
Comments Egglaying, with recorded clutches of 3–9; often laid communally. Over 60 hatchlings are recorded from one site.

Tussock Skink
Leiolopisma entrecasteauxii
(Duméril and Bibron, 1839)
Photo 510

Description Variably patterned member of *L. baudini* group comprising distinct strongly and weakly patterned forms. These may constitute separate taxa.

Strongly patterned form: Dorsal ground colour brown, olive-brown to brownish grey. Narrow dark brown to blackish vertebral stripe extends from nape to base of tail. Scattered blackish flecks, and paravertebral and dorsal series of whitish dashes or broken lines may be present. Narrow cream to white dorsolateral stripe (sometimes margined above and below by narrow dark lines) extends from temple, becoming diffuse on base of tail. Broad upper lateral stripe of ground colour or darker (sometimes enclosing a paler median line) commences as a streak on snout, extending onto tail. This often breaks into a series of large flecks beyond hips. Pale midlateral stripe (often margined by blackish lines) extends from lips, becoming diffuse on base of tail. Lower lateral zone greyish, variably flecked with darker pigment. Head often tinged with copper. On breeding males, pale midlateral and (when present) upper lateral stripes become bright reddish orange. Ventral surfaces silvery grey, pale olive to white. SVL 65 mm.

Weakly patterned form: All aspects of dark and pale striping become diffuse to virtually absent, particularly on adults. Dorsal ground colour dark brown to almost black. Dark vertebral stripe present or absent. Obscure pale dorsolateral line usually present; most prominent above forelimb. Upper flanks black. Obscure narrow pale midlateral stripe extends from upper lip, fading before hindlimb. Breeding males develop a reddish orange flush over ventral surfaces; occasionally restricted to throat only. Red midlateral stripe may develop on some populations; often confined to anterior flanks.

Distinguished from *L. duperreyi*, *L. platynotum* and *L. metallicum* by nature of frontoparietal scales (divided vs fused to form a single shield). Differs from *L. coventryi* in usually bearing more complex pattern, including dark and pale stripes (vs a brown dorsum and darker flanks). Breeding males differ further in bearing reddish pigment.

Preferred habitat Highland and lowland dry sclerophyll forests, woodlands, swamplands, and heathlands, favouring a ground cover of tussock grasses and sedges. Extends from scattered highland areas of NSW (as far north as Barrington Tops), through southern Vic. and south-eastern SA (including Kangaroo Island, and Pearson Islands off west coast of Eyre Peninsula) to Bass Strait islands and Tas.

Microhabitat Shelters beneath fallen timber, stones, mats of dead vegetation, and in grass tussocks. Though both forms may ascend tussocks, rocks and timber to bask and forage, strongly patterned form appears more consistently terrestrial.

Comments Though both forms are sympatric over much of range, several trends are apparent. Strongly patterned form occurs further north in NSW and into Tas. Weakly patterned form extends further west in Vic. and SA. In southern highlands of NSW and Vic. weakly patterned form extends into higher altitudes. Breeding colours appear from spring to late autumn, though this is subject to considerable local variation. Females store sperm over winter, producing litters of 1–7 young in late February or early March.

Leiolopisma greeni Rawlinson, 1975
Photo 511

Description Member of *L. spenceri* group with ground colour of black; paler on head and side of neck. Scales weakly glossed, bearing greenish to copper iridescence when viewed obliquely. Pattern consists of numerous small greenish yellow, greyish green to pale olive dashes and dots over head, body, limbs and tail, tending to align longitudinally on body. Distal half of tail suffused with black. Ventral surfaces greenish grey. SVL 70 mm.

Preferred habitat Occurs on rocky edges of streams and swamps above the tree-line in alpine areas of Tas. at altitudes over 1000 m.

Microhabitat Shelters in cracks and crevices of dark rocks protruding from, or lining edges of streams or swamps, basking and foraging on exposed surfaces. Burrows are excavated in waterlogged soil beneath rocks along water's edge.

Comments This is the only reptile restricted to mainland Tas. If alarmed, individuals will not hesitate to swim or seek shelter beneath submerged rocks, despite water temperatures as low as 5°C. *L. greeni* is forced to hibernate over winter, as much of its habitat is subject to heavy snowfall. Livebearing with recorded litters of 2–3 young, born in late February.

Leiolopisma jigurru Covacevich, 1984
Photo 512

Description Member of *L. spenceri* group. Dorsal ground colour coppery brown, prominently dotted with black. Each dot is margined posteriorly by a conspicuous transversely oriented cream dash. Pale markings cluster on dorsolateral region to form a ragged-edged broken stripe from nape to hips. Narrow black upper lateral zone extends from snout to hindlimb. This may enclose obscure paler flecks. Broken white midlateral stripe (composed of a series of dashes) extends from side of neck to hindlimb. Lower lateral zone black, merging to greyish brown on ventrolateral region. Top of head rich copper, sharply contrasting with dark upper lateral zone. Tail suffused with grey and prominently dotted with black. Ventral surfaces whitish. Soles of feet black. SVL 70 mm.

Preferred habitat Known only from near the summit of Mt Bartle Frere in north-eastern Qld, between altitudes 1440 and 1620 m. This area consists of granite outcrops surrounded by dense rainforest; significantly cooler than surrounding lowlands and often enshrouded in mist.

Microhabitat Forages on exposed rock surfaces. Shelters in crevices and beneath exfoliations.

Comments Occurs 1500 km north of nearest congeners, and is probably a relict from past cooler climates. Otherwise as for species group.

Metallic Skink
Leiolopisma metallicum (O'Shaughnessy, 1874)
Photo 513

Description Member of *L. baudini* group with bronze-brown dorsal ground colour. Dorsal pattern (if present) consists of longitudinally aligned dark and pale flecks or streaks. Narrow dark vertebral stripe, and complete or broken paravertebral stripes are rarely present. Narrow pale copper dorsolateral line sometimes present. Upper lateral surfaces, from behind eye to base of tail, dark grey to black enclosing numerous pale flecks. Lower lateral surfaces greyish smudged with darker pigment; sometimes delineated from upper lateral zone by an obscure pale midlateral stripe. Ventral surfaces cream to pinkish brown, often bearing a pinkish red flush from level of forelimbs to base of tail. SVL 65 mm.

Distinguished from *L. coventryi* and *L. entrecasteauxii* by nature of frontoparietal scales (fused to form a single shield vs divided). Differs further from *L. coventryi* in attaining larger maximum size (SVL 65 vs 50 mm). Differs further from *L. entrecasteauxii* in usually lacking dark and pale stripes. Differs from *L. pretiosum* in bearing fewer midbody scale rows (24–28 vs 30–42). Differs from *L. duperreyi* in lacking a prominent white midlateral stripe and in bearing pale flecks within upper lateral zone.
Preferred habitat Wet and dry sclerophyll forests, woodlands, heathlands, and rock outcrops of cool areas of south-eastern Vic. and Tas.
Microhabitat Shelters in cracks in logs, beneath rocks and fallen timber. Basks and forages on logs, lower branches and trunks, rocks and leaf-litter.
Comments Commonest and most widely distributed skink in Tas. Livebearing. Mating occurs in autumn, and females store sperm over winter. Litters of 1–8 young are born from early to mid-February. Otherwise as for species group.

Ocellated Skink
Leiolopisma ocellatum (Gray, 1845)
Photo 514

Description Member of *L. spenceri* group. Ground colour dark bronze-brown to coppery brown, marked over body and limbs with numerous cream to silvery grey dark-edged blotches. These often coalesce to form transversely aligned variegations. Dark-edged blotches on flanks are larger and more sparse, approximating ocelli. Top of head dotted with dark and pale pigment. Tail bears numerous obscure pale irregular bars. Ventral surfaces cream. SVL 70 mm.
Preferred habitat Rocky areas associated with woodlands, heathlands and shrublands in lowland Tas. and eastern islands of Bass Strait. Widespread in the cool temperate zone, becoming scarce in sub-alpine and alpine regions.
Microhabitat Normally shelters in narrow rock

crevices, though loose bark and cracks in logs provide alternative sites. Basks on exposed rock surfaces or fallen logs.
Comments Mating occurs in autumn, female storing sperm over winter. Litters of 2–4 young are born from mid- to late February.

Pedra Branca Skink
Leiolopisma palfreymani (Rawlinson, 1974)
Photo 515

Description Member of *L. spenceri* group. Largest Australian member of genus. Dorsal ground colour blackish brown to black, densely flecked with grey and brown. Narrow (often broken) dorsolateral line commences above eye, breaking on tail. Flanks black, sometimes bearing paler flecks or spots. Ventral surfaces grey. SVL 95 mm.
Preferred habitat Known only from Pedra Branca Rock, approximately 40 km south of Tasmania. This comprises 1.4 ha of rugged sandstone supporting no vegetation.
Microhabitat Shelters in crevices, foraging and basking on exposed rock surfaces.
Comments This is Australia's most southerly occurring wholly terrestrial vertebrate. Apparently feeds almost entirely on regurgitated fish, scavenged from the island's cohabitants, Australasian gannets and albatrosses. Littoral crustaceans may also be consumed. Skinks are active when the ambient temperature rises above 15°C. Basking lizards cluster together, forming a large dark heat-absorbent mass. This appears an efficient means of raising body temperatures in cool windy conditions, and is mirrored by New Zealand's Fiordland skink *(Leiolopisma acrinasum)*, and to a lesser extent by *L. spenceri*.

Red-throated Skink
Leiolopisma platynotum (Peters, 1881)
Photos 507, 516

Description Large member of *L. baudini* group with dorsal ground colour of pale silvery grey, brownish grey to dark grey. Dorsal scales may be narrowly margined with dark pigment, forming a fine reticulum or indistinct lines. Broad dark grey to black upper lateral stripe (sometimes margined by a narrow pale dorsolateral line) commences as a streak on snout, extending well onto tail. Lower lateral zone ground colour or paler (each scale dark-edged), sometimes delineated from upper lateral stripe by an indication of a pale midlateral line. Head usually tinged with copper. Ventral surfaces whitish. Throat usually tinged with orange-red on individuals of both sexes at all ages. This is most intense on breeding males. SVL 80 mm.

Distinguished from *L. duperreyi* in lacking a prominent white midlateral stripe. Differs from *L. coventryi* and *L. entrecasteauxii* in usually bearing a reddish flush on throat. Differs further from *L.*

coventryi in lacking pale dorsal flecks, and further from *L. entrecasteauxii* by nature of frontoparietal scales (fused to form a single shield vs divided).

Preferred habitat Lowland and highland dry sclerophyll forests, woodlands and heathlands, favouring a ground cover of tussock grasses. Extends along Great Dividing Range from Granite Belt of south-eastern Qld in north, to north-eastern Vic.

Microhabitat Shelters and forages among leaf-litter, fallen timber, grass tussocks, rocks and surface debris.

Comments Normally an arthropod feeder, though recorded to take skink eggs, which are swallowed whole. Egglaying, with recorded clutches of 3–9 eggs laid in midsummer. Hatchlings appear during mid-autumn.

Leiolopisma pretiosum (O'Shaughnessy, 1874)
Photo 517

Description Member of *L. spenceri* group with dorsal ground colour of dark olive-brown to brown. Narrow blackish vertebral line sometimes extends from nape to base of tail. Remainder of dorsal surface obscurely marked with small scattered dark and pale flecks. Narrow ragged-edged yellowish brown to whitish dorsolateral zone or stripe extends from nape to hips, often breaking posteriorly. Broad dark brown to black upper lateral zone, commencing as streak on snout, extends to hindlimb or well onto tail. This may be immaculate or enclose scattered pale flecks. Lower lateral zone, from side of neck to base of tail, grey with numerous paler and darker flecks and spots. Ventral surfaces whitish, marked with small dark longitudinally aligned flecks on throat. Sexually mature individuals may bear a pinkish flush over posterior ventral surfaces and base of tail. SVL 70 mm.

Distinguished from *L. metallicum* in bearing more midbody scale rows (30–42 vs 24–28).

Preferred habitat Occurs in most well-timbered and rocky areas of highland and lowland Tas. Abundant in cool temperate zones, though less common in alpine regions.

Microhabitat Shelters beneath rocks, logs, leaf-litter, surface debris and in crevices. Basks and forages on fallen timber, lower trunks and exposed rocks.

Comments Mating occurs in autumn, females storing sperm over winter. Litters of 1–4 young are born in late summer.

Leiolopisma spenceri (Lucas and Frost, 1894)
Photo 518

Description Moderately small member of *L. spenceri* group with dorsal ground colour of olive-brown to coppery brown. Broad black ragged-edged laterodorsal stripe (sometimes sufficiently broad to obscure all but an indistinct narrow vertebral line of ground colour) extends from head or

shoulders, merging with its opposite on base of tail. This usually encloses 1 or 2 series of pale dots and dashes. Prominent cream dorsolateral stripe commences above eye, becoming suffused with grey on base of tail and often tinged with copper anteriorly. Broad black upper lateral stripe commencing as a streak on snout becomes ragged-edged or diffuse on base of tail. This is immaculate, or encloses numerous fine scattered cream dots on body. Narrow whitish midlateral stripe (wavy anteriorly) extends from lips to hindlimb. Lower lateral surfaces dark grey. Top of head coppery brown, finely ornamented with dark pigment. Ventral surfaces pale grey. SVL 65 mm.

Preferred habitat Humid montane areas of south-eastern Australia, favouring wet sclerophyll forests, and rock outcrops in subalpine woodlands. Extends disjunctly from Blue Mountains, NSW, to eastern Vic., with isolated populations occurring in Gisborne district and Otway Ranges, Vic.

Microhabitat Forages on exposed sunlit surfaces of trees and rocks, sheltering beneath exfoliating bark or rock.

Comments With its dorsally depressed build and preference for vertical surfaces, *L. spenceri* resembles *Cryptoblepharus* spp., occupying an equivalent cool temperate highland niche. Hibernates over winter, and aggregations of approximately 20–50 individuals are recorded. Mating occurs in late summer, females storing sperm over winter. Livebearing with recorded litters of 1–4 (usually 2) young, born in midsummer.

Three-lined Skink
Leiolopisma trilineatum (Gray, 1838)
Photo 519

Description Drab member of *L. baudini* group with dorsal ground colour of dark brown to dark brownish grey. Narrow blackish vertebral, dorsal and laterodorsal stripes may extend from nape to base of tail. Narrow greyish white dorsolateral stripe usually discernible from nape to base of tail. Dark grey to blackish brown upper lateral stripe (commencing as streak on snout and often obscure on side of head) extends to hindlimb, becoming diffuse on tail. Obscure whitish midlateral stripe sometimes present. Lower lateral zone grey, each scale margined and/or flecked with black. Head usually tinged with copper. Ventral surfaces pale grey. Adult males and females may display a reddish tinge on chin and throat; the intensity varying according to locality and season. SVL 70 mm.

Distinguished from *L. baudini* in bearing a weaker pattern, and by nature of frontoparietal scales (fused to form a single shield vs divided).

Preferred habitat Usually associated with swamplands and drainage systems on sandy soils of south-western WA, from just north of Perth, southeast to Israelite Bay.

Microhabitat Shelters among dense vegetation, leaf-litter, and beneath fallen timber, adjacent to wetlands.

Comments Egglaying with recorded clutches of 3–6. Otherwise as for species group.

Leiolopisma zia Ingram and Ehmann, 1981
Photo 520

Description Distinctive small short-limbed member of *L. baudini* group with depressed pointed snout. Dorsal ground colour pale to dark brown, bearing scattered dark brown to black, and greyish yellow flecks. Obscure narrow pale yellowish brown dorsolateral line extends from behind eye onto base of tail. This is sharply edged below by a narrow dark zone extending forward to snout and breaking behind hindlimb. Flanks pale reddish brown to dark greyish brown, marked with scattered pale flecks. Tail suffused with reddish brown. Ventral surfaces bright yellow from chest to vent, fading to whitish on base of tail and reddish brown towards tip. Chin, throat and neck speckled with black. SVL 55 mm.

Preferred habitat Favours highland rainforests and antarctic beech forests *(Nothofagus moorei)* along Great Dividing Range of south-eastern Qld and adjacent NSW. Extends from Cunningham's Gap south to Armidale district.

Microhabitat Shelters beneath logs and stones, foraging among leaf-litter on edges of sunny clearings.

Comments Lays 3–6 eggs in a shallow depression beneath moss, rocks or fallen timber during midsummer. Mating probably occurs in spring, and/or after laying. It appears likely that females store sperm over winter. Otherwise as for species group.

Genus *LERISTA* Bell, 1833

Endemic; second largest genus of Australian lizards, containing 57 species. Additional taxa await description. Most successful in arid to subhumid sandy areas, though a few species (*L. bougainvillii*, *L. arenicola* and *L. microtis*) are restricted to cooler, more humid areas of south-east and south-west.

Small to medium-sized elongate skinks with fragile tails and minute ear openings. Some retain 4 small widely spaced limbs, each bearing 5 digits. Progressive loss of limbs and digits reaches its extreme in 2 fossorial species (*L. apoda* and *L. ameles*) which have lost all trace. Fingers (when present) are always equal to or fewer than toes. Head-shape variable, with fusion of head-scales and protrusion of snout beyond lower jaw occurring on many specialised burrowing *Lerista*. Eyelid movable, bearing a transparent disc; or fused to form an immovable spectacle. Eye completely covered by a transparent ocular scale on *Lerista apoda*. Scales smooth. Pattern, when present, tends to comprise simple stripes and/ or longitudinally aligned dots or dashes.

Crepuscular to nocturnal, though considerable time may be spent foraging beneath cover by day. Terrestrial, leaf-litter inhabiting to fossorial. Excepting the above-mentioned southern species, all are egglayers, producing small clutches. Small arthropods, their eggs and larvae probaby constitute the bulk of diets.

Members have adapted to cryptozoic or fossorial lifestyles in widely varying degrees. In many areas several species occur in sympatry, each usually favouring different levels in the leaf-litter and upper soil profiles. Those with well-developed limbs and little or no reduction of digits tend to forage and shelter in a variety of situations: in or under fallen logs, beneath rocks resting on loose soil or among leaf-litter. Species with reduced limbs or toes and protrusive snouts prefer lower layers of humus and soft upper layers of soil or sand.

The genus offers an excellent model for evolutionary study, as it comprises the most complete limb reduction series within Australian vertebrates. Eight species groups are recognised. One distinctive species, *L. stictopleura*, has not been allocated to any of those groups due to its unique combination of characteristics (blunt, non-protrusive snout, immovable lower eyelid, 1 finger and 2 toes, and a pattern including orange-brown laterodorsal stripes.

L. elegans group Comprises 19 taxa of small slender *Lerista*, each bearing 4 well-developed limbs; forelimb about half as long as hindlimb. Fingers 3–5; toes equal in number. Lower eyelid movable or fused. Snout not markedly protrusive. Pattern often includes white midlateral and dark upper lateral stripes. Tails of juveniles (occasionally adults) are often flushed with red. Most are leaf-litter inhabiting, rather than burrowers. Diversity is greatest in semi-arid and subhumid zones of southern Australia, on sandy, stony and heavy soils. Members are *L. aericeps aericeps*, *L. aericeps taeniata*, *L. arenicola*, *L. bougainvillii*, *L. chalybura*, *L. christinae*, *L. distinguenda*, *L. dorsalis*, *L. elegans*, *L. flammicauda*, *L. fragilis*, *L. frosti*, *L. haroldi*, *L. microtis*, *L. muelleri*, *L. orientalis*, *L. separanda*, *L. terdigitata* and *L. xanthura*.

L. lineata group Represented by one species bearing 4 limbs; forelimb much less than half length of hindlimb. Fingers 2; toes 3. Eyelid immovable. Snout slightly protrusive. Pattern consists of prominent stripes. Restricted to pale sands on subhumid lower west coast of WA.

L. planiventralis group Contains one species bearing 4 limbs (forelimb much less than half length of hindlimb) and a prominent ventrolateral flange. Fingers 2; toes 3. Eyelid movable. Snout slightly protrusive. A specialised sand-swimmer, restricted to subhumid and semi-arid midwest coasts of WA.

L. walkeri group Contains 3 medium-sized moderately robust *Lerista* bearing 4 limbs; forelimb about half length of hindlimb. Fingers 1 or 2; toes 2 or 3. Eyelid movable. Snout slightly protrusive.

Pattern consists entirely of small dark spots. Members inhabit leaf-litter, lower humus layers and soft upper soil layers at bases of trees or shrubs, and beneath rocks. Restricted to semi-arid to subhumid Kimberley region, WA. Members are *L. borealis*, *L. kalumburu* and *L. walkeri*.

L. macropisthopus group   Contains 8 taxa of large to very large robust *Lerista* bearing 4 limbs; forelimb much less than half length of hindlimb. Digits variable; forelimb stylar, or with 1, 2 or 3 fingers; toes 2 or 3. Eyelid movable. Snout slightly protrusive. Pattern absent, or comprises longitudinally aligned dots or narrow dark lines. Members favour lower humus layers, soft upper soil layers, or in and beneath decomposing timber. Best represented in arid to semi-arid woodlands and shrublands of southern Australia. Group contains *L. desertorum*, *L. gerrardii*, *L. macropisthopus*, *L. neander*, *L. picturata baynesi*, *L. picturata edwardsae*, *L. picturata picturata* and *L. punctatovittata*.

L. lineopunctulata group   Comprises one very large robust *Lerista* with forelimb reduced to a style, or absent and represented by a groove. Toes 1 or 2. Eyelid movable. Snout slightly protrusive. Pattern absent; or consisting of longitudinally aligned dots or dashes. Inhabits lower humus layers and soft upper soil layers in sandy areas of subhumid to semi-arid west coast of WA.

L. bipes group   Contains 19 taxa. Small to medium-sized, moderate to very slender *Lerista* with no forelimbs (often represented by a groove; very rarely a stump) and 1 or 2 toes. Eyelid movable or immovable. Snout very protrusive, usually wedge-shaped. Pattern variable, often including longitudinally aligned dorsal rows of dots or dashes, and a dark lateral stripe. Best represented in sandy coastal and desert regions. Sand-swimmers, usually dwelling in soft upper soil layers beneath leaf-litter and humus. Their distinctive meandering tracks are often visible in open sandy areas. Members are *L. allanae*, *L. bipes*, *L. carpentariae*, *L. connivens*, *L. gascoynensis*, *L. greeri*, *L. griffini*, *L. humphriesi*, *L. ips*, *L. karlschmidti*, *L. labialis*, *L. nichollsi nichollsi*, *L. nichollsi petersoni*, *L. onsloviana*, *L. praefrontalis*, *L. praepedita*, *L. simillima*, *L. uniduo*, *L. varia* and *L. vermicularis*.

L. wilkinsi group   Contains 7 species of small slender *Lerista*. Forelimbs absent without trace. Hindlimbs present or absent, never bearing more than 2 digits. Eyelid movable in all but 1 species (eye of *L. apoda* covered by a transparent ocular scale). Snout strongly protrusive. Pattern (when present) usually consists of dark longitudinal dashes, which may join to form narrow lines. Members inhabit upper soil layers beneath leaf-litter and soft sandy soil or humus beneath rocks and logs. The group includes Australia's most specialised fossorial *Lerista*. Restricted to subhumid northern Australia, with greatest diversity occurring in north-east Qld. Members are *L. ameles*, *L. apoda*, *L. cinerea*, *L. storri*, *L. stylis*, *L. vittata* and *L. wilkinsi*.

Lerista is distinguished from *Hemiergis* (excluding the aberrant *H. graciloides* and *H. maccoyi*) in possessing an exposed ear opening (vs reduced to a dimple), and in usually lacking orange to yellow ventral pigments. Differs from *Anomalopus* and *Sphenomorphus* by nature of lower eyelid (movable and bearing a transparent disc, or fused to form an immovable spectacle, vs movable and scaly). *Lerista* with 5 fingers and toes, and immovable lower eyelids differ from sympatric *Proablepharus* by size of ear opening (minute vs relatively large and prominent) and eye (usually small vs very large and surrounded by granular scales). Those with immovable lower eyelids differ from *Menetia* in never possessing a digital formula of 4 + 5, and in bearing a much smaller eye.

Lerista aericeps Storr, 1986
Photos 521, 522

Description   Small slender member of *L. elegans* group with immovable lower eyelid and 4 well-developed limbs, each bearing 4 digits. Two subspecies recognised.

L. a. aericeps   Ground colour pale greyish brown, sometimes flushed with coppery red on head and usually with yellow on tail. Pattern obscure; each scale finely dark-edged and marked with faint dark flecks. Dark upper lateral stripe very obscure, its presence indicated by a blackish brown streak between nostril and eye and several series of dark spots on body. Ventral surfaces whitish, each scale finely dark-edged. SVL 45 mm.

L. a. taeniata Storr, 1986   Differs from nominate form in bearing stronger pattern. Each scale finely dark-edged. Dark dashes align to form 4 longitudinal lines (paravertebrals and dorsals). Blackish brown upper lateral stripe sharply defined. SVL 45 mm.

Distinguishable from *L xanthura* in having faint dark spots on back and tail, and fewer preocular scales (1 vs 2). *L. a. taeniata* differs further in bearing a prominent dark upper lateral stripe.

Preferred habitat   Arid eastern Australia, from southern NT to south-western Qld and north-western NSW. *L. a. taeniata* occupies the far western portion of this range, occurring in Tanami Desert, NT. Both subspecies inhabit sandy areas dominated by hummock grass *(Triodia)*.

Microhabitat   Shelters beneath leaf-litter and *Triodia*.

Comments   See species group.

Lerista allanae (Longman, 1937)
Photo 523

Description   Largest member of *L. bipes* group with a movable lower eyelid. Forelimb represented by a groove; hindlimb bearing one digit. Ground colour grey to greyish brown. Darkened edges or centres of each dorsal and lateral scale form narrow lines or series of spots or dashes. Ventral surfaces whitish, each scale bearing a dark brown spot; boldest beneath tail. SVL 90 mm.

Preferred habitat Subhumid to semi-arid central-eastern interior of Qld, from Emerald district north to Charters Towers. Favours sandy soils supporting woodlands and shrublands. Populations from Charters Towers area occur among basalt outcrops.

Microhabitat Shelters in loose upper layers of sand beneath rocks, and under leaf-litter at bases of trees and shrubs.

Comments As for species group.

Lerista ameles Greer, 1979
Photo 524

Description Small completely limbless member of *L. wilkinsi* group with movable lower eyelid. Forelimbs absent without trace. Hindlimbs represented merely by depressions. Dorsal ground colour dark silvery grey to greyish brown, becoming grey on tail. Six darker longitudinal lines (one per dorsal scale row) extend from nape onto tail. Flanks and ventral surfaces dark brown to dark grey. SVL 58 mm.

Preferred habitat Known only from a granite outcrop in eucalypt woodland, in the vicinity of Mt Surprise in subhumid north-eastern Qld.

Microhabitat Shelters in soft soil beneath rocks.

Comments As for species group.

Lerista apoda Storr, 1976
Photo 525

Description Slender completely limbless member of *L. wilkinsi* group with short abruptly terminating tail. Eye covered by a transparent ocular scale. Snout flat and sharp; protruding well beyond mouth. Dorsal surfaces whitish, marked with 4 longitudinal series of obscure brown dots, extending onto tail. Flanks and ventral surfaces dark brown, spotted with darker brown. Chin and throat whitish. Anterior half of tail whitish, sparsely spotted with brown. SVL 75 mm.

Preferred habitat Restricted to Dampier Land, in semi-arid west Kimberley region, WA. Most abundant along *Acacia*-dominated transition zone between consolidated coastal dunes and open Pindan country.

Microhabitat Shelters in soft upper layers of sand beneath leaf-litter. Retreats to insect holes (such as those of ants) when disturbed.

Comments Complete loss of limbs, and presence of a covering over eye, suggest *L. apoda* to be an advanced fossorial *Lerista*.

Lerista arenicola Storr, 1972
Photo 526

Description Large member of *L. elegans* group with movable lower eyelid, 5 fingers and toes.

Dorsal ground colour pale grey, lacking pattern on western populations. Those from eastern portion of range bear narrow dark vertebral and paravertebral lines. Blackish brown upper lateral stripe (narrow in west; broader in east) extends from behind ear to base of tail. Broad white midlateral stripe extends from snout; breaking up on base of tail. This is bordered below by a narrow indistinct lower lateral line, extending from forelimb to base of tail. Hindlimbs and tail suffused with pink. Ventral surfaces white; pinkish beneath tail. SVL 55 mm.

Western populations are distinguished from *L. microtis* by nature of colour and pattern (paler, with obscure more simple pattern, including a narrower dark upper lateral stripe) and in attaining larger maximum size (SVL 55 vs 50 mm). Differs from *L. dorsalis* in bearing more digits on each foot (5 vs 4).

Preferred habitat Pale coastal sands on Great Australian Bight, from Twilight Cove, WA, to Nuyts Archipelago, SA.

Microhabitat Shelters among leaf-litter at bases of coastal shrubs.

Comments Previously treated as a subspecies of *L. microtis*. Livebearing. Regarded as a primitive *Lerista*. See species group, and *L. bougainvillii*.

Lerista bipes (Fischer, 1882)
Photo 527

Description Member of *L. bipes* group with movable lower eyelid. Forelimbs absent without trace; hindlimbs bear 2 toes. Snout depressed; protruding well beyond lower jaw. Dorsal ground colour pale reddish brown to yellowish brown. Paravertebral series of small dark dots usually extend from nape to tail-tip. Broad dark brown to black upper lateral stripe extends from nostril, through eye almost to tail-tip; often ragged-edged and diffuse beyond hips. Tail flushed with grey to yellow, and often flecked with dark brown. Ventral surfaces whitish. SVL 65 mm.

Distinguished from *L. greeri* and *L. labialis* in bearing fewer upper labial scales (5 vs 6). Differs from *L. griffini* by build (relatively slender vs robust) and nature of snout (flatter and more protrusive). Differs from *L. vermicularis* by nature of lower eyelid (movable vs immovable). Differs from *L. simillima* in bearing supraciliary scales.

Preferred habitat Reddish sands supporting hummock grass associations from arid interior of NT and north-western SA to north-west coast and offshore islands of WA.

Microhabitat Shelters in loose upper layers of sand beneath leaf-litter, low shrubs and grass hummocks. Forages just beneath surface in open sandy areas, leaving conspicuous meandering tracks.

Comments As for species group.

Lerista borealis Storr, 1971
Photo 528

Description Relatively robust member of *L.*

walkeri group with a movable lower eyelid, 2 fingers, and 3 toes. Dorsal and upper lateral ground colour reddish brown to greyish brown, obscurely flecked or dotted with dark brown. Upper lips may be heavily barred with dark brown. Lower flanks and ventral surfaces pale brown to dull pink; flecked with dark brown beneath tail. SVL 50 mm.

Distinguished from *L. walkeri* in bearing more numerous toes (3 vs usually 2), in attaining smaller maximum size (SVL 50 vs 60 mm) and in bearing less prominent pattern. Differs from *L. kalumburu* in bearing more numerous fingers (2 vs 1).

Preferred habitat Favours alluvial soils, though occurs less commonly on adjacent rocky hills and outcrops, in subhumid to semi-arid central and eastern Kimberley region, WA.

Microhabitat Shelters in loose sand under rocks, and beneath sand and leaf-litter at bases of boulders, trees and shrubs.

Comments As for species group.

Lerista bougainvillii (Gray, 1839)
Photos 529, 530

Description Largest member of *L. elegans* group with movable lower eyelid and 4 well-developed limbs, each bearing 5 digits. Subject to geographic variation; attaining greatest size in south of range. Dorsal ground colour pale brown to greyish brown. Four longitudinal series of blackish dashes (sometimes coalesced to form lines) usually extend from nape well onto tail. Broad black lateral stripe extends from snout, through eye onto base of tail, breaking into oblique bars toward tip. Lower lateral zone white to grey, streaked with black. Tail often suffused with brown, yellow or red. Ventral surfaces white, flushed beneath tail with yellow to red. Northern populations may bear dense black spotting over chest and belly. SVL 70 mm.

Distinguished from *L. dorsalis* in bearing more digits on each foot (5 vs 4).

Preferred habitat Humid to subhumid south-eastern Australia, from western slopes of Great Dividing Range in mideastern NSW, through southern Vic. to north-eastern Tas. and south-eastern SA. Apparently isolated population occurs on Eyre Peninsula, SA. Favours rock outcrops and hard to stony soils supporting dry sclerophyll forests or woodlands.

Microhabitat Shelters beneath rocks, fallen timber, leaf-litter, and in soil cracks.

Comments Possibly comprises several distinct taxa. Populations from Tas. and Kangaroo Island bear live young. Those from Eyre Peninsula and most of mainland are egglayers. Individuals from southern Vic. are somewhat intermediate. In Tas. mating occurs in autumn and females store sperm over winter. Young are born from mid- to late February. Regarded as a primitive *Lerista* due to its restriction to cool southern areas and the absence of

any strong development towards a fossorial lifestyle; limbs are long, no digits have been lost, and little or no fusion of head shields has occurred. Otherwise as for species group.

Lerista carpentariae Greer, 1983
Photo 531

Description Slender member of *L. bipes* group with movable lower eyelid, and forelimb absent without trace. Hindlimb stylar, or bearing one clawed digit. Snout angular and slightly protrusive. Dorsal ground colour pale yellowish brown. Narrow dark brown paravertebral lines extend from nape, and broader dark brown lateral stripes commence in front of eyes, all becoming diffuse toward tail-tip. Ventral surfaces pinkish white. SVL 65 mm.

Distinguished from *L. stylis* in bearing fewer mid-body scale rows (16 vs 18). Differs from *L. karlschmidti* by build (relatively more slender) and nature of lateral pattern (a broad dark stripe vs narrow lines).

Preferred habitat Known only from poor sandy soils supporting shrublands and exfoliating sandstones on Groote Eylandt and islands of Sir Edward Pellew Group, in Gulf of Carpentaria, NT.

Microhabitat As for species group.

Comments As for species group.

Lerista chalybura Storr, 1985
Photo 532

Description Member of *L. elegans* group with movable lower eyelid and 4 fingers and toes. Dorsal ground colour coppery brown without pattern. Prominent narrow blackish brown upper lateral stripe, its upper edge sharply defined and its lower edge deeply notched and merging with lower flanks, extends from snout to hindlimb. Lower flanks brown to dark brown, with up to 5 longitudinal rows of obscure dark spots. Tail grey to blue (brightest on juveniles), spotted with blackish brown. Ventral surfaces whitish to pale brown with dark spots beneath tail. SVL 50 mm.

Distinguished from *L. flammicauda* by tail colour (bluish vs reddish) and width of dark upper lateral stripe (less than 1 scale wide, its lower edge diffuse, vs more than 1 scale wide and sharply defined). Differs from *L. muelleri* in bearing a movable lower eyelid (vs immovable) and more fingers and toes (4 vs 3).

Preferred habitat Occurs in Hamersley Range in arid Pilbara region of north-western WA. Appears to be strongly associated with major drainage systems, especially gorges.

Microhabitat Recorded sheltering beneath flood debris deposited among roots of paperbarks (*Melaleuca*) and eucalypts lining the bottoms of gorges.

Comments As for species group.

Lerista christinae Storr, 1979
Photo 533

Description Slender boldly striped member of *L. elegans* group with immovable lower eyelid and 4 well-developed limbs, each bearing 4 digits. Dorsal ground colour silvery grey to almost white. Prominent, moderately broad paravertebral stripe extends from nape onto base of tail, breaking into dashes on head and beyond middle of tail. Black upper lateral stripe commences on snout as a streak, becoming broad from eye onto base of tail, and breaking into irregular series of blackish brown dots toward middle of tail. Broad white midlateral stripe extends from upper lip to base of tail. Narrow black lower lateral stripe extends from forelimb to hindlimb. Tail flushed with pale pink. Ventral surfaces white. SVL 35 mm.

Preferred habitat Restricted to undulating pale sand plains and laterites supporting complex heathlands on subhumid lower west coast of WA; in the vicinity of Badgingarra and Eneabba.

Microhabitat As for species group.

Comments As for species group.

Lerista cinerea Greer, McDonald and Lawrie, 1983
Photo 534

Description Member of *L. wilkinsi* group with movable lower eyelid. Forelimb absent without trace; hindlimb bears one clawed digit. Dorsal ground colour grey to silvery brown, suffused with yellow on tail. Six narrow (often obscure) dark longitudinal lines composed of dashes on each dorsal scale extend from nape well onto tail. Indication of dark upper lateral suffusion present. Tails of juveniles are tinged with red. Ventral surfaces greyish white. SVL 65 mm.

Distinguished from *L. wilkinsi* in bearing 1 toe (vs 2). Differs from *L. karlschmidti*, *L. storri* and *L. vittata* in possessing a distinct prefrontal scale. Differs further from *L. karlschmidti* in bearing more numerous midbody scale rows (18 vs 16).

Preferred habitat Restricted to subhumid northeastern interior of Qld. Recorded from 5 distinct habitats: semi-evergreen vine thicket on dark clay-loam; open hillside supporting introduced buffel grass (*Cenchrus* sp.) on coarse sandy yellow soil; low *Acacia* woodland on grey sandy soil with lateritic outcrops; eucalypt woodland with grassy understorey on red loam soil; and a granite outcrop beside a creek in eucalypt woodland.

Microhabitat As for species group.

Comments As for species group.

Lerista connivens Storr, 1971
Photo 535

Description Large robust member of *L. bipes* group with movable lower eyelid, forelimb represented by a groove (rarely a stump), and 2 toes. Dorsal ground colour pale greyish brown to almost white. Broad dark vertebral stripe (composed of paravertebral series of blackish transversely elongate spots enclosing a darker shade of ground colour) extends from head or nape to tail-tip. Blackish brown upper lateral stripe extends from snout, through eye to tail-tip. Upper lips cream, barred with brown. Ventral and lower lateral surfaces pale yellow. SVL 80 mm.

Distinguished from *L. nichollsi*, *L. uniduo*, *L. gascoynensis* and *L. onsloviana* by nature of lower eyelid (movable vs fused). Differs from *L. varia* in usually bearing a much stronger pattern and more midbody scale rows (usually 22 vs usually 20).

Preferred habitat Sandy areas supporting *Acacia* shrublands and red loams vegetated with eucalypts on subhumid to semi-arid midwest coast of WA, from mouth of Murchison River north to Gnaraloo and Mia Mia Stations.

Microhabitat Shelters in loose upper layers of sand beneath leaf-litter at bases of trees and shrubs.

Comments As for species group.

Lerista desertorum (Sternfeld, 1919)
Photo 536

Description Moderately robust member of *L. macropisthopus* group with movable lower eyelid, 2 fingers, and 3 toes. Dorsal ground colour pale brown to yellowish brown. Paravertebral (and sometimes dorsal) lines, composed of series of dark dashes, usually extend from nape to tail-tip. Prominent broad blackish brown upper lateral stripe extends from snout, through eye to base of tail, tending to break into spots or narrow lines beyond hips. Tail flushed with grey, yellow to reddish brown. Lower lateral and ventral surfaces pale yellow, dotted with dark brown beneath tail. SVL 90 mm.

Distinguished from *L. picturata* in bearing a greater number of toes (3 vs 2).

Preferred habitat Favours woodlands and *Acacia* shrublands on reddish sandy or loamy soils from arid south-eastern interior of WA to adjacent NT and SA.

Microhabitat As for species group.

Comments As for species group.

Lerista distinguenda (Werner, 1910)
Photo 537

Description Member of *L. elegans* group with immovable lower eyelid and 4 well-developed limbs, each bearing 4 digits. Dorsal ground colour pale olive-grey, olive-brown to silvery brown, usually marked with 2 or 4 longitudinal series of dark dots (paravertebrals and dorsals) from nape onto tail. Black upper lateral and white midlateral stripes extend from snout onto tail. Ventrolateral zone clouded with grey; contrasting with white midlateral stripe. Tail usually suffused with red; boldest on juveniles and fading to yellow with age. Ventral surfaces white to pinkish brown, sparsely dotted with dark brown beneath tail. SVL 45 mm.

Distinguished from *L. elegans* in bearing more numerous midbody scale rows (18 vs 16). Differs from *L. dorsalis* by nature of lower eyelid (fused vs movable).

Preferred habitat Occupies a variety of habitats in subhumid southern and south-western WA, from Greenough River in north to Twilight Cove in east, and inland to Northam.

Microhabitat Often encountered in abandoned stick-ant nests *(Iridomyrmex conifer)*. Otherwise as for species group.

Comments As for species group.

Lerista dorsalis Storr, 1985
Photo 538

Description Large member of *L. elegans* group with movable lower eyelid and 4 fingers and toes. Dorsal ground colour pale olive-brown to pale olive-grey, marked with 2 or 4 narrow black stripes or equivalent series of dots, dashes or spots. Prominent broad black upper lateral stripe extends from snout, nearly to tail-tip. This is often narrowly edged above and below with white. Flanks greyish white with 0–3 (usually 2) narrow dark lines or series of dots. Tail usually tinged with reddish brown, each scale dark-edged. Ventral surfaces whitish, scales usually edged with grey. Beneath tail pink, unmarked or occasionally sparsely spotted with brown. SVL 70 mm.

Differs from *L. bougainvillii, L. microtis* and *L. arenicola* in bearing fewer digits on each foot (4 vs 5), and from *L. terdigitata* in having more digits (4 vs 3). Differs from *L. distinguenda* by nature of lower eyelid (movable vs immovable).

Preferred habitat Subhumid to semi-arid southern Australia, from Norseman in WA, east to lower Murray River in south-eastern SA, including many offshore islands in eastern parts of range. Occurs in a variety of shrubland and woodland habitats.

Microhabitat As for species group.

Comments Populations from eastern parts of range attain greatest size. Otherwise as for genus and species group.

Lerista elegans (Gray, 1845)
Photo 539

Description Member of *L. elegans* group with immovable lower eyelid and 4 well-developed limbs, each bearing 4 digits. Dorsal ground colour olive-brown to olive-grey. Paravertebral series of dark dashes usually extend from nape onto tail. On Rottnest Island population these may form prominent stripes. Black upper lateral and white midlateral stripes extend from snout, nearly to tail-tip. Ventrolateral zone clouded with grey. Tail often suffused

with red; boldest on juveniles. Ventral surfaces whitish, sometimes clouded with grey; usually dotted with greyish brown beneath tail. SVL 40 mm.

Distinguished from *L. distinguenda* in bearing fewer midbody scale rows (16 vs 18). Differs from *L. flammicauda* by nature of lower eyelid (immovable vs movable).

Preferred habitat Sandy coastal plain and offshore islands along subhumid to arid north-west and midwest coasts of WA, from Barrow Island south to Perth and inland to Watheroo.

Microhabitat As for species group.

Comments As for species group.

Lerista flammicauda Storr, 1985
Photo 540

Description Member of *L. elegans* group with movable lower eyelid and 4 fingers and toes. Dorsal ground colour brown. Prominent blackish brown upper lateral stripe extends from snout to hindlimb. Flanks pale brown, each scale dark-edged, occasionally with 1 or 2 series of longitudinally aligned dark spots. Tail orange-red (brightest on juveniles), densely dotted with dark brown. Ventral surfaces whitish. SVL 55 mm.

Distinguished from *L. chalybura* by nature of dark upper lateral stripe (sharply defined and more than 1 scale wide vs lower edge diffuse and less than 1 scale wide) and by tail colour (reddish vs bluish). Differs from *L. elegans* and *L. muelleri* by nature of lower eyelid (movable vs immovable), and further from *L. muelleri* in having more digits on each limb (4 vs 3).

Preferred habitat Hamersley and Barlee Ranges in arid Pilbara region of north-western WA. Apparently favours minor watercourses lined with *Acacia* and *Eucalyptus* over a *Triodia*-dominated ground cover on stony soils.

Microhabitat Shelters beneath leaf-litter, *Triodia* hummocks, rocks and logs.

Comments As for species group.

Lerista fragilis (Günther, 1876)
Photo 541

Description Large member of *L. elegans* group with movable lower eyelid and 4 well-developed limbs, each bearing 3 digits. Dorsal ground colour olive-brown to dark greyish brown. Paravertebral and dorsal series of dark dashes usually form 4 narrow lines from nape, well onto tail. Blackish upper lateral stripe extends from snout to middle or tip of tail. Tail often flushed with red; particularly on juveniles. Ventral surfaces whitish, each scale dark-edged. Fine dotting usually present beneath tail. SVL 45 mm.

Distinguished from *L. muelleri* by nature of lower eyelid (movable vs immovable).

Preferred habitat Semi-arid to subhumid interior of south-east Qld, usually on sandy soils supporting dry sclerophyll forests, woodlands or shrublands.

Microhabitat Shelters in soil beneath rocks and logs. See species group.
Comments As for species group.

Lerista frosti (Zietz, 1920)
Photo 542

Description Member of *L. elegans* group with movable lower eyelid and 4 well-developed limbs, each bearing 4 digits. Dorsal ground colour olive-grey, olive-brown to copper. Two or 4 rows of faint dots or dashes may extend from nape to base, or nearly to tip of tail. Narrow dark upper lateral stripe extends from nostril onto tail, often enclosing a series of pale spots. This is sharply defined and sometimes pale-edged above; notched or fading with lateral colour below. Lower flanks dark brown, mottled with pale brown. Lips narrowly barred with dark brown. Ventral surfaces whitish, each scale edged or spotted with dark brown. SVL 60 mm.

Distinguished from *L. muelleri* in bearing more digits (4 vs 3), and by nature of lower eyelid (movable vs immovable).
Preferred habitat Rocky ranges of arid southern NT.
Microhabitat As for species group.
Comments As for species group.

Lerista gascoynensis Storr, 1986
Photo 543

Description Large strongly patterned member of *L. bipes* group with immovable lower eyelid, no trace of forelimbs and 2 toes. Dorsal ground colour brownish white. Broad dark brown to black vertebral stripe extends from nape well onto tail. Broad dark brown to black upper lateral stripe extends from nostril to tail-tip. Lips barred with dark brown. Lower flanks and ventral surfaces whitish. SVL 70 mm.

Distinguished from *L. connivens* by nature of lower eyelid (immovable vs movable). Differs from *L. nichollsi* and *L. uniduo* in attaining greater maximum size (SVL 70 vs 60 and 55 mm, respectively), and further from *L. uniduo* by more robust build and stronger pattern. Differs further from *L. nichollsi* in bearing fewer supraciliary scales (3 vs 4).
Preferred habitat Known only from Gascoyne River valley, from Mt Clere west to Winderie in arid midwestern interior of WA.
Microhabitat As for species group.
Comments Very closely related to *L. nichollsi*, differing only in minor scale characters. It may prove to be a subspecies. Otherwise as for species group.

Lerista gerrardii (Gray, 1864)
Photo 544

Description Small strongly patterned member of *L. macropisthopus* group with movable lower eyelid.

Forelimb usually bears 1 (rarely 2) clawed digit; occasionally reduced to a style. Hindlimb bears 2 toes. Dorsal ground colour pale yellowish brown. Prominent broad black vertebral stripe (sometimes forked at nape) extends to base of tail. This becomes diffuse on tail, forming narrow paravertebral lines or series of spots to tip. Prominent broad black upper lateral stripe extends from in front of eye to tail-tip, becoming diffuse and ragged beyond hips. Lower lateral and ventral surfaces cream to yellow. SVL 85 mm.

Distinguished from *L. nichollsi* by nature of lower eyelid (movable vs fused), presence (vs absence) of a forelimb, and in attaining greater maximum size (SVL 85 vs 70 mm or less).
Preferred habitat Semi-arid south-western interior of WA, extending into coastal areas between Kalbarri and Geraldton. Occurs on hard reddish soils supporting woodlands, and sands and loams supporting shrublands adjacent to rock outcrops.
Microhabitat Shelters beneath logs or leaf-litter, and in soft upper soil layers at bases of trees and shrubs.
Comments As for species group.

Lerista greeri Storr, 1982
Photo 545

Description Member of *L. bipes* group with movable lower eyelid, forelimb absent without trace, and 2 toes. Dorsal ground colour pale brown to pale reddish brown. Paravertebral series of small dark dots (sometimes coalesced to form narrow lines) extend from nape, nearly to tail-tip. Less conspicuous laterodorsal series present or absent. Broad dark brown upper lateral stripe extends from nostril, through eye to tail-tip. Lower lateral and ventral surfaces whitish. SVL 60 mm.

Distinguished from *L. bipes* in bearing more numerous upper labial scales (6 vs 5). Differs from *L. labialis* by number of supraocular scales contacting frontal scale (2 vs 1). Differs from *L. griffini* by build (relatively more slender), and from *L. vermicularis* by nature of lower eyelid (movable vs fused). Differs from *L. simillima* in possessing supraciliary scales.
Preferred habitat Sandy and loamy soils of semi-arid south and east Kimberley region, WA. Known only from scattered localities.
Microhabitat Shelters in loose sand beneath leaf-litter accumulated in depressions, and at bases of trees and shrubs.
Comments As for species group.

Lerista griffini Storr, 1982
Photo 546

Description Robust member of *L. bipes* group with movable lower eyelid, forelimbs absent without trace, and 2 toes. Dorsal ground colour reddish brown to brown. Paravertebral series of small dark dashes form narrow lines from top of head, nearly to tail-tip. A weaker and more broken laterodorsal series may extend to base of tail. Broad dark brown upper lateral stripe extends from snout to tail-tip, becoming diffuse beyond hips. Tail flushed with grey and finely peppered with dark brown. Lower lateral and ventral surfaces pinkish white. SVL 65 mm.

Distinguished from *L. greeri*, *L. labialis*, *L. simillima* and *L. bipes* by build (relatively robust vs slender) and colouration (usually darker).

Preferred habitat Disjunct populations occur in sandy areas of semi-arid Dampier Land in west Kimberley region, WA, and lower Ord Valley of subhumid east Kimerley region, extending into adjacent north-western NT.

Microhabitat Usually dwells in sand and leaf-litter at bases of trees, shrubs and rock outcrops, or in loose sand beneath fallen timber.

Comments As for species group.

Lerista haroldi Storr, 1983
Photo 547

Description Short-tailed moderately robust member of *L. elegans* group with immovable lower eyelid and 4 well-developed limbs, each bearing 3 digits. Ground colour pale yellowish brown. Back and flanks finely speckled with brownish grey. Dark streak extends from nostril to eye. Fine markings on dorsal surface of tail tend to form transverse curves, following the scale margins. Those on sides of tail are more obscure, shorter, and oriented longitudinally. Ventral surfaces whitish. SVL 39 mm.

Distinguished from *L. muelleri* by more robust build and in bearing pale, almost patternless colouration.

Preferred habitat Only known specimen was collected on coastal dunes vegetated with *Spinifex longifolius* at Gnaraloo Station, on semi-arid upper west coast of WA.

Microhabitat As for species group.

Comments As for species group.

Lerista humphriesi Storr, 1971
Photo 548

Description Slender member of *L. bipes* group with movable lower eyelid, forelimb absent without trace, and hindlimb reduced to a minute style. Dorsal ground colour pale brownish grey. Paravertebral series of dark dashes form narrow broken lines from nape almost to tail-tip. Less conspicuous and more broken laterodorsal lines terminate at hips. Broad dark brown upper lateral stripe extends from in front of eye almost to tail-tip, often becoming narrower, ragged-edged and diffuse beyond hips. Head flushed with orange, and tail with greyish white. Ventral and ventrolateral surfaces white, occasionally bearing dark edges to ventrolateral scales. Dark edges may coalesce to form narrow irregular lines.

SVL 65 mm.

Distinguished from *L. praepedita* in bearing more numerous dorsal lines (laterodorsal series present vs absent) and paler ventral surfaces.

Preferred habitat *Acacia*-dominated sand plains on semi-arid midwest coast of WA between Shark Bay and lower Murchison River.

Microhabitat Shelters beneath rotting stumps and in loose sand beneath leaf-litter at bases of *Acacia* shrubs.

Comments A gravid female has been collected in December. Otherwise similar to closely allied *L. praepedita*. See species group.

Lerista ips Storr, 1980
Photo 549

Description Small robust member of *L. bipes* group with movable lower eyelid, forelimb absent without trace, and 2 toes. Snout strongly depressed, wedge-shaped, and protruding well beyond lower jaw. Ground colour pinkish brown, each scale bearing an obscure brown spot. Tip of snout whitish. Ventral surfaces pinkish white. SVL 60 mm.

Distinguished from all other members of *L. bipes* group in virtually lacking pattern.

Preferred habitat Arid red sand ridges vegetated with hummock grasses in Great Sandy and Gibson Deserts, in interior of WA and south-western NT. Known only from scattered localities.

Microhabitat Shelters in loose sand beneath hummock grasses and under litter beneath scattered shrubs.

Comments As for species group.

Lerista kalumburu Storr, 1976

Description Small member of *L. walkeri* group with movable lower eyelid, 1 finger and 3 toes. Ground colour brown, each scale bearing a darker brown central spot. Spots on lateral surfaces tend to coalesce, forming obscure longitudinal lines. Lips barred with dark brown. Ventral surfaces whitish, sparsely spotted with pale brown towards tail-tip. SVL 50 mm.

Distinguished from *L. walkeri* and *L. borealis* in bearing fewer fingers (1 vs 2).

Preferred habitat Only known from one specimen, collected in the vicinity of Napier Broome Bay in humid northern Kimberley region, WA.

Microhabitat No data available, presumably similar to *L. borealis*.

Comments As for species group.

Lerista karlschmidti (Marx and Hosmer, 1959)
Photo 550

Description Member of *L. bipes* group with movable lower eyelid, forelimb absent without trace, and hindlimb bearing one clawed digit. Ground colour olive-brown to greyish brown. Blackish streaks through each dorsal and lateral scale form series of narrow lines from nape to tail-tip. Ventral surfaces whitish to dull pink. SVL 70 mm.

Distinguished from *L. carpentariae* and *L. vittata* in lacking a broad dark upper lateral stripe. Differs further from *L. carpentariae* by build (relatively more robust). Differs from *L. cinerea*, *L. storri* and *L. stylis* in bearing fewer midbody scale rows (16 vs 18–20).
Preferred habitat Woodlands and rock outcrops of subhumid northern Australia, from north-eastern NT, through Gulf of Carpentaria to north-eastern Qld.
Microhabitat Shelters in soft sandy soil beneath rocks, logs or mats of leaf-litter.
Comments As for species group.

Lerista labialis Storr, 1971
Photo 551

Description Slender member of *L. bipes* group with movable lower eyelid, forelimb absent without trace, and 2 toes. Snout depressed, protruding well beyond lower jaw. Dorsal ground colour pale brown, yellowish brown to reddish brown. Paravertebral series of small dark dots may extend from nape well onto tail. Broad dark brown to black upper lateral stripe extends from nostril, through eye well onto tail, usually becoming diffuse and ragged-edged beyond hips. Tail flushed with pale grey. Ventral surfaces white to pinkish. SVL 60 mm.

Distinguished from *L. bipes* in bearing more numerous upper labial scales (6 vs 5). Differs from *L. griffini* in attaining smaller maximum size (SVL 60 vs 65 mm), and by more slender build. Differs from *L. greeri* and *L. simillima* by number of supraocular scales contacting frontal (1 vs 2). Differs from *L. vermicularis* by nature of lower eyelid (movable vs fused).
Preferred habitat Widely distributed through arid areas of south-west Qld, western NSW, southern NT, northern SA and south-eastern interior of WA. Disjunct populations occur in north-western interior of WA. Favours reddish sands and loams, particularly where hummock grasslands are present.
Microhabitat Shelters in soft upper soil layers beneath leaf-litter and low vegetation.
Comments See species group.

Lerista lineata Bell, 1833
Photo 552

Description Small slender *Lerista*. Sole member of *L. lineata* group, with slightly protrusive snout,

immovable lower eyelid, very small forelimbs bearing 2 fingers, and relatively long hindlimbs bearing 3 toes. Dorsal ground colour brownish grey; darker and browner on vertebral region. Prominent blackish brown paravertebral lines extend from nape, breaking into series of short dashes towards tail-tip. Broad blackish brown upper lateral stripe extends from snout, through eye almost to tail-tip. Narrow greyish white midlateral stripe extends from rear of upper lip to base of tail. Lower lateral and ventral surfaces dotted or flushed with grey, particularly along ventrolateral zone and beneath tail. SVL 55 mm.

Distinguished from members of *L. elegans* group in bearing fewer fingers than toes (2 fingers and 3 toes vs fingers 3–5 and toes equal in number).
Preferred habitat Restricted to pale sands supporting heathlands and shrublands on subhumid lower west coast of WA, from Mandurah north to southern suburbs of Perth, and on adjacent Garden and Rottnest Islands.
Microhabitat Dwells in accumulated leaf-litter and upper layers of loose sand at bases of coastal shrubs.
Comments Somewhat intermediate between *L. elegans* and *L. bipes* groups in both form and habits. Possibly threatened, due to its restriction to areas undergoing rapid urban development.

Lerista lineopunctulata
(Duméril and Bibron, 1839)
Photo 553

Description Very large robust *Lerista*. Sole member of *L. lineopunctulata* group; subject to considerable geographic variation. Lower eyelid movable. Forelimb absent in north (indicated by a groove), and represented as a clawless stump in south. Hindlimb bears one clawed digit in north; 2 in south. Ground colour in north usually pale yellowish brown, with little pattern except for an obscure pale brown margin to each scale, dark brown to black bars on upper lip, and dark greyish brown flush on head. Ground colour in south pale greyish brown to grey, prominently to obscurely marked with 6 or more series of longitudinally aligned (occasionally transversely elongate or squarish) dots or dashes (1 per scale row) from nape to tail-tip. Lips bear dark bars. Ventral surfaces whitish. Individuals from Shark Bay combine characteristics of northern and southern populations, though the head is seldom as dark as in north, or pattern as prominent as in south. SVL 100 mm.

Distinguished from sympatric populations of *L. macropisthopus* in bearing fewer toes (1 or 2 vs 3). Juveniles may be confused with adult unstriped *L. varia*, but differ in bearing more supraciliary scales (5 vs 4).
Preferred habitat Coastal dunes and sand plains along subhumid to arid west coast of WA, from Perth to North West Cape.

Microhabitat Inhabits soft upper layers of loose sand, usually beneath leaf-litter at bases of coastal shrubs.

Comments An accomplished sand-swimmer, regularly traversing considerable distances between leaf-litter deposits.

Lerista macropisthopus (Werner, 1903)
Photo 554

Description Robust member of *L. macropisthopus* group with movable lower eyelid, usually 2 fingers, and 3 toes. Populations from lower Murchison River district bear 1 finger and 2 toes. Ground colour dull pink, brown, brownish grey to purplish grey. Pattern usually absent. Dorsal and lateral scales may be obscurely dark-margined or finely flecked with dark grey. Head may be darker with whitish to cream lips. Ventrolateral and ventral surfaces whitish, yellowish to pale pink, often in more or less sharp contrast to darker upper flanks. SVL 90 mm.

Distinguished from *L. lineopunctulata* and *L. neander* in lacking pattern (within zones of overlap) and bearing a greater number of toes (3 vs 2 or fewer).

Preferred habitat Semi-arid to arid midwest coast and interior of WA, favouring sandy to loamy soils supporting *Acacia* shrublands or woodlands. An apparently isolated population occurs on North West Cape.

Microhabitat Shelters beneath leaf-litter and loose sand at bases of trees and shrubs.

Comments Taxonomic investigation is required to clarify its relationship with *L. neander*. Otherwise as for species group.

Lerista microtis (Gray, 1845)
Photo 555

Description Member of *L. elegans* group with movable lower eyelid and 4 well-developed limbs, each bearing 5 digits. Dorsal ground colour grey to coppery grey. Dorsal pattern (when present) consists of a narrow ragged-edged blackish vertebral line and broader paravertebral lines, extending from nape to base of tail. Broad blackish brown upper lateral stripe extends from snout to about middle of tail, breaking and becoming diffuse beyond hips. White midlateral stripe extends from upper lip onto base of tail. Narrow black lower lateral stripe extends from about ear onto base of tail. Tail greyish brown to reddish brown, peppered with blackish brown. Ventral surfaces white; reddish beneath tail. SVL 50 mm.

Distinguished from *L. arenicola* in bearing darker colouration and stronger pattern, including a broader dark upper lateral stripe. Differs further in attaining a smaller maximum size (SVL 50 vs 55 mm). Differs from *L. dorsalis* in possessing a greater number of digits on each foot (5 vs 4).

Preferred habitat Cool temperate coastal heathlands and wet sclerophyll forest margins on sandy

and lateritic soils of lower south-western WA, from Dwellingup east to Israelite Bay.

Microhabitat Shelters among leaf-litter or other dead surface vegetation, beneath logs or stones, and in abandoned stick-ant nests *(Iridomyrmex conifer)*.

Comments Livebearing. Regarded as a primitive *Lerista*. See species group and *L. bougainvillii*.

Lerista muelleri (Fischer, 1881)
Photos 556–558

Description Variable member of *L. elegans* group with immovable lower eyelid and 4 well-developed limbs, each bearing 3 digits. Possibly comprises several taxa as currently defined. Dorsal ground colour grey, greyish brown, coppery brown to yellowish brown. Paravertebral and dorsal series of blackish dashes form 4 narrow (sometimes broken) lines from nape to base or middle of tail. Prominent to obscure black upper lateral stripe (sometimes reduced to a concentration of dark flecks) extends from snout to base or tip of tail. Lower lateral surfaces paler shade of ground colour, sometimes bearing dark margins to each scale. Tail may be flushed with red to yellow, particularly on juveniles. Ventral surfaces whitish; immaculate or speckled with black. SVL 55 mm.

Distinguished from *L. fragilis*, *L. flammicauda*, *L. chalybura* and *L. frosti* by nature of lower eyelid (immovable vs movable). Differs further from *L. frosti*, *L. orientalis*, *L. flammicauda*, *L. chalybura* and *L. xanthura* in bearing fewer digits (3 vs 4), and from *L. haroldi* by darker colouration and stronger pattern.

Preferred habitat Favours arid and semi-arid areas of all mainland States, penetrating into cooler highlands in the Granite Belt of New England area, NSW, and adjacent south-eastern Qld. Occurs in dry sclerophyll forest, woodland and shrubland associations, on sandy to stony soils.

Microhabitat Shelters beneath mats of leaf-litter, stumps and surface debris, and in abandoned ant nests and soil cracks.

Comments As for species group.

Lerista neander Storr, 1971
Photo 559

Description Small moderately slender member of *L. macropisthopus* group with movable lower eyelid. Fingers and toes usually 2. Dorsal and upper lateral ground colour greyish brown. Centre of each dorsal and upper lateral scale bears a squarish blackish brown spot. These form 8 longitudinal series, coalescing into obscure transverse bars on nape. Pattern extends onto ventrolateral portion of tail. Tail yellowish brown. Lower lateral and ventral surfaces whitish to yellowish, marked with longitudinally aligned dark brown dots beneath tail. SVL 85 mm.

Distinguished from *L. macropisthopus* in bearing a spotted pattern (vs uniform).

Preferred habitat Arid areas dominated by woodlands, shrublands and hummock grasslands in Opthalmia and east Hamersley Ranges of Pilbara region, WA. Favours loams, usually associated with drainage systems.

Microhabitat Shelters in loose soil and leaf-litter at bases of trees and shrubs.

Comments Taxonomic investigation required to clarify its relationship with *L. macropisthopus*. Otherwise as for species group.

Lerista nichollsi (Loveridge, 1933)
Photos 560, 561

Description Large member of *L. bipes* group with immovable lower eyelid, forelimb absent (represented by a groove), and 2 toes. Two subspecies recognised.

L. n. nichollsi Dorsal ground colour pale grey, pale brown to almost white. Moderately broad dark vertebral stripe (composed of approximately 2 series of small dark spots mixed with dark brown pigment) extends from base of head to tail-tip. Broad dark brown upper lateral stripe extends from snout to tail-tip. Upper lips barred with brown. Ventral surfaces yellowish. SVL 65 mm.

L. n. petersoni Storr, 1976 Differs from nominate form in bearing a broader vertebral stripe (enclosing approximately 4 series of dark spots) and in attaining greater size. SVL 70 mm.

Distinguished from *L. connivens* and *L. varia* by nature of lower eyelid (immovable vs movable). Differs from *L. uniduo, L. gascoynensis* and *L. onsloviana* in bearing a greater number of supraciliary scales (4 vs 3, 3 and 2, respectively).

Preferred habitat Sands or loams dominated by low *Acacia* woodlands and shrublands, from semi-arid lower mid-western interior of WA *(L. n. nichollsi)*, to upper west and midwest coasts and adjacent interior *(L. n. petersoni)*.

Microhabitat Shelters beneath sand and leaf-litter at bases of trees and shrubs, and under embedded stumps.

Comments As for species group.

Lerista onsloviana Storr, 1984
Photo 562

Description Large member of *L. bipes* group with immovable lower eyelid, forelimb absent (represented by a groove), and 2 toes. Dorsal ground colour brownish white. Narrow to moderately broad dark vertebral stripe (composed of paravertebral series of spots or longitudinally elongate dashes, enclosing a brown to pale brown strip) extends from nape onto tail. Moderately narrow dark brown upper lateral stripe (with ragged lower edge) extends from nostril to tail-tip. Upper lips barred with dark brown. Lower lateral and ventral surfaces yellow. SVL 70 mm.

Distinguished from *L. connivens, L. nichollsi* and *L. uniduo* in usually bearing fewer supraciliary scales (2 vs 4, 4 and 3, respectively). Differs further from *L. connivens* by nature of lower eyelid (fused vs movable).

Preferred habitat Reddish sands and loams on north-west coastal plains, and white coastal dunes at Onslow. Extends from Onslow south to Giralia Station and Barradale, WA.

Microhabitat Shelters beneath leaf-litter and loose sand at bases of trees and shrubs.

Comments As for species group.

Lerista orientalis (De Vis, 1889)
Photo 563

Description Member of *L. elegans* group with immovable lower eyelid and 4 well-developed limbs, each bearing 4 digits. Dorsal ground colour brownish grey, brown to coppery brown. Four longitudinal rows of dots (one per scale) extend from nape to base of tail. Broad blackish upper lateral stripe extends from snout to base of tail. Lower lateral zone pale brown, each scale bearing a dark margin. Tail often flushed with red, particularly on juveniles. Ventral surfaces whitish, marked with scattered dark dots beneath tail. SVL 45 mm.

Distinguished from *L. muelleri* in bearing greater number of digits on each foot (4 vs 3). Superficially similar to *Sphenomorphus cracens* of north-eastern Qld, differing in bearing fewer digits (4 vs 5) and by nature of lower eyelid (immovable vs movable and scaly).

Preferred habitat Pale sands supporting heathlands on eastern interior of Cape York Peninsula, Qld, and on heavier soils supporting woodlands and shrublands through Gulf of Carpentaria to north-eastern NT.

Microhabitat Populations living on loose sands in north-east of range are accomplished sand-swimmers. Otherwise as for species group.

Comments Cape York population may constitute a distinct taxon. See species group.

Lerista picturata (Fry, 1914)
Photos 564–566

Description Member of *L. macropisthopus* group with movable lower eyelid. Forelimb stylar, or bearing 1 or 2 clawed digits; hindlimb bears 2 digits. Three subspecies recognised.

L. p. picturata Bears 2, 1 or 0 digits on forelimb. Dorsal ground colour pale grey to yellowish brown, marked with 4 narrow blackish lines: paravertebrals and laterodorsals. These commence on nape, often breaking into series of dashes beyond middle of tail. Broad blackish brown upper lateral stripe extends from in front of eye onto base of tail, continuing to tip as oblique dashes. Lower lateral and ventral surfaces pale yellow. SVL 90 mm.

L. p. baynesi Storr, 1971 Differs from nominate

form in bearing weaker limbs (0 or 1 digit on forelimb), greyer colouration and reduced pattern. Dorsal lines indistinct or absent. Upper lateral stripe relatively narrow and grey, flecked with blackish and occasionally split into 2 or 3 separate lines. Ventral surfaces pale yellow to greyish white. SVL 90 mm.

L. p. edwardsae Storr, 1982 Differs from both other forms in bearing weaker limbs (forelimb reduced to a tubercle) and fewer dorsal lines. Dorsal ground colour pale brownish grey to silvery brown, prominently marked with narrow dark paravertebral lines from nape to tail-tip. A broken series of dorsal lines commences on hips. Broad blackish brown upper lateral stripe extends from in front of eye to tail-tip. Lower lateral and ventral surfaces yellow. SVL 95 mm.

Distinguished from *L. desertorum* in bearing fewer toes (2 vs 3).
Preferred habitat Restricted to semi-arid to arid southern Australia. *L. p. picturata* favours woodlands on sandy loams in southern interior of WA, from Kalgoorlie and Norseman east to Zanthus. *L. p. baynesi* is restricted to pale sands along coast of Great Australian Bight, from Twilight Cove east to far western SA. *L. p. edwardsae* occurs in woodlands of southern SA, west of Flinders and Mt Lofty Ranges.
Microhabitat All subspecies dwell in soft upper layers of sandy soil beneath leaf-litter at bases of trees and shrubs.
Comments As for species group.

Lerista planiventralis (Lucas and Frost, 1902)
Photos 567, 568

Description Medium-sized *Lerista*. Sole member of *L. planiventralis* group, with depressed protrusive snout, movable lower eyelid, very small forelimbs bearing 2 digits, relatively long hindlimbs bearing 3 digits, and a distinctive ventrolateral keel from neck to hips. Two subspecies recognised.
L. p. planiventralis Dorsal ground colour brownish grey, olive-grey to pale brownish red. Four narrow blackish dorsal lines commence on nape. Most prominent inner pair extend onto tail. Outer pair tends to break into series of dots, extending only to hips. Narrow dark brown to blackish lateral stripe extends from snout, through eye to tail-tip; becoming broader, darker and dorsolaterally oriented posteriorly. Remaining lateral surfaces whitish, sometimes enclosing a midlateral series of brown dots which form an obscure line between forelimb and hindlimb. Ventral surfaces white. SVL 70 mm.
L. p. decora Storr, 1978 Differs in bearing much paler brown to pale grey dorsal ground colour. Lines on dorsum tend to be more prominent, and upper lateral stripe is broader. Tail suffused with yellow.

Both subspecies are distinguished from all other sympatric *Lerista* in bearing a strong ventrolateral keel.
Preferred habitat Restricted to sand plains and dunes on subhumid to arid mid- and lower west coasts of WA. *L. p. planiventralis* occurs on whitish, yellowish and reddish sands from North West Cape, south to outer Shark Bay Peninsula. *L. p. decora* occurs on whitish to yellowish sands from inner Shark Bay Peninsula south to about Watheroo.
Microhabitat Shelters deep beneath embedded stumps, or in soft upper layers of sand beneath accumulated leaf-litter at bases of shrubs and small trees. Often sand-swims considerable distances between leaf-litter deposits.
Comments Diurnal. During warmer months activity is usually restricted to early morning and late afternoon. An adept sand-swimmer, leaving conspicuous meandering tracks. Individuals have been observed to periodically raise their heads above the surface while foraging. Purposes of the ventrolateral keel are unclear. It may serve to streamline the body or aid traction.

Lerista praefrontalis Greer, 1986

Description Member of *L. bipes* group with movable lower eyelid. Forelimb absent without trace; hindlimb bears 2 toes. Dorsal ground colour pale greyish brown. Four rows of dark brown dashes (paravertebrals and dorsals) extend from nape to base of tail. Broad dark brown lateral stripe extends from snout well onto tail, becoming ragged-edged beyond hips. Lower lateral and ventral surfaces opalescent white. SVL 67 mm.

Distinguished from all sympatric members of *L. bipes* group in possessing prefrontal scales.
Preferred habitat Known only from King Hall Island in Yampi Sound, north-western Kimberley region, WA.

Microhabitat Collected in litter and sand at base of a cliff.
Comments Known from only 1 specimen. See species group.

Lerista praepedita (Boulenger, 1887)
Photo 569

Description Slender, virtually limbless member of *L. bipes* group with movable lower eyelid, forelimb absent without trace, and hindlimb reduced to a minute style. Dorsal ground colour pale silvery brown to yellowish brown. Each paravertebral scale bears a blackish brown dash, forming prominent to obscure narrow lines from nape, usually to tail-tip. Broad blackish brown upper lateral stripe extends from head, through eye to tail-tip. Tail flushed with grey, and usually flecked with blackish brown. Ventral surfaces greyish white, each scale edged anteriorly with blackish brown. SVL 65 mm.

Distinguished from *L. humphriesi* in bearing fewer dorsal lines (paravertebrals only vs paravertebrals and laterodorsals).

Preferred habitat Pale sands supporting heathlands and woodlands along subhumid to arid coast, hinterland and offshore islands of mid to lower west coasts of WA. Extends from just south of Perth to North West Cape.

Microhabitat Shelters in loose sand beneath leaf-litter at bases of shrubs, under coastal limestones, and deep beneath rotting stumps.

Comments Though an accomplished sand-swimmer, *L. praepedita* penetrates deep into the upper soil profiles more effectively than most sympatric *Lerista*. See species group.

Lerista punctatovittata (Günther, 1867)
Photo 570

Description Largest member of *L. macropisthopus* group. Lower eyelid movable. Forelimbs minute, bearing one clawed digit. Hindlimbs bear 2 toes. Dorsal ground colour pale yellowish brown, brown to greyish brown, becoming greyer on flanks and tail. Hind-edge of each dorsal and lateral scale bears a black to brown dot; becoming larger, darker and more prominent on tail. Head shields usually margined with blackish brown. Lips barred with brown. Ventral surfaces white to dull pink, heavily spotted and flecked with dark brown beneath tail. SVL 100 mm.

Preferred habitat Semi-arid to arid south-eastern interior of Australia, from southern-central Qld, through interior of NSW to north-west corner of Vic. and adjacent SA. Occurs in a variety of woodlands, favouring sandy to loamy soils supporting a ground cover of hummock grasses or chenopod shrubs.

Microhabitat Shelters in sand beneath leaf-litter and shrubs, or in and under decaying timber.

Comments As for species group.

Lerista separanda Storr, 1976

Description Slender member of *L. elegans* group with immovable lower eyelid and long limbs, each bearing 4 digits. Dorsal ground colour pale pinkish brown, each scale finely edged with brown. Obscure dark brown median streak extends from top of head to foreback. Dark brown upper lateral stripe extends from snout to base of tail. Tail flushed with reddish brown. Ventral surfaces whitish. SVL 30 mm.

Distinguished from *L. xanthura* by nature of

pattern (more prominent upper lateral stripe, and reddish vs yellow flush on tail), and in bearing fewer supraciliary scales (4 vs 5).

Preferred habitat Known from Dampier Land, in semi-arid south-west Kimberley region of WA.

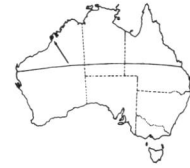

Microhabitat Holotype was collected under green bird flower bushes *(Crotalaria cunninghamii)* growing in pale sand at the base of a coastal dune.

Comments Status uncertain, possibly representing north-western variant of *L. xanthura*. See species group.

Lerista simillima Storr, 1984
Photo 571

Description Small member of *L. bipes* group with movable lower eyelid, forelimb absent without trace, and 2 toes. Snout depressed, protruding well beyond lower jaw. Dorsal ground colour pale brown. Paravertebral lines of small dark brown dots or dashes extend from nape, well onto tail. Broad blackish brown upper lateral stripe extends from nostril, through eye to tail-tip. Lower lateral and ventral surfaces white. SVL 50 mm.

Distinguished from *L. greeri* and *L. bipes* in lacking supraciliary scales. Differs from *L. griffini* in possessing a preocular scale, by build (relatively more slender), and in attaining smaller maximum size (SVL 50 vs 65 mm). Differs from *L. labialis* by dorsal colour (brown vs usually reddish) and number of supraocular scales contacting frontal scale (2 vs 1).

Preferred habitat Semi-arid interior of south-western Kimberley region, WA. Occurs on red sandy loams vegetated with woodlands and *Acacia* thickets (pindan).

Microhabitat As for species group.

Comments As for species group.

Lerista stictopleura Storr, 1985
Photo 572

Description Medium-sized, moderately robust *Lerista* of undetermined species group. Snout blunt and not protrusive. Eyelid immovable. Limbs present; forelimb bears 1 finger, hindlimb bears 2 toes. Dorsal ground colour orange-brown. Four series of blackish brown dashes (paravertebrals and dorsals) extend from nape onto tail, becoming paler beyond hips. Pale orange-yellow laterodorsal stripe extends from nape well onto tail. This is margined above by the outer row of dark dashes, and below by a narrow black upper lateral stripe which extends from

behind eye nearly to tail-tip. Flanks orange-brown (becoming paler towards venter) marked with 3–5 series of angular black spots. Lips white barred with dark brown. Ventral surfaces whitish. SVL 55 mm.
Preferred habitat Known only from sparse *Acacia* shrublands on pale red sands surrounding Mt Augustus in arid western interior of WA.
Microhabitat Shelters in litter, and in soil beneath logs and stumps.
Comments As for genus.

Lerista storri
Greer, McDonald and Lawrie, 1983
Photo 573

Description Member of *L. wilkinsi* group with movable lower eyelid, forelimb absent without trace, and hindlimb bearing one clawed digit. Ground colour brown to pale silvery grey. Broken dark brown longitudinal lines extend over dorsum, from nape to tail-tip. SVL 70 mm.

Distinguished from *L. cinerea* in lacking a distinct prefrontal scale. Differs from *L. vittata* in lacking a dark lateral stripe, and from *L. karlschmidti* in bearing more midbody scale rows (18–20 vs 16).
Preferred habitat Recorded on sandy soils supporting eucalypt woodlands over grassy understorey, and from loose soil supporting low shrubs at the base of a limestone outcrop. Known only from the vicinity of Chillagoe, in subhumid north-east Qld.
Microhabitat As for species group.
Comments Holotype contained 2 eggs. Otherwise as for species group.

Lerista stylis (Mitchell, 1955)
Photo 574

Description Large member of *L. wilkinsi* group with movable lower eyelid and forelimb absent without trace. Hindlimb short and stylar, or bearing one clawed digit. Snout slightly protrusive. Dorsal ground colour pale greyish brown, yellowish brown, reddish brown to rich brown. Paravertebral (and occasionally dorsal) scales each bear a blackish streak, forming more or less continuous narrow lines from nape well onto tail. Faint broken laterodorsal stripe may be present, especially anteriorly. Prominent black upper lateral stripe begins on snout, extending almost to tail-tip. Scales on lower flanks may be flecked with dark brown. Ventral surfaces white. SVL 60 mm.

Distinguished from *L. carpentariae* and *L. karlschmidti* in bearing more midbody scale rows (18 vs 16).
Preferred habitat Favours woodlands along coast and hinterland of western Gulf of Carpentaria, NT.
Microhabitat Shelters in upper layers of soft sand, and beneath leaf-litter at bases of trees, shrubs and rock outcrops.
Comments As for species group.

Lerista terdigitata (Parker, 1926)
Photo 575

Description Large member of *L. elegans* group with movable lower eyelid and 4 well-developed limbs, each bearing 3 digits. Dorsal ground colour olive-grey to olive-brown, marked with 4 longitudinal series of black to dark brown dots or dashes from nape onto tail. Blackish lateral stripe extends from snout, through eye onto base of tail. Lower lateral and ventral surfaces whitish, bearing longitudinal series of blackish dots. SVL 60 mm.

Distinguished from *L. muelleri* by nature of lower eyelid (movable vs fused). Differs from *L. dorsalis* in bearing fewer digits (3 vs 4).
Preferred habitat Arid and semi-arid regions of southern Australia, from Adelaide area west to Ooldea district and north to Musgrave Ranges, SA. An apparently isolated population occurs in southeastern WA. Favours sandy and limestone-based soils, usually vegetated with mallee woodlands and chenopod shrublands.
Microhabitat As for species group.
Comments As for species group.

Lerista uniduo Storr, 1984
Photo 576

Description Member of *L. bipes* group with immovable lower eyelid, forelimb represented by a groove, and 2 toes. Dorsal ground colour brownish white to greyish white. Narrow to moderately broad, pale to dark brown vertebral stripe (composed of 2 or 4 series of dark angular spots mixed with fine peppering) extends from nape to tail-tip. Broad dark brown upper lateral stripe extends from snout or temple to tail-tip. Upper lips barred anteriorly with dark brown. Lower lateral and ventral surfaces yellow. SVL 55 mm.

Distinguished from *L. connivens* and *L. varia* by nature of lower eyelid (immovable vs movable). Differs from *L. nichollsi* and *L. onsloviana* by number of supraciliary scales (3 vs 4 and 2, respectively). Differs further from *L. nichollsi* and *L. onsloviana*, and from *L. gascoynensis*, by smaller size (SVL 55 vs 65, 70 and 70 mm, respectively). Differs further from *L. gascoynensis* by more slender build and weaker pattern.
Preferred habitat Pale coastal sands, or reddish dunes and sandy loams supporting open *Acacia* shrublands over ground cover of *Triodia*, *Plectrachne* or soft grasses, on semi-arid to arid midwest coast of WA.
Microhabitat Shelters beneath leaf-litter and loose sand at bases of trees and shrubs, and under rotting stumps.
Comments As for species group.

Lerista varia Storr, 1986
Photo 577

Description Large robust variably patterned

member of *L. bipes* group with movable lower eyelid, no trace of forelimb and 2 toes. Ground colour pale brown to brown. Broad, usually obscure, dark vertebral stripe may be present, enclosing 0, 2 or 4 series of prominent to obscure brown spots. Brown upper lateral stripe, when present, is narrow and obscure on body; often more strongly developed on side of head. Lips barred with brown. Lower lateral and ventral surfaces whitish, suffused with greyish brown on chin. SVL 75 mm.

Distinguished from *L. nichollsi* and *L. uniduo* by nature of lower eyelid (movable vs immovable). Differs from *L. connivens* in usually bearing a much weaker pattern and having fewer midbody scale rows (usually 20 vs usually 22). Unstriped individuals may bear superficial resemblance to young *L. lineopunctulata*, differing by fewer supraciliary scales (4 vs 5).
Preferred habitat Known only from Shark Bay region (including Dirk Hartog Island) on semi-arid midwest coast of WA, extending south to Cooloomia Station.
Microhabitat Recorded in sand beneath leaf-litter.
Comments As for species group.

Lerista vermicularis Storr, 1982
Photo 578

Description Small slender member of *L. bipes* group with immovable lower eyelid, no trace of forelimb, 2 toes and an anterior ventrolateral keel. Snout depressed, protruding well beyond lower jaw. Dorsal ground colour pale reddish brown to pale yellowish brown. Dorsal pattern (when present) consists of paravertebral series of small dark dots extending from nape, nearly to tail-tip. Dorsal series may be present, terminating at hips. Dots on tail tend to be larger and more closely spaced. Dark brown upper lateral stripe (broken on head, variably defined on body, and boldest on tail) extends nearly to tail-tip. Lower lateral and ventral surfaces whitish. SVL 40 mm.

Distinguished from *L. bipes*, *L. greeri*, *L. griffini* and *L. labialis* by nature of lower eyelid (fused vs movable) and in bearing an anterior ventrolateral keel.
Preferred habitat Crests of red sand ridges in Great Sandy Desert, north-western interior of WA.
Microhabitat Shelters in loose upper layers of sand beneath hummock grasses and shrubs.
Comments As for species group.

Lerista vittata
Greer, McDonald and Lawrie, 1983
Photo 579

Description Small member of *L. wilkinsi* group with movable lower eyelid, forelimb absent without trace, and hindlimb bearing one clawed digit. Dor-

sal ground colour silvery brown to silvery grey. Four narrow dark longitudinal lines (formed by dashes on each dorsal scale) usually extend from nape well onto tail, becoming less regular beyond hips. Prominent dark brown lateral stripe extends from in front of eye to tail-tip. This becomes fragmented on tail; represented by upper and lower margins only. Tails of juveniles and subadults are flushed with bright reddish orange. Ventral surfaces pinkish white. SVL 60 mm.

Distinguished from all other members of *L. wilkinsi* group, and from *L. karlschmidti*, in bearing a prominent dark lateral stripe.
Preferred habitat Known from yellowish red coarse sandy soil supporting deciduous vine thickets and open patches of low vegetation, extending onto adjacent heavier soils supporting woodlands, on Mt Cooper Station, north-east Qld. This distinctive habitat originally occupied approximately 6000 ha, but was reduced in 1980 to approximately 2000 ha.
Microhabitat Shelters in soft upper soil layer, usually beneath logs; occasionally under leaf-litter.
Comments As for species group.

Lerista walkeri (Boulenger, 1891)
Photo 580

Description Largest member of *L. walkeri* group with movable lower eyelid, 2 fingers, and 2 or 3 toes. Ground colour dark greyish brown. Centre of each dorsal scale bears a small obscure blackish brown spot. These tend to align longitudinally, becoming larger and darker on posterior body and tail. Ventral surfaces whitish, each scale obscurely edged with dark brown. Blackish brown spots present beneath tail. SVL 63 mm.

Distinguished from *L. borealis* and *L. kalumburu* in attaining greater maximum size (SVL 63 vs 50 mm), and in bearing fewer toes (usually 2 vs 3). Differs further by colour and pattern (darker and more heavily spotted).
Preferred habitat Coast and islands of west and north-west Kimberley region, WA.
Microhabitat Recorded to shelter beneath sandstone boulders.
Comments As for species group.

Lerista wilkinsi (Parker, 1926)
Photo 581

Description Moderately large member of *L. wilkinsi* group with movable lower eyelid, forelimb absent without trace, and hindlimb bearing 2 clawed digits. Dorsal ground colour silvery grey to silvery brown. Each dorsal scale bears a brown dot or fleck. These form 6 narrow longitudinal lines or series of dots from nape to tail-tip. Flanks silvery grey, each lateral scale bearing a prominent brown spot. Obscure dark brown streak usually extends from nostril, through eye onto neck or anterior body. Tails of juveniles and subadults are flushed with bright reddish orange. Ventral surfaces greyish, heavily spotted with brown beneath tail. SVL 75 mm.

Distinguished from *L. karlschmidti*, and from all other members of *L. wilkinsi* group, in bearing more numerous toes (2 vs 0 or 1).
Preferred habitat Rocky ranges and adjacent sandy to loamy soils supporting woodlands in sub-humid to semi-arid north-eastern interior of Qld.
Microhabitat Shelters in loose sand under rocks or logs, and beneath leaf-litter and sand at bases of trees or shrubs.
Comments As for species group.

Lerista xanthura Storr, 1976

Description Slender long-tailed member of *L. elegans* group with a large eye bearing an immovable lower eyelid, and 4 long limbs, each bearing 4 digits. Ground colour pale grey to pinkish brown, each scale finely edged with brown. Tail flushed with yellow, and often irregularly marked with transversely oriented dark and pale flecks. Ventral surfaces whitish; yellowish beneath tail. SVL 35 mm.

Distinguished from *L. separanda* by nature of colour and pattern (upper lateral stripe weaker and tail flushed with yellow), and in bearing more numerous supraciliary scales (5 vs 4). Differs from *L. aericeps* in bearing more preocular scales (2 vs 1), and further from *L. aericeps taeniata* in lacking a dark upper lateral stripe. Differs from *L. muelleri* in bearing more digits (4 vs 3).
Preferred habitat Sand plains supporting hummock grass associations. Known from only one locality in Gibson Desert of eastern WA.

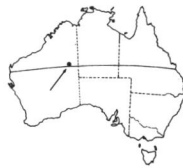

Microhabitat Shelters beneath hummock grasses.
Comments Relationship with *L. separanda* is uncertain. Otherwise as for species group.

Genus *MENETIA* Gray, 1845

Endemic genus containing Australia's smallest reptiles. Seven species recognised. Widespread throughout subhumid to arid regions west of Great Dividing Range, reaching the east coast in mideastern Qld. Extends into more humid areas in southwestern WA. Absent from Tas., most of east coast and far northern Qld.

Tiny skinks with moderately well-developed limbs, bearing 4 fingers and 5 toes. Lower eyelid immovable, fused to form a large transparent spectacle. Ear opening minute to absent, lacking lobules. Tail fragile. Scales smooth and shiny. Pattern includes dark flecks, and often a dark upper lateral and white midlateral stripe.

Diurnal. Terrestrial and secretive; foraging among leaf-litter and rarely venturing into open spaces. Highly active arthropod feeders which consume large quantities of food relative to body weight. Egglayers, producing small clutches.

Distinguished from *Proablepharus* and members of *Lerista elegans* species group in possessing 4 fingers and 5 toes (vs 5 fingers and toes, and 3–5 fingers with an equal number of toes, respectively). Differs from *Carlia* by nature of ear opening (minute to absent, lacking lobules, vs relatively prominent, bearing lobules). Differs further from *Carlia* (except *C. foliorum*) by nature of lower eyelid (fused to form a spectacle vs movable, bearing a transparent disc).

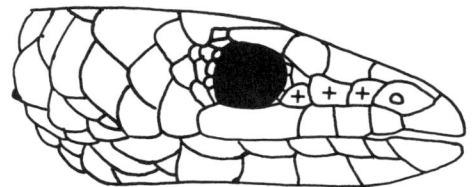

(a) *M. maini* (3)

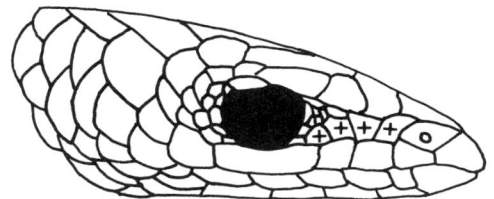

(b) *M. surda* (4)

Variation in number of scales in a line between eye and nasal scale on *Menetia*

Menetia alanae Rankin, 1979
Photo 582

Description Dorsal ground colour pale brown; paler on tail. Pattern obscure, consisting of sparse paravertebral series of fine blackish longitudinally aligned flecks, most prominent posteriorly. Upper lateral zone dark greyish brown and poorly defined from dorsum (black and sharply defined on juveniles), merging to paler grey on lower lateral zone. Upper lips white, speckled with dark brown. Ventral surfaces white to pale grey; darker to yellow beneath tail. SVL 30 mm.

Distinguished from *M. concinna* and *M. greyii* in lacking a pale midlateral stripe (vs present, at least anteriorly). Indistinguishable from *M. maini* except by scale characters: 4 scales in a line between eye and nasal scale (vs 3).

Preferred habitat Subhumid to humid north-western NT, usually on sandy coastal and alluvial soils supporting various forest types or woodlands.
Microhabitat As for genus.
Comments As for genus.

Menetia amaura Storr, 1978

Description Ground colour dark brown; paler on tail. Flanks pale brown, each scale marked with a pale fleck. Lips whitish, flecked with dark brown. Ventral surfaces cream. SVL 25 mm.

Distinguished from *M. greyii* in lacking an ear opening and lateral stripes. Differs from *M. surda* in bearing one supraciliary scale (vs 3 or 4).
Preferred habitat Known only from Edel Land, western peninsula of Shark Bay, WA. Recorded in ecotonal zone between chenopod-dominated flats, coastal dunes and heathlands.

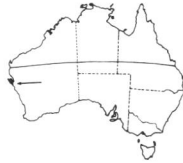

Microhabitat Holotype was collected beneath a limestone slab.
Comments Status uncertain; possibly representing an aberrant *M. greyii*. Additional specimens are required to determine the true identity of this species.

Menetia concinna Sadlier, 1984
Photo 583

Description Dorsal ground colour pale brownish grey, marked with fine darker spotting on each scale; most prominent on vertebral zone. Broad blackish brown upper lateral stripe extends from snout to hindlimb, becoming diffuse on tail. Prominent white midlateral stripe extends from upper lip through ear, fading at mid or posterior body; sharper and continuous to hindlimb on juveniles. This is margined below by a fine line of dark flecks between ear and forelimb, continuing as brown and cream mottling to hindlimb. Ventral surfaces white. SVL 30 mm.

Distinguished from *M. alanae* and *M. maini* in bearing dark and pale lateral stripes; at least anteriorly. Differs from *M. greyii*, and further from *M. maini*, by number of scales in a line between eye and nasal scale (4 vs 3).
Preferred habitat Known only from East Alligator River drainage on western edge of Arnhem Land Escarpment, NT. Favours sandy, alluvial soils supporting woodlands with ground cover of dense leaf-litter. One individual recorded from a sandstone outcrop. In contrast, sympatric population of *M. greyii* appears to favour woodlands on lateritic soils

with understorey of tall speargrass.
Microhabitat As for genus.
Comments As for genus.

Menetia greyii Gray, 1845
Photo 584

Description Variably patterned *Menetia* with dorsal ground colour of pale or dark brownish grey to grey, usually tinged with bronze or copper. Two to 5 series of longitudinally aligned dashes (sometimes forming broken lines) usually extend from nape onto tail. Broad dark brown to blackish upper lateral stripe (often narrowly margined above by a fine paler line) extends from snout, through eye to midbody, hindlimb, or well onto tail. Broad white midlateral stripe extends from lips, beneath eye to above forelimb, hindlimb, or onto tail. This is finely edged below by a black lower lateral stripe or series of dashes. Tail ground colour, occasionally flushed with bright blue to bluish grey in far northern NT. Ventral surfaces white (yellow on breeding males), usually bearing dark spots beneath tail. SVL 35 mm.

Distinguished from all other *Menetia* except *M. concinna* in bearing dark and pale upper and midlateral stripes, at least anteriorly. Differs further from *M. amaura* and *M. surda* in possessing an ear opening. Differs from *M. concinna*, and further from *M. alanae* and *M. timlowi* by number of scales in a line between eye and nasal scale (3 vs 4).
Preferred habitat Widespread through subhumid and arid regions of all mainland States, on a variety of soils and open vegetation types. Absent from subhumid to humid north-west and north-east, humid south-east and deep south-west.
Microhabitat As for genus.
Comments Clutches of 2 or 3 eggs are laid in summer. See genus.

Menetia maini Storr, 1976
Photo 585

Description Dorsal ground colour pale or dark coppery brown to greyish brown, each scale bearing dark streaks or flecks. Indistinct pale dorsolateral line sometimes discernible anteriorly. Upper lateral zone dark greyish brown to black, often bearing darker and paler flecks. Obscure pale midlateral line sometimes present anteriorly. Lower lateral surfaces pale grey. Lips and side of neck pale grey, flecked or spotted with blackish brown. Ventral surfaces white to pale grey, darker beneath tail, and sometimes throat. SVL 25 mm.

Distinguished from *M. greyii* and *M. concinna* in lacking prominent dark and pale lateral stripes. Differs further from *M. concinna*, and from *M. alanae* and *M. timlowi* by scale characters: 3 scales in a line between eye and nasal scale (vs 4).
Preferred habitat Humid to arid northern Australia, from Kimberley region of WA, through northern half of NT to interior of Qld. Occurs in a

variety of habitats, from woodlands to hummock grasslands. Also recorded from monsoon forest margins in far northern NT.

Microhabitat As for genus.

Comments As for genus.

Menetia surda Storr, 1976
Photo 586

Description Ground colour glossy pale to dark brown, fading to greyish brown laterally, with little or no indication of pattern. Palest individuals of northern population may bear obscure indications of dark upper lateral and pale midlateral stripes. Southern individuals usually bear a dark median streak on each dorsal and lateral scale, forming obscure lines to tail-tip. Ventral surfaces whitish. SVL 30 mm.

Distinguished from *M. amaura* in bearing more supraciliary scales (3 or 4 vs one). Differs from *M. greyii* in lacking an ear-opening, and in usually bearing a weaker pattern.

Preferred habitat Semi-arid to arid coast and adjacent interior of central-western WA. Occurs on sandy to stony soils supporting *Acacia* shrublands or low woodlands in association with hummock grasses and/or heathlands.

Microhabitat As for genus.

Comments As for genus.

Menetia timlowi Ingram, 1977
Photo 587

Description Ground colour dark brown to grey, darker on flanks; iridescent bluish green when viewed obliquely. Individual scales are often marked with obscure alternating dark and pale streaks. Fine dark spotting usually present on flanks and sides of tail. Lips whitish, obscurely barred with dark brown to black. Breeding males develop reddish orange flush on tail. Ventral surfaces white to pale grey, sparsely flecked with brown on belly; densely beneath tail. SVL 25 mm.

Distinguished from *M. greyii* in lacking dark and pale lateral stripes. Differs further from *M. greyii*, and from *M. maini* by scale characters: 4 scales in a line between eye and nasal scale (vs 3).

Preferred habitat Subhumid to semi-arid areas in eastern interior of Qld, from Chinchilla in south to southern Cape York Peninsula. Occurs in a variety of woodland types.

Microhabitat As for genus.

Comments Generic status uncertain. It may be more closely related to the small secretive members of the genus *Carlia*, allied to *C. foliorum* and *C. macfarlani*. Breeding males share with these skinks a reddish orange flush on tail.

Snake-eyed Skinks, Fire-tailed Skinks
Genus MORETHIA Gray, 1845

Endemic genus comprising 8 species. Widespread through subhumid to arid areas of all mainland States. Absent from cool moist south-east, Tas., higher altitudes of Great Dividing Range and humid areas of east coast.

Small skinks with well-developed limbs, each bearing 5 digits. Ear opening present. Eye large bearing an immovable transparent spectacle. Tail fragile. Scales smooth and shiny.

Diurnal. Swift terrestrial sun-loving skinks inhabiting margins of leaf-litter and low vegetation at bases of trees, shrubs and rock outcrops. Arthropod feeders. Egglaying.

Two species groups are apparent, separable largely on colour, pattern and distribution. Members of both groups usually bear a pale spot on posterior base of hindlimb.

***M. lineoocellata* group** Contains 5 species of medium to large *Morethia*. Colour and pattern variable, usually including dark dashes, variegations or ocelli on dorsal surfaces, and a pale midlateral stripe. Head usually tinged with copper. Tails of juveniles may be flushed with reddish brown, fading with age. Males display prominent red to orange throats during breeding season. Largely restricted to southern Australia. Group comprises *M. adelaidensis*, *M. butleri*, *M. boulengeri*, *M. lineoocellata* and *M. obscura*.

***M. taeniopleura* group** Comprises 4 taxa of small to medium-sized *Morethia*. Colour and pattern includes dark brown to glossy black body, prominent pale dorsolateral stripes, and dull to bright red flush on hips and tail. Popularly known as fire-tailed skinks. Largely restricted to northern Australia. Reddish breeding colours develop on only 1 species (*M. storri*). Group comprises *M. ruficauda ruficauda*, *M. ruficauda exquisita*, *M. storri* and *M. taeniopleura*.

Morethia is distinguished from *Leiolopisma*, *Lampropholis* and *Carlia* (except *C. foliorum*) by nature of lower eyelid (an immovable transparent spectacle vs movable, bearing a transparent disc). Differs further from *Carlia*, and from *Menetia* in bearing 5 (vs 4) fingers. Differs from *Notoscincus* by nature of head shields (frontoparietals and interparietal fused to form a single large shield vs interparietal free). Differs from *Cryptoblepharus* in bearing a deeper head and body (vs strongly dorsally depressed) and by restriction to terrestrial habitats (vs vertical surfaces of trees and rocks).

Morethia adelaidensis Peters, 1874
Photo 588

Description Member of *M. lineoocellata* group. Dorsal ground colour grey, olive-grey to brown, sometimes tinged with reddish brown. Dorsum usually marked with scattered darker dashes which tend to form broken longitudinal lines. Obscure broken pale dorsolateral stripe sometimes present, extending from above eye to base of tail. Broad dark brown fragmented upper lateral stripe (enclosing pale flecks) extends from eye onto base of tail.

Wavy-edged pale midlateral stripe (when present) extends from lips onto base of tail. Weak and broken dark lower lateral stripe (often absent to barely discernible anteriorly) extends from about lower jaw to hindlimb. Ventral surfaces white. Breeding males develop an orange flush around edges of venter, extending onto inner surfaces of limbs, vent and anterior portion of tail. SVL 50 mm.

Distinguished from *M. boulengeri* by pattern (fragmented; with or without an obscure pale wavy-edged midlateral stripe vs well-defined, including a straight-edged pale midlateral stripe). Differs further from *M. boulengeri*, and from *M. obscura* in bearing sharply keeled (vs bluntly keeled to rounded) subdigital lamellae. Differs further from *M. obscura* by dorsal pattern (dark flecks which tend to form irregular longitudinal lines vs absent or composed of dark-edged pale spots). Differs from *M. butleri* by number and arrangement of supraciliary scales (5, the 3rd, 4th and 5th largest; vs 6, the 1st largest, decreasing in size posteriorly). Differs further by nature of dark upper lateral stripe (fragmented and ragged-edged vs prominent and straight-edged).

Preferred habitat Subhumid to arid southern Australia, from north-western Vic., western NSW and south-western Qld, through most of SA (including several offshore islands) to coast and interior of south-eastern WA. Favours chenopod-dominated ground cover, often in association with woodlands, particularly mallee eucalypts. Often occurs on loamy or saline soils.

Microhabitat As for genus.

Comments A communal laying site containing 20 eggs is recorded on Reevesby Island, SA. Otherwise as for genus.

Morethia boulengeri (Ogilby, 1890)
Photo 589

Description Member of *M. lineoocellata* group. Dorsal ground colour coppery brown, dark olive, greyish brown to grey. Dorsal pattern (when present) consists of dark dashes which form longitudinal lines, or scattered dark and pale flecks. Pattern is often strongest on posterior body and base of tail. Broad black upper lateral stripe extends from eye or temple to groin. Broad prominent white midlateral stripe extends from upper lip to groin. This is usually edged below with a narrow (often broken) black line. Lower lateral zone pale grey. Tail of juveniles flushed with reddish brown, fading to ground colour with age. Ventral surfaces white. Breeding males display reddish orange wash on chin and throat. SVL 45 mm.

Distinguished from *M. butleri* in bearing a black line on lower edge of white midlateral stripe (vs often absent posteriorly), and by nature of supraciliary scales (a ragged border between supraciliaries and supraoculars vs a straight border). Differs from *M. adelaidensis* by pattern (well defined, and invariably including a straight-edged pale midlateral

stripe, vs fragmented, and with or without an obscure wavy-edged midlateral stripe). Differs from *M. taeniopleura* by extent of black upper lateral stripe (not extending beyond temple or eye vs extending to snout), and by nature of pale dorsolateral stripe (weak to absent vs prominent).

Preferred habitat Subhumid to arid areas from south-eastern interior of WA, through most of SA to northern Vic., NSW and southern interior of Qld, west of Great Dividing Range. Extends to east coast through Brisbane Valley, Qld. Favours heavy soils supporting a variety of vegetation types, including dry sclerophyll forests, woodlands and shrublands.

Microhabitat As for genus.

Comments Males display breeding colours from August to mid-January. Mating occurs in spring, with clutches of 1–6 eggs laid in summer. Juveniles have been observed during autumn.

Morethia butleri (Storr, 1963)
Photo 590

Description Member of *M. lineoocellata* group. Dorsal ground colour coppery brown, greyish brown to dark olive-brown, each scale usually bearing a narrow dark margin. Obscure blackish flecks or blotches occasionally present, aligned to form indistinct lines. Broad black upper lateral stripe commences as an obscure streak on snout, extending to base of tail. White midlateral stripe extends from upper lip to forelimb; usually ill-defined to absent on body. Tail flushed with red to reddish brown on juveniles, fading to brown with age. Lower lateral and ventral surfaces greyish white. Breeding males develop a reddish orange wash on chin and throat. SVL 55 mm.

Distinguished from *M. boulengeri* by lateral pattern (pale midlateral stripe weak to absent on body vs prominent with a dark lower edge). Differs further from *M. boulengeri*, and from *M. adelaidensis* by nature of supraciliary scales (the 1st largest, decreasing in size posteriorly, vs the 1st and 3rd largest, and the 3rd, 4th and 5th largest, respectively). Differs further from *M. adelaidensis* by nature of dark upper lateral zone (straight-edged vs ragged-edged).

Preferred habitat Subhumid to semi-arid southern WA, north to Shark Bay and extending east to Eyre Peninsula, SA. Favours eucalypt and *Acacia* woodlands, often in association with chenopod shrublands.

Microhabitat As for genus.

Comments Mating takes place in spring. Clutches of 2–5 eggs are laid in late summer. Otherwise as for genus.

Morethia lineoocellata
(Duméril and Bibron, 1839)
Photo 591

Description Member of *M. lineoocellata* group.

Ground colour olive-grey, coppery brown to olive-brown, usually marked over body and limbs with prominent white-centred black ocelli. These often fragment into longitudinally aligned dark and/or pale spots. Narrow broken pale vertebral and dorsolateral stripes may extend from nape to base of tail. Dark upper lateral stripe extends from eye to base of tail. Prominent white midlateral stripe extends from upper lip to hindlimb, margined by a narrow dark lower lateral stripe. Ventral surfaces white. Breeding males develop a prominent reddish orange flush on throat and lower lips. SVL 45 mm.

Distinguished from *M. obscura* in bearing a more complex pattern, including a prominent white midlateral stripe (vs midlateral stripe weakly developed to absent). Differs further in attaining smaller maximum size (SVL 45 vs 55 mm).

Preferred habitat West coast and offshore islands of WA, north on mainland to arid North West Cape and south to Lake Jasper in humid lower southwest. Also present on Barrow and Monte Bello Islands off north-west coast. Occurs in a wide variety of habitats from coastal dunes and limestones to samphire flats, woodlands and margins of dry sclerophyll forests. In north of range, where *Triodia*-clad red desert dunes abut white coastal dunes it occurs on both substrates.

Microhabitat As for genus.

Comments Males develop breeding colours during September. Otherwise as for genus.

Morethia obscura Storr, 1972
Photo 592

Description Large variable member of *M. lineoocellata* group. Ground colour olive-brown to olive-grey. Pattern present to absent (usually obscure), consisting of white-centred black ocelli or dark flecks, tending to be more numerous on (or restricted to) posterior body and tail. Indistinct pale dorsolateral stripe rarely present. Obscure blackish brown upper lateral zone may extend from behind eye to base of tail. Obscure narrow, ragged-edged greyish white midlateral stripe (when present) extends from upper lip to base of tail; occasionally margined above and below by broken blackish lines. Lower lateral zone greyish brown. Top of head coppery brown. Ventral surfaces white. Breeding males display a reddish orange wash on chin and throat. SVL 55 mm.

Distinguished from *M. lineoocellata* in bearing a less complex pattern (pale midlateral stripe ill-defined to absent vs prominent). Differs further in attaining greater maximum size (SVL 55 vs 45 mm). Differs from *M. adelaidensis* by nature of dorsal pattern (dark-edged pale spots vs dark flecks which tend to form irregular longitudinal lines).

Preferred habitat Occurs in a wide variety of vegetation types, including woodlands, heathlands and shrublands on sandy to heavy soils in subhumid to semi-arid southern Australia and offshore islands.

Extends from southern WA to north-western Vic. and south-western NSW.

Microhabitat As for genus.

Comments Mating occurs during spring. Clutches of 1–5 eggs are recorded. Otherwise as for genus.

Morethia ruficauda (Lucas and Frost, 1895)
Photos 593, 594

Description Brightly coloured member of *M. taeniopleura* group. Two subspecies recognised.

M. r. ruficauda Ground colour glossy black. Dorsum usually immaculate, occasionally bearing faint indication of a pale vertebral stripe. Prominent broad cream to white dorsolateral stripe extends back to base of tail and forward to meet its opposite on tip of snout. Lower back to hips flushed with red, becoming more intense on tail. Limbs reddish, hindlimbs most intense. Ventral surfaces white. SVL 35 mm.

M. r. exquisita Storr, 1972 Differs from nominate form in bearing a prominent white to cream vertebral stripe from snout or top of head to hips.

Distinguished from *M. storri* by extent of dorsolateral stripe (extending continuously to snout vs obscure between eye and snout).

Preferred habitat Subhumid to arid north-western Australia, encompassing most of NT, northern half of WA and far north-western SA. Represented by *M. r. exquisita* south of Great Sandy Desert, WA, from Pilbara to Gascoyne regions. Favours margins of rock outcrops and heavy to stony soils.

Microhabitat Shelters and forages among rocks and leaf-litter. Otherwise as for genus.

Comments Often active during high midday temperatures. A swift and agile skink, diving beneath leaf-litter when disturbed. Two individuals of *M. r. exquisita* were observed to face one another from a distance of 10 cm, whipping their tails horizontally. Solitary individuals are also reported to wave their tails. These actions possibly represent sexual or territorial responses.

Morethia storri Greer, 1980
Photo 595

Description Member of *M. taeniopleura* group. Dorsal ground colour pale or dark brown to olive-brown, usually lacking pattern. Obscure paler and darker stripes sometimes present. Prominent cream dorsolateral stripe (sometimes suffused anteriorly with copper) extends from above eye to base of tail; indistinct and broken between eye and snout. Broad dark brown to black upper lateral stripe extends from snout, through eye to hindlimb. Broad white lower lateral stripe extends from lips to hindlimb; margined below by a narrow dark ventrolateral stripe. Bright to dull reddish flush extends over lower back, hips and hindlimbs, intensifying to deep red on tail. Ventral surfaces white, flushed with red beneath tail. Breeding males bear a pinkish orange wash on throat. SVL 35 mm.

Distinguished from *M. ruficauda* by extent of dorsolateral stripe (obscure between eye and snout vs extending continuously to snout). Breeding males differ further in developing reddish flush on throat.

Preferred habitat Coast (including some offshore islands) and adjacent interior of subhumid northern NT. An apparently isolated population occurs on Dampier Land, in semi-arid west Kimberley region, WA. Known from lateritic and sandy soils supporting woodlands and vine thickets.

Microhabitat Observed to bury itself beneath loose sand when pursued. Otherwise as for genus.

Comments Clutches of 2 and 3 eggs are recorded. Otherwise as for genus.

Morethia taeniopleura (Peters, 1874)
Photo 596

Description Member of *M. taeniopleura* group. Dorsal ground colour rich brown to grey-brown; immaculate to flecked with darker brown. Prominent pale dorsolateral stripe extends from about nostril, above eye to base of tail. Broad black lateral stripe extends from snout, through eye to behind hindlimb. Broad white lower lateral stripe extends from lips to hindlimb; edged below by a narrow dark ventrolateral stripe. Hips and base of tail suffused with orange-red to reddish brown, becoming more intense on tail. This is brightest on juveniles, occasionally fading to brown on adults. Ventral surfaces white. SVL 35 mm.

Distinguished from *M. boulengeri* by extent of black upper lateral stripe (extending continuously to snout vs to temple or eye), and by nature of pale dorsolateral stripe (prominent vs weak to absent).

Preferred habitat Subhumid eastern Qld, from Cape York south to just west of Brisbane and to islands of Moreton Bay. Favours dry sclerophyll forests and woodlands (occasionally heathlands), with shrub- or tussock-dominated ground cover on stony to sandy soils.

Microhabitat As for species group.

Comments As for genus.

Genus *NOTOSCINCUS* Fuhn, 1969

Endemic genus containing 3 species. Restricted to subhumid to arid northern half of Australia, excluding northern Cape York Peninsula, Qld.

Small moderately slender to robust skinks with well-developed limbs, each bearing 5 digits. Eye large with round pupil. Eyelid immovable, fused to form a transparent spectacle. Ear opening moderately large, with or without anterior lobules. Scales smooth.

Diurnal and terrestrial. Egglaying. Arthropod feeders.

Distinguished from *Carlia* and *Menetia* in bearing more fingers (5 vs 4). Differs from *Ctenotus*, and further from all *Carlia* except *C. foliorum*, by nature of lower eyelid (fused to form a spectacle vs movable). Differs from *Morethia* by arrangement of head-shields (interparietal free vs fused with fronto-parietals to form a single large shield). Differs further from members of *M. taeniopleura* group in lacking a reddish flush on tail. Differs from *Proablepharus* in bearing a greatly enlarged first supraocular scale (vs not noticeably larger than remainder).

Notoscincus butleri Storr, 1979
Photo 597

Description Large striped *Notoscincus* with dorsal ground colour of pale coppery brown. Black vertebral stripe extends from nape well onto tail. Black dorsal stripes extend from nape, fading on base of tail. Broader black upper lateral stripe extends from in front of eye well onto tail; bordered below by a white midlateral stripe extending from lips and becoming diffuse on base of tail. Narrow blackish stripe extends from behind ear (turning downwards at forelimb), well onto tail. This is margined below by a white ventrolateral stripe. Ventral surfaces whitish. SVL 40 mm.

Preferred habitat Arid rocky near-coastal Pilbara region, WA. Only known from 2 localities in the vicinity of Dampier and Roebourne. Specimens were collected from sandy *Triodia*-dominated areas associated with creek and river margins.

Microhabitat Original specimens were collected beneath the fallen nest of a wedge-tailed eagle (*Aquila audax*). Otherwise shelters in *Triodia* hummocks, leaf-litter, and beneath surface debris.

Comments As for genus.

Notoscincus ornatus (Broom, 1896)
Photo 598

Description Small *Notoscincus* with dorsal ground colour of coppery brown to bronze-brown. Dorsal pattern (if present) consists of vertebral and paravertebral series of black dots and/or dashes from nape to base of tail. Vertebral series may coalesce on tail to form narrow irregular line, extending almost to tip. Black upper lateral zone commences as a streak on tip of snout, breaking on body into a series of dark squarish bars alternating with ground colour and continuing on tail as a series of blotches. Prominent to obscure white midlateral stripe extends from lips to hindlimb, becoming diffuse on base of tail. This is margined below by a narrow blackish line, often broken into series of irregular dashes. Ventral surfaces whitish. SVL 35 mm.

Distinguished from *N. wotjulum* in bearing a much more broken pattern, especially on dark upper lateral zone (represented by a series of blotches vs a broad unbroken stripe).

Preferred habitat Subhumid to arid northern

Australia, including some offshore islands. Extends from Pilbara and southern Kimberley regions of WA, through southern NT and far northern SA to north-eastern interior of Qld, as far east as Charters Towers district. Favours sandy flats and dunes with an open ground cover of hummock grasses, cane-grass or shrubs.

Microhabitat Shelters beneath low vegetation, leaf-litter and surface debris. Forages widely in open spaces between vegetation.

Comments As for genus.

Notoscincus wotjulum (Glauert, 1959)
Photo 599

Description Small moderately robust *Notoscincus* with dorsal ground colour of coppery brown to olive-grey. Vertebral series of large black spots usually extends from nape or midbody for various lengths onto tail. Broad sharply demarcated black upper lateral stripe extends from snout, through eye to hindlimb; represented on tail by a series of dark spots or angular blotches. This sometimes encloses 1 or 2 series of small whitish dots on body. White midlateral stripe, margined below by an obscure narrow dark stripe, extends from lips to hindlimb. Ventral surfaces whitish. SVL 35 mm.

Distinguished from *N. ornatus* in bearing a more simple pattern, especially on flanks (a broad un-broken dark upper lateral stripe vs a series of dark squarish bars).

Preferred habitat Subhumid to semi-arid Kimberley region, WA, to northern NT, including Groote Eylandt and Sir Edward Pellew Islands. Usually associated with woodlands on sandy to stony substrates.

Microhabitat Shelters in leaf-litter, beneath fallen timber, loose stones and surface debris, rarely venturing far from cover.

Comments Formerly treated as a subspecies of *N. ornatus*. Both are sympatric on Groote Eylandt, NT. *N. wotjulum* does not forage in open areas to the same degree as *N. ornatus*. Otherwise as for genus.

Genus OPHIOSCINCUS Peters, 1873

Endemic genus containing 3 species. Restricted to coastal and near-coastal eastern Australia, from north-eastern NSW to south-eastern Qld.

Elongate skinks with limbs reduced to minute styles (*O. truncatus*) or absent. Eye very small with a movable scaly lower eyelid. Ear-aperture absent, represented by a depression. Snout tipped with an opaque dermis. Scales smooth, glossy.

Fossorial skinks which dwell in or beneath rotting logs, under leaf-litter or in loose soil, wherever moist conditions prevail. Egglayers. Arthropod feeders.

Distinguished from *Anomalopus* and *Coeranoscincus* in bearing fewer upper labial scales (5 vs 6). Differs further from sympatric *Coeranoscincus reticulatus* by greater reduction of limbs (absent or stylar vs present, bearing 3 digits).

Ophioscincus cooloolensis
Greer and Cogger, 1985
Photo 600

Description Small completely limbless *Ophioscincus*. Dorsal ground colour silvery grey, black on tail-tip, marked with 2–4 longitudinal series of black spots, one per scale. Broad black to dark brown lateral stripe, sharp-edged and contrasting strongly with dorsal and ventral surfaces, extends from side of head onto tail. Ventral surfaces yellow to orange, black beneath tail. SVL 65 mm.

Distinguished from *O. ophioscincus* in being smaller (SVL 65 vs 95 mm), bearing fewer midbody scales (18–19 vs 20–24) and in lacking prefrontal scales.

Preferred habitat White sands supporting heath-lands, eucalypt and *Banksia* woodlands and rain-forests at Cooloola and adjacent Fraser Island, south-east Qld. Apparently isolated population occurs on Kroombit Tops.

Microhabitat As for genus.

Comments Gravid female containing 3 eggs collected in January. Otherwise as for genus.

Ophioscincus truncatus (Peters, 1876)
Photo 601

Description Small *Ophioscincus* with 4 very small stylar limbs. Dorsal ground colour brown, pinkish brown, greyish brown to grey; darker grey to black on tail. Each scale marked with a darker spot or dash; aligned in longitudinal series, and occasionally coalescing to form narrow broken lines. Those on flanks may join to form a broader stripe. Lower flanks paler, merging to cream or bright yellow on ventral surfaces. Throat whitish. Distal portion of tail dark brown to black. SVL 60 mm.

Preferred habitat South-eastern Qld and north-eastern NSW, from Maleny area in Qld, south to about Macksville. Mainland populations favour rainforests and wet sclerophyll forests of coastal ranges. Those from islands of Moreton Bay, Qld, occur in more open habitats: woodlands and heath-lands on sandy soils.

Microhabitat See genus.

Comments As for genus.

Ophioscincus ophioscincus Boulenger, 1887
Photo 602

Description Completely limbless *Ophioscincus*. Dorsal ground colour pale brownish grey to silvery white, marked with 4 or 6 longitudinal rows of dashes; reducing to 2 or 4 on tail. Broad black lateral stripe extends from neck to tail-tip, sharply contrasting with dorsum. Ventral surfaces yellow to orange. Throat grey to black. Tail-tip black. SVL 80 mm.

Preferred habitat Wet sclerophyll forests and rainforests of south-eastern Qld, from Brisbane area, north to Bulburin State Forest.

Microhabitat As for genus.

Comments Females containing 2 or 3 well-developed eggs are encountered near the surface during late summer. Otherwise as for genus.

Genus *PROABLEPHARUS* Fuhn, 1969

Endemic genus containing 3 species occurring in subhumid to arid north, west and eastern interior of Australia.

Very small slender skinks with short slender limbs, each bearing 5 digits. Eye large with round pupil. Eyelid immovable, fused to form a transparent spectacle. Ear opening small, lacking lobules. Tail fragile. Scales smooth. Pattern uniform, or consisting of small dark spots arranged in longitudinal series; coalesced to form prominent stripes on one species.

Diurnal. Terrestrial, cryptozoic leaf-litter inhabitants which rarely venture into open spaces. Egglaying. Arthropod feeders.

Distinguished from *Menetia* and *Carlia* in bearing more fingers (5 vs 4), and further from all *Carlia* except *C. foliorum* by nature of lower eyelid (immovable vs movable). Differs from *Lerista* in possessing a combination of immovable eyelid, and a digital formula of 5 + 5. All *Lerista* with fused eyelids have fewer than 5 digits. Differs from *Notoscincus* by size of first supraocular scale (not noticeably larger than remainder vs considerably larger).

Proablepharus kinghorni (Copland, 1947)
Photo 603

Description Large striped *Proablepharus* with ground colour of brownish white to pale grey. Dorsal and lateral scales may bear fine dark brown to blackish posterior margins. Broader dark lateral margins coalesce to form 9 dark stripes: vertebral, dorsals and laterodorsals extend from base of head, and 2 upper laterals extend from eye, all fading on base of tail. On obscurely marked individuals these are most prominent anteriorly. Tip of snout pinkish. Lips and side of neck white. Tail dull to bright reddish orange. Ventral surfaces white. SVL 45 mm.

Preferred habitat Favours deeply cracking black-soil plains and heavy red loams supporting ground cover of low tussock grasses in far western Qld, adjacent NT and upper Murray/Darling Basin of western NSW.

Microhabitat Shelters in deep soil cracks and cavities at bases of stumps, and beneath leaf-litter and surface debris.

Comments As for genus.

Proablepharus reginae (Glauert, 1960)
Photo 604

Description Moderately large *Proablepharus* with long tail and large eye. Ground colour brown, coppery brown to olive-brown, fading laterally. Scales are dark-edged, forming an obscure reticulum. Some individuals bear a dark anterior spot on each scale, often tending to spread over most of scale surface, particularly on lizards from Barrow Island, WA. Top of head usually suffused with dark brown to black; paler on snout. Lips, margin of eye, sides of neck and anterior flanks (occasionally base of forelimb) whitish. Ventral surfaces whitish; brown beneath toes. SVL 40 mm.

Distinguished from *P. tenuis* in possessing more supraocular scales (4 vs 3). Differs further in usually bearing a whitish margin or patch around eye.

Preferred habitat Recorded from scattered localities in semi-arid to arid northern Pilbara, Great Sandy Desert, southern Kimberley region, and southern interior of WA. Also known from south-western NT and adjacent SA. Favours sandy to stony areas dominated by hummock grassland associations. Central Australian populations are normally associated with gorges along the major drainage systems.

Microhabitat Shelters in leaf-litter, rock crevices, hummock grasses, and beneath surface debris, occasionally ascending fallen timber to bask.

Comments Infrequently encountered on the mainland, despite its broad distribution. Abundant on Barrow Island off the north-west coast, possibly because the superficially similar genus *Menetia* is absent from that area.

Proablepharus tenuis (Broom, 1896)
Photo 605

Description Small *Proablepharus* with ground colour of coppery brown, olive-brown to olive-grey. Dorsal and lateral scales dark-edged or -centred, forming an obscure reticulum. Lips and lower surfaces of neck and forebody brownish white. Tail suffused with grey. Ventral surfaces whitish; dark grey beneath tail and brown on fingers and toes. SVL 30 mm.

Distinguished from *P. reginae* in bearing fewer supraocular scales (3 vs 4). Differs further in lacking a whitish margin or patch around eye (vs present on most *P. reginae*).

Preferred habitat Subhumid to semi-arid zones from Kimberley Region, WA, and northern NT to north-eastern interior of Qld. Normally occurs in woodlands with ground cover dominated by hummock grass or spear grass.

Microhabitat Shelters in leaf-litter, soil cracks and beneath fallen timber, rocks and surface debris.

Comments As for genus.

Genus *SAIPHOS* Gray, 1831

Endemic monotypic genus restricted to humid mideastern Australia.

Moderately small elongate skink with long thick fragile tail. Limbs short, weak and widely separated, each bearing 3 digits. Ear opening covered by scales; represented by a depression. Lower eyelid movable and scaly. Scales smooth and glossy.

Crepuscular to nocturnal. Terrestrial and cryptozoic. Egglaying.

Distinguished from *Hemiergis* by nature of lower eyelid (scaly vs bearing a transparent disc). Differs from *Calyptotis* in bearing fewer digits (3 vs 5). Differs from *Anomalopus* in bearing a digital formula of 3 + 3 (vs digits absent, or toes fewer than fingers).

Three-toed Skink
Saiphos equalis (Gray, 1825)
Photo 606

Description Dorsal ground colour bronze-brown, coppery brown to grey-brown. Each dorsal scale usually bears a blackish dash; aligned to form lines or longitudinal series. Flanks, sides of head and tail blackish brown to black, contrasting sharply with dorsal colour. Obscure pale flecks on sides of head and anterior body tend to align longitudinally. Ventral surface, from chest to base of tail, yellow to bright yellowish orange. Scales on chin and throat narrowly to very broadly margined with black. Throats of some individuals are entirely black. Tip of tail black. SVL 75 mm.

Preferred habitat Occurs in wet and dry sclerophyll forests, woodlands, subalpine tussock grasslands and occasionally rainforests. Extends from south-eastern NSW north to Kroombit Tops, Qld, becoming increasingly altitude dependent northwards.

Microhabitat Shelters and forages beneath rocks, logs and surface debris, wherever damp conditions prevail.

Comments Regarded as an egglayer though embryos are well developed and hatch shortly after laying. Clutch of 3 recorded in early autumn.

Genus *SPHENOMORPHUS* Fitzinger, 1843

Large and extremely diverse genus distributed through Asia, Indo-Malayan Archipelago, New Guinea and islands of the western Pacific. Represented in Australia by 22 species. Diversity is greatest in the east, particularly north-eastern Qld. Additional taxa extend across northern Australia, and 1 species is isolated in south-western WA. Best represented in humid habitats, particularly rainforests. Subhumid to semi-arid areas support fewer species, usually associated with margins of drainage systems.

Small to moderately large, slender to robust skinks with moderate to very long fragile tails. Head deep and blunt, to weakly depressed and wedge shaped. Limbs long, to very short and widely spaced, each bearing 5 digits. Eye moderately small to large, with round pupil and black iris. Lower eyelid movable and scaly. Ear opening present, lacking lobules. Scales smooth and glossy.

Diurnal to nocturnal. Terrestrial to arboreal, rock-inhabiting or semi-aquatic. Predominantly arthropod feeders, though large species are known to prey on smaller skinks. Frogs and possibly fish may also be consumed. Egglaying or livebearing.

Relationships within *Sphenomorphus* are poorly understood. Some species clearly form distinct natural groups, others are less easily placed. Eight species groups are tentatively recognised here, based largely on behaviour, habitat preferences, distribution, ecology and proportions (particularly limb length and elongation of body).

***S. amplus* group** Contains 1 very large robust species with deep head and long limbs (overlapping when pressed to side of body). Pattern includes irregular narrow pale bands and a dark blotch centred on shoulder. Diurnal. Restricted to rainforests of mideastern Qld.

***S. murrayi* group** Comprises 2 large robust *Sphenomorphus* with deep heads and moderately long limbs (overlapping when pressed to side of body). Pattern variable, including small sharp pale dots on flanks. Crepuscular to diurnal. Often encountered basking in diffuse sunlight on buttresses or fallen logs, particularly after rain. Territorial; only juveniles or members of the opposite sex are tolerated within home range. Intruders are warned by vigorous waving of tails. When fighting occurs, individuals bite each other about the head and body until one (usually the challenger) retreats. Capable of vocalisation: a short sharp squeak emitted when fighting or during handling. Livebearing, producing litters of 3–5 offspring. Restricted to rainforests and wet sclerophyll forests of north-eastern NSW and mideastern Qld. Contains *S. luteilateralis* and *S. murrayi*.

***S. quoyii* group (water skinks)** Contains 4 large robust *Sphenomorphus* with deep heads and long limbs (broadly overlapping when pressed to side of body). Pattern variable, typically including bronze-brown dorsum, and dark flanks enclosing prominent white to yellow spots. Pale dorsolateral stripe usually present. Dark vertebral and/or dorsal stripes present or absent. Active sun-loving skinks, favouring basking sites adjacent to creeks, rivers or swamps. Members will not hesitate to enter water when pursued. Most are strongly territorial; savage fighting may ensue if home ranges are encroached upon. Livebearing, producing litters of 2–5 young. Restricted to eastern Australia, from south-eastern

SA to northern Qld. Members are *S. kosciuskoi, S. leuraensis, S. quoyii* and *S. tympanum*. One species awaits description.

***S. isolepis* group** Comprises 3 medium-sized to moderately large *Sphenomorphus* with moderately short limbs (barely overlapping or just failing to overlap when pressed to side of body). Predominantly crepuscular to nocturnal. Terrestrial. Distributed through subhumid to humid northern NT and northern WA, tending to favour well-vegetated margins of drainage systems or swamps in woodlands. Members are *S. brongersmai, S. douglasi* and *S. isolepis*.

***S. crassicaudus* group** Contains 7 taxa. Very small to medium-sized *Sphenomorphus*. Body elongate. Limbs very small and widely spaced, failing to overlap when pressed to side of body. Crepuscular to nocturnal. Cryptozoic, sheltering in loose soil beneath leaf-litter, rocks or fallen timber. Widespread in northern Australia, favouring moist microhabitats associated with woodlands or monsoon forests. Comprises *S. cracens, S. crassicaudus, S. darwiniensis, S. pardalis, S. pumilus pumilus, S. pumilus arnhemicus* and *S. punctulatus*.

***S. australis* group** Contains one small slender *Sphenomorphus* with slightly depressed head, elongate body, very small widely-spaced limbs (failing to overlap when pressed to side of body) and very long tail. Nocturnal. Cryptozoic, sheltering in moist conditions beneath leaf-litter or fallen logs. Isolated in humid south-western WA.

***S. tenuis* group** Comprises 2 species of medium-sized *Sphenomorphus* with long slender limbs and well-clawed digits (overlapping when pressed to side of body). Pattern variable, including brown dorsum bearing darker flecks or blotches. Upper lateral zone black; ragged-edged or broken into vertical bars. Predominantly diurnal; one species is often crepuscular. Arboreal and rock-inhabiting. Livebearing. Restricted to eastern Australia, from mideastern NSW to northern Qld. Contains *S. tenuis* and *S. tigrinus*.

***S. nigricaudis* group** Contains 3 moderately small to medium-sized *Sphenomorphus* with deep heads and moderate to very short limbs (failing to overlap when pressed to side of body). Pattern includes brown ground colour and irregular transversely aligned dark flecks or blotches on nape and anterior body. An anterior series of pale dorsolateral blotches present on 2 species. Crepuscular to nocturnal. Terrestrial. Egglaying. Restricted to northern Qld, 1 favouring woodland habitats, the others rainforests. Contains *S. fuscicaudis, S. mjobergi* and *S. nigricaudis*.

Sphenomorphus is distinguished from *Calyptotis* in usually attaining much greater maximum size (SVL 55 mm or greater vs 55 mm or less), and in lacking a combination of yellow and pink ventral pigments (present on all mature *Calyptotis* except *C. thorntonensis*). Differs from *Ctenotus* and *Egernia* in lack-

ing anterior ear lobules. Differs further from *Ctenotus*, and from *Eremiascincus* in favouring humid (vs subhumid to arid) habitats. Differs further from *Eremiascincus* by nature of pattern (never consisting of simple dark bands), and dorsal scales (smooth vs longitudinally ridged on hips and base of tail). Differs from *Hemiergis, Lerista, Leiolopisma* and *Lampropholis* by nature of lower eyelid (movable and scaly vs bearing a transparent disc; fused to form a spectacle on some *Lerista*).

Sphenomorphus amplus
Covacevich and McDonald, 1980
Photo 607

Description Large *Sphenomorphus*; sole member of *S. amplus* group. Ground colour dark olive-brown. Numerous pale yellowish brown scales align transversely to form irregular narrow bands on body and tail. These may become broken or less regular on flanks. Prominent dark patch present above forelimb. Side of neck and lower lateral surfaces bluish grey, each scale finely dark-edged. Lips marked with irregular dark blotches. Ventral surfaces lemon yellow, bearing dark edges to chin shields and dark flecks on throat. SVL 110 mm.

Preferred habitat Known only from rainforests of mideastern Qld: in Conway State Forest, and between 300 and 900 m at Eungella National Park.

Microhabitat Eungella population normally occurs on and among large tumbled granite boulders beside streams, sometimes sleeping at night on exposed rock faces. Conway State Forest population dwells among boulders, or roots and buttresses of large trees, particularly figs (*Ficus* spp.).

Comments Diurnal. Predominantly rock-inhabiting. Captured or fighting individuals are able to emit a loud sharp squeak. Livebearing, with recorded litter of 5; well-developed embryos in oviducts during January.

Sphenomorphus australis (Gray, 1839)
Photo 608

Description Sole member of *S. australis* group. Dorsal ground colour pale to dark brown, marked with continuous to broken vertebral or paravertebral stripes from nape onto tail. Black (often ragged-edged) dorsolateral line, usually enclosing white spots, extends from snout onto side of tail. Flanks grey, finely reticulated with black and spotted with white from neck to tail-tip. Side of head grey. Lips barred with black. Ventral surfaces, from chest to behind vent, yellow. Throat white. Under surface of tail white, heavily mottled with black. SVL 90 mm.

Preferred habitat Restricted to humid south-western WA, from Collie south-east to Cheyne Bay. Occurs in wet sclerophyll forests, coastal heathlands and swamp margins.

Microhabitat Shelters beneath rotting logs, mats

of leaf-litter, and in abandoned stick-ant nests *(Iridomyrmex conifer)*, wherever conditions are damp.

Comments Most isolated member of genus, occurring over 1000 km south of nearest congener. Livebearing. Litters of 2–6 recorded.

Sphenomorphus brongersmai Storr, 1972
Photo 609

Description Large robust member of *S. isolepis* group with dorsal ground colour of pale to dark reddish brown. Dorsum patternless, or marked with 4–6 longitudinal series of dark dashes, forming broken lines from nape onto tail. Irregular blackish brown upper lateral streak extends from snout through eye, fading on forebody. Flanks reddish brown to pale brown, heavily dotted or flecked with dark brown to black, and spotted with white. Lips obscurely barred with dark brown. Ventral surfaces whitish. SVL 95 mm.

Distinguished from *S. isolepis* in attaining much larger maximum size (SVL 95 vs 70 mm), bearing fewer upper labial scales (6 vs 7), and by sharper contrast between dorsal and lateral pattern.

Preferred habitat Inhabits river margins in humid north-western Kimberley region, WA.

Microhabitat Shelters among tree roots and beneath logs, rocks or low dense vegetation.

Comments As for species group.

Sphenomorphus cracens Greer, 1985
Photo 610

Description Member of *S. crassicaudus* group. Dorsal ground colour pale to dark brown; immaculate or marked with 2–4 longitudinal series of small dark spots between nape and base of tail. Broad black upper lateral stripe extends from snout to beyond hips, breaking into heavy dark mottling on sides of tail. Lower flanks grey marked with small dark spots, becoming larger and confluent with mottling on sides of tail. Ventral surfaces cream to pale yellow, usually lightly spotted with black beneath tail. Scales on throat may be dark-edged, forming broken longitudinal lines. SVL 55 mm.

Distinguished from *S. pumilus* in having 1 (vs 2) lower labial scales contacting postmental scale. Differs from superficially similar *Lerista orientalis* in having more digits (5 vs 4).

Preferred habitat Subhumid areas around and to the west of Atherton Plateau and Windsor Tableland in north-eastern Qld. Occurs in woodlands, dry sclerophyll forests and rock outcrops.

Microhabitat Dwells in loose substrates beneath logs, stones and leaf-litter.

Comments As for species group.

Sphenomorphus crassicaudus
(Duméril and Duméril, 1851)
Photo 611

Description Member of *S. crassicaudus* group.

Dorsal ground colour yellowish brown to coppery brown. Narrow dark brown to black paravertebral lines or series of dots (sometimes coalesced to form a broad vertebral stripe) extend from nape onto tail, tending to break or fade beyond hips. Dark brown to black upper lateral stripe extends from snout well onto tail. This may be prominent and sharp-edged, or ill-defined with a ragged edge; enclosing pale flecks or composed of concentrated dark and pale flecks. Lower flanks pale greyish brown, often spotted with dark brown. Lips sometimes barred with dark brown. Ventral surfaces cream to pale yellow with dark flecking on throat and prominent spotting beneath tail. SVL 55 mm.

Difficult to distinguish from *S. pumilus* using external characters. Midbody scales usually more (20–24 vs 20–22) and presacral vertebrae fewer (29–32 vs 32–36).

Preferred habitat Subhumid to humid areas from northern Cape York Peninsula to islands of Torres Strait. Extralimital in New Guinea. Recorded in monsoon rainforests and adjacent woodlands.

Microhabitat Shelters beneath fallen timber and in loose upper layer of sand beneath leaf-litter.

Comments Egglaying, clutches of 1–4 recorded. The status of this species and *S. pumilus* is yet to be resolved. See species group and *S. pumilus*.

Sphenomorphus darwiniensis Storr, 1967
Photos 612, 613

Description Member of *S. crassicaudus* group with pale to dark brown dorsal ground colour; paler and greyer on flanks. Pattern (when present) consists of broad darker vertebral stripe; often forked anteriorly by a paler median line, or broken to form vertebral or paravertebral series of small blotches and spots. Dorsolateral zone composed of fine concentrated dark dots usually extends from neck well onto tail, becoming diffuse on flanks. Lips ground colour to whitish, barred with dark brown. Ventral surfaces whitish. SVL 55 mm.

Distinguished from *S. pumilus arnhemicus* in bearing shorter toes (fewer than 19 subdigital lamellae under 4th toe vs more than 18), and in usually bearing a stronger pattern.

Preferred habitat Occurs in a variety of habitats, from monsoon forests to woodlands, particularly along creek margins or river floodplains in subhumid zones of northern NT and far northern WA.

Microhabitat Shelters beneath leaf-litter or fallen timber, wherever moist conditions prevail.

Comments As for species group.

Sphenomorphus douglasi Storr, 1967
Photo 614

Description Moderately large member of *S. isolepis* group. Dorsal ground colour brown to dark brown, marked with numerous dark streaks or spots from nape onto base of tail. Broad black upper lateral zone extends from eye onto anterior body or hips. Lateral surfaces, from side of neck onto base of tail, pale brown to rich burnt orange enclosing numerous prominent small white dots and dark brown flecks. Lips narrowly barred with dark brown. Ventral surfaces white. SVL 90 mm.

Distinguished from *S. isolepis* by build (robust vs relatively more slender), attaining larger maximum size (SVL 90 vs 70 mm), bearing a prominent black upper lateral streak (at least anteriorly), and sharper contrast between dorsal and lateral pattern.

Preferred habitat Extends widely through woodland habitats, though favours margins of rivers, swamps and lagoons. Occurs in subhumid northern NT.

Microhabitat Shelters in abandoned burrows, beneath logs or dense low vegetation.

Comments In addition to consuming invertebrate prey, individuals have been observed scavenging morsels of meat from bones of larger animals. Otherwise as for species group.

Sphenomorphus fuscicaudis Greer, 1979
Photo 615

Description Moderately large member of *S. nigricaudis* group. Dorsal ground colour pale to dark brown (darker on tail), marked with numerous darker, wavy to broken bands. These are most prominent anteriorly, breaking into diffuse spotting or flecking on posterior body. Pattern becomes more complex to form a reticulum on side of neck, often enclosing an irregular dorsolateral series of small cream to yellow blotches from neck to midbody. Flanks pinkish brown to greyish brown, marked with an irregular and fragmented continuation of dorsal pattern. Forelimbs ground colour streaked with black. Hindlimbs and tail glossy dark brown to black. Ventral surfaces pale yellow; most prominent and occasionally flushed with pink, posteriorly. Tail white to bluish grey, sometimes flushed with pink beneath base. SVL 90 mm.

Distinguished from *S. nigricaudis* in bearing a dorsolateral series of cream to pale yellow blotches, and in attaining larger maximum size (SVL 90 vs 75 mm). Differs further in preferring rainforest (vs woodland) habitats. Differs from *S. mjobergi* in possessing much longer limbs, and less elongate body.

Preferred habitat Montane and lowland rainforests of north-eastern Qld, from just south of Cooktown to southern end of Atherton Tableland. Apparently isolated population occurs further north, in the McIlwraith Range.

Microhabitat Shelters beneath rotting logs and damp leaf-litter.

Comments Occasionally encountered active on surface during day. Clutches of 2–4 eggs recorded. Otherwise as for species group.

Sphenomorphus isolepis (Boulenger, 1887)
Photo 616

Description Small member of *S. isolepis* group. Dorsal ground colour pale or dark brown to rich reddish brown, prominently to obscurely marked with numerous darker irregularly shaped flecks and dashes, often aligned longitudinally. These tend to become more intense dorsolaterally, forming a dark zone. Flanks darker shade of ground colour, heavily flecked with blackish brown and spotted with pale yellowish brown. Lips barred with cream and brown. Ventral surfaces white. SVL 70 mm.

Distinguished from *S. brongersmai* and *S. douglasi* in lacking a prominent black upper lateral zone, and by weak (vs strong) contrast between dorsal and lateral surfaces. Differs further from both in attaining smaller maximum size (SVL 70 vs 95 and 90 mm, respectively).

Preferred habitat Most abundant along river floodplains, margins of swamps, lagoons or rocky gorges, particularly where dense vegetation such as *Pandanus* or paperbark *(Melaleuca)* thickets occurs. Occurs in subhumid to semi-arid areas from northern NT to Kimberley region, WA. Isolated populations occur in arid western Pilbara region and offshore islands of WA.

Microhabitat Shelters beneath rocks, logs, accumulated dead vegetation and surface debris.

Comments See species group.

Alpine Water Skink
Sphenomorphus kosciuskoi (Kinghorn, 1932)
Photos 617, 618

Description Member of *S. quoyii* group, comprising 2 distinct populations.

Southern form: Dorsal ground colour olive-brown. Narrow black vertebral and laterodorsal stripes and yellowish brown dorsolateral stripes, extend from nape to base of tail. Flanks black, enclosing vertically aligned series of cream to yellow spots; represented on tail as a series of black blotches. Lower flanks pale yellow to olive-grey, sometimes bearing black scales arranged to form irregular vertical bars. Ventral surfaces pale grey to yellow, bearing grey clouding on throat, and usually numerous small black flecks on chest and belly. SVL 80 mm.

Northern form: Vertebral (and sometimes laterodorsal) stripe weak to absent.

Southern form differs from *S. tympanum* and *Sphenomorphus* sp. (1) (see photo 635) in possessing a vertebral stripe, and in bearing a shorter tail. Northern form differs from *S. quoyii* by head-shape (relatively deeper with blunter snout), shorter tail, and in usually lacking dark dorsal blotches. Differs further in preferring cooler, higher altitudes.

Preferred habitat Restricted to high altitudes (southern form often occurs above 1000 m) in woodlands, heathlands and tussock grasslands. Often associated with sphagnum bogs lining creeks. Southern form occurs in highlands of southern NSW and north-eastern Vic. Northern form occurs on New England plateau and Barrington Tops, north-eastern NSW.

Microhabitat Basks on fallen timber, and low vegetation such as tussocks. Shelters beneath rocks, logs or dense vegetation.

Comments Southern form hibernates during winter months, when much of the habitat may be covered by snow. Observations on captive individuals (northern form) show several distinct displays, including head-bobbing (widespread among lizards, but infrequently observed in skinks) and a 'challenge display' consisting of lowering head and expanding throat, accompanied by audible opening and closing of mouth. Southern form produces litters of 2–5 young during summer. Otherwise as for species group.

Blue Mountains Water Skink
Sphenomorphus leuraensis
(Wells and Wellington, 1983)
Photo 619

Description Small member of *S. quoyii* group with dorsal ground colour of very dark brown to black. Narrow sharp-edged (sometimes broken) pale yellow paravertebral and dorsolateral lines extend from nape to base of tail, breaking into series of spots beyond hips. Flanks black, enclosing numerous yellow spots; becoming larger and tending to coalesce on lower lateral surfaces. Top of head coppery brown, variegated with black. Side of head black, marked with a series of yellow spots beneath eye, coalescing to form a streak on neck. Yellow stripe on lower lips extends to forelimb. Ventral surfaces bright yellow, marked with coarse longitudinally aligned variegations. SVL 70 mm.

Distinguished from other members of *S. quoyii* group in bearing a very dark dorsum and pale paravertebral lines.

Preferred habitat Swampy heathland over sandstone. Known only from Wentworth Falls, Leura and Newnes Plateau in the Blue Mountains, NSW.

Microhabitat Ascends dense grass tussocks to bask, readily taking shelter beneath them or in burrows (possibly including those of freshwater crustaceans) when disturbed.

Comments Regarded as at risk because of restricted habitat and encroaching development. Otherwise as for species group.

Sphenomorphus luteilateralis
Covacevich and McDonald, 1980
Photo 620

Description Member of *S. murrayi* group. Dorsal ground colour rich brown to bronze-brown, marked with scattered darker scales or flecks. Obscure dark suffusion may be present on upper flanks. Remaining lateral surfaces, from forelimb to hindlimb, burnt orange enclosing numerous prominent white spots. Large dark patch present above forelimb. Smaller dark patches present on side of neck and above ear. Ventral surfaces whitish. SVL 90 mm.

Preferred habitat Known only from rainforest above 900 m in Eungella National Park, mideastern Qld.

Microhabitat Shelters beneath litter such as fallen fronds at bases of palms, or under rotting logs.

Comments As for species group.

Sphenomorphus mjobergi
(Lönnberg and Andersson, 1915)
Photo 621

Description Elongate short-limbed member of *S. nigricaudis* group. Dorsal ground colour rich brown, bearing a black spot or streak on each scale. Dorsolateral series of cream blotches mixed with larger dark blotches extends from above ear to about forelimb. Flanks greyish brown, flecked with black. Ventral surfaces whitish, each scale margined with dark brown beneath throat, and flecked with dark brown beneath posterior portion of tail. SVL 90 mm.

Distinguished from *S. pumilus* in attaining much larger maximum size (SVL 90 vs 55 mm), and in bearing pale dorsolateral blotches. Differs from *S. fuscicaudis* in bearing a more elongate body and shorter limbs.

Preferred habitat Restricted to montane rainforests (above 650 m) of north-eastern Qld, from about Mt Bartle Frere south to Ravenshoe area.

Microhabitat Shelters in and beneath rotting logs.

Comments Crepuscular to nocturnal. See species group.

Sphenomorphus murrayi (Boulenger, 1887)
Photo 622

Description Member of *S. murrayi* group with dorsal ground colour of golden brown to coppery brown. Dark margins to individual scales may form short irregular transverse bars or a variegated pattern. Upper lateral zone may bear a prominent to obscure dark suffusion. Sides of neck, body, and sometimes tail black, prominently marked with numerous fine white to bluish white dots and occasionally enclosing a few small yellow blotches. Head scales finely edged with dark brown. Lips dark brown barred with cream. Ventral surfaces pale to deep yellow, usually spotted or flecked with brown towards vent and beneath tail. SVL 85 mm.

Preferred habitat Rainforests and wet sclerophyll forests (usually above 150 m) from mideastern NSW to south-eastern Qld; north to Conondale Ranges.

Microhabitat Shelters in and under rotting timber or accumulated leaf-litter. Often observed resting with head protruding from hollows in buttresses or fallen logs.

Comments Largely insectivorous, though smaller skinks such as *Lampropholis* spp. are recorded as prey items. Otherwise as for species group.

Sphenomorphus nigricaudis (Macleay, 1877)
Photo 623

Description Moderately small member of *S. nigricaudis* group with ground colour of pale to rich brown. Irregular dark brown flecks and blotches usually coalesce to form narrow wavy bands from nape to midbody. Posterior dorsum usually lacks pattern. Pale lateral margins to scales may form obscure lines. Anterior flanks bear a continuation of dorsal pattern. Posterior flanks obscurely spotted or flecked with dark brown. Lips prominently barred with cream and dark brown. Ventral surfaces white to cream, often marked with sparse dark brown streaks or flecks on sides of throat. SVL 75 mm.

Distinguished from *S. fuscicaudis* in lacking a dorsolateral series of cream to pale yellow blotches, and in preferring woodland (vs rainforest) habitats. Differs from *S. pardalis* in bearing irregular dark dorsal bands (vs scattered to longitudinally aligned dark spots).

Preferred habitat Woodlands (extending into margins of monsoon rainforests and vine thickets) of humid to subhumid northern and eastern Cape York Peninsula, Qld. Extralimital in southern New Guinea.

Microhabitat Shelters beneath rocks, logs or leaf-litter.

Comments As for species group.

Sphenomorphus pardalis (Macleay, 1877)
Photo 624

Description Moderately large robust member of *S. crassicaudus* group. Dorsal ground colour pale golden brown to rich dark brown, marked with irregularly shaped dark brown to black flecks (densely scattered over dorsum, or sparse and centred on vertebral zone) from nape or top of head onto tail. Flanks paler shade of ground colour to grey, heavily spotted with dark brown to black. These markings tend to concentrate (occasionally coalescing) on dorsolateral zone, becoming sparser on lower lateral surfaces. Lips prominently barred with cream and dark brown. Ventral surfaces cream, sometimes bearing dark margins to scales on chin and throat. SVL 70 mm.

Distinguished from *S. nigricaudis* by nature of dorsal pattern (scattered to longitudinally aligned dark spots vs irregular bands). Differs from *S. pumilus* in attaining much larger size (SVL 70 vs 55 mm), by build (robust vs very slender), and in lacking a vertebral stripe, paravertebral lines or series of dashes.

Preferred habitat Occurs in a variety of woodland habitats, extending into monsoon forests. Restricted to northern Qld, extending south to about Cairns area.

Microhabitat Shelters in soft soil beneath rocks, logs, leaf-litter and surface debris.

Comments Some uncertainty exists as to the mode of reproduction. A dissected female contained 3 well-developed eggs while a captive individual apparently gave birth to 4 young. Otherwise as for species group.

Sphenomorphus pumilus (Boulenger, 1887)
Photo 625

Description Member of *S. crassicaudus* group. Two subspecies recognised. Their relationship is uncertain.

S. p. pumilus Pattern variable; both strongly and weakly patterned individuals occur. Dorsal ground colour yellowish brown to coppery brown. Narrow dark brown to black paravertebral lines or series of spots (occasionally coalesced to form a broad vertebral stripe) extend from nape onto tail, tending to break or fade beyond hips. Broad black upper lateral stripe, sharply defined with a straight edge to poorly defined and ragged-edged, extends from snout well onto tail. Lower flanks greyish brown, usually spotted with dark brown. Lips may be barred with dark brown. Ventral surfaces cream to pale yellow usually marked with dark spots, most prominent beneath tail. SVL 55 mm.

S. p. arnhemicus Storr, 1967 Differs from nominate form in bearing much weaker pattern, particularly the absence of a prominent dark upper edge on its darkened flanks, and the absence of a dark vertebral stripe. Differs further in having more lamellae beneath 4th toe (19 or more vs 19 or fewer).

S. p. pumilus is distinguished from *S. cracens* in having 2 (vs 1) lower labial scales contacting postmental scale. Differs from *S. mjobergi* and *S. pardalis* by much more slender build, attaining smaller maximum size (SVL 55 vs 90 and 70 mm, respectively), and in usually bearing a dark vertebral stripe, paravertebral lines or series of dashes. Difficult to distinguish from *S. crassicaudus* using external characters. Midbody scales usually fewer (20–22 vs 20–24) and more presacral vertebrae (32–36 vs 29–32). *S. p. arnhemicus* differs from *S. darwiniensis* in bearing weaker pattern (though virtually patternless individuals of *S. darwiniensis* occur) and more lamellae beneath 4th toe (more than 18 vs fewer than 18).

Preferred habitat *S. p. pumilus* occurs in northeastern Qld, from south-west of Cairns to Cape York Peninsula. *S. p. arnhemicus* occurs in northeastern NT. Both subspecies occupy a variety of habitats, from woodlands and coastal dunes to vine thickets and margins of rainforests.

Microhabitat Sites beneath leaf-litter and in soft soil beneath rocks, fallen timber or surface debris are

utilised, particularly where moist conditions prevail.
Comments *S. p. pumilus* is recorded as an egglayer. Clutch of 3 recorded. Both subspecies are poorly defined. In scalation, colouration and pattern *S. p. pumilus* is virtually indistinguishable from *S. crassicaudus* and the status of these taxa is unresolved. Their relationship with *S. p. arnhemicus* similarly requires investigation, as does the affinity between *S. p. arnhemicus* and *S. darwiniensis. S. p. arnhemicus* was originally described as a subspecies of *S. crassicaudus* because at the time the status of the far northern *S. crassicaudus* and the widespread *S. pumilus* was poorly understood, and the former name was generally applied to all Qld populations. *S. p. arnhemicus* is tentatively regarded herein as a subspecies of *S. pumilus* rather than of *S. crassicaudus*. See species group.

Sphenomorphus punctulatus (Peters, 1871)
Photo 626

Description Moderately large robust member of *S. crassicaudus* group. Ground colour brownish grey to pale or rich brown. Pattern absent, or consisting of one or more dark flecks or spots on each dorsal and lateral scale. Heavy dark flecking sometimes extends along upper lateral zone, forming an indistinct streak. Side of head heavily spotted with dark brown to black. Lips whitish, barred with dark brown to black. Ventral surfaces cream to yellow, bearing dark longitudinally aligned dots on chin and throat. SVL 50 mm.
Preferred habitat Favours woodlands and vine thickets, particularly those on sandy soils. Occurs in subhumid mideastern Qld.
Microhabitat Shelters beneath leaf-litter, fallen timber and surface debris. Also recorded beneath rocks on sandy beaches and dunes.
Comments Egglaying. Clutch of 3 recorded. Otherwise as for species group.

Eastern Water Skink
Sphenomorphus quoyii
(Duméril and Bibron, 1839)
Photos 627, 628

Description Largest Australian *Sphenomorphus.* Member of *S. quoyii* group with dorsal ground colour of brown, coppery brown, golden brown to grey-brown. Dorsum occasionally immaculate, though usually marked with small irregular black flecks or blotches. These may coalesce to form a narrow (often broken) black vertebral line, particularly on posterior body and base of tail. Narrow pale brown to yellow dorsolateral stripe (edged above with black) extends from above eye to midbody, or base of tail. Prominent black upper lateral zone (occasionally obscure on inland populations), usually enclosing numerous small scattered to verti-

cally aligned cream to pale brown spots, extends from side of neck onto base of tail. This breaks on tail into small black blotches. Lower lateral zone white, grey to yellow, bearing numerous scattered to vertically aligned black spots or variegations. Ventral surfaces white to yellow, often bearing longitudinal series of black to dark grey lines from throat onto chest or belly. SVL 115 mm.

Distinguished from *Sphenomorphus* sp. (1) (see below) in bearing more prominent pale dorsolateral stripes. Differs from *S. kosciuskoi* in bearing a longer snout and tail, and in favouring warmer lower altitudes. Differs further from both in attaining greater maximum size (SVL 115 vs 90 and 80 mm, respectively).
Preferred habitat Wide variety of habitats, from margins of wet sclerophyll forests or rainforests to woodlands. Favours edges of rivers, creeks or swamps, particularly where rocks or fallen logs are present. Frequently encountered in moist areas some distance from water. Extends from Cairns district, Qld, south along coast and ranges to south-eastern NSW. Penetrates semi-arid interior of NSW to north-western Vic. and south-eastern SA via Darling and Murray River drainage systems.
Microhabitat Basks on exposed surfaces of rocks or logs, readily seeking shelter beneath them when disturbed. Populations dwelling along Darling and Murray Rivers shelter and forage among the root systems of large riverside eucalypts.
Comments In addition to a broad range of invertebrates, smaller skinks are regularly included on diet. Displays such as head-bobbing have been observed. Litters of 2 and 3 young are recorded. Otherwise as for species group.

Sphenomorphus tenuis (Gray, 1831)
Photos 629–632

Description Highly variable member of *S. tenuis* group, probably comprising a complex of taxa. Dorsal ground colour pale to rich brown (silvery brown on some populations from southern Qld), marked with small black blotches from nape to hips. In southern parts of range these may be densely scattered to transversely aligned. In mideastern Qld they tend to coalesce on paravertebral region, leaving a narrow vertebral stripe or zone. Broad ragged-edged upper lateral stripe commences as a streak between snout and eye, extending to hips. This may enclose small vertically aligned pale grey dots, or break to form a series of vertically elongate blotches. Mid to lower lateral surfaces pale grey, sparsely to densely variegated with black, occasionally in combination with obscure pale spots or flecks. Lips prominently to obscurely barred with black, and pale brown to white. Tail prominently marked with narrow ragged-edged black bands or transversely aligned blotches. Ventral surfaces white, pale grey to pale yellow. Chin shields dark-edged, and throat obscurely variegated with grey. SVL 70 mm.

Preferred habitat Occurs in a wide variety of habitats on east coast and ranges, from Sydney region, NSW, to southern Cape York Peninsula, Qld. Most abundant in wet sclerophyll forests, well-watered rock outcrops, vine thickets, rainforests, or moist conditions in dry sclerophyll forests or woodlands.

Microhabitat Most populations are rock-inhabiting, sheltering in horizontal and vertical crevices on rock outcrops, in caves or human dwellings. In some areas cracks, hollows or beneath the bark of fallen or standing timber, are favoured.

Comments Some sympatric or adjacent populations appear to occupy distinctive niches. In southern Qld, heavily blotched individuals bearing broad, often unbroken upper lateral stripes occur among rocks or fallen logs adjacent to animals with reduced and broken upper lateral stripes which favour elevated arboreal microhabitats. Similarly, densely blotched forms extend into isolated moist pockets (such as Blackdown Tableland) of mideastern Qld, surrounded by subhumid areas which support populations bearing distinct paravertebral blotches. Detailed taxonomic and ecological work throughout the range of this unwieldy complex is required to clarify the status of its members. The name 'brachysoma' (type locality Atherton, Qld) is widely used and may prove valid for the northern population.

Sphenomorphus tigrinus (De Vis, 1888)
Photo 633

Description Large member of *S. tenuis* group. Dorsal ground colour pale golden brown to dark brown, usually without pattern. Juveniles (occasionally adults) are marked with black blotches, coalesced to form narrow irregular bands from nape onto tail. Prominent dorsolateral series of alternating black, and cream to yellow or orange blotches extend from side of neck to hips or onto tail. Flanks greyish brown, bearing irregular to vertically aligned black flecking or bars. Lips white to yellow, sometimes marked with prominent dark brown bars. Ventral surfaces white, yellow to pale green, often variegated with brown on throat. SVL 80 mm.

Preferred habitat Known only from rainforests and high altitude heathlands of north-eastern Qld, between Bloomfield and Kirrama. Extends from sea-level to 1600 m.

Microhabitat Shelters in hollows, or beneath bark of fallen or standing timber, and among epiphytes or moss-covered boulders. Often encountered resting with head protruding from cover.

Comments Diurnal to crepuscular. Predominantly arboreal. Capable of emitting a sharp squeak if handled, or when fighting. Otherwise as for species group.

Southern Water Skink
Sphenomorphus tympanum
(Lönnberg and Andersson, 1913)
Photo 634

Description Member of *S. quoyii* group. Dorsal ground colour golden brown or dark brown to almost black, irregularly blotched with black from top of head onto tail. Upper lateral zone (from upper lip to hips) black, enclosing numerous small white to yellow spots, commencing on neck. This zone is represented on tail by irregular black spots or blotches. Lower lateral zone pale grey, spotted with white and sparsely dotted with black. White to pale grey stripe extends from lower lip, curving up to lower portion of, or over, ear. Ventral surfaces, from chest to base of tail, cream to yellow flecked with black. Throat white to pale grey, with or without darker clouding. SVL 85 mm.

Distinguished from *Sphenomorphus* sp. (1) (see below) in lacking prominent dark blotches on throat, and in bearing dark markings on belly. Differs further by alignment of white lower labial stripe (curving up to or over ear vs extending below ear). Differs from southern form of *S. kosciuskoi* in lacking a dark vertebral stripe.

Preferred habitat Variety of well-timbered habitats, usually along creek, river or swamp margins or on well-watered slopes. Overlaps broadly with *Sphenomorphus* sp. (1), favouring cooler conditions (higher altitudes or more shaded sides of gullies). Extends from southern and eastern Vic. to highlands of southern NSW.

Microhabitat Basks on exposed surfaces of rocks or logs. Shelters in cracks in fallen timber, beneath logs, stones, tree roots and low vegetation.

Comments Mating occurs in spring, and litters of 2–5 young are born in summer. See species group.

Sphenomorphus sp. (1)
Photo 635

Description Member of *S. quoyii* group. Dorsal ground colour pale to dark bronze-brown, sparsely to densely marked from head onto base of tail with numerous small black blotches. Narrow obscure pale dorsolateral line may extend from above eye to midbody. Upper flanks black spotted with white; represented on side of tail by black mottling. Mid to lower flanks pale grey to white, finely variegated with black and spotted with white. Side of head black, or ground colour blotched with black. Lower lips white. Ventral surfaces white to yellow, blotched with black on chin and throat. SVL 90 mm.

Distinguished from *S. tympanum* in bearing prominent black blotches on throat, and in lacking black markings on belly. Differs further by alignment of white labial streak (extending below ear vs curving up to or over ear). Differs from *S. quoyii* in attaining smaller maximum size (SVL 90 vs 115 mm), usually bearing a weaker pale dorsolateral stripe, and a more prominent white stripe on lower lips. Differs from sympatric population of *S. kosciuskoi* in lacking a dark vertebral stripe.

Preferred habitat Occurs along creek, river and swamp margins associated with a wide variety of habitats, from edges of wet and dry sclerophyll forests to woodlands and heathlands. Extends from central and eastern Vic. (excluding alpine areas) north to Blue Mountains, NSW. Isolated populations occur in south-eastern SA.

Microhabitat Forages among waterside vegetation and basks on exposed surfaces of rocks and logs. Shelters among tree roots or beneath stones, fallen timber and low vegetation.

Comments This undescribed species is well known, and referred to in previous publications as *Sphenomorphus tympanum* (warm-temperate form). Feeds on a broad range of invertebrate prey, and occasionally smaller skinks. Mating occurs in spring, with litters of 2–5 young born in summer. See species group and *S. tympanum*.

Blue-tongued Lizards, Shingleback
Genus *TILIQUA* Gray, 1825

Represented in Australia by 6 species. Widespread through all Australian States. Extralimital in New Guinea and eastern Indonesia.

Moderately large to very large robust skinks, each with a broad head, distinct from neck. Limbs small, each bearing 5 short digits of approximately equal length; 4th toe not noticeably longer. Tail short and non-fragile; slender and pointed to bulbous and blunt. Lower eyelid movable and scaly. Ear opening present, usually bearing anterior lobules. Tongue broad and fleshy; bright blue to dark purple. Scales smooth to extremely rugose.

Diurnal. Terrestrial, sheltering beneath low vegetation and surface debris, or in hollow logs and abandoned burrows. Omnivorous, feeding on a broad range of arthropods, gastropods, bird eggs, carrion, flowers and fruit. Livebearing, producing small to very large litters. These slow-moving skinks are a distinctive element of Australia's reptile fauna. They occur well within the suburbs of all Australian cities. When harassed, blue-tongued lizards inflate and deflate their bodies, while hissing loudly. Mouth is opened to display bright pink interior and conspicuous blue tongue is protruded.

Distinguished from *Cyclodomorphus* by nature of tail (short and non-fragile vs relatively long and fragile), and by head-shape (triangular; distinct from neck vs not noticeably distinct from neck on all *Cyclodomorphus* except *C. gerrardii*). Differs from *Egernia* by nature of digits (short and approximately equal in length vs 4th toe noticeably longer).

Tiliqua adelaidensis (Peters, 1863)
Photo 636

Description Smallest *Tiliqua*, with a deep short pointed head, short robust body, short slender tail and smooth scales. Ground colour (in preservative) pale yellowish brown to pale bluish grey. Pattern consists of irregular narrow, transversely and longitudinally aligned blackish streaks, forming a broken dark vertebral zone. Remainder of dorsum is often unmarked. Side of head, flanks and base of tail bear fine to coarse dark variegations, usually alternating with scattered pale scales. Ventral surfaces yellowish grey. SVL 95 mm.

Preferred habitat Apparently restricted to a small area north and east of Adelaide, SA. Believed to occur on sandy to loamy plains and low hills, vegetated with low woodlands over a chenopod-dominated ground cover.

Microhabitat Virtually unknown; one specimen recorded under a stone. See genus.

Comments Possibly extinct. The last specimen was collected approximately 25 years ago. Listed as 'rare and endangered'. Dissection of preserved specimens reveals a diet of small cockroaches, beetles and vegetation, and 1 litter of 2. Otherwise as for genus.

Centralian Blue-tongued Lizard
Tiliqua multifasciata Sternfeld, 1919
Photo 637

Description Robust *Tiliqua* with short slightly depressed angular head, very short body, short slender tail and smooth scales. Ground colour pale grey to greyish brown, bearing approximately 9–12 orange to yellowish brown bands (broader than pale interspaces) between nape and hips, and 8–10 on tail. Prominent broad black stripe extends from eye to above ear. Ventral surfaces white to cream, often bearing dark variegations on throat. SVL 250 mm.

Preferred habitat Semi-arid to arid red sand plains, dunes or stony hills vegetated with hummock grass associations. Extends from north-western WA, through central Australia to interior of Qld.

Microhabitat As for genus.

Comments Mating occurs in spring, with litters of 4–10 young born in summer. A common food item and totem for central Australian Aborigines. Otherwise as for genus.

Southern or Blotched Blue-tongued Lizard
Tiliqua nigrolutea (Quoy and Gaimard, 1824)
Photos 638, 639

Description Large *Tiliqua* with deep short head, long robust body, relatively long thick tail and smooth scales. Dorsal ground colour dark brown to black. Pattern variable, consisting of large oblong-shaped whitish, yellowish, pale brown, orange to reddish blotches; occasionally bluish grey in southern highlands and Tas. These may be scattered, or aligned in transverse or longitudinal series on body; almost invariably coalescing to form bands on tail. Anterior blotches sometimes coalesce to form broad longitudinal bars on nape and shoulders. Those on flanks are larger and paler, leaving an irregular coarse reticulum of ground colour. Top of head brownish to olive, usually mottled to flecked with darker pigment. Side of head flushed with yellow to orange. Populations from north of range are largest and darkest, bearing redder markings. Ventral surfaces cream to yellow, with or without dark variegations. SVL 300 mm.

Preferred habitat Restricted to cool temperate south-eastern Australia, from northern Tas., through far south-eastern SA and southern Vic. to Blue Mountains, NSW. Widespread in most lowland habitats in south of range, becoming increasingly altitude dependent northwards.

Microhabitat As for genus.

Comments Litters of 3–10 (usually 4 or 5) large young are born in summer. Otherwise as for genus.

Western Blue-tongued Lizard
Tiliqua occipitalis (Peters, 1863)
Photo 640

Description Slender *Tiliqua* with long slightly depressed head, elongate body, long slender tail and smooth scales. Ground colour pale yellowish brown to pale greyish brown, marked with approximately 4–6 broad dark brown bands on body, and 3–4 on tail. These may enclose scattered pale spots, occasionally aligned to form large irregular open circles on dorsal surface. Pale interspaces may enclose additional narrow incomplete bands, particularly on flanks. Broad blackish stripe extends from eye to about ear. Ventral surfaces cream to white, sometimes bearing obscure extensions of lateral bands. Those on tail form complete rings. SVL 270 mm.

Differs from *T. scincoides* by number of supraocular scales contacting frontal scale (1 vs 2), and in usually bearing fewer and broader bands on body.

Preferred habitat Subhumid to arid southern Australia, from north-western Vic. and south-western NSW, through SA and south-western NT to Carnarvon, WA. Favours open sandy areas supporting mallee/hummock grass associations and heathlands. Inhabits red sand ridges in NT, and pale dunes in coastal regions.

Microhabitat Usually shelters in shallow burrows beneath dead vegetation and surface debris. Otherwise as for genus.

Comments Litters of 4–10 (usually about 5) large young are born in summer. Otherwise as for genus.

Shingleback, Bob-tail, Sleepy Lizard or Boggi
Tiliqua rugosa (Gray, 1825)
Photos 641–644

Description Large, very robust *Tiliqua* with a broad deep triangular head and short blunt tail. Scales extremely large, irregularly shaped and rugose. Four subspecies tentatively recognised.

T. r. rugosa Tail relatively long and slender. Ground colour pale to dark brown, olive-brown, grey to black, usually marked with irregular, broad to narrow cream, yellow, orange to pale grey bands on body and tail. Head usually paler than ground colour, often boldly flushed with orange. Ventral surfaces cream to white, usually bearing irregular greyish to brownish stripes, bands or blotches. SVL 290 mm.

T. r. konowi (Mertens, 1958) Differs from nominate form in attaining a smaller maximum size, and bearing a narrower head, more slender body, longer tail and less rugose body scales. Ground colour dark grey, marked with obscure pale bands, each composed of dense peppering. Ventral surfaces dark grey, bearing obscure irregular dark markings or fine peppering. SVL 250 mm.

T. r. asper (Gray, 1845) Differs from nominate form in attaining larger maximum size, and bearing a broader head, more robust body, shorter broader tail, and larger more rugose body scales. Colour and pattern highly variable; usually shades of dark brown, grey to black, irregularly flecked, spotted and/or banded with paler pigment. Ventral surfaces usually ground colour without pattern. SVL 310 mm.

T. r. tropisurus (Péron, 1807) Differs from nominate form in bearing a deeper longer head and a smaller ear opening. Tail often tapers to a point. Pattern usually includes scattered pale flecks or blotches over a dark grey to brown ground colour. Ventral surface pale brown, usually without pattern; occasionally clouded with darker brown. SVL 290 mm.

Preferred habitat Subhumid to arid southern Australia. *T. r. rugosa* occurs in south-west of range, from about western edge of Nullarbor Plain to lower west coast. Encountered in all terrestrial habitats, though uncommon in wet sclerophyll forests and swamplands. *T. r. konowi* is restricted to Rottnest Island, WA, on pale sands and limestones supporting low woodland/heathland associations. *T. r. asper* extends through remaining eastern portion of range, occurring in a wide variety of habitats, from dry sclerophyll forests to hummock grasslands, chenopod shrublands and sparsely vegetated coastal dunes. *T. r. tropisurus* is restricted to midwest coast of WA, extending north to Carnarvon.

Microhabitat As for genus.

Comments The number of regional common names indicates the degree of familiarity Australians have with this well-known and distinctive lizard. Usually produces 2 (occasionally 1 or 3; rarely 4) large young during summer. A slow-moving lizard, possibly an ecological equivalent, in terms of form, diet and habitat preferences, to terrestrial tortoises

(Testudinidae) of other continents. Often encountered basking on roads, where mortality is high. Reported to exceed 20 years in age.

Common, Eastern and Northern Blue-tongued Lizard
Tiliqua scincoides (White, 1790)
Photos 645, 646

Description Very large robust *Tiliqua* with narrow, moderately depressed head, elongate body, long thick tail and smooth scales. Largest member of genus. Among largest of the world's skinks. Two subspecies recognised.

T. s. scincoides Ground colour highly variable, ranging through shades of yellow, brown, silvery grey to black. Pattern usually includes approximately 6–9 irregular (usually dark-edged) paler bands between nape and hips, and 7–10 on tail. These may be complete, or alternate on either side of body, displaced along midline. Bands are often suffused with orange to brown on flanks. Dark lateral margins to scales may form narrow longitudinal lines within pale interspaces. Broad prominent dark stripe usually present from eye to about ear. Ventral surfaces white, grey to yellow, often mottled with pale brown. SVL 300 mm. Larger sizes are attained in Cooktown district, and on islands of Moreton Bay, Qld.

T. s. intermedia Mitchell, 1955 Differs from nominate form in attaining larger maximum size, and in bearing distinctive pattern. Bands obscure, often broken into variegations or heavy mottling on dorsum. Flanks flushed with yellow to orange, alternating with black vertical bars (extensions of dorsal bands). In west of range, top of head is prominently peppered with black. Dark temporal stripe usually absent; obscure when present. SVL 320 mm.

T. s. scincoides is distinguished from *T. occipitalis* by number of supraocular scales contacting frontal scale (2 vs 1), and in usually bearing more numerous and narrower bands on body.

Preferred habitat Occurs in virtually all habitats throughout eastern and northern Australia. Absent from high altitudes, and humid environments such as rainforests. *T. s. scincoides* occupies eastern portion of range, west to about Mt Isa area, Qld. *T. s. intermedia* occupies remainder.

Microhabitat As for genus.

Comments Litters of 5–25 small young are born in summer. Otherwise as for genus.

Genus *TROPIDOPHORUS*
Duméril and Bibron, 1839

Widespread through South-East Asia. One species occurs in Australia; restricted to rainforests in northeast Qld. The inclusion of this species in *Tropidophorus* is tentative. Its affinities may lie closer to *Sphenomorphus*.

Medium-sized robust skink with a moderately long fragile tail and well-developed limbs, each bearing 5 digits. Eye moderately large with a dark iris and a movable scaly lower eyelid. Ear opening large, lacking lobules. Dorsal, lateral and ventral scales (including those on throat) strongly keeled, giving skin a rough and granular appearance. Scales of lips, chin and snout smooth and glossy.

Crepuscular and nocturnal. Terrestrial. Livebearing. Invertebrate feeder.

Prickly Forest Skink
Tropidophorus queenslandiae De Vis, 1890
Photo 647

Description Ground colour brown, dark brown to rich purplish brown. Raised and pointed tip of each keeled scale, black. Pattern most prominent on juveniles; obscure to absent on adults. Numerous irregular, narrow and broken pale bands or transversely aligned blotches extend from nape onto limbs and tail. Pattern often restricted to, or most prominent on, flanks. Scales surrounding eyes, lips, tip of snout and throat are glossy dark brown to black. Lips usually spotted with cream to white. Ventral surfaces cream to pale yellowish brown, flecked, spotted or blotched with brown. These markings sometimes coalesce on midventral region to form an obscure stripe. SVL 80 mm.

Preferred habitat Highland and lowland rainforests of north-eastern Qld, from near Rossville south to Kirrama.

Microhabitat Shuns direct sunlight, sheltering and foraging in and beneath rotting logs, stones and leaf-litter, where damp shaded conditions prevail.

Comments Secretive; rarely observed active on the forest floor. Litters of 1 or 2 young are recorded; born throughout the year. Slugs, snails and worms are probably included on diet. Extremely heat sensitive, with a lower preferred body temperature than most sympatric reptiles.

LIZARDS
(suborder SAURIA)

DRAGON LIZARDS
Family AGAMIDAE

1. Some dragons are able to remain active in hot weather by angling their bodies into the sun to reduce heat absorption. *Tympanocryptis tetraporophora*. Camooweal, Qld. (M. Hanlon)

2 *Caimanops amphiboluroides*. Mangaroon Station, WA. (G. Harold)

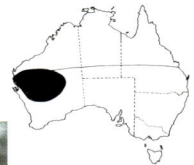

3 *Chelosania brunnea*. Nabarlek, NT. (G. Harold)

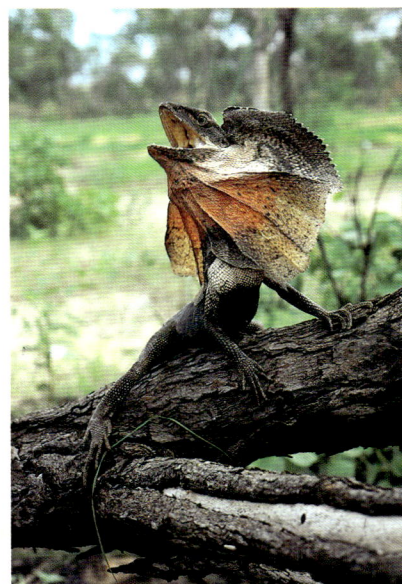

4 *Chlamydosaurus kingii* (enacting defensive display). Beagle Bay Mission, WA. (D. Knowles)

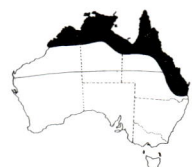

5 *Chlamydosaurus kingii* (juvenile in typical cryptic posture). Kununurra, WA. (S. Wilson)

6 *Cryptagama aurita*. Wave Hill, NT. (P. Horner)

7 *Ctenophorus caudicinctus caudicinctus* (adult male). Warambie Station, WA. (G. Harold)

8 *Ctenophorus caudicinctus mensarum* (female). Yeelirrie Station, WA. (P. Griffin)

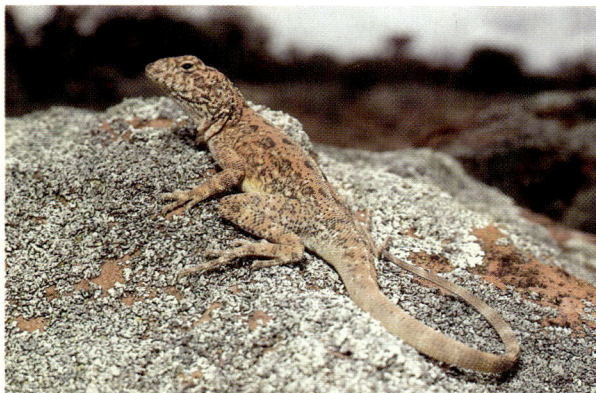

9 *Ctenophorus caudicinctus infans*. Laverton area, WA. (G. Harold)

10 *Ctenophorus caudicinctus slateri* (male). Barrow Creek, NT. (S. Wilson)

11 *Ctenophorus caudicinctus macropus*
(male). Halls Creek, WA.
(G. Harold)

12 *Ctenophorus caudicinctus macropus*
(female). Typical posture adopted
during hot weather. Turkey Creek
area, WA. (S. Wilson)

13 *Ctenophorus clayi*. Manberry Station,
WA. (P. Griffin)

14 *Ctenophorus
cristatus*.
Nundroo area,
SA. (S.
Wilson)

15 *Ctenophorus decresii* (mature male
of southern population). Adelaide
Hills, SA. (M. Hanlon)

16 *Ctenophorus femoralis*. Exmouth,
WA. (G. Harold)

17 *Ctenophorus fionni* (adult male of northern form). Bookaloo, SA. (G. Harold)

18 *Ctenophorus fionni* (adult male of central form). Darke Peak, SA. (M. Hanlon)

19 *Ctenophorus fionni* (female of central form). Darke Peak, SA. (M. Hanlon)

20 *Ctenophorus fionni* (adult male of western form). Streaky Bay area, SA. (M. Hanlon)

21 *Ctenophorus fordi* (male). Menzies area, WA. (S. Wilson)

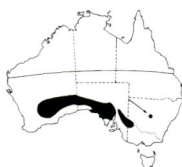

22 *Ctenophorus gibba*. Oodnadatta, SA. (G. Schmida)

23 *Ctenophorus isolepis isolepis* (male).
Nanutarra, WA. (G. Harold)

24 *Ctenophorus isolepis citrinus* (male).
Dedari, WA. (D. Knowles)

25 *Ctenophorus isolepis gularis* (male).
Big Shot Bore, WA. (G. Harold)

26 *Ctenophorus isolepis gularis* (female).
Laverton area, WA. (M. Hanlon)

27 *Ctenophorus maculatus maculatus.*
Tamala Station, WA. (D. Knowles)

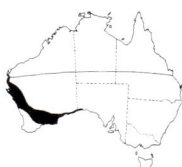

28 *Ctenophorus maculatus badius.*
Doorawarrah Station area, WA.
(G. Harold)

29 *Ctenophorus maculatus griseus* (male).
McDermid Rock, WA. (G. Harold)

30 *Ctenophorus maculatus dualis* (male).
Eucla area, WA. (M. Hanlon)

31 *Ctenophorus maculatus dualis*
(female). Eucla area, WA.
(M. Hanlon)

32 *Ctenophorus maculosus*. Lake Eyre,
SA. (R. Jenkins)

33 *Ctenophorus mckenziei*. Colona
Station, SA. (P. Canty)

34 *Ctenophorus nuchalis*. Fort Grey area,
NSW. (M. Swan)

210

35 *Ctenophorus ornatus* (adult male of southern and western form). Farrell Grove, WA. (S. Wilson)

36 *Ctenophorus ornatus* (adult male of wheat-belt form). Maranalgo Station, WA. (D. Knowles)

37 *Ctenophorus ornatus* (female of wheat-belt form). Ravensthorpe area, WA. (S. Wilson)

38 *Ctenophorus ornatus* (adult male of northern form). Paynes Find area, WA. (G. Harold)

39 *Ctenophorus ornatus* (adult male of Hospital Rocks form). Hospital Rocks, WA. (G. Harold)

40 *Ctenophorus pictus* (breeding male). Lake Amadeus, NT. (M. Gillam)

41 *Ctenophorus pictus* (female). Little
Desert National Park, Vic.
(S. Wilson)

42 *Ctenophorus reticulatus* (mature
male). Carnarvon area, WA.
(G. Harold)

43 *Ctenophorus reticulatus* (female).
Leonora area, WA. (P. Rankin)

44 *Ctenophorus rubens* (adult male).
Mardathuna Station, WA.
(G. Harold)

45 *Ctenophorus rufescens* (mature
female). Everard Ranges, SA.
(B. Miller)

46 *Ctenophorus salinarum* (breeding
male). Dedari, WA. (D. Knowles)

47 *Ctenophorus scutulatus.* Wooleen
Station, WA. (S. Wilson)

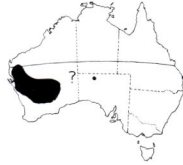

48 *Ctenophorus vadnappa* (adult male)
Flinders Ranges, SA. (J. Weigal)

49 *Ctenophorus yinnietharra* (adult
male). Yinnietharra Station, WA.
(G. Harold)

50 *Diporiphora albilabris albilabris.*
Drysdale River Station, WA.
(S. Wilson)

51 *Diporiphora albilabris sobria.* Adelaide
River area, NT. (G. Husband)

52 *Diporiphora arnhemica.* Nicholson
Station, WA. (R. Johnstone)

213

53 *Diporiphora australis*. Brisbane, Qld. (S. Wilson)

54 *Diporiphora bennettii* (adult male approaching breeding condition). Manning Creek Gorge, WA. (S. Wilson)

55 *Diporiphora bilineata*. Darwin, NT. (S. Wilson)

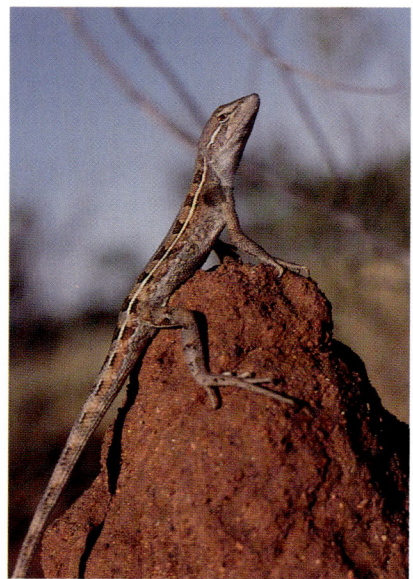

56 *Diporiphora lalliae*. Three Ways. NT. (S. Wilson)

57 *Diporiphora linga* (male). Immarna, SA. (B. Miller)

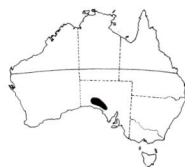

58 *Diporiphora magna* (mature male). Gibb River area, WA. (J. Weigal)

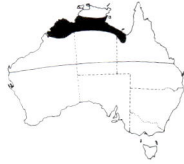

59 *Diporiphora pindan*. Fitzroy Crossing, WA. (G. Harold)

60 *Diporiphora reginae* (breeding male). Buningonia Spring, WA. (G. Harold)

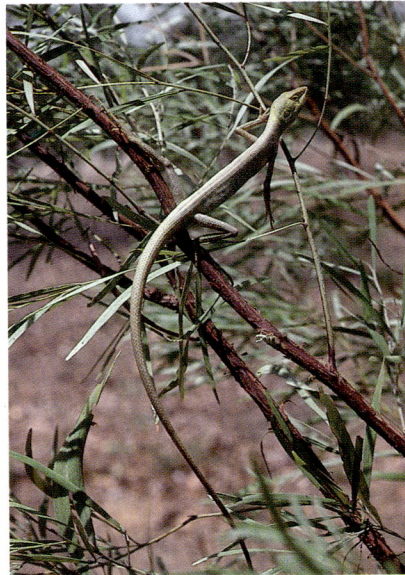

61 *Diporiphora superba*. Manning Creek Gorge, WA. (S. Wilson)

62 *Diporiphora valens*. Marandoo area, WA. (R. Johnstone)

63 *Diporiphora winneckei*. Yardie Creek, WA. (S. Wilson)

64 *Diporiphora* sp. (1), closely related to *D. bilineata* (mature male). Tip of Cape York, Qld. (S. Wilson)

65 *Diporiphora* sp. (2). Edward River, Qld. (J. Wombey)

66 *Gemmatophora gilberti gilberti* (typical colouration and form of females and juveniles). Mt North, WA. (G. Harold)

67 *Gemmatophora gilberti centralis* (mature male). Moonie district, Qld. (D. Knowles)

68 *Gemmatophora longirostris.* Port Hedland, WA. (G. Schmida)

69 *Gemmatophora muricata.* You Yangs, Vic. (S. Wilson)

70 *Gemmatophora nobbi nobbi* (breeding male). Crows Nest National Park, Qld. (D. Knowles)

71 *Gemmatophora nobbi coggeri.* Warrumbungle Mountains, NSW. (J. Bevan)

72 *Gemmatophora norrisi.* Eyre, WA. (G. Harold)

73 *Gemmatophora temporalis.* Weipa, Qld. (D. Knowles)

74 *Hypsilurus boydii.* Cairns, Qld.
(P. Horner)

75 *Hypsilurus spinipes.* Lamington
Plateau, Qld. (S. Wilson)

76 *Hypsilurus spinipes* (juvenile).
Cunningham's Gap, Qld.
(D. Knowles)

77 *Moloch horridus.* Kalbarri, WA.
(G. Schmida)

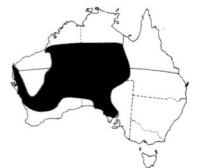

78 *Physignathus lesueurii lesueurii.*
Ourimbah, NSW. (S. Swanson)

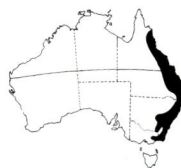

79 *Physignathus lesueurii howittii.*
Kangaroo Valley, NSW.
(G. Schmida)

80 *Pogona barbata* (mature male in
defensive posture). Kerang, Vic.
(M. Swan)

81 *Pogona microlepidota.* Prince Regent
River area, WA. (R. Johnstone)

82 *Pogona minor minor.* Forrestonia
area, WA. (P. Griffin)

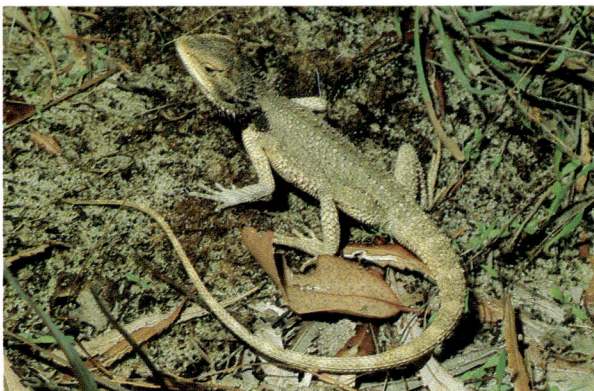

83 *Pogona minor minima.* Houtman
Abrolhos Islands, WA.
(G. Harold)

84 *Pogona minor mitchelli.* Bedford
Downs Station, WA. (S. Wilson)

85 *Pogona nullarbor*. Cocklebiddy area, WA. (J. Wombey)

86 *Pogona vitticeps* (in defensive stance). Wilcannia district, NSW. (M. Swan)

87 *Pogona* sp. Moderately small very robust *Pogona* with poorly developed 'beard'. Apparently restricted to deeply cracking clay soils (black-soil plains) in interior of Qld. Winton, Qld. (P. Horner)

88 *Tympanocryptis adelaidensis adelaidensis*. Perth area, WA. (S. Wilson)

89 *Tympanocryptis adelaidensis chapmani*. Eucla area, WA. (S. Wilson)

90 *Tympanocryptis butleri*. Steep Point, WA. (G. Harold)

91 *Tympanocryptis cephalus*. Mount Jackson, WA. (G. Harold)

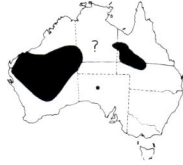

92 *Tympanocryptis cephalus* (in cryptic posture). Twin Peaks Station, WA (S. Wilson)

93 *Tympanocryptis diemensis*. Gosford, NSW.

94 *Tympanocryptis diemensis*. Flinders Island, Tas. (G. Shea)

95 *Tympanocryptis intima*. Marree, SA. (G. Harold)

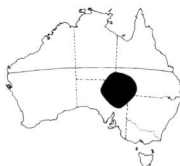

96 *Tympanocryptis lineata centralis*. Davenport Range, NT. (P. Horner)

97 *Tympanocryptis lineata houstoni.*
Cocklebiddy, WA. (M. Hanlon)

98 *Tympanocryptis lineata lineata.* Fort
Grey area, NSW. (M. Swan)

99 *Tympanocryptis lineata macra.* Mt
North, WA. (G. Harold)

100 *Tympanocryptis parviceps.* North
West Cape, WA. (S. Wilson)

101 *Tympanocryptis tetraporophora.*
Hughenden area, Qld.
(D. Knowles)

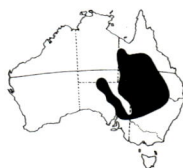

102 *Tympanocryptis uniformis.* Top
Springs, NT. (B. Miller)

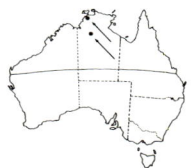

GECKOS
Family GEKKONIDAE

103 Australian geckos are largely nocturnal, with most activity occurring during the first few hours after sunset. Spiny-tailed gecko (*Diplodactylus ciliaris*). (M. Hanlon)

104 *Carphodactylus laevis*. Lake Barrine, Qld. (H. Cogger)

105 *Crenadactylus ocellatus horni* (with regenerated tail). East Yuna Nature Reserve, WA. (P. Griffin)

106 *Crenadactylus ocellatus ocellatus*. Darlington, WA. (J. Wombey)

107 *Crenadactylus ocellatus rostralis* (with regenerated tail). Halls Creek, WA. (P. Horner)

223

108 *Cyrtodactylus louisiadensis* (common form). Trevethan Range, Qld. (S. Crane)

109 *Diplodactylus alboguttatus* (with regenerated tail). Marchagee Reserve, WA. (S. Wilson)

110 *Diplodactylus assimilis*. Kalgoorlie, WA. (J. Weigal)

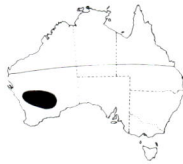

111 *Diplodactylus byrnei*. Roto, NSW. (H. Cogger)

112 *Diplodactylus ciliaris ciliaris*. Katherine, NT. (G. Schmida)

113 *Diplodactylus ciliaris aberrans*. North West Cape, WA. (P. Griffin)

114 *Diplodactylus conspicillatus.* Giralia Station, WA. (D. Knowles)

115 *Diplodactylus damaeus* (with regenerated tail). Developing egg clearly visible. Laverton district, WA. (S. Wilson)

116 *Diplodactylus elderi.* Coombah area, NSW. (G. Shea)

117 *Diplodactylus fulleri* (with regenerated tail). Lake Disappointment, WA. (G. Barron)

118 *Diplodactylus galeatus.* Alice Springs, NT. (P. Rankin)

119 *Diplodactylus granariensis* (northern form). Mt Jackson, WA. (S. Wilson)

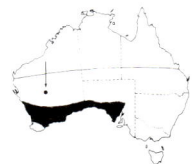

120 *Diplodactylus granariensis* (southern form). Eucla, WA. (G. Harold)

121 *Diplodactylus intermedius*. Iron Knob, SA. (S. Wilson)

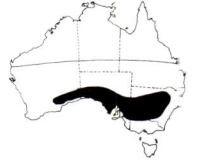

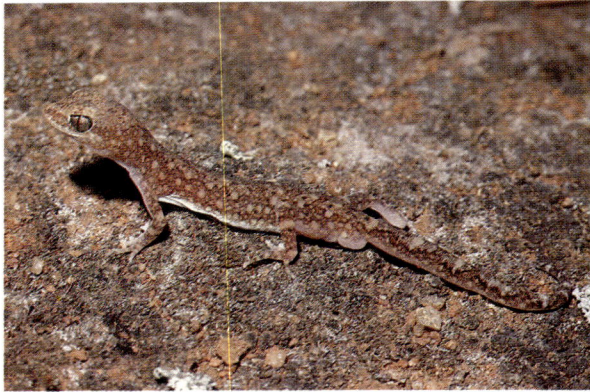

122 *Diplodactylus maini*. Mt Jackson, WA. (G. Harold)

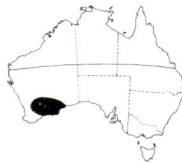

123 *Diplodactylus mcmillani*. Mt Barnett Station, WA. (J. Weigal)

124 *Diplodactylus michaelseni* (with regenerated tail). Marchagee Reserve, WA. (P. Griffin)

125 *Diplodactylus mitchelli*. North West Cape, WA. (P. Griffin)

126 *Diplodactylus occultus*. Kapalga, NT. (J. Wombey)

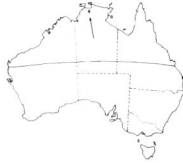

127 *Diplodactylus ornatus*. Cararang Station, WA. (D. Knowles)

128 *Diplodactylus polyophthalmus*. Kalamunda, WA. (M. Hanlon)

129 *Diplodactylus pulcher*. Diemals, WA. (S. Wilson)

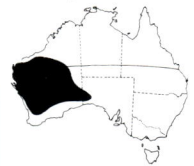

130 *Diplodactylus pulcher*. Edah Station, WA. (G. Harold)

131 *Diplodactylus rankini* (in typical cryptic posture adopted during daylight hours). North West Cape, WA. (S. Wilson).

132 *Diplodactylus savagei*. Pannawonica, WA. (S. Wilson)

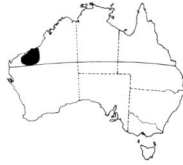

133 *Diplodactylus spinigerus* (white-eyed form). Shark Bay, WA. (D. Knowles)

134 *Diplodactylus spinigerus* (yellow-eyed form) cleaning eye. Yanchep, WA. (S. Wilson)

135 *Diplodactylus squarrosus*. Thundelarra Station, WA. (S. Wilson)

136 *Diplodactylus steindachneri*. Edungalba, Qld. (M. Hanlon)

137 *Diplodactylus stenodactylus* (widespread form with bold pattern). Giralia Station, WA. (D. Knowles)

138 *Diplodactylus stenodactylus* (eastern form). St George district, Qld. (J. Weigal)

139 *Diplodactylus strophurus*. North West Cape, WA. (J. Weigal)

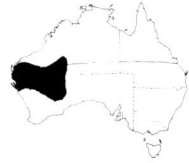

140 *Diplodactylus taeniatus*. Lissadell Station, WA. (P. Griffin)

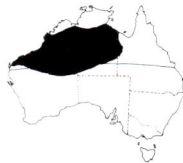

141 *Diplodactylus taenicauda*. St George area, Qld. (J. Weigal)

142 *Diplodactylus tessellatus*. Renner Springs, NT. (G. Harold)

143 *Diplodactylus tessellatus*. Glenmorgan, Qld. (D. Knowles)

144 *Diplodactylus vittatus.*
Warrumbungle National Park,
NSW. (S. Wilson)

145 *Diplodactylus wellingtonae.* Wiluna,
WA. (M. Hanlon)

146 *Diplodactylus williamsi.*
Warrumbungle National Park,
NSW. (D. Knowles)

147 *Diplodactylus wilsoni* (holotype).
Waldburg Station, WA.
(S. Wilson)

148 *Diplodactylus wombeyi.* Nullagine
district, WA. (G. Harold)

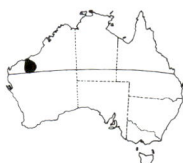

149 *Diplodactylus* sp. (1). Member of
D. strophurus group, allied to *D.
ciliaris.* Diamantina Lakes, Qld.
(D. Knowles)

150 *Gehyra australis*. Halls Creek, WA. (S. Wilson)

151 *Gehyra baliola*. Murray Island, Qld. (H. Cogger)

152 *Gehyra borroloola*. Limmen Bight River, NT. (D. Knowles)

153 *Gehyra catenata*. Lochnager Station, Qld. (T. Low)

154 *Gehyra dubia* (with regenerated tail). Westmar, Qld. (S. Wilson)

155 *Gehyra minuta*. Barry Caves, NT. (S. Wilson)

156 *Gehyra montium.* Davenport Ranges, NT. (P. Horner)

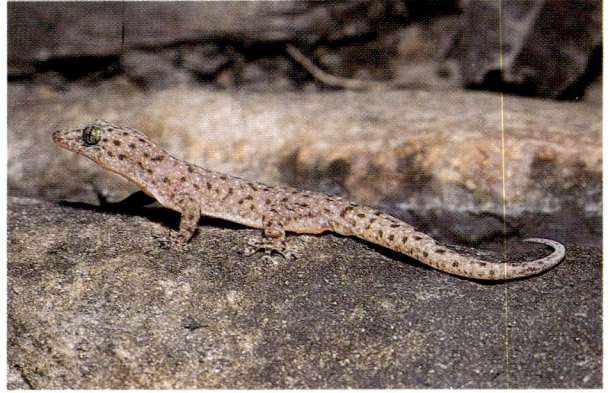

157 *Gehyra nana.* Mt Daglish, WA. (G. Harold)

158 *Gehyra occidentalis* (with portion of tail regenerated). Mt Daglish, WA. (G. Harold)

159 *Gehyra oceanica* (with regenerated tail). Nadi, Fiji. (M. Hanlon)

160 *Gehyra pamela.* Nabarlek, NT. (G. Harold)

161 *Gehyra pilbara* (adult with obscure pattern). Warroora Station, WA. (G. Harold)

162 *Gehyra punctata*. Wittenoom
Gorge, WA. (G. Harold)

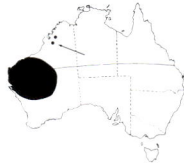

163 *Gehyra punctata* (boldly marked
southern form). Wooramel River,
WA. (D. Knowles)

164 *Gehyra purpurascens*. Davenport
Ranges, NT. (P. Horner)

165 *Gehyra robusta*. Cloncurry, Qld.
(S. Wilson)

166 *Gehyra robusta*. Winton area, Qld.
(D. Knowles)

167 *Gehyra variegata* (eastern form).
Cobar, NSW. (G. Schmida)

168 *Gehyra variegata* (western form). White Cliffs Station, WA. (J. Weigal)

169 *Gehyra xenopus* (with regenerated tail). Mitchell Plateau, WA. (P. Griffin)

170 *Gehyra* sp. (1). Arboreal. Lissadell Station, WA. (S. Wilson)

171 *Gehyra* sp. (2). Arboreal. Berri Springs, NT. (S. Wilson)

172 *Gehyra* sp. (3). Arboreal and rock-inhabiting. Tip of Cape York Peninsula, Qld. (D. Knowles)

173 *Hemidactylus frenatus*. Darwin, NT. (S. Wilson)

234

174 *Heteronotia binoei*. Maranalgo Station, WA. (D. Knowles)

175 *Heteronotia binoei*. Drysdale River Station, WA. (S. Wilson)

176 *Heteronotia binoei*. Mueller's Range, Qld. (D. Knowles)

177 *Heteronotia binoei*. Westmar, Qld. (S. Wilson)

178 *Heteronotia spelea*. Pannawonica, WA. (S. Wilson)

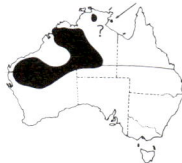

179 *Lepidodactylus lugubris* (containing well-developed egg). Tip of Cape York Peninsula, Qld. (D. Knowles).

180 *Lepidodactylus pumilus*. Torres Strait, Qld. (A. Greer)

181 *Nactus arnouxii*. Tip of Cape York Peninsula, Qld. (S. Wilson)

182 *Nactus galgajuga*. Trevethan Range. Qld. (M. Golding)

183 *Nephrurus asper* (enacting threat posture typical of genus). Moura, Qld. (D. Knowles)

184 *Nephrurus deleani*. Mt Gunson area, vicinity of Pernatty Lagoon, SA. (G. Shea)

185 *Nephrurus laevissimus*. Laverton area, WA. (D. Knowles)

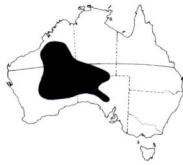

186 *Nephrurus levis levis*. Kulgera, NT.
(G. Harold)

187 *Nephrurus levis occidentalis*. Male is endeavouring to copulate,
while female (with regenerated tail) is enacting a defensive
response to the photographer. Size disparity reflects
individual variation rather than sexual dimorphism. Cardabia
Station, WA. (D. Knowles)

188 *Nephrurus levis pilbarensis* (cleaning
eye). De Grey River, WA.
(S. Wilson)

189 *Nephrurus stellatus* (western form).
Mt Holland area, WA.
(D. Knowles)

190 *Nephrurus stellatus* (eastern form).
Kimba area, SA. (S. Wilson)

191 *Nephrurus vertebralis*. Morawa,
WA. (P. Griffin)

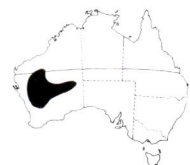

192 *Nephrurus wheeleri wheeleri*. Ned's
Creek Station, WA. (S. Wilson)

193 *Nephrurus wheeleri cinctus*.
Pannawonica, WA. (G. Harold)

194 *Oedura castelnaui* (with regenerated
tail). Chillagoe, Qld. (D. Knowles)

195 *Oedura coggeri*. Chillagoe, Qld.
(D. Knowles)

196 *Oedura filicipoda* (holotype).
Mitchell Plateau, WA.
(J. Wombey)

197 *Oedura filicipoda*. Detail of unique
fringed toes. (J. Wombey)

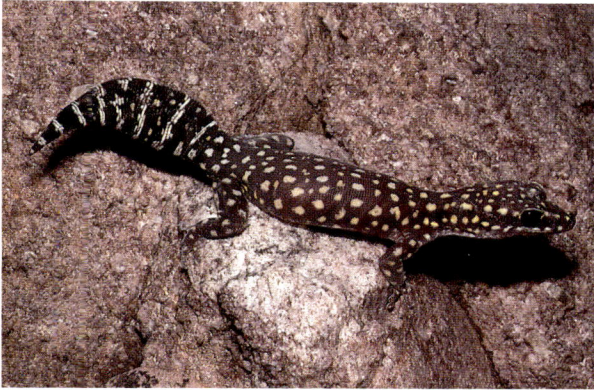

198 *Oedura gemmata*. E1 Sharana area, NT. (S. Wilson)

199 *Oedura gracilis*. Mt Daglish area, WA. (G. Harold)

200 *Oedura lesueurii*. Amiens, Qld. (G. Harold)

201 *Oedura marmorata*. Westmar, Qld. (D. Knowles)

202 *Oedura marmorata*. Edah Station, WA. (S. Wilson)

203 *Oedura monilis* (with regenerated tail). Warrumbungle National Park, NSW. (D. Knowles)

204 *Oedura obscura.* Mt Daglish area, WA. (G. Harold)

205 *Oedura reticulata* (with regenerated tail). Lake Cronin, WA. (R. Jenkins)

206 *Oedura rhombifer.* Cracow, Qld. (M. Stewart-Jones)

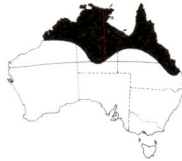

207 *Oedura robusta* (rock-inhabiting population). Isla Gorge National Park, Qld. (S. Wilson)

208 *Oedura tryoni.* Mt Nebo, Qld. (D. Knowles)

209 *Oedura* sp. (1) (with regenerated tail). Allied to *O. rhombifer.* Beerwah district, Qld. (S. Wilson)

210 *Phyllodactylus marmoratus marmoratus* (with regenerated tail). Boundary Bend, Vic. (S. Wilson)

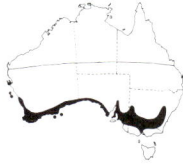

211 *Phyllodactylus marmoratus marmoratus*. Perth, WA. (P. Griffin)

212 *Phyllodactylus marmoratus alexanderi*. Eucla, WA. (G. Harold)

213 *Phyllurus caudiannulatus* (northern form). Eungella National Park, Qld. (T. Helder)

214 *Phyllurus caudiannulatus* (southern form). Bulburin State Forest, Qld. (S. Wilson)

215 *Phyllurus cornutus* (southern form). Mt Warning, NSW. (D. Knowles)

216 *Phyllurus cornutus* (Granite Belt form, with regenerated tail). Girraween National Park, Qld. (S. Wilson)

217 *Phyllurus cornutus* (northern form, with regenerated tail). The disruptive pattern and outline effectively camouflage these geckos against the variegated surfaces on which they forage. Kuranda, Qld. (D. Knowles)

218 *Phyllurus platurus*. Sydney, NSW. (S. Wilson)

219 *Phyllurus salebrosus* (with regenerated tail). Blackdown Tableland National Park, Qld. (D. Knowles)

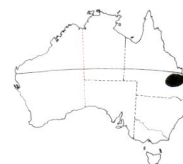

220 *Pseudothecadactylus australis*. Lockerbie Scrub, Cape York Peninsula, Qld. (D. Knowles)

221 *Pseudothecadactylus lindneri lindneri*. E1 Sharana district, NT. (S. Wilson)

223 *Rhynchoedura ornata* (cleaning eye).
Paynes Find, WA. (D. Knowles)

222 *Pseudothecadactylus lindneri cavaticus*. Mitchell Plateau, WA.
(R. Johnstone)

224 *Underwoodisaurus milii*. White
Cliffs Station, WA. (J. Weigal)

225 *Underwoodisaurus sphyrurus*
(enacting threat response).
Amiens, Qld. (M. Hanlon)

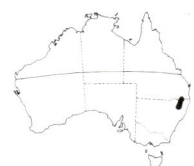

LEGLESS LIZARDS
Family PYGOPODIDAE

226 Active mimicry of snakes is practised by several pygopodids, including *Paradelma orientalis*. The obvious ear opening and thick fleshy tongue provide clues to its true identity. Cracow, Qld. (S. Wilson)

227 *Aclys concinna concinna*. Mt Peron, WA. (S. Wilson)

228 *Aprasia haroldi*. False Entrance Well, WA. (G. Harold)

229 *Aprasia inaurita* (with portion of tail regenerated). Billiatt National Park, SA. (J. Wombey)

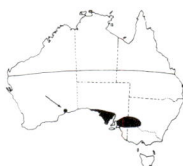

230 *Aprasia parapulchella*. Coppins Crossing, ACT. (D. Knowles)

231 *Aprasia pseudopulchella*. Mt Bryan area, SA. (G. Schmida)

232 *Aprasia pulchella*. Perth, WA. (M. Hanlon)

233 *Aprasia repens*. Koondoola, WA. (G. Harold)

234 *Aprasia rostrata fusca*. Bullara Station, WA. (P. Griffin)

p.36–40

ARS6

235 *Aprasia smithi*. Coolamia Station, WA. (G. Harold)

236 *Aprasia striolata* (typical striped form of eastern Australia). Port Lincoln area, SA. (J. Wombey)

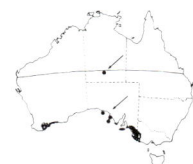

237 *Aprasia striolata* (patternless form of WA). Emu Point, WA. (G. Harold)

238 *Delma australis*. Lort River, WA. (P. Griffin)

239 *Delma borea*. Mt Isa, Qld. (S. Wilson)

240 *Delma butleri*. Yuinmery, WA. (G. Harold)

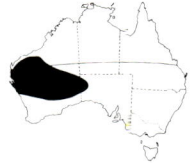

241 *Delma elegans*. Paraburdoo district, WA. (G. Harold)

242 *Delma fraseri*. Melaleuca Park, WA. (S. Wilson)

243 *Delma grayii*. Green Head, WA. (G. Harold)

244 *Delma haroldi*. Barradale, WA. (R. Johnstone)

245 *Delma impar*. Deer Park, Vic. (J. Bevan)

246 *Delma inornata*. Big Desert, Vic. (J. Bevan)

247 *Delma molleri*. Adelaide, SA.
(G. Shea)

248 *Delma nasuta*. The use of the tongue to clean the eye or snout is unique to legless lizards and geckos. North West Cape, WA.
(D. Knowles)

249 *Delma pax*. Marble Bar, WA.
(G. Harold)

250 *Delma plebeia* (northern population). Westmar, Qld.
(D. Knowles)

251 *Delma tincta*. Northampton, WA.
(G. Harold)

252 *Delma tincta* with reduced head pattern. The Range Station, WA.
(P. Griffin)

253 *Delma torquata* (with portion of tail regenerated). Mt Crosby, Qld. (S. Wilson)

254 *Lialis burtonis.* Cracow, Qld. (S. Wilson)

255 *Lialis burtonis.* North West Cape, WA. (D. Knowles)

256 *Lialis burtonis.* Nanutarra, WA. (G. Harold)

257 *Lialis burtonis.* King Leopold Ranges, WA. (J. Weigal)

258 *Ophidiocephalus taeniatus.* Abminga, SA. (D. Knowles)

259 *Paradelma orientalis.* Cracow, Qld. (S. Wilson)

260 *Pletholax gracilis gracilis.* Winchester, WA. (G. Harold)

261 *Pygopus lepidopodus* (heathland form). McDermid Rock, WA. (G. Harold)

262 *Pygopus lepidopodus* (plain form) Mt Nebo, Qld. (S. Wilson)

263 *Pygopus nigriceps schraderi.* Wilcannia, NSW. (P. Rankin)

264 *Pygopus nigriceps* (intermediate form). Wyndham, WA. (G. Harold)

SKINKS
Family SCINCIDAE

265 *Anomalopus brevicollis* (with regenerated tail-tip). Cracow, Qld. (S. Wilson)

266 *Anomalopus gowi* (with regenerated tail-tip). Forty Mile Scrub, Qld. (H. Cogger).

267 *Anomalopus leuckartii*. Bakers Creek, New England Tablelands, NSW. (D. Knowles)

268 *Anomalopus mackayi*. Oakey district, Qld. (S. Wilson)

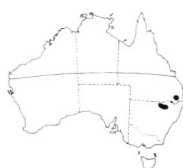

269 *Anomalopus pluto*. Heathlands area, Qld. (H. Cogger)

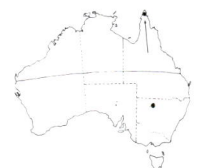

270 *Anomalopus swansoni*. Denman, NSW. (S. Wilson).

271 *Anomalopus verreauxii*. Oakey area, Qld. (D. Knowles)

272 *Calyptotis lepidorostrum*. Kroombit Tops, Qld. (S. Wilson)

273 *Calyptotis ruficauda*. Brinerville, NSW. (G. Shea)

274 *Calyptotis scutirostrum*. Mt Nebo, Qld. (S. Wilson)

275 *Calyptotis temporalis*. Yeppoon area, Qld. (D. Knowles)

276 *Calyptotis thorntonensis*. Thornton
Peak, Qld. (S. Wilson)

277 *Carlia aerata*. Mt Mulligan, Qld.
(S. Wilson)

278 *Carlia amax*. E1 Sharana, NT.
(S. Wilson)

279 *Carlia bicarinata* (male). Cairns,
Qld. (S. Wilson)

280 *Carlia coensis*. Coen area, Qld.
(D. Knowles)

281 *Carlia dogare* (male approaching
breeding condition). Lizard Island,
Qld. (Queensland Museum)

282 *Carlia dogare* (female). Lizard
Island, Qld. (Queensland
Museum)

283 *Carlia foliorum*. Peak Ranges, Qld.
(D. Knowles)

284 *Carlia gracilis* (male approaching
breeding colouration). South
Alligator River, NT. (S. Wilson)

285 *Carlia jarnoldae* (mature male).
Petford, Qld. (S. Wilson)

286 *Carlia jarnoldae* (female).
Chillagoe, Qld. (D. Knowles)

287 *Carlia johnstonei* (breeding male).
Manning Creek, WA. (S. Wilson)

288 *Carlia laevis* (breeding male).
Kuranda, Qld. (S. Wilson)

289 *Carlia longipes* (breeding male).
Tip of Cape York Peninsula, Qld.
(D. Knowles)

290 *Carlia macfarlani* (male approaching
breeding condition). Tip of Cape
York Peninsula, Qld. (D. Knowles)

291 *Carlia macfarlani* (female or non-
breeding male). Tip of Cape York
Peninsula, Qld. (S. Wilson)

292 *Carlia munda* (breeding male with regenerated tail). Kapalga, NT. (J. Wombey)

293 *Carlia mundivensis*. Chillagoe, Qld. (D. Knowles)

294 *Carlia pectoralis* (male approaching breeding colouration). Murgon, Qld. (S. Wilson)

295 *Carlia pectoralis* (female). Carnarvon National Park, Qld. (S. Wilson)

296 *Carlia rhomboidalis* (male, and female or non-breeding male of southern form). Eungella, Qld. (D. Knowles)

297 *Carlia rhomboidalis* (northern form). Thornton Peak, Qld. (S. Wilson)

298 *Carlia rimula*. Coen area, Qld. (Queensland Museum)

299 *Carlia rostralis* (breeding male). Kuranda, Qld. (D. Knowles)

300 *Carlia rufilatus* (breeding male). Nabarlek, NT. (G. Harold)

302 *Carlia schmeltzii prava*. Chillagoe, Qld. (D. Knowles)

301 *Carlia schmeltzii schmeltzii* (mature male). (G. Schmida)

303 *Carlia scirtetis*. Black Mountain, Qld. (D. Knowles)

304 *Carlia tetradactyla* (breeding male). Oakey, Qld. (M. Stewart-Jones)

305 *Carlia triacantha* (breeding male). Kapalga, NT. (J. Wombey)

306 *Carlia vivax* (male approaching breeding colouration). Stradbroke Island, Qld. (D. Knowles)

307 *Carlia vivax* (female). Fraser Island, Qld. (D. Knowles)

308 *Carlia* sp. (1). Rock-inhabiting. Chillagoe, Qld. (S. Wilson)

258

309 *Carlia* sp. (2). Small leaf-litter inhabiting species, favouring monsoon forests and vine thickets of northern Cape York Peninsula, Qld. Closely related to *C. aerata*, *C. laevis* and *C. macfarlani*. Lockerbie Scrub, Qld. (D. Knowles)

310 *Carlia* sp. (3). Small leaf-litter inhabiting species favouring woodlands and dry sclerophyll forests of south-eastern Cape York Peninsula, Qld. Closely related to *C. aerata*, *C. laevis* and *C. macfarlani*. Cooktown, Qld. (S. Wilson)

311 *Coeranoscincus frontalis*. Mt Spec, Qld. (D. Knowles)

312 *Coeranoscincus frontalis* (juvenile). Western slopes of Mt Bartle Frere, Qld. (Queensland Museum)

313 *Coeranoscincus reticulatus* (adult and juvenile). Cunningham's Gap, Qld. (S. Wilson)

314 *Cryptoblepharus carnabyi*. Westmar, Qld. (D. Knowles)

315 *Cryptoblepharus fuhni.* Cape Melville, Qld. (Queensland Museum collection)

316 *Cryptoblepharus litoralis.* Tip of Cape York Peninsula, Qld. (S. Wilson)

317 *Cryptoblepharus megastictus.* Glenroy Station, Qld. (D. Knowles)

318 *Cryptoblepharus plagiocephalus.* Nicholson area, WA. (M. Hanlon)

319 *Cryptoblepharus plagiocephalus.* Collie, WA. (G. Harold)

320 *Cryptoblepharus virgatus virgatus.* Tip of Cape York Peninsula, Qld. (S. Wilson)

321 *Cryptoblepharus virgatus clarus* (with portion of tail regenerated). Eucla, WA. (G. Harold)

322 *Ctenotus alacer* (with portion of tail regenerated). Alice Springs, NT. (G. Harold)

323 *Ctenotus alleni*. Yuna district, WA. (A. Burbidge)

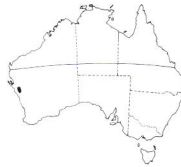

324 *Ctenotus allotropis*. Hollymount Station, Qld. (D. Knowles)

325 *Ctenotus arcanus*. Kroombit Tops, Qld. (S. Wilson)

326 *Ctenotus arcanus*. Stradbroke Island, Qld. (S. Wilson)

261

327 *Ctenotus ariadnae* (with regenerated tail-tip). Ethabuka Station, Qld. (G. Shea)

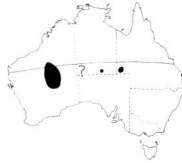

328 *Ctenotus arnhemensis*. Kakadu National Park, NT. (J. Wombey)

329 *Ctenotus astarte*. Boulia, Qld. (J. Weigal).

330 *Ctenotus atlas* (with portion of tail regenerated). Mt Jackson, WA. (G. Harold)

331 *Ctenotus borealis*. Bathurst Island, NT. (P. Horner).

332 *Ctenotus brachyonyx* (with portion of tail regenerated). Lake Mungo area, NSW. (G. Shea)

333 *Ctenotus brooksi brooksi.* Comet Vale, WA. (G. Harold)

334 *Ctenotus brooksi euclae.* Eucla, WA. (G. Harold)

335 *Ctenotus brooksi iridis* (with portion of tail regenerated). Big Billy Bore, Vic. (M. Swan)

336 *Ctenotus burbidgei* (with portion of tail regenerated). Mt Daglish area, WA. (G. Harold)

337 *Ctenotus calurus.* George Gill Ranges, NT. (P. Horner)

338 *Ctenotus capricorni.* Jericho district (type locality), Qld. (D. Knowles)

339 *Ctenotus catenifer*. Emu Point, WA. (G. Harold)

340 *Ctenotus coggeri*. Obiri Creek, Kakadu National Park, NT. (J. Wombey).

341 *Ctenotus colletti nasutus*. White Cliffs Station, WA. (P. Rankin)

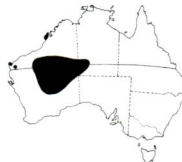

342 *Ctenotus colletti rufescens*. Giralia Station, WA. (M. Hanlon)

343 *Ctenotus decaneurus*. Muellers Range, Winton District, Qld. (D. Knowles)

344 *Ctenotus delli*. Kalamunda, WA. (S. Wilson)

345 *Ctenotus duricola.* Yardie Creek, WA. (D. Knowles)

346 *Ctenotus dux.* Alice Springs area, NT. (R. Jenkins)

347 *Ctenotus essingtonii brevipes.* Chillagoe district, Qld. (S. Crane)

348 *Ctenotus essingtonii essingtonii.* Darwin, NT. (S. Wilson)

349 *Ctenotus eurydice.* Walcha, NSW. (G. Shea)

350 *Ctenotus eutaenius.* Magnetic Island, Qld. (D. Knowles)

351 *Ctenotus fallens*. Rottnest Island, WA. (S. Wilson)

352 *Ctenotus gagudju*. Nourlangie, Kakadu National Park, NT. (J. Wombey).

353 *Ctenotus gemmula*. Wanneroo area, WA. (S. Wilson)

354 *Ctenotus grandis grandis* (with regenerated tail-tip). Laverton district, WA. (D. Knowles)

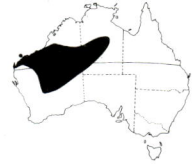

355 *Ctenotus grandis titan*. Pannawonica, WA. (G. Harold)

356 *Ctenotus greeri*. Mt Linden, WA. (G. Harold)

357 *Ctenotus hanloni*. Giralia Station, WA. (G. Harold)

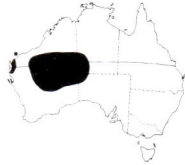

358 *Ctenotus hebetior hebetior* (holotype). Fermoy Station, Qld. (G. Harold)

359 *Ctenotus hebetior* (subsp. ?). Mary Kathleen Dam, Qld. (D. Knowles)

360 *Ctenotus helenae*. Giralia Station, WA. (S. Wilson)

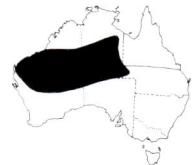

361 *Ctenotus hilli*. Darwin, NT. (S. Wilson)

362 *Ctenotus iapetus*. Exmouth, WA. (G. Harold)

363 *Ctenotus impar.* Israelite Bay, WA. (G. Harold)

364 *Ctenotus ingrami.* Hollymount Station, Qld. (D. Knowles)

365 *Ctenotus inornatus.* Lissadell Station, WA. (P. Griffin)

366 *Ctenotus joanae.* Avon Downs Station area, NT. (H. Ehmann)

367 *Ctenotus kurnbudj.* Kapalga area, NT. (J. Wombey)

368 *Ctenotus labillardieri* (northern form). Mt Dale, WA. (S. Wilson)

369 *Ctenotus lancelini*. Lancelin Island, WA. (R. Johnstone)

370 *Ctenotus lateralis* (with portion of tail regenerated). Mt Isa, Qld. (P. Rankin)

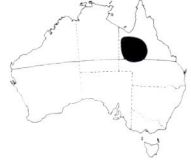

371 *Ctenotus leae*. Ethabuka Station, Qld. (G. Shea)

372 *Ctenotus leonhardii*. Zanthus district, WA. (G. Harold)

373 *Ctenotus leonhardii* (?). Diamantina Lakes Station, Qld. (D. Knowles)

374 *Ctenotus lesueurii*. Dirk Hartog Island, WA. (G. Harold)

269

375 *Ctenotus mastigura*. Mitchell
Plateau, WA. (P. Griffin)

376 *Ctenotus militaris*. Lissadell Station,
WA. (P. Griffin)

377 *Ctenotus mimetes* (with portion of
tail regenerated). Yellowdine
district, WA. (G. Harold)

378 *Ctenotus monticola*. Mareeba, Qld.
(S. Wilson)

379 *Ctenotus pantherinus calx*. Coolibah
Station, NT. (M. Hanlon)

380 *Ctenotus pantherinus ocellifer*. White
Cliffs Station, WA. (G. Harold)

381 *Ctenotus pantherinus pantherinus* (with portion of tail regenerated). Jurien Bay district, WA. (P. Griffin)

382 *Ctenotus piankai*. Lissadell Station, WA. (P. Griffin)

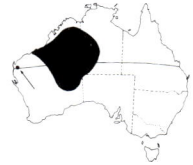

383 *Ctenotus pulchellus*. Mt Isa district, Qld. (D. Knowles)

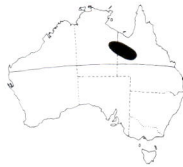

384 *Ctenotus quattuordecimlineatus* (with regenerated tail-tip). Big Shot Bore, WA. (G. Harold)

335 *Ctenotus quinkan*. Laura area, Qld. (G. Harold)

386 *Ctenotus rawlinsoni*. (S. Donnellan)

271

387 *Ctenotus regius*. St George district, Qld. (S. Wilson)

388 *Ctenotus robustus* (from north-west of range). The reddish colouration behind the forelimb is a colony of mites. Mitchell Plateau, WA. (G. Harold)

389 *Ctenotus robustus* (from central-east of range). Girraween National Park, Qld. (S. Wilson)

390 *Ctenotus robustus* (inornate east coast and island form). Harrington, NSW. (P. Rankin)

391 *Ctenotus rubicundus*. Mt Herbert, WA. (G. Harold)

392 *Ctenotus rutilans*. Joffre Falls, Hamersley Ranges, WA. (D. Knowles)

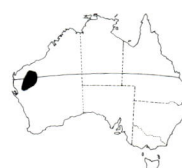

393 *Ctenotus saxatilis*. North West Cape, WA. (S. Wilson)

394 *Ctenotus schevilli*. Muttaburra area, Qld. (H. Cogger)

395 *Ctenotus schomburgkii* (western form). Yalgoo district, WA. (P. Griffin)

396 *Ctenotus schomburgkii* (south-western form). Hyden area, WA. (S. Wilson)

397 *Ctenotus schomburgkii* (eastern form). Big Shot Bore, WA. (G. Harold)

398 *Ctenotus serotinus* (holotype). Spring Valley Station, Qld. (D. Knowles)

273

399 *Ctenotus serventyi*. Fitzroy Crossing, WA. (P. Griffin)

400 *Ctenotus severus* (with portion of tail regenerated). Paynes Find district, WA. (G. Harold)

401 *Ctenotus spaldingi*. Tip of Cape York Peninsula, Qld. (D. Knowles)

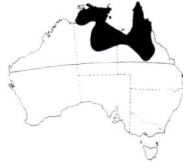

402 *Ctenotus spaldingi*. Chillagoe, Qld. (D. Knowles)

403 *Ctenotus spaldingi*. Wrotham Park Station, Qld. (S. Wilson)

404 *Ctenotus storri*. Mandorah, NT. (S. Wilson)

405 *Ctenotus strauchii strauchii.*
Belyando Star, Qld. (S. Wilson)

406 *Ctenotus strauchii varius* (with
regenerating tail-tip). Oodnadatta,
SA. (P. Rankin)

407 *Ctenotus striaticeps.* Mt Isa district,
Qld. (D. Knowles)

408 *Ctenotus taeniolatus.* Sydney, NSW.
(S. Wilson)

409 *Ctenotus taeniolatus.* Cooloola
National Park, Qld. (S. Wilson)

410 *Ctenotus tanamiensis.* Tanami
Desert, NT. (Australian Museum
collection, G. Shea)

411 *Ctenotus tantillus*. Kununurra district, WA. (S. Wilson)

412 *Ctenotus uber johnstonei* (holotype, with regenerating tail-tip). Balgo, WA. (R. Johnstone)

413 *Ctenotus uber orientalis*. Middle Beach, SA. (G. Shea)

414 *Ctenotus uber uber*. Lake Goongarrie, WA. (G. Harold)

415 *Ctenotus vertebralis*. UDP Falls, NT. (S. Wilson)

416 *Ctenotus xenopleura*. Bungalbin, WA. (G. Harold)

417 *Ctenotus yampiensis*. Mt Elizabeth Station area, WA. (H. Ehmann)

418 *Ctenotus youngsoni* (with regenerated tail). Tamala Station, WA. (G. Harold)

419 *Ctenotus zastictus* (holotype). Hamelin Pool area, WA. (G. Harold)

420 *Ctenotus zebrilla*. Chillagoe district, Qld. (J. Weigal)

421 *Ctenotus* sp. (1). Member of *C. leonhardii* group. Herbert Downs Station, Qld. (D. Knowles)

422 *Ctenotus* sp. (2). Member of *C. lesueurii* group. Occurs on deeply cracking clay soils in central Qld. Aramac, Qld. (S. Wilson).

423 *Ctenotus* sp. (3). Species group indeterminate. Granite Gorge, Mareeba area, Qld. (S. Wilson)

424 *Ctenotus* sp. (4). Member of *C. lesueurii* group. Isabella Falls, Cooktown area, Qld. (D. Knowles)

425 *Ctenotus* sp. (5). Member of *C. lesueurii* group, closely allied to *C. brachyonyx*. Charleville area, Qld. (D. Knowles)

426 *Ctenotus* sp. (6). Member of *C. lesueurii* group. Hinchinbrook Island, Qld. (S. Wilson)

427 *Ctenotus* sp. (7). Member of *C. atlas* group. Winton area, Qld. (D. Knowles)

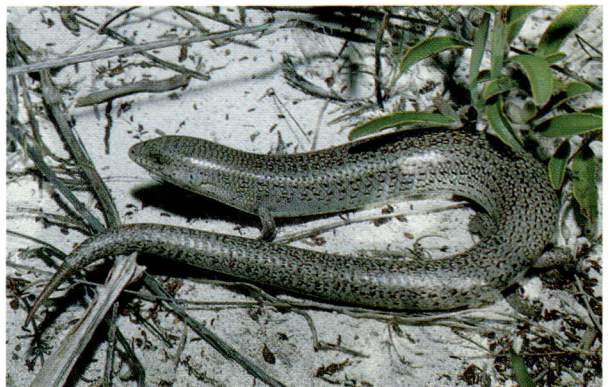

428 *Cyclodomorphus branchialis*. Green Head, WA. (S. Wilson)

278

429 *Cyclodomorphus casuarinae.* Gosford, NSW. (J. Weigal)

430 *Cyclodomorphus gerrardii.* Cairns area, Qld. (G. Schmida)

431 *Cyclodomorphus maximus.* Mitchell Plateau, WA. (P. Griffin)

433 *Cyclodomorphus melanops* (juvenile). Brooking Springs Station, WA. (P. Griffin)

432 *Cyclodomorphus melanops.* Millstream, WA. (S. Wilson)

279

434 *Cyclodomorphus* sp. A common, though undescribed species from south-eastern SA. Port Pirie, SA. (G. Shea)

435 *Egernia coventryi*. Boneo, Vic. (J. Wombey)

436 *Egernia cunninghami cunninghami* (northern NSW and south-east Qld Granite Belt form). Girraween National Park, Qld. (S. Wilson)

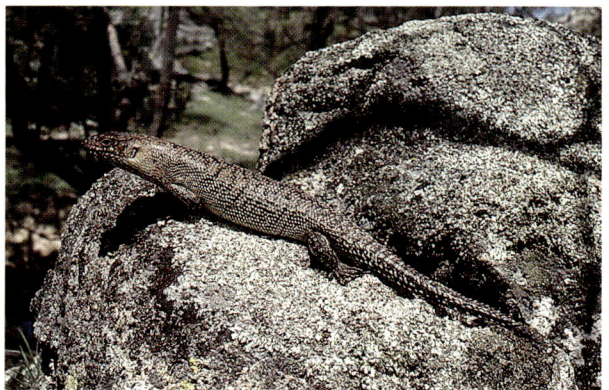

437 *Egernia cunninghami cunninghami* (widespread southern form). Collector, NSW. (J. Weigal)

438 *Egernia cunninghami krefftii*. Gosford area, NSW. (J. Weigal)

439 *Egernia depressa* (southern form). Meadow Station, WA. (J. Weigal)

440 *Egernia depressa* (northern form).
Urala Station, WA. (P. Griffin)

441 *Egernia formosa* (southern form).
White Cliffs Station, WA.
(G. Harold)

442 *Egernia formosa* (Pilbara form).
Joffre Gorge, WA. (D. Knowles)

443 *Egernia frerei*. Mt Glorious, Qld.
(S. Wilson)

444 *Egernia frerei*. Weipa, Qld.
(D. Knowles)

445 *Egernia hosmeri*. Mt Isa, Qld.
(J. Weigal)

446 *Egernia inornata* (with portion of tail regenerated). Yellowdine district, WA. (D. Knowles)

447 *Egernia kingii*. Houtman Abrolhos Islands, WA. (G. Harold)

448 *Egernia kintorei*. Tanami Desert, NT. (G. Harold)

449 *Egernia luctuosa*. Perth, WA. (S. Wilson)

450 *Egernia major*. Gosford, NSW. (G. Schmida)

451 *Egernia margaretae margaretae*. George Gill Ranges, NT. (J. Wombey)

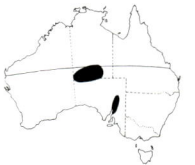

452 *Egernia margaretae personata.*
Wilpena Pound, Flinders Ranges,
SA. (H. Ehmann)

453 *Egernia modesta.* Tamworth, NSW.
(S. Wilson)

454 *Egernia multiscutata bos.* Lake
Cronin, WA. (S. Wilson)

455 *Egernia napoleonis.* Cape Leeuwin,
WA. (P. Rankin)

456 *Egernia pilbarensis.* Port Hedland
area, WA. (H. Cogger)

457 *Egernia pulchra pulchra.* Worsley,
WA. (G. Harold)

458 *Egernia pulchra longicauda.*
Favourite Island, Jurien Bay, WA.
(D. Knowles)

459 *Egernia richardi.* Lake Cronin, WA.
(S. Wilson)

460 *Egernia rugosa.* (G. Schmida)

461 *Egernia saxatilis saxatilis.*
Warrumbungle Mountains, NSW.
(J. Weigal)

462 *Egernia saxatilis intermedia.*
Blackheath, NSW. (G. Husband)

463 *Egernia slateri slateri.* Alice Springs,
NT. (P. Rankin)

464 *Egernia stokesii stokesii*. West Wallabi Island, Houtman Abrolhos, WA. (M. Hanlon)

465 *Egernia stokesii badia*. Mullewa, WA. (D. Knowles)

466 *Egernia stokesii* (eastern form). Bookaloo, SA. (M. Hanlon)

467 *Egernia striata*. Alice Springs area, NT. (J. Weigal)

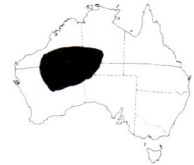

468 *Egernia striolata*. Nebo area, mideastern Qld. (D. Knowles)

469 *Egernia whitii whitii*. New England National Park, NSW. (S. Wilson)

470 *Egernia whitii whitii.* Mt Kosciusko, NSW. (M. Swan)

471 *Egernia* sp. (1). Member of *E. striolata* group, known only from a small outcrop in Mt Kaputar National Park, in north–eastern interior of NSW. (G. Shea)

472 *Egernia* sp. (2). Member of *E. frerei* group, occurring on the Arnhem Land Escarpment and its outliers. Little Nourlangie Rock, NT. (S. Swanson)

473 *Egernia* sp. (3). Member of *E. striolata* group. Dorrigo Plateau, NSW. (D. Knowles).

474 *Emoia atrocostata irrorata.* Somerset, Qld. (S. Wilson)

475 *Emoia longicauda.* Lockerbie Scrub, Cape York Peninsula, Qld. (D. Knowles)

476 *Eremiascincus fasciolatus* (with portion of tail regenerated). Exmouth, WA. (G. Harold)

477 *Eremiascincus richardsonii*. Yalgoo, WA. (P. Griffin)

478 *Eugongylus rufescens*. Lockerbie Scrub, Cape York Peninsula, Qld. (S. Wilson)

479 *Hemiergis decresiensis continentis*. Adelaide, SA. (G. Harold)

480 *Hemiergis decresiensis decresiensis*. Kangaroo Island, SA. (B. Miller)

481 *Hemiergis decresiensis talbingoensis*. Lake Eildon, Vic. (G. Fyfe) NPIAW

482 *Hemiergis graciloides*. Boreen Point, Qld. (S. Wilson)

483 *Hemiergis initialis brookeri*. Eucla, WA. (G. Harold)

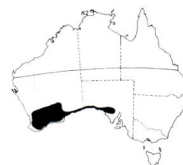

484 *Hemiergis initialis initialis*. Mt Jackson, WA. (G. Harold)

485 *Hemiergis maccoyi* (widespread form with regenerated tail-tip). The Grampians, Vic. (G. Harold)

486 *Hemiergis maccoyi* (Illawarra form with regenerated tail-tip). Nowra district, NSW. (D. Knowles)

487 *Hemiergis millewae*. Blanchetown area, SA. (G. Shea)

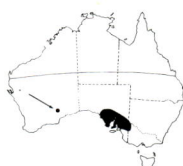

488 *Hemiergis peronii*. Toolinna Rock
Hole, WA. (G. Harold)

489 *Hemiergis quadrilineata*. Rottnest
Island, WA. (S. Wilson)

490 *Lampropholis amicula*. Mt Nebo,
Qld. (S. Wilson)

491 *Lampropholis basiliscus*. Curtain Fig
National Park, Qld. (D. Knowles)

492 *Lampropholis caligula*. Polblue,
Barrington Tops, NSW. (G. Shea)

493 *Lampropholis challengeri*.
Cunningham's Gap National Park,
Qld. (D. Knowles)

494 *Lampropholis challengeri.* Mt
Glorious, Qld. (S. Wilson)

495 *Lampropholis challengeri* (breeding
male). Lamington National Park,
Qld. (S. Wilson)

496 *Lampropholis czechurai* (male
approaching breeding condition).
Ravenshoe area, Qld.
(D. Knowles)

497 *Lampropholis delicata.* Eumundi,
Qld. (D. Knowles)

498 *Lampropholis guichenoti.* Walhalla,
Vic. (S. Wilson)

499 *Lampropholis mirabilis.* Magnetic
Island, Qld. (T. Helder)

500 *Lampropholis mustelina.* Walhalla, Vic. (S. Wilson)

501 *Lampropholis tetradactyla* (gravid female with developing egg visible). Curtain Fig National Park, Qld. (S. Wilson)

502 *Lampropholis* sp. (1). Small slender member of *L. challengeri* group occurring on east coast of NSW, from Sydney to the Qld border. Bellingen area, NSW. (G. Shea)

503 *Lampropholis* sp. (2). Moderately small member of *L. delicata* group occurring in isolated moist pockets in Carnarvon Gorge National Park, Qld. (S. Wilson)

504 *Lampropholis* sp. (3). Member of *L. delicata* group restricted to cool high altitudes of north-eastern Qld. Thornton Peak (1200 m), Qld. (D. Knowles)

505 *Lampropholis* sp. (4). Member of *L. delicata* group restricted to rainforests of north-eastern Qld. Thornton Peak (650 m), Qld. (S. Wilson)

506 *Lampropholis* sp. (5). Large member of *L. delicata* group, widespread in well-watered habitats of south to mideastern Qld. Eungella National Park, Qld. (D. Knowles)

507 *Leiolopisma platynotum* (showing red throat colouration typical of many members of *L. baudini* species group). Oberon, NSW. (D. Knowles)

508 *Leiolopisma coventryi*. Mt St Leonard, Vic. (H. Cogger)

509 *Leiolopisma duperreyi* (displaying reddish flush on throat and side of neck). Osterley, Tas. (S. Wilson)

510 *Leiolopisma entrecasteauxii* (breeding male of strongly patterned form). Blackheath, NSW. (S. Wilson)

511 *Leiolopisma greeni*. Breona district, Tas. (G. Shea)

512 *Leiolopisma jigurru*. Mt Bartle Frere, Qld. (R. Jenkins)

513 *Leiolopisma metallicum*. Northern Tas. (G. Shea)

514 *Leiolopisma ocellatum*. Launceston, Tas. (S. Wilson)

515 *Leiolopisma palfreymani*. Pedra Branca Rock, Tas. (R. Jenkins)

516 *Leiolopisma platynotum*. Girraween National Park, Qld. (S. Wilson)

517 *Leiolopisma pretiosum*. Mt Hartz National Park, Tas. (S. Wilson)

518 *Leiolopisma spenceri*. Mt Baw Baw, Vic. (M. Swan)

519 *Leiolopisma trilineatum*. Perth, WA. (G. Harold)

520 *Leiolopisma zia*. Styx River State Forest, NSW. (H. Ehmann)

521 *Lerista aericeps aericeps*. Kinchega National Park, NSW. (J. Wombey)

522 *Lerista aericeps taeniata* (holotype). The Granites area, NT. (R. Johnstone)

523 *Lerista allanae*. Red Falls, Charters Towers area, Qld. (G. Shea)

524 *Lerista ameles*. Mt Surprise, Qld.
(H. Cogger)

525 *Lerista apoda*. Broome, WA.
(D. Knowles)

526 *Lerista arenicola*. Eyre, WA.
(G. Harold)

527 *Lerista bipes*. Western NT.
(H. Cogger)

528 *Lerista borealis*. Smoke Creek, WA.
(G. Harold)

529 *Lerista bougainvillii*. Pomonal, Vic.
(G. Harold)

530 *Lerista bougainvillii.* Adelaide, SA.
(D. Knowles)

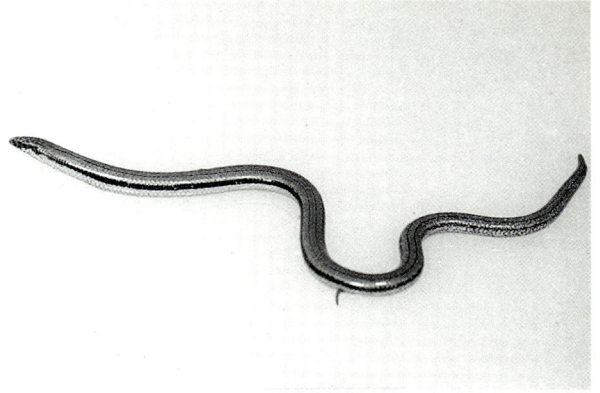

531 *Lerista carpentariae.* Centre Island,
Sir Edward Pellew Group (type
locality), NT. (A. Greer)

532 *Lerista chalybura.* Dale Gorge, WA.
(S. Wilson)

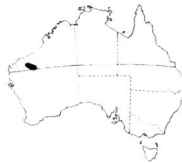

533 *Lerista christinae* (with regenerated
tail). Badgingarra, WA.
(G. Harold)

534 *Lerista cinerea.* Mt Cooper Station,
Qld. (S. Wilson)

535 *Lerista connivens.* Galena, WA.
(M. Hanlon)

536 *Lerista desertorum*. Big Shot Bore,
WA. (G. Harold)

537 *Lerista distinguenda*. Israelite Bay,
WA. (G. Harold)

538 *Lerista dorsalis*. Eucla, WA.
(G. Harold)

539 *Lerista elegans*. Perth, WA.
(P. Griffin)

540 *Lerista flammicauda*. Paraburdoo,
WA. (G. Harold)

541 *Lerista fragilis*. Moura, Qld.
(G. Shea)

542 *Lerista frosti*. Alice Springs, NT.
(G. Harold).

543 *Lerista gascoynensis* (holotype).
Gascoyne Junction area, WA.
(G. Harold)

544 *Lerista gerrardii*. Mt Jackson, WA.
(G. Harold)

545 *Lerista greeri*. Debesa Station,
Derby area, WA. (D. Mead–
Hunter)

546 *Lerista griffini*. Kununurra, WA. ·
(G. Harold)

547 *Lerista haroldi* (holotype). Gnaraloo
Station, WA. (G. Harold)

548 *Lerista humphriesi*. Murchison River Station, WA. (G. Harold)

549 *Lerista ips*. Sandfire area, WA. (H. Ehmann)

550 *Lerista karlschmidti*. South Alligator River, NT. (P. Horner)

551 *Lerista labialis*. Alice Springs, NT. (G. Harold)

552 *Lerista lineata* (with regenerated tail-tip). Singleton Beach, WA. (G. Harold)

553 *Lerista lineopunctulata*. Perth, WA. (P. Griffin)

554 *Lerista macropisthopus*. Waldburg Station, WA. (S. Wilson)

555 *Lerista microtis*. Emu Point, WA (G. Harold)

556 *Lerista muelleri*. Westmar, Qld. (S. Wilson)

557 *Lerista muelleri*. Yeelirrie Station, WA. (P. Griffin)

558 *Lerista muelleri* (with regenerated tail). Yinnietharra Station, WA. (S. Wilson)

559 *Lerista neander*. Capricorn, WA. (G. Harold)

560 *Lerista nichollsi nichollsi* (with portion of tail regenerated). Yalgoo, WA. (G. Harold)

561 *Lerista nichollsi petersoni* (with portion of tail regenerated). Mangaroon Station, WA. (G. Harold)

562 *Lerista onsloviana*. Onslow, WA. (G. Harold)

563 *Lerista orientalis*. Chillagoe, Qld. (D. Knowles)

564 *Lerista picturata baynesi*. Eucla, WA. (M. Hanlon)

565 *Lerista picturata edwardsae*. Yalata, SA. (M. Hanlon)

566 *Lerista picturata picturata* (with portion of tail regenerated). Caiguna, WA. (M. Hanlon)

567 *Lerista planiventralis decora.* Kalbarri, WA. (S. Wilson)

568 *Lerista planiventralis planiventralis.* North West Cape, WA. (P. Griffin)

569 *Lerista praepedita.* Swanbourne, WA. (G. Shea)

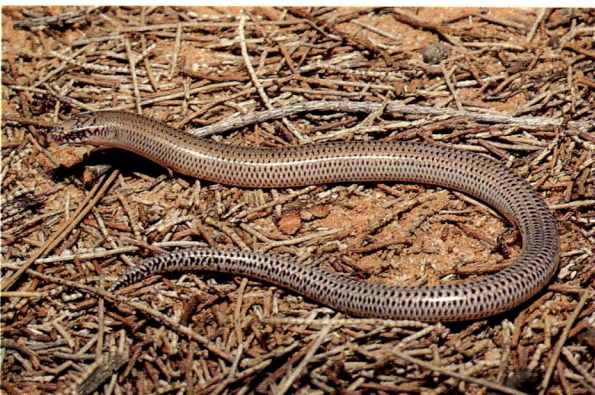

570 *Lerista punctatovittata.* Westmar, Qld. (S. Wilson)

571 *Lerista simillima* (with broken tail-tip). Ellendale Station, WA. (G. Harold)

572 *Lerista stictopleura* (holotype). Mt Augustus area, WA. (G. Harold).

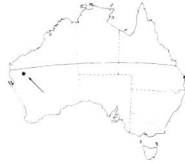

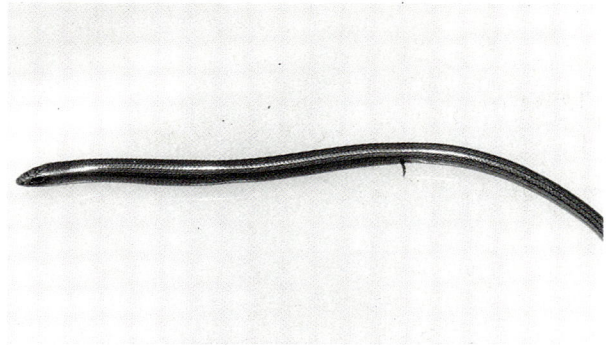

573 *Lerista storri*. Chillagoe (type locality), Qld. (A. Greer)

574 *Lerista stylis*. Kakadu, NT. (J. Wombey)

575 *Lerista terdigitata*. Streaky Bay, SA. (G. Harold)

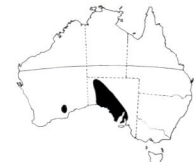

576 *Lerista uniduo*. Gnaraloo Station, WA. (G. Harold)

577 *Lerista varia* (holotype). Denham, WA. (G. Harold)

578 *Lerista vermicularis*. Great Sandy Desert, WA. (H. Ehmann)

579 *Lerista vittata*. Mt Cooper Station, Qld. (D. Knowles)

580 *Lerista walkeri*. Sale River, WA. (G. Harold)

581 *Lerista wilkinsi* (subadult). Warrigal Range, Qld. (D. Knowles)

582 *Menetia alanae*. Jabiru, NT. (J. Wombey)

583 *Menetia concinna*. Jabiluka area, NT. (A. Greer)

584 *Menetia greyii*. Westmar district, Qld. (D. Knowles)

585 *Menetia maini*. Mt Isa district, Qld. (D. Knowles)

586 *Menetia surda*. East Yuna Reserve, WA. (P. Griffin)

587 *Menetia timlowi*. Chinchilla area, Qld. (S. Wilson)

588 *Morethia adelaidensis*. Eucla, WA. (M. Hanlon)

589 *Morethia boulengeri*. Dutton Bluff, SA. (G. Harold)

590 *Morethia butleri.* Yeelirrie Station, WA. (P. Griffin)

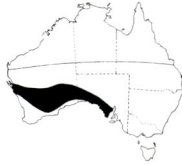

591 *Morethia lineoocellata* (breeding male). Rottnest Island, WA. (S. Wilson)

592 *Morethia obscura* (breeding male with portion of tail regenerated). Mindarie, SA. (G. Harold)

593 *Morethia ruficauda exquisita.* Barradale, WA. (G. Harold)

594 *Morethia ruficauda ruficauda* (with regenerated tail). Twin Falls, NT. (J. Wombey)

595 *Morethia storri.* Kakadu National Park, NT. (J. Wombey)

596 *Morethia taeniopleura*. Cracow, Qld. (S. Wilson)

597 *Notoscincus butleri* (with regenerating tail-tip). Cooya Pooya Station, WA. (G. Harold)

598 *Notoscincus ornatus*. Mt Cooper Station, Qld. (D. Knowles)

599 *Notoscincus wotjulum*. Kununurra area, WA. (S. Wilson)

600 *Ophioscincus cooloolensis*. Cooloola National Park, Qld. (S. Wilson)

601 *Ophioscincus truncatus*. Conondale Ranges, Qld. (S. Wilson)

602 *Ophioscincus ophioscincus*. Mt Glorious, Qld. (D. Knowles)

603 *Proablepharus kinghorni*. Brunette Downs Station, NT. (H. Cogger)

604 *Proablepharus reginae*. Ormiston Gorge, NT. (H. Cogger)

605 *Proablepharus tenuis*. Kununurra area, WA. (S. Wilson)

606 *Saiphos equalis*. Yangan, Qld. (D. Knowles)

607 *Sphenomorphus amplus* (with portion of tail regenerated). Finch Hatton Gorge, Qld. (D. Knowles)

608 *Sphenomorphus australis.* Albany, WA. (S. Wilson)

609 *Sphenomorphus brongersmai.* Mitchell Plateau, WA. (P. Griffin)

610 *Sphenomorphus cracens.* Chillagoe, Qld. (D. Knowles)

611 *Sphenomorphus crassicaudus.* Tip of Cape York Peninsula, Qld. (D. Knowles)

612 *Sphenomorphus darwiniensis* (weakly patterned individual). Bynoe Harbour, NT. (S. Wilson)

613 *Sphenomorphus darwiniensis.* Jabiru, NT. (R. Jenkins)

614 *Sphenomorphus douglasi*. Humpty Doo, NT. (S. Wilson)

615 *Sphenomorphus fuscicaudis*. Lake Barrine, Qld. (S. Wilson)

616 *Sphenomorphus isolepis*. Millstream, WA. (S. Wilson)

617 *Sphenomorphus kosciuskoi* (southern form). Thredbo area, NSW. (R. Jenkins)

618 *Sphenomorphus kosciuskoi* (northern form). New England National Park, NSW. (S. Wilson)

619 *Sphenomorphus leuraensis*. Wentworth Lake; NSW. (D. Knowles)

620 *Sphenomorphus luteilateralis.* Eungella National Park, Qld. (G. Shea)

621 *Sphenomorphus mjobergi.* Ravenshoe area, Qld. (G. Schmida)

622 *Sphenomorphus murrayi.* Barrington Tops, NSW. (D. Knowles)

623 *Sphenomorphus nigricaudis.* Tip of Cape York Peninsula, Qld. (D. Knowles)

624 *Sphenomorphus pardalis.* Edward River, Qld. (J. Wombey)

625 *Sphenomorphus pumilus pumilus.* Somerset, Cape York Peninsula, Qld. (D. Knowles)

626 *Sphenomorphus punctulatus.* Townsville, Qld. (T. Helder)

627 *Sphenomorphus quoyii.* Wallaman Falls National Park, Qld. (T. Helder)

628 *Sphenomorphus quoyii.* All members of this species group readily enter water to forage or if alarmed, and are known popularly as water skinks. Blackdown Tableland National Park, Qld. (D. Knowles)

629 *Sphenomorphus tenuis* (northern form). Chillagoe, Qld. (D. Knowles)

630 *Sphenomorphus tenuis* (mideastern Qld form). Gayndah, Qld. (S. Wilson)

631 *Sphenomorphus tenuis* (southern Qld arboreal form). Pomona area, Qld. (S. Wilson)

632 *Sphenomorphus tenuis* (southern
Qld, heavily blotched form).
Conondale Ranges, Qld.
(S. Wilson)

633 *Sphenomorphus tigrinus* (with
regenerated tail). Curtain Fig
National Park, Qld. (D. Knowles)

634 *Sphenomorphus tympanum.* Buchan,
Vic. (G. Harold)

635 *Sphenomorphus* sp. (1) (with
portion of tail regenerated).
Wentworth Lake, Blue Mountains,
NSW. (D. Knowles)

636 *Tiliqua adelaidensis.* Presumably
Buschfelde, near Gawler, SA.
(G. Shea)

637 *Tiliqua multifasciata.* Newman area,
WA. (D. Knowles)

638 *Tiliqua nigrolutea.* Launceston, Tas. (S. Wilson)

639 *Tiliqua nigrolutea* (juvenile). Tumbarumba, NSW. (G. Schmida)

640 *Tiliqua occipitalis* (showing defence response typical of the genus). Mick's Camp area, SA. (J. Weigal)

641 *Tiliqua rugosa rugosa.* Kelmscott, WA. (S. Wilson)

642 *Tiliqua rugosa konowi.* Rottnest Island, WA. (S. Wilson)

643 *Tiliqua rugosa asper.* Grampians, Vic. (G. Harold)

644 *Tiliqua rugosa tropisurus*. Tamala
Station, WA. (D. Knowles)

645 *Tiliqua scincoides scincoides*.
Brisbane, Qld. (S. Wilson)

646 *Tiliqua scincoides intermedia*.
Ellendale Station, WA. (P. Griffin)

647 *Tropidophorus queenslandiae*.
Curtain Fig National Park, Qld.
(S. Wilson)

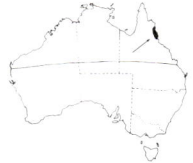

GOANNAS
Family VARANIDAE

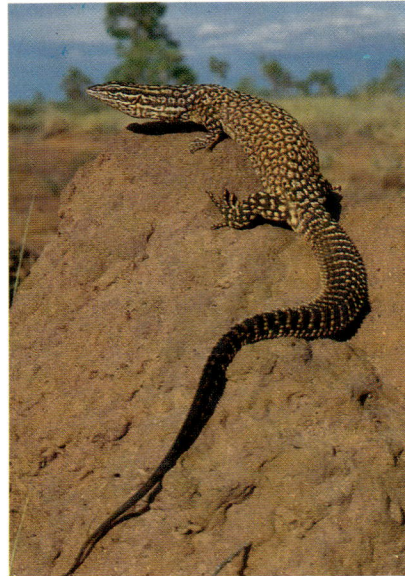

648 *Varanus acanthurus.* Mt Isa district, Qld. (J. Weigal)

649 *Varanus acanthurus* (drab reddish colouration from south-west of range). Upper Gascoyne region, WA. (S. Wilson)

650 *Varanus brevicauda.* Marillana Station, WA. (S. Wilson)

651 *Varanus caudolineatus.* Twin Peaks Station, WA. (S. Wilson)

652 *Varanus eremius.* Alice Springs area, NT. (J. Weigal)

653 *Varanus giganteus*. Alice Springs, NT. (S. Wilson)

655 *Varanus glauerti*. Mitchell Plateau, WA. (G. Harold)

654 *Varanus gilleni*. Kingoonya, SA. (G. Husband)

656 *Varanus glebopalma*. Mt Daglish, WA. (G. Harold)

657 *Varanus gouldii*. Mt Dale, WA. (G. Harold)

658 *Varanus indicus*. Lockerbie Scrub, Cape York Peninsula, Qld. (S. Wilson)

659 *Varanus kingorum*. Turkey Creek, WA. (G. Harold)

660 *Varanus mertensi*. Berri Springs, NT. (G. Schmida)

661 *Varanus mitchelli*. Kununurra, WA. (G. Schmida)

662 *Varanus panoptes panoptes* (enacting defensive response typical of many large terrestrial monitors). Napier Downs Station, WA. (J. Weigal)

663 *Varanus panoptes rubidus* (juvenile). Wooleen Station, WA. (S. Wilson)

664 *Varanus pilbarensis*. Chichester Ranges, WA. (S. Wilson)

665 *Varanus prasinus* (showing distended throat typical of many monitor defensive displays). South-western New Guinea. (G. Schmida)

666 *Varanus primordius* (juvenile). Howard Springs, NT. (G. Husband)

▲ **667** *Varanus rosenbergi*. Ravensthorpe WA. (M. Swan)

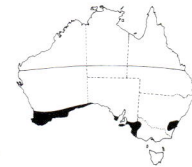

668 *Varanus scalaris*. Kununurra, WA. (G. Harold)

669 *Varanus scalaris*. Cairns area, Qld. (G. Schmida)

670 *Varanus semiremex* (northern form). Weipa, Qld. (S. Wilson)

671 *Varanus spenceri*. Boulia district, Qld. (G. Husband)

672 *Varanus storri storri*. Pentland, Qld. (S. Wilson)

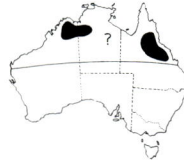

673 *Varanus storri ocreatus*. Smoke Creek, WA. (G. Harold)

674 *Varanus tristis* (black-headed form). Mt Jackson, WA. (G. Harold)

675 *Varanus tristis* ('freckled' form). Theodore district, Qld. (S. Wilson)

676 *Varanus tristis* ('freckled' form). Mt Isa district, Qld. (D. Knowles)

677 *Varanus varius* (common form). Eurimbula National Park, Qld. (C. Vye)

678 *Varanus varius* (Bell's form). Chinchilla, Qld. (G. Schmida)

679 *Varanus* sp. Widespread from Gulf of Carpentaria to south-western Qld. Diamantina Lakes Station, Qld. (D. Knowles)

SNAKES
(suborder OPHIDIA)

FILE SNAKES
Family ACROCHORDIDAE

680 *Acrochordus arafurae*. Adelaide River area, NT. (G. Husband)

681 *Acrochordus granulatus*. Darwin, NT. (P. Horner)

PYTHONS
Family BOIDAE

682 Pythons are the only snakes to possess cloacal spurs. These are all that remain of hindlimbs, and are used by males to stimulate females during copulation. *Bothrochilus fuscus*. (S. Wilson)

683 *Aspidites melanocephalus*. Great Sandy Desert, WA. (S. Wilson)

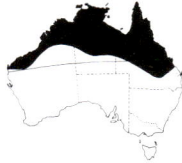

684 *Aspidites ramsayi*. (S. Swanson)

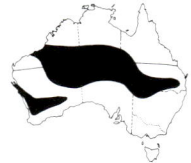

685 *Bothrochilus childreni* emerging from abandoned nest of Fairy Martin (*Cecropis ariel*). Kununurra, WA. (S. Wilson)

686 *Bothrochilus fuscus*. Cairns district, Qld. (D. Knowles)

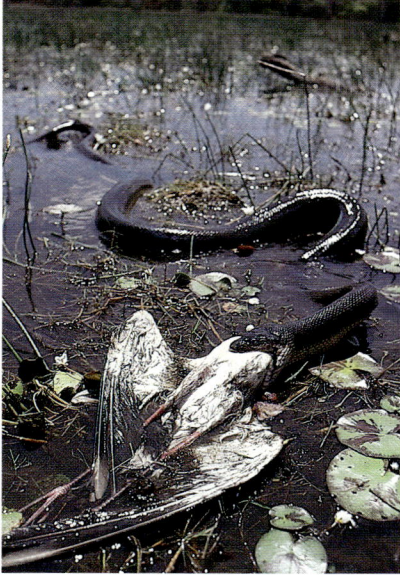

687 *Bothrochilus fuscus* feeding on masked plover (*Vanellus miles*). Fogg Dam, NT. (M. Hanlon)

688 *Bothrochilus maculosus*. Cairns district, Qld. (J. Weigal)

689 *Bothrochilus olivaceus olivaceus*. Mt Isa district, Qld. (D. Knowles)

690 *Bothrochilus perthensis*. Mt Nicholay, south-east of Wooleen Station, WA. (P. Griffin)

691 *Bothrochilus stimsoni stimsoni*. Northam, WA. (S. Wilson)

692 *Chondropython viridis*. Iron Range,
Qld. (S. Wilson)

694 *Morelia bredli*. Alice Springs, NT
(G. Harold)

693 *Morelia amethistina*. Atherton
Tablelands area, Qld. (J. Weigal)

695 *Morelia carinata* (holotype).
Admiralty Gulf, WA. (Western
Australian Museum collection)

696 *Morelia oenpelliensis*. Arnhem Land
Escarpment, NT. (D. Knowles)

697 *Morelia spilota spilota*. Pythons of all species coil round their eggs in this manner. Gosford, NSW. (J. Weigal)

698 *Morelia spilota variegata* (eastern population). Mt Glorious, Qld. (S. Wilson)

699 *Morelia spilota variegata* (north-east Qld population). Palmerston National Park, Qld. (S. Wilson)

700 *Morelia spilota variegata* (northern NT/Kimberley population). Nightcliff, NT. (G. Husband)

701 *Morelia spilota imbricata*. Serpentine, WA. (S. Wilson)

SOLID-TOOTHED and REAR-FANGED SNAKES Family COLUBRIDAE

702 Many homalopsine snakes, such as the bockadam (*Cerberus rynchops*), bear slightly protrusive eyes, directed upwards. This is an adaptation for an aquatic lifestyle. Darwin, NT. (M. Hanlon)

703 *Boiga irregularis* (eastern form). Brisbane, Qld. (S. Wilson)

704 *Boiga irregularis* ('night tiger' form). Katherine, NT. (M. Hanlon)

705 *Cerberus rynchops*. Buffalo Creek, Darwin, NT. (S. Wilson)

706 *Dendrelaphis calligastra*. Lockerbie Scrub, Cape York Peninsula, Qld. (D. Knowles)

707 *Dendrelaphis punctulata* (widespread northern colour form). Darwin, NT. (S. Wilson)

708 *Dendrelaphis punctulata* (eastern colour form). Brisbane, Qld. (S. Wilson)

709 *Dendrelaphis punctulata* (uncommon blue colour form). Brisbane, Qld. (S. Wilson)

710 *Enhydris polylepis*. Darwin, NT. (P. Horner)

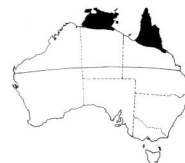

711 *Enhydris polylepis*. Chillagoe, Qld. (G. Shea)

712 *Fordonia leucobalia*. Darwin, NT. (P. Horner)

713 *Fordonia leucobalia.* Elcho Island, NT. (R. Jenkins)

714 *Myron richardsonii.* Buffalo Creek, Darwin, NT. (G. Shea)

715 *Stegonotus cucullatus.* Darwin, NT. (S. Wilson)

716 *Styporhynchus mairii.* Cairns, Qld. (M. Hanlon)

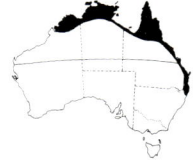

FRONT-FANGED
LAND SNAKES
Family ELAPIDAE

717 *Acanthophis antarcticus.* Sydney, NSW. (G. Schmida)

718 *Acanthophis praelongus.* Katherine, NT. (S. Wilson)

719 *Acanthophis pyrrhus.* Anna Plains Station, WA. (P. Griffin)

720 *Austrelaps superbus* (lowland form). Stony Rises, Vic. (M. Swan)

721 *Austrelaps superbus* (highland form
showing strongly barred lips).
Taralga, NSW. (D. Knowles)

722 *Austrelaps superbus* (Adelaide Hills/
Kangaroo Island form). Adelaide
Hills, SA. (P. Mirtschin)

723 *Cacophis harriettae* (pale individual
in foreground is aberrantly
coloured and patterned). Brisbane,
Qld. (D. Knowles)

724 *Cacophis krefftii*. Brisbane, Qld.
(S. Wilson)

725 *Cacophis squamulosus* (in defensive
posture). Dorrigo, NSW. (C. Vye)

726 *Cacophis* sp. Occurs in rainforests from Atherton Tablelands to Bluewater Range and Mt Spec, Qld. Millaa Millaa, Qld. (S. Wilson)

727 *Cryptophis nigrescens.* Coffs Harbour district, NSW. (C. Vye)

728 *Cryptophis pallidiceps.* Darwin, NT. (P. Horner)

729 *Demansia atra.* Beerwah, Qld. (S. Wilson)

730 *Demansia calodera.* Tamala Station, WA. (P. Griffin)

731 *Demansia olivacea.* Fitzroy Crossing, WA. (P. Griffin)

732 *Demansia papuensis melaena.* Cox
River, NT. (M. Gillam)

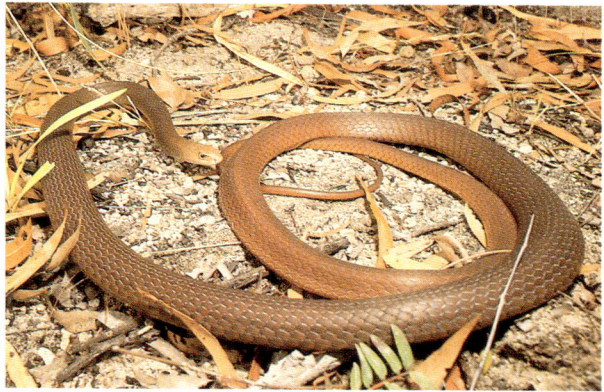

733 *Demansia papuensis papuensis.* Iron
Range, Qld. (J. Weigal)

734 *Demansia psammophis psammophis.*
Brisbane, Qld. (D. Knowles)

735 *Demansia psammophis reticulata.*
Wialki, WA. (S. Wilson)

736 *Demansia psammophis cupreiceps.*
Gascoyne Junction area, WA.
(G. Harold)

737 *Demansia rufescens.* Roebourne
area, WA. (G. Harold)

333

738 *Demansia simplex*. Forrest River Mission, WA. (Australian Museum collection, G. Shea)

739 *Demansia torquata*. Magnetic Island, Qld. (T. Helder)

740 *Demansia* sp. (closely related to *D. torquata*). Davenport Downs Station, Qld. (G. Shea)

741 *Denisonia atriceps* (holotype). Lake Cronin, WA. (D. Knowles)

742 *Denisonia devisi*. Glenmorgan, Qld. (S. Wilson)

743 *Denisonia fasciata*. Nanutarra area, WA. (P. Griffin)

744 *Denisonia maculata*. Moura area, Qld. (G. Shea)

745 *Denisonia ordensis*. Gordon Downs Station, WA. (P. Horner)

746 *Denisonia suta*. Oakey, Qld. (S. Wilson)

747 *Denisonia suta*. Iona Station, Qld. (D. Knowles)

748 *Drysdalia coronata*. Emu Point, WA. (G. Harold)

749 *Drysdalia coronoides*. Oatlands, Tas. (S. Wilson)

750 *Drysdalia mastersii.* Eucla, WA.
(M. Hanlon)

751 *Drysdalia rhodogaster.* Bermagui
Nature Reserve, NSW.
(J. Wombey)

752 *Echiopsis curta* (south-western
population). Albany, WA.
(G. Harold)

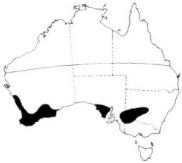

753 *Echiopsis curta* (eastern population).
Bidura, NSW. (T. Helder)

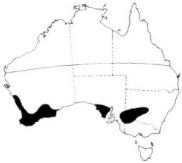

754 *Elapognathus minor.* Rocky Gully,
WA. (S. Wilson)

755 *Furina diadema.* Warrumbungle
National Park, NSW.
(D. Knowles)

756 *Furina ornata*. Sandfire, WA.
(G. Harold)

757 *Glyphodon barnardi*. Opalton, Qld.
(J. Wombey)

758 *Glyphodon dunmalli*. Lake
Broadwater, Qld. (D. Knowles)

759 *Glyphodon tristis*. Weipa, Qld.
(G. Shea)

760 *Hemiaspis damelii*. Glenmorgan,
Qld. (D. Knowles)

761 *Hemiaspis signata* (dark form).
Lamington National Park, Qld.
(D. Knowles)

337

762 *Hoplocephalus bitorquatus*. Oakey
district, Qld. (D. Knowles)

763 *Hoplocephalus bungaroides*.
Springwood, NSW. (H. Cogger)

764 *Hoplocephalus stephensii* (banded
form). Mt Glorious, Qld.
(D. Knowles)

765 *Hoplocephalus stephensii* (unbanded
form). Kroombit Tops, Qld.
(D. Knowles)

766 *Neelaps bimaculatus*. Yanchep, WA.
(D. Knowles)

767 *Neelaps calonotus*. Lancelin, WA.
(G. Shea)

768 *Notechis ater ater.* Wilmington area SA. (R. Jenkins)

769 *Notechis ater humphreysi.* Tas. (J. Weigal)

770 *Notechis ater niger.* Coffin Bay, Eyre Peninsula, SA. (B. Miller)

771 *Notechis ater serventyi.* Chappell Island, Tas. (S. Wilson)

772 *Notechis scutatus scutatus.* (D. Knowles)

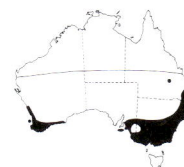

773 *Notechis scutatus occidentalis.* Ravensthorpe, WA. (T. Helder)

774 *Oxyuranus microlepidotus* (pale summer colour phase in defensive stance). Goyder's Lagoon, SA. (D. Knowles)

775 *Oxyuranus scutellatus*. Cairns area, Qld. (S. Wilson)

776 *Pseudechis australis*. (S. Swanson)

777 *Pseudechis butleri* (subadult). Sandstone area, WA. (S. Wilson)

778 *Pseudechis butleri* (juvenile). Yalgoo, WA. (S. Wilson)

779 *Pseudechis colletti*. Nonda, Qld. (D. Knowles)

780 *Pseudechis guttatus*. Forest Hill, Qld. (D. Knowles)

781 *Pseudechis porphyriacus*. Dalby area, Qld. (D. Knowles)

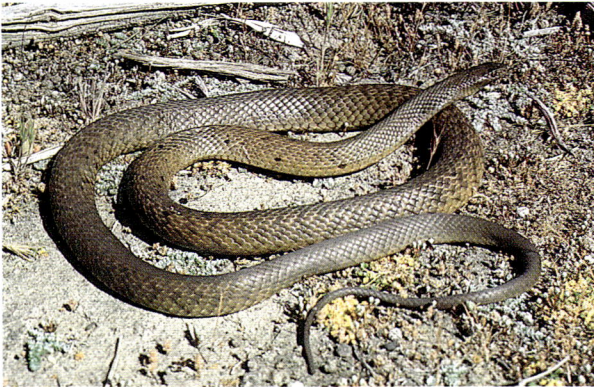

782 *Pseudonaja affinis affinis*. Hyden area, WA. (S. Wilson)

783 *Pseudonaja affinis* subsp. Rottnest Island, WA. (D. Knowles)

784 *Pseudonaja guttata*. Avon Downs, NT. (M. Gillam)

785 *Pseudonaja ingrami*. (D. Knowles)

786 *Pseudonaja modesta*. Tamala Station, WA. (G. Harold)

787 *Pseudonaja nuchalis* (banded form). Bourke area, NSW. (G. Shea)

788 *Pseudonaja nuchalis* (black-headed form). Onslow, WA. (G. Harold)

789 *Pseudonaja textilis textilis* (remnant juvenile banding is visible on reddish individual). Canberra, ACT. (J. Wombey)

790 *Pseudonaja textilis textilis* (juvenile). Brisbane, Qld. (D. Knowles)

791 *Pseudonaja textilis inframacula*. (P. Mirtschin)

792 *Rhinoplocephalus bicolor* (consuming *Leiolopisma trilineata*). Denmark, WA. (P. Rankin)

793 *Rhinoplocephalus bicolor* (juvenile). Two People Bay, WA. (S. Wilson)

794 *Rhinoplocephalus boschmai*. Oakey, Qld. (S. Wilson)

795 *Rhinoplocephalus dwyeri*. Westmar, Qld. (D. Knowles)

796 *Rhinoplocephalus flagellum*. You Yangs, Vic. (S. Wilson)

797 *Rhinoplocephalus gouldii*. Scarborough, WA. (G. Shea)

798 *Rhinoplocephalus monachus*. Mt Linden, WA. (G. Harold)

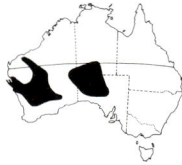

799 *Rhinoplocephalus nigriceps*. Lort River, WA. (P. Griffin)

800 *Rhinoplocephalus nigrostriatus*. Weipa, Qld. (G. Shea)

801 *Rhinoplocephalus punctatus*. Minderoo Station, WA. (P. Griffin)

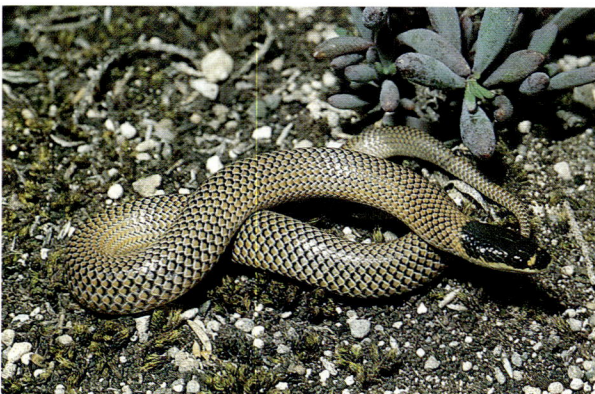

802 *Rhinoplocephalus spectabilis nullarbor*. Eucla, WA. (M. Hanlon)

803 *Rhinoplocephalus spectabilis spectabilis*. Port Wakefield area, SA. (G. Shea)

804 *Simoselaps anomalus.* Giralia
Station, WA. (D. Knowles)

805 *Simoselaps approximans.* Mt Bruce,
WA. (P. Griffin)

806 *Simoselaps australis.* Charters
Towers, Qld. (S. Wilson)

807 *Simoselaps bertholdi.* Edah Station,
WA. (D. Knowles)

808 *Simoselaps fasciolatus fasciolatus.*
Leeman, WA. (M. Hanlon)

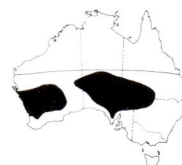

809 *Simoselaps fasciolatus fasciata.*
George Gill Ranges, NT.
(P. Horner)

810 *Simoselaps incinctus.* Alice Springs, NT. (P. Horner)

811 *Simoselaps littoralis.* Exmouth, WA. (D. Knowles)

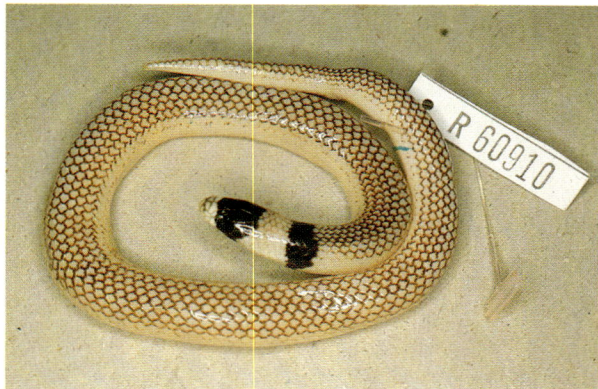

812 *Simoselaps minimus.* Coulomb Point, WA. (West Australian Museum collection, G. Harold)

813 *Simoselaps roperi.* Elliot, NT. (G. Husband).

814 *Simoselaps roperi.* Jabiru, NT. (G. Shea)

815 *Simoselaps semifasciatus semifasciatus.* Perth area, WA. (D. Knowles)

816 *Simoselaps warro*. Townsville district, Qld. (G. Shea)

817 *Simoselaps* sp. Known from Groote Eylandt and Nabarlek in northern NT. Nabarlek, NT. (G. Harold)

818 *Tropidechis carinatus*. NSW. (G. Schmida)

819 *Vermicella annulata annulata* (showing distinctive defensive stance: a contortion of the body into loops). Mt Nebo, Qld. (S. Wilson)

820 *Vermicella annulata snelli*. Darwin, NT. (P. Horner)

821 *Vermicella multifasciata*. Darwin, NT. (P. Horner)

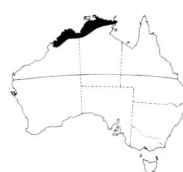

BLIND SNAKES
Family TYPHLOPIDAE

822 Blind snakes feed exclusively on termites and the eggs, larvae and pupae of ants. This usually takes place beneath cover, hence is rarely observed. (J. Weigal)

823 *Ramphotyphlops affinis*. Aramac, Qld. (S. Wilson)

824 *Ramphotyphlops australis*. Darling Range, WA. (P. Griffin)

825 *Ramphotyphlops bituberculatus*. Coober Pedy, SA. (S. Wilson)

826 *Ramphotyphlops braminus*. Darwin, NT. (S. Wilson)

827 *Ramphotyphlops broomi.* Scone, NSW. (Australian Museum collection, G. Shea)

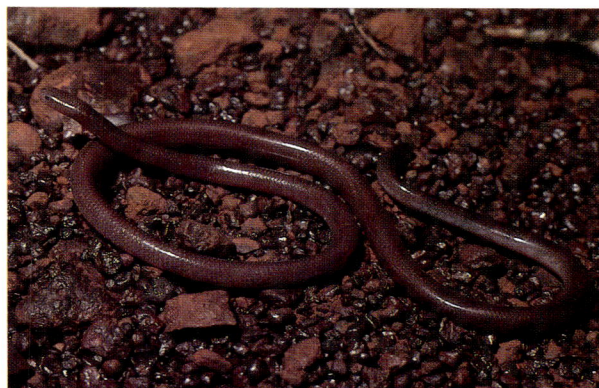

828 *Ramphotyphlops diversus ammodytes.* Yandicoogina Station, WA. (G. Harold)

829 *Ramphotyphlops diversus diversus.* Darwin area, NT. (S. Wilson)

830 *Ramphotyphlops endoterus.* Strzelecki-track, SA. (B. Miller)

831 *Ramphotyphlops grypus.* Carnarvon, WA. (S. Wilson)

832 *Ramphotyphlops guentheri.* Lissadell Station, WA. (G. Harold)

833 *Ramphotyphlops hamatus*. Meka Station, WA. (G. Harold)

834 *Ramphotyphlops howi* (holotype). Admiralty Gulf, WA. (P. Griffin)

835 *Ramphotyphlops leptosoma*. Coolamia Station, WA. (H. Ehmann)

836 *Ramphotyphlops ligatus*. Forty Mile Scrub National Park, Qld. (H. Cogger)

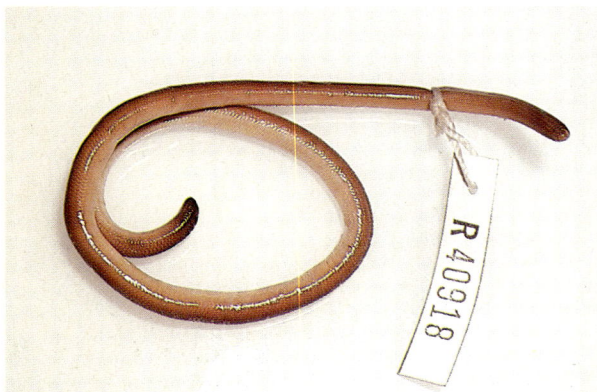

837 *Ramphotyphlops minimus*. Lake Evella, NT. (Australian Museum collection, G. Shea)

838 *Ramphotyphlops nigrescens*. Mt Glorious, Qld. (S. Wilson)

839 *Ramphotyphlops nigrescens* (showing the marked change in colour prior to sloughing). Mt Glorious, Qld. (D. Knowles)

840 *Ramphotyphlops pinguis*. Canning Dam, WA. (S. Wilson)

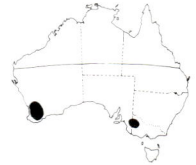

841 *Ramphotyphlops polygrammicus*. Somerset area, Cape York Peninsula, Qld. (D. Knowles)

842 *Ramphotyphlops proximus*. NSW. (G. Shea)

843 *Ramphotyphlops tovelli*. Humpty Doo area, NT. (S. Wilson)

844 *Ramphotyphlops waitii*. Coorow, WA. (G. Harold)

845 *Ramphotyphlops wiedii.*
Glenmorgan, Qld. (S. Wilson)

846 *Ramphotyphlops yirrikalae*
(holotype). Yirrikala Mission, NT.
(Australian Museum collection, G.
Shea)

847 *Ramphotyphlops* sp. Cooktown,
Qld. (S. Wilson).

MONITORS or GOANNAS
Family VARANIDAE

A small Old World family comprising approximately 31 species, all currently contained in the genus *Varanus*. Range encompasses Africa, Asia, Indo-Malayan Archipelago, New Guinea and Australia.

Varanidae includes the world's largest lizard, the komodo dragon (*V. komodoensis*) of eastern Indonesia, which may exceed TL 3.0 m and weigh up to 100 kg. The Australian perenty (*V. giganteus*) ranks about third, while the short-tailed monitor (*V. brevicauda*) is the world's smallest varanid, rarely exceeding TL 0.2 m.

Australia is the stronghold of the family with 24 species. Greatest diversity occurs in northern and arid regions. Absent from Tas. and alpine areas of eastern highlands.

Genus *VARANUS* Merrem, 1820

Moderately small to extremely large lizards (TL 0.23 to 2.5 m) with long head and neck and narrow snout. Eye well developed with round pupil and movable scaly lower eyelid. Tongue long, slender and deeply forked. Limbs well developed, each with 5 strongly clawed digits. Tail non-fragile, slender to robust, and laterally compressed to round in cross-section. Skin thick and loose-fitting with small juxtaposed scales (occasionally spinose on tail; never on body).

The tail varies in shape and proportions according to function. Larger species may use their powerful tails as defensive weapons. Occasionally they are used in conjunction with the hindlimbs to form a tripod, enabling some terrestrial monitors to stand erect for extended periods. Many smaller rock-inhabiting monitors have robust tails bearing rings of strongly keeled to spinose scales. These are used to block entrances to crevices or shallow burrows. Tails of semi-aquatic monitors are strongly laterally compressed to aid swimming while the tail of the arboreal emerald monitor (*V. prasinus*) has a prehensile tip to assist climbing.

The long slender tongue plays a part in the sense of smell. Flicking movements of the tongue collect and transfer air-borne particles to Jacobson's Organ, located in the roof of the mouth, where they are savoured.

Diurnal; occasionally crepuscular in hot weather. Most large monitors are terrestrial, ascending trees only when alarmed. Juveniles and small species tend to be secretive; usually arboreal and rock-inhabiting. Large monitors are conspicuous open foragers with few natural predators. Individuals may cover several kilometres per day in search of food, moving with a distinctive unhurried waddling gait.

Monitors are predators and scavengers. Diets include arthropods, small lizards, snakes, bird eggs and carrion. The teeth are long, sharp and recurved to ensure a secure grip on struggling prey or to tear flesh from carcasses. Food is consumed with a characteristic jerking motion of the head and neck. The diversity of Australian monitors may be due to lack of competition from mammalian carnivores and scavengers, present throughout their extralimital range.

Egglayers, producing parchment-shelled eggs. Receptive females of large, highly mobile species appear to use scent to attract males. Large numbers of males may gather together, vying for the right to mate with a single female. Ritualised combat often occurs in these situations. Combat consists of both participants standing erect and grasping each other about the body with their forelimbs, each attempting to unbalance the other by various contortions. Hissing and biting may precede or follow combat. Elaborate rituals are well documented in large monitors but poorly known in small species. This is probably a result of their cryptic habits.

Spiny-tailed Monitor
Varanus acanthurus Boulenger, 1885
Photos 648, 649

Description Medium-sized robust monitor with thick, strongly spinose tail; depressed at base and round to triangular in cross-section distally. Ground colour black, dark brown to dull or rich reddish brown, often paler on vertebral region. Pattern usually prominent throughout most of range, becoming obscure and flushed with red southwestwards. Numerous transverse rows of pale reddish, yellow to cream ocelli extend over back, flanks and occasionally top of neck. Individuals from Arnhem Escarpment, NT, are distinctively marked with pale flecks and large blackish spots or bars. Neck usually marked with cream to yellowish stripes or series of spots. Broad pale-edged dark reddish brown to black stripe extends from snout through eye to forelimb. Another extends from lip. Limbs ground colour spotted with pale reddish brown, cream to white. Anterior three-quarters of tail ground colour, narrowly banded with cream to white. Remainder dark with little indication of pattern. Ventral surfaces pale brown to yellow, spotted with brown on throat, belly, hindlimbs and base of tail. SVL 0.23 m. TL 0.6 m.

Distinguished from *V. primordius* and *V. storri* in possessing stripes on neck, narrow bands on tail and generally sharper pattern. Differs further in attaining greater size (TL 0.6 vs 0.25 and 0.4 m respectively) and bearing more strongly spinose tail.

Preferred habitat Subhumid to arid north-western two-thirds of Australia. Favours hard soils and rocky areas supporting woodlands and shrublands with dominant ground cover of tussock or hummock grasses.

Microhabitat Shelters in rock crevices, beneath abandoned termitaria or in shallow burrows excavated beneath rocks, logs or dense low vegetation.

Comments Terrestrial and rock-inhabiting. Spinose tail is used to block entrance to shelter. Severed tails of several individuals were encountered during field work in northern WA; probably a result of a predator discarding the least palatable part of its prey. Eight newborn young recorded in a tunnel filled with soft earth in central-eastern NT during January.

Short-tailed Monitor
Varanus brevicauda Boulenger, 1898
Photo 650

Description An extremely small robust short-limbed monitor. Tail short, thick and depressed at base; round in cross-section distally and bearing strongly keeled scales. Ground colour reddish brown to yellowish brown, marked on body and limbs with faint darker flecks or reticulum, and obscure darker and paler spots. Dark streak usually present, extending from snout through eye to above ear. Tail marked with larger dark spots. Ventral surfaces pale brown to pale reddish brown, occasionally spotted with brown on throat; rarely on belly. SVL 0.11 m. TL 0.23 m.

Preferred habitat Arid north-west and interior of Australia, from Great Sandy Desert, WA, to south-western Qld. Favours sand plains, sand ridges or stony and loamy flats vegetated with hummock grasses.

Microhabitat Shelters in shallow burrows, usually beneath hummock grasses. May excavate its own burrow or utilise those of other lizards.

Comments World's smallest monitor. Terrestrial, foraging in open spaces between hummocks. Feeds largely on arthropods, though reptile eggs and small lizards are also taken. Mating probably commences in early spring. Clutches of 2–3 eggs recorded. Extremely shy, dashing to burrow or into hummocks when disturbed.

Stripe-tailed Monitor
Varanus caudolineatus Boulenger, 1885
Photo 651

Description Small moderately dorsally depressed monitor. Tail thick and relatively short; round in cross-section, bearing keeled scales. Ground colour shades of grey to brown, often with reddish brown dorsal flush. Pattern consists of scattered blackish

brown to dark reddish brown spots and blotches, each usually margined by paler shade of ground colour. These extend from head to proximal quarter to third of tail. Remainder of tail bears 4–5 prominent dark stripes. Short dark streak extends from eye to above ear. Ventral surfaces greyish white to brownish white, peppered with brown on chin and throat; occasionally undersurface of limbs and tail. SVL 0.13 m. TL 0.32 m.

Distinguished from *V. gilleni* by spotted (vs banded) dorsal pattern.

Preferred habitat Arid midwest coast and interior of WA. Favours hard soils and stony regions dominated by mulga (*Acacia aneura*) woodlands and shrublands.

Microhabitat Shelters in tree hollows and rock crevices or beneath bark of dead trees. Disused termitaria are utilised to a lesser extent.

Comments Arboreal. Infrequently ventures far from shelter. Individuals or pairs are sometimes seen basking on dead trees during mild weather. Geckos, particularly *Gehyra* spp., are favoured prey though arthropods, especially cockroaches and grasshoppers, are also taken. Juveniles appear to feed largely on the severed tails of geckos. Clutches of 4–5 eggs recorded; laid during summer.

Desert Pygmy Monitor
Varanus eremius Lucas and Frost, 1895
Photo 652

Description Small monitor; tail triangular in cross-section, bearing keeled scales. Ground colour pale reddish brown to bright orange-brown patterned with yellowish to greyish brown spots or flecks over neck, body and limbs. These are usually mixed with dark-edged pale brown to cream spots. Head streaked with dark brown and cream. Pale-edged dark stripe extends from eye to ear. Tail bears 4 dark brown longitudinal stripes. Ventral surfaces whitish, clouded with grey on throat. SVL 0.16 m. TL 0.46 m.

Preferred habitat Arid to semi-arid western interior of Australia, from south-west Kimberley region of WA, through southern NT and northern SA to south-western Qld. Favours reddish sands or sandy loams vegetated with hummock grasses, particularly *Triodia*.

Microhabitat Shelters in deep burrows, located at bases of hummock grasses or low shrubs.

Comments Terrestrial. Extremely wary and infrequently observed despite abundance of tracks in some areas. Forages widely (up to a kilometre or more per day), investigating all burrows and fresh diggings it encounters. Feeds largely on lizards, though arthropods such as grasshoppers are also taken. Active throughout year. Mating occurs during spring and clutches of 3–6 eggs are laid in late summer.

Perenty
Varanus giganteus (Gray, 1845)
Photo 653

Description Extremely large long-necked monitor with angular brow and slender, strongly laterally compressed tail. Ground colour whitish to cream, densely speckled with rich to dull brown or black. Pattern usually prominent; pale pigment tending to darken with age. Transverse rows of large circular dark-edged cream to yellow or pale brown spots extend over neck, body and limbs, tending to coalesce into irregular bands on tail. Those on back are usually dark-centred. Side of head, neck and throat paler shade of ground colour to white, usually prominently marked with coarse black reticulum. Tip of tail cream to yellow. Ventral surfaces whitish, spotted or reticulated with black to grey. SVL 0.8 m. TL 2.5 m.

Preferred habitat Arid interior of Australia from western Qld to north-west coast of WA. Most abundant in the vicinity of rock outcrops, ranges and gorges. Also occurs on stony soils supporting sparse *Acacia* shrublands or woodlands and on sand plains or sand ridges dominated by hummock grasses.

Microhabitat Shelters in cavities beneath boulders or in deep burrows. One such burrow in open sandy country measured over a metre in depth and 7–8 m in length. This may have been a modified mammal burrow. Hopping mice (*Notomys* spp.) occur in sandy areas and are known to excavate tunnels of similar dimensions.

Comments Australia's largest lizard, third largest in the world. Feeds on reptiles, birds, mammals and carrion. Apparently inactive from May to August (at least in central Australia). Capable of attaining great speeds, occasionally ascending trees when pursued. When harassed and cornered, raises body on hindlimbs and distends throat, exhaling noisily. Will bite if provoked. Tail may be used defensively. A lash recorded to break both forelimbs of a dog.

Gillen's Pygmy Monitor
Varanus gilleni Lucas and Frost, 1895
Photo 654

Description Small moderately dorsally depressed monitor with thick tail, relatively short and round in cross-section, bearing keeled scales. Ground colour reddish brown, yellowish brown to greyish brown marked on back and proximal third to half of tail with narrow darker bands. Remainder of tail bears 5 narrow dark stripes. Snout marked with narrow dark bands, tending to form reticulum on head, and irregular stripes on neck. Short dark streak extends from eye to above ear. Limbs sparsely spotted with dark pigment. Ventral surfaces whitish, spotted with brown on throat; occasionally on belly. SVL 0.16 m. TL 0.38 m.

Distinguished from *V. caudolineatus* by banded (vs spotted) dorsal pattern.

Preferred habitat Arid north-western and central Australia, from Great Sandy Desert, WA, south nearly to Port Augusta, SA. Favours loams and sand plains, particularly where mulga (*Acacia aneura*) woodlands and shrublands are present, and interdunes supporting desert oak (*Casuarina decaisneana*).

Microhabitat Shelters beneath loose bark or in hollows of dead, standing or fallen trees.

Comments Arboreal. Secretive, rarely encountered active. Feeds largely on geckos (*Gehyra* spp.) though other lizards and arthropods are also taken. Juveniles appear to include severed tails of geckos as a significant part of their diet. Ritualised combat recorded between captive males in the presence of a female. Opponents distend throats and tilt dorsally flattened bodies towards each other, presumably to convey an apparent increase in size. They embrace vent to vent or side to side, clasping each other's trunk with fore- and hindlimbs, each attempting to push the other off balance. Their contorted bodies rise to arched postures, supported only by tails and snouts. Biting does not occur until a position of superiority is established, in which case the victor bites the loser about body and hips. Clutch of 4 eggs recorded; laid in September and hatching in late December. When cornered distends throat, laterally compresses body and lashes with tail.

Glauert's Monitor
Varanus glauerti Mertens, 1957
Photo 655

Description Medium-sized slender strongly dorsally depressed monitor with very long thin tail. Ground colour reddish brown, bearing numerous large bluish grey to olive ocelli arranged in regular transverse rows between neck and base of tail. Top and sides of head olive-grey to bluish grey. Pale-edged dark stripe extends through eye to above ear. Limbs pale to dark grey, prominently to obscurely spotted with cream. Tail narrowly banded with blackish brown and cream; irregularly on base, becoming sharper and more prominent on remainder. Ventral surfaces whitish, banded with bluish grey to brown. SVL 0.22 m. TL 0.78 m.

Preferred habitat Rocky gorges and escarpments in subhumid areas of northern Kimberley region, WA, and adjacent far northern NT. Disjunct population occurs on Arnhem Land Escarpment, NT.

Microhabitat Shelters in deep narrow crevices from which it is virtually impossible to extract.

Comments Rock-inhabiting. An extremely wary monitor, seldom venturing far from shelter. Feeds on lizards and arthropods.

Varanus glebopalma Mitchell, 1955
Photo 656

Description Moderately large slender monitor

with angular brow, long neck and limbs. Tail long, thin and weakly laterally compressed. Ground colour pale or dark grey to reddish brown marked with obscure narrow blackish brown transverse lines. These are usually joined to form reticulum on body, neck, side of head and base of tail. Top of head flecked with blackish brown. Sides of head and neck paler shade of ground colour, accentuating reticulum. Limbs blackish spotted with yellow to white. Proximal three-fifths of tail blackish brown. Remainder pale brown, yellow to white; narrow dark bands extend to tip on juveniles. Ventral surfaces brownish white, clouded with grey on abdomen, limbs and base of tail. Chest and throat marked with coarse dark reticulum. Palms and soles of feet black. SVL 0.35 m. TL 1.0 m.

Preferred habitat Gorges and escarpments (particularly sandstones) of far northern Australia from Kimberley region, WA, to Mt Isa district, Qld.

Microhabitat Shelters in caves, crevices and cavities between boulders.

Comments Rock-inhabiting. An alert agile monitor, capable of making well-coordinated leaps between boulders. Moves with ease over sheer rock faces. Crepuscular in hot weather. Individuals observed active in caves after dark.

Gould's Goanna or Sand Monitor
Varanus gouldii (Gray, 1838)
Photo 657

Description Moderate to large variably patterned monitor with long laterally compressed tail. Three major forms occur, varying in size and colouration. These tend to intergrade in several areas. TL to 1.65 m.

Widespread southern form: Ground colour dark brown to almost black, densely to sparsely flecked or spotted with reddish brown, yellow to white. Larger pale spots, ocelli or clusters of dots form transverse rows (leaving variable amounts of ground colour) between neck and base of tail. Head ground colour, lacking pattern above and variably spotted with yellow to white on sides. Prominent pale-edged dark stripe extends from eye onto neck. Limbs ground colour bearing large (often dark-edged) pale spots. Tail marked with narrow pale bands. Distal quarter to third yellow or white without pattern; occasionally dark or with obscure dark bands on juveniles. Ventral surfaces yellow to white marked with grey V-shape on chin, streaks or clouding on throat, and spots on belly. Intermediate in size.

Sandy desert form: Differs by redder colouration and tendency for paler markings to fragment, forming rosettes or ocelli. Chin and throat marked with dark V-shape or spots. Smallest form.

Northern form: Ground colour dark reddish brown heavily flecked with black. Pale spots are dull; relatively large and sparse. Ventral surfaces, from snout to abdomen, heavily spotted with black

to brown. Largest form.

Distinguished from *V. panoptes* in lacking alternating dorsal rows of dark and pale spots and transverse ventral rows of dark spots. Differs further from *V. p. panoptes* and from *V. rosenbergi* in lacking dark bands on tail-lip (except occasionally on juveniles). Differs from *V. varius* in possessing pale-edged dark streak behind eye and attaining much smaller maximum size (TL 1.65 vs 2.0 m).

Preferred habitat Widespread throughout sub-humid to arid areas of all mainland States. Occurs in virtually all open habitat types, favouring sandy soils. Northern form occurs in tropical woodlands of far north. Desert form occupies arid interior to north-west coast. Common form occupies remainder of range.

Microhabitat Terrestrial. Excavates sloping burrow, with expanded terminal cavity, at base of low vegetation. Several burrows may provide shelter for one individual.

Comments Most widespread Australian monitor. Terrestrial. Forages widely (up to 2 km per day), stopping to dig for prey in any small burrows it encounters. Feeds on small vertebrates (particularly lizards), arthropods and carrion. Desert form lays 5–8 eggs from late November to mid-December, hatching in late January to early February. Inactive during cooler months (from March to August) in southern part of range. Active throughout year in north. When disturbed, dashes to nearest burrow or (rarely) ascends tree. When cornered distends throat, raises body with arched back, hissing and occasionally lunging at aggressor. Frequently raises body on hindlimbs and tail; either as defensive stance or to gain a better view of surroundings.

Mangrove Monitor
Varanus indicus (Daudin, 1802)
Photo 658

Description Moderately large distinctively patterned monitor with strongly laterally compressed tail. Ground colour black, prominently marked with fine yellow, or yellow and greenish blue spots over head, body, limbs and tail. Ventral surfaces greenish white to cream, bearing densely clustered black scales which tend to align transversely on belly. SVL 0.5 m. TL 1.2 m.

Preferred habitat North-west coast of NT, northern Cape York Peninsula and islands of Torres Strait, Qld. Extralimital on islands of western Pacific, New Guinea and Indo-Malayan Archipelago. Inhabits estuarine mangrove associations and monsoon vine forests.

Microhabitat Frequently encountered basking on branches overhanging water. Shelters in hollow limbs and trunks.

Comments Terrestrial and arboreal. A powerful swimmer, taking to water or ascending trees when alarmed. Clutch of 8 eggs recorded.

Long-tailed Rock Monitor
Varanus kingorum Storr, 1980
Photo 659

Description Small moderately dorsally depressed monitor with long slender tail bearing keeled scales. Ground colour dull greyish brown to rich reddish brown marked with small blackish spots. These usually coalesce to form fine reticulum over head, body, limbs and most of tail; occasionally joining to form obscure stripes on distal quarter of tail. Ventral surfaces pale yellowish brown, dotted with blackish brown on throat and belly. SVL 0.11 m. TL 0.33 m.
Preferred habitat Rock outcrops in semi-arid southern Kimberley region, WA, and adjacent north-western NT.
Microhabitat Most abundant in vertical crevices of low outcrops. Also shelters beneath slabs.
Comments Terrestrial and rock-inhabiting. Extremely wary, rarely venturing far from shelter. Feeds on lizards and arthropods.

Mertens' Water Monitor
Varanus mertensi Glauert, 1951
Photo 660

Description Moderately large monitor; tail long and extremely laterally compressed, bearing double-keeled vertebral ridge. Ground colour dark olive-brown to olive-grey marked with numerous very small dark-edged pale grey to pale yellow spots on body, limbs and base of tail. Lips and side of neck yellowish brown. Lips barred indistinctly with brown. Ear opening rimmed with pale yellowish brown. Tail ground colour or darker, sometimes marked with indistinct yellowish brown and blackish brown flecks. Ventral surfaces whitish to pale yellow, irregularly barred, spotted or reticulated with brownish grey on abdomen, hindlimbs and base of tail. SVL 0.47 m. TL 1.1 m.

Distinguished from *V. mitchelli* in attaining larger maximum size (TL 1.1 vs 0.7 m). Differs further by build (robust vs slender) and absence of dark bars beneath throat.
Preferred habitat Margins of watercourses, swamps and lagoons in far northern Australia, from Kimberley region, WA, to far northern Qld.
Microhabitat Usually encountered along water's edge, especially among roots of trees along bank. Basks on overhanging branches or partly submerged rocks and timber.
Comments Semi-aquatic and arboreal, seldom venturing far from water. Feeds on a broad range of small vertebrates. As pools contract during Dry Season, large numbers of fish are easily caught and consumed. When pursued, either ascends trees or drops into water below, sometimes from a great height. If cornered, raises body on hindlimbs and inflates throat while arching neck and hissing. Clutches of 10–14 eggs are laid, hatching during Wet Season.

Mitchell's Water Monitor
Varanus mitchelli Mertens, 1958
Photo 661

Description Medium-sized slender monitor with strongly laterally compressed tail. Ground colour dark grey to dark olive-grey. Neck, body, limbs and base of tail bear numerous small whitish to yellow or orange dots or dark-centred ocelli, mixed with obscure darker spots or flecks. Sides of head and neck flushed with dull yellowish orange and marked with dark-centred ocelli or spots. Lips barred with ground colour. Tip of tail lacks pattern. Ventral surfaces pale yellow, marked with pale to dark grey bands; greyish brown without pattern on tail. SVL 0.24 m. TL 0.7 m.

Distinguished from *V. mertensi* in attaining smaller maximum size (TL 0.7 vs 1.1 m). Differs further by build (slender vs robust) and presence of dark bars on throat.
Preferred habitat Margins of watercourses, swamps and lagoons of northern Australia from Kimberley region, WA, to far north-western Qld. Irrigation channels of eastern Kimberley region support particularly high numbers.
Microhabitat Shelters and forages among waterside vegetation, particularly *Pandanus*. Occasionally encountered in hollow limbs or beneath loose bark of overhanging trees.
Comments Arboreal and semi-aquatic. Feeds on small reptiles, fish, arthropods, frogs and tadpoles. Readily takes to water when pursued.

Varanus panoptes Storr, 1980
Photos 662, 663

Description Large robust monitor with strongly laterally compressed tail. Two subspecies recognised.
V. p. panoptes Ground colour blackish brown, dark brown to dull reddish brown, finely variegated with darker pigment. Pattern prominent to obscure, consisting of transverse rows of black to blackish brown spots over neck, body, limbs and proximal third to two-thirds of tail. These are sometimes pale-edged and alternate with rows of dark-edged white to pale yellow spots. Top of head darker shade of ground colour. Pale-edged dark streak extends through eye to side of neck. Another extends from lip, tending to break into large oblong black spots. Distal portion of tail yellow to pale brown, banded with dark brown. Ventral surfaces white to yellow with small dark spots on throat and abdomen, aligned with those on dorsal and lateral surfaces. SVL 0.5 m. TL 1.4 m.
V. p. rubidus Storr, 1980 Differs from nominate form by redder colouration and uniformly yellow tail-tip.

Distinguished from *V. gouldii* by pattern: transverse rows of dark dorsal spots are continuous onto ventral surface. *V. p. panoptes* differs further in possessing dark banded tail-tip.

Preferred habitat *V. p. panoptes* occurs in a variety of woodland to grassland habitats, usually on heavy stony soils, of subhumid to arid northern Australia. Extends from Kimberley region, WA, to north and interior of Qld. Extralimital in southern New Guinea. *V. p. rubidus* occurs in arid western interior of WA, extending to north-west coast and Barrow Island. Favours heavy to stony soils supporting hummock grasses or *Acacia* woodlands and shrublands.

Microhabitat Excavates burrow at bases of dense low vegetation or beneath boulders.

Comments Terrestrial. Poorly documented due to long-standing confusion with *V. gouldii*. Presumably similar in many respects.

Pilbara Rock Monitor
Varanus pilbarensis Storr, 1980
Photo 664

Description Medium-sized slender monitor with long neck and very long thin tail. Ground colour greyish to bright reddish brown, sometimes tinged dorsally with olive. Transverse rows of greyish spots or ocelli extend over back, fading on neck and hips. Sides of head and neck marked with coarse dark reddish brown reticulum, extending onto throat. Limbs reddish brown to greyish bearing large pale spots or ocelli. Distal two-thirds of tail cream, prominently marked with pairs of narrow blackish brown rings. Ventral surfaces whitish, obscurely banded or clouded with grey; reticulated with grey beneath limbs. SVL 0.16 m. TL 0.5 m.

Distinguished from *V. tristis* in possessing prominent bands on tail. Differs further by longer neck and snout and more slender tail.

Preferred habitat Rocky hills, cliff faces and gorges of arid Pilbara region, WA.

Microhabitat Shelters in crevices or cavities among piled boulders.

Comments Rock-inhabiting. A swift agile monitor, able to make well-coordinated leaps between boulders.

Emerald Monitor
Varanus prasinus (Schlegel, 1839)
Photo 665

Description Medium-sized extremely slender long-limbed monitor with very long thin prehensile tail. All known Australian individuals are black, with the area from snout to about eyes, pale bluish green. Short yellowish bar may extend from above ear opening to behind eye. Ground colour of extralimital populations (particularly on mainland New Guinea) may be vivid green marked with narrow irregular blackish brown bands. These often combine with longitudinal lines to form obscure reticu-

lum. Ventral surfaces pale yellowish green. Palms and soles of feet black. SVL 0.25 m. TL 0.5 m.

Preferred habitat Australian specimens are known only from in or near vine forests (especially riverine) at altitudes of 60–540 m in McIlwraith Range on eastern Cape York Peninsula and Torres Strait Islands, Qld. Extralimital in New Guinea and associated islands.

Microhabitat Arboreal. Appears to dwell largely in foliage of upper canopy.

Comments Possibly Australia's most consistently arboreal monitor, as indicated by prehensile tail and soft black, almost sticky tissue on soles of feet. Common name is derived from vivid green hues of some New Guinea populations. Reports of 'green' emerald monitors in Australia have usually been attributed to *V. indicus*, observed in poor lighting conditions. Though the possibility exists for a green *V. prasinus* to be discovered in this poorly surveyed area, black Australian populations conform to a general extralimital trend: an increase in melanism towards outlying populations.

Varanus primordius Mertens, 1942
Photo 666

Description Small robust monitor with thick weakly spinose tail, depressed at base and round to triangular in cross-section distally. Ground colour dark olive-grey to dark reddish brown, obscurely patterned over head, body, limbs and base of tail with fine dark reticulum (often broken into spots and flecks) mixed with paler flecks. Obscure dark streak may extend from eye to above ear. Ventral surfaces pale brownish grey; darkest beneath throat, hips and limbs. SVL 0.13 m. TL 0.25 m.

Distinguished from *V. acanthurus* and *V. storri* in possessing weakly (vs strongly) spinose tail. Differs further from *V. acanthurus* by much smaller maximum size (TL 0.25 vs 0.6 m) and weak (vs usually strong) pattern.

Preferred habitat Rocky ranges, outcrops and woodlands of far north-western NT.

Microhabitat Shelters in rock crevices, fallen hollow timber, shallow burrows and beneath stones or logs.

Comments Terrestrial and rock-inhabiting. Spinose tail is used to block entrance to shelter. Feeds on arthropods and small lizards.

Rosenberg's Monitor
Varanus rosenbergi Mertens, 1957
Photo 667

Description Large monitor with long laterally compressed tail. Ground colour dark grey to black, peppered with yellow to grey. Pattern prominent to obscure, consisting of transversely aligned yellow spots or narrow blackish bands; approximately 4 on neck (each curving forward laterally) and approximately 12 on body. Head blackish bearing pale-edged black streak from in front of eye to above and behind ear. Lips barred with blackish brown and greyish white. Limbs black, spotted with yellow to cream. Tail dull yellow marked with approximately 25 pairs of narrow dark bands extending to tip; occasionally tip uniformly dark. Ventral surfaces yellowish to cream, marked with black to dark grey reticulum; occasionally broken to form bands or chevron on chin and throat. SVL 0.39 m. TL 1.3 m.

Distinguished from *V. gouldii* in possessing banded or uniformly dark tail-tip (vs unbanded and pale), reticulated to banded ventral surfaces (vs spotted or streaked) and darker colouration. From *V. varius* by nature of pattern on tail (narrow bands vs very broad bands), presence of pale-edged dark streak behind eye and smaller maximum size (TL 1.3 vs 2.0 m).

Preferred habitat Humid to semi-arid heathlands and woodlands (extending into wet sclerophyll forests in far south-west of range), favouring sandy soils. Extends from southern WA, north to about Perth and east to SA border. Isolated populations occur from south-eastern SA to Big Desert, Vic., and in Goulburn, Nowra and Sydney areas, NSW.

Microhabitat Excavates shallow, slightly curved burrow with expanded terminal cavity, usually adjacent to dense low vegetation.

Comments Terrestrial. Forages widely in search of reptiles, arthropods, birds, mammals and carrion. On Kangaroo Island, SA, monitors are active throughout year. This is in contrast to winter hibernation of *V. gouldii* on nearby mainland and is probably assisted by dark, heat absorbent colouration. Clutches of 10–19 eggs are laid in termitaria from November to February.

Spotted Tree Monitor
Varanus scalaris Mertens, 1941
Photos 668, 669

Description Medium-sized monitor with long tail, round in cross-section and bearing keeled scales. Ground colour brownish grey to black. Pattern variable, usually including prominent transversely aligned series of white to yellow or pale grey dark-centred ocelli (sometimes broken or wavy-edged; occasionally reduced to spots) from shoulders to hips, fading and breaking on flanks. Head and neck spotted to densely flecked with pale pigment. Pale-edged dark streak may extend from eye to above ear or side of neck. Limbs spotted to ocellated with pale pigment. Tail marked with pale individual scales, aligned to form irregular bands (at least on proximal half; often nearly to tip). Ventral surfaces whitish (often flushed with yellow on throat and lower flanks), sometimes bearing transverse rows of darker spots. SVL 0.25 m. TL 0.6 m.

Distinguished from *V. tristis* by head-shape (weakly depressed and blunt snouted vs strongly depressed and relatively sharp snouted). Differs from *V. semiremex* by nature of tail (round in cross-section vs laterally compressed distally).

Preferred habitat Variety of subhumid to humid habitats of northern Australia from Kimberley region, WA, to mideast coast of Qld. Favours woodlands throughout most of range, extending into rainforests in east.

Microhabitat Shelters in hollow trunks and limbs and occasionally beneath loose bark.

Comments Arboreal. Forages widely in search of arthropods and small vertebrates, including bird eggs and fledglings. Previously regarded as conspecific with *V. timorensis* (Gray, 1831) from Timor, eastern Indonesia.

Rusty Monitor
Varanus semiremex Peters, 1869
Photo 670

Description Medium-sized monitor with moderately short tail, round at base and laterally compressed distally. Two distinct colour forms occurs.

Eastern form: Ground colour greyish brown marked with sparse to dense blackish flecks, often forming reticulum over neck, body and limbs. Top of head smooth and glossy; darker shade of ground colour. Side of head paler with dark brown bars on lips. Limbs ground colour variegated with blackish brown and spotted with cream. Tail dark greyish brown bearing little discernible pattern. Ventral surfaces white to pale yellow irregularly banded with brown. SVL 0.23 m. TL 0.6 m.

Northern form: Differs by darker ground colour and stronger pattern. This includes reddish brown to white transversely aligned ocelli on body and neck.

Distinguished from *V. scalaris* and *V. tristis* by nature of tail (laterally compressed distally vs round in cross-section).

Preferred habitat Subhumid north to north-eastern coast and hinterland of Qld. Eastern form extends from Yeppoon north to southern Cape York Peninsula. Northern form occupies the remainder of Cape York Peninsula. Favours coastal and estuarine mangrove communities or *Melaleuca*-dominated margins of swamps, creeks, lakes or rivers.

Microhabitat Shelters in hollow trunks or limbs, occasionally beneath loose bark.

Comments Arboreal and semi-aquatic. Feeds on arthropods, crustaceans (especially crabs) and small vertebrates (including fish). A capable swimmer, readily taking to water or ascending trees when disturbed.

Spencer's Monitor
Varanus spenceri Lucas and Frost, 1903
Photo 671

Description Moderately large robust blunt-headed monitor. Tail short; round at base and laterally compressed distally. Ground colour pale or dark grey to greyish brown (occasionally dull reddish brown), marked with pale bands narrower or approximately equal in width to dark interspaces. Three or 4 V-shaped bands extend from base of head to shoulders and approximately 20–50 bands extend from shoulders to tail-tip. Bands are prominent and sharp-edged on juveniles, becoming diffuse with age. Top of head and neck ground colour; often grey (in noticeable contrast to ground colour) on individuals from central Qld. Lips paler, barred with dark grey to black. Ventral surfaces pale grey, sometimes bearing darker grey to brown spots, particularly on throat. SVL 0.5 m. TL 1.2 m.

Preferred habitat Occurs on semi-arid to arid deeply cracking dark clay (black soil) plains vegetated with Mitchell grass (*Astrebla* spp.), sometimes extending into adjacent reddish loams. Ranges from western interior of Qld to central-eastern NT.

Microhabitat Usually shelters in deep soil cracks, and cavities beneath rocks. Occasionally excavates burrows or utilises those of other animals.

Comments Terrestrial. Forages widely on hot still days. Activity is reduced during strong winds which prevail throughout its range. Feeds on a variety of small vertebrates, arthropods and carrion. Clutches of 11–31 eggs are laid during spring. Raises body on hindlimbs when threatened, or to survey surroundings when foraging.

Ridge-tailed Monitor
Varanus storri Mertens, 1966
Photos 672, 673

Description Small robust monitor with thick spinose tail, dorsally depressed at base and rounded to triangular in cross-section distally. Two subspecies recognised.

V. s. storri Ground colour pale or dark brown to reddish brown (often paler on vertebral region) marked with obscure fine darker reticulum or ocelli over body, limbs and usually head. These often fragment into irregular flecks. Dark streak (sometimes pale-edged) extends from eye to above ear. Lips may bear irregular dark vertical bars. Tail spotted with blackish brown. Ventral surfaces whitish to pale brown. SVL 0.13 m. TL 0.4 m.

V. storri ocreatus Storr, 1980 Differs from nominate form by longer limbs and tail, and presence of enlarged scales beneath distal portion of hindlimb.

Distinguished from *V. acanthurus* by pattern (weak, without stripes on neck vs strong, usually including stripes on neck) and much smaller maximum size (TL 0.4 vs 0.6 m). Differs from *V. primordius* by ground colour (reddish vs greyish) and nature of tail (strongly vs weakly spinose).

Preferred habitat Rocky ranges and outcrops of subhumid to semi-arid far northern Australia. *V. s. storri* occurs in north-eastern interior of Qld, parti-

cularly among low scattered rock outcrops. *V. s. ocreatus* occupies similar habitats in Kimberley region, WA, and adjacent NT, extending onto black soil plains in these areas.

Microhabitat Terrestrial and rock-inhabiting. Shelters in rock crevices or in shallow oblique U-shaped burrows excavated beneath rocks.

Comments Usually locally abundant. Spinose tail is used to block entrance to shelter. Feeds largely on arthropods though lizards are also taken. Clutches of 5–7 eggs are recorded.

Black-headed Monitor or Freckled Monitor
Varanus tristis (Schlegel, 1839)
Photos 674–676

Description Medium-sized monitor with long slender tail; round in cross-section and bearing strongly keeled scales. Two distinct forms occur, varying in colour of head and neck, and extent of anterior pattern. These have been described as subspecies: (black-headed form) *V. t. tristis* and ('freckled' form) *V. t. orientalis* Fry, 1913. These names have not been applied here due to the extent of intergradation between them.

'Freckled' form: Ground colour pale or dark brown, reddish brown to blackish brown, usually with prominent pattern. Numerous greyish white transversely aligned ocelli extend from base of head onto base of tail. These tend to be most prominent (flushed with yellow to red) posteriorly. Top of head paler to darker shade of ground colour, spotted to flecked with pale greyish brown. Obscure pale-edged dark streak extends from eye to above ear. Lips usually pale, mottled to obscurely barred with brown. Limbs bear pale grey, yellow to reddish spots or ocellations. Anterior half of tail narrowly banded to variegated with pale pigment. Remainder dark brown to black, usually without pattern. Ventral surfaces whitish, spotted to irregularly barred with darker pigment. SVL 0.28 m. TL 0.75 m.

Black-headed form: Ocelli tend to become smaller and more fragmented; mixed with fine dark reticulum. Pattern seldom extends on to neck (if so, it is represented by small obscure spots). Head, neck and all but base of tail, blackish brown to black without pattern. Adults from far south-west of range are uniformly dark, virtually lacking pattern.

Distinguished from *V. scalaris* by head-shape (strongly depressed and relatively sharp snouted vs weakly depressed and blunt snouted). Differs from *V. pilbarensis* by shorter head, neck and tail, and absence of bands on tail-tip. Differs from *V. semiremex* by nature of tail (round in cross-section vs laterally compressed distally).

Preferred habitat Widespread through subhumid to arid woodlands, rocky ranges and outcrops from WA and SA (excluding south) to NT, Qld (excluding far south-east corner and humid areas of north-east) and north-western NSW. Black-headed form is predominantly western and southern in distribution, extending to central Australia. 'Freckled' form is predominantly eastern, extending to central Australia and northern NT.

Microhabitat Arboreal and rock-inhabiting. Shelters in hollow trunks and limbs, beneath loose bark, in rock crevices and under slabs. In some areas, mud nests of swallows and martins are frequently utilised.

Comments Terrestrial, arboreal and rock-inhabiting. Active throughout year in north. Inactive from autumn to late winter in south. Forages widely (up to 2 km per day) in search of food, ascending trees to investigate all likely hollows or crevices. Feeds largely on lizards, though arthropods and other small vertebrates (particularly birds, their nestlings and eggs) are also taken. In southern WA breeding probably takes place in September. Clutches of 5–17 eggs are laid, probably in late spring.

Lace Monitor
Varanus varius (White, 1790)
Photos 677, 678

Description Extremely large monitor with long slender tail, round in cross-section at base and strongly laterally compressed distally. Two distinct colour forms occur.

Common widespread form: Pattern prominent on juveniles, darkening to virtual absence on adults. Ground colour of juveniles pale bluish grey spotted with yellow. Approximately 5 narrow black bands (each curving forward laterally to form U shape) extend across neck, and approximately 8 pairs of bands extend between shoulders and hips. Top of head blackish, mottled or spotted with yellow. Snout prominently banded with black and yellow, each band extending onto chin. Lips yellow bearing broad black bar from beneath eye onto chin. Forelimbs narrowly banded with black and yellow. Hindlimbs black, spotted with yellow. Tail banded with black and yellow to cream; narrowly on base, broadly on distal two-thirds. Ventral surfaces yellow banded with black. Adults are dark grey to dull bluish black, usually retaining some indication of bands and/or pale spots. Yellow and black chin markings are almost invariably retained.

Banded or Bell's form: Ground colour yellowish brown to bright yellow, finely mottled with black and marked with very broad irregular dark brown to black bands between shoulders and tail-tip. Top of head black, blotched with yellow; dark pigment usually continuous with broad black U-shaped band

on neck. Limbs and ventral surfaces banded with black and yellow. SVL 0.7 m. TL 2.0 m.

Distinguished from *V. gouldii* and *V. rosenbergi* by pattern: prominent broad bars across throat, no pale-edged dark streak behind eye and very broad (vs narrow) bands on tail. These extend to tail-tip on *V. varius* and *V. rosenbergi* but not on *V. gouldii*. Differs further in possessing longer, more slender tail and attaining greater maximum size (TL 2.0 vs 1.65 m or less).

Preferred habitat Subhumid to humid eastern Australia from south-eastern Cape York Peninsula, Qld, to south-eastern SA. Occurs in a variety of habitats, from woodlands to wet sclerophyll and rainforests. Common form extends continuously throughout range. Bell's form appears restricted to subhumid areas from northern NSW to mideastern Qld.

Microhabitat Regularly forages on ground, dashing to nearest tree when disturbed. Shelters in hollow trunks, limbs and logs.

Comments Terrestrial and arboreal. Australia's second largest lizard. Forages extensively in search of food, investigating all suitable hollows or crevices it encounters. Feeds on a wide variety of vertebrates (including fish), arthropods, bird eggs and carrion. Often shot by poultry farmers for stealing eggs. Juveniles less than TL 0.75 m are rarely encountered. As size increases lizards become bolder due to reduced predation and many picnic areas are regularly patrolled by large resident monitors scavenging for scraps. During breeding season (early summer in NSW, midsummer in southern Vic.) large numbers of males may aggregate in the vicinity of a receptive female. Spectacular chases and ritual combat between rivals are common at these times. Mating is preceded by a dominant male approaching the female with vigorous shaking movements of head. Female lies prostrate and male explores her dorsal and lateral surfaces with flickering tongue, eventually positioning himself above her. Female then raises hips enabling copulation to occur. Clutches of 8–12 eggs are recorded. These are almost invariably laid in arboreal termitaria. Termites seal nest over eggs, providing effective incubation. If cornered, distends throat and hisses noisily. May rear on hindlimbs and lash with powerful tail. Recorded to lash tail at attacking birds. These no doubt recognise the lizards as major predators of their eggs and nestlings, harassing them at every opportunity.

See also photo 679, which shows an undescribed *Varanus* taxon widespread from Gulf of Carpentaria to south-western Queensland.

SNAKES

(Order Squamata, Suborder Ophidia)

Seven families of snakes occur in Australia. Two of these, the sea snakes (Hydrophiidae) and sea kraits (Laticaudidae), differ from the families discussed in bearing paddle-shaped tails. They are adapted to a marine environment, and are not dealt with here. The remaining five families are restricted to the land, rivers and mangrove communities. These encompass 36 genera and 136 described species:

Acrochordidae (file snakes): 1 genus and 2 species.

Boidae (pythons): 4 genera and 14 species.

Colubridae (solid-toothed and rear-fanged snakes): 8 genera and 10 species.

Elapidae (front-fanged snakes): 22 genera and 80 species.

Typhlopidae (blind snakes): 1 genus and 30 species.

Snakes are distinguished from lizards in bearing some (usually all) of the following characters:
- no limbs
- no ear-openings
- long slender deeply forked tongues
- eyes covered by transparent spectacles (unable to blink)
- short tails, usually much less than SVL, and
- ventral scales greatly enlarged to form transverse plates

Although some of these characteristics are shared with lizards, only those lizards which have lost or partially lost their limbs (flap-footed lizards and some skinks) are likely to pose problems of identification to a layperson.
- Limbs are absent on snakes, though vestigal hind-limbs, in the form of short spurs, are present on all pythons. In addition, both pythons and blind snakes retain a rudimentary pelvis, suggesting their ancestors resembled conventional lizards. Lizards lacking limbs or bearing weak limbs differ from snakes in most of the other characters listed above.
- Snakes invariably lack ears, but are very sensitive to vibration. Some dragon lizards, flap-footed lizards and skinks also lack an external ear-opening, though a scaly depression usually indicates its position.
- All snakes possess forked tongues, a character shared only with monitor lizards, and several lizard families occurring outside Australia.
- Eyelids are invariably absent on snakes, replaced by an immovable transparent spectacle. Blind snakes differ in that the rudimentary eye is covered by a transparent ocular scale. Geckos, flap-footed lizards and some skinks also have immovable spectacles.
- Tails are shorter than the SVL on all snakes. With the exception of the colubrid snake, the keelback (Styporhynchus mairii), tails are non-fragile on all Australian species. The keelback may easily lose the tail-tip if handled roughly, though it is unable

to regenerate a replacement. In contrast, lizard tails (when undamaged) are usually considerably longer than the SVL.
- With the exception of blind snakes and file snakes, ventral scales are enlarged to form transverse plates which are noticeably larger than remaining scales. Those of blind snakes and file snakes are more or less equal in size to surrounding body scales.

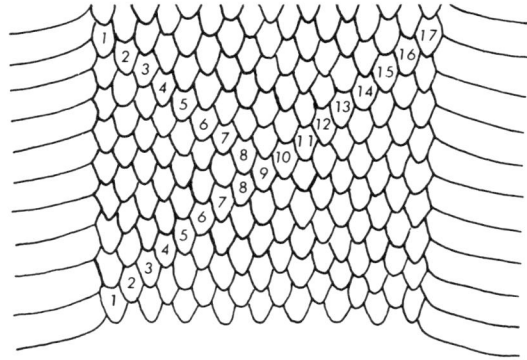

Midbody scale rows are counted diagonally. Note that the expanded ventral scales are not counted

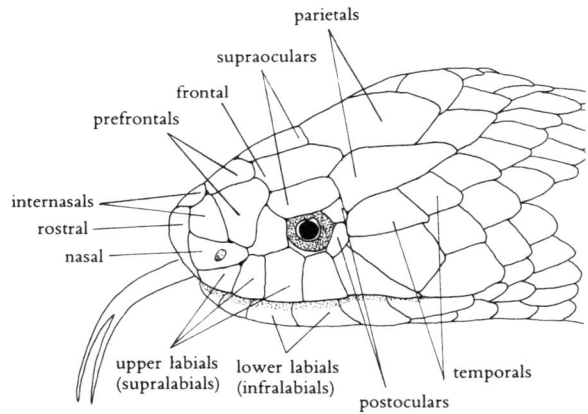

Arrangement of head shields on a typical elapid snake (Notechis scutatus)

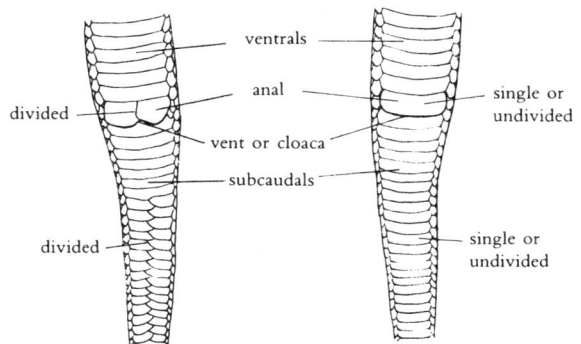

Variation in scalation beneath the tail of Australian snakes

FILE SNAKES
Family ACROCHORDIDAE

Contains a single genus of 3 distinctive non-venomous aquatic snakes extending from India, through South-East Asia, Indo-Malayan Archipelago and New Guinea to Australia. Represented in northern Australia by 2 species.

Genus *ACROCHORDUS*
Hornstedt, 1787

Characterised by large to very large robust body and rough rasp-like, loose to baggy skin. Snout blunt. Eye small and slightly protrusive with vertically elliptic pupil. Nostril valvular. Tail narrow and prehensile. Scales tiny, finely keeled or pointed, in 80 or more rows at midbody. Ventral scales not noticeably enlarged.

Nocturnal and diurnal wholly aquatic snakes preying almost entirely on fish. Long sharp teeth and rough scales aid in holding and constricting struggling prey. Livebearing. Harmless, though bites from large individuals may cause lacerations. Aborigines consider adults of both species to be a delicacy.

Arafura File Snake
Acrochordus arafurae McDowell, 1979
Photo 680

Description Large robust loose-skinned file snake with ground colour of brown to olive-brown. Pattern brightest on juveniles, becoming darker and more obscure with age. Coarse dark reticulum enclosing pale brown, olive to whitish blotches extends over dorsal and ventral surfaces. This tends to be finest anteriorly, often coalescing to form broad line on vertebral region. Head spotted and mottled anteriorly, merging with reticulum on temple and neck. Lips whitish to yellowish. Ventral surfaces yellowish white. Tail blackish, spotted with yellow. TL 1.5 m.

Distinguished from *A. granulatus* in attaining larger maximum size (TL 1.5 vs 1.2 m). Differs further by build (robust vs relatively slender), tail-shape (weakly vs strongly compressed) and pattern (reticulated vs regular bands), and preference for fresh (vs brackish to saline) water.

Preferred habitat Favours freshwater habitats, particularly *Pandanus*-lined lagoons and sheltered riverbanks. Associated with major drainage systems of far northern Australia, from north-west NT to western Cape York Peninsula, Qld. Extralimital in southern New Guinea, occurring in rivers connected to Arafura Sea.

Microhabitat Shelters beneath submerged detritus, among aquatic vegetation and under overhanging root-bound banks.

Comments Previous common name 'Javan file snake' results from long-term confusion with the extralimital species *A. javanicus*. When foraging, flickers long deeply forked tongue slowly. Fish are captured with a surprisingly rapid gaping strike. During Wet Season flooding, file snakes are able to disperse widely through ephemeral waterways. As these dry, large numbers may be found together in shrunken pools. Males are recorded to aggregate, forming a writhing ball while attempting to mate with a single female.

Little File Snake
Acrochordus granulatus (Schneider, 1799)
Photo 681

Description Small relatively slender file snake with ground colour of dark grey to dark brown. Pattern prominent on juveniles, becoming obscure and darker with age. Narrow whitish, pale grey to pale brown bands (continuous or alternating on each side of body) usually extend onto ventral surfaces. Ventral surfaces are usually a paler shade of ground colour, merging to blackish brown on tail. TL 1.2 m.

Distinguished from *A. arafurae* in attaining smaller maximum size (TL 1.2 vs 1.5 m). Differs further by build (slender vs relatively robust), tail-shape (strongly vs weakly compressed) and pattern (regular bands vs reticulum).

Preferred habitat Favours saline water, particularly where mangroves are present, though occasionally enters freshwater. Occurs in estuaries and along coastline of northern Australia, from far northern Kimberley region, WA, to north-east Qld. Extralimital from New Guinea to South-East Asia.

Microhabitat Shelters among mangrove roots and submerged debris. Occasionally encountered swimming in intertidal creeks or basking on exposed mudflats.

Comments Litters of 2–12 young recorded. Gestation period of 5–8 months is among longest recorded for snakes. Females apparently do not breed each year, probably following a biennial cycle. Otherwise as for genus.

PYTHONS
Family BOIDAE

A widespread family which includes the world's largest snakes. Diversity is greatest in tropical areas. Though several subfamilies are recognised, most species are contained in Boinae (boas) and Pythoninae (pythons). The distributions of these groups are mostly mutually exclusive. Boas occur in the New World, extending to islands of the western Pacific, New Guinea, India, Madagascar and Africa. These are absent from Australia. Pythons occur from Africa, through Asia to islands of the western Pacific. Four genera comprising 14 species are represented in Australia. The genus *Aspidites* is endemic.

Non-venomous snakes, characterised in Australia by small to extremely large size (TL 0.5 to a maximum of 8.0 m), presence of heat-sensitive pits in some lower labial scales (occasionally in some upper labials and rostral) on all genera except *Aspidites*, and a thorn-like spur on either side of the cloaca. Scales small and numerous, in 30 or more rows at midbody. Anal scale single. Subcaudal scales divided, single or a combination of both. Head scales fragmented, or enlarged to form shields. Ventral scales comprise transverse plates; considerably larger than adjacent scales, though never extending fully across belly. With exception of *Aspidites*, the head is broad; distinct from neck. Tail usually prehensile.

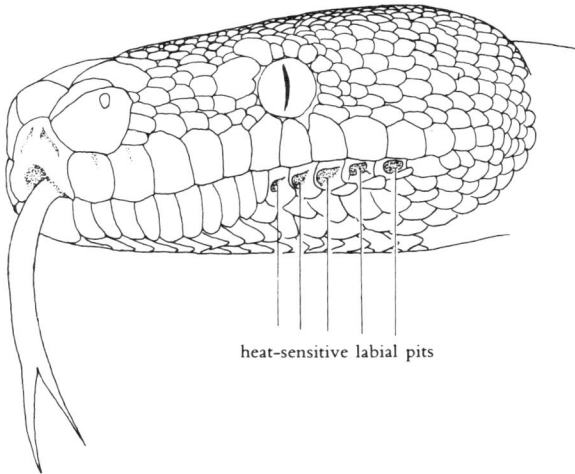

heat-sensitive labial pits

Lateral view of *Morelia spilota imbricata* showing heat receptors

Pythons are predominantly nocturnal, though often encountered basking in mild weather, particularly when digesting large meals. Most are adept climbers, equally at home in trees, rock outcrops or on the ground. One species is semi-aquatic, though most others enter water on occasions.

Diets are composed entirely of vertebrates. Heat-sensitive pits aid in locating warm-blooded animals. Pythons asphyxiate their prey by constricting it in tight coils, rather than crushing it to death as is popularly believed. They are best known for their ability to consume large prey items many times their own girth and to endure extended fasts; sometimes a year or more. Though several extra-limital pythons, particularly the reticulated python (*Python reticulatus*), are occasionally reported to prey on humans, no Australian snakes attain sufficient size to do so. Most large species have long been food items prized by Aborigines.

Pythons are the only Australian snakes to possess both a pelvis and vestigial hindlimbs (cloacal spurs): see photo 682 of *Bothrochilus fuscus*. These spurs are used by males to stimulate females during copulation. Pythons lay parchment-shelled eggs, often adhered to form a cluster. Females cease feeding prior to laying and remain coiled around the eggs during incubation. They are able to slightly raise their body temperature during this period by producing muscular spasms (shivering).

Although non-venomous, pythons are equipped with numerous sharp backward-curving teeth and may deliver a painful bite if harassed.

Taxonomy of Australian pythons at the generic level is unresolved. We have tentatively recognised *Bothrochilus* and *Morelia*, though captive individuals of *M. spilota* and *B. fuscus* have produced hybrid offspring, suggesting a close affinity between them.

Genus *ASPIDITES*   Peters, 1876

Endemic genus containing 2 widespread species occurring through subhumid north and arid interior of Australia.

Large moderately robust pythons, each with a narrow head barely distinct from neck. Eye small, with dark iris and vertically elliptic pupil. Head scales enlarged to form symmetrical shields. Heat-sensitive labial pits absent. Tail not prehensile. Scales smooth in 50–65 rows at midbody. Subcaudal scales single anteriorly, divided posteriorly.

Pattern includes numerous dark bands on body and tail.

Nocturnal, though occasionally encountered basking during mild weather. Terrestrial and rock-inhabiting pythons which feed on mammals, birds and reptiles, including venomous snakes. May be pugnacious when harassed, raising head and fore-body to form an S shape, hissing loudly and striking repeatedly.

Distinguished from all other Australian pythons

in lacking heat-sensitive pits on lower labial scales, and in possessing a narrow head (vs broad, distinct from neck).

Black-headed Python
Aspidites melanocephalus (Krefft, 1864)
Photo 683

Description Largest *Aspidites*. Ground colour cream, pale yellowish brown to reddish brown; palest bearing sharpest pattern in far west of range (west Kimberley region, WA, south-westwards). Numerous dark brown to blackish bands (usually narrower than pale interspaces) extend between neck and tail-tip. These may be disjunct, or coalesced to form a dark suffusion along vertebral line. Head, neck and throat glossy black. Ventral surfaces cream to pale yellow, often bearing obscure blotches or smudges. These represent lower extremes of dark bands. TL 2.5 m.

Distinguished from *A. ramsayi* by head colour (black vs pale).

Preferred habitat Woodlands, rocky ranges and outcrops of subhumid to humid northern Australia. Absent from extremely arid areas, and from cracking clay soils of western Qld and adjacent NT. Extends from North West Cape, WA, through northern NT (as far south as Tea-Tree) to Qld (south on coast to Gladstone district).

Microhabitat Shelters in hollow logs, crevices, caves and abandoned burrows of monitors and mammals.

Comments Glossy black head and nape (uncommon among large Australian snakes) may enable maximum heat absorption while exposing minimum body surface. Clutches of 8 and 11 eggs are recorded. Otherwise as for genus.

Woma
Aspidites ramsayi (Macleay, 1882)
Photo 684

Description Ground colour pale brown, yellowish brown, reddish brown to pale olive, marked with numerous irregular darker brown to reddish brown bands. These may be slightly narrower to broader than pale interspaces and often coalesce on dorsum to form a darker vertebral zone. All aspects of pattern become obscure to absent with age. Juveniles bear a conspicuous dark patch above each eye. This characteristic may be retained to adulthood, especially in populations from south-eastern interior of Qld. Ventral surfaces cream to pale yellow, bearing irregular brownish blotches. TL 2.0 m.

Distinguished from *A. melanocephalus* by head colour (pale vs black).

Preferred habitat Subhumid to arid interior of Australia from north-west coast of WA, through all mainland States except Vic., to southern Qld, east to Moonie district. Favours sandy substrates supporting hummock grasslands, woodlands, shrub-lands or heathland associations.

Microhabitat Shelters largely in abandoned monitor and mammal burrows.

Comments Captive womas have been observed to subdue their prey by pressing it against the walls of their enclosures; possibly an adaptation to hunting within the confines of burrow systems. This feeding strategy may enable prey to retaliate, contributing to the high proportion of scarred adults encountered. The tail-tip has been reported to function as a lure, which may explain the frequency of individuals with damaged tails. Isolated population of womas on sand plains of southern WA has not been seen for many years and may be considered endangered or extinct in that region. Land-clearing and predation on young snakes by feral animals have probably contributed to this decline. Clutch of 22 eggs is recorded. Otherwise as for genus.

Genus *BOTHROCHILUS*
Fitzinger, 1843

Represented in Australia by 6 species. Widespread through most of continent, excepting cool areas of eastern highlands and extreme south. Extralimital in New Guinea and eastern Indonesia.

Very small to very large pythons. Head narrow, distinct from neck. Eye bears a pale iris and vertically elliptic pupil. Head scales enlarged to form symmetrical shields. Heat sensitive pits present in some lower labial scales. Scales smooth; weakly to strongly glossed in 31–80 rows at midbody.

Predominantly terrestrial and rock-inhabiting. Two species groups are recognised.

B. olivaceus **group** Comprises 3 taxa of large pythons (up to TL 6.5 m), lacking all trace of dorsal pattern. Restricted to northern Australia. Members are *B. fuscus*, *B. olivaceus barroni* and *B. olivaceus olivaceus*.

B. childreni **group** Comprises 5 taxa of small to very small pythons (up to TL 1.05 m), possibly including the world's smallest species. Pattern (when present) consists of dark blotches on a pale ground colour. Excepting the dwarf *B. perthensis* which feeds mainly on geckos, members consume a broad range of small birds, mammals and lizards. Large numbers of these snakes are often encountered in caves supporting colonies of bats. Members are *B. childreni*, *B. maculosus*, *B. perthensis*, *B. stimsoni orientalis* and *B. stimsoni stimsoni*.

Bothrochilus is distinguished from *Morelia* (excepting the very large, distinctive *M. amethistina*) by nature of head shields (large and symmetrical vs small and fragmented).

Children's Python
Bothrochilus childreni (Gray, 1842)
Photo 685

Description Large member of *B. childreni* group

with ground colour of pale yellowish brown to dark purplish brown. Pattern usually obscure, occasionally absent, comprising numerous relatively small dark smooth-edged blotches. These are mostly circular, rarely transversely elongate. Dark streak usually present from nostril through eye to temple. Ventral surfaces whitish with an opalescent sheen. TL 1.02 m.

Distinguished from *B. stimsoni* by nature of pattern (weak to absent vs strong).

Preferred habitat Humid to subhumid areas of northern Australia, from the Kimberley region of WA through northern NT to north-western Qld. Occurs in a variety of habitats from rock outcrops and escarpments to monsoon forests and woodlands.

Microhabitat Shelters in caves, rock crevices, hollow timber, abandoned burrows, termitaria and surface debris.

Comments See species group.

Water Python
Bothrochilus fuscus (Peters, 1873)
Photos 686, 687

Description Member of *B. olivaceus* group. Ground colour dark olive-brown, olive-grey to almost black (iridescent bluish grey when viewed obliquely), fading to yellow on lower lateral surfaces. Lips and throat cream to white. Ventral surfaces of body dull to bright yellow, brightest anteriorly. Subcaudal scales dorsal colour. TL 2.0 m. Individuals of 3.0 m recorded.

Distinguished from *B. olivaceus* in possessing glossy, highly iridescent scales, and yellow (vs cream) ventral surfaces.

Preferred habitat Freshwater swamps, lagoons, creeks and river margins (including man-made dams and reservoirs) of northern Australia. Extends from Broome area to Drysdale River region in WA, thence across northern NT to northern Qld, ranging as far south as St Lawrence district. Extralimital in southern New Guinea and eastern Lesser Sunda Islands.

Microhabitat Shelters in hollow logs, stumps, abandoned burrows, rock crevices and beneath mats of vegetation.

Comments Predominantly nocturnal. Terrestrial and semi-aquatic, entering water more frequently than other Australian pythons. Feeds largely on waterbirds. Adults are reported to prey on young freshwater crocodiles (*Crocodylus johnstoni*). Clutches of 9–16 eggs are recorded.

Bothrochilus maculosus (Peters, 1873)
Photo 688

Description Large member of *B. childreni* group with ground colour of pale yellowish brown to cream, marked with numerous ragged-edged darker brown to purplish brown blotches. These tend to

coalesce along vertebral region, especially anteriorly and posteriorly, to form a coarse wavy stripe. Ventrolateral stripe of ground colour may be present, often poorly defined or absent. Head marked with dark blotches, and usually bearing a dark streak from nostril through eye to temple. Dark sutures usually present between upper labial scales. Ventral surfaces whitish with an opalescent sheen. TL 1.05 m.

Distinguished from *B. stimsoni orientalis* by nature of pattern (blotches ragged-edged and tending to coalesce along vertebral line, especially anteriorly and posteriorly, vs smooth-edged, tending to coalesce transversely).

Preferred habitat Humid to subhumid areas of eastern Qld and far north-eastern NSW. Occurs in a variety of habitats, from rainforest margins to sclerophyll forests and woodlands. Rock outcrops, particularly where caves are present, are favoured.

Microhabitat Shelters in hollow timber, abandoned burrows and termitaria, beneath rock slabs, in caves and under surface debris.

Comments An individual recorded to have consumed an adult of the large powerful skink, *Egernia frerei*. Clutches of 4–20 eggs recorded. See species group.

Olive Python
Bothrochilus olivaceus (Gray, 1842)
Photo 689

Description Largest member of *B. olivaceus* group with moderately glossed scales, bearing a milky sheen. Two subspecies are recognised.

B. o. olivaceus Ground colour dark olive, yellowish brown to olive-brown, fading laterally. Lips, side of throat, neck and ventral surfaces white to cream. Lips may be finely dotted with darker pigment. TL 2.5 m (average).

B. o. barroni (Smith, 1981) Differs from nominate form in possessing fewer midbody scale rows (58–63 vs 61–80), more numerous ventral scales (374–411 vs 355–377), and in attaining larger average size. Individuals up to 6.5 m reported, but this is yet to be verified.

Distinguished from *B. fuscus* in bearing cream (vs yellow) ventral surfaces, and weakly glossed (vs highly iridescent) body scales.

Preferred habitat Arid to humid areas of northern Australia. Often encountered along drainage systems, especially those associated with rocky areas. *B. o. olivaceus* extends from Broome area, WA, across northern NT to western half of Qld; as far south as Windorah district. *B. o. barroni* is restricted to Pilbara region, WA; separated from nominate form by Great Sandy Desert.

Microhabitat Shelters in deep rock crevices, caves and abandoned burrows.

Comments Terrestrial and rock-inhabiting. Feeds on mammals, birds and reptiles. Adults often consume mammals as large as rock wallabies. These may be ambushed along regularly used trails to water, or captured while drinking. Clutch of 11 eggs recorded.

Pygmy Python
Bothrochilus perthensis (Stull, 1932)
Photo 690

Description Member of *B. childreni* group. Australia's (possibly the world's) smallest python. Ground colour pale brown to pale reddish brown, obscurely marked with irregularly sized darker blotches and spots. These decrease in size laterally, often breaking to leave an obscure midlateral stripe of ground colour. Obscure dark streak extends from eye to corner of mouth. Ventral surfaces cream. TL 0.5 m.

Distinguished from all sympatric pythons in attaining a smaller maximum size (TL 0.6 vs 0.75 m or greater) and bearing fewer midbody scale rows (31–35 vs 37 or more).

Preferred habitat Arid north-west coast and interior of WA, from southern Great Sandy Desert south to Mullewa district. Favours rock outcrops and hard to stony soils supporting *Acacia*-dominated woodlands and shrublands.

Microhabitat Shelters beneath rocks, in crevices, soil cracks, termitaria and abandoned burrows.

Comments Nocturnal. Predominantly terrestrial, occasionally ascending low shrubs. Appears to feed largely on geckos, particularly *Gehyra* spp. An inoffensive snake, rarely attempting to bite when handled. The name 'perthensis' is derived from erroneous locality data, as the species does not extend as far south as Perth.

Bothrochilus stimsoni (Smith, 1985)
Photo 691

Description Medium-sized member of *B. childreni* group with 2 recognised subspecies.

B. s. stimsoni Ground colour pale brown, yellowish brown to whitish, irregularly marked with darker brown to reddish brown blotches. These may be elongate and/or circular. Pale ventrolateral line of ground colour extends from side of neck for varying lengths along body. Head blotched, and usually bearing a dark streak from nostril, through eye to side of neck. Dark sutures usually present between upper labial scales. Ventral surfaces whitish with an opalescent sheen. TL 0.87 mm.

B. s. orientalis (Smith, 1985) Similar in most respects to *B. s. stimsoni*, differing by arrangement of pattern: dark blotches tend to be transversely elongate, smoother edged, and interdigitated with those on opposing side. At least some, often many, coalesce with opposites to form transverse and oblique bars. Differs further in having fewer ventral scales (243–284 vs 260–302).

Both subspecies differ from *B. childreni* by nature of pattern (contrasting strongly with ground colour vs weak to absent). *B. s. orientalis* differs from *B. maculosus* by arrangement of pattern (blotches smooth-edged, tending to coalesce transversely vs ragged-edged and tending to coalesce longitudinally along vertebral line, especially anteriorly and posteriorly). *B. s. stimsoni* differs from *B. perthensis* in attaining much greater size (0.87 vs 0.6 m), having more ventral scales (260–302 vs 212–250) and more midbody scale rows (39–47 vs 31–35).

Preferred habitat Wide variety of habitats in sub-humid to arid areas, tending to favour rock outcrops or, in sparsely vegetated regions, woodlands lining drainage systems. *B. s. stimsoni* is restricted to WA, extending from Perth area north to Dampier Land in south-west Kimberley region. In arid eastern interior it merges with *B. s. orientalis* which extends through southern NT, northern SA, far western NSW to eastern interior of Qld, on western side of Great Dividing Range.

Microhabitat Shelters in hollow limbs, rock crevices and caves, abandoned burrows, termitaria and surface debris.

Comments See species group.

Genus *CHONDROPYTHON*
Meyer, 1874

Monotypic genus restricted in Australia to far northern and north-eastern Qld. Extralimital in New Guinea.

Moderately small python, with body roughly triangular in cross-section. Head large, bulbous at base and distinct from neck. Head scales fragmented and granular. Eye bears pale iris and vertically elliptic pupil. Heat sensitive pits present on some labial scales. Tail prehensile. Midbody scales smooth, in 50–75 rows.

Nocturnal and arboreal. Feeds on birds and mammals.

Green Python
Chondropython viridis (Schlegel, 1872)
Photo 692

Description Ground colour of adults, dull to bright emerald green. Broken or nearly continuous vertebral row of white scales (occasionally tinged with yellow or blue) extends from nape to tail. Sparsely scattered white, blue or yellow scales and narrow transverse blue lines are occasionally present on flanks. Tip of tail very slender and tinged with blue. Ground colour of juveniles bright yellow, orange or brick red, occasionally black or deep blue. Pale-centred purplish brown streak extends through eye. Purplish brown vertebral line or series of blotches extends to tail, often in combination with dark bars or blotches on upper flanks. Juvenile colour and pattern is apparently retained for approximately 3 years. Transition to green may reach completion over a period of several weeks. Ventral surfaces cream to bright yellow. TL 1.8 m.

Preferred habitat Rainforests, monsoon forests and bamboo thickets of north-eastern Cape York Peninsula and Torres Strait Islands, south to Iron Range, Qld. Extralimital in New Guinea.

Microhabitat Rests in a distinctive coil (see photograph) on a branch or vine in dense foliage.

Comments Undoubtedly one of Australia's most strikingly beautiful snakes. It illustrates an excellent example of convergent evolution, its mirror being the Emerald Tree Boa (*Corallus caninus*) of South America. Both species are bright yellow or orange at birth, changing to brilliant green as they mature, both are arboreal snakes which feed mainly on birds and both loop their bodies into the same distinctive symmetrical coils when at rest. *C. viridis* is reported to vibrate its thin bluish tail to lure prey, and to drink water collected in its coils after rain. Clutches of 11–25 eggs recorded.

Genus *MORELIA*   Gray, 1842

Contains 7 taxa. Widespread through most of Australia. Absent from west coast and interior of WA, alpine and subalpine regions, southern Vic. and Tas. Extralimital in southern New Guinea and the Moluccas.

Moderate to very large, slender to robust pythons. Body round in cross-section. Head moderately long and usually broad at base; distinct from neck. Eye bears pale to dark iris and vertically elliptic pupil. Head scales usually small, irregular and fragmented. Heat-sensitive pits present on lips. Tail prehensile. Subcaudal scales divided or mostly divided. Pattern prominent, usually including coarse irregular reticulum of blotches and/or spots.

Nocturnal, though often encountered basking during day. Predominantly arboreal and rock-inhabiting, though most species are regularly encountered on the ground. Diets consist largely of birds and mammals.

With the exception of the distinctive *M. amethistina*, *Morelia* differs from *Bothrochilus* by nature of head shields (small and fragmented vs large and symmetrical).

Amethyst or Scrub Python
Morelia amethistina (Schneider, 1801)
Photo 693

Description Australia's largest snake. Relatively slender *Morelia* with large elongate head, bearing enlarged plate-like head shields. Scales bear a milky iridescent sheen which has given rise to common and scientific names. Ground colour pale yellowish brown to brown, marked with numerous irregular angular dark brown to black bands, blotches and streaks. Those on anterior body may form elongate

streaks, while those on lower flanks often coalesce into one or more broken stripes. All aspects of pattern become obscure on posterior body and tail. Dark streak extends from eye down to corner of mouth. Juveniles are less glossy than adults, with a weaker pattern. Lips and ventral surfaces cream to white. TL 3.5 m, though individuals over 8 m are recorded.

Preferred habitat Rainforests, monsoon forests and vine thickets (occasionally dry sclerophyll forests and woodlands) in north-eastern Qld; from Townsville district north to Cape York Peninsula and islands of Torres Strait. Extralimital in New Guinea and the Moluccas.

Microhabitat Shelters in hollow timber, rock crevices, caves, abandoned buildings and beneath dense thickets of vegetation.

Comments Large individuals are predominantly terrestrial. Feeds mostly on mammals, and distended individuals containing prey as large as wallabies are occasionally encountered basking during the day. Clutches of 7 and 12 eggs are recorded.

Morelia bredli (Gow, 1981)
Photo 694

Description Ground colour rich orange-red to dark brown, marked with numerous irregular dark-edged cream to dull yellow blotches, bands and spots. These tend to align transversely, and are boldest, often forming bands, on posterior body and tail. Pale streak extends from eye to base of head. Lips, side of neck and ventral surfaces cream to pale yellowish brown, bearing irregular dark anterior margins on each ventral scale. All aspects of pattern are heightened in juveniles. TL 2.5 m.

Preferred habitat Rocky ranges, outcrops and associated drainage systems of arid southern NT.

Microhabitat Shelters in hollow trunks and limbs (especially those of eucalypts bordering rivers), or in rock crevices and caves associated with gorges.

Comments Predominantly arboreal and rock-inhabiting. Clutches of 13 and 47 eggs are recorded.

Morelia carinata (Smith, 1981)
Photo 695

Description Moderately slender large-eyed *Morelia*; sole member of genus bearing keeled dorsal scales. Ground colour brownish white, marked with numerous large angular dark brown transversely elongate blotches and coarse variegations. Ground colour fades and pattern darkens posteriorly, heightening contrast. Obscure pale streak extends from in front of eye to rear of head. Lips and ventral surfaces cream, every second to fifth scale smudged with brown. TL 2.0 m.

Preferred habitat Only 2 known specimens recorded from Mitchell River Falls on dissected sandstone plateau of Admiralty Gulf, north-west Kimberley region, WA.

Microhabitat Holotype was collected in a patch of monsoon vine forest at the base of falls.
Comments No data available. See genus.

Oenpelli Rock Python
Morelia oenpelliensis (Gow, 1977)
Photo 696

Description Large slender *Morelia* with ground colour of pale brown to pale olive-brown, fading to pale grey on lower flanks. Pattern consists of longitudinal series of dark brown to dark brownish grey blotches. These are largest dorsally, decreasing in size laterally and fading posteriorly. Occasionally some dorsal scales are dark-edged, tending to coalesce on tail to form an obscure reticulum. Dark brown streak extends from snout or eye to corner of jaw. Labial scales white, narrowly edged with dark brown. Ventral surfaces cream to dull yellow. TL 3.5 m.
Preferred habitat Arnhem Land Escarpment and adjacent outliers, northern NT.
Microhabitat Shelters in deep rock crevices and caves.
Comments Predominantly rock-inhabiting. Adults feed largely on mammals, particularly rock wallabies and possums. Clutch of 10 large eggs is recorded. Aborigines have regularly portrayed this large snake in rock art.

Diamond and Carpet Pythons
Morelia spilota (Lacépède, 1804)
Photos 697–701

Description Three subspecies are currently recognised, though a number of distinctly patterned populations occur. Differences between these appear as significant as those between the described subspecies.
Morelia s. spilota (**diamond python**) Ground colour dark grey to black. Most individual scales bear a cream spot. Clusters of all cream or predominantly cream scales form roughly diamond-shaped blotches over dorsal and lateral surfaces. Lips cream, lightly to heavily barred with black. Ventral surfaces cream to greenish white, marbled to blotched with dark grey. TL 2.5 m.
M. s. variegata Gray, 1842 (**carpet python**) Extremely variable, comprising at least 4 distinct forms:

Widespread eastern populations: Ground colour pale or dark brown to olive-green, marked with numerous irregular dark-edged cream to pale yellowish brown blotches. These tend to be transversely elongate on dorsum, while those on anterior flanks usually coalesce to form a stripe. Intergrades with nominate race in Northern Rivers district of NSW.

North-eastern Qld population: Ground colour blackish brown to black, prominently marked with yellow blotches, bands and/or stripes. Though sympatric with widespread eastern populations, little or no hybridisation appears to occur.

Murray/Darling population: Ground colour shades of grey with a reddish brown dorsal flush. Dorsal series of nearly circular, roughly paired, broadly dark-edged pale grey blotches extend from nape to tail. Those on flanks coalesce to form a broad broken stripe.

Northern NT/Kimberley population: Ground colour reddish brown to blackish brown, fading on lower flanks. Pattern consists of simple dark-edged yellowish brown to cream bands, 3–4 scales wide.

Ventral surfaces of all forms similar to those of nominate race. TL up to 2.5 m though individuals of 4 m have been recorded.
M. s. imbricata (Smith, 1981) Ground colour brown to blackish brown with variable pattern; similar to that of *M. s. variegata* (widespread eastern form).
Preferred habitat Occupies almost all habitats within its broad distribution. *M. s. spilota* occurs on south-east coast and ranges, from north-eastern Vic. to Northern Rivers region, NSW. Eastern population of *M. s. variegata* extends from Northern Rivers region to Cape York Peninsula and Torres Strait Islands, Qld. Extralimital in southern New Guinea. North-east Qld population occurs in rainforest on ranges and tablelands of that region. Murray/Darling population is associated with rock outcrops and large eucalypts along those drainage systems. NT/Kimberley form is restricted to northern parts of these areas. *M. s. imbricata* occurs in south-western WA and on some offshore islands, from Houtman Abrolhos Islands, Geraldton and Yalgoo districts south-east to Mt Le Grand.
Microhabitat Shelters in hollow trunks and limbs, disused burrows, caves, rock crevices and beneath boulders. Often encountered on rafters and in ceilings of buildings, including those in many urban areas.
Comments Australia's most familiar python. Largely nocturnal though individuals are commonly encountered basking or foraging during day. Arboreal, terrestrial and rock-inhabiting. Feeds largely on mammals and birds though lizards are occasionally taken. Combat has been observed between males during spring. Small numbers may aggregate for this purpose, fighting daily. Bodies are intertwined with heads raised more than a metre above the ground. Though this is largely ritualised, combatants may savagely bite each other, causing severe lacerations. Clutches of 9–52 eggs have been recorded. Individuals differ markedly in temperament. Some hiss loudly and strike with mouth agape when approached while others readily allow themselves to be handled.

SOLID-TOOTHED and REAR-FANGED SNAKES
Family COLUBRIDAE

Large cosmopolitan family containing over 1600 species in approximately 300 genera. Colubrids comprise a major proportion of the world's snake fauna. Members are highly variable and have radiated broadly to occupy most available habitats, from deserts and rainforests to rivers and coastlines. Numerous arboreal, fossorial and aquatic forms occur.

The family is probably a relatively recent arrival in Australia, invading via land bridges from New Guinea. This is indicated by the dominance of elapid snakes, the predominantly northern colubrid distribution, and the absence of endemic colubrids. Only 5 genera comprising 10 species occur here, all of which are extralimital at least as far as New Guinea, and in some cases India. Three widespread species extend south to NSW. Two subfamilies occur in Australia.

Subfamily Colubrinae contains 4 genera comprising 6 terrestrial and arboreal species. It includes both solid-toothed and weakly venomous rear-fanged forms. Solid-toothed colubrines include tree snakes (*Dendrelaphis*), keelbacks (*Styporhynchus*) and slaty-grey snakes (*Stegonotus*). The brown tree snake (*Boiga*) is Australia's only rear-fanged colubrine.

Subfamily Homalopsinae contains 4 genera (each represented by 1 species) of rear-fanged weakly venomous aquatic snakes. *Cerberus, Fordonia* and *Myron* inhabit salt to brackish water lined with mangroves. In Australia *Enhydris* is confined to fresh water. Homalopsines are widespread through the Orient and are restricted in Australia to the far north.

Distinguished from sea snakes (Hydrophiidae and Laticaudidae) in possessing a more or less cylindrical tail (vs laterally compressed to form a paddle).

Many homalopsine snakes, such as the bockadam (*Cerberus rynchops*) in photo 702, bear slightly protrusive eyes directed upwards. This is an adaptation for an aquatic lifestyle.

Genus *BOIGA*   Fitzinger, 1826

(Subfamily Colubrinae)

Widespread genus occurring in Africa, Asia, Indo-Malayan Archipelago, Philippine Islands, New Guinea and islands of the western Pacific. Represented in Australia by one species restricted to the north and east.

Moderately large slender weakly venomous rear-fanged snake with bulbous head and narrow neck. Eye large bearing vertically elliptic pupil. Scales smooth in 19–23 rows at midbody; vertebral series enlarged. Anal scale single; subcaudals divided.

Nocturnal. Arboreal and rock-inhabiting. Egg-laying.

Brown Tree Snake or Night Tiger
Boiga irregularis (Merrem, 1802)
Photo 703, 704

Description Two regionally distinct colour forms occur. Northern 'night tiger' form is cream to pale reddish brown bearing prominent broad and irregular dark reddish brown to rich reddish bands from nape to tail-tip. Eastern form is pale yellowish brown, grey-brown to rich reddish brown marked with numerous, prominent to obscure, narrow dark irregular bands or variegations. Scales may be finely edged with dark brown or black. Ventral surfaces cream to salmon pink. TL 2.0 m.

Preferred habitat Eastern form occurs in woodlands, wet and dry sclerophyll forests, rainforests and rock outcrops of subhumid to humid eastern Australia. Extends from Illawarra Scrub of southern NSW to Cape York and islands of Torres Strait, Qld. Extralimital from New Guinea to eastern Indonesia. Northern 'night tiger' form occurs in woodlands, vine thickets and monsoon forests, favouring rock outcrops, gorges and escarpments. Extends from Kimberley region, WA, through northern NT to Gulf of Carpentaria, Qld.

Microhabitat Shelters in hollow trunks and limbs, termitaria, rock crevices and caves. Often encountered among rafters of suburban buildings.

Comments Small mammals, birds and eggs constitute major prey items, although lizards are frequently taken, especially by juveniles. Clutches of 4–6 eggs recorded. Individuals may aggregate in caves and buildings, often littering surroundings with sloughed skins. Aggressive if threatened, holding body in a series of S-shaped loops and striking repeatedly. Not regarded as dangerous to humans.

Genus *CERBERUS*   Cuvier, 1829

Subfamily Homalopsinae

Widespread through India. South-East Asia, Indo-Malayan Archipelago, Philippine Islands and New Guinea. One species occurs in Australia, restricted to northern coastline.

Robust weakly venomous rear-fanged snake with small eye; protrusive and directed upwards, bearing vertically elliptic pupil. Nostril valvular. Head broad and distinct from neck. Scales moderately strongly keeled in 25 (occasionally 23) rows at midbody. Anal and subcaudal scales single.

Nocturnal, amphibious and livebearing.

Distinguished from *Myron* by pattern (bars, blotches or occasionally longitudinal markings vs numerous bands) and build (robust vs relatively slender). Differs further in attaining greater maximum size (TL 1.0 vs 0.6 m).

Bockadam
Cerberus rynchops (Schneider, 1799)
Photos 702, 705

Description Ground colour pale grey, shades of brown to brick red, prominently to obscurely marked with narrow irregular blackish bars, transversely aligned blotches or occasionally longitudinal streaks. Dark streak extends from snout, through eye to side of neck. Another extends from corner of mouth to side of neck or anterior body. Ventral surfaces whitish, yellow to pinkish; banded and blotched with black to dark brown. TL 1.0 m.

Preferred habitat Salt to brackish water on coastline, tidal creeks, rivers and estuaries margined with mangrove communities. Known from isolated localities from western Kimberley region, WA, to tip of Cape York Peninsula, Qld.

Microhabitat Shelters among mangrove roots and beneath submerged detritus. Forages in shallows along water's edge or adjacent to sandbars or mudflats.

Comments Predominantly nocturnal, though occasionally basks on mudflats. Feeds largely on fish. Litters of 1–7 young are recorded. Pugnacious if provoked, striking repeatedly and emitting a foul odour from anal glands. Not regarded as dangerous.

Tree Snakes
Genus *DENDRELAPHIS*
Boulenger, 1890

(Subfamily Colubrinae)

Widespread through India, South-East Asia, Indo-Malayan Archipelago, Philippine Islands, New Guinea and islands of the western Pacific. Represented in northern and eastern Australia by 2 species.

Slender long-tailed non-venomous snakes with large eye and round pupil. Midbody scales in 13 (occasionally 15) rows; vertebral series enlarged. Lateral edges of each ventral scale longitudinally ridged. Anal and subcaudal scales divided.

Swift, alert, diurnal, predominantly arboreal snakes which feed largely on frogs; located by keen eyesight. Lizards are also taken, especially by juveniles. Some individuals bear prominent lumps beneath their skin. These are parasites, acquired from the frogs they have eaten. Egglayers, producing 5–12 elongate eggs per clutch.

Northern Tree Snake
Dendrelaphis calligastra (Günther, 1867)
Photo 706

Description Extremely slender tree snake with ground colour of olive, olive-grey to pale or rich brown. Ragged-edged (sometimes broken) black streak extends from snout through eye to forebody, contrasting sharply with white to yellowish scales of upper lip. Juveniles may exhibit numerous narrow irregular dark bands or variegations; boldest anteriorly. Lower lateral and ventral surfaces white to yellow, usually marked with darker flecks. TL 0.8 m.

Distinguished from *D. punctulata* in possessing dark anterior lateral streak. Differs further by build (extremely slender vs relatively more robust) and eye size (very large vs moderately large).

Preferred habitat Rainforests, monsoon forests and vine thickets, especially along margins of waterways, from Townsville district north to Cape York Peninsula and islands of Torres Strait, Qld. Extralimital in New Guinea.

Microhabitat Inhabits dense foliage, often descending to ground when foraging.

Comments Swiftest, most consistently arboreal Australian tree snake. When cornered, forebody is inflated (to lesser extent than in *D. punctulata*), accompanied by hissing. Harmless. Otherwise as for genus.

Green or Common Tree Snake
Dendrelaphis punctulata (Gray, 1826)
Photos 707–709

Description Moderately slender tree snake. Several distinct colour forms occur. Ground colour may be black (common in Townsville district, Qld), bright yellow to yellowish brown merging to pale bluish grey on head and neck (predominant through northern Australia), olive-green, dull green to blue-green (common eastern Australian form) and pale to sky blue (uncommon, though widespread). Ventral surfaces usually yellow (occasionally greenish to whitish), generally most intense on anterior body. TL 1.2 m.

Distinguished from *D. calligastra* in lacking dark anterior lateral streak. Differs further by build (relatively more robust vs slender) and eye size (relatively smaller vs large).

Preferred habitat Semi-arid to humid areas of northern Australia, from Kimberley region, WA, to Cape York and Torres Strait Islands, Qld, extending south on east coast to Illawarra Scrub of south-eastern NSW. Extralimital in New Guinea. Occurs in a wide variety of habitats from woodlands to vine thickets, wet and dry sclerophyll forests and rainforests. Populations in dry areas usually occur along watercourses.

Microhabitat Shelters among foliage, in hollow limbs, rock crevices and caves. Common in many suburban areas throughout range.

Comments Large aggregations recorded over-wintering in hollow trees, disused buildings and caves. When cornered, neck and forebody are distended to display brightly coloured blue skin between scales; inhales and exhales sharply with loud hissing. Harmless. Otherwise as for genus.

Genus *ENHYDRIS*
Sonnini and Latreille, 1802

(Subfamily Homalopsinae)

Widespread through India, Asia, South-East Asia, Indo-Malayan Archipelago and New Guinea. One species occurs in northern Australia.

Moderately robust weakly venomous rear-fanged snake with small eye, set on top of head and bearing vertically elliptic pupil. Nostril valvular. Scales smooth in 21–23 rows at midbody. Anal and sub-caudal scales divided.

Nocturnal to diurnal. Livebearing. Restricted in Australia to freshwater habitats. Amphibious.

Macleay's Water Snake
Enhydris polylepis (Fischer, 1886)
Photos 710, 711

Description Dorsal and upper lateral ground colour shades of brown, olive to grey; iridescent shining purple when viewed obliquely. Pattern variable, and usually weaker on adults. Broad darker vertebral stripe may extend back from head, occasionally breaking into 2 paravertebral stripes on anterior body. Many Qld individuals (particularly juveniles) are marked with a dorsal series of irregular short dark transverse bars (1 or 2 scales wide) on posterior body. Dark lateral stripe may extend from snout, through eye onto body; often breaking into spots towards tail. Yellow lower lateral stripe (often broken into series of spots, blotches or variegations) extends from neck, becoming diffuse posteriorly. This is margined by a narrow ventrolateral stripe of ground colour; each scale often bearing paler centre or edge. Ventral surfaces cream to yellow; often mottled with black anteriorly, and on lateral edges of ventral scales. Tail may bear black median stripe, or each subcaudal scale may be black, edged posteriorly with yellow. TL 0.7 m.

Preferred habitat Associated with freshwater lakes, lagoons, swamps, rivers and creeks of northern Australia, from northern Kimberley region, WA, to north-eastern Qld. Extralimital in New Guinea.

Microhabitat Shelters among aquatic vegetation or beneath submerged root-tangles, leaf-litter and other detritus.

Comments Common name derives from confusion with *Enhydris macleayi* (Ogilby, 1890), the status of which is uncertain. Closer examination of specimens from Qld may be necessary to determine whether all Australian populations are conspecific. Feeds on small aquatic vertebrates, particularly fish. Appears to rely largely upon ambush to capture prey. Individuals observed camouflaged among submerged roots probably use these as supports from which to strike at passing prey. Often widely dispersed as a result of Wet Season sheet-flooding, contracting to permanent pools during dry periods. Harmless.

Genus *FORDONIA*   Gray, 1842

(Subfamily Homalopsinae)

Monotypic genus restricted in Australia to northern coastline. Extralimital in New Guinea, Philippine Islands, Indo-Malayan Archipelago and South-East Asia.

Moderately robust weakly venomous rear-fanged snake with broad head and rounded snout. Eye small with round pupil. Nostril valvular. Scales smooth in 23–29 rows at midbody. Anal and sub-caudal scales divided (occasionally a few subcaudals single).

Nocturnal to diurnal, amphibious snake which feeds largely on crabs.

White-bellied Mangrove Snake
Fordonia leucobalia (Schlegel, 1837)
Photos 712, 713

Description A number of distinctive forms occur, ranging from black through shades of brown to reddish brown or cream. Pattern prominent to absent. Dark individuals may be uniform or marked with white to greyish bands, blotches, spots or combinations of these. Markings tend to be most prominent on lower lateral surfaces. Reddish brown to cream individuals may bear vertebral and lower lateral series of large bluish grey, brown to blackish spots and blotches. Brown individuals may be marked laterally with dark red and pink blotches or variegations. Ventral surfaces and adjacent 1–4 lower lateral scale rows white, yellowish to pink. Dark median stripe usually present beneath tail. TL 0.6 m.

Preferred habitat Salt to brackish waters of coastline, tidal creeks and estuaries in northern Australia. Known from isolated localities in WA, from Nickol Bay in the Pilbara region to Wyndham in the east Kimberley region, then more or less continuously to north-eastern Qld.

Microhabitat Forages in mangrove-lined tidal channels and on mudflats, sheltering in crab burrows and among root-tangles.

Comments Feeds almost exclusively on crabs, pressing them against substrate with its coils and immobilising them by biting off legs and claws before consuming them. Harmless.

Genus *MYRON* Gray, 1849
(Subfamily Homalopsinae)

Monotypic genus restricted to northern Australia and New Guinea.

Small relatively slender weakly venomous rear-fanged snake. Eye small, slightly protrusive and directed upwards. Nostril valvular. Scales weakly keeled, in 21–23 rows at midbody. Anal and subcaudal scales divided.

Nocturnal and amphibious.

Distinguished from *Cerberus* by pattern (irregular bands vs bars, blotches and occasionally longitudinal markings) and build (relatively slender vs robust). Differs further in attaining smaller maximum size (TL 0.6 vs 1.0 m).

Richardson's Mangrove Snake
Myron richardsonii Gray, 1849
Photo 714

Description Smallest Australian homalopsine snake. Ground colour brown, olive-brown to grey. Pattern consists of numerous narrow irregular blackish to dark brown bands, of roughly equal width to pale interspaces. These usually extend onto ventral surfaces. Head tends to be darker shade of ground colour, with a prominent to obscure blackish streak from snout, through eye to temple or side of neck. Ventral surfaces yellow to cream with black anterior edge to each ventral and subcaudal scale. TL 0.6 m.

Preferred habitat Salt to brackish water of estuaries and tidal creeks on coast and islands of northern Australia. Known from 2 localities in the Kimberley region of WA (Derby and Wyndham), extending along coast of NT to Gulf of Carpentaria.

Microhabitat Shelters among mangrove roots, beneath submerged detritus and in crab burrows. Forages in shallows and on mudflats.

Comments Feeds on small fish. Infrequently encountered. Harmless.

Genus *STEGONOTUS* Duméril, Bibron and Duméril, 1854
(Subfamily Colubrinae)

Widespread through Philippine Islands, New Guinea and Moluccas. Two species occur in northern Australia.

Moderately large slender square-snouted non-venomous snakes. Eye moderately small with black iris. Scales smooth and glossy in 17–19 rows at midbody. Anal scale single, subcaudals divided.

Nocturnal. Predominantly terrestrial. Egglaying.

Slaty-grey Snake
Stegonotus cucullatus (Duméril, Bibron and Duméril, 1854)
Photo 715

Description Ground colour dark brown to very dark grey, becoming paler on flanks; shining iridescent purple when viewed obliquely. Upper lips cream to pale brown. Ventral surfaces white to cream, sometimes marked with black flecks, particularly on lateral portion of posterior ventral scales. TL 1.3 m.

Distinguished from *S. parvus* by pattern (pale upper lip less sharply defined) and greater size (TL 1.3 vs 0.8 m).

Preferred habitat Favours damp margins of creeks, rivers, swamps and lagoons, extending into a variety of woodland, monsoon forest and rainforest habitats from northern NT to northern Qld.

Microhabitat Shelters beneath logs, rocks, low vegetation and in abandoned burrows. May also be encountered climbing in low foliage or on steep rock faces.

Comments Partially arboreal and semi-aquatic. Feeds largely on frogs though reptiles and warm-blooded prey are also taken. Pugnacious when provoked, striking repeatedly. Harmless.

Stegonotus parvus (Meyer, 1874)

Description Ground colour brown, flushed with darker brown to black on vertebral region and fading to pale brown on lower flanks. Lips white to pale brown, often contrasting sharply with ground colour. Ventral surfaces white to pale yellow. TL 0.8 m.

Distinguished from *S. cucullatus* in possessing more sharply defined pale upper lip and attaining smaller maximum size (TL 0.8 vs 1.3 m).

Preferred habitat Poorly known. Restricted in Australia to Murray Island, in Torres Strait, Qld. Extralimital in New Guinea.

Microhabitat Not documented, presumably similar to *S. cucullatus*.

Comments Snake and lizard eggs constitute a significant portion of diet. Lizards are also taken.

Genus *STYPORHYNCHUS* Peters, 1863
(Subfamily Colubrinae)

Widespread through eastern Indonesia and New Guinea. One species extends to northern and mideastern Australia.

Moderately robust non-venomous snake with strongly keeled dorsal and lateral scales. Eye moderately large with round pupil. Tail semi-fragile. Midbody scales in 15 (rarely 17) rows. Anal and subcaudal scales divided.

Diurnal to nocturnal. Terrestrial and semi-aquatic. Egglaying.

Superficially similar to highly venomous rough-scaled snake (*Tropidechis carinatus*), differing in possessing fewer midbody scale rows (15 vs 23), and by nature of anal and subcaudal scales (divided vs single).

Freshwater Snake or Keelback
Styporhynchus mairii (Gray, 1841)
Photo 716

Description Ground colour variable, ranging through shades of dull grey, olive to almost black, or rich reddish brown to yellow. Pattern prominent to obscure, usually including irregular narrow dark bands, spots or variegations, mixed with dark and pale flecks on skin between scales. These are often masked by darker ground colour on posterior body and tail. Lips whitish. Ventral scales cream, pale brown, pink to olive; often edged laterally with black. TL 0.7 m.

Preferred habitat Extends across subhumid to humid northern Australia, from Kimberley region, WA, to northern Qld and south to north-eastern NSW. Favours well-watered habitats such as creek, river, lagoon, swamp and lake margins.

Microhabitat Shelters among low vegetation, beneath fallen timber or in abandoned burrows.

Comments Often encountered foraging or basking in warm weather. Regularly enters water, sometimes spending a considerable time submerged. Feeds largely on frogs, though tadpoles, small lizards and fish are also taken. Apparently able to prey on young of the introduced and poisonous cane toad (*Bufo marinus*), its tadpoles and eggs, without ill-effect. However, individuals are reported to die after attempting to consume large toads. In southern Qld mating takes place between early October and early December. Males are recorded to indulge in combat during this period. Clutches of 5–15 (average 8) eggs are laid, hatching after 12–15 weeks, from February to April. When cornered, head and forebody are raised with neck flattened while lunging feebly at aggressor. Tail is readily discarded if handled roughly. Capable of emitting an unpleasant odour from anal glands as a further deterrent. Will bite if provoked. Harmless, though easily confused with highly venomous rough-scaled snake (*Tropidechis carinatus*), with which it is sympatric over part of range. See genus (and *T. carinatus*) for distinguishing features.

FRONT-FANGED VENOMOUS LAND SNAKES
Family ELAPIDAE

Large family containing approximately 200 species in 50 genera. Very well represented in Australia by 80 species in 22 genera. Australian elapids appear only distantly related to their extralimital counterparts, and the subfamily Oxyuraninae has been proposed to accommodate all Australo-Papuan members.

Australian elapids range in size from TL 0.25–4.0 m. All possess a pair of relatively short fangs in the front of the upper jaw. These are hollow or deeply grooved, functioning in the same way as a hypodermic syringe. They are enclosed in a fleshy sheath, and each is connected by a duct to a venom gland situated in the side of the head. Eye very small to large with round or vertically elliptic pupil, and pale or dark iris. Head scales enlarged to form symmetrical shields. Body scales usually smooth (occasionally keeled), overlapping in 15–23 rows at midbody. Ventral scales enlarged to form transverse plates. Anal scale single or divided. Subcaudal scales single, divided, or a combination of both.

Elapids occur widely throughout the continent, and few undisturbed habitats are without at least one species. Few Australian elapids have exploited arboreal niches. Only the broad-headed snakes (*Hoplocephalus stephensii* and *H. bitorquatus*) can be considered arboreal although the rough-scaled snake (*Tropidechis carinatus*) regularly ascends low vegetation. No truly aquatic elapids occur here though several, including black snakes (*Pseudechis porphyriacus*) and tiger snakes (*Notechis* spp.), frequently dwell beside bodies of fresh water, and will not hesitate to enter it in search of food, or if disturbed.

Two modes of reproduction occur in Australian Elapidae. Species with undivided subcaudal scales are livebearers. Young may be free-born, or enclosed in membranous sacs from which they emerge shortly after birth. Snakes with divided subcaudal scales lay parchment-shelled eggs. The relationship between reproductive strategy and nature of subcaudal scales is not clear though it appears consistent in Australia. The majority of livebearers occur in cooler climates.

Elapids feed exclusively on vertebrates. Small snakes tend to prey mainly on lizards and frogs while large elapids include mammals, birds, and other snakes on their diets. Several specialise on particular prey types. Taipans (*Oxyuranus* spp.) feed on warm-blooded animals (especially mammals), *Neelaps calonotus* consumes burrowing skinks of the genus *Lerista*, bandy bandys (*Vermicella* spp.) prey only on blind snakes (Typhlopidae), and members of the *Simoselaps semifasciatus* group consume reptile eggs. Invertebrates or plant material may be incidentally ingested with prey.

Australian elapids occupy niches utilised in other parts of the world by the largest and most widely distributed family Colubridae; represented here by only 10 species. Many elapid genera have extralimital colubrid equivalents. Large-eyed slender diurnal snakes of the genus *Demansia* resemble the African rear-fanged colubrids, *Psammophis*. Members of the *Simoselaps semifasciatus* species group share with some African *Prosymna* an acute-edged shovel-shaped snout, burrowing habits, and a diet dominated by squamate eggs. Death adders (*Acanthophis* spp.) appear to have evolved convergently with some vipers (Viperidae), sharing robust bodies, angular heads, sedentary habits, and a predation strategy involving ambush.

In Australia, elapids outnumber all other terrestrial snake families combined. This is the only continent where venomous snakes are more numerous than non-venomous species. It must be remembered that most Australian elapids are too small to be regarded as harmful. The remaining minority includes some of the world's most dangerously venomous land snakes. Regardless of size or venom toxicity, all species avoid confrontations with humans whenever possible and must be trodden on or otherwise harassed before they resort to biting in self-defence. The primary function of venom is to subdue prey, not to attack animals too large to be consumed.

The following elapids have delivered fatal bites, or are believed capable of doing so (* = one recorded fatality, [†] = no recorded fatalities):

Death adders. *Acanthophis antarcticus, A. praelongus*[†] and *A. pyrrhus*[†].

Copperhead. *Austrelaps superbus.*

Small-eyed snake. *Cryptophis nigrescens*.*

Tiger snakes. *Notechis ater* and *N. scutatus.*

Taipans. *Oxyuranus microlepidotus*[†] and *O. scutellatus.*

Black snakes. *Pseudechis australis, P. butleri*[†], *P. colletti*[†], *P. guttatus*[†] and *P. porphyriacus*.*

Brown snakes. *Pseudonaja affinis, P. guttata*[†], *P. ingrami*[†], *P. nuchalis* and *P. textilis.*

Rough-scaled snake. *Tropidechis carinatus**

Bites from the following species may, or are known to, produce severe symptoms. Tolerance to snake-bite varies between individuals. Some snakes not included here may, under certain circumstances, deliver a serious bite.

Golden crowned snake. *Cacophis squamulosus.*

Whip snakes. *Demansia atra, D. psammophis* and *D. papuensis.*

Denisonia atriceps, D. devisi, D. fasciata, D. maculata, D. suta and presumably *D. ordensis.*

Bardick. *Echiopsis curta.*

Glyphodon dunmalli and *G. tristis.*

Broad-headed snakes. *Hoplocephalus bitorquatus, H. bungaroides* and *H. stephensii.*

Ringed brown snake. *Pseudonaja modesta.*

Death Adders
Genus *ACANTHOPHIS* Daudin, 1803

Small genus containing 3 Australian species. Widespread throughout continent, excepting lower south-west and most of Vic. Extralimital in New Guinea and eastern Indonesia.

Very robust short-bodied snakes each with a broad triangular head and abruptly thin tail, segmented at tip and terminating in a small curved spur. Eye small with vertically elliptic pupil and pale iris. Scales smooth to keeled, non-glossy, in 17–23 rows at midbody. Anal scale single. Subcaudal scales mostly single; a few divided posteriorly. Patern consists of prominent to obscure bands.

Taxonomic work in WA reveals the presence of 3 species, with no apparent gene flow between them. Some eastern populations appear significantly different, and it is likely that an Australia-wide revision will reveal the presence of additional taxa and redefine those already recognised.

Sluggish terrestrial snakes; nocturnal to diurnal according to temperature. Death adders feed on reptiles, small mammals, birds and frogs. These are captured by a unique method of ambush. Snake lies motionless, half buried by sand, leaf-litter, or beneath overhanging foliage of low vegetation. Body is held in a loose coil with the tail resting a short distance in front of snout. At the approach of a potential prey item the segmented tail-tip is wriggled convulsively, in mimicry of a worm or caterpillar. As prey moves closer to investigate, the snake strikes with lightning speed. Livebearers, producing small to very large litters.

When threatened the body is flattened and held in a rigid coil, from which the snake may strike repeatedly. Despite stories in local folklore, death adders are unable to 'leap'. Fangs are long and capable of administering large quantities of powerfully neurotoxic venom.

Distinguished from all other elapids by combination of triangular head, robust body, and slender segmented tail-tip terminating in a curved spur.

Common Death Adder
Acanthophis antarcticus (Shaw and Nodder, 1802)
Photo 717
Description Large robust death adder with smooth to moderately rugose dorsal scales and head shields. Considerable variation occurs throughout broad distribution. Ground colour pale or dark grey, brown to reddish brown. Series of irregular narrow (often finely dark-edged) pale bands usually extend from nape to tail. Broad dark V shape may be present on base of head, the free edges usually extending back to neck. White to cream edges of dark labial scales form prominent bars on lips. Segmented tail-tip white to cream, or black. Ventral surfaces whitish, dotted with black or brown. Midbody scales in 21 (rarely 23) rows. TL 0.7 m throughout most of range. Individuals from Barkly Tableland, NT, may exceed 1.0 m.

Distinguished from *A. praelongus* and *A. pyrrhus* by build (very robust vs moderately robust to relatively slender) and nature of scales (smooth vs moderately to strongly keeled).

Preferred habitat Wide variety of habitats, including rainforests and wet sclerophyll forests, woodlands, chenopod-dominated shrublands and coastal heathlands. Widespread; disjunct populations occur through most of southern and eastern Australia, including some islands but excluding lower south-west and south-east. Penetrates Vic. only in far east and north-west.

Microhabitat As for genus.

Comments Death adders appear to be declining in numbers in many parts of range, probably due to disturbance of habitats. Qld and northern NSW populations have suffered further; a result of attempted predation on poisonous cane toads (*Bufo marinus*). Dead individuals have been found with dead toads in their mouths. Females appear to reproduce biennially. Litters range from 2 to 33 young. DANGEROUSLY VENOMOUS. Otherwise as for genus.

Northern Death Adder
Acanthophis praelongus Ramsay, 1877
Photo 718

Description Moderately robust death adder with poorly keeled body scales and weakly rugose head shields. Supraocular scales often raised to form sharp ridge, particularly on populations from far northern Qld. Ground colour variable, ranging from grey to dark brown or reddish brown. Approximately 50 dark-edged pale bands extend from neck to tail. Head ground colour or darker, to almost black. Cream to white margins to labial scales may form prominent bars on lips. Tail-tip cream, yellow or black. Ventral surfaces whitish spotted with black. Midbody scales in 23 (occasionally 21) rows. TL 0.65 m.

Intermediate between other death adders. Differs from *A. antarcticus* in possessing keeled (vs smooth) scales, usually in 23 (vs usually 21) rows at midbody. Differs from *A. pyrrhus* in possessing weakly keeled (vs strongly keeled) scales, usually in 23 (vs 17–21) rows at midbody. Differs further from *A.*

pyrrhus by nature of head shields (weakly vs strongly rugose) and presence of prominent bars on lips.

Preferred habitat Grasslands, woodlands, rocky ranges and outcrops of humid to subhumid far northern Australia.

Microhabitat As for genus.

Comments DANGEROUSLY VENOMOUS. See genus.

Desert Death Adder
Acanthophis pyrrhus Boulenger, 1898
Photo 719

Description Relatively slender death adder with strongly keeled dorsal scales and very rugose head shields. Ground colour pale reddish brown to rich red, marked with transversely aligned dark flecks, alternating with 50–70 narrow cream to yellow bands. These are composed of pale pigment on base of each scale. Pale pigment on labial scales may occasionally form obscure bars. Segmented tail-tip cream, yellow or black. Midbody scales in 19–21 (rarely 17) rows. Ventral surfaces whitish. TL 0.75 m.

Distinguished from *A. antarcticus* and *A. praelongus* in possessing strongly keeled dorsal scales (vs smooth or weakly keeled, respectively), slender build (vs very robust or moderately robust, respectively), and fewer midbody scale rows (19–21, rarely 17 vs 21–23).

Preferred habitat Arid regions through western Qld, southern NT and north and interior of SA to north-west coast of WA. Favours hummock grasslands on sand ridges, sandy or stony flats, and rock outcrops.

Microhabitat Shelters beneath hummock grasses and in abandoned burrows. See genus.

Comments Feeds largely on lizards, particularly skinks and dragons. Litter of 13 young is recorded. When flattening body during defensive display the skin is distended, bringing pale bands into sharp contrast. DANGEROUSLY VENOMOUS. See genus.

Copperheads
Genus *AUSTRELAPS* Worrell, 1963

Endemic genus. Currently regarded as monotypic, though several forms may constitute distinct taxa. Restricted to south-eastern Australia, including Tas.

Moderately small to very large robust elapid. Eye large with round pupil and pale iris. Scales smooth and weakly glossed, in 15–17 rows at midbody; lower lateral row noticeably enlarged. Anal and subcaudal scales single.

Terrestrial, Diurnal. Livebearing.

Distinguished from *Notechis* and *Pseudechis* in possessing enlarged series of lower lateral scales. Differs further from *Pseudechis* in bearing undivided subcaudal scales (vs divided posteriorly).

Copperhead
Austrelaps superbus (Günther, 1858)
Photos 720–722

Description Subject to considerable geographic and local variation. Three forms recognised.

Lowland form: Ground colour variable, ranging through shades of brown, reddish brown, grey to almost black. Dark nuchal bar and narrow dark vertebral stripe may be present. Lower lateral scales usually paler than dorsals; cream to yellow on pale snakes, and salmon pink to orange on dark snakes. Lips and side of head prominently to obscurely marked with dark and pale bars. Ventral surfaces white, yellow to grey. TL 1.25 m on mainland; 1.7 m on Flinders and King Islands, Bass Strait.

Highland form: Ground colour dark brown, grey to black. Vertebral stripe indistinct to absent. Lower lateral scales white to cream. Lips and side of head prominently marked with dark and pale bars. Ventral surfaces grey. TL 1.1 m.

Adelaide Hills/Kangaroo Island form: Ground colour pale brown to pale or dark grey. Narrow dark vertebral stripe present or absent. Dark transverse bar often present, located 4 or 5 scales behind head. Lips and side of head prominently barred with cream. Ventral surfaces cream, yellow, dark grey to almost black. TL 0.65 m.

Preferred habitat Closely associated with fresh water or moist low-lying areas in dry sclerophyll forests, woodlands or heathlands. Especially common where tussock grasses occur. Extends from New England Tablelands, NSW, disjunctly through higher altitudes of Great Dividing Range to south-eastern NSW, then more or less continuously from eastern and southern Vic., Bass Strait islands and Tas. to south-eastern SA. Highland form is restricted to highlands of NSW and eastern Vic. Adelaide Hills/Kangaroo Island form is isolated in that region of SA.

Microhabitat Shelters beneath rocks, low vegetation and surface debris, or in hollow logs.

Comments Most cool-adapted Australian snake. Often encountered basking tightly coiled in sheltered sunlit areas, at temperatures which would render most other reptiles inactive. Adults feed largely on frogs; juveniles on skinks. Mating occurs in spring and autumn, during which time males may be observed in combat. Litters of 6–20 young are born after a gestation period of 14–16 weeks, attaining sexual maturity at approximately 2 years. When cornered, copperheads hiss loudly with neck flattened and raised in a low curve, presenting broadest aspect to aggressor. DANGEROUSLY VENOMOUS.

Crowned Snakes
Genus *CACOPHIS* Günther, 1863

Endemic genus containing 3 described species. Restricted to moist habitats in eastern Australia.

Small to medium-sized snakes. Eye small, bearing round to vertically elliptic pupil and pale iris. Scales smooth and glossy, in 15 rows at midbody. Anal and subcaudal scales divided. Pattern includes pale band or collar on nape.

Nocturnal. Terrestrial. Egglayers. Cryptozoic snakes which shelter beneath rocks, rotting logs or leaf-litter, wherever damp conditions prevail. Crowned snakes feed on skinks, particularly the diurnal genera *Lampropholis* and *Leiolopisma*. These are probably captured while inactive. Not regarded as dangerous.

Distinguished from *Furina* in possessing white, yellow to pale brown (vs red to orange) nuchal bar, and pale (vs dark) iris.

White Crowned Snake
Cacophis harriettae Krefft, 1869
Photo 723

Description Ground colour glossy dark grey to almost black. Cream to pale grey dots and dashes may be present on dorsal and lateral scales, forming series of pale striae. Broad immaculate white band (4 or more scales wide) curves across nape. This extends forward (becoming invaded by numerous dark flecks) onto side of head and snout. Top of head glossy black. Ventral surfaces pale grey. TL 0.25 m.

Distinguished from *C. krefftii* and *C. squamulosus* in possessing broad white collar (vs narrow yellow collar, and broad broken yellow to pale brown collar, respectively).

Preferred habitat Wet sclerophyll forests, rainforests and well-watered urban areas, on coast and ranges from far north-eastern NSW to mideastern Qld.

Microhabitat Frequently uncovered in garden compost heaps throughout suburbs of Brisbane, Qld. Otherwise as for genus.

Comments Between 2 and 10 eggs are laid in summer, hatching in late summer or early autumn. When disturbed, raises forebody with head angled acutely, and strikes repeatedly with mouth closed. Rarely, if ever, attempts to bite. See genus.

Dwarf Crowned Snake
Cacophis krefftii Günther, 1863
Photo 724

Description Smallest *Cacophis*. Ground colour dark grey to almost black. Narrow pale yellow to cream band (½–2 scales wide) curves across nape. This extends forward (becoming broader, paler and invaded by dark flecks) onto side of head, enclosing snout. Ventral surfaces pale yellow. Ventral scales laterally dark-edged, forming angular ragged junction of lateral and ventral colours. Dark median line present beneath tail. TL 0.2 m.

Distinguished from *C. harriettae* and *C. squamulosus* in possessing narrow yellow to cream collar (vs broad white collar, and broad broken yellow to pale brown collar, respectively).

Preferred habitat Rainforests and wet sclerophyll forests (occasionally well-watered urban areas) on coast and ranges from Gosford area, NSW, north to mideastern Qld.

Microhabitat As for genus.

Comments Clutches of 2–5 eggs are laid in summer. When threatened, raises forebody rigidly off ground with head angled acutely, and strikes repeatedly with mouth closed. See genus.

Golden Crowned Snake
Cacophis squamulosus (Duméril, Bibron and Duméril, 1854)
Photo 725

Description Largest *Cacophis*, with angular head distinct from neck. Ground colour dark brown to dark grey. Pale dots or dashes may be present on each scale, forming series of pale striae. Broad pale brown to yellow streak encompasses snout, extending back on either side of head, through eyes onto neck; failing to form complete bar. Lips prominently barred with dark brown. Ventral surfaces pink to pinkish brown, bearing numerous longitudinally aligned brown blotches. Dark median line present beneath tail. TL 0.7 m.

Distinguished from *C. harriettae* and *C. krefftii* in possessing broad incomplete pale yellow to brown collar (vs broad white collar, and narrow yellow collar, respectively). Differs further in attaining larger maximum size (TL 0.7 vs 0.25 m or less), presence of pinkish ventral pigment, and distinctive defensive posture (see photo).

Preferred habitat Rainforests and wet sclerophyll forests or well-watered rock outcrops (particularly sandstones), on coast and ranges from Wollongong area, NSW, north to mideastern Qld.

Microhabitat As for genus.

Comments Up to 12 eggs (usually about 6) are laid in summer, hatching in autumn. When threatened, raises forebody in a tight S shape with head held at an acute angle to neck, thrashing wildly and striking repeatedly with mouth closed. Though not considered dangerously venomous, care should be taken with large individuals. See genus.

Photo 726 depicts an undescribed species of *Cacophis* which occurs from the Atherton Tableland to Bluewater Range and Mt Spec, north-east Qld.

Genus *CRYPTOPHIS* Worrell, 1961

Endemic genus containing 2 species, occurring in northern Kimberley region of WA, northern NT and eastern Australia. Recent chromosomal work suggests relationships between them may be sufficiently distant to warrant generic reclassification.

Small to medium-sized moderately robust snakes, each with a relatively narrow depressed head. Eye small with black iris. Scales smooth and glossy, in 15 rows at midbody. Anal and subcaudal scales single. Ground colour brown to black with little indication of pattern.

Terrestrial and nocturnal. Livebearing.

Distinguished from *Glyphodon* by nature of anal and subcaudal scales (single vs divided). Differs from subadult *Pseudechis* in possessing fewer midbody scale rows (15 vs 17 or more), and from *Denisonia* by nature of eye (very small with dark iris vs moderately large with pale iris).

Eastern Small-Eyed Snake
Cryptophis nigrescens (Günther, 1862)
Photo 727

Description Ground colour glossy bluish black to black, without pattern. Ventral surfaces pale pink, sometimes flecked and blotched with black. TL 0.6 m (average) to 1.2 m.

Distinguished from superficially similar juvenile red-bellied black snakes (*Pseudechis porphyriacus*) in possessing very small (vs large) eye, and by restriction of pinkish pigment to ventral scales (vs pinkish red to red pigment brightest on ventrolateral scale row). Differs from sympatric *Rhinoplocephalus* spp. in bearing darker ground colour (black vs brown to reddish brown or greyish brown).

Preferred habitat Favours humid areas of east coast and ranges, extending into subhumid regions west of Great Dividing Range at several localities. Widespread from west of Melbourne, Vic., north to Cairns district, Qld, in a variety of habitats including rainforests and wet sclerophyll forests, woodlands, heathlands and rock outcrops.

Microhabitat Shelters beneath rocks, fallen timber, surface debris and in crevices. Frequently encountered beneath bark of logs.

Comments Feeds largely on reptiles such as skinks, blind snakes and other small elapids (including its own species). Juveniles feed almost exclusively on skinks. Combat has been observed between males in spring. Litters range from 2 to 8; usually 4 or 5. Thrashes and strikes wildly when disturbed. Venom toxicity appears to vary geographically, and some populations may be considered potentially DANGEROUSLY VENOMOUS. One recorded fatality.

Northern Small-eyed Snake
Cryptophis pallidiceps (Günther, 1858)
Photo 728

Description Ground colour glossy black, dark grey to brown; paler on head. Each lower lateral scale is tinged with orange, and bears dark brown suffusion on base. Lips and side of head whitish to pale brown. Ventral surfaces white, pale grey to pink, often bearing dark flecks on posterior ventral scales and along middle of tail. TL 0.5 m.

Preferred habitat Subhumid woodlands of northern NT and northern Kimberley region, WA.

Microhabitat Shelters beneath rocks, fallen timber, surface debris and in abandoned burrows or termitaria.

Comments Reported to feed predominantly on skinks. Otherwise as for genus.

Whip Snakes
Genus *DEMANSIA*   Günther, 1858

Contains 11 described taxa and several undescribed forms occurring widely through tropical, temperate to arid areas. Absent from south-east (including Tas.), deep south-west and wet forests of east coast. Extralimital in southern New Guinea.

Slender long-tailed elapids, each with a deep narrow head, and a very large eye bearing pale iris and round pupil. Scales smooth and non-glossy, in 15 rows at midbody. Anal and subcaudal scales divided. Pattern (when present) includes dark and/or pale comma-shaped marking encircling eye, and occasionally a dark nuchal band.

Swift terrestrial, diurnal snakes which use keen vision to locate their prey. Most feed on diurnal lizards, chased and captured on the run. Egglayers. Whip snakes favour open areas, seeking shelter beneath surface debris and in low vegetation such as grasses and dense shrubs. Threat displays are not normally employed; they rely on speed to escape danger. Because of their small size most are not considered dangerous, though bites from the 3 largest species (*D. atra*, *D. papuensis* and *D. psammophis*) may require attention.

Distinguished from *Pseudonaja* and *Oxyuranus* in possessing fewer midbody scale rows (15 vs 17–21 and 21–23, respectively) and nature of ventral pattern (uniform vs blotched with orange to brown).

Black Whip Snake
Demansia atra (Macleay, 1884)
Photo 729

Description Large moderately robust whip snake, possibly comprising several taxa. Ground colour black, dark brown, reddish brown to dark grey, often flushed with reddish brown on posterior body and tail. Individual scales may bear black posterior margin or blotch, forming reticulated or spotted pattern. Prominent pale flecks on lateral margins of anterior body scales may be present, contrasting sharply with black skin between them. Posterior half to third of body usually without pattern. Eastern populations usually bear small dark blotches on top and sides of head. These are absent on western populations. Indication of pale and/or dark rim usually present around eye, particularly on lateral margins. Ventral surfaces pale to dark grey or greenish grey, often suffused with yellow, pink to white on chin and throat, and reddish beneath tail. Each anterior ventral scale edged with black. TL 1.5 m.

Distinguished from *D. papuensis* in possessing dark-edged anterior ventral scales, fewer ventral and subcaudal scales (280 or less vs 280 or more), and in attaining smaller maximum size (TL 1.5 vs 1.8 m). Western populations differ further in lacking dark spots on head. Differs from *D. psammophis* in lacking a narrow dark line across front of snout.

Preferred habitat Subhumid woodlands and heathlands of far northern Australia, extending south on east coast to Ipswich area, Qld, and northeast to Ord River drainage in the Kimberley region of WA.

Microhabitat As for genus.

Comments In addition to skinks, frogs are included on diet. Appears to breed throughout year; probably a result of uniformly high temperatures over most of range. Combat has been observed between males. From 4 to 13 eggs (depending on size of female) are laid per clutch. Bites from large individuals should be regarded as potentially dangerous. Otherwise as for genus.

Demansia calodera Storr, 1978
Photo 730

Description Small whip snake with ground colour of olive-grey to olive-brown. Base of each scale bears black spot, forming obscure dotted to reticulated pattern. Broad pale-edged dark nuchal bar present. Top of head brown blotched with darker brown. Eye narrowly margined with dark brown, sweeping back as comma-shaped streak to corner of mouth. Lips and side of head cream to white. Narrow pale-edged dark line extends across snout, through each nostril to dark eye-margin. Ventral surfaces cream, occasionally with indication of dark longitudinal streak on either side of chin. TL 0.45 m.

Distinguished from *D. rufescens* by ground colour (olive-grey to olive-brown vs brown to reddish brown).

Preferred habitat Semi-arid to arid midwest coast, from North West Cape south to Shark Bay, and a few larger offshore islands of WA. Occurs on reddish sands and loams supporting woodlands, heathlands and *Acacia* shrublands.

Microhabitat As for genus.

Comments As for genus.

Marble-headed Whip Snake
Demansia olivacea (Gray, 1842)
Photo 731

Description Small slender whip snake with ground colour of greyish brown, yellowish brown to brown; sometimes darker and redder on neck. Individual scales may bear variably sized dark spots. Top and sides of head usually marked with irregularly sized dark blotches. These are usually pale-edged, and may occasionally coalesce to form an obscure nuchal bar. Eye rimmed with dark brown, continuous with broad dark streak which sweeps back to corner of mouth. This is broadly margined with cream to white. Narrow pale-edged dark line extends across front of snout from nostril to nostril; occasionally to eye. Side of head often suffused with reddish brown. Ventral surfaces white to very pale grey or brown, variegated with brown on lips and chin. TL 0.85 m.

Distinguished from *D. torquata* in lacking a pale-edged dark nuchal bar. Differs from *D. psammophis* by ventral colouration (dark variegations vs usually immaculate) and in bearing dark blotches on head.

Preferred habitat Extends widely across northern Australia from central Qld to south-west Kimberley region, WA. Favours subhumid to semi-arid woodlands and grasslands.

Microhabitat As for genus.

Comments Mating occurs throughout year, with 3 or 4 eggs laid per clutch. Otherwise as for genus.

Demansia papuensis (Macleay, 1877)
Photos 732, 733

Description Largest whip snake, comprising 2 subspecies.

D. p. melaena Storr, 1978 Ground colour dark grey, blackish brown to almost black, becoming paler and redder posteriorly. Top of head marked with irregular scattered dark spots. Eye may be narrowly margined with cream to white. Ventral surfaces grey becoming paler on lips, chin and throat, and redder beneath tail. TL to 1.8 m.

D. p. papuensis Differs in bearing paler colouration and more numerous ventral scales (usually more than 220 vs 220 or fewer).

Distinguished from *D. atra* in lacking dark edges on anterior ventral scales, and in possessing more numerous ventral and subcaudal scales (280 or more vs 280 or fewer). Differs further in attaining greater maximum size (TL 1.8 vs 1.5 m), and possessing dark spots on head. These are absent from western populations of *D. atra*. Distinguished from *D. psammophis* in attaining much greater size (TL 1.8 vs 1.0 m) and bearing weaker head pattern; no dark transverse line across front of snout, and little or no indication of markings around eye.

Preferred habitat Favours subhumid grassy woodlands of far northern Australia. *D. p. melaena* extends from north-west Kimberley region, WA, to northern NT. *D. p. papuensis* occurs on Cape York Peninsula, Qld, extending north to southern New Guinea.

Microhabitat As for genus.

Comments Little is documented on this relatively common snake, due to long-standing confusion with *D. atra*. Clutches of 9–20 eggs are laid throughout year. Because of its large size, a bite should be treated promptly. Otherwise as for genus.

Yellow-faced Whip Snake
Demansia psammophis (Schlegel, 1837)
Photos 734–736

Description Moderately large whip snake comprising 3 subspecies. These may require further investigation as there are many examples of pattern intergradation.

D. p. psammophis Ground colour pale grey, bluish grey, olive to brownish grey. Scales usually finely pale-edged laterally, forming obscure flecks. Dark skin may be visible between scales, producing an obscure reticulated pattern. Reddish brown paravertebral flush usually extends from behind neck to anterior third to half of body. Eye enclosed by dark comma-shaped mark, which curves back to corner of mouth. This is broadly margined by cream to white. Narrow pale-edged dark line extends across front of snout between nostrils or eyes. Ventral surfaces greyish, becoming yellowish posteriorly. Broad bluish green median stripe may extend from throat onto tail. TL 1.0 m.

D. p. reticulata (Gray, 1842) Ground colour pale or dark olive-brown to olive. Each scale margined with dark brown to black, forming prominent reticulum.

D. p. cupreiceps Storr, 1978 Similar to *D. p. reticulata*. Head, anterior body and tail flushed with orange to copper.

Distinguished from *D. atra* and *D. papuensis* in possessing a narrow dark line across front of snout, and more prominent markings around eye. Differs from *D. olivacea* in lacking dark markings on venter. Differs from *D. torquata* in lacking a pale-edged dark nuchal bar, and from *D. rufescens* (within zone of overlap) by ground colour (shades of grey to olive vs reddish brown).

Preferred habitat Widely distributed through humid to arid mainland Australia, excluding Cape York Peninsula in Qld, northern NT, most of Kimberley and Great Sandy Desert regions of WA, extreme south and south-east, and subalpine to alpine areas. Occurs in a variety of habitats, including dry sclerophyll forests, woodlands, heathlands, hummock grasslands and margins of rainforests and wet sclerophyll forests. Penetrates very arid regions via eucalypt-lined watercourses. *D. p. psammophis* occurs in eastern Australia, extending west as far as the Goldfields of WA. *D. p. reticulata* is restricted to south-west coast and adjacent interior of WA. *D. p. cupreiceps* occupies remaining arid interior to midwest coast and north-west of WA. A population occuring in subhumid south-west Kimberley region may be isolated.

Microhabitat As for genus.

Comments (For *D. p. psammophis*). Mating takes place in spring, when large numbers of individuals aggregate, returning to the same areas each year. From 3 to 9 eggs are laid per clutch, sometimes at communal sites. One such site, containing approximately 500–600 eggs, was apparently used repeatedly over consecutive seasons. A bite from a large individual may produce painful local reactions, but not normally considered dangerous. Otherwise as for genus.

Rufous Whip Snake
Demansia rufescens Storr, 1978
Photo 737

Description Small slender whip snake with ground colour of reddish brown to coppery brown. Dorsal and lateral scales dark-margined, variably suffused with pale brownish grey on anterior edges. Pale suffusions tend to disappear on hindbody and tail. Head and neck olive-grey to dark grey; paler on top of snout. Pale-edged dark line extends from snout through eye, curving back to corner of mouth. Tail suffused with grey. Ventral surfaces white. TL 0.65 m.

Distinguished from all sympatric *Demansia* by prominent reddish brown colouration.

Preferred habitat Stony hills and plains supporting hummock grasses, often in association with low open woodlands and shrublands, in arid Pilbara region of WA. Extends from coastal plain (including Dolphin and Barrow Islands) through Hamersley Ranges south-east to Mt Newman.

Microhabitat Associated with rocks and *Triodia* hummocks. See genus.

Comments Previously treated as a subspecies of *D. olivacea*. See genus.

Demansia simplex Storr, 1978
Photo 738

Description Small robust short-tailed whip snake with uniform brownish grey ground colour. Eye usually edged with dark brown, and broadly margined with yellow. Short dark brown streak curves back from below eye to corner of mouth. Ventral surfaces cream, contrasting sharply with darker flanks. TL 0.45 m.

Preferred habitat Grassy woodlands in subhumid areas of northern Kimberley region of WA, and Katherine district of NT.

Microhabitat Probably as for genus.

Comments Poorly known. See genus.

Collared Whip Snake
Demansia torquata (Günther, 1862)
Photo 739

Description Very slender whip snake with

ground colour of pale brown, olive-brown to greyish brown; often flushed with reddish brown. Lower lateral scales may each bear a darker base or smudge, forming obscure spots or stripe; most prominent anteriorly. Top of head darker shade of ground colour to black, with or without prominent blackish brown blotches. Eye broadly rimmed laterally with cream. Broad dark streak curves back from lower margin of eye to corner of mouth. Narrow dark line usually extends across front of snout, from nostril to nostril. Dark brown to black bar (narrowly margined with yellow, cream to pale grey) extends across base of head and neck. Ventral surfaces whitish, usually irregularly spotted to blotched with blackish on throat. These markings tend to align into 2 longitudinal series on anterior body. TL 0.7 m.

Distinguished from *D. olivacea* in possessing dark nuchal bar.

Preferred habitat Occurs in open subhumid to arid habitats, including grassy woodlands, heathlands and hummock grasslands. Extends from east coast of Qld (Rockhampton district to Cape York Peninsula), south-east to northern interior of NSW, and west to central NT. Most abundant on islands off mideast coast of Qld.

Microhabitat As for genus.

Comments Clutches of 2–8 eggs are laid during spring. Some aspects of description and distribution probably apply to an undescribed, closely related species. Otherwise as for genus.

See also photo 740, which depicts an undescribed taxon, probably closely related to *Demansia torquata*.

Genus *DENISONIA* Krefft, 1869

Endemic genus containing 6 species. Widespread throughout subhumid to arid areas of Australia.

Small to medium-sized, moderately slender to very robust elapids, each with a relatively broad depressed head. Eye moderately large with pale iris and vertically elliptic pupil. Scales smooth; matt to glossy in 17–21 rows at midbody. Anal and subcaudal scales single.

Nocturnal. Terrestrial. Livebearing. Favoured shelter sites include beneath rocks or logs, in soil cracks, and in disused burrows or termitaria. Pugnacious by nature, flattening body, thrashing and striking wildly when provoked.

Distinguished from *Rhinoplocephalus, Furina, Glyphodon* and *Cryptophis* by iris colour (pale vs dark). Differs from superficially similar juvenile *Pseudonaja* and *Pseudechis* by nature of subcaudal scales (undivided vs divided at least posteriorly), and shape of pupil (vertically elliptic vs round). Differs from *Acanthophis* in lacking slender segmented tail-tip. Differs from *Hemiaspis* by nature of anal scale (undivided vs divided), and shape of pupil (vertical-

ly elliptic vs round). Differs from *Echiopsis* (in zone of overlap) in possessing a dark hood.

Denisonia atriceps (Storr, 1980)
Photo 741

Description Moderately slender *Denisonia* with ground colour of matt brown. Head and nape black. Lips narrowly barred with white. First row of scales bordering nape are tinged with pale brown. Ventral surfaces very pale reddish brown. Chin and throat dark grey streaked with white. Midbody scales in 19 rows. TL 0.49 m.

Preferred habitat Known only from the vicinity of Lake Cronin, a small ephemeral freshwater lake surrounded by eucalypt woodland and *Melaleuca* thickets on sandy loam in semi-arid south-western interior of WA.

Microhabitat No data available.

Comments Known from very few specimens. Only known bite produced severe symptoms, hence the species may be regarded as potentially DANGEROUSLY VENOMOUS.

De Vis' Banded Snake
Denisonia devisi Waite and Longman, 1920
Photo 742

Description Robust *Denisonia*, closely related to *D. maculata*. Ground colour yellowish brown, reddish brown to olive. Pattern usually prominent, consisting of numerous irregular dark brown bands. These may be broken along vertebral line, especially on forebody. Large dark blotch present on top of head. Dark streak often extends from nostril, beneath eye onto temple. Lips whitish prominently barred with dark brown. Ventral surfaces cream. Midbody scales in 17 rows. TL 0.48 m.

Distinguished from *D. maculata* by pattern on body (banded vs uniform).

Preferred habitat Interior of Qld and NSW, favouring low-lying moist areas associated with shrublands or woodlands.

Microhabitat As for genus.

Comments Known locally as 'mud adder'. Feeds predominantly on frogs though geckos are sometimes taken. Produces 3–9 young per litter. Not regarded as dangerous though a bite from a large individual may require medical attention. Otherwise as for genus.

Rosén's Snake
Denisonia fasciata Rosén, 1905
Photo 743

Description Ground colour orange-brown, yellowish brown to pale olive-grey. Pattern usually prominent, comprising numerous irregular blackish to dark brown bands or transversely aligned blotches. Top of head blotched and spotted. Dark streak extends from nostril, through eye to temple or side of neck. Lips paler shade of ground colour to white. Ventral surfaces cream to white, sometimes bearing dark streaks on chin. Midbody scales in 17 (rarely 19) rows. TL 0.5 m.

Preferred habitat Subhumid to arid interior and north-west coast of WA, on sandy to loamy (often stony) soils supporting shrublands or woodlands. Areas dominated by *Acacia* spp., particularly mulga (*Acacia aneura*), are favoured.

Microhabitat As for genus.

Comments Appears to prey almost entirely on sleeping diurnal lizards, particularly dragons. Litters of 2–7 young are recorded. Not regarded as dangerous though a bite from a large individual could require medical attention. Otherwise as for genus.

Ornamental Snake
Denisonia maculata (Steindachner, 1867)
Photo 744

Description Extremely robust *Denisonia*, closely related to *D. devisi*. Ground colour dark greyish brown, grey to almost black. Lower lateral scales paler, bearing dark posterior edges, flecks or streaks. Top of head blackish brown to black; from first few scale rows on nape almost to tip of snout. Tip of snout, sides of head and foreneck, pale grey to pale greyish brown, finely peppered with dark brown to black. Lips whitish prominently barred with black. Ventral surfaces cream. Outer edges of throat and ventral scales marked with black flecks or spots. Midbody scales in 17 rows. TL 0.5 m.

Distinguished from *D. devisi* by pattern on body (uniform vs banded).

Preferred habitat Mideastern Qld, in the Dawson River drainage system south-west of Rockhampton. Favours margins of fresh water, and moist
low-lying areas associated with woodlands.

Microhabitat As for genus.

Comments Feeds almost exclusively on frogs. Litters of 3–11 young are recorded. A bite may produce severe local symptoms. Otherwise as for genus.

Denisonia ordensis Storr, 1984
Photo 745

Description Large *Denisonia*, closely related to *D. suta*. Ground colour brown to greyish brown, each scale finely dark-edged. Top of head may be black on juveniles, to ground colour or sightly darker (obscurely spotted with dark brown) on adults. Upper lip bears dark-edged cream stripe or series of blotches. Ventral surfaces whitish, flushed with grey on anterior half of each ventral and subcaudal scale, and on chin. Midbody scales in 19 rows. TL 0.75 m.

Distinguished from *D. suta* by duller pattern: dark hood and pale ocular stripe obscure to absent (vs usually prominent). Differs further in bearing dark

bands on ventral surfaces.

Preferred habitat Subhumid to arid far eastern Kimberley region, WA, and adjacent NT. Extends from Argyle Downs Station south to Gordon Downs Station, WA, and east to Wave Hill, NT. Inhabits cracking clays (black-soil plains) associated with major drainage systems.

Microhabitat Presumably shelters in soil cracks.

Comments As for genus.

Myall or Curl Snake
Denisonia suta (Peters, 1863)
Photos 746, 747

Description Small to large *Denisonia* (increasing in size from south to north), closely related to *D. ordensis*. Ground colour pale greyish brown, brown, yellowish brown to reddish brown; each scale dark-edged. Juveniles from some areas may be uniform dark grey. Top of head and first 5–8 scale rows on nape, dark greyish brown to black. This may be barely discernible on dark individuals. White to yellow or pale brown stripe extends from snout, through eye to temple. This is margined below by an irregular (often broken) blackish brown streak. Lips and ventral surfaces cream, smudged with grey on chin. Greyish brown midventral stripe may be present in some populations. Midbody scales in 17–21 (usually 19) rows. TL 0.88 m.

Distinguished from *D. ordensis* by brighter pattern: dark hood and pale ocular stripe usually prominent (vs weak to absent). Differs further in lacking dark bands on ventral surfaces.

Preferred habitat Widespread through subhumid to arid eastern interior of Australia; from northern Vic and eastern SA, north to Weipa, Qld, northern NT, and far eastern Kimberley region, WA. Isolated population occurs in southern NT and far northern SA. Favours heavy soils (particularly deeply cracking clays) supporting shrublands, though also occurs on a variety of other soil types (rarely soft sands) vegetated with woodlands and grasslands.

Microhabitat As for genus.

Comments Common name 'curl snake' is derived from its defensive posture. Body is curled into a tight coil, from which it thrashes and strikes wildly. Feeds largely on lizards, though frogs are also taken. Litter of 6 young is recorded. Large individuals could be considered potentially DANGEROUSLY VENOMOUS.

Genus *DRYSDALIA* Worrell, 1961

Endemic genus containing 4 species, restricted to cool temperate southern Australia.

Small moderately slender snakes, each with a relatively narrow deep head. Eye large with pale iris and round pupil. Scales smooth and matt, in 15 rows at midbody. Anal and subcaudal scales single.

Terrestrial. Predominantly diurnal. Usually encountered foraging or basking in mild sunlight close to cover; particularly logs, rocks, or low vegetation such as tussock grasses. Most feed largely on skinks, located by eyesight and captured on the run. Livebearing. Not considered dangerous to humans.

Distinguished from *Hemiaspis* in possessing single (vs divided) anal scale, and from *Elapognathus* (within zone of overlap) in possessing a nuchal bar (vs oblique pale bar on side of neck).

Crowned Snake
Drysdalia coronata (Schlegel, 1837)
Photo 748

Description Large robust *Drysdalia* with ground colour of grey, greyish brown, yellowish brown to olive. Top of head bluish grey, margined behind by broad black nuchal bar. Black streak extends from snout through lower portion of eye, joining nuchal bar on side of neck. This is margined below by a prominent white streak. Ventral surfaces cream, grey to pinkish brown. Anterior edges of ventral scales darker. TL 0.6 m.

Distinguished from *D. mastersii* in possessing dark (vs pale) nuchal bar and unspotted lips.

Preferred habitat Coastal woodlands, heathlands and swamps of southern and south-western WA (including some offshore islands). Extends northwards on west coast to Perth area, and east to Great Australian Bight.

Microhabitat Shelters beneath rocks, particularly coastal granites, and in abandoned stick-ant nests (*Iridomyrmex conifer*). Otherwise as for genus.

Comments Feeds largely on frogs, and to a lesser extent skinks. Mating occurs from late spring to early summer; 3 or 4 young are born from March to April. See genus.

White-lipped Snake
Drysdalia coronoides (Günther, 1858)
Photo 749

Description Ground colour variable: olive, reddish brown, pale or dark grey to almost black. Prominent white stripe (edged above with black) extends from nostril, through upper lip to side of neck. Some individuals from Tas. may bear an additional white stripe from temple to neck. Ventral surfaces usually pink to orange, occasionally cream, yellowish to olive. TL 0.45 m.

Distinguished from *D. rhodogaster* and *D. mastersii* in lacking pale nuchal bar. Differs further from *D. rhodogaster* in possessing white stripe on lower lip.

Preferred habitat Extends from Tas., through islands of Bass Strait to southern Vic., south-eastern SA and south-eastern NSW. Disjunct population occurs in highlands of north-eastern NSW. Most abundant where ground cover is dominated by tussocks, usually in association with heathlands, wood-

lands, dry sclerophyll forests or margins of wet sclerophyll forests.

Microhabitat As for genus.

Comments Skinks constitute over 80 per cent of diet, though skink eggs, frogs, and even a small mammal have been recorded. Mating occurs in spring. From 2 to 10 young are born in late summer to midautumn. Mainland females give birth each year while those from Tas. produce a litter every 2–3 years. See genus.

Masters' Snake
Drysdalia mastersii (Krefft, 1866)
Photo 750

Description Ground colour pale yellowish brown, olive-brown to grey; darker on juveniles. Head dark grey to black, margined behind by yellow to whitish nuchal band; often narrowly broken on midline. Black streak extends from snout to side of neck, edged below by white streak through lips. This may enclose darker peppering. Ventral surfaces orange (red on juveniles) centrally; grey speckled with black along outer edges. TL 0.31 m.

Distinguished from *D. coronoides* in possessing a nuchal bar. Differs from *D. coronata* in bearing a pale (vs dark) nuchal bar.

Preferred habitat Semi-arid southern Australia, from south-east coast of WA to southern Eyre Peninsula, SA. Disjunct populations occur in southern Yorke Peninsula, SA, and from south-eastern interior of SA to adjacent Little Desert area, Vic. Occurs on coastal dunes and limestones, or on sand plains supporting heathlands or mallee/*Triodia* associations.

Microhabitat As for genus.

Comments Litters of 2 or 3 young are recorded. See genus.

Drysdalia rhodogaster (Jan and Sordelli, 1873)
Photo 751

Description Ground colour brown, olive-brown to olive-grey (darker on juveniles); often finely peppered with paler pigment. Top of head very dark grey to black, fading to ground colour and peppered with black on snout and side of head. Orange to yellow nuchal band usually prominent, occasionally reduced to obscure pale patch. Narrow dark line usually extends from nostril to eye; often continuous with longitudinal series of dark spots from eye to side of neck. Ventral surfaces yellow to orange. TL 0.45 m.

Distinguished from *D. coronoides* in bearing a pale nuchal band, and in lacking a white stripe on upper lip.

Preferred habitat Coast and ranges of southern NSW, north to Blue Mountains. Favours woodlands, heathlands or dry sclerophyll forests; usually with tussock-dominated ground cover.

Microhabitat As for genus.
Comments Litters of 2–6 young are born in late summer. See genus.

Genus *ECHIOPSIS* Fitzinger, 1843

Endemic monotypic genus restricted to southern Australia.

Medium-sized robust snake with large bulbous head distinct from neck. Eye moderately large with vertically elliptic pupil and pale iris. Scales smooth and matt, in 17–21 (usually 19) rows at midbody. Anal and subcaudal scales single.

Terrestrial. Nocturnal to diurnal. Livebearing.

Distinguished from *Acanthophis* in possessing uniform ground colour (vs banded pattern), in lacking a slender segmented tail-tip, and by build (robust, vs very robust, at least within zone of overlap). Differs from superficially similar *Denisonia atriceps* in lacking a prominent black hood, and by build (robust vs relatively more slender).

Bardick
Echiopsis curta (Schlegel, 1837)
Photos 752, 753

Description Ground colour olive-grey, brown, yellowish brown to rich reddish brown. Pattern obscure to absent. Side of head and neck may be flecked with white, particularly on eastern populations. Diffuse pale streak may be present from eye to side of neck, particularly on western populations. Individuals from midwest coast may bear distinctly dark grey heads. Ventral surfaces pale grey, cream to yellow. Chin and side of throat may be dark grey, spotted with white. Ventral scales may each bear a dark grey base. TL 0.62 m.
Preferred habitat Three isolated populations occur in southern Australia: south-western WA from the Greenough River south-east to the Great Australian Bight, on Eyre Peninsula area in SA, and from south-eastern SA to adjacent Vic. and NSW. Favours heathlands, woodlands and mallee/*Triodia* associations, on sandy to loamy soils. In some areas individuals inhabit semi-consolidated coastal dunes, occasionally foraging onto beach.
Microhabitat Shelters among leaf-litter, and beneath overhanging foliage of shrubs, grass hummocks or tussocks.
Comments Sedentary; usually encountered basking fully stretched in open areas close to shelter. Lizards comprise most regular prey items, followed by frogs (especially in WA), mammals and occasionally birds. These are probably captured by ambush. Litters of 3–14 large young are born from late summer to autumn. Pugnacious when harassed. Not regarded as dangerous although a bite may cause severe local symptoms.

Genus *ELAPOGNATHUS* Boulenger, 1896

Endemic monotypic genus restricted to humid south-western corner of WA.

Small moderately robust snake with relatively narrow deep head. Eye large, bearing round pupil and dark grey iris. Scales smooth and matt, in 15 rows at midbody. Anal and subcaudal scales single.

Terrestrial. Diurnal. Livebearing.

Distinguished from *Drysdalia* (within zone of overlap) in possessing oblique pale bar on side of neck (vs unbroken collar).

Elapognathus minor (Günther, 1863)
Photo 754

Description Ground colour pale to dark grey; flushed with reddish brown to bright red on tail. Side of head white to pale grey. Rear margins of upper labial scales may be pigmented, forming narrow dark bars. Broad orange-yellow bar (widest ventrolaterally) sweeps upward on side of neck, failing to meet its opposite on nape. This is separated from orange-yellow ventrolateral flush on rear of neck, by oblique bar of ground colour to black. Ventral surfaces bright yellow, darkening to orange laterally and posteriorly. Base of each ventral scale black, forming distinct bands. TL 0.4 m.
Preferred habitat Cool humid south-western corner of WA, from Two Peoples Bay area extending north-west (apparently disjunctly) to Busselton. Favours heathlands margining swamps, though also known from wet sclerophyll forests.
Microhabitat Shelters in low dense vegetation such as tussocks and sedges.
Comments Poorly documented. Uncommon, probably due to competition from the more abundant *Drysdalia coronata*. Not considered dangerous.

Genus *FURINA* Duméril, 1853

Endemic genus containing 2 species. Widespread throughout most of Australia, excepting cool temperate south.

Small, slender to moderately robust snakes with glossy scales, weakly depressed heads and small black eyes. Scales smooth, in 15–17 rows at midbody. Anal and subcaudal scales divided. Pattern usually prominent (weak on large adults), consisting of fine dark reticulum, glossy black head and neck, and red to orange nuchal bar or blotch.

Terrestrial and nocturnal, sheltering beneath rocks, logs, mats of dead vegetation, and in soil cracks, ant nests or termitaria. Both species feed almost exclusively on skinks. Diurnal prey is probably taken while sleeping. Egglaying. When disturbed, snake raises forebody high off ground, mock striking with mouth closed. A bite from an adult of the largest species (*F. ornata*) may produce a mild local reaction.

Distinguished from *Glyphodon* (with which it is closely allied and possibly congeneric), *Cacophis*, *Denisonia* and *Rhinoplocephalus* in possessing a prominent red to orange nuchal bar or blotch (often weakly defined on aged individuals). This is yellow, pale brown or absent on *Glyphodon*; white, yellow to pale brown on *Cacophis*, and absent on *Denisonia* and *Rhinoplocephalus*. Differs further from *Cacophis* and *Denisonia* by iris colour (dark vs pale), and from *Glyphodon* by nature of nasal scale (undivided vs divided).

Red-naped Snake
Furina diadema (Schlegel, 1837)
Photo 755

Description Small *Furina* with ground colour of dark brown, orange-brown to reddish brown, fading to cream or pale yellowish brown on flanks. Each dorsal scale is usually marked with a pale anterior blotch. Dorsal and lateral scales prominently dark-edged, forming fine reticulum. Head and neck glossy black, enclosing bright orange-red crescent-, diamond- or oval-shaped nuchal blotch. Pattern may become obscure with age. Lips and ventral surfaces white to cream; occasionally black on chin. Scales normally in 15 rows at midbody. TL 0.35 m.

Distinguished from *F. ornata* by shape of reddish nuchal mark (crescent-, diamond- or oval-shaped vs usually represented as a broad unbroken band), and in attaining smaller maximum size (TL 0.35 vs 0.6 m).

Preferred habitat Humid to arid areas from mid-eastern Qld, through much of NSW to eastern interior of SA. Occupies most habitats except rainforests. Rock outcrops are particularly favoured.

Microhabitat As for genus.

Comments Coastal and near-coastal populations feed largely on skinks of the genus *Lampropholis*. Mating occurs during late spring and summer. Clutches of 1–5 eggs are recorded, hatching in late summer. Populations from Qld may produce more than one clutch per year. Otherwise as for genus.

Orange-naped Snake
Furina ornata (Gray, 1842)
Photo 756

Description Large *Furina* with ground colour of reddish brown, orange-brown to yellowish brown. Scales dark-edged, forming reticulum. Head and neck glossy dark brown to black, enclosing narrow to broad (usually conspicuous) orange-red to orange-brown band. This may become obscure to absent with age. Lips, ventral and lower lateral surfaces white to cream. Midbody scales in 15–17 rows. TL 0.6 m.

Distinguished from *F. diadema* by shape of reddish nuchal mark (usually represented as a broad unbroken band vs crescent-, diamond- or oval-shaped), and in attaining greater maximum size (0.6 vs 0.35 m).

Preferred habitat Widespread throughout sub-humid to arid areas of northern Australia, extending south into southern interior of WA. Occurs in a variety of habitats, including woodlands, shrublands and hummock grasslands, on sandy to stony soils.

Microhabitat As for genus.

Comments Relationship between *F. ornata* and *Glyphodon barnardi* is unclear. Clutches of 3–6 eggs are recorded. See genus.

Genus *GLYPHODON* Günther, 1858

Small genus containing 3 species, extending from south-eastern interior of Qld to Cape York Peninsula and islands of Torres Strait. Extralimital in New Guinea.

Medium-sized moderately robust snakes each with a weakly depressed head and small black eyes. Scales smooth and glossy, in 15–21 rows at midbody. Anal and subcaudal scales divided.

Terrestrial and nocturnal, sheltering beneath rocks, logs, mats of dead vegetation, and in soil cracks, ant nests, termitaria and abandoned burrows. Diet appears to consist largely or entirely of skinks. Egglaying.

Distinguished from *Furina* by nature of nasal scale (divided vs undivided) and nuchal band (absent, or pale brown to yellow vs red to orange). Differs from *Cryptophis*, *Denisonia* and *Rhinoplocephalus* in possessing divided (vs undivided) anal and subcaudal scales. Differs further from *Denisonia* by iris colour (dark vs pale).

Yellow-naped Snake
Glyphodon barnardi Kinghorn, 1939
Photo 757

Description Ground colour dark brown, dark grey to black, each scale bearing an obscure pale blotch or margin, forming reticulum. Broad diffuse pale brown to yellow band extends across nape and base of head. This darkens to absence with age. Ventral surfaces white to cream. Midbody scales in 15 rows. TL 0.5 m.

Preferred habitat Woodlands and rock outcrops of mid-eastern to north-eastern coast and interior of Qld.

Microhabitat As for genus.

Comments Poorly documented. May represent a variant of *Furina ornata*, indicating the uncertain grounds on which these genera are separated. Clutches of 7–10 eggs are recorded. When harassed flattens neck and raises forebody, rocking from side to side.

Dunmall's Snake
Glyphodon dunmalli Worrell, 1955
Photo 758

Description Ground colour pale or dark olive-grey to blackish brown, fading on lower flanks. Pattern absent, except for a few diffuse pale blotches on upper lips. Ventral surfaces whitish. Midbody scales in 21 rows. TL 0.7 m.

Distinguished from superficially similar *Rhinoplocephalus boschmai* in possessing more numerous midbody scale rows (21 vs 15).

Preferred habitat Woodlands and dry sclerophyll forests, particularly those dominated by brigalow (*Acacia harpophylla*), in subhumid south-eastern interior of Qld, extending north to Yeppoon.

Microhabitat As for genus.

Comments Rarely encountered, possibly due to its apparent association with brigalow scrub, little of which remains intact. The tree skink *Egernia striolata* is a recorded prey item. Inoffensive even when harassed, though a single known bite produced a marked reaction.

Brown-headed Snake
Glyphodon tristis Günther, 1858
Photo 759

Description Large *Glyphodon* with ground colour of dark purplish brown to almost black, fading on lower flanks. Each scale narrowly pale-edged, forming reticulum; particularly on flanks. Broad pale brown to cream band extends across nape, darkening to brown or black on head. Ventral surfaces white to cream; each ventral scale bearing brown patch on outer edge. Midbody scales in 17 rows. TL 1.0 m.

Preferred habitat Woodlands, monsoon forests and vine thickets of north-eastern Cape York Peninsula and Torres Strait Islands, Qld, Extralimital in southern New Guinea.

Microhabitat As for genus.

Comments Appears to feed largely on skinks of the genus *Sphenomorphus*. Clutch of 6 eggs is recorded. Extremely nervous, thrashing wildly when provoked. Not regarded as dangerous, though care should be taken with large individuals.

Genus *HEMIASPIS* Fitzinger, 1860

Endemic genus containing 2 species. Restricted to eastern Australia; one between the Great Dividing Range and the coast, the other penetrating the subhumid eastern interior.

Small relatively slender snakes, each with a deep narrow head. Eye large, bearing round pupil and pale iris. Scales smooth and weakly glossed, in 17 rows at midbody. Anal scale divided. Subcaudal scales single.

Diurnal or crepuscular. Livebearing. Terrestrial snakes which shelter beneath rocks, logs, low vegetation and in soil cracks or disused burrows; usually in the vicinity of watercourses. One species (*H. signata*) is a diurnal predator of skinks and frogs while the other (*H. damelii*) is a crepuscular frog specialist. Not regarded as dangerous.

Distinguished from *Drysdalia*, *Denisonia* and *Rhinoplocephalus* in possessing divided (vs undivided) anal scale. Differs further from *Rhinoplocephalus* by large (vs small) eye bearing pale (vs dark) iris, and further from *Denisonia* by round (vs vertically elliptic) pupil.

Grey Snake
Hemiaspis damelii (Günther, 1876)
Photo 760

Description Ground colour pale or dark grey to olive-grey; paler on flanks. Each scale may be finely dark-edged. Top of head and first few scale rows on nape black on juveniles, contracting to form a nuchal blotch or bar (occasionally fading completely) on adults. Ventral surfaces white to cream, usually flecked with dark grey. TL 0.6 m.

Preferred habitat Extends from interior of NSW north to coastal districts in the vicinity of Rockhampton, Qld. Favours woodlands, usually on heavy soils.

Microhabitat As for genus.

Comments Crepuscular to nocturnal. Litters of 4–16 young are recorded, born in summer. See genus.

Black-bellied Swamp Snake or Marsh Snake
Hemiaspis signata (Jan, 1859)
Photo 761

Description Two colour forms occur: brown to olive-brown, and dark olive-grey to black. Rarely pinkish brown individuals are encountered. Head ground colour or darker on pale forms; pale yellow on dark forms. Narrow dark-edged white, cream to yellow streak extends from snout or eye to side of neck. Similar streak extends from snout, through upper lip to corner of mouth. Ventral surfaces dark grey to black; paler on throat. TL 0.6 m.

Preferred habitat Humid east coast and ranges from south-eastern NSW to south-eastern Qld. Disjunct populations occur at Finch Hatton Gorge in mideastern Qld, and in north-eastern Qld from Mt Spec north to Thornton Peak. Most abundant on margins of creeks or swamps, though in humid habitats such as rainforests or wet sclerophyll forests individuals may be found well away from permanent water.

Microhabitat As for genus.

Comments Predominantly diurnal; crepuscular to

nocturnal in hot weather. Litters of 4–20 (usually 10–12) young are recorded. Not regarded as dangerous though a bite from a large individual may require attention. See genus.

Genus *HOPLOCEPHALUS*
Wagler, 1830

Endemic genus containing 3 species restricted to eastern Australia.

Medium-sized moderately slender snakes, each with a broad depressed head distinct from neck. Eye moderately large with round pupil and pale iris. Scales smooth in 19–21 rows at midbody. Ventral scales laterally keeled or notched. Anal and subcaudal scales single.

Nocturnal. Unusual among Australian elapid snakes in being arboreal and rock-climbing. Livebearers, tending to give birth biennially to small litters of large offspring. Pugnacious when provoked, flattening head and raising forebody into a rigid S-shape from which they may strike repeatedly with mouth agape. Bites may cause severe symptoms.

Pale-headed Snake
Hoplocephalus bitorquatus (Jan, 1859)
Photo 762

Description Ground colour pale brown, shades of grey to almost black. Scales may be narrowly dark-edged, forming obscure reticulum. Head and nape pattern very distinctive: a broad white, cream, pale grey to pale brown nuchal band is bordered posteriorly by a continuous to broken black bar, and anteriorly by a narrow dark edge, or angular dark blotches. Top of head pale grey, usually blotched with dark grey. Lips cream, usually barred with dark grey. Ventral surfaces cream to pale grey, sometimes bearing darker flecks. Midbody scales in 19–21 rows. TL 0.8 m.

Distinguished from *H. stephensii* in lacking banded pattern (though patternless individuals of *H. stephensii* occur), and in possessing a pale nuchal band.

Preferred habitat Favours dry sclerophyll forests and woodlands (occasionally rainforests or wet sclerophyll forests) along coast and eastern interior, from just north of Sydney to mideastern Qld. Disjunct population occurs in north-eastern Qld.

Microhabitat Usually encountered beneath loose bark, or in hollow trunks and limbs of dead timber; especially in the vicinity of watercourses.

Comments Feeds largely on frogs (particularly tree frogs, *Litoria* spp.), though lizards and mammals are also taken. Mating occurs in spring, with litters of 2–11 young (usually about 5) born in late summer. See genus.

Broad-headed Snake
Hoplocephalus bungaroides (Schlegel, 1837)
Photo 763

Description Strongly patterned *Hoplocephalus* with black ground colour. Numerous bright yellow scales align to form narrow irregular bands. These are boldest anteriorly, darkening and breaking posteriorly. Those on lower flanks may align longitudinally to form a wavy broken stripe. Top of head spotted, and lips barred, with yellow. Ventral surfaces grey to dark grey, often blotched with yellow. Midbody scales in 21 rows. TL 0.9 m.

Preferred habitat Restricted to sandstone outcrops and escarpments of eastern NSW. Extends from about Sydney, inland to Blue Mountains and south to Nowra area.

Microhabitat Shelters in wind-blown sandstone caves or beneath boulders and slabs resting on bare rock.

Comments Rock-inhabiting. An adept climber, able to negotiate sheer cliff faces with apparent ease. Feeds largely on lizards, particularly skinks and geckos. Mating occurs in late spring, and 4–8 young are born in late summer. Though once relatively abundant throughout southern areas of Sydney, indiscriminate collecting and the removal of sandstone slabs for gardens has largely restricted the species to isolated ridges. See genus.

Stephens' Banded Snake
Hoplocephalus stephensii Krefft, 1869
Photos 764, 765

Description Largest *Hoplocephalus* with ground colour of dark grey to black. Pattern usually consists of numerous narrow brown, orange-brown to cream bands; becoming obscure and often broken posteriorly. Some populations (and occasional individuals throughout range) lack all trace of banded pattern. Top of head usually bears large brown blotch. Side of head white, blotched or barred with black; even on patternless individuals. Ventral surfaces cream to white, each scale suffused with grey. Dark blotches may also be present. Midbody scales in 21 rows. TL 1.2 m.

Distinguished from *H. bitorquatus* in lacking a broad pale nuchal band, and in usually possessing banded pattern on body.

Preferred habitat Coastal ranges from Gosford area, NSW, north to Kroombit Tops, Qld. Occurs in a variety of habitats, from rainforests and wet or dry sclerophyll forests to rock outcrops.

Microhabitat Shelters beneath loose bark, in hollow trunks, limbs and rock crevices, or under slabs.

Comments Though predominantly nocturnal, individuals may occasionally be encountered basking in sheltered sites during mild weather. Feeds on lizards, frogs, mammals, and presumably birds. Mating occurs from late spring to early summer, and 3–8 offspring are born during February and March. See genus.

Genus *NEELAPS* Günther, 1863

Endemic genus containing 2 species, occurring in subhumid to arid western half of southern Australia.

Very small slender snakes, each with a depressed head and rounded snout. Eye small and dark. Scales smooth, in 15 rows at midbody. Anal and subcaudal scales divided. Pattern includes prominent dark nuchal bar, blotch on head.

Nocturnal. Fossorial; inhabiting soft upper soil layers under leaf-litter or overhanging foliage of shrubs or tussocks, and beneath logs or stumps. May be encountered foraging on surface during hot summer nights. Both species feed exclusively on skinks, particularly small fossorial *Lerista* spp. Egg-layers, producing small clutches. When harassed, forebody is raised, head angled acutely. Harmless.

Distinguished from *Simoselaps* (within zone of overlap) in lacking bands on body. Differs from *Rhinoplocephalus* in possessing a prominent dark nuchal bar, and divided (vs single) anal and subcaudal scales.

Neelaps bimaculatus
(Duméril, Bibron and Duméril, 1854)
Photo 766

Description Large slender *Neelaps* with ground colour of brown to bright orange-brown. Each scale bears cream blotch or base, forming reticulum. Mid to lower lateral surfaces are cream, usually without pattern. Broad black bands extend across nape, and across head forward to level of eyes. Snout and ventral surfaces white to cream. TL 0.4 m.

Distinguished from *N. calonotus* in lacking dark vertebral stripe (vs usually present, at least on tail).
Preferred habitat Extends from subhumid to semi-arid lower west coast, through arid southern interior of WA, east disjunctly to Kingoonya area, SA. Occurs in a wide variety of habitats, particularly sandy soils supporting low open vegetation. Sparsely distributed inland; more common in coastal and near-coastal areas.
Microhabitat See genus.
Comments Clutches of 2–5 eggs are recorded.

Black-striped Snake
Neelaps calonotus (Duméril, Bibron and Duméril, 1854)
Photo 767

Description Australia's smallest elapid snake. Ground colour bright orange-red, each scale bearing cream centre. Bluish black vertebral stripe (1–3 scales wide) enclosing cream to white spots, extends from nape to tip of tail. This may be broken to absent, although indications almost always remain on tail. Broad black crescent-shaped band extends

across nape. Narrow black bar extends across tip of snout, and broad black bar across top of head, forward to level of eyes. Interspaces white to cream. Ventral surfaces white. TL 0.25 m.

Distinguished from *N. bimaculatus* in possessing a dark vertebral stripe, at least on tail.
Preferred habitat Pale coastal and near-coastal dunes and sand plains, vegetated predominantly with heathlands and/or eucalypt/*Banksia* woodlands in the vicinity of Perth, WA. Extends from Rockingham north to Lancelin. An inland locality of 'Yorke' requires confirmation.
Microhabitat See genus.
Comments Feeds largely on *Lerista praepedita*, the smallest burrowing skink occurring in its range. Clutches of 2–5 eggs are recorded. Potentially endangered because of increasing urban and industrial development in its restricted distribution. See genus.

Tiger Snakes
Genus *NOTECHIS* Boulenger, 1896

Endemic genus containing 6 taxa. Restricted to cool temperate southern Australia, including Tas. and many offshore islands.

Large robust snakes, each with a broad blunt head. Eye moderately small, bearing dark iris and round pupil. Scales smooth in 17–21 rows at midbody. Anal and subcaudal scales single. Pattern (when present) consists of ragged-edged bands.

Terrestrial. Predominantly diurnal. Livebearing, producing large litters. Tiger snakes feed on birds, mammals, lizards and frogs. Venom is highly toxic, considered to be among the most potent of the world's land snakes.

Distinguished from *Austrelaps* in possessing more numerous midbody scale rows (17–21 vs almost invariably 15, rarely 17), and in lacking dark and pale bars on lips. Differs from *Pseudechis* and *Pseudonaja* by nature of anal scale (single vs divided) and subcaudal scales (single vs divided posteriorly, and all divided respectively). Differs further from all (except some *Pseudonaja* spp.) in frequently bearing body bands.

Black Tiger Snakes
Notechis ater (Krefft, 1866)
Photos 768–771

Description Large robust tiger snake, currently regarded as comprising 4 subspecies. Some of these may represent clinal variants.
N. a. ater Dorsal surfaces uniform shiny black. Pattern (when present) consists of paler bands. These are usually present on juveniles, and occasionally retained by adults, particularly on lower flanks. Body scales often widely spaced, with grey to black skin visible between them. Ventral surfaces pale to dark grey. Midbody scales in 17 rows. TL 1.0 m.
N. a. humphreysi Worrell, 1963 Large robust sub-

species. Ground colour dark brown to black, often bearing darker flecks. Bands present to absent; usually tinged with yellow. Midbody scales in 17 (occasionally 15) rows. TL 1.5 m.

N. a. niger Kinghorn, 1921   Adults black, usually without pattern. Juveniles usually bear whitish bands. Ventral surfaces dark grey to black; occasionally reddish on Kangaroo Island, SA. Midbody scales in 17–19 (rarely 21) rows. TL 1.1 m throughout most of range; 0.85 m on Roxby Island, SA.

N. a. serventyi Worrell, 1963   Largest subspecies. Adults dark brown, dark grey to black, occasionally bearing some indication of bands. Lower lateral scales may be noticeably paler than dorsum. Juveniles usually banded. Midbody scales in 17 rows. TL 1.8 m, though individuals exceeding 2.0 m have been recorded.

Preferred habitat   N. a. ater occurs in Flinders Ranges, SA, from Wilmington area north to Melrose area. Favours rocky creek margins. N. a. humphreysi ranges from Tas. to King and adjacent islands of western Bass Strait. Occurs in a variety of habitats, from wet and dry sclerophyll forests to coastal heathlands and tussock grasslands. N. a. niger occurs on Kangaroo Island, Sir Joseph Banks group, and lower parts of Eyre and Yorke Peninsulas, SA. Inhabits tussock- or shrub-dominated coastal dunes, woodlands, dry sclerophyll forests and chenopod shrublands. N. a. serventyi occurs on Chappell and Badger Islands of Furneaux Group, Bass Strait.

Microhabitat   N. a. serventyi, Bass Strait populations of N. a. humphreysi, and some island populations of N. a. niger inhabit muttonbird colonies (Puffinus tenuirostris). They rely on burrows for shelter and may be encountered basking coiled among adjacent low tussocks. Throughout remainder of range favours conditions similar to N. scutatus.

Comments   Snakes inhabiting muttonbird colonies feed on young chicks. These are small enough to be consumed only early in breeding season, and some populations are believed to fast for the remainder of year, living on fat reserves. On some islands of SA, snakes include petrel chicks (Pelagodroma marina) on their diets. Those living in forested areas and swamp, creek or river margins feed largely on frogs, mammals and lizards. Juveniles prey on small skinks and frogs. Island populations tend to occur in high density. Up to 30 or more may be encountered during an hour's walk on a sunny morning on some of the Bass Strait islands. When harassed, a defensive stance similar to that of N. scutatus may be employed. Large adults are often extremely sluggish by nature and may offer no resistance when approached or handled. DANGEROUSLY VENOMOUS.

Mainland or Eastern Tiger Snake and Western Tiger Snake
Notechis scutatus (Peters, 1861)
Photos 772, 773

Description   Two subspecies recognised. Status of western form is uncertain; regarded here as being a subspecies of N. scutatus.

N. s. scutatus   Ground colour extremely variable, ranging from pale grey through shades of brown, olive, reddish brown to black. Pattern usually consists of narrow ragged-edged pale bands; boldest anteriorly. Some individuals lack pattern. Ventral surfaces cream, pale yellow, olive to grey; often darker grey on throat and beneath tail. Midbody scales in 17–19 (rarely 15) rows. TL 1.5 m.

N. s. occidentalis Glauert, 1948   Darker than nominate form (usually black) bearing yellow bands, and yellow ventrolateral and anterior ventral surfaces.

Preferred habitat   Favours margins of swamps, rivers or other bodies of fresh water, in cool to mild climates over much of southern Australia. N. s. scutatus occupies eastern portion of range. Isolated populations occur as far north as highlands of the Carnarvon Ranges in central-eastern Qld. Extends southward down east coast of NSW to Vic. (excluding sandy semi-arid regions in north-west), and west into south-eastern SA. Penetrates semi-arid areas of north-western Vic. and south-western NSW, along Murray River and associated drainage systems. N. s. occidentalis occurs in south-western WA from Point Malcolm in east to Jurien in north. Abundant on Carnac and Garden Islands, near Fremantle. Both subspecies are common in many suburban areas.

Microhabitat   Shelters beneath rocks, logs or surface debris, and in abandoned burrows (including those of large crustaceans) beside creeks and other well-watered areas. Carnac Island population usually shelters in shearwater and penguin burrows.

Comments   Largely diurnal. Active at night in hot weather. Though normally terrestrial, seasonal flooding in some parts of range drives many individuals to higher ground; into bushes and low trees. Under favourable conditions local populations may reach particularly high numbers. Frogs constitute the bulk of diet, though lizards, mammals, birds and fish are also taken. Individuals are known to climb into low vegetation to capture birds. Normally about 30 young are produced per litter, though litters of over 100 are recorded. Tiger snakes attempt to flee if disturbed. When cornered the head is slightly raised with neck flattened and held in a low curve, presenting broadest aspect to aggressor. Hisses loudly, striking somewhat clumsily. Venom powerfully neurotoxic. DANGEROUSLY VENOMOUS.

Taipans
Genus *OXYURANUS*   Kinghorn, 1923

Contains 2 species, restricted to far northern, eastern interior and north-eastern Australia. One subspecies is endemic to New Guinea.

Very large moderately slender snakes, each with a deep narrow head and smooth or weakly keeled scales. Eye large with round pupil and orange-brown or blackish iris. Midbody scales in 21–23 rows. Anal scale single; subcaudals divided.

Terrestrial. Diurnal. Taipans feed entirely on warm-blooded prey, particularly mammals. These are captured by a rapid strike and release strategy, which is probably an adaptation for prey capable of retaliating when bitten. This distinctive behaviour is shared by the highly toxic African mambas (*Dendroaspis* spp.) which bear a superficial resemblance to taipans. Egglaying, producing moderately large clutches. *Oxyuranus* includes some of the world's most dangerously venomous land snakes.

Distinguished from *Pseudechis*, *Demansia* and *Pseudonaja* by nature of anal scale (single vs divided). Differs further (except from Qld populations of *Pseudonaja guttata*) in bearing more numerous midbody scale rows (21 or more vs 19 or fewer).

Small-scaled Snake, Western Taipan, Inland Taipan or 'Fierce Snake'
Oxyuranus microlepidotus (McCoy, 1879)
Photo 774

Description Moderately robust *Oxyuranus* with blackish iris. Ground colour variable, ranging from pale yellowish grey, yellowish brown, brown to rich dark brown. Individuals are paler during summer, becoming noticeably darker during winter. Most dorsal and lateral scales bear blackish edges, forming irregular speckled and/or herring-bone pattern. Head and neck uniform glossy black in winter, fading to shades of brown in summer. Lower lateral and ventral surfaces cream to yellow, occasionally bearing orange blotches. Ventral scales bear dark posterior edges. Scales at midbody in 23 (rarely 25) rows. TL 2.0 m.

Superficially similar to black-headed forms of the western brown snake (*Pseudonaja nuchalis*), differing in possessing more numerous midbody scale rows (23 or rarely 25 vs 17).

Preferred habitat Largely associated with Diamantina River and Cooper Creek drainage systems in arid south-western Qld and north-eastern SA. Additional records exist from far eastern NT, far northern NSW, and junction of Murray and Darling Rivers in far northern Vic. Favours low undulating gibber plains and loams (known locally as 'ashy downs') supporting sparse chenopod shrubs.

Microhabitat Shelters in deep soil cracks and in extensive burrow systems of the long-haired rat (*Rattus villosissimus*).

Comments Forages on surface in summer, for brief periods during midmorning. Feeds almost exclusively on long-haired rats (*Rattus villosissimus*), which occur in plagues following heavy rains. Large numbers of prey are consumed when rats are plentiful, but feeding virtually ceases when numbers

drop. Clutches of 12–20 eggs are laid. Venom is the most toxic known for any terrestrial snake; about 3 times that of the taipan (*O. scutellatus*). Despite lethal status and unflattering name of 'fierce snake', *O. microlepidotus* is shy and rarely attempts to bite, even when provoked. DANGEROUSLY VENOMOUS.

Taipan
Oxyuranus scutellatus (Peters, 1867)
Photo 775

Description Very large moderately slender *Oxyuranus* with orange-brown iris, and long head bearing sharply angular brow. Scales weakly keeled, at least on neck. Ground colour yellowish brown, brown, reddish brown, dark brown to almost black, fading on head. Juveniles usually bear numerous darker flecks; occasionally retained on adults. Head cream on juveniles, darkening with age. On large adults cream colouration may be restricted to snout. Ventral surfaces cream, bearing scattered orange spots or blotches. Scales in 21 or 23 rows at midbody. TL 2.0 m (individuals to 4.0 m recorded).

Preferred habitat Disjunct populations extend from northern Kimberley region (including Koolan Island), WA, through northern NT to northern Qld, then more or less continuously down east coast to Grafton area, north-eastern NSW. Occurs in a wide variety of habitats, from woodlands to dry sclerophyll forests and monsoon forests. Most abundant on well-timbered grassy slopes. Cultivation of sugar cane has provided additional favourable habitats.

Microhabitat Shelters in abandoned mammal burrows, hollow logs or stumps, and beneath surface debris.

Comments Diurnal (occasionally nocturnal in hot weather), generally foraging in early morning and late afternoon. Feeds on mammals, particularly rats, though prey as large as the bandicoot (*Isoodon macrourus*) are also taken. Mating probably occurs from July to December, and combat has been observed during this period. Clutches of 6–25 eggs are laid from October to February, hatching after approximately 60–70 days. Young taipans grow quickly, reaching sexual maturity as early as 16 months (males) to 28 months (females). Taipans are swift, extremely alert snakes with keen vision, and hence are infrequently encountered. When cornered and harassed, however, they will readily defend themselves, and may deliver multiple bites in rapid succession. DANGEROUSLY VENOMOUS.

Genus *PSEUDECHIS* Wagler, 1830

Contains 5 species distributed throughout Australia. Absent only from lower south-west, Nullarbor Plain, far south-eastern Vic. and Tas. A 6th species is endemic to southern New Guinea, and another

(*P. australis*) may extend to that region.

Very large robust elapids, each with a broad depressed head. Eye moderately small, bearing round pupil and pale to dark iris. Scales smooth in 17–19 rows at midbody. Anal scale usually divided. Subcaudal scales usually single anteriorly and divided posteriorly.

Terrestrial. Predominantly diurnal; crepuscular to nocturnal in hot weather. Some bear live young (born in membranous sacs), others are egglayers. Diet consists of a wide variety of vertebrate prey.

Distinguished from *Oxyuranus* and *Pseudonaja* in usually possessing undivided anterior subcaudal scales (vs all divided). Differs further from *Oxyuranus* in possessing fewer midbody scale rows (17–19 vs 21–23). Differs from *Denisonia, Notechis* and *Austrelaps* by nature of posterior subcaudal scales (divided, occasionally all single on *P. australis*, vs all single), and further from *Austrelaps* in bearing more numerous midbody scale rows (17–19 vs 15, rarely 17).

King Brown or Mulga Snake
Pseudechis australis (Gray, 1842)
Photo 776

Description Largest *Pseudechis*. Ground colour highly variable; pale brown, olive, rich reddish brown to coppery brown. Populations from southern parts of range may be darker to almost black. Individual scales usually bear paler bases, tending to form reticulated pattern. Ventral surfaces cream to white. Iris reddish brown. Midbody scales in 17 rows. Subcaudal scales usually single anteriorly and divided posteriorly; occasionally all single. TL 2.0 m, though individuals over 3 m have been recorded.

Distinguished from *P. guttatus* in possessing fewer midbody scale rows (17 vs 19) and cream (vs dark grey) ventral colouration. Differs from *P. butleri* in bearing weak, uniform to reticulated pattern (vs usually prominent; consisting of pale-centred scales mixed with clusters of black scales). Differs further in lacking black base to each ventral scale, and (within zone of overlap) fewer ventral scales (189–207 vs 204–216).

Preferred habitat Widespread throughout Australia, excepting humid and subhumid eastern and southern areas. May be encountered in virtually all subhumid to arid habitats throughout its range; from woodlands and monsoon forests to gibber and sand-ridge deserts. Possibly extralimital in New Guinea.

Microhabitat Shelters in any terrestrial sites available; abandoned burrows, soil cracks or hollow logs, and beneath surface debris.

Comments Nocturnal to diurnal according to temperature. Preys on a broad range of vertebrates, including other snakes. Reproductive data have been somewhat contradictory, with reports of livebearing and egglaying. A litter of 22 young and clutches of 11–16 eggs have been recorded. If cornered and provoked, hisses loudly with neck and forebody flattened, raised in an oblique curve. DANGEROUSLY VENOMOUS.

Pseudechis butleri Smith, 1982
Photos 777, 778

Description Ground colour dark grey to black. Most scales enclose a prominent pale grey, cream to yellow blotch; these become larger on flanks. These are mixed with irregular clusters of black scales. Top of head and nape dark with few, if any, pale spots. Snout and side of head reddish brown. Juveniles are dark bluish grey and obscurely patterned. Ventral surfaces cream to bright yellow, each ventral scale irregularly edged, and occasionally flecked, with black. Midbody scales in 17 rows. TL 1.5 m.

Distinguished from *P. australis* by pattern (prominent; pale-centred scales mixed with clusters of black scales; vs weak; uniform to reticulated). Differs further in bearing a black base to each ventral scale and (within zone of overlap) more numerous ventral scales (204–216 vs 189–207).

Preferred habitat Arid midwestern interior of WA, on heavy (often stony) soils dominated by mulga (*Acacia aneura*) woodlands and shrublands.

Microhabitat Shelters in abandoned burrows, beneath dead vegetation, and in wind- or water-worn caves of breakaways, extensive throughout range.

Comments Diurnal to nocturnal. Feeds on mammals and reptiles. Clutches of 9–12 eggs recorded. DANGEROUSLY VENOMOUS.

Collett's Snake
Pseudechis colletti Boulenger, 1902
Photo 779

Description Ground colour shades of grey, brown to dark reddish brown, marked with numerous broken and irregular cream, pinkish to red bands or transversely aligned blotches. These merge on mid to lower flanks, excluding most or all of ground colour. Ventral surfaces cream to pink. Colour is boldest, and pattern most prominent, on juveniles. Iris dark brown. Midbody scales in 19 rows. TL 1.5 m.

Preferred habitat Deeply cracking clays (blacksoil) in arid interior of Qld south to Tambo area.

Microhabitat Shelters in soil cracks.

Comments Nocturnal to diurnal according to temperature. Usually encountered foraging after rain. Probably feeds largely on reptiles and mammals. Clutches of 6–19 eggs are recorded. When harassed, inflates and deflates body, hissing loudly. DANGEROUSLY VENOMOUS.

Spotted Black Snake or Blue-bellied Black Snake
Pseudechis guttatus De Vis, 1905
Photo 780

Description Ground colour black, shades of grey to pale brown, with or without prominent to obscure paler grey, brown or cream spots. Some individuals may be cream with black tipped scales. Ventral surfaces grey to bluish grey, sometimes bearing whitish blotches. Iris black. Midbody scales in 19 rows. TL 1.5 m.

Distinguished from *P. porphyriacus* and *P. australis* in bearing more numerous midbody scale rows (19 vs 17). Differs further from *P. porphyriacus* in lacking pink lower lateral flush, and further from both by darker ventral colour.

Preferred habitat Variety of subhumid habitats, including river floodplains, dry sclerophyll forests and woodlands. Extends from mid-eastern NSW to south-eastern Qld. Most widespread west of Great Dividing Range, though occurring further east near Brisbane, Qld and Newcastle, NSW.

Microhabitat Shelters beneath fallen timber, in abandoned burrows or soil cracks.

Comments Predominantly diurnal, nocturnal in hot weather. Feeds on mammals, reptiles and frogs. Recorded clutches of 7–13 eggs, and a litter of newborn young in transparent membranous sacks (found beside adult beneath a log), suggest 2 modes of reproduction may occur. When provoked, arches forebody and flattens neck, hissing loudly. DANGEROUSLY VENOMOUS.

Red-bellied Black Snake
Pseudechis porphyriacus (Shaw, 1794)
Photo 781

Description Ground colour uniform glossy purplish black. Individuals with reddish ground colour or bearing scattered reddish scales are rarely encountered. Tip of snout usually suffused with pale brown. Ventrolateral and adjacent lateral edges of ventral scales pink to rich red. Belly cream to pink; black beneath tail. Iris black. Midbody scales in 17 rows. TL 1.5–2.0 m though individuals of 2.5 m have been recorded.

Distinguished from *P. guttatus* by ventral colour (cream to pink vs grey to bluish grey) and fewer midbody scale rows (17 vs 19). Juveniles differ from the small-eyed snake (*Cryptophis nigrescens*) by eye size (large vs very small), more numerous midbody scale rows (17 vs 15), and nature of ventral colour (pinkish red pigment brightest on ventrolateral scale row vs restricted to ventral scales).

Preferred habitat Widespread along east coast and ranges from south-eastern Cape York Peninsula, Qld, to south-eastern SA. Favours well-watered habitats such as swamps, riverbanks or edges of wet sclerophyll forests and rainforests.

Microhabitat Shelters in abandoned burrows and hollow logs, or beneath rocks and surface debris.

Comments One of eastern Australia's most familiar elapid snakes. Diurnal. Frogs probably constitute bulk of diet though mammals, reptiles and fish

(including eels) are also taken. Mating occurs in spring, and combat between rival males has been observed during this period. Bodies are intertwined with heads raised, each apparently attempting to place its own above that of opponent. Between 5 and 40 young are born from January to March. These are enclosed in membranous sacs from which they emerge shortly after birth. Though once abundant throughout most of range, Qld and northern NSW populations appear to have declined dramatically. This has been attributed to the spread of introduced cane toads (*Bufo marinus*). Toads are extremely poisonous, and there have been many reports of snakes dying suddenly while attempting to devour them. Quick to flee when disturbed, but when provoked, the red-bellied black snake will hiss loudly with neck flattened, and head and forebody raised, presenting broadest aspect to aggressor. The species may be regarded as DANGEROUSLY VENOMOUS, though only one human fatality has been recorded.

Brown Snakes
Genus *PSEUDONAJA* Günther, 1858

Contains 8 described taxa distributed throughout most of Australia. Absent only from rainforests and wet sclerophyll forests of east, alpine areas, south-eastern Vic. and Tas. Extralimital in southern New Guinea. It appears likely that with future work more taxa will be recognised.

Moderately small to very large, relatively slender elapids, each with a narrow head (not noticeably distinct from neck) and angular brow. Eye large, bearing round pupil and usually a pale iris. Scales smooth and weakly glossed, in 17–21 rows at midbody. Anal and subcaudal scales divided. Colour and pattern are extremely variable, though juveniles of most species (excepting *P. guttata*) bear a black blotch on top of head; usually separated by a narrow strip of ground colour from a black nuchal bar or blotch.

Fast-moving diurnal (nocturnal in hot weather) terrestrial snakes which rely on keen vision to locate their prey: mammals, birds, lizards and occasionally other snakes. These are usually subdued by a combination of envenomation and constriction. Egg-laying. Brown snakes shelter beneath logs, rocks or surface debris, and in abandoned burrows or hollow logs. With the exception of *P. modesta* all are DANGEROUSLY VENOMOUS.

Distinguished from *Oxyuranus* by nature of anal scale (divided vs single), and in usually bearing fewer midbody scale rows (17–21 vs 21–23). Differs from *Demansia* in bearing more numerous midbody scale rows (17–21 vs 15) and from *Notechis* and *Denisonia* by nature of anal and subcaudal scales (divided vs single). Differs from *Pseudechis* in possessing divided subcaudal scales (vs anterior subcaudals single). Juveniles differ from black-headed members of *Rhinoplocephalus gouldii* species group by pattern (dark nuchal bar or blotch, separated from dark hood by a narrow band of ground colour vs dark hood restricted to head or extending onto nape). Juveniles differ further by head-shape and eye size (deep head bearing a very large eye vs depressed head with a small eye).

Dugite
Pseudonaja affinis Günther, 1872
Photos 782, 783

Description Large *Pseudonaja* comprising 2 subspecies.

P. a. affinis Ground colour variable; yellowish brown, pale or dark brown, grey to almost black. Many individuals bear scattered black scales. Heavily marked snakes from southern coastal areas are known as 'Kabadas'. Juveniles bear a black head and nape, and dark flecks on body, forming herringbone pattern. Ventral surfaces pale brown to greyish white, blotched with orange to brown. Iris usually orange-brown. Midbody scales in 19 rows. TL 2.0 m.

P. a. tanneri (Worrell, 1961) Differs from nominate race by smaller size and uniformly dark colouration (including ventral surfaces). TL 1.0 m.

Distinguished from *P. nuchalis*, *P. modesta* and *P. textilis inframacula* in possessing more numerous midbody scale rows (19 vs 17).

Preferred habitat *P. a. affinis* is widespread through south-western Australia, from Cervantes area, WA, south-east to western SA. Occupies virtually all habitats, including coastal dunes, semi-arid woodlands or shrublands, and wet sclerophyll forests. *P. a. tanneri* is known from some islands of Recherche Archipelago off southern coast of WA. An undescribed dwarf subspecies occurs on Rottnest Island off Fremantle. These islands are vegetated with woodlands and heathlands over pale sands and limestones.

Microhabitat As for genus.

Comments *P. a. affinis* is occasionally cannibalistic. Recorded to lay 13 and 20 eggs, hatching in February. When provoked, raises forebody in S-shape, hissing loudly and striking repeatedly. Heavily blotched 'Kabada' form has been noted as more excitable than other variants. DANGEROUSLY VENOMOUS. Otherwise as for genus.

Speckled Brown Snake
Pseudonaja guttata (Parker, 1926)
Photo 784

Description Ground colour orange-yellow, pale yellowish brown to pale greyish brown. Unbanded and banded forms occur.

Unbanded form: Lateral edges of most scales black, forming speckled pattern. Head and nape uniform, bearing dark peppering, and occasionally a dark brown nuchal blotch.

Banded form bears 9–12 evenly spaced broad reddish brown to dark brown bands. These may be narrower, equal to, or wider than pale interspaces. Dark speckling may align to form up to 3 narrow transverse lines between each dark band.

Juveniles appear to lack the prominent black head and nape markings on young of all other *Pseudonaja*. Ventral surfaces of both forms are white to yellow, often bearing an orange median flush. Intense orange peppering usually present, becoming obscure posteriorly. Occasionally individuals bear large closely packed orange blotches. These become smaller and less dense posteriorly. Iris reddish yellow; inner margin narrowly edged with contrasting white. Midbody scales in 19 (NT) or 21 (Qld) rows. TL 1.4 m.

Distinguished from *P. nuchalis*, *P. ingrami* and *P. textilis* in possessing more midbody scale rows (19–21 vs 17). Differs further from *P. ingrami* by iris colour (pale vs dark), and further from *P. textilis* by colour of mouth-lining (bluish black vs pink).

Preferred habitat Restricted to arid black-soil plains supporting *Astrebla* grasslands of mideastern NT, far north-western SA and interior of Qld.

Microhabitat Shelters in deep soil cracks.

Comments Diurnal. Captive individuals show a preference for lizards over mammals. Many adults bear damaged tails; possibly a result of leaving them exposed when sheltering in soil cracks. When harassed the speckled brown snake raises its forebody and flattens its neck to form a conspicuous hood. DANGEROUSLY VENOMOUS. Otherwise as for genus.

Ingram's Brown Snake
Pseudonaja ingrami (Boulenger, 1908)
Photo 785

Description Five distinct colour forms occur: glossy blackish brown, golden brown, pale olive-brown, dark brown fading posteriorly to golden brown, and pale to rich yellowish brown (bearing darker brown, greyish brown to almost black head and nape). Scales of all forms are dark-tipped. Ventral surfaces pale or bright yellow to orange, often fading to cream on chin and lower lips. Two large orange spots usually present on each ventral scale, increasing posteriorly to 4 or more, before fusing to form narrow edge to each scale. This is subject to considerable variation. Iris dull orange-brown, superficially appearing black. Midbody scales in 17 rows. TL 1.7 m.

Distinguished from all other *Pseudonaja* by iris colour (dark vs pale). Differs further from *P. guttata* in possessing fewer midbody scale rows (17 vs 19–21), and from *P. textilis* by colour of mouth-lining (predominantly black vs pink). Differs further from *P. textilis*, and from *P. nuchalis* in possessing more lower labial scales (7 vs 6).

Preferred habitat Arid black-soil plains supporting *Astrebla* grasslands, from interior of Qld to central NT. Disjunct population occurs in subhumid Kununurra area, WA. Favours low-lying, seasonally flooded habitats.

Microhabitat Shelters in deep soil cracks.

Comments Feeds largely on mammals, including long-haired rats (*Rattus villosissimus*) when these are abundant. Clutch of 10 eggs recorded in early summer. Defensive stance is similar to that described for *P. guttata*. DANGEROUSLY VENOMOUS. Otherwise as for genus.

Ringed Brown Snake
Pseudonaja modesta (Günther, 1872)
Photo 786

Description Smallest *Pseudonaja*. Ground colour pale grey, yellowish brown, brown to rich reddish brown. Juveniles display bright colouration and sharp markings while adults may be virtually patternless. Individual scales often bear obscure pale bases and darker centres, forming a lightly flecked pattern. From 4 to 12 evenly spaced narrow dark bands are usually present between nape and tail-tip. These may be pale-edged on juveniles. Black patch on top of head extends through eye to upper lip or chin, separated from black nuchal bar by a narrow strip of cream to ground colour. Side of head ground colour to cream. Ventral surfaces cream to white, usually flecked with orange. Iris orange-brown. Midbody scales in 17 rows. TL 0.6 m.

Distinguished from all other *Pseudonaja* in possessing fewer ventral scales (less than 177 vs more than 185), and in attaining very small maximum size (0.6 m; scarcely larger than juveniles of other species).

Preferred habitat Semi-arid to arid central and western interior of Australia, from north-western NSW and western Qld to west coast of WA. Occurs in virtually all habitats (with the possible exception of black-soil plains) throughout its broad distribution.

Microhabitat Often shelters in abandoned lizard burrows, particularly those of the central netted dragon (*Ctenophorus nuchalis*). Otherwise as for genus.

Comments Nocturnal to diurnal. Feeds largely on diurnal skinks. Clutches of 7–11 eggs are recorded. When threatened, the ringed brown snake adopts a defensive stance similar to that of *P. affinis*. Not considered dangerous though large individuals should be treated with caution.

Western Brown Snake or Gwardar
Pseudonaja nuchalis Günther, 1858
Photo 787, 788

Description Extremely variable *Pseudonaja*, probably comprising several species. A bewildering array of colour forms occur; at least 16 have been listed from NT alone. These and their intermediate variants are too numerous and complex to cover in every detail, though several trends predominate.

(a) Ground colour pale yellowish brown to dark brown, paler on head and usually nape. Black scales on nape may be scattered or aligned to form V- or W-shape.

(b) Orange-brown to dark brown. Dark edges to scales form prominent reticulum or herring-bone pattern. Head and nape glossy black.

(c) Orange-brown to dark brown, bearing prominent reticulum or herring-bone pattern. Top of head glossy black; paler to white on sides, and bordered posteriorly by a pale brown collar, and a disjunct black mark on nape.

(d) Orange-brown to olive-brown with 10–18 broad black bands. Pale interspaces may enclose 3 narrow irregular transverse lines. In northern parts of range forebody may lack bands.

(e) Uniform rich brown, paler on snout.

(f) Olive-brown, paler on head and nape, and bearing prominent reddish brown vertebral line.

(g) Pale to dark brown, bearing darker brown to black reticulum and a black nuchal band.

(h) Olive-brown, densely marked with scattered black scales.

(i) Dark greyish brown, bearing darker head and pale tip to snout.

Colour pattern is further complicated by a tendency for southern populations to become paler in warm months. Ventral surfaces of all forms cream to bright yellow, marked with scattered orange blotches; tending to fade posteriorly. Iris red, forming broken circle. Midbody scales usually in 17 rows. TL 1.45 m.

Distinguished from *P. affinis* and *P. guttata* in possessing fewer midbody scale rows (17 vs 19, and 9–21, respectively). Differs from *P. ingrami* in bearing fewer lower labial scales (6 vs 7) and by iris colour (pale reddish iris vs dull orange-brown, superficially appearing black). Differs from *P. textilis* by colour of mouth-lining (blackish vs pink). Black-headed forms closely resemble inland taipans (*Oxyuranus microlepidotus*), differing in possessing fewer midbody scale rows (17 vs 23; rarely 25).

Preferred habitat Extends through virtually all subhumid to arid areas of Australia. Absent from east coast and ranges, Tas., most of Vic., south-eastern SA, southern Eyre Peninsula, SA, Great Australian Bight and south-western WA. Occupies all habitats in its broad distribution, possibly excepting black-soil plains of eastern NT and western Qld.

Microhabitat As for genus.

Comments Karyological work supports the recognition of several taxa in this unwieldy complex and resurrection of several old names from synonymy may prove justified. Feeds largely on lizards, mammals, and occasionally other snakes. Clutches of 13–22 eggs are recorded. Cornered individuals rear in a defensive stance similar to that of *P. affinis*. DANGEROUSLY VENOMOUS.

Common or Eastern Brown Snake
Pseudonaja textilis (Duméril, Bibron and Duméril, 1854)
Photos 789–791

Description Largest *Pseudonaja*. Two subspecies recognised.

P. t. textilis Ground colour yellowish brown, brown, reddish brown, greyish brown to almost black. Dark individuals often bear significantly paler heads. Pattern usually absent; occasionally composed of dark and/or pale flecking or mottling. Juveniles bear a black blotch on head, a black nuchal band, and (in some areas) prominent narrow black bands on body. Ventral surfaces cream, yellow to orange, marked with scattered orange to brown blotches. Iris very pale brown. Midbody scales in 17 rows. TL 2.0 m, though individuals exceeding this are occasionally encountered.

P. t. inframacula (Waite, 1925) Similar to *P. t. textilis*. Differs in usually bearing scattered black scales, and dark grey ventral surfaces. TL 1.5 m.

Distinguished from all other *Pseudonaja* by colour of mouth-lining (pink vs bluish black). Differs further from *P. affinis* and *P. guttata* in possessing fewer midbody scale rows (17 vs 19 and 19–21), and further from *P. ingrami* by iris colour (pale brown vs dull orange-brown, superficially appearing black).

Preferred habitat *P. t. textilis* is widespread through subhumid to arid eastern Australia, extending disjunctly to north-eastern WA. Extralimital in southern New Guinea. *P. t. inframacula* extends from Eyre Peninsula, SA, along southern coast of SA to about Eucla area, WA. Both subspecies occupy virtually all habitats except rainforests or wet sclerophyll forests and alpine areas. Land clearing has apparently proven beneficial, as brown snakes seem to be most abundant in agricultural regions.

Microhabitat As for genus.

Comments Possibly eastern Australia's most frequently encountered dangerously venomous snake. Relationships between the subspecies are obscure, as *P. t. inframacula* more closely resembles *P. affinis*. Feeds largely on lizards, mammals and birds. Abundance in rural areas is probably due to the presence of numerous house mice (*Mus musculus*), which provide a valuable food source. Clutches of 10–35 eggs are recorded; laid in late spring. Males have been observed in combat during this period. A litter may contain both banded and unbanded individuals. Extremely swift, alert and nervous; quick to retaliate if provoked, readily adopting a defensive stance similar to that of *P. affinis*. DANGEROUSLY VENOMOUS.

Genus *RHINOPLOCEPHALUS* Müller, 1885

Contains 10 species. Widespread throughout Australia, particularly in south and east. One species extends north to New Guinea.

Small elapids, each with a broad depressed head. Eye small with round pupil and black iris. Scales smooth and glossy, in 15–17 rows at midbody. Anal and subcaudal scales single.

Terrestrial, nocturnal and livebearing. Individuals shelter beneath logs, rocks, dead vegetation and in soil cracks. Lizards (mainly skinks) constitute major prey items though smaller snakes are occasionally taken. Foraging snakes probably capture sleeping diurnal prey. Most appear to remain active throughout year. Bites from most species may cause local pain and swelling. Not considered dangerously venomous.

Three species groups are tentatively recognised.

R. bicolor **group** Contains one species. Only member of genus to lack internasal scales. Ground colour drab greyish brown without pattern. Restricted to humid lower south-west of WA.

R. gouldii **group (hooded or black-headed snakes)** Contains 9 taxa. Ground colour reddish brown to greyish brown, usually with prominent black blotch or hood on top of head. Widespread across southern and eastern Australia. Frenetic thrashing defence strategy of some species results in alternative common name of whip snakes (not to be confused with true whip snakes, *Demansia* spp.). Comprises *R. dwyeri*, *R. flagellum*, *R. gouldii*, *R. monachus*, *R. nigriceps*, *R. nigrostriatus*, *R. spectabilis spectabilis*, *R. spectabilis nullarbor*, and tentatively *R. boschmai*.

R. punctatus **group** Contains one species with reddish ground colour and prominent dark spots or blotches on head and nape. Widespread through northern arid regions.

Rhinoplocephalus is distinguished from *Hemiaspis* and juvenile *Pseudonaja* by eye size (very small vs large). Differs further from these, and from *Glyphodon*, by nature of anal and subcaudal scales (single vs divided). Differs further from juvenile *Pseudonaja* spp., and from *Furina* and *Neelaps* by nature of black hood. If present, this is restricted to head or extends continuously onto nape (vs separated from black nape by a pale interspace or blotch). Eastern and southern species differ from the small-eyed snake (*Cryptophis nigrescens*) in bearing paler ground colour (brown to reddish brown or greyish brown vs black). Differs from *Denisonia* by nature of eye (small and black vs slightly protrusive, bearing pale iris and vertically elliptic pupil).

Müller's Snake
Rhinoplocephalus bicolor Müller, 1885
Photos 792, 793

Description Moderately robust *Rhinoplocephalus*; sole member of *R. bicolor* group. Ground colour glossy dark brown to dark grey. Mid to lower flanks bright to dull orange. Juveniles pale bluish grey with darker patch on head, occasionally an obscure narrow yellow vertebral line and pale lemon yellow flanks. Ventral surfaces white. Midbody scales in 15 rows. TL 0.4 m.

Distinguished from all sympatric elapids in lacking internasal scales. These are present on all other Australian species except the northern bandy bandy (*Vermicella multifasciata*).

Preferred habitat Restricted to humid and sub-humid areas in lower south-west of WA, from Busselton in west to Thomas River in east. Favours sandy, seasonally saturated areas supporting ground cover of low shrubs.

Microhabitat Usually encountered in disused stick-ant nests (*Iridomyrmex conifer*). Also recorded beneath granite slabs (when these occur in suitable low-lying areas), and under fallen grass trees (*Xanthorrhoea* spp.).

Comments On mild winter days individuals ascend to warmer upper levels of ant nests. In dry summer weather snakes are infrequently encountered, presumably penetrating deeper into adjacent swamps. Though one individual is known to have consumed a frog, diet consists largely of skinks. All species recorded as prey items frequently utilise ant nests as shelter sites. Litter of 4 young recorded. Hatchlings have been found in May. When threatened, head is raised, accompanied by hissing and striking with mouth closed. Rarely (if ever) attempts to bite, even when handled.

Carpentaria Whip Snake
Rhinoplocephalus boschmai (Brongersma and Knaap-van Meeuwen, 1961)
Photo 794

Description Member of *R. gouldii* group lacking the glossy black hood present on other members. Ground colour pale yellowish brown, brown to dark orange-brown. Dark vertebral suffusion may be present; occasionally in sharp contrast to lateral colouration. Scales bear black basal blotch and paler posterior margins. Top of head pale to dark brown. Side of head, neck and forebody, paler shade of ground colour. Ventral surfaces white. Midbody scales in 15 rows. TL 0.45 m.

Distinguished from *R. dwyeri* in lacking well-defined black hood, and from *Glyphodon dunmalli* in possessing fewer midbody scale rows (15 vs 21).

Preferred habitat Subhumid to arid regions, usually on hard soils supporting a variety of open vegetation-types. Extends from south-east Qld, through eastern interior to Gulf of Carpentaria.

Microhabitat As for genus.

Comments As for genus.

Dwyer's Snake
Rhinoplocephalus dwyeri (Worrell, 1956)
Photo 795

Description Member of *R. gouldii* group with ground colour of yellowish brown, brown to orange-brown; rarely with a dark vertebral suffusion. Each scale bears blackish base. Scales on nape and anterior flanks may be tinged with brighter orange. Lower lateral surfaces yellowish. Top of head and first 4–6 scale rows on nape bear a glossy black hood. Lips, tip of snout, and area in front of eye, cream to pale yellowish brown. Ventral surfaces cream. Midbody scales in 15 rows. TL 0.4 m.

Distinguished from *R. boschmai* in possessing well-defined black hood, and from *R. nigriceps* in lacking dark vertebral stripe.

Preferred habitat Dry sclerophyll forests, woodlands and rock outcrops; usually associated with heavy soils. Occurs from south-eastern interior of Qld, through interior of NSW (west of Great Dividing Range, reaching coast through Hunter Valley) to Seymour district, central Vic., and far eastern SA.

Microhabitat As for genus.

Comments Mating takes place during spring and autumn (at least in New England area, NSW). Otherwise as for genus.

Little Whip Snake
Rhinoplocephalus flagellum (McCoy, 1878)
Photo 796

Description Small member of *R. gouldii* group with ground colour of dull greyish brown, pale brown to rich reddish brown. Base of each scale generally blackish; posterior edge a paler shade of ground colour. Top of head and first 6 or 7 scale rows on nape bear a glossy black hood. Side of head yellowish brown to cream. Broad pale bar extends over snout, between nostril and eye. On some south-eastern highland populations dark hood is reduced to large blotch on top of head. Ventral surfaces cream. TL 0.4 m.

Distinguished from all other *Rhinoplocephalus* in possessing more numerous midbody scale rows (17 vs 15).

Preferred habitat Highland and lowland cool temperate woodlands, dry sclerophyll forests, granite outcrops and basalt plains. Extends from ACT, south (on western side of Great Dividing Range) to western suburbs of Melbourne, and through remainder of southern Vic. to south-eastern SA. An isolated population occurs on St Francis Island in the Nuyts Archipelago near Ceduna, SA.

Microhabitat As for genus.

Comments A litter of 4 has been recorded in September. Adults are often found in pairs. If provoked, flattens body to form tight coils, thrashing abruptly when touched. Otherwise as for genus.

Rhinoplocephalus gouldii (Gray, 1841)
Photo 797

Description Member of *R. gouldii* group with ground colour of orange-brown to reddish brown.

Scales narrowly edged with black, forming a fine reticulum. Top of head and first 4–9 scale rows on nape glossy black, broken by variably sized pale orange-brown mark in front of each eye. Lips and ventral surfaces white. Midbody scales in 15 rows. TL 0.5 m.

Distinguished from *R. nigriceps* in lacking dark vertebral stripe or zone. Differs from *R. spectabilis* in possessing a dark edge to each dorsal scale (vs dark blotch on base of each scale), and in attaining greater maximum size (TL 0.5 vs 0.4 m).

Preferred habitat Heathlands, woodlands, shrublands, dry sclerophyll forests and rock outcrops of south-western WA, with an apparently isolated population further north in the Murchison district. Absent from humid deep south-west.

Microhabitat Shelters beneath rock slabs, surface debris, and loose bark at bases of trees. See genus.

Comments Litters of 3–7 young are recorded. Otherwise as for genus.

Hooded or Monk Snake
Rhinoplocephalus monachus (Storr, 1964)
Photo 798

Description Relatively slender member of *R. gouldii* group with ground colour of orange-brown to bright brick red. Top of head bears glossy black to very dark brown hood; barely extending onto nape. Lips and ventral surfaces white. Midbody scales in 15 rows. TL 0.53 m.

Preferred habitat Favours hard red soils supporting *Acacia*-dominated woodlands and shrublands. Often associated with rock outcrops. Occurs in semi-arid to arid regions, from west coast (apparently absent from lower Gascoyne, western Pilbara and North West Cape regions) to interior of WA, south to northern Nullarbor Plain. Apparently isolated population extends from far eastern WA to south-western NT and north-western SA.

Microhabitat Often shelters in disused termitaria. Otherwise as for genus.

Comments See genus.

Short-tailed Snake
Rhinoplocephalus nigriceps (Günther, 1863)
Photo 799

Description Large member of *R. gouldii* group with prominent dark grey to black vertebral stripe or zone. Upper lateral scales reddish to purplish brown bearing pale posterior margins. Mid to lower lateral scales paler. Head and nape glossy greyish black to black, continuous with vertebral stripe. Lips and ventral surfaces whitish. Midbody scales in 15 rows. TL 0.6 m.

Distinguished from all other southern *Rhinoplocephalus* in possessing prominent dark vertebral stripe or zone.

Preferred habitat Associated largely with gra-

nites of Darling Range in far west of distribution, extending through a variety of semi-arid habitats (particularly mallee communities) from southern WA to southern SA (apparently excluding chenopod-dominated border region), north-western Vic. and south-western NSW.

Microhabitat As for genus.

Comments In addition to skinks, other small elapids (including own kind) and blind snakes are recorded as prey items. Litters of 3 or 4 are recorded. Otherwise as for genus.

Black-striped Snake
Rhinoplocephalus nigrostriatus (Krefft, 1864)
Photo 800

Description Slender long-tailed large-eyed member of *R. gouldii* group with dark brown to black vertebral stripe or suffusion from nape to tip of tail. Ground colour dark brown, dull reddish brown to bright pinkish red, usually fading on lower flanks. Head glossy black, occasionally dark brown to brown. Side of head, neck and forebody cream to pinkish. Ventral surfaces white. Midbody scales in 15 rows. TL 0.5 m.

Preferred habitat Eastern Qld, from islands of Torres Strait south at least to Rockhampton district, and possibly to Bundaberg area. Favours dry sclerophyll forests and woodlands on variety of soil-types. Extralimital in New Guinea.

Microhabitat As for genus.

Comments As for genus.

Little Spotted Snake
Rhinoplocephalus punctatus (Boulenger, 1896)
Photo 801

Description Sole member of *R. punctatus* group, with ground colour of yellowish brown, brown to rich reddish brown. Base of each scale usually smudged with dark brown. Smudges may become larger and darker on lower lateral scale row, forming a narrow broken stripe. Vertebral scales may be dark-edged, forming an obscure suffusion. Head ground colour to yellow with highly variable dark brown to black markings. Typically these include: a spot on tip of snout, a streak from nostril through or under eye to base of head (breaking into a series of large blotches on side of neck), small to large scattered spots on top of head, and occasionally a pair of nuchal blotches. Ventral surfaces white. Midbody scales in 15 rows. TL 0.52 m.

Preferred habitat Widespread across subhumid to arid northern Australia, from interior of Qld, through NT to Kimberley region, WA. Population on north-west coast and adjacent interior of WA is isolated by Great Sandy Desert. Favours sandy and loamy soils supporting woodlands or hummock grasslands.

Microhabitat As for genus.

Comments Feeds largely on sleeping diurnal lizards, particularly skinks and dragons. Blind snakes are also recorded prey items. Produces 2–5 young per litter. Otherwise as for genus.

Rhinoplocephalus spectabilis (Krefft, 1869)
Photos 802, 803

Description Small member of *R. gouldii* group comprising 2 subspecies.

R. s. spectabilis Ground colour greyish brown, occasionally tinged with orange. Each scale bears dark brown blotch on base. Top of head and first 4–7 scale rows on nape are glossy black. Broad pale brown transverse bar extends across snout, often broken to form spectacle-shaped markings. Conspicuous pale brown area behind each eye is continuous with pale upper lips. Upper lips and ventral surfaces white. Midbody scales in 15 rows. TL 0.4 m.

R. s. nullarbor (Storr, 1981) Differs from nominate form in bearing reduced pale markings on head, and longer tail.

Distinguished from *R. gouldii* by ground colour (greyish brown vs reddish brown), and pattern (dark blotch on base of each scale vs dark edges). Differs from *R. nigriceps* in lacking dark vertebral stripe or zone, and further from both in attaining smaller maximum size (TL 0.4 vs 0.5 and 0.6 m, respectively). Differs from *R. flagellum* by fewer midbody scale rows (15 vs 17).

Preferred habitat *R. s. spectabilis* occurs on sands and heavy soils supporting open eucalypt and chenopod associations on Eyre and upper Yorke Peninsula regions, SA. *R. s. nullarbor* replaces nominate form on Nullarbor Plain of south-western SA and south-eastern WA, inhabiting limestone-based heavy soils vegetated with extensive chenopod shrublands. A distinctive population occurs north of Esperance (Scadden area) in south-western WA.

Microhabitat *R. s. nullarbor* frequently shelters beneath chunks of limestone. Otherwise as for genus.

Comments As for genus.

Burrowing Snakes
Genus *SIMOSELAPS* Jan, 1859

Endemic genus containing 11 species. Certain taxa are poorly defined; some of which may be distinct species, others local variants. Widespread throughout subhumid to arid areas of Australia. Absent from most of east coast, eastern highlands, southeast, Tas. and lower south-west. At least one taxon awaits description.

Small, moderate to robust short-tailed elapids. Snout rounded to acutely shovel-shaped; protruding beyond mouth. Eye small, bearing round to vertically elliptic pupil and pale or dark iris. Scales smooth; weakly to strongly glossed, in 15 or 17 rows at midbody. Anal and subcaudal scales divided (a few single anterior subcaudals occasionally present). Pattern invariably includes a dark nuchal bar or blotch. Dark head blotch and numerous bands or rings on body are usually present.

Semi-fossorial to fossorial, sometimes ascending to surface at night. Egglaying. Harmless.

Tentatively divisible into 4 species groups.

S. bertholdi group Contains 4 species. Snout depressed and rounded, lacking sharp cutting edge. Eye bears pale or dark iris and vertically elliptic pupil. Bands (present on all except *S. minimus*) form complete rings. Largely restricted to sandy areas in western half of continent. Members are usually sand-swimmers, sheltering in loose upper substrate levels beneath overhanging foliage of shrubs or grasses. They feed on burrowing skinks (*Lerista* spp.), which are constricted in a series of tight coils. Comprises *S. anomalus*, *S. bertholdi*, *S. littoralis* and *S. minimus*.

S. semifasciatus group Contains 7 taxa. Snout upturned and shovel-shaped, bearing acute anterior cutting edge. Iris dark. Bands (present on all species except *S. incinctus*) never form complete rings. Widespread throughout range of genus, particularly on hard loams and stony soils. Members burrow into soil cracks, insect burrows, and beneath stumps or rocks. Most feed exclusively on squamate eggs, though *S. australis* also preys on skinks. Comprises *S. approximans*, *S. australis*, *S. incinctus*, *S. roperi*, *S. semifasciatus campbelli*, *S. semifasciatus semifasciatus* and *S. semifasciatus woodjonesii*.

S. fasciolatus group Contains one large, relatively robust species comprising 2 subspecies. Snout depressed with moderately sharp cutting edge. Iris dark. Bands narrow and irregular, often broken to form transverse series of spots; never complete rings. Pale interspaces usually enclose scattered spots. Distributed through subhumid to arid southern Australia, inhabiting rock outcrops, hard loams and soft sandy soils. Populations occurring on soft substrates are largely sand-swimmers. Shelters beneath loose sand and leaf-litter, in soil cracks and bases of stumps. Feeds on skinks and squamate eggs. Comprises *S. fasciolatus fasciolatus* and *S. fasciolatus fasciata*.

S. warro group Contains one divergent species (so much so that its inclusion in *Simoselaps* is only tentative) with depressed snout, lacking cutting edge. Iris pale. Bands absent. Dark-edged scales form a reticulum. Feeds on skinks. Restricted to subhumid north-eastern Qld.

Simoselaps is distinguished from *Vermicella* in attaining much smaller maximum size (TL 0.5 vs TL 1.0 m), and by pattern not consisting of black and white rings. Differs from *Neelaps* (in zone of overlap) by pattern (bands or rings on body vs bands restricted to head and nape).

Desert Banded Snake
Simoselaps anomalus (Sternfeld, 1919)
Photo 804

Description Member of *S. bertholdi* group with dark iris. Ground colour yellowish orange to reddish orange; rarely with darker lateral edges to each scale. Approximately 24–40 black rings (equal to or narrower than pale interspaces) extend between nape and tail-tip. Head black, bearing complete to broken narrow white bar across level of nostrils; continuous with white patch on side of snout. Broad black nuchal ring present, separated from black head by interspace of cream, white, or occasionally ground colour. Ventral surfaces paler shade of ground colour to white. Midbody scales in 15 rows. TL 0.2 m.

Distinguished from *S. bertholdi* and *S. littoralis* by head-pattern (glossy black patch vs dark mottling and/or flecking).
Preferred habitat Red sand ridges and interdunes vegetated with hummock grasses, from arid northwest coast of WA to southern NT and northwestern SA.
Microhabitat As for species group.
Comments As for species group.

Simoselaps approximans (Glauert, 1954)
Photo 805

Description Member of *S. semifasciatus* group. Ground colour grey to dark greyish brown, marked with 51–96 very narrow (less than one scale wide) cream to pale grey interspaces between nape and tail-tip. These may be reduced to transverse series of spots. Top of head dark greyish brown. Snout cream, pale brown to orange-brown. Broad dark nuchal band (5–8 scales wide) may be continuous with head blotch, or separated by narrow pale interspace. Ventral surfaces cream. Midbody scales in 17 rows. TL 0.36 m.

Distinguished from *S. semifasciatus* and *S. roperi* by nature of pattern (dark bands at least 5 times broader than pale interspaces vs considerably less than 5 times broader). Differs further from *S. semifasciatus* in bearing more upper labial scales (6 vs 5).
Preferred habitat Arid north-western interior, coast and some islands of WA, from Broome area south to Shark Bay and Yalgoo. Favours heavy (often stony) reddish soils dominated by *Acacia* woodlands and shrublands.
Microhabitat As for species group.
Comments As for species group.

Coral Snake
Simoselaps australis (Krefft, 1864)
Photo 806

Description Member of *S. semifasciatus* group. Ground colour pink, pale reddish brown to brick red. Approximately 50–60 narrow ragged-edged bands (each composed of a transverse series of dark-edged cream to pale grey scales) extend from behind nape to tail-tip. Broad black to dark grey band extends across head, separated from broad pale-edged nuchal band by a narrow strip of ground colour. Ventral surfaces cream. Midbody scales in 17 rows. TL 0.5 m.

Distinguished from *S. semifasciatus* by nature of pattern (narrow bands composed of dark-edged pale scales vs broader bands composed of wholly pigmented scales).
Preferred habitat Subhumid to arid eastern interior of Australia, from north-eastern Qld, through interior of NSW and far north-western Vic. to Port Augusta area, SA. Occupies a wide variety of habitats from woodlands and shrublands to hummock grasslands and rock outcrops. Red sands are favoured.
Microhabitat As for species group.
Comments Clutch of 4–6 eggs is recorded. Otherwise as for species group.

Jan's Banded Snake
Simoselaps bertholdi (Jan, 1859)
Photo 807

Description Member of *S. bertholdi* group with pale iris. Ground colour yellow to reddish orange, marked from nape to tail-tip with 18–31 black rings of approximately equal width. Scales in pale interspaces usually bear darker lateral edges, fading to absence on lower flanks. Head white to very pale grey, densely flecked with blackish brown. Flecks coalesce on base of head to form diffuse dark blotch. Ventral surfaces white to pale pink, rarely bearing a series of dark midventral blotches between black rings. Midbody scales in 15 rows. TL 0.3 m.

Distinguished from *S. anomalus* by head-pattern (dark flecks and/or mottling vs glossy black blotch). Differs from *S. littoralis* by width of nuchal ring (broader than 4 scales vs narrower),· and in bearing narrow longitudinal lines formed by dark edges to scales in pale interspaces.
Preferred habitat Humid to arid sandy areas from mid- to lower west coast of WA (absent from Darling Range) to eastern SA and southern NT. Occurs in a variety of habitats, from coastal dunes to woodlands, heathlands and rock outcrops.
Microhabitat As for species group.
Comments Though predominantly nocturnal, individuals have been observed active on surface during day, even in hot weather. Clutches of 1–8 eggs are recorded. Otherwise as for species group.

Narrow-banded Burrowing Snake
Simoselaps fasciolatus (Günther, 1872)
Photos 808, 809

Description Sole member of *S. fasciolatus* group, comprising 2 subspecies.
S. f. fasciolatus Ground colour white, cream to

very pale grey or pink, marked with numerous narrow irregular ragged-edged dark brown to black bands. Pale interspaces bear scattered to transversely aligned reddish to blackish spots. Snout reddish brown. Prominent black to dark brown blotch on top of head is separated from a broad black nuchal blotch (7–15 scales wide) by a narrow band of reddish brown. Ventral surfaces white. Midbody scales in 17 rows. TL 0.4 m.

S. f. fasciata (Stirling and Zietz, 1893) differs from nominate race in bearing a narrower nuchal blotch (3½–5½ scales wide).

Preferred habitat Widespread through subhumid to arid southern interior of Australia, from lower west coast of WA, through southern NT and northern SA to south-western Qld and north-western NSW (east to Curra Bulla Bore). Occupies a variety of habitats (usually sandy). *S. f. fasciolatus* occurs in western portion of range, extending east to about Laverton district, WA; most abundant on pale coastal dunes. *S. f. fasciata* occupies eastern portion of range, extending west as far as Warburton Ranges, WA. This subspecies penetrates rocky and stony areas to a greater extent than nominate form.

Microhabitat As for species group.

Comments As for species group.

Simoselaps incinctus (Storr, 1968)
Photo 810

Description Member of *S. semifasciatus* group lacking bands. Ground colour pink to brown, fading on lower flanks. Each scale dark-edged, forming reticulum. Dark grey to black blotch extends forward from base of head to level of eyes. This is widely separated from a broad dark nuchal bar by a band of ground colour. Ventral surfaces cream. Midbody scales in 17 rows. TL 0.3 m.

Preferred habitat Arid north-eastern interior of Australia, from southern NT to Gulf of Carpentaria and interior of Qld. Associated with heavy clays, loams, stony soils and rock outcrops, supporting woodlands, shrublands or hummock grasslands.

Microhabitat As for species group.

Comments As for species group.

Simoselaps littoralis (Storr, 1968)
Photo 811

Description Member of *S. bertholdi* group with pale iris. Ground colour very pale yellowish orange, pale yellow to almost white, marked with 20–42 narrow black rings; usually much narrower than pale interspaces. Head white, flecked and lightly blotched with black, and bordered by a narrow nuchal band which rarely forms a complete ring. Ventral surfaces white. Midbody scales in 15 rows. TL 0.34 m.

Distinguished from *S. anomalus* by head-pattern (dark flecks and/or mottling vs glossy black blotch). Differs from *S. bertholdi* in lacking narrow lines

formed by dark lateral edges to scales in pale interspaces. Differs further from both by width of nuchal band or ring (fewer than 4 scales wide vs greater).

Preferred habitat Subhumid to arid mid- to lower west coast of WA and some offshore islands. Favours pale coastal dunes and limestones vegetated with shrubs and beach spinifex (*Spinifex longifolius*), occasionally extending into adjacent hummock grass associations.

Microhabitat Island populations often shelter in soil beneath limestone rocks. Otherwise as for species group.

Comments As for species group.

Simoselaps minimus (Worrell, 1960)
Photo 812

Description Member of *S. bertholdi* group lacking bands. Ground colour (in preservative) cream, each dorsal and upper lateral scale edged with dark reddish brown, forming fine reticulum. Snout ground colour. Broad black band extends across head, widely separated from a narrower black nuchal band. Ventral surfaces white. Midbody scales in 15 rows. TL 0.2 m.

Preferred habitat Known only from Dampier Land, south-western Kimberley region, WA. Occurs on coastal dunes and sandy ecotonal zone between dunes and adjacent 'pindan' country.

Microhabitat One individual recorded in soil at the edge of a *Melaleuca*-fringed near-coastal freshwater swamp.

Comments Represented in museum collections by only 2 specimens. Ecology is presumably similar to other members of species group.

Simoselaps roperi (Kinghorn, 1931)
Photos 813, 814

Description Relatively robust, variably patterned member of *S. semifasciatus* group with strongly protrusive snout bearing sharp cutting edge. Ground colour orange, reddish-brown to shades of grey, marked with 34–63 dark brown to black bands on body and 4–11 on tail. Interspaces of ground colour are always narrower, and occasionally reduced to transverse rows of pale spots. Broad dark brown blotch on head encompasses eyes; separated from broad dark nuchal bar by strip of ground colour. Ventral surfaces cream. Midbody scales in 15 rows (Roper River, NT); usually 17 in Kimberley region in WA and invariably 17 in Tennant Creek area in NT. TL 0.37 m.

Distinguished from *S. approximans* by pattern: dark bands are considerably less than 3 times broader than pale interspaces vs at least 5 times broader. Differs from *S. semifasciatus* in bearing fewer upper labial scales (5 vs 6).

Preferred habitat Subhumid to semi-arid areas of south-western Kimberley region, WA, extending to northern NT, as far south as Tea Tree. Favours heavy soils and rocky ranges.

Microhabitat As for species group.

Comments Formerly treated as a subspecies of *S. semifasciatus*. It may in fact be closely related to the eastern subspecies of that taxon (*S. s. campbelli* and *S. s. woodjonesii*).

Half-girdled Snake
Simoselaps semifasciatus (Günther, 1863)
Photo 815

Description Relatively robust, variable member of *S. semifasciatus* group with strongly protrusive snout bearing sharp cutting edge. Comprises 3 described subspecies; though eastern races are inadequately diagnosed.

S. s. semifasciatus Ground colour orange to reddish brown, fading on lower flanks. Approximately 45–80 dark brown, dark grey to almost black bands (slightly narrower to slightly broader than pale interspaces) extend from nape to tail-tip. These are broadest and most numerous (with narrowest pale interspaces) in north and interior of range. Broad dark band on head encompasses eyes. This is separated from broad nuchal band (4–10 scales wide) by a band of ground colour. Ventral surfaces cream. Midbody scales in 17 rows. TL 0.35 m.

North Qld populations represent 2 described subspecies: *S. s. campbelli* (Kinghorn, 1929) and *S. s. woodjonesii* (Thompson, 1934). Both were named from small series (a holotype, and holotype and paratype, respectively). Specimens collected subsequently do not conform to the diagnoses outlined in original descriptions and more material is required to ascertain their true status. Midbody scales in 17 rows (*S. s. campbelli*) and 15 rows (*S. s. woodjonesii*).

Distinguished from *S. approximans* by pattern; dark bands are considerably less than 5 times broader than pale interspaces (vs at least 5 times broader). *S. s. semifasciatus* differs further from *S. approximans*, and from *S. roperi*, in possessing fewer lower labial scales (5 vs 6). Differs from *S. australis* by nature of dark bands (composed of wholly pigmented scales vs dark-edged pale scales).

Preferred habitat *S. s.. semifasciatus* occurs in subhumid to arid southern WA, extending into southern NT and western SA. Occupies a wide variety of habitats, from pale coastal sand plains supporting heathland/*Banksia* associations, to heavy loams vegetated with *Acacia* spp., and sand ridges supporting hummock grasses. *S. s. campbelli* is known from Almaden, Qld. *S. s. woodjonesii* was collected on the lower Archer River, Cape York Peninsula, Qld. Collective distribution of eastern subspecies encompasses Cape York Peninsula south to Almaden and west to Gregory Downs Station.

Microhabitat As for species group.

Comments *S. s. campbelli* and *S. s. woodjonesii* are treated tentatively as subspecies of *S. semifasciatus*.

They may prove more closely associated with *S. roperi*. Otherwise as for species group.

Simoselaps warro (De Vis, 1884)
Photo 816

Description Sole member of *S. warro* group. Ground colour cream, pale orange to orange-brown, each scale bearing darker edge, forming reticulum. Head cream, densely flecked to blotched with dark pigment, and usually separated from broad dark brown to black nuchal blotch by a broad to narrow cream zone. Ventral surfaces cream. Dark median stripe may be present beneath tail. TL 0.4 m.

Preferred habitat Subhumid north-eastern Qld, from Townsville district north to Weipa area and west to Karumba. The type locality (Warro Station near Gladstone, Qld) is believed to be an error. Usually associated with sandy soils supporting dry sclerophyll forests and woodlands with grassy understorey.

Microhabitat Shelters beneath leaf-litter, logs and stumps.

Comments Feeds on skinks. Otherwise little known. See species group.

Photo 817 shows an apparently undescribed *Simoselaps* taxon known from Groote Eylandt and Nabarlek, NT.

Genus *TROPIDECHIS* Günther, 1863

Endemic monotypic genus occurring in mideastern and north-eastern Australia.

Moderately robust snake with broad distinct head. Eye moderately large with pale iris and round pupil. Scales very strongly keeled, in 23 rows at midbody. Anal and subcaudal scales single.

Nocturnal to diurnal. Terrestrial to semi-arboreal. Livebearing. DANGEROUSLY VENOMOUS.

Rough-scaled or Clarence River Snake
Tropidechis carinatus (Krefft, 1863)
Photo 818

Description Ground colour yellowish brown, brown, olive-brown, dark brown to almost black. Irregular darker bands or transverse series of blotches extend from nape for various distances along body, fading posteriorly. These are most prominent on juveniles, and often obscure to absent on adults. Ventral surfaces cream, olive to grey, usually with darker blotches. TL 0.9 m.

Distinguished from the superficially similar harmless colubrid snake, the keelback (*Styporhynchus mairii*), in possessing more numerous midbody scale rows (23 vs 15, rarely 17).

Preferred habitat Wet sclerophyll forests, rainforests, swamps and creek margins on coast and ranges, from Barrington Tops, mideastern NSW, to Fraser Island area, Qld. Disjunct population occurs in north-eastern Qld, from Mt Spec north to Thornton Peak, including Atherton Tablelands region and adjacent coastline.

Microhabitat Shelters among dense vegetation, beneath fallen timber, and in soil cracks or cavities.

Comments Predominantly terrestrial, frequently ascending low foliage to bask or forage. Feeds largely on frogs and small mammals, though birds and lizards are occasionally taken. Produces 5–18 relatively large young during late summer and autumn. Generally pugnacious if cornered. DANGER-OUSLY VENOMOUS.

Bandy Bandys
Genus *VERMICELLA* Günther, 1858

Endemic genus containing 2 species. Widespread throughout Australia, excepting lower south-east and lower half of WA.

Medium-sized elapids, each with a cylindrical body, short blunt tail, and narrow depressed head. Eye small, bearing dark iris. Scales smooth, in 15 rows at midbody. Anal and subcaudal scales divided. Pattern comprises simple black and white rings.

Nocturnal. Fossorial, sheltering in loose soil beneath rocks or logs, in soil cracks and termitaria. Usually encountered on surface during or after rain in warm weather. Diets appear to consist entirely of blind snakes (*Ramphotyphlops* spp.). Egglaying. When agitated, the body is contorted into one or more vertically oriented loops. This peculiar stance is changed and repeated with abrupt thrashing movements. Not regarded as dangerous.

Distinguished from banded *Simoselaps* spp. by colour and pattern (invariably consisting of black and white rings vs black and orange or yellow rings, or brown to reddish brown bands). Differs further in attaining much greater maximum size (TL 1.0 vs 0.5 m or less).

Common Bandy Bandy
Vermicella annulata (Gray, 1841)
Photos 819, 820

Description Robust *Vermicella*, comprising 2 subspecies.

V. a. annulata Pattern typically comprises approx-imately 30 bluish black to dark brown rings with narrower white interspaces; commencing with dark-tipped snout and white band between nostril and eye. Ventral surfaces similar to dorsal. TL 1.0 m.

V. a. snelli Storr, 1968 Differs from nominate form in possessing more numerous ventral scales (254–313 vs 180–243), and usually a greater number of rings (34–66). TL 0.5 m.

Distinguished from *V. multifasciata* by nature of pattern (fewer black rings separated by relatively broad pale interspaces vs numerous black rings separated by very narrow pale interspaces). Differs further in possessing free internasal scales (vs fused with prefrontal scales).

Preferred habitat *V. a. annulata* occupies virtually all habitats, from deserts to rainforests, through eastern Australia; south to south-eastern NSW, northern Vic. and southern SA (excluding lower south-east, Eyre Peninsula and south-west). *V. a. snelli* occupies central and western portion of range, extending disjunctly through NT to Pilbara region of WA.

Microhabitat As for genus.

Comments Females of *V. a. annulata* are sexually mature at 2 years; males at 3. Clutches of 2–13 eggs are laid, depending on size of female. In eastern States, young are first seen in autumn. Otherwise as for genus.

Northern Bandy Bandy
Vermicella multifasciata (Longman, 1915)
Photo 821

Description Relatively slender *Vermicella*, marked with 46–83 narrow black rings, enclosing narrower white interspaces. Though these usually encircle body, they tend to be narrower on flanks and paler below. Pattern commences with black-tipped snout and a narrow white band behind nostril. TL 0.53 m.

Distinguished from *V. annulata* by nature of pattern (numerous black rings separated by very narrow pale interspaces vs fewer black rings separated by relatively broad pale interspaces). Differs further by nature of scales on tip of snout (internasal scales absent, fused with prefrontal scales, vs present).

Preferred habitat Humid to semi-arid areas of Kimberley region, WA, to north-western NT, occupying all available habitats.

Microhabitat As for genus.

Comments Little known. Presumably similar to *V. annulata*. See genus.

BLIND or WORM SNAKES
Family TYPHLOPIDAE

Large family containing approximately 150 species in 2 genera. Widespread, extending from Africa through Asia to islands of western Pacific. Represented in Australia by 30 species all contained in a single genus.

Genus *RAMPHOTYPHLOPS* Fitzinger, 1843

Extremely slender to robust worm-like snakes, each with a blunt head (indistinct from neck) and a very short tail terminating abruptly in small spur. Eye greatly reduced in size and covered by a scale. Mouth small, set beneath a protrusive snout. Vestigial pelvis present. Body scales (including ventrals) small, equal in size, highly polished and overlapping. Head shields enlarged, symmetrical and few in number. Ground colour ranges from pink to blackish brown and pattern is usually simple to absent. Scales may bear dark streaks, aligned to form lines. Lateral colour may fade into ventral colour, or meet it with a ragged margin. A few species bear dark heads and tails.

Most species cannot be accurately identified in the field, requiring microscopic examination. Major clues to identification are: number of midbody scale rows (including ventrals); shape of rostral scale; shape of snout (rounded, weakly angular to trilobed

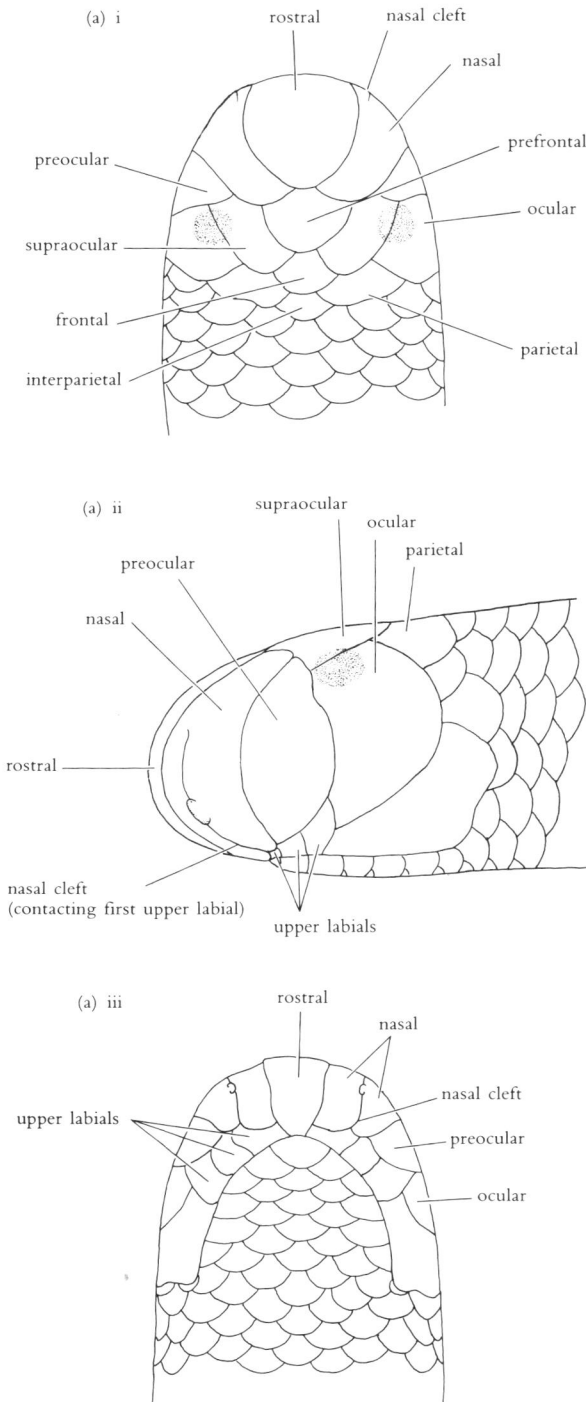

Variations in snout shape of Australian blind snakes
(a) *Ramphotyphlops nigrescens*   i. snout rounded from above
    ii. snout rounded in profile   iii. snout rounded from below
(b) *R. bituberculatus*   snout strongly trilobed from above
(c) *R. grypus*   snout beak-like in profile

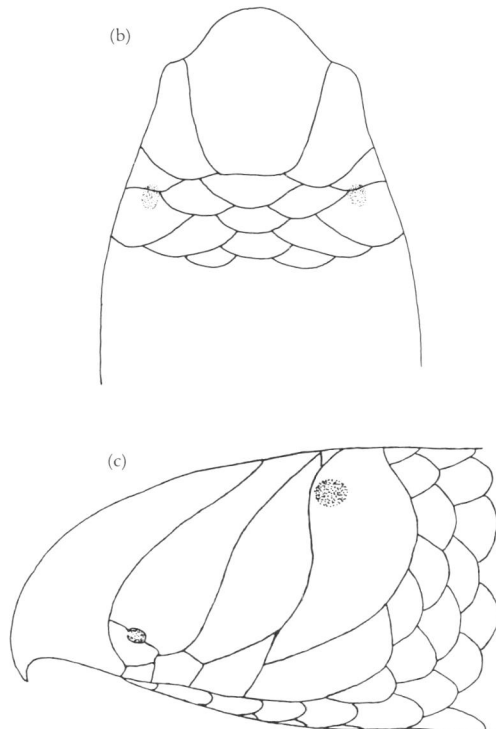

from above, and rounded, sharply angular or recurved with a transverse cutting edge in profile) and position of nasal cleft (contacting first or second upper labial or preocular scale, whether it is visible from above, and whether it extends to rostral scale, completely dividing nasal scale). Many of these characters are subject to variation, particularly the arrangement of the nasal cleft. The descriptions provided apply to most individuals.

Blind snakes are fossorial, sheltering in ant nests, termitaria or soil beneath leaf-litter, rocks and logs. Differences in build and snout-shape represent adaptations to various conditions. Those with angular snouts bearing sharp transverse cutting edges are probably best suited to burrowing in heavier soils or deep in soft soils. Individuals are occasionally encountered active on the surface at night, particularly during or after summer rain.

Blind snakes apparently feed exclusively on termites and the eggs, larvae and pupae of ants. See photo 822. This usually takes place beneath cover, hence is rarely observed. Several appear specialised to a particular prey type, dwelling in the chambers and galleries of their nests. Blind snakes are regarded as egglayers, though this has been positively confirmed for few species. *Ramphotyphlops braminus* (Australia's only introduced snake) is unusual in being parthenogenetic. Its inclusion within *Ramphotyphlops* (separable from extralimital *Typhlops* by examination of male genitalia) is therefore tentative.

Blind snakes are completely harmless, relying on cryptic habits and their ability to emit an unpleasant odour from anal glands to deter predation. Though these offer limited protection from many predators, burrowing elapids of the genus *Vermicella* (bandy bandys) feed exclusively on blind snakes.

Many of Australia's 30 blind snakes are known from single specimens or from single isolated localities. Unfortunately they have not attracted a great deal of interest from herpetologists due to their cryptic habits, the similarity between species and the absence of easily visible external characteristics with which to identify them. There can be little doubt that future work will reveal the presence of more species and redefine the distributions of others. With this in mind we have not attempted to provide diagnoses for similar sympatric species.

Ramphotyphlops affinis (Boulenger, 1889)
Photo 823

Description Ground colour dark brown; paler on head. Ventral surfaces yellowish, cream to pinkish white, merging with ground colour on lower flanks. Midbody scales in 18 rows. Snout rounded from above, and bluntly angular in profile. Nasal cleft extends from second upper labial scale to rostral scale. Not visible from above. TL 150 mm. Maximum 220 mm.
Preferred habitat Coast, ranges and eastern in-

terior from south-eastern NSW north to Cape York Peninsula, Qld. Presumed to be extralimital in the Solomon Islands.
Microhabitat As for genus.
Comments As for genus.

Ramphotyphlops australis (Gray, 1845)
Photo 824

Description Moderately large blind snake with moderate to very robust build. Ground colour purplish brown (adults) to purplish pink (juveniles). Ventral surfaces cream. Junction of lateral and ventral colouration usually prominent and jagged. Midbody scales in 22 rows. Snout rounded from above, and rounded to weakly angular in profile. Nasal cleft extends from second upper labial scale (occasionally from junction of first and second, second and preocular, or from preocular) to between nostril and rostral scale. Not or scarcely visible from above. TL 200 mm. Maximum 415 mm.
Preferred habitat Widespread in humid to arid areas of southern Australia. Extends from deep south-west of WA, through SA and southern NT to western Vic. and interior of NSW. Occupies a variety of habitats, from wet sclerophyll forests to rock outcrops, mallee/hummock grass associations and chenopod shrublands.
Microhabitat As for genus.
Comments Taxonomic status of eastern population unresolved. Members of this population recorded to emit an audible squeak if handled roughly.

Ramphotyphlops bituberculatus (Peters, 1863)
Photo 825

Description Moderate to slender blind snake with ground colour of dark purplish brown to almost black, fading to whitish on lower flanks and ventral surfaces. Midbody scales in 20 rows. Snout strongly trilobed from above and slightly angular in profile. Nasal cleft extends from second upper labial scale to between nostril and rostral scale. Not visible from above. TL 300 mm. Maximum 450 mm.
Preferred habitat Subhumid to arid areas of southern Australia, from southern Qld through interior of NSW and north-western Vic. to southern interior of WA.
Microhabitat As for genus.
Comments As for genus.

Flower Pot Snake
Ramphotyphlops braminus (Daudin, 1803)
Photo 826

Description Very small, moderate to slender blind snake. Ground colour dark purplish brown to almost black, paler on snout and sometimes tail-tip. Ventral surfaces pale brown. Midbody scales in 20 rows. Snout rounded from above and in profile.

Nasal cleft extends from preocular scale to rostral scale. TL 120 mm. Maximum 170 mm.

Preferred habitat Known only from Darwin area, NT, and islands of Torres Strait, Qld. Extra-limital through New Guinea, South-East Asia and India. NT population rarely occurs outside suburban gardens.

Microhabitat Shelters in moist soil beneath garden debris, among rockeries, beneath compost and (as common name suggests) under flower pots.

Comments Australia's only introduced snake, presumed to have arrived recently (1960s) from South-East Asia, probably in cargo. Parthenogenetic. Otherwise as for genus.

Ramphotyphlops broomi (Boulenger, 1898)
Photo 827

Description Small blind snake with medium to moderately robust build. Ground colour pale brown, merging to dark grey on tail. Dark reddish brown centres to dorsal scales align to form narrow longitudinal streaks. Ventral surfaces whitish. Midbody scales in 20 rows. Snout rounded from above and in profile. Nasal cleft extends from second upper labial scale to rostral scale. Not or scarcely visible from above. TL 180 mm. Maximum 250 mm.

Preferred habitat Extends from northern NT to northern and eastern Qld, interior of NSW, north-western Vic. and adjacent SA.

Microhabitat As for genus.

Comments As for genus.

Ramphotyphlops centralis Storr, 1984

Description Moderately slender blind snake with ground colour of purplish brown, fading on lower flanks. Midbody scales in 20 rows. Snout short and rounded from above; beak-like in profile. Nasal cleft extends from second upper labial scale to nostril or a little beyond. Not visible from above. TL 305 mm.

Preferred habitat Known only from Alice Springs area in arid southern NT.

Microhabitat As for genus.

Comments As for genus.

Ramphotyphlops diversus (Waite, 1894)
Photos 828, 829

Description Moderate to slender blind snake comprising 2 subspecies.

R. d. diversus Ground colour dark pinkish brown to purplish brown (occasionally with a darker head, posterior body and tail) fading to cream or pale brown ventrally. Midbody scales in 20 rows. Snout rounded from above and in profile. Nasal cleft extends from preocular scale to rostral scale, or nearly so. Visible from above. TL 250 mm. Maximum 350 mm.

R. d. ammodytes (Montague, 1914) Differs from nominate form in possessing a narrow (vs moderately broad) rostral scale. Nasal cleft extends further onto top of head.

Preferred habitat *R. d. diversus* extends widely across subhumid to arid northern Australia, from southern Kimberley region, WA, to eastern Qld. *R. d. ammodytes* occurs on North West Cape and in the Pilbara region of WA, including some offshore islands.

Microhabitat As for genus.

Comments As for genus.

Ramphotyphlops endoterus (Waite, 1918)
Photo 830

Description Ground colour brown, dark purplish brown to reddish brown; paler on snout. Ventral surfaces cream. Junction of lateral and ventral colouration prominent and jagged. Midbody scales in 22 rows. Snout weakly trilobed from above, and angular in profile with a weak transverse cutting edge. Nasal cleft extends from preocular scale to nostril, a little beyond, or to rostral scale. Not visible from above. TL 230 mm. Maximum 375 mm.

Preferred habitat Arid interior of Australia, from south-western Qld and adjacent NSW, through northern SA and southern NT to Great Sandy and Gibson Deserts of WA.

Microhabitat As for genus.

Comments As for genus.

Ramphotyphlops grypus (Waite, 1918)
Photo 831

Description Extremely slender blind snake with ground colour of pinkish brown to dark reddish brown. Snout cream. Head and neck ground colour or paler than body colour to black. Tail black. Ventral surfaces cream; blackish on throat. Midbody scales in 18 rows. Snout angular from above, and weakly to strongly beak-like in profile. Nasal cleft extends from second upper labial scale (occasionally from preocular, junction of preocular and second labial, or from first labial) to or towards rostral scale. Not visible from above. TL 350 mm. Maximum 415 mm.

Preferred habitat Subhumid to arid northern interior of Australia from north-west coast of WA to north-western Qld.

Microhabitat Usually shelters in termitaria and abandoned nests of red meat ants (*Iridomyrmex* sp.). See genus.

Comments As for genus.

Ramphotyphlops guentheri (Peters, 1865)
Photo 832

Description Moderate to slender blind snake with ground colour of purplish brown. Snout pale brown. Remainder of head and neck dark purplish brown. Tail prominently tipped with blackish brown. Lower lateral and ventral surfaces cream. Midbody scales in 18 rows. Snout round. Nasal cleft extends from second upper labial scale to between nostril and rostral scale. Not visible from above. TL 250 mm. Maximum 290 mm.
Preferred habitat Subhumid to semi-arid northern Australia from northern NT to southern and eastern Kimberley region, WA.
Microhabitat As for genus.
Comments As for genus.

Ramphotyphlops hamatus Storr, 1981
Photo 833

Description Ground colour brownish black (adults) to pinkish brown (juveniles). Ventral surfaces cream. Junction of lateral and ventral colouration prominent and jagged. Midbody scales in 22 rows. Snout weakly trilobed from above and weakly to strongly angular with a transverse cutting edge in profile. Nasal cleft usually extends from second upper labial scale (occasionally from preocular, first upper labial, or junction of first and second upper labial scales) to nostril or a little beyond. Not visible from above. TL 418 mm.
Preferred habitat Extends from semi-arid midwest coast to arid western interior of WA. Favours heavy loams and stony soils dominated by *Acacia* woodlands and shrublands.
Microhabitat As for genus.
Comments As for genus.

Ramphotyphlops howi Storr, 1984
Photo 834

Description Moderately slender blind snake with ground colour of dark brown; darkening on head and neck, and fading to brown on lower lateral and ventral surfaces. Midbody scales in 18 rows. Snout round from above and in profile. Nasal cleft extends from second upper labial scale to rostral. Not visible from above. TL 210 mm.
Preferred habitat Known only from stony clay-based soil on the coast of Admiralty Gulf in subhumid north-western Kimberley region of WA.
Microhabitat As for genus.
Comments As for genus.

Ramphotyphlops kimberleyensis Storr, 1981

Description Slender blind snake with ground colour of dark brown, fading on lower lateral and ventral surfaces. Snout cream. Midbody scales in 22 rows. Head depressed. Snout rounded from above

and in profile. Nasal cleft extends from second upper labial scale to above nostril. Visible from above. TL 295 mm.
Preferred habitat Known only from Bigge and Koolan Islands, and Napier Broome Bay in humid to subhumid north-western Kimberley region, WA.

Microhabitat As for genus.
Comments As for genus.

Ramphotyphlops leptosoma Robb, 1972
Photo 835

Description Very slender blind snake with ground colour of pink to purplish brown, fading on lower lateral and ventral surfaces. Snout paler. Midbody scales in 16 (rarely 18) rows. Snout weakly trilobed from above, and angular in profile with a weak to sharp transverse cutting edge. Nasal cleft extends from second upper labial scale to rostral scale. Not visible from above. TL 240 mm. Maximum 375 mm.
Preferred habitat Restricted to midwest coast of WA, from Wooramel River south to Geraldton. Favours sandy soils.
Microhabitat One individual recorded in sand beneath thick accumulations of *Acacia* leaf-litter. Otherwise as for genus.
Comments As for genus.

Ramphotyphlops leucoproctus
(Boulenger, 1889)

Description Small slender blind snake with ground colour of dark purplish brown over dorsal and ventral surfaces. Midbody scales in 20 rows. Snout round from above and in profile. Nasal cleft extends from second upper labial scale, failing to reach rostral. Visible from above. TL 180 mm. Maximum 250 mm.
Preferred habitat Extends from eastern Cape York Peninsula to islands of Torres Strait, Qld. Extralimital in southern New Guinea.

Microhabitat As for genus.
Comments As for genus.

Ramphotyphlops ligatus (Peters, 1879)
Photo 836

Description Very large robust blind snake with

ground colour of dark greyish brown to dark purplish brown. Ventral surfaces cream to dull pink, sharply delineated from dorsal colour. Midbody scales in 24 rows. Snout rounded from above and in profile. Nasal cleft extends from first upper labial scale, almost to rostral scale. Visible from above. TL 320 mm. Maximum 500 mm.

Preferred habitat Widespread in subhumid to arid areas from northern interior of Qld to western interior of NSW and adjacent SA. Disjunct population extends from north-western NT to eastern Kimberley region, WA.

Microhabitat As for genus.

Comments As for genus.

Ramphotyphlops margaretae Storr, 1981

Description Very slender blind snake with ground colour of pink to purplish grey. Snout pale yellowish brown. Ventral surfaces pale grey. Midbody scales in 18 rows. Snout trilobed from above, and angular in profile. Nasal cleft extends from second upper labial scale to between nostril and rostral scale. Not visible from above. TL 305 mm.

Preferred habitat Known only from Lake Throssell in arid south-eastern interior of WA.

Microhabitat As for genus.

Comments As for genus.

Ramphotyphlops micromma Storr, 1981

Description Slender blind snake with very small eyes. No data on colour available. Midbody scales in 18 rows. Snout rounded from above and in profile. Nasal cleft extends from second upper labial scale to rostral scale. Visible from above. TL 205 mm.

Preferred habitat Known only from Leopold Downs Station in semi-arid south-western interior of Kimberley region, WA.

Microhabitat As for genus.

Comments Represented by a single faded specimen collected in 1924.

Ramphotyphlops minimus (Kinghorn, 1929)
Photo 837

Description Small, very slender blind snake with

ground colour of pale brown to reddish brown. Tail-tip (and occasionally head) blackish. Ventral surfaces white. Midbody scales in 16 rows. Snout rounded from above and in profile. Nasal cleft extends from second upper labial scale to a little beyond nostril. Visible from above. TL 200 mm.

Preferred habitat Apparently restricted to sandy soils in subhumid north-eastern NT. Known only from Groote Eylandt, and from Lake Evella near Waraga Settlement on the mainland.

Microhabitat As for genus.

Comments As for genus.

Ramphotyphlops nigrescens (Gray, 1845)
Photos 838, 839

Description Very large moderately robust blind snake with ground colour of pinkish brown (juveniles) to dark purplish brown or almost black (adults). Base of each scale usually paler, forming an obscure reticulum. Ventral surfaces pinkish white, occasionally with a few scattered dark scales and dark patch on either side of vent. Midbody scales in 22 rows. Snout round from above and in profile. Nasal cleft extends from first upper labial scale nearly to rostral. Visible from above. TL 380 mm. Maximum 750 mm.

Preferred habitat Humid to subhumid east coast and ranges, from south-eastern Qld to northern Vic. Occurs in a variety of habitats, from rainforests to woodlands and rock outcrops.

Microhabitat Frequently encountered beneath rocks or logs resting on soft moist soil. See genus.

Comments Taxonomy unclear. A complex of species may be involved. Clutch of 19 eggs is recorded; laid in February. Occasionally numerous individuals are encountered sharing a shelter-site. Otherwise as for genus.

Ramphotyphlops pinguis (Waite, 1897)
Photo 840

Description Large, extremely robust blind snake with ground colour of dark greyish brown. Pale smudge may be present on each scale, aligning to form longitudinal series on anterior body. Ventral surfaces whitish; sharply to weakly contrasting with upper lateral colour. Midbody scales in 20 rows. Snout weakly trilobed from above, and slightly angular in profile. Nasal cleft extends from second upper labial scale to between nostril and rostral scale. Not visible from above. TL 350 mm. Maximum 445 mm.

Preferred habitat Known from widely separated localities: humid to subhumid south-western WA, and in semi-arid areas from western Vic. to adjacent SA. Occurs in dry sclerophyll forests and woodlands.

Microhabitat As for genus.

Comments As for genus.

Ramphotyphlops polygrammicus
(Schlegel, 1839)
Photo 841

Description Moderately robust blind snake with ground colour of pinkish brown to dark greyish brown; paler on snout and usually tail-tip. Each scale narrowly pale-edged. Ventral surfaces cream to yellowish. Midbody scales in 22 rows. Snout round from above and in profile. Nasal cleft extends from second upper labial, nearly to rostral scale. Visible from above. TL 250 mm. Maximum 400 mm.
Preferred habitat Occurs in a variety of habitats, including woodlands, monsoon forests and vine thickets, from mideastern Qld north to Cape York Peninsula and islands of Torres Strait. Extralimital in New Guinea and eastern Indonesia.
Microhabitat As for genus.
Comments As for genus.

Ramphotyphlops proximus (Waite, 1893)
Photo 842

Description Very large blind snake with ground colour of pinkish brown, greyish brown to rich brown, fading to yellowish brown or cream on lower lateral and ventral surfaces. Small dark patch may be present on either side of vent. Midbody scales in 20 rows. Snout weakly trilobed from above and weakly angular in profile. Nasal cleft extends from first upper labial scale. Visible from above. TL 500 mm. Maximum 750 mm.
Preferred habitat Occurs in subhumid to semi-arid areas from north-eastern Qld, through interior of NSW to northern Vic.
Microhabitat As for genus.
Comments As for genus.

Ramphotyphlops tovelli (Loveridge, 1945)
Photo 843

Description Very small blind snake with ground colour of dark pinkish brown, merging to dark grey or black on tail. Each scale bears a darker centre, forming obscure narrow lines. Ventral surfaces pale pinkish grey. Midbody scales in 20 rows. Snout rounded from above and in profile. Nasal cleft extends from preocular scale to just beyond nostril. Not visible from above. TL 122 mm.
Preferred habitat Known only from vicinity of Darwin, NT. The individual pictured was collected in a vine thicket margining a creek.
Microhabitat As for genus.
Comments As for genus.

Ramphotyphlops troglodytes Storr, 1981

Description Very slender blind snake with depressed head. Ground colour brown, fading to off-white on snout, tail-tip and ventral surfaces. Midbody scales in 22 rows. Snout round from above

and in profile. Nasal cleft extends from second upper labial scale to rostral scale. Visible from above. TL 402 mm.

Preferred habitat The only known specimen was collected in Tunnel Cave in the Napier Range, semi-arid southern Kimberley region, WA.
Microhabitat As for genus.
Comments As for genus.

Ramphotyphlops unguirostris (Peters, 1867)

Description Large, moderate to slender blind snake with ground colour of dark olive-brown. Ventral surfaces cream, in moderately sharp contrast to lower lateral colour. Midbody scales in 24 rows. Snout weakly trilobed from above, and sharply angular in profile. Nasal cleft extends from first upper labial scale to rostral scale. Barely or not visible from above. TL 400 mm. Maximum 700 mm.
Preferred habitat Widespread through subhumid to semi-arid areas from the Kimberley region of WA, through northern NT and eastern Qld to interior of NSW, northern Vic. and south-eastern SA.

Microhabitat As for genus.
Comments As for genus.

Ramphotyphlops waitii (Boulenger, 1895)
Photo 844

Description Large, extremely slender blind snake with ground colour of yellowish brown to dark purplish brown, often paler on snout, and gradually fading to cream on ventral surfaces. Snout trilobed from above, and beak-like in profile. Nasal cleft extends from second upper labial scale nearly to rostral. Not visible from above. TL 340 mm. Maximum 610 mm.
Preferred habitat Subhumid to arid southern WA, from Hamersley Range in Pilbara region to Eastern Goldfields in south and Warburton Ranges in east. Favours pale sand plains and heavy red loams.
Microhabitat Usually encountered in galleries of ant nests. Otherwise as for genus.
Comments See genus.

Ramphotyphlops wiedii (Peters, 1867)
Photo 845

Description Small, moderate to slender blind snake with ground colour of pinkish brown, brown to blackish brown, fading to cream on ventral surfaces. Midbody scales in 20 rows. Snout round from above and in profile. Nasal cleft extends from second upper labial scale nearly to rostral. Visible from above. TL 200 mm. Maximum 300 mm.
Preferred habitat Widespread through subhumid areas of northern NT and eastern Australia; from Cape York Peninsula, south to northern Vic. Extralimital in New Guinea.
Microhabitat As for genus.
Comments As for genus.

Ramphotyphlops yampiensis Storr, 1981

Description Small slender blind snake with ground colour of brown; darker on head and tail. Snout pale yellowish brown. Ventral surfaces pale brown. Midbody scales in 18 rows. Snout round from above and in profile. Nasal cleft extends from preocular to rostral scale. Not visible from above. TL 128 mm.
Preferred habitat Known only from Koolan Island in Yampi Sound, in subhumid north-western Kimberley region, WA.

Microhabitat As for genus.
Comments As for genus.

Ramphotyphlops yirrikalae (Kinghorn, 1942)
Photo 846

Description Small, moderately slender blind snake with ground colour of brown, fading to whitish on ventral surfaces. Midbody scales in 24 rows. Snout round from above and in profile. Nasal cleft extends from first upper labial scale to between nostril and rostral scale. TL 200 mm.
Preferred habitat Known only from subhumid north-eastern tip of Arnhem Land, NT.
Microhabitat As for genus.
Comments As for genus.

Photo 847 shows a *Ramphotyphlops*, probably undescribed, from Cooktown, Qld.

Appendix 1

FIRST AID TREATMENT OF SNAKEBITE

An unprovoked snake will rarely attempt to bite. However, accidents do occur and prompt first aid is essential. The Commonwealth Serum Laboratories, in their recent publication *First Aid for Snakebite in Australia*, give the following information.

- At least 95 per cent of bites occur on the limbs. Perhaps 75 per cent involve the lower limbs.
- Sometimes no venom is injected, even if fangs have made holes in the skin.
- The venom is injected quite deeply. It was shown many years ago that very little venom is removed by incision or excision.
- Recent research has shown that firm pressure applied over the bitten area significantly delays the movement of venom. When pressure is combined with immobilising the limb very little venom reaches the blood stream.

First aid should therefore be given as follows:

1. Immediately apply a broad firm bandage around the limb to cover the bitten area. It should be as tight as one would bind a sprained ankle. As much of the limb should be bound up as possible. Crepe bandages are ideal but any flexible material can be used, e.g., tear up clothing or old towels into strips.
2. The limb must be kept as still as possible. Bind some type of splint to the limb, e.g. piece of timber, spade, any rigid object.
3. Bring transport to the victim whenever possible.
4. Leave the bandages and splint on until medical care is reached.

Do not cut or excise the bitten area.

Arterial tourniquets are no longer recommended for snake-bite.

Do not wash the bitten area. The snake involved may be identified by the detection of venom on the skin.

If the snake can be safely killed bring it in to hospital with the victim.

The injection of venom can have the following effects:

anticoagulant—slowing down or stopping blood clotting
coagulant—causing blood clotting
cytolytic—causing the breakdown of cells
haemolytic—causing the breakdown of red blood cells
neurotoxic—toxic to the peripheral nervous system (not the brain)

The venom of the most dangerous snakes in Australia is predominantly neurotoxic. Typical symptoms are vomiting, sweating, drowsiness, pallor, loss of consciousness, and tender and enlarged lymph nodes. Muscle paralysis may develop at a later stage resulting in difficulty in seeing or double vision, and difficulty in swallowing, speaking or breathing.

The venom may also affect the blood system and destroy cells, resulting in bleeding at the site of a bite, bruising, passing of blood in the urine, and impairment of kidney function.

Snakes capable or believed capable of delivering a bite fatal to humans are listed on p. 378.

Appendix 2

A CHECKLIST OF AUSTRALIAN LIZARDS AND NON-MARINE SNAKES

The taxonomy applied here is current to early 1988. Many new species are still being discovered and named, and relationships between some well-known taxa have yet to be resolved. In cases where taxonomists differ in their interpretation of a standardised nomenclature we have had to make our own assessments. For the most part, names have been derived from the major works of Drs H. G. Cogger and G. M. Storr.

AGAMIDAE
CAIMANOPS
amphiboluroides
CHELOSANIA
brunnea
CHLAMYDOSAURUS
kingii
CRYPTAGAMA
aurita
CTENOPHORUS
caudicinctus caudicinctus
c. graafi
c. infans
c. macropus
c. mensarum
c. slateri
clayi
cristatus
decresii
femoralis
fionni
fordi
gibba
isolepis citrinus
i. gularis
i. isolepis
maculatus badius
m. dualis
m. griseus
m. maculatus
maculosus
mckenziei
nuchalis
ornatus
pictus
reticulatus
rubens
rufescens
salinarum
scutulatus
vadnappa
yinnietharra
DIPORIPHORA
albilabris albilabris
a. sobria
arnhemica
australis
bennettii
bilineata

convergens
lalliae
linga
magna
pindan
reginae
superba
valens
winneckei
GEMMATOPHORA
gilberti centralis
g. gilberti
longirostris
muricata
nobbi coggeri
n. nobbi
norrisi
temporalis
HYPSILURUS
boydii
spinipes
MOLOCH
horridus
PHYSIGNATHUS
lesueurii howittii
l. lesueurii
POGONA
barbata
microlepidota
minor minima
m. minor
m. mitchelli
nullarbor
vitticeps
TYMPANOCRYPTIS
adelaidensis adelaidensis
a. chapmani
butleri
cephalus
diemensis
intima
lineata centralis
l. houstoni
l. lineata
l. macra
l. pinguicolla
parviceps
tetraporophora
uniformis

GEKKONIDAE
CARPHODACTYLUS
laevis
CRENADACTYLUS
ocellatus horni
o. naso
o. ocellatus
o. rostralis
CYRTODACTYLUS
louisiadensis
DIPLODACTYLUS
alboguttatus
assimilis
byrnei
ciliaris aberrans
c. ciliaris
conspicillatus
damaeus
elderi
fulleri
galeatus
granariensis
intermedius
maini
mcmillani
michaelseni
mitchelli
occultus
ornatus
polyophthalmus
pulcher
rankini
savagei
spinigerus
squarrosus
steindachneri
stenodactylus
strophurus
taeniatus
taenicauda
tessellatus
vittatus
wellingtonae
williamsi
wilsoni
wombeyi
GEHYRA
australis
baliola

borroloola
catenata
dubia
minuta
montium
nana
occidentalis
oceanica
pamela
pilbara
punctata
purpurascens
robusta
variegata
xenopus
HEMIDACTYLUS
frenatus
HETERONOTIA
binoei
spelea
LEPIDODACTYLUS
lugubris
pumilus
NACTUS
arnouxii
galgajuga
NEPHRURUS
asper
deleani
laevissimus
levis levis
l. occidentalis
l. pilbarensis
stellatus
vertebralis
wheeleri cinctus
w. wheeleri
OEDURA
castelnaui
coggeri
filicipoda
gemmata
gracilis
lesueurii
marmorata
monilis
obscura
reticulata
rhombifer
robusta
tryoni
PHYLLODACTYLUS
marmoratus alexanderi
m. marmoratus
PHYLLURUS
caudiannulatus
cornutus
platurus
salebrosus

PSEUDOTHECADACTYLUS
australis
lindneri cavaticus
l. lindneri
RHYNCHOEDURA
ornata
UNDERWOODISAURUS
milii
sphyrurus

PYGOPODIDAE

ACLYS
concinna concinna
c. major
APRASIA
aurita
haroldi
inaurita
parapulchella
pseudopulchella
pulchella
repens
rostrata fusca
r. rostrata
smithi
striolata
DELMA
australis
borea
butleri
elegans
fraseri
grayii
haroldi
impar
inornata
molleri
nasuta
pax
plebeia
tincta
torquata
LIALIS
burtonis
OPHIDIOCEPHALUS
taeniatus
PARADELMA
orientalis
PLETHOLAX
gracilis edelensis
g. gracilis
PYGOPUS
lepidopodus
nigriceps nigriceps
n. schraderi

SCINCIDAE
ANOMALOPUS
brevicollis
gowi
leuckartii
mackayi
pluto
swansoni
verreauxii
CALYPTOTIS
lepidorostrum
ruficauda
scutirostrum
temporalis
thortonensis
CARLIA
aerata
amax
bicarinata
coensis
dogare
foliorum
gracilis
jarnoldae
johnstonei
laevis
longipes
macfarlani
munda
mundivensis
pectoralis
rhomboidalis
rimula
rostralis
rufilatus
schmeltzii prava
s. schmeltzii
scirtetis
tetradactyla
triacantha
vivax
COERANOSCINCUS
frontalis
reticulatus
CRYPTOBLEPHARUS
carnabyi
fuhni
litoralis
megastictus
plagiocephalus
virgatus clarus
v. virgatus
CTENOTUS
alacer
alleni
allotropis
arcanus
ariadnae
arnhemensis
astarte

atlas
borealis
brachyonyx
brooksi aranda
b. brooksi
b. euclae
b. iridis
b. taeniatus
burbidgei
calurus
capricorni
catenifer
coggeri
colletti colletti
c. nasutus
c. rufescens
decaneurus
delli
duricola
dux
ehmanni
essingtonii brevipes
e. essingtonii
eurydice
eutaenius
fallens
gagudju
gemmula
grandis grandis
g. titan
greeri
hanloni
hebetior hebetior
h. schuettleri
helenae
hilli
iapetus
impar
ingrami
inornatus
joanae
kurnbudj
labillardieri
lancelini
lateralis
leae
leonhardii
lesueurii
mastigura
militaris
mimetes
monticola
pallescens
pantherinus acripes
p. calx
p. ocellifer
p. pantherinus
piankai
pulchellus
quattuordecimlineatus

quinkan
rawlinsoni
regius
robustus
rubicundus
rutilans
saxatilis
schevilli
schomburgkii
serotinus
serventyi
severus
spaldingi
storri
strauchii strauchii
s. varius
striaticeps
taeniolatus
tanamiensis
tantillus
uber johnstonei
u. orientalis
u. uber
vertebralis
xenopleura
yampiensis
youngsoni
zastictus
zebrilla
CYCLODOMORPHUS
branchialis
casuarinae
gerrardii
maximus
melanops
EGERNIA
coventryi
cunninghami cunninghami
c. krefftii
depressa
douglasi
formosa
frerei
hosmeri
inornata
kingii
kintorei
luctuosa
major
margaretae margaretae
m. personata
modesta
multiscutata bos
m. multiscutata
napoleonis
pilbarensis
pulchra longicauda
p. pulchra
richardi
rugosa

saxatilis intermedia
s. saxatilis
slateri slateri
s. virgata
stokesii aethiops
s. badia
s. stokesii
striata
striolata
whitii moniligera
w. whitii
EMOIA
atrocostata irrorata
longicauda
EREMIASCINCUS
fasciolatus
richardsonii
EUGONGYLUS
rufescens
HEMIERGIS
decresiensis continentis
d. davisi
d. decresiensis
d. talbingoensis
graciloides
initialis brookeri
i. initialis
maccoyi
millewae
peronii
quadrilineata
LAMPROPHOLIS
amicula
basiliscus
caligula
challengeri
czechurai
delicata
guichenoti
mirabilis
mustelina
tetradactyla
LEIOLOPISMA
baudini
coventryi
duperreyi
entrecasteauxii
greeni
jigurru
metallicum
ocellatum
palfreymani
platynotum
pretiosum
spenceri
trilineatum
zia
LERISTA
aericeps aericeps
a. taeniata

417

allanae
ameles
apoda
arenicola
bipes
borealis
bougainvillii
carpentariae
chalybura
christinae
cinerea
connivens
desertorum
distinguenda
dorsalis
elegans
flammicauda
fragilis
frosti
gascoynensis
gerrardii
greeri
griffini
haroldi
humphriesi
ips
kalumburu
karlschmidti
labialis
lineata
lineopunctulata
macropisthopus
microtis
muelleri
neander
nichollsi nichollsi
n. petersoni
onsloviana
orientalis
picturata baynesi
p. edwardsae
p. picturata
planiventralis decora
p. planiventralis
praefrontalis
praepedita
punctatovittata
separanda
simillima
stictopleura
storri
stylis
terdigitata
uniduo
varia
vermicularis
vittata
walkeri
wilkinsi
xanthura

MENETIA
alanae
amaura
concinna
greyii
maini
surda
timlowi
MORETHIA
adelaidensis
boulengeri
butleri
lineoocellata
obscura
ruficauda exquisita
r. ruficauda
storri
taeniopleura
NOTOSCINCUS
butleri
ornatus
wotjulum
OPHIOSCINCUS
cooloolensis
ophioscincus
truncatus
PROABLEPHARUS
kinghorni
reginae
tenuis
SAIPHOS
equalis
SPHENOMORPHUS
amplus
australis
brongersmai
cracens
crassicaudus
darwiniensis
douglasi
fuscicaudis
isolepis
kosciuskoi
leuraensis
luteilateralis
mjobergi
murrayi
nigricaudis
pardalis
pumilus arnhemicus
p. pumilus
punctulatus
quoyii
tenuis
tigrinus
tympanum
TILIQUA
adelaidensis
multifasciata
nigrolutea

occipitalis
rugosa asper
r. konowi
r. rugosa
r. tropisurus
scincoides intermedia
s. scincoides
TROPIDOPHORUS
queenslandiae

VARANIDAE
VARANUS
acanthurus
brevicauda
caudolineatus
eremius
giganteus
gilleni
glauerti
glebopalma
gouldii
indicus
kingorum
mertensi
mitchelli
panoptes panoptes
p. rubidus
pilbarensis
prasinus
primordius
rosenbergi
scalaris
semiremex
spenceri
storri ocreatus
s. storri
tristis
varius

ACROCHORDIDAE
ACROCHORDUS
arafurae
granulatus

BOIDAE
ASPIDITES
melanocephalus
ramsayi
BOTHROCHILUS
childreni
fuscus
maculosus
olivaceus barroni
o. olivaceus
perthensis
stimsoni stimsoni
s. orientalis
CHONDROPYTHON
viridis

MORELIA
amethistina
bredli
carinata
oenpelliensis
spilota imbricata
s. spilota
s. variegata

COLUBRIDAE

BOIGA
irregularis
CERBERUS
rynchops
DENDRELAPHIS
calligastra
punctulata
ENHYDRIS
polylepis
FORDONIA
leucobalia
MYRON
richardsonii
STEGONOTUS
cucullatus
parvus
STYPORHYNCHUS
mairii

ELAPIDAE

ACANTHOPHIS
antarcticus
praelongus
pyrrhus
AUSTRELAPS
superbus
CACOPHIS
harriettae
krefftii
squamulosus
CRYPTOPHIS
nigrescens
pallidiceps
DEMANSIA
atra
calodera
olivacea
papuensis melaena
p. papuensis
psammophis cupreiceps
p. psammophis
p. reticulata
rufescens
simplex
torquata
DENISONIA
a*riceps
devisi
fasciata
maculata

ordensis
suta
DRYSDALIA
coronata
coronoides
mastersii
rhodogaster
ECHIOPSIS
curta
ELAPOGNATHUS
minor
FURINA
diadema
ornata
GLYPHODON
barnardi
dunmalli
tristis
HEMIASPIS
damelii
signata
HOPLOCEPHALUS
bitorquatus
bungaroides
stephensii
NEELAPS
bimaculatus
calonotus
NOTECHIS
ater ater
a. humphreysi
a. niger
a. serventyi
scutatus occidentalis
s. scutatus
OXYURANUS
microlepidotus
scutellatus
PSEUDECHIS
australis
butleri
colletti
guttatus
porphyriacus
PSEUDONAJA
affinis affinis
a. tanneri
guttata
ingrami
modesta
nuchalis
textilis inframacula
t. textilis
RHINOPLOCEPHALUS
bicolor
boschmai
dwyeri
flagellum
gouldii
monachus

nigriceps
nigrostriatus
punctatus
spectabilis nullarbor
s. spectabilis
SIMOSELAPS
anomalus
approximans
australis
bertholdi
fasciolatus fasciata
f. fasciolatus
incinctus
littoralis
minimus
roperi
semifasciatus campbelli
s. semifasciatus
s. woodjonesii
warro
TROPIDECHIS
carinatus
VERMICELLA
annulata annulata
a. snelli
multifasciata

TYPHLOPIDAE

RAMPHOTYPHLOPS
affinis
australis
bituberculatus
braminus
broomi
centralis
diversus ammodytes
d. diversus
endoterus
grypus
guentheri
hamatus
howi
kimberleyensis
leptosoma
leucoproctus
ligatus
margaretae
micromma
minimus
nigrescens
pinguis
polygrammicus
proximus
tovelli
troglodytes
unguirostris
waitii
wiedii
yampiensis
yirrikalae

Glossary

The definitions below apply to the context in which the words have been used in this book. They have been adapted, in part, from the following works:

R. J. Lincoln, G. A. Boxshall & P. F. Clark (1982). *A Dictionary of Ecology, Evolution and Systematics*. Cambridge University Press, Cambridge.

E. Mayr (1969). *Principles of Systematic Zoology*. McGraw-Hill Book Co., New York and London.

J. A. Peters (1964). *A Dictionary of Herpetology*. Hafner Publishing Co., New York and London.

H. G. Cogger (1983). *Reptiles and Amphibians of Australia*. Revised edn. A. H. & A. W. Reed, Sydney.

H. Heatwole (1976). *Reptile Ecology*. University of Queensland Press, St. Lucia.

G. M. Storr, L. A. Smith & R. E. Johnstone (1981). *Lizards of Western Australia, I. Skinks*. University of Western Australia Press and Western Australian Museum, Perth.

G. M. Storr, L. A. Smith & R. E. Johnstone (1983). *Lizards of Western Australia, II. Dragons and Monitors*. Western Australian Museum, Perth.

aberrant   diverging from the normal type.

ACT   Australian Capital Territory.

aggregation   a number of animals occupying a communal shelter, or densely populating a small area; usually a seasonal occurrence associated with mating, egglaying or exploitation of a prime over-wintering site.

allopatric   of populations or species, occupying mutually exclusive (but usually adjacent) geographical areas.

amphipod   small marine crustacean of order Amphipoda, e.g., sandhopper.

anal   one or more enlarged scales along the anterior margin of the vent.

anterior   situated at the front or head-end of the body; opposite to posterior.

apical   at or near the tip of a structure.

arboreal   dwelling in trees or shrubs.

arthropod   an animal of the phylum Arthropoda, with segmented body and jointed limbs, e.g., insect, spider, centipede, scorpion, crustacean.

association   a naturally occurring group of plants or animals, usually named after the dominant species or genus.

autotomy   spontaneous or reflexive separation of the tail from the body.

band   a colour marking which extends more or less continuously across the body, tail or limbs.

bandicoot   a marsupial of the family Peramelidae.

bar   a short band or stripe.

basal   at or near the base of a structure.

bicarinate   bearing two keels or ridges.

biennial   lasting or recurring every two years.

billabong   a river branch isolated to form a waterhole, usually replenished during wet seasons.

bipedal gait   of dragon lizards, running only on the hindlimbs with the body erect and the forelimbs held off the ground.

blotch   an irregular patch of colour, not circular enough to call a spot.

calcareous-shelled   of eggs, bearing brittle calcified shells like those of birds.

canegrass   a member of the genus *Zygochloa* (family Poaceae) found in eastern sandridge deserts.

carinate   bearing one or more keels or ridges.

caudal   pertaining to the tail.

cavernicolous   cave-inhabiting.

chenopod (adj. chenopodiaceous)   herb or shrub belonging to the family Chenopodiaceae, often growing in saline conditions, e.g., *Atriplex, Maireana*.

chevron   an inverted V-shaped marking.

chromosome   a structure in the cell nucleus composed of DNA and containing the genes which determine the characteristics of an organism.

clinal   pertaining to a graded geographic sequence of differences within species.

cloaca (pl. cloacae)   the common chamber into which the reproductive, intestinal and urinary ducts open in reptiles, amphibians and birds. *See* vent and p. 365.

cloacal spurs   one or more enlarged, often spinose scales lying beside the vent, on either side of the base of the tail.

clutch   the number of eggs laid by an individual.

community   a group of animals or plants living or growing together in a given area.

complex   a term for a group of related taxa, most commonly involving units in which the taxonomy is difficult or confusing.

composite species   an informal term applied to unrecognised species which, pending taxonomic assessment, are included under one name.

congeneric   belonging to the same genus.

conspecific   belonging to the same species.

crepuscular   active in twilight: at dusk, dawn or in deeply shaded conditions.

crest   longitudinal row of relatively high, usually spinose scales along neck, back or tail.

cryptozoic   living in hidden or darkened places, e.g., under stones, logs, leaf-litter, etc.

dashes   short narrow longitudinal or transverse markings.

detritus   an aggregate of loosened fragments of vegetation and/or rock.

didactyle   bearing two digits.

distal   situated away from the body or point of attachment, and towards the tip of an appendage or structure; opposite to proximal.

diurnal   active by day.

dorsal   pertaining strictly to the back, broadly to all upper surfaces.

dorsally depressed   tending to be flattened from the top.

dorsolateral   pertaining to the boundary between upper and lateral surfaces.

dorsoventral   pertaining to the boundary between upper and lower surfaces.

dorsum   back or upper surface.

ear lobules   pointed or rounded, usually pale scales lining the ear opening, especially the front edge. *See* p.105.

ecology   branch of biology dealing with relationships between organisms and their environment.

ecotone   a transition zone between two or more distinct communities—e.g., between forest and grassland—often containing elements of the adjoining communities.

endemic   confined to a particular region.

envenomation   injection of venom, and subsequent effects. *See* venom.

epiphyte   a plant growing on another plant, without being parasitic.

eucalypts   shrubs or trees of the genus *Eucalyptus* (Myrtaceae), forming the dominant species in many woodlands and sclerophyll forests.

extralimital   pertaining to the distribution of a species, genus or family outside a prescribed area (here, Australia).

family   a formal group of closely related genera, its name formed by adding the suffix '-idae' to the stem name of one of the included genera (e.g., *Acrochordus*/Acrochordidae).

femoral pore   the opening of a duct or pit in a scale on the lower surface of the thigh, usually more well developed on males. The pore usually exudes a waxy cellular material which may protrude well above the surface of the scale. Its function is unclear. *See* preanal pore and p. 28.

form   an informal term for a subspecies or other variant of a species.

fossorial   adapted for digging or burrowing into the substrate in contrast to living only in burrows or natural cavities.

free   pertaining to scales or head-shields not contacting each other.

frontal   a large shield or scale situated on top of the head between the eyes of most snakes and lizards. Usually much longer than wide. *See* pp. 96, 105, 365, 407.

frontoparietals   paired shields or scales on top of the head between the frontal and interparietal. *See* p. 105.

gastropod   any member of the class Gastropoda, including snails and slugs.

gene-flow   the normal reproductive process by which genetic material is exchanged within or between populations or organisms.

generic   pertaining to a genus.

genus (pl. genera)   a group of closely related species and species groups.

gestation   the period between conception and birth.

gravid   pregnant.

ground colour   background colour, as distinct from markings or pattern.

gular   pertaining to the throat.

gular fold   transverse fold of skin across the throat immediately in front of the forelimbs, separating the throat and chest regions. *See* p. 28.

gular pouch   that part of the throat which is loose, or capable of erection or expansion. Usually applied to dragon lizards and monitors.

habitat   the environment where an animal or plant lives and grows.

herpetologist   one who studies herpetology.

herpetology   the study of reptiles and amphibians.

heterogeneous   the condition where the scales are of mixed size and/or form.

hibernation   spending winter in a dormant state.

holotype   the single specimen chosen as the basis for description and further reference of a new species. Also referred to as the type specimen.

home range   an area, including favoured sheltering and foraging sites, in which an animal habitually dwells.

homogeneous   the condition where the scales are more or less similar in size and form.

hood   a large marking covering the top of the head, and sometimes neck.

imbricate   of scales, overlapping as in roof tiles.

immaculate   lacking spots or other markings.

infralabials   see lower labials.

intergradation zone   the area where distinctive geographical populations of a species meet, and where characteristics of each population occur or merge.

internasals   scales situated on top of the snout between the nasal scales on the majority of lizards and snakes. *See* p. 365.

interparietal   a scale situated centrally on top of the head of lizards, separating the parietal scales, and sometimes containing the 'parietal eye'. *See* pp. 365, 407.

interspaces   the spaces between major elements of pattern, such as bands.

invertebrate   an animal lacking a backbone or spinal column.

juxtaposed   pertaining to scales which lie side by side, as opposed to imbricate.

karyology   the study of chromosomes and chromosome complements.

keel   a narrow longitudinal ridge, especially on scales; also applies to a low crest or other body flange.

labial   of the lips; particularly longitudinal series of scales along the upper and lower lips.

lateral   pertaining to the sides.

laterally compressed   tending to be flattened from side to side.

laterodorsal   on the outer part of the back. Usually refers to a dark stripe along the inner edge of a pale dorsolateral stripe. *See* p. 105.

lateroventral   on the outer part of the ventral surfaces.

littoral   pertaining to the shoreline.

livebearing   giving birth to fully developed young, as opposed to egglaying.

longitudinal   arranged along the body, rather than across it.

loreal   pertaining to those scales on the side of the snout, between the nostril and the eye.

lower labials   a series of scales along the lower lips. Also known as infralabials. *See* pp. 105 and 365.

lower lateral   on the lower half of the sides of body and tail, between midlateral and ventrolateral areas.

lunate   crescent-shaped.

marbling   irregular mottling and streaks, as in some kinds of marble.

median   along the middle.

melanism   the condition of having a high content of dark pigment.

membranous   pertaining to pliable, thin, sheetlike tissue.

microhabitat   the space occupied by an animal within a given habitat, e.g., shelter sites, foraging areas, etc.

midbody scales   the scales counted along an imaginary line around the middle of the body, excluding the enlarged ventral scales of snakes. Midbody scales are most easily counted obliquely. *See* p. 365.

midlateral   on the middle of the sides along body and tail.

mimicry   the close resemblance of one organism or part thereof (the mimic) to another (the model) to deceive a third and thus enhance protection or concealment.

monodactyle   bearing one digit.

monotypic   pertaining to a genus containing a single species.

morphological   of form and structure.

nape   back of the neck.

nasal   the scale enclosing or bordering the nostril.

nasal cleft   the suture extending from the nostril of a blind snake.

neurotoxic   pertaining to venoms injurious to nerve tissue. *See* venom.

New World   North and South America.

niche   in ecology, the position and role a species occupies in a community, including where it lives, what it feeds on, its relationship with its predators and what limits the growth of its population.

nocturnal   active during the night.

nomenclature   of taxonomy, a system of names.

nominate form   the subspecies originally described; recognised by having the same specific and subspecific names, e.g., *Ctenotus grandis grandis* as opposed to *C. g. titan*.

non-fragile   of tails, not easily broken due to lack of specialised cleavage points, and virtually incapable of regeneration if severed.

NSW   New South Wales.

NT   Northern Territory.

nuchal   pertaining to the nape, including markings, ornamentations or scales thereon.

ocellated   having pattern consisting of eye-like markings known as ocelli.

ocular   (a) pertaining to the eye, (b) a transparent scale covering the eye of a blind snake. *See* p. 407.

Old World   the eastern hemisphere, e.g., Europe, Asia, Africa, Australia, etc.

ontogenetic variation   variation related to growth and development; differences in colour, pattern and form between juveniles and adults.

oviduct   one of a pair of tubes along which an egg passes from the ovary to the cloaca.

palmar   pertaining to the soles of the front feet.

paratype   one or more specimens excluding the holotype, comprising the type series, upon which the description of a new species is based.

paravertebral scales   the longitudinal series of scales on either side of the dorsal midline.

paravertebral stripe   the line or stripe (usually pale) on either side of the vertebral stripe (usually dark). *See* p. 105.

parchment-shelled   of eggs, bearing pliable, rather than brittle and calcareous, shells.

parietals   paired scales at the back of the head, partly or wholly separated by the interparietal scale. *See* pp. 105, 365 and 407.

parthenogenesis (adj. parthenogenetic)   reproduction without fertilisation by a male.

plates   of scales: usually referring to laterally expanded scales on the bellies of most snakes, or the enlarged scales on the soles and digits of feet.

Plectrachne   *see* spinifex.

polychaetes   predominantly marine segmented worms of the class Polychaeta.

polyphyletic   originating from more than one evolutionary line.

postauricular fold   an oblique fold of skin immediately behind the ear on some dragon lizards. *See* p. 28.

posterior   towards the rear of the body, appendage or structure. Opposite of anterior.

postocular   one or more scales lying along the hind edge of the eye.

preanal pore   one or more pores identical in structure to femoral pores, situated in front of the cloaca. *See* femoral pores and p. 28.

prefrontal   one or more scales lying on top of the snout, immediately in front of the frontal scale. *See* pp. 105, 365 and 407.

proteaceous   pertaining to plants of the family Proteaceae, including the genera *Banksia, Grevillea* and *Hakea*.

proximal   towards the point of attachment of an appendage or structure. Opposite of distal.

Qld   Queensland.

race   *see* subspecies.

rafting   the process by which organisms disperse across large bodies of water on floating vegetation.

range   (a) extent of distribution of a given taxon, (b) a series of hills or mountains.

reticulum   a net-like pattern.

rhomboid   of pattern, diamond-shaped.

rings   of pattern, bands of colour completely encircling the body or tail.

rosette   circular arrangement of scales, usually surrounding a tubercle.

rostral   the scale situated on the tip of the snout, its lower edge bordering the mouth. *See* pp. 96, 105, 365 and 407.

rugose   of scales, bearing a wrinkled or uneven surface.

SA   South Australia.

scapular fold   continuation of gular fold up onto shoulder.

sclerophyll   a hard stiff leaf, as in that of a eucalypt.

serrated   of pattern, markings with indented or tooth-like margins, as on a saw.

sexual dichromatism   differences in colour between the sexes of a species.

sexual dimorphism   differences in form and/or size between the sexes of a species.

shields   the larger scales on the head, which are individually or group-named and do not overlap.

slough   the cast-off skin of a reptile.

sp. (pl. spp.)   abbreviation for species.

species   a formal group, subordinate in classification to genus and subgenus. Groups of actually or potentially interbreeding natural populations genetically isolated from other such groups. The name follows that of the genus or subgenus and is italicised with the first letter in lower case.

species group   a group of closely related species within a given genus.

spectacle   the fixed transparent scale covering the eyes on snakes and those lizards which lack movable lower eyelids.

spine   (a) an enlarged raised scale with a sharp, more or less erect point, (b) the long pointed tip of certain scales, usually the prolongation of a sharp, strong keel.

spinifex   (a) a genus of coastal tussock grasses of the family Poaceae, (b) a common name applied to spiny-leafed grasses of the genera *Triodia* and *Plectrachne*, which form prickly hummocks.

spinose   bearing spines.

squamate   pertaining to members of the order Squamata, e.g., lizards and snakes.

stick-ant nest   the nest of the ant *Iridomyrmex conifer*, consisting of a loose mound of soil particles mixed with finely chopped grass, and slender leaves, such as those of *Casuarina* spp.

striae (sing. stria)   fine shallow grooves on the surfaces of some scales; usually parallel and longitudinally oriented.

striate   bearing striae.

stripe   a long, narrow and continuous longitudinal marking.

style (adj. stylar)   a slender, rod-like vestigial limb in which none of the normal parts (joints, digits, claws) are distinct externally.

subfamily   a formal group of closely related genera, subordinate in classification to family. Subfamilies are designated by the addition of the suffix -inae to the stem name of one of the included genera (e.g., *Diplodactylus*/Diplodactylinae).

subgenus   a formal group of species, subordinate in classification to genus. The name is italicised and the first letter is capitalised. It is enclosed in brackets immediately following the genus, e.g., *Diplodactylus (Strophurus) ciliaris* (abbr. *D.(S.) ciliaris*).

suboculars   a series of scales beneath the eye.

subspecies   a formal classification for part of a species which in isolation has acquired some distinct characteristics of its own.

supraciliaries   a longitudinal series of small scales between the supraocular scales and the eye. *See* p. 105.

supralabials   see upper labials.

supraoculars   a longitudinal series of large scales between the frontal and supraciliaries. *See* pp. 105, 365 and 407.

surface debris   used here to denote rubbish discarded by humans, e.g., sheets of iron, piled soil, vegetation, timber, etc.

suture   the groove between non-overlapping scales.

sympatric   of populations or species, occurring together in the same geographic region.

synonym   a name proposed for a taxon described as new, but later shown to be already named. The new name, the synonym, becomes invalid.

Tas.   Tasmania.

taxon (pl. taxa)   a basic unit of classification in taxonomy, e.g., species, genus, family, etc.

taxonomy   the study of animal and plant classification, its principles and the means by which formation of species, etc., takes place.

temporals   large scales on the side of the head between eye and ear, bounded by the parietal scale, the postoculars and the upper labials. *See* pp. 105 and 365.

termitarium (pl. termitaria)   a nest or mound of termites.

thermo-regulation: the means by which a reptile regulates its body temperature, e.g., basking, shuttling between sun and shade, or bringing the body into contact with warm surfaces.

transparent disc   a small spectacle set within the movable lower eyelid of certain skinks. Also known as palpebral disc. *See* p. 104.

tricarinate   bearing three keels.

tridactyle   bearing three digits.

trilobed   having three lobes, as in the snouts of some blind snakes.

Triodia   see spinifex.

tristriate   bearing three striae.

tussock grass   any grass that grows in tufts, bunches or clumps, e.g., Mitchell grasses (*Astrebla* spp.)

tympanum ear drum, visible externally on many lizards.

type locality the locality from which the type specimen was collected. *See* holotype.

understorey a general term to include grasses, shrubs, and small trees which are below the canopy.

undescribed of a taxon, not yet formally named and described in the literature.

upper labials the series of scales along the upper lip. Also known as supralabials. *See* pp. 105, 365 and 407.

upper lateral pertaining to the upper half of the sides of the body and tail, between the dorsolateral and midlateral areas. Often represented as a broad dark stripe or zone.

valvular pertaining to a structure which enables the nostrils of some aquatic and marine snakes to be closed during submersion in water.

venom a protein mixture capable of producing a toxic reaction. Produced in specialised glands and used to immobilise prey or for defence.

vent the transverse external opening of the cloaca. *See* cloaca

and p. 365.

ventral pertaining strictly to the belly (of scales), or broadly to all lower surfaces.

ventrolateral pertaining to the boundary between lower and lateral surfaces.

vermiculations short wavy lines, like the tracks of small worms.

vertebral (a) pertaining to the spine or vertebral column, (b) a dark median stripe or line extending from the nape for varying distances along the back or tail. *See* p. 105.

vertebrate an animal with a backbone and spinal cord.

vestigial term describing a reduced and functionless structure representing what was once useful and developed.

Vic. Victoria.

vs abbreviation for versus; usually used in comparative diagnoses.

WA Western Australia.

wombat a large, robust burrowing marsupial (family Vombatidae).

Selected Bibliography

Readers wanting further information on various aspects of lizard and snake classification and biology are referred to the following selected references. The list was compiled with a bias towards works published in the last three decades.

Additional references are included in the bibliographies accompanying these works, and a comprehensive bibliography of the Australian herpetofauna is supplied in H. G. Cogger, E. E. Cameron & H. M. Cogger (1983), Amphibia and Reptilia, *Zoo. Cat. Aust. 1*.

GENERAL WORKS ON LIZARDS AND SNAKES

Brooker, M. G. & Wombey, J. C. (1978). Some notes on the herpetofauna of the western Nullarbor Plain, Western Australia. *West. Aust. Nat.* 14 (2): 36–41.

Burbidge, A. A. (1983). Amphibians and reptiles. *In* Burbidge, A. A. and McKenzie, N. L. (Eds) 'Wildlife of the Great Sandy Desert, Western Australia'. pp. 109–120. (Wild. Res. Bull. West. Aust. N. 12) (Dept. Fish. Wildl.: Perth).

Bush, B. (1981). *Reptiles of the Kalgoorlie-Esperance region*. Vanguard Press, Perth.

Bustard, H. R. (1968). The reptiles of the Merriwindi State Forest, Pilliga West, Northern New South Wales, Australia. *Herpetologica* 24: 131–140.

Cogger, H. G. (1967). *Australian Reptiles in Colour*, A. H. and A. W. Reed, Sydney.

Cogger, H. (1968). Reptiles of the Pellew Islands. *Mimag* December 1968: 21–23.

Cogger, H. G. (1983). *Reptiles and Amphibians of Australia*. Revised edn. A. H. and A. W. Reed, Sydney.

Cogger, H. G., Cameron, E. E. & Cogger, H. M. (1983). Amphibia and Reptilia. *Zoo. Cat. Aust.* 1: 78–240.

Cogger, H. & Lindner, D. A. (1974) Frogs and reptiles. *In* Fauna survey of the Port Essington District, Cobourg Peninsula, Northern Territory of Australia. Frith, H. J. & Calaby, J. H. (eds.) *CSIRO Div. Wildl. Res. Tech. Pap.* 28: 63–107.

Covacevich, J. & McDonald, K. R. (1984). Frogs and reptiles of tropical and subtropical eastern Australian rainforests: distribution patterns and conservation, pp. 361–382. *In* Werren, G. L. and Kershaw, A. P., (eds). *Australian National Rainforest Study Report to the World Wildlife Fund (Australia) Volume 1. Proceedings of a workshop on the past, present and future of Australian rainforests*. Griffith University, December; 1983, Geography Department, Monash University, for the Australian Conservation Foundation.

Czechura, G. V. (1976). Additional notes on the Conondale Range herpetofauna. *Herpetofauna* 8 (2): 2–4.

Czechura, G. V. (1984). The Blackall-Conondale Range: frogs, reptiles and fauna conservation. Pp. 384–395 *in* Werren, G. L. and Kershaw, A. P., (eds). *Australian National Rainforest Study Report to the World Wildlife Fund (Australia) Volume 1. Proceedings of a workshop on the past, present and future of Australian rainforests*. Griffith University, December, 1983, Geography Department, Monash University, for the Australian Conservation Foundation.

Dwyer, P. D., Kikkawa, J. & Ingram, G. J. (1979). The vertebrate fauna of Australian heathlands—an evolutionary perspective. Pp. 231–279 *in* Specht, R. L. (ed.). *Ecosystems of the World 9A. Heathlands and Related Shrublands*. Elsevier, Amsterdam.

Ehmann, H. F. W. (1976). The reptiles of the Mt Lofty Ranges, South Australia. Part 1. *Herpetofauna* 8 (1): 2–5.

Ehmann, H. F. W. (1976). The reptiles of the Mt Lofty Ranges, South Australia. Part 2. *Herpetofauna* 8 (2): 5–13.

Ford, J. (1963) The reptilian fauna of the islands between Dongara and Lancelin, Western Australia. *W. Aust. Nat.* 8: 135–142.

Fyfe, G. (1980). The effect of fire on lizard communities in central Australia. *Herpetofauna* 12 (1): 1–9.

Gillam, M. W., Cawood, I. S. & Honner, G. J. (1978). New reptile records from Central Australia, Northern Territory. *Herpetofauna* 9 (2): 18–25.

Gow, G. (1981). Checklist of reptiles and amphibians of the southern sector of the NT. *N. Territory Nat.* 4: 14–16.

Gow, G. (1981). Checklist of reptiles and amphibians of the northern sector of the NT. *N. Territory Nat.* 4: 16–19.

Gow, G. (1981). Herpetofauna of Groote Eylandt, Northern Territory. *Aust. J. Herp.* 1 (2): 62–70.

Green, D. (1973). The reptiles of the outer north-western suburbs of Sydney. *Herpetofauna* 6 (2): 2–5.

Harlow, P. & Van der Straaten, M. (1976). Reptiles of the Oxford Falls area. *Herpetofauna* 8 (1): 6–7.

Heatwole, H. (1976). *Reptile Ecology*, University of Queensland Press, St. Lucia.

Houston, T. F. (1973). Reptiles of South Australia. Extract from *South Australian Year Book*, 1973. 11 pp.

Jacobson, K. (1973). Reptiles of the Tamworth area. *Herpetofauna* 6 (1): 20–22.

Jenkins, R. & Bartell, R. (1980). *A Field Guide to Reptiles of the Australia High Country*. Inkata Press, Melbourne.

Johnston, G. R. & Ellins, P. (1979). The reptiles of the Sir Joseph Banks Islands, South Australia. *Herpetofauna* 10 (2): 9–12.

Limpus, C. J. (1982). The reptiles of Lizard Island. *Herpetofauna* 13 (2): 1–6.

Low, T. (1978). The reptiles of Magnetic Island, Nth Queensland. *Herpetofauna* 9 (2): 10–14.

Martin, K. (1975). Reptiles of the Alice Springs area. *Herpetofauna* 7 (2): 6–7.

Morris, K. D. & Rice, G. E. (1981). Some vertebrates recorded on a visit to Queen Victoria Spring in December 1977. *West. Aust. Nat.* 15 (1): 11–13.

Pailes, R. (1978). Reptiles of the Ballarat region, Victoria. *Herpetofauna* 10 (1): 26–28.

Pianka, E. R. (1968). Habitat specificity, speciation and species density in Australian desert lizards. *Ecology* 50 (3): 498–502.

Pianka, E. R. (1972). Zoogeography and speciation of Australian desert lizards. An ecological perspective. *Copeia* 1972 (1): 127–144.

Rawlinson, P. A. (1969). The reptiles of east Gippsland. *Proc. R. Soc. Vict.* 82: 113–128.

Rawlinson, P. A. (1971). The reptiles of west Gippsland. *Proc. R. Soc. Vict.* 84: 37–52.

Rawlinson, P. A. (1974). Biogeography and ecology of the reptiles of Tasmania and the Bass Strait area. Chapt 11, pp. 291–338 *in* Williams, W. D. (ed.) *Biogeography and Ecology in Tasmania*. The Hague: Junk.

Richardson, P. (1975). Snakes of the Bundaberg region. *Herpetofauna* 7 (2): 16–20.

Richardson, P. (1976). Freshwater tortoises and lizards of the Bundaberg region. *Herpetofauna* 8 (2): 14–15.

Schwaner, T. D. & Miller, B. (1984). Range extensions of reptiles in South Australia. *Trans. R. Soc. S. Aust.* 108 (4): 215–216.

Schwaner, T. D. & Miller, B. (1984). Reptiles new to the fauna of South Australia. *Trans. R. Soc. S. Aust.* 108 (4): 217–218.

Schwaner, T. D., Miller, B. and Tyler, M. J. (1985). Reptiles and

Amphibians. 13: 159–168. *In Natural History of Eyre Peninsula. Trans. R. Soc. S. Aust.*

Smales, I. (1981). The herpetofauna of Yellingbo State Faunal Reserve, *Vict. Nat.* 98: 234–246.

Smith, L. A. & Johnstone, R. E. (1979). Amphibians and reptiles. *In* McKenzie, N. L. and Burbidge, A. A. (Eds) 'The wildlife of some existing and proposed Nature Reserves in the Gibson, Little Sandy and Great Victoria Deserts, Western Australia'. (Wildl. Res. Bull. West. Aust. No. 8) (Dept. Fish. Wildl.: Perth).

Smith, L. A. & Johnstone, R. E. (1981). Amphibians and reptiles of Mitchell Plateau and adjacent coast and lowland, Kimberley Region, WA. *In* 'Biological survey of Mitchell Plateau and Admiralty Gulf, Western Australia' pp. 215–227 (WA Museum: Perth)

Storr, G. M. (1964). Some aspects of the geography of Australian reptiles. *Senck. Biol.*, 45: 577–589.

Storr, G. M. (1978). Taxonomic notes on the reptiles of the Shark Bay region, Western Australia. *Rec. West. Aust. Mus.* 6 (3): 303–318.

Storr, G. M. & Hanlon, T. M. S. (1980). Herpetofauna of the Exmouth region, Western Australia. *Rec. West. Aust. Mus.* 8 (3): 423–439.

Storr, G. M., Hanlon, T. M. S. & Dunlop, J. N. (1983). Herpetofauna of the Geraldton region, Western Australia. *Rec. West. Aust. Mus.* 10 (3): 215–234.

Storr, G. M., Hanlon, T. M. S. & Harold, G. (1981). Herpetofauna of the shores and hinterland of the Great Australian Bight, Western Australia. *Rec. West. Aust. Mus.* 9 (1): 23–38.

Storr, G. M. & Harold, G. (1978). Herpetofauna of the Shark Bay region, Western Australia. *Rec. West. Aust. Mus.* 6 (4): 449–466.

Storr, G. M. & Harold, G. (1980). Herpetofauna of the Zuytdorp Coast and hinterland, Western Australia. *Rec. West. Aust. Mus.* 8 (3): 359–375.

Storr, G. M. & Harold G. (1984). Herpetofauna of the Lake MacLeod region, Western Australia. *Rec. West. Aust. Mus.* 11(2): 173–189.

Storr, G. M. and Harold, G. (1985). Herpetofauna of the Onslow Region, Western Australia. *Rec. West Aust. Mus.* 12 (3): 277–291.

Storr, G. M. & Johnstone, R. E. (1983). Amphibians and reptiles. *In* McKenzie, N. L. (Ed.) Wildlife of the Dampier Peninsula, South-west Kimberley, Western Australia, pp. 70–74. (Wildl. Res. Bull. West. Aust. No. 11) (Dept. Fish. Wildl.: Perth).

Storr, G. M. & Smith, L. A. (1974). Amphibians and reptiles of the Prince Regent River Reserve, North-western Australia. *In* Miles, J. M. and Burbidge, A. A. (Eds) 'A biological survey of the Prince Regent River Reserve north-west Kimberley, Western Australia in August, 1974', pp. 85–88 (Wildl. Res. Bull. West. Aust. No. 3) (Dept. Fish. Wildl.: Perth).

Storr, G. M. & Smith, L. A. (1975). Amphibians and reptiles of the Drysdale River National Park North Kimberley, Western Australia. *In* Kabay, E. D. & Burbidge, A. A. (Eds). 'A biological survey of the Drysdale River National Park, North Kimberley, Western Australia in August 1975', pp. 97–101. (Wildl. Res. Bull. West. Aust. No. 6) (Dept. Fish. Wildl.: Perth).

Storr, G. M. & Smith, L. A. (1981). Amphibians and reptiles. *In* Mckenzie, N. L. (Ed.). 'Wildlife of the Edgar Ranges area, south-west Kimberley, Western Australia', pp. 54–57. (Wildl. Res. Bull. West Aust. No. 10) (Dept. Fish. Wildl.: Perth).

Swanson, S. (1979). Some rock-dwelling reptiles of the Arnhem Land escarpment. *N. Territory Nat.* 1 (2): 14–18.

Wells, R. (1979). New reptile records for the Northern Territory. *N. Territory Nat.* 1 (2): 3–4.

White, J. (1976). Reptiles of the Corunna Hills. *Herpetofauna* 8 (1): 21–23.

White, J. (1979). The road to Mokari. *Herpetofauna* 11 (1): 13–16.

Worrell, E. (1963). *Reptiles of Australia*, Angus & Robertson, Sydney.

LIZARDS

General Works on Lizards

Bustard, H. R. (1970). *Australian Lizards*. Collins, Sydney and London.

Glauert, L. (1961). *A Handbook of the Lizards of Western Australia*. WA Naturalists Club, Perth.

Swanson, S. (1976). *Lizards of Australia*. Angus & Robertson, Sydney.

Dale, D. F. (1973). *Forty Queensland Lizards*. Queensland, Museum, Brisbane.

Family Agamidae (Dragon Lizards)

General

Gumbold, N. (1979). Thermoregulation in Agamids. *Herpetofauna* 10 (2): 14–15.

Houston, T. F. (1978). *Dragon Lizards and Goannas of South Australia*. South Australian Museum, Adelaide.

Storr, G. M. (1982). Revision of the bearded dragons (Lacertilia: Agamidae) of Western Australia with notes on the dismemberment of the genus *Amphibolurus. Rec. West. Aust. Mus.* 10 (2): 199–214.

Storr, G. M., Smith, L. A. & Johnstone, R. E. (1983). *Lizards of Western Australia, II. Dragons and Monitors*. Western Australian Museum, Perth.

Witten, G. J. (1982). Phyletic groups within the family Agamidae (Reptilia: Lacertilia) in Australia. *In Evolution of the flora and fauna of arid Australia* (Eds W. R. Barker & P. J. M. Greenslade), pp. 225–8. Peacock Publications.

Genera and Species

Caimanops

Storr, G. M. (1974). Agamid lizards of the genera *Caimanops*, *Physignathus* and *Diporiphora* in Western Australia and Northern Territory. *Rec. West. Aust. Mus.* 3: 121–146.

Chelosania

Husband, G. (1979). Range extension for *Chelosania brunnea. Herpetofauna* 10 (2): 29–30.

Pengilley, R. (1982). Note on the reproductive biology of the Ring-tailed dragon (*Chelosania brunnea*). *N. Territory Nat.* 5: 6.

Cryptagama

Storr, G. M. (1981). Three new agamid lizards from Western Australia. *Rec. West. Aust. Mus.* 8: 599–607.

Witten, G. J. (1984). Relationships of *Tympanocryptis aurita* Storr, 1981. *Rec. West. Aust. Mus.* 11 (4): 399–401.

Ctenophorus

Bradshaw, S. D. (1971). Growth and mortality in a field population of *Amphibolurus* lizards exposed to seasonal cold and aridity. *J. Zool.* 165: 1–25.

Cogger, H. G. (1974). Thermal regulations of the mallee dragon, *Amphibolurus fordi* (Lacertilia: Agamidae). *Aust. J. Zool.* 22: 319–339.

Cogger, H. G. (1978). Reproductive cycles, fat body cycles and socio-sexual behaviour in the mallee dragon, *Amphibolurus fordi* (Lacertilia: Agamidae). *Aust. J. Zool.* 26: 653–672.

Gibbons, J. R. H. (1979). The hind leg push up display of the *Amphibolurus decresii* species complex (Lacertilia: Agamidae). *Copeia* 1979: 29–40.

Gibbons, J. R. H. & Lillywhite, H. B. (1981). Ecological segregation, colour matching, and speciation in lizards of the *Amphibolurus decresii* species complex. (Lacertilia: Agamidae). *Ecology* 62: 1573–1584.

Gillam, M. W., Cawood, I. S. & Honner, G. J. (1978). New reptile records from Central Australia, Northern Territory. *Herpetofauna* 9: 18–25.

Heatwole, H. (1970). Thermal ecology of the desert dragon *Amphibolurus inermis*. *Ecol. Monogr.* 40: 425–457.

Houston, T. F. (1974). Revision of the *Amphibolurus decresii* complex (Lacertilia: Agamidae) of South Australia. *Trans. R. Soc. S. Aust.* 98: 49–60.

Houston, T. F. (1974). *Amphibolurus gibba*, a new dragon lizard (Lacertilia: Agamidae) from northern South Australia. *Trans. R. Soc. S. Aust.* 98: 209–212.

Hudson, P. (1979). Notes on the behavioural antics of the painted dragon *Amphibolurus pictus* Peters. *Herpetofauna* 11: 25–26.

Mitchell, F. J. (1948). A revision of the lacertilian genus *Tympanocryptis Rec. S. Aust. Mus.* 9: 57–86.

Mitchell, F. J. (1965). The affinities of *Tympanocryptis maculosa* Mitchell (Lacertilia: Agamidae). *Rec. S. Aust. Mus.* 15: 179–191.

Mitchell, F. J. (1973). Studies on the ecology of the agamid lizard *Amphibolurus maculosus* (Mitchell). *Trans. R. Soc. S. Aust.* 97: 47–76.

Pianka, E. R. (1971). Ecology of the agamid lizard *Amphibolurus isolepis* in Western Australia. *Copeia* 1971: 527–536.

Pianka, E. R. (1971). Notes on the biology of *Amphibolurus cristatus* and *Amphibolurus scutulatus*. *West. Aust. Nat.* 12: 36–41.

Pianka, E. R. (1971). Comparative ecology of two lizards. *Copeia* 1971: 129–138.

Rankin, P. R. (1977). Burrow plugging in the Netted Dragon, *Amphibolurus nuchalis*, with reports on the occurrence in three other Australian agamids. *Herpetofauna* 9 (1): 18–22.

Storr, G. M. (1965). The *Amphibolurus maculatus* species-group (Lacertilia: Agamidae) in Western Australia. *J. R. Soc. West. Aust.* 48: 45–54.

Storr, G. M. (1966). The *Amphibolurus reticulatus* species-group (Lacertilia: Agamidae) in Western Australia. *J. R. Soc. West. Aust.* 49: 17–25.

Storr, G. M. (1967). Geographic races of the agamid lizard *Amphibolurus caudicinctus*. *J. R. Soc. West. Aust.* 50: 49–56.

Storr, G. M. (1981). Three new agamid lizards from Western Australia. *Rec. West. Aust. Mus.* 8: 599–607.

Diporiphora

Francis, M. (1981). Observations on heat regulating behaviour in captive specimens of *Diporiphora winneckei* (Lucas and Frost). *Herpetofauna* 12 (2): 35–36.

Glauert, L. (1959). A new agamid lizard from Queen Victoria Springs, Western Australia. *Diporiphora reginae*, sp. nov. *Proc. R. Zool. Soc. N.S.W.* 1957–58: 10.

Houston, T. F. (1977). A new species of *Diporiphora* from South Australia and geographic variation in *D. winneckei* Lucas and Frost (Lacertilia: Agamidae). *Trans. R. Soc. S. Aust.* 101: 199–206.

Storr, G. M. (1974). Agamid lizards of the genera *Caimanops, Physignathus* and *Diporiphora* in Western Australia and Northern Territory. *Rec. West. Aust. Mus.* 3: 121–146.

Storr, G. M. (1979). Two new *Diporiphora* (Lacertilia: Agamidae) from Western Australia. *Rec. West. Aust. Mus.* 7: 255–263.

Gemmatophora

Groom, S. (1973). Notes on the keeping and distribution of the jacky lizard (*Amphibolurus muricatus*). *Herpetofauna* 5: 3–5.

Groom, S. (1973). Further notes on the jacky lizard (*Amphibolurus muricatus*), in captivity. *Herpetofauna* 6 (1): 6.

Storr, G. M. (1974). Agamid lizards of the genera *Caimanops, Physignathus* and *Diporiphora* in Western Australia and Northern Territory. *Rec. West. Aust. Mus.* 3: 121–146.

Witten, G. J. (1972). A new species of *Amphibolurus* from eastern Australia. *Herpetologica* 28: 191–195.

Witten, G. J. (1974). Population movements of the agamid lizard, *Amphibolurus nobbi. Aust. Zool.* 18: 129–132.

Witten, G. J. & Coventry, A. J. (1984). A new lizard of the genus *Amphibolurus* (Agamidae) from southern Australia. *Proc. R. Soc. Vict.* 96 (3): 155–159.

Hypsilurus

Wells, R. (1972). Notes on *Goniocephalus boydii* (Macleay). *Herpetofauna* 5: 24.

Moloch

Bentley, P. J. & Blumer, W. F. C. (1962). Uptake of water by the lizard, *Moloch horridus. Nature* 194: 699–700.

Hudson, P. (1977). An account of egg laying by the Thorny Devil (*Moloch horridus*) Gray. (Squamata: Agamidae) *Herpetofauna* 9 (1): 23–24.

Johnston, G. R. (1981). A note on *Moloch horridus* Gray, 1841. *Herpetofauna* 13 (1): 29.

Pianka, E. R. & Pianka, H. D. (1970). The ecology of *Moloch horridus* (Lacertilia: Agamidae) in Western Australia. *Copeia* 1970: 90–103.

Sporn, C. C. (1955). The breeding of the mountain devil in captivity. *West. Aust. Nat.* 5: 1–5.

Sporn, C. C. (1958). Further observations of the mountain devil in captivity. *West. Aust. Nat.* 6: 136–137.

Sporn, C. C. (1965). Additional observations on the life history of the mountain devil, *Moloch horridus*, in captivity. *West. Aust. Nat.* 9: 157–159.

Physignathus

Australian Herpetological Society Members (1976). Observations on the eastern water dragon *Physignathus lesueurii* in the natural state and in captivity. *Herpetofauna* 8 (2): 20–22.

Smith, J. (1979). Notes on incubation and hatching of eggs of the eastern water dragon. *Herpetofauna* 10: 12–14.

Pogona

Badham, J. A. (1976). The *Amphibolurus barbatus* species-group (Lacertilia: Agamidae). *Aust. J. Zool.* 24: 423–443.

Brattstrom, B. H. (1971). Social and thermoregulatory behaviour of the bearded dragon, *Amphibolurus barbatus. Copeia* 1971: 484–497.

Carpenter, C. C., Badham, J. A. & Kimble, B. (1970). Behaviour patterns of three species of *Amphibolurus* (Agamidae). *Copeia* 1970: 497–505.

Johnston, G. R. (1979). The eggs, incubation and young of the bearded dragon *Amphibolurus vitticeps* Ahl. *Herpetofauna* 11: 5–8.

Pickworth, B. (1981). Observations of behaviour patterns displayed by a pair of bearded dragons, *Amphibolurus barbatus* Cuvier. *Herpetofauna* 12 (2): 13–15.

Smith, J. & Schwaner, T. D. (1980). Notes on reproduction by captive *Amphibolurus nullarbor* (Sauria: Agamidae). *Trans. R. Soc. S. Aust.* 105 (4): 215–216.

Storr, G. M. (1982). Revision of the bearded dragons (Lacertilia: Agamidae) of Western Australia with notes on the dismemberment of the genus *Amphibolurus. Rec. West. Aust. Mus.* 10 (2): 199–214.

Tympanocryptis

Kent, D. S. (1987). Notes on the biology and osteology of *Amphibolurus diemensis* (Gray, 1841), the mountain dragon. *Vic. Nat.* 104 (4): 101–104.

Mitchell, F. J. (1948). A revision of the lacertilian genus *Tympanocryptis. Rec. S. Aust. Mus.* 9: 57–86.

Storr, G. M. (1964). The agamid lizards of the genus *Tympanocryptis* in Western Australia. *J. R. Soc. West. Aust.* 47: 43–50.

Storr, G. M. (1977). The *Amphibolurus adelaidensis* species group (Lacertilia: Agamidae) in Western Australia. *Rec. West. Aust. Mus.* 5: 73–81.

Storr. G. M. (1982). Taxonomic notes on the genus *Tympanocryptis* Peters (Lacertilia: Agamidae). *Rec. West. Aust. Mus.* 10 (1): 61–66.

Storr, G. M. (1984). Note on *Tympanocryptis lineata macra* (Lacertilia: Agamidae). *Rec. West. Aust. Mus.* 11 (3): 317.

Tasoulis, T. (1980). Range extension for *Amphibolurus diemensis. Herpetofauna* 11 (2): 27.

Family Gekkonidae (Geckos)

General

Bustard, H. R. (1965). Observations on Australian geckos. *Herpetologica* 21 (4): 294–302.

Pianka, E. R. & Pianka, H. D. (1976). Comparative ecology of twelve species of nocturnal lizards (Gekkonidae) in the Western Australian Desert. *Copeia* 1976: 125–142.

Genera and Species

Crenadactylus
Dixon, J. R. & Kluge, A. G. (1964). A new gekkonid genus from Australia. *Copeia* 1964: 174–180.

Storr, G. M. (1978). Seven new gekkonid lizards from Western Australia. *Rec. West. Aust. Mus.* 6: 337–352.

Diplodactylus
Bustard, H. R. (1964). Defensive behaviour shown by Australian geckos, genus *Diplodactylus*. *Herpetologica* 20 (3): 198–200.

Bustard, H. R. (1968). Temperature dependent activity in the Australian gecko *Diplodactylus vittatus*. *Copeia* 1968: 606–612.

Bustard, H. R. (1969). The ecology of the Australian geckoes *Diplodactylus williamsi* and *Gehyra australis* in northern New South Wales. *Proc. K. Ned. Akad. Wet. (C)* 72: 451–477.

Ehmann, H. (1980). Diurnal perching by the southern spiny-tailed gecko, *Diplodactylus intermedius*. *Herpetofauna* 12: 37.

King, M. (1977). Chromosomal and morphometric variation in the gecko *Diplodactylus vittatus* Gray. *Aust. J. Zool.* 25: 43–57.

King, M., Braithwaite, R. W. & Wombey, J. C. (1982). A new species of *Diplodactylus* (Reptilia: Gekkonidae) from the Alligator Rivers Region, Northern Territory. *Trans. R. Soc. S. Aust.* 106 (1): 15–18.

Kluge, A. G. (1962). A new species of gekkonid lizard, genus *Diplodactylus* from the Carnarvon region, Western Australia. *West. Aust. Nat.* 8: 73–75.

Kluge, A. G. (1962). A new species of gekkonid lizard, genus *Diplodactylus* (Gray) from southern interior of Western Australia. *West. Aust. Nat.* 8: 97–101.

Kluge, A. G. (1963). Three new species of the gekkonid lizard genus *Diplodactylus* Gray from Australia. *Rec. S. Aust. Mus.* 14: 545–553.

Kluge, A. G. (1963). A new species of gekkonid lizard, genus *Diplodactylus* Gray, from eastern Australia. *Proc. Linn. Soc. N.S.W.* 88: 230–234.

Kluge, A. G. (1967). Systematics, phylogeny, and zoogeography of the lizard genus *Diplodactylus* Gray (Gekkonidae). *Aust. J. Zool.* 15: 1007–1108.

Richardson, K. C. & Hinchcliffe, P. M. (1983). Caudal glands and their secretions in the Western Spiny-Tailed Gecko, *Diplodactylus spinigerus*. *Copeia* 1983 (1), 161–169.

Shea, G. M. (1984). Egg Deposition Site in the gecko *Diplodactylus williamsi*. *Vict. Nat.* 101 (5): 198–199.

Storr, G. M. (1978). Seven new gekkonid lizards from Western Australia. *Rec. West. Aust. Mus.* 6: 337–352.

Storr, G. M. (1979). The *Diplodactylus vittatus* complex (Lacertilia: Gekkonidae) in Western Australia. *Rec. West. Aust. Mus.* 7: 391–402.

Storr, G. M. (1979). Five new lizards from Western Australia. *Rec. West. Aust. Mus.* 8: 134–142.

Storr, G. M. (1983). Two new lizards from Western Australia (Genera *Diplodactylus* and *Lerista*). *Rec. West. Aust. Mus.* 11 (1): 59–62.

Storr, G. M. (1988). The *Diplodactylus ciliaris* complex (Lacertilia: Gekkonidae) in Western Australia. *Rec. West Aust. Mus.* (In press).

Storr, G. M. & Ford, J. R. (1967). Rediscovery and taxonomic status of the Western Australian gecko *Diplodactylus michaelseni*. *West. Aust. Nat.* 10: 160–162.

Gehyra
Bustard, H. R. (1965). The systematic status of the Australian geckos *Gehyra variegata* (Duméril and Bibron, 1836) and *Gehyra australis* Gray, 1845. *Herpetologica* 20 (4): 259–272.

Bustard, H. R. (1965). The systematic status of the Australian gecko *Gehyra variegata punctata* (Fry). *Herpetologica* 21: 157–158.

Bustard, H. R. (1967). Activity cycle and thermoregulation in the Australian gecko *Gehyra variegata*. *Copeia* 1967: 753–758.

Bustard, H. R. (1968). The ecology of the Australian gecko *Gehyra variegata*, in northern New South Wales. *J. Zool.* 154: 113–138.

Bustard, H. R. (1969). The ecology of the Australian geckoes *Diplodactylus williamsi* and *Gehyra australis* in northern New South Wales. *Proc. K. Ned. Akad. Wet. (C)* 72: 451–477.

Bustard, H. R. (1969). Population ecology of the gekkonid lizard (*Gehyra variegata* [Duméril & Bibron]) in exploited forests in northern New South Wales. *J. Anim. Ecol.* 38: 35–51.

King, M. (1979). Karyotypic evolution in *Gehyra* (Gekkonidae: Reptilia) I. The *Gehyra variegata–punctata* complex. *Aust. J. Zool.* 27: 373–393.

King, M. (1981). Notes on the distribution of *Gehyra nana* Storr and *Gehyra punctata* (Fry) in Australia. *Aust. J. Herp.* 1 (2): 55–56.

King, M. (1982). Karyotypic evolution in *Gehyra* (Gekkonidae: Reptilia) II. A new species from the Alligator Rivers Region in northern Australia. *Aust. J. Zool.* 30: 93–101.

King, M. (1982). A new species of *Gehyra* (Reptilia: Gekkonidae) from Central Australia. *Trans. R. Soc. S. Aust.* 106 (4): 155–158.

King, M. (1983). Karyotypic evolution in *Gehyra* (Gekkonidae: Reptilia). III. The *Gehyra australis* complex. *Aust. J. Zool.* 31: 723–741.

King, M. (1983). The *Gehyra australis* species complex (Sauria: Gekkonidae). *Amphibia-Reptilia.* 4: 147–169.

King, M. (1984). A new species of *Gehyra* (Reptilia: Gekkonidae) from northern Western Australia. *Trans. R. Soc. S. Aust.* 108 (2): 113–117.

Low, T. (1979). A new species of gecko, genus *Gehyra* (Reptilia: Gekkonidae) from Queensland. *Vict. Nat.* 96: 190–196.

Mitchell, F. J. (1965). Australian geckos assigned to the genus *Gehyra* Gray. (Reptilia: Gekkonidae). *Senckenberg. Biol.* 46: 287–319.

Storr, G. M. (1978). Seven new gekkonid lizards from Western Australia. *Rec. West. Aust. Mus.* 6 (3): 337–352.

Storr, G. M. (1982). Two new *Gehyra* (Lacertilia: Gekkonidae) from Australia. *Rec. West. Aust. Mus.* 10: 53–59.

Hemidactylus
Fyfe, G. (1981). Range extension for *Hemidactylus frenatus*, the Asian house gecko. *Herpetofauna* 13: 33.

Heteronotia
Bustard, H. R. (1968). The ecology of the Australian gecko *Heteronotia binoei* in northern New South Wales. *J. Zool.* 156: 483–497.

Bustard, H. R. (1970). The population ecology of the Australian gekkonid lizard *Heteronotia binoei* in an exploited forest. *J. Zool.* 162: 31–42.

Kluge, A. G. (1963). A review of the gekkonid lizard genus *Heteronota* Gray, with a description of a new species from Western Australia. *J. R. Soc. West. Aust.* 46: 63–67.

Moritz, C. (1983). Parthenogenesis in the endemic Australian lizard *Heteronotia binoei* (Gekkonidae). *Science* 220: 735–737.

Lepidodactylus
Brown, W. C. & Parker, F. (1977). Lizards of the genus *Lepidodactylus* (Gekkonidae) from the Indo-Australian Archipelago and the islands of the Pacific, with descriptions of new species. *Proc. Calif Acad Sci. (4)* 41: 253–265.

Nactus
Ingram, G. J. (1978). A new species of gecko, genus *Cyrtodactylus*, from Cape York Peninsula, Queensland, Australia, *Vict. Nat.* 95: 142–146.

Kluge, A. G. (1983). Cladistic relationships among Gekkonid lizards. *Copeia* 1983 (2): 465–475.

Nephrurus
Delean, S. (1983). (Unpublished manuscript). Ecology of a new species of *Nephrurus* from South Australia.

Delean, S. & Harvey, C. (1981). Some observations on the knob-tailed gecko, *Nephrurus laevissimus* in the wild. *Herpetofauna* 13: 1–3.

Delean, S. & Harvey, C. (1984). Notes on the reproduction of *Nephrurus deleani* (Reptilia: Gekkonidae). *Trans. R. Soc. S. Aust.* 108 (4): 221–222.

Galliford, M. (1981). Notes on the starred knob-tailed gecko, *Nephrurus stellatus*, caught spotlighting. *Herpetofauna* 12: 33–34.

Gow, G. (1979). Notes on the biology of *Nephrurus asper*. *N. Territory Nat.* 1: 19–20.

Harvey, C. (1983). A new species of *Nephrurus* (Reptilia: Gekkonidae) from South Australia. *Trans. R. Soc. S. Aust.* 107 (4): 231–235.

Storr, G. M. (1963). The gekkonid genus *Nephrurus* in Western Australia, including a new species and three new sub-species. *J. R. Soc. West. Aust.* 46: 85–90.

Storr, G. M. (1968). *Nephrurus stellatus*, a new knob-tailed gecko from southern Australia. *West. Aust. Nat.* 10: 180–182.

Oedura

Bustard, H. R. (1966). The *Oedura tryoni* complex: east Australian rock dwelling geckos (Reptilia: Gekkonidae). *Bull. Brit. Mus. Nat. Hist.* 14: 1–14.

Bustard, H. R. (1967). Reproduction in the Australian gekkonid genus *Oedura* Gray, 1842. *Herpetologica* 23: 276–284.

Bustard, H. R. (1969). *Oedura reticulata*, a new velvet gecko from south-west Western Australia. *West. Aust. Nat.* 11: 82–86.

Bustard, H. R. (1970). *Oedura marmorata* a complex of Australian geckos (Reptilia: Gekkonidae). *Senckenberg. Biol.* 51: 21–40.

Bustard, H. R. (1971). A population study of the eyed gecko, *Oedura ocellata* Boulenger, in northern New South Wales, Australia. *Copeia* 1971 (4): 658–669.

Cogger, H. G. (1957). Investigations in the gekkonid genus *Oedura* Gray. *Proc. Linn. Soc. N.S.W.* 82: 167–179.

King, M. (1984). Three new species of *Oedura* (Reptilia: Gekkonidae) from the Mitchell Plateau of North Western Australia. *Amphibia-Reptilia* 5: 329–337.

King, M. & Gow, G. (1983). A new species of *Oedura* (Gekkonidae: Reptilia) from the Alligator Rivers Region of Northern Australia. *Copeia*, 1983 (2): 445–449.

Milton, D. (1980). An example of community egglaying in *Oedura tryoni* (De Vis). *Herpetofauna* 11: 19–23.

Phyllodactylus

King, M. & Rofe, R. (1976). Karyotypic variation in the Australian gecko *Phyllodactylus marmoratus* (Gray) (Gekkonidae: Reptilia). *Chromosoma (Berl.)* 54: 75–87.

King, M. & King, D. (1977). An additional chromosome race of *Phyllodactylus marmoratus* (Gray) (Reptilia: Gekkonidae) and its phylogenetic implications. *Aust. J. Zool.* 25: 667–672.

King, M. (1977). Reproduction in the Australian gecko *Phyllodactylus marmoratus* (Gray). *Herpetologica* 33: 7–13.

Storr, G. M. (1987). The genus *Phyllodactylus* (Lacertilia: Gekkonidae) in Western Australia. *Rec. West Aust. Mus.* 13(2): 275–284.

Phyllurus

Covacevich, J. (1975). A review of the genus *Phyllurus* (Lacertilia: Gekkonidae). *Mem. Q. Mus.* 17: 293–303.

Green, D. (1973). Observations on the southern leaf-tailed gecko *Phyllurus platurus* (Shaw). *Herpetofauna* 6: 21–24.

Pseudothecadactylus

Cogger, H. G. (1975). New lizards of the genus *Pseudothecadactylus* (Lacertilia: Gekkonidae) from Arnhem Land and north-western Australia. *Rec. Aust. Mus.* 30: 87–97.

Swanson, S. (1979). Some rock-dwelling reptiles of the Arnhem Land Escarpment. *N. Territory Nat.* 1: 14–18.

Underwoodisaurus

Strong, B. W. & Gillam, M. W. (1983). A new record for the Northern Territory of the Thick-tailed Gecko (*Underwoodisaurus milii*). *N. Territory Nat.* 6: 18–19.

Family Pygopodidae (Legless Lizards)

General

Kluge, A. G. (1974). A taxonomic revision of the lizard family Pygopodidae. *Misc. Publ. Mus. Zool. Univ. Mich.* 147: 1–221.

Genera and Species

Aprasia

Parker, H. W. (1956). The lizard genus *Aprasia*, its taxonomy and temperature correlated variation. *Bull. Brit. Mus. Nat. Hist. (Zool.)* 3: 365–385.

Rankin, P. R. (1976). A note on a possible diversionary defence mechanism in the worm lizard, *Aprasia inaurita* Kluge. *Herpetofauna* 8 (2): 18–19.

Storr, G. M. (1970). *Aprasia smithi*, a new worm-lizard (Pygopodidae) from Western Australia. *West. Aust. Nat.* 11: 141.

Storr, G. M. (1978). Taxonomic notes on the reptiles of the Shark Bay region, Western Australia. *Rec. West. Aust. Mus.* 6: 303–318.

Storr, G. M. (1979). Five new lizards from Western Australia. *Rec. West. Aust. Mus.* 8: 134–142.

Delma

Ludowici, P. A. (1975). Notes on an undescribed species of legless lizard. *Herpetofauna* 7 (2): 20–21.

Sonnemann, N. (1974). Notes on *Delma fraseri* in the north-east of Victoria. *Herpetofauna* 7 (1): 15.

Storr, G. M. (1987). Three new legless lizards (Pygopodidae) from Western Australia. *Rec. West Aust. Mus.* (In press).

Lialis

Bradshaw, S. D., Gans, C. & Saint Girons, H. (1980). Behavioural thermoregulation in a pygopodid lizard, *Lialis burtonis*. *Copeia* 1980: 738–743.

Neill, W. T. (1957). Notes on the pygopodid lizards, *Lialis burtoni* and *L. jicari*. *Copeia* 1957: 230–232.

Ophidiocephalus

Ehmann, H. (1981). The natural history and conservation of the bronzeback (*Ophidiocephalus taeniatus* Lucas and Frost) (Lacertilia, Pygopodidae). Pp. 7–13 *in* Banks, C. B. & Martin, A. A. (Eds.) *Proceedings of the Melbourne Herpetological Symposium*, 1980. Zoological Board of Victoria, Melbourne.

Ehmann, H., Metcalfe, D. (1978). The rediscovery of *Ophidiocephalus taeniatus* Lucas and Frost (Pygopodidae, Lacertilia)—The Bronzeback. *Herpetofauna* 9 (2): 8–10.

Pletholax

Storr, G. M. (1978). Taxonomic notes on the reptiles of the Shark Bay region, Western Australia. *Rec. West. Aust. Mus.* 6: 303–318.

Pygopus

Husband, G. (1980). Unusual burrowing behaviour in *Pygopus lepidopodus*. *Herpetofauna* 12 (1): 36.

Wells, R. & Husband, G. (1979). Comments on the reproduction of *Pygopus lepidopodus* (Lacépède). *Herpetofauna* 11: 22–25.

Family Scincidae (Skinks)

General

Czechura, G. V. (1983). Limb reduction in skinks. Queensland Museum Information Sheet, 83/9.

Greer, A. E. (1976). A most successful invasion: the diversity of Australia's skinks. *Aust. Nat. Hist.* 18 (12): 428–433.

Storr, G. M., Smith, L. A. & Johnstone, R. E. (1981). *Lizards of Western Australia. 1. Skinks.* University of Western Australia Press and Western Australia Museum, Perth.

Greer, A. E. and Cogger, H. G. (1985). Systematics of the reduce-limbed and limbless skinks currently assigned to the genus *Anomalopus* (Lacertilia: Scincidae). *Rec. Aust. Mus.* 37 (1): 11–54.

Genera and Species

Anomalopus

Ingram, G. J. (1977). A new species of legless skink *Anomalopus pluto* from Cape York, Queensland. *Vict. Nat.* 94: 52–53.

Calyptotis

Greer, A. E. (1983). The Australian scincid genus *Calyptotis*, De Vis: resurrection of the name, description of four new species, and discussion of relationships. *Rec. Aust. Mus.* 35: 29–59.

Carlia

Covacevich, J. & Ingram, G. J. (1975). Three new species of rainbow skinks of the genus *Carlia* from northern Queensland. *Vict. Nat.* 92: 19–22.

Greer, A. E. (1975). Notes on the systematics of the genus *Carlia* (Lacertilia: Scincidae). I. *Carlia melanopogon* Gray, 1845. *Herpetologica* 31: 70–75.

Greer, A. E. (1976). Notes on the systematics of the genus *Carlia* (Lacertilia: Scincidae). II. *Carlia peroni* (Duméril and Bibron 1839). *Herpetologica* 32: 371–377.

Ingram, G. J. (1985). Implicit technique in taxonomy: The skinks of Cape York Peninsula. (Unpublished Ph.D. thesis): University of Queensland.

Ingram, G. J. & Covacevich, J. (Unpublished manuscript). Skinks of the genus *Carlia* (Lacertilia: Scincidae) in Australia and Papua.

Ingram, G. J. & Covacevich, J. (1980). Two new lygosomine skinks endemic to Cape York Peninsula. Pp. 45–48 *in* Stevens, N. C. & Bailey, A. (Eds) *Contemporary Cape York*. Royal Society of Queensland, Brisbane.

Mitchell, F. J. (1953). A brief revision of the four-fingered members of the genus *Leiolopisma* (Lacertilia). *Rec. S. Aust. Mus.* 11: 75–90.

Storr, G. M. (1974). The genus *Carlia* (Lacertilia: Scincidae) in Western Australia and Northern Territory. *Rec. West. Aust. Mus.* 3: 151–165.

Wells, R. (1975). Notes on an unidentified skink of the genus *Carlia* from Black Mountain, north-east Queensland. *Herpetofauna* 7 (2): 11.

Wilhoft, D. C. (1963). Reproduction in the tropical Australian skink, *Leiolopisma rhomboidalis*. *Am. Midl. Nat.* 70: 442–461.

Coeranoscincus

Czechura, G. V. (1974). A new south-east locality for the skink *Anomalopus reticulatus*. *Herpetofauna* 7 (1): 24–25.

McDonald, K. R. (1977). Observations on the skink *Anomalopus reticulatus* (Günther) (Lacertilia: Scincidae). *Vict. Nat.* 94: 99–103.

Cryptoblepharus

Cook, R. (1973). The wall lizard, *Cryptoblepharus boutonii virgatus*. *Herpetofauna* 6: 15–16.

Covacevich, J. & Ingram, G. J. (1978). An undescribed species of rock dwelling *Cryptoblepharus* (Lacertilia: Scincidae). *Mem. Qd. Mus.* 18: 151–154.

Horner, P. G. (1984). Notes on the scincid lizard *Cryptoblepharus litoralis* (Mertens, 1958) in the Northern Territory. *N. Territory Nat.* 7: 4–7.

Storr, G. M. (1961). *Ablepharus boutonii clarus*, a new skink from the Esperance District, Western Australia. *West. Aust. Nat.* 7: 176–178.

Storr, G. M. (1976). The genus *Cryptoblepharus* (Lacertilia: Scincidae) in Western Australia. *Rec. West. Aust. Mus.* 4: 53–63.

Ctenotus

Borner, A. R. (1981). A new subspecies of the *Ctenotus leonhardii* complex. *Misc. Articles in Saurology* 7: 1–10.

Czechura, G. V. (1986). Skinks of the *Ctenotus schevillii* species group. *Mem. Qd Mus.* 22 (2): 289–297.

Czechura, G. V. & Wombey, J. (1982). Three new striped skinks, (*Ctenotus*, Lacertilia, Scincidae) from Queensland. *Mem. Qd. Mus.* 20 (3): 639–645.

Ford, J. (1969). Distribution and variation of the skink *Ctenotus labillardieri* (Gray) of southwestern Australia. *J. Proc. R. Soc. West. Aust.* 51: 68–75.

Horner, P. and King, M. (1985). A new species of *Ctenotus* (Scincidae: Reptilia) from the Northern Territory. *The Beagle. Occ. Pap. of the NT Mus. of Arts and Sciences.* 2 (1): 143–148.

Ingram, G. J. (1979). Two new species of skinks, genus *Ctenotus* (Reptilia: Lacertilia: Scincidae), from Cape York Peninsula, Queensland, Australia. *J. Herpet* 13: 279–282.

Pianka, E. R. (1969). Sympatry of desert lizards (*Ctenotus*) in Western Australia. *Ecology* 50: 1012–1030.

Rankin, P. R. (1978). A new species of lizard (Lacertilia: Scincidae) from the Northern Territory, closely allied to *Ctenotus*

decaneurus Storr. *Rec. Aust. Mus.* 31: 395–407.

Rankin, P. R. & Gillam, M. W. (1979). A new lizard in the genus *Ctenotus* (Lacertilia: Scincidae) from the Northern Territory with notes on its biology. *Rec. Aust. Mus.* 32: 501–511.

Sadlier, R. (1985). A new Australian scincid lizard, *Ctenotus coggeri*, from the Alligator Rivers Region, Northern Territory. *Rec. Aust. Mus.* 36: 153–156.

Sadlier, R., Wombey, J. C. and Braithwaite, R. W. (1985). *Ctenotus kurnbudj* and *Ctenotus gagudju*, two new lizards (Scincidae) from the Alligator Rivers Region of the Northern Territory. *The Beagle. Occ. Pap. of the NT Mus. of Arts and Sciences.* 2 (1): 95–103.

Storr, G. M. (1964). *Ctenotus*, a new generic name for a group of Australian skinks. *West. Aust. Nat.* 9: 84–85.

Storr, G. M. (1969). The genus *Ctenotus* (Lacertilia: Scincidae) in the Eastern Division of Western Australia. *J. R. Soc. West. Aust.* 51: 97–109.

Storr, G. M. (1970). The genus *Ctenotus* (Lacertilia: Scincidae) in the Northern Territory. *J. R. Soc. West. Aust.* 52: 97–108.

Storr, G. M. (1971). The genus *Ctenotus* (Lacertilia: Scincidae) in South Australia. *Rec. S. Aust. Mus.* 16: 1–15.

Storr, G. M. (1974). The genus *Ctenotus* (Lacertilia: Scincidae) in the South-west and Eucla Divisions of Western Australia. *J. R. Soc. West. Aust.* 56: 86–93.

Storr, G. M. (1975). The genus *Ctenotus* (Lacertilia: Scincidae) in the Kimberley and North-west Divisions of Western Australia. *Rec. West. Aust. Mus.* 3: 209–243.

Storr, G. M. (1978). *Ctenotus rubicundus*, a new scincid lizard from Western Australia. *Rec. West. Aust. Mus.* 6: 333–335.

Storr, G. M. (1978). Notes on the *Ctenotus* (Lacertilia: Scincidae) of Queensland. *Rec. West. Aust. Mus.* 6: 319–332.

Storr, G. M. (1979). Five new lizards from Western Australia. *Rec. West. Aust. Mus.* 8: 134–142.

Storr, G. M. (1979). *Ctenotus greeri*, a new scincid lizard from Western Australia. *Rec. West. Aust. Mus.* 8: 143–146.

Storr, G. M. (1980). The *Ctenotus grandis* species-group (Lacertilia: Scincidae). *Rec. West. Aust. Mus.* 8: 415–422.

Storr, G. M. (1980). A new *Lerista* and two new *Ctenotus* (Lacertilia: Scincidae) from Western Australia. *Rec. West. Aust. Mus.* 8: 441–447.

Storr, G. M. (1981). Ten new *Ctenotus* (Lacertilia: Scincidae) from Australia. *Rec. West. Aust. Mus.* 9: 125–146.

Storr, G. M. (1984). A new *Ctenotus* (Lacertilia: Scincidae) from Western Australia. *Rec. West. Aust. Mus.* 11 (2): 191–193.

Cyclodomorphus

Field, R. (1980). The pink-tongued skink (*Tiliqua gerrardii*) in captivity. *Herpetofauna* 11: 6–10.

Rankin, P. R. (1973). Lizard mimicking a snake—juvenile *Tiliqua casuarinae*. *Herpetofauna* 5: 13–14.

Shea, G. M. (Ed.) (1982). Observations on some members of the genus *Tiliqua*. *Herpetofauna* 13: 18–20.

Stephenson, G. (1977). Notes on *Tiliqua gerrardii* in captivity. *Herpetofauna* 9 (1): 4–5.

Storr, G. M. (1976). The genus *Omolepida* (Lacertilia: Scincidae) in Western Australia. *Rec. West. Aust. Mus.* 4: 163–170.

Egernia

Bustard, H. R. (1970). A population study of the scincid lizard *Egernia striolata* in northern New South Wales. *Proc. K. Ned. Akad. Wet.* 73C: 186–213.

Cogger, H. G. (1960). The ecology, morphology, distribution and speciation of a new species and subspecies of the genus *Egernia* (Lacertilia: Scincidae). *Rec. Aust. Mus.* 25: 95–105.

Day, K. (1980). Notes on the birth of the pygmy spiny tailed skink, *Egernia depressa* (Günther) in captivity. *Herpetofauna* 11: 29.

Ford, J. (1963). The distribution and variation of the skinks *Egernia pulchra* and *E. bos* in Western Australia. *West. Aust. Nat.* 9: 25–29.

Ford, J. (1965). The skink *Egernia pulchra* in the Stirling Range. *West. Aust. Nat.* 9: 175–176.

Glauert, L. (1956). A new skink from West Kimberley. *Egernia striolata douglasi ssp. nov. West. Aust. Nat.* 5: 117–119.

Hickman, J. L. (1960). Observations on the skink lizard *Egernia whitii* (Lacépède). *Pap. Proc. R. Soc. Tasm.* 94: 111–118.

Mitchell, F. J. (1950). The scincid genera *Egernia* and *Tiliqua* (Lacertilia). *Rec. S. Aust. Mus.* 9: 275–308.

Pianka, E. R. & Giles, W. F. (1982). Notes on the biology of two species of nocturnal skinks, *Egernia inornata* and *Egernia striata*, in the Great Victoria Desert. *West. Aust. Nat.* 15: 8–13.

Storr, G. M. (1960). *Egernia bos*, a new skink from the south coast of Western Australia. *West. Aust. Nat.* 7: 99–103.

Storr, G. M. (1968). Revision of the *Egernia whitei* species-group (Lacertilia: Scincidae). *J. R. Soc. West. Aust.* 51: 51–62.

Storr, G. M. (1978). The genus *Egernia* (Lacertilia: Scincidae) in Western Australia. *Rec. West. Aust. Mus.* 6: 147–187.

Swanson, S. (1979). Some rock-dwelling reptiles of the Arnhem Land escarpment. *N. Territory Nat.* 1 (2): 14–18.

Wells, R. (1972). On the occurrence of the skink *Egernia saxatilis intermedia* Cogger in the Blue Mountains west of Sydney, NSW with additional notes on its behaviour in captivity. *Herpetofauna* 5: 2–4.

Webber, P. (1979). Burrow density, position and relationship of burrows to vegetation coverage shown by Rosén's desert skink *Egernia inornata* (Lacertilia: Scincidae). *Herpetofauna* 10: 16–20.

Emoia

Alcala, A. C. & Brown, W. A. (1967). Population ecology of the tropical scincoid lizard, *Emoia atrocostata*, in the Philippines. *Copeia* 1967: 596–604.

Brown, W. C. (1954). Notes on several lizards of the genus *Emoia*, with descriptions of new species from the Solomon Islands. *Fieldiana Zool.* 34: 263–276.

Ingram, G. J. (1979). The occurrence of lizards of the genus *Emoia* (Lacertilia: Scincidae) in Australia. *Mem. Qd. Mus.* 19: 431–437.

Eremiascincus

Greer, A. E. (1979). *Eremiascincus*, a new generic name for some Australian sand-swimming skinks (Lacertilia: Scincidae). *Rec. Aust. Mus.* 32: 321–338.

Storr, G. M. (1967). The genus *Sphenomorphus* (Lacertilia: Scincidae) in Western Australia and the Northern Territory. *J. R. Soc. West. Aust.* 50: 10–20.

Storr, G. M. (1974). Revision of the *Sphenomorphus richardsonii* species-group (Lacertilia: Scincidae). *Rec. West. Aust. Mus.* 3: 66–70.

Hemiergis

Copland, S. J. (1946). Geographic variation in the lizard *Hemiergis decresiensis* (Fitzinger). *Proc. Linn. Soc. N.S.W.* 70: 62–92.

Coventry, A. J. (1976). A new species of *Hemiergis* (Scincidae: Lygosominae) from Victoria. *Mem. Natl. Mus. Vict.* 37: 23–26.

Crome, B. (1981). The diet of some ground-layer lizards in three woodlands of the New England Tableland of Australia. *Herpetofauna* 13: 4–11.

Czechura, G. V. (1981). The rare scincid lizard, *Nannoscincus graciloides*: a reappraisal. *J. Herpet.* 15: 315–320.

Robertson, P. (1981). Comparative reproductive ecology of two south-eastern Australian skinks. Pp. 25–37 *in* Banks, C. B. & Martin, A. A. (Eds) *Proceedings of the Melbourne Herpetological Symposium*. Melbourne: Zoological Board of Victoria.

Smyth, M. (1968). The distribution and life history of the skink, *Hemiergis peronii* (Fitzinger). *Trans. R. Soc. S. Aust.* 92: 51–58.

Smyth, M. (1974). Changes in the fat stores of the skinks *Morethia boulengeri* and *Hemiergis peronii* (Lacertilia). *Aust. J. Zool.* 22: 135–145.

Smyth, M. & Smith, M. J. (1968). Obligatory sperm storage in the skink *Hemiergis peronii*. *Science* 161: 575–576.

Storr, G. M. (1975). The genus *Hemiergis* (Lacertilia: Scincidae) in Western Australia. *Rec. West. Aust. Mus.* 3: 251–260.

Lampropholis

Clarke, C. J. (1965). A comparison between some Australian five-fingered lizards of the genus *Leiolopisma* Duméril and Bibron (Lacertilia: Scincidae). *Aust. J. Zool.* 13: 577–592.

Crome, B. (1981). The diet of some ground-layer lizards in three woodlands of the New England Tablelands of Australia. *Herpetofauna* 13: 4–11.

Greer, A. E. & Kluge, A. G. (1980). A new species of *Lampropholis* (Lacertilia: Scincidae) from the rainforests of northeastern Queensland. *Occ. Pap. Mus. Zool. Univ. Mich.* 691: 1–12.

Humphreys, W. F. (1976). Spider induced egg mortality in a skink population. *Copeia* 1976: 404.

Ingram, G. J. & Rawlinson, P. (1981). Five new species of skinks (genus *Lampropholis*) from Queensland and New South Wales. *Mem. Qd. Mus.* 20: 311–317.

Milton, D. (1980). Some aspects of the population dynamics of *Lampropholis guichenoti* in Toohey Forest near Brisbane. *Herpetofauna* 11: 19–23.

Powell, H., Heatwole, H. & Heatwole, M. (1979). Winter aggregation of *Leiolopisma guichenoti*. *Br. J. Herpet.* 5: 789–791.

Wells, R. W. (1979). A large aggregation of skink eggs. *Herpetofauna* 11: 19–20.

Wells, R. W. (1981). Utilisation of the same site for communal egg-laying by *Lampropholis delicata* and *L. guichenoti*. *Aust. J. Herp.* 1: 35–36.

Leiolopisma

Covacevich, J. (1984). A biogeographically significant new species of *Leiolopisma* (Scincidae) from north eastern Queensland. *Mem. Qd. Mus.* 21 (2): 404–411.

Greer, A. E. (1974). The generic relationships of the scincid lizard genus *Leiolopisma* and its relatives. *Aust. J. Zool. Suppl. Ser.* 31: 1–67.

Greer, A. E. (1982). A new species of *Leiolopisma* (Lacertilia: Scincidae) from Western Australia, with notes on the biology and relationships of other Australian species. *Rec. Aust. Mus.* 34 (12): 549–573.

Ingram, G. J. & Ehmann, H. (1981). A new species of scincid lizard of the genus *Leiolopisma* (Scincidae: Lygosominae) from south eastern Queensland and north eastern New South Wales. *Mem. Qd. Mus.* 20: 307–310.

Rawlinson, P. A. (1974). Revision of the endemic southeastern Australian lizard genus *Pseudemoia* (Scincidae: Lygosominae). *Mem. Natl. Mus. Vict.* 35: 87–96.

Rawlinson, P. A. (1975). Two new lizard species from the genus *Leiolopisma* (Scincidae: Lygosominae) in southeastern Australia and Tasmania. *Mem. Natl. Mus. Vict.* 36: 1–16.

Lerista

Greer, A. E. (1967). A new generic arrangement for some Australian scincid lizards. *Breviora* 267: 1–19.

Greer, A. E. (1979). A new species of *Lerista* (Lacertilia: Scincidae) from northern Queensland, with remarks on the origin of the genus. *Rec. Aust. Mus.* 32: 383–388.

Greer, A. E. (1983). A new species of *Lerista* from Groote Eylandt and the Sir Edward Pellew Group in northern Australia. *J. Herp.* 17 (1): 48–53.

Greer, A. E. (1986). Diagnosis of the *Lerista bipes* species-group (Lacertilia: Scincidae), with a description of a new species and an updated diagnosis of the genus. *Rec. West. Aust. Mus.* 13 (1): 121–127.

Greer, A. E., McDonald, J. R. & Lawrie, B. C. (1983). Three new species of *Lerista* (Scincidae) from northern Queensland with a diagnosis of the *wilkinsi* species group. *J. Herp.* 17 (3): 247–55.

Smyth, M. and Smith, M. J. (1974). Aspects of the natural history of three Australian skinks, *Morethia boulengeri*, *Menetia greyii* and *Lerista bougainvillii*. *J. Herpet.* 8: 329–336.

Storr, G. M. (1971). The genus *Lerista* (Lacertilia: Scincidae) in Western Australia. *J. R. Soc. West. Aust.* 54: 59–75.

Storr, G. M. (1976). Revisionary notes on the genus *Lerista* (Lacertilia: Scincidae) of Western Australia. *Rec. West. Aust. Mus.* 4: 241–256.

Storr, G. M. (1978). Taxonomic notes on the reptiles of the Shark Bay region, Western Australia. *Rec. West. Aust. Mus.* 6: 303–318.

Storr, G. M. (1979). Five new lizards from Western Australia.

Rec. West. Aust. Mus. 8: 134–142.

Storr, G. M. (1980). A new *Lerista* and two new *Ctenotus* (Lacertilia: Scincidae) from Western Australia. *Rec. West. Aust. Mus.* 8: 441–447.

Storr, G. M. (1982). Four new *Lerista* (Lacertilia: Scincidae) from Western and South Australia. *Rec. West. Aust. Mus.* 10 (1): 1–9.

Storr, G. M. (1983). Two new lizards from Western Australia (genera *Diplodactylus* and *Lerista*). *Rec. West. Aust. Mus.* 11 (1): 59–62.

Storr, G. M. (1984). Revision of the *Lerista nichollsi* complex (Lacertilia: Scincidae). *Rec. West. Aust. Mus.* 11 (2): 109–118.

Storr, G. M. (1984). A new *Lerista* (Lacertilia: Scincidae) from Western Australia. *Rec. West. Aust. Mus.* 11 (3): 287–290.

Storr, G. M. (1985). Revision of *Lerista frosti* and allied species (Lacertilia: Scincidae). *Rec. West. Aust. Mus.* 12 (3): 307–316.

Storr, G. M. (1986). A new species of *Lerista* (Lacertilia: Scincidae) with two subspecies from central Australia. *Rec. West. Aust. Mus.* 13 (1): 145–149.

Storr, G. M. (1986). Two new members of the *Lerista nichollsi* complex (Lacertilia: Scincidae). *Rec. West. Aust. Mus.* 13 (1): 47–52.

Menetia

Bush, B. (1983). Notes on reproduction in captive *Menetia greyii* (Lacertilia: Scincidae). *West. Aust. Nat.* 15 (6): 130–131.

Ingram, G. J. (1977). Three species of small lizards—two of them new. *Vict. Nat.* 94: 184–187.

Rankin, P. R. (1979). A taxonomic revision of the genus *Menetia* (Lacertilia: Scincidae) in the Northern Territory. *Rec. Aust. Mus.* 32: 491–499.

Sadlier, R. A. (1984). A new Australian scincid lizard, *Menetia concinna*, from the Alligator Rivers Region, Northern Territory. *Rec. Aust. Mus.* 36 (2) 45–49.

Smyth, M. & Smith, M. J. (1974). Aspects of the natural history of three Australian skinks, *Morethia boulengeri, Menetia greyii* and *Lerista bougainvillii*. *J. Herpet.* 8: 329–336.

Storr, G. M. (1976). The genus *Menetia* (Lacertilia: Scincidae) in Western Australia. *Rec. West. Aust. Mus.* 4: 189–200.

Storr, G. M. (1978). Taxonomic notes on the reptiles of the Shark Bay region, Western Australia. *Rec. West. Aust. Mus.* 6: 303–318.

Wells, R. W. (1979). New reptile records for the Northern Territory. *N. Territory Nat.* 1 (2): 3–4.

Morethia

Greer, A. E. (1980). A new species of *Morethia* (Lacertilia: Scincidae) from northern Australia, with comments on the biology and relationships of the genus. *Rec. Aust. Mus.* 33: 89–122.

Rawlinson, P. A. (1976). The endemic Australian lizard genus *Morethia* (Scincidae: Lygosominae) in southern Australia. *Mem. Natl. Mus. Vict.* 37: 27–41.

Smyth, M. (1972). The genus *Morethia* (Lacertilia: Scincidae) in South Australia. *Rec. S. Aust. Mus.* 16: 1–14.

Smyth, M. & Smith, M. J. (1974). Aspects of the natural history of three Australian skinks, *Morethia boulengeri, Menetia greyii* and *Lerista bougainvillii*. *J. Herpet.* 8: 329–336.

Storr, G. M. (1963). *Ablepharus butleri*. A new scincid lizard from Australia. *West. Aust. Nat.* 9: 46–47.

Storr, G. M. (1972). The genus *Morethia* (Lacertilia: Scincidae) in Western Australia. *J. R. Soc. West. Aust.* 55: 73–79.

Notoscincus

Storr, G. M. (1974). The genus *Notoscincus* (Lacertilia: Scincidae) in Western Australia and Northern Territory. *Rec. West. Aust. Mus.* 3: 111–114.

Storr, G. M. (1979). Five new lizards from Western Australia. *Rec. West. Aust. Mus.* 8: 134–142.

Wells, R. W. (1979). New reptile records for the Northern Territory. *N. Territory Nat.* 1 (2): 3–4.

Ophioscincus

Copland, S. J. (1952). A mainland race of the scincid lizard *Lygosoma truncatum* (Peters). *Proc. Linn. Soc. N.S.W.* 77: 126–131.

Proablepharus

Bradshaw, B. J. (1976). Discovery of *Proablepharus reginae,* a small member of Scincidae at Ormiston Gorge and Pound Scenic Reserve, NT. *Ranger Review.* 11.

Storr, G. M. (1975). The genus *Proablepharus* (Scincidae: Lacertilia) in Western Australia. *Rec. West. Aust. Mus.* 3: 335–338.

Wells, R. (1979). New reptile records for the Northern Territory. *N. Territory Nat.* 1 (2): 3–4.

Saiphos

Bustard, H. R. (1964). Reproduction in the Australian rain forest skinks, *Saiphos equalis* and *Sphenomorphus tryoni*. *Copeia* 1964: 715–716.

Sphenomorphus

Bustard, H. R. (1964). Reproduction in the Australian rain forest skinks, *Saiphos equalis* and *Sphenomorphus tryoni*. *Copeia* 1964: 715–716.

Covacevich, J. & McDonald, K. R. (1980). Two new species of skinks from mid-eastern Queensland rainforest. *Mem. Qd. Mus.* 20: 95–101.

De Lissa, G. (1981). Notes on the skink *Sphenomorphus tenuis*. *Herpetofauna* 13: 33.

Done, B. S. & Heatwole, H. (1977). Social behaviour of some Australian skinks. *Copeia* 1977: 419–430.

Greer, A. E. (1979). A new *Sphenomorphus* (Lacertilia: Scincidae) from the rainforests of northeastern Queensland. *Rec. Aust. Mus.* 32: 373–383.

Greer, A. E. (1985). A new species of *Sphenomorphus* from northeastern Queensland. *J. Herp.* 19 (4): 469–473.

Greer, A. E. & Parker, F. (1974). The *fasciatus* species group of *Sphenomorphus* (Lacertilia: Scincidae): notes on eight previously described species and descriptions of three new species. *Papua New Guinea Sci. Soc. Proc.* 25: 31–61.

Rankin, P. R. (1973). The barred sided skink *Sphenomorphus tenuis tenuis* (Gray) in the Sydney region. *Herpetofauna* 6: 8–14.

Rankin, P. R. (1978). Notes on the biology of the skink *Sphenomorphus pardalis* (Macleay) including a captive breeding record. *Herpetofauna* 10: 4–7.

Shea, G. M. & Peterson, M. (Manuscript in press). The Blue Mountains Water Skink, *Sphenomorphus leuraensis* (Lacertilia: Scincidae): A redescription, with notes on its natural history.

Spellerberg, I. F. (1972). Thermal ecology of allopatric lizards (*Sphenomorphus*) in southeast Australia. I. The environment and lizard critical temperatures. *Oecologia* 9: 371–383.

Storr, G. M. (1967). The genus *Sphenomorphus* (Lacertilia: Scincidae) in Western Australia and the Northern Territory. *J. R. Soc. West. Aust.* 50: 10–20.

Storr, G. M. (1972). Revisionary notes on the *Sphenomorphus isolepis* complex (Lacertilia: Scincidae). *Zool. Meded.* 47: 1–5.

Tiliqua

Bull, C. M. & Satrawaha, R. (1981). Dispersal and social organisation in *Trachydosaurus rugosus*. P. 24 in Banks, C. B. & Martin, A. A. (Eds). *Proceedings of the Melbourne Herpetological Symposium*. Zoological Board of Victoria, Melbourne.

Christian, T. (1977). Notes on centralian bluetongues (*Tiliqua multifasciata*). *Vict. Herp. Soc. Newsletter* 1: 8–9.

Ehmann, H. (1982). The natural history and conservation status of the Adelaide pygmy bluetongue lizard *Tiliqua adelaidensis*. *Herpetofauna* 14 (1): 61–76.

Mitchell, F. J. (1950). The scincid genera *Egernia* and *Tiliqua* (Lacertilia). *Rec. S. Aust. Mus.* 9: 275–308.

Satrawaha, R. & Bull, C. M. (1981). The area occupied by an omnivorous lizard *Trachydosaurus rugosus*. *Aust. Wildl. Res.* 8: 435–442.

Shea, G. (1981). Notes on the reproductive biology of the eastern blue-tongue skink, *Tiliqua scincoides* (Shaw). *Herpetofauna* 12: 16–23.

Shea, G. (Ed.) (1982). Observations on some members of the genus *Tiliqua*. *Herpetofauna* 13: 18–20.

Shea, G. & Peterson, M. (1981). Observations on sympatry of the social lizards *Tiliqua multifasciata* Sternfeld and *T. occipitalis* (Peters). *Aust. J. Herp.* 1: 27–28.

Tropidophorus

Naylor, L. M. (1980). The maintenance of a group of prickly forest skinks (*Tropidophorus queenslandiae* deVis), in captivity. *Thylacinus, J. Aust. Soc. Zookeepers* 5: 5–6.

Family Varanidae (Goannas or Monitor Lizards)

Genus and Species

Varanus

Bartlett, R. D. (1982). Initial observations on the captive reproduction of *Varanus storri*, Mertens. *Herpetofauna* 13 (2): 6–7.

Christian, T. (1979). Notes on Spencer's monitor (*Varanus spenceri*). *Vict. Herp. Soc. Newsletter* 14: 13–14.

Christian, T. (1981). *Varanus tristis*—a variable monitor. *Herpetofauna* 12: 7–12.

Czechura, G. V. (1980). The emerald monitor *Varanus prasinus* (Schlegel): an addition to the Australian mainland herpetofauna. *Mem. Qd. Mus.* 20: 103–109.

Dunson, W. A. (1974). Salt gland secretion in a mangrove monitor lizard. *Comp. Biochem. Physiol.* 47A: 1245–1255.

Fyfe, G. (1979). Notes on the black-headed monitor (*Varanus tristis*). *Vict. Herp. Soc. Newsletter* 13: 17–18.

Gillam, M. W., Cawood, I. S. and Honner, G. J. (1978). New reptile records from Central Australia, Northern Territory. *Herpetofauna* 9 (2): 18–25.

Gow, G. F. (1982). Notes on the reproductive biology of the Pygmy Mulga Goanna *Varanus gilleni* Lucas & Frost, 1895. *N. Territory Nat.* 5: 4–5.

Green, B. (1972). Water loss in the sand goanna (*Varanus gouldii*) in its natural environment. *Ecology* 53: 452–457.

Green, B. & King, D. (1978). Home range and activity patterns of the sand goanna, *Varanus gouldii* (Reptilia: Varanidae). *Aust. Wildl. Res.* 5: 417–424.

Hermes, N. (1981). Mertens water monitor feeding on trapped fish. *Herpetofauna* 13: 34.

Houston, T. F. (1978). *Dragon lizards and goannas of South Australia*. South Australian Museum, Adelaide.

Husband, G. A. (1979). Notes on a nest and hatchlings of *Varanus acanthurus*. *Herpetofauna* 11: 29–30.

Johnson, C. R. (1976). Some behavioural observations on wild and captive sand monitors, *Varanus gouldii* (Sauria: Varanidae). *Zool. J. Linn. Soc.* 59: 377–380.

King, D. (1980). The thermal biology of free-living sand goannas (*Varanus gouldii*) in southern Australia. *Copeia* 1980: 755–767.

King, D. & Green, B. (1979). Notes on the diet and reproduction of the sand goanna, *Varanus gouldii rosenbergi*. *Copeia* 1979: 64–70.

Mitchell, M. & Mitchell, L. A. (1976). A further analysis of the combat ritual of the pygmy mulga monitor, *Varanus gilleni* (Reptilia: Varanidae). *Herpetologica* 32: 35–40.

Murphy, J. B. & Lamoreaux, W. E. (1978). Threatening behaviour in Merten's water monitor *Varanus mertensi* (Sauria: Varanidae). *Herpetologica* 34: 202–205.

Murphy, J. B. & Mitchell, L. A. (1974). Ritualised combat behaviour of the pygmy mulga monitor lizard, *Varanus gilleni* (Sauria: Varanidae). *Herpetologica* 30: 90–97.

Pengilley, R. (1981). Notes on the biology of *Varanus spenceri* and *V. gouldii*, Barkly Tablelands, Northern Territory. *Aust. J. Herp.* 1: 23–26.

Peters, U. (1973). A contribution to the ecology of *Varanus* (*Odatria*) *storri*. *Koolewong* 2: 12–13.

Pianka, E. R. (1968). Notes on the biology of *Varanus eremius*. *West. Aust. Nat.* 11: 39–44.

Pianka, E. R. (1969). Notes on the biology of *Varanus caudolineatus* and *Varanus gilleni*. *West. Aust. Nat.* 11: 76–82.

Pianka, E. R. (1970). Notes on *Varanus brevicauda*. *West. Aust. Nat.* 11: 113–116.

Pianka, E. R. (1970). Notes on the biology of *Varanus gouldi flavirufus*. *West. Aust. Nat.* 11: 141–144.

Pianka, E. R. (1971). Notes on the biology of *Varanus tristis*. *West. Aust. Nat.* 11: 180–182.

Pianka, E. R. (1982). Observations on the ecology of *Varanus* in the Great Victoria Desert. *West. Aust. Nat.* 15: 1–8.

Storr, G. M. (1966). Rediscovery and taxonomic status of the Australian lizard, *Varanus primordius*. *Copeia* 1966: 583–584.

Storr, G. M. (1980). The monitor lizards (genus *Varanus* Merrem, 1820) of Western Australia. *Rec. West. Aust. Mus.* 8: 237–293.

Swanson, S. (1979). Some rock-dwelling reptiles of the Arnhem Land escarpment. *N. Territory Nat.* 1: 14–18.

SNAKES

General Works on Snakes

Covacevich, J. (1968). *The Snakes of Brisbane*. Queensland Museum, Brisbane.

Covacevich, J. (1974). An unusual aggregation of snakes following major flooding in the Ipswich–Brisbane area, south-eastern Queensland. *Herpetofauna* 7 (1): 21–24.

Glauert, L. (1960). *A Handbook of Snakes of Western Australia*. 2nd edn, Western Australian Naturalists' Club, Perth.

Gow, G. F. (1976). *Snakes of Australia*. Angus & Robertson, Sydney.

Hoser, R. T. (1980). Further records of aggregations of various species of Australian snakes. *Herpetofauna* 12: 16–22.

Parker, H. W. & Grandison, A. G. C. (1977). *Snakes: a natural history*. 2nd edn, University of Queensland Press, St Lucia.

Storr, G. M., Smith, L. A. and Johnstone, R. E. (1986). *Snakes of Western Australia*. Western Australian Museum, Perth.

Family Acrochordidae (File Snakes)

Genus and Species

Acrochordus

Magnusson, W. A. (1979). Production of an embryo by an *Acrochordus javanicus* isolated for seven years. *Copeia* 1979: 744–745.

McDowell, S. B. (1979). A catalogue of the snakes of New Guinea and the Solomons, with special reference to those in the Bernice P. Bishop Museum. Part III. Boinae and Acrochordoidea (Reptilia: Serpentes). *J. Herpet.* 13: 1–92.

Family Boidae (Pythons)

Genera and Species

Aspidites

Fyfe, G. & Harvey, C. (1981). Some observations on the woma (*Aspidites ramsayi*) in captivity. *Herpetofauna* 18: 23–25.

Smith, L. A. (1981). A revision of the python genera *Aspidites* and *Python* (Serpentes: Boidae) in Western Australia. *Rec. West. Aust. Mus.* 9: 211–226.

Bothrochilus

Banks, C. & Schwaner, T. D. (1984). Two cases of interspecific hybridisation among captive Australian boid snakes. *Zoo. Biol.* 3: 221–227.

Delean, S. & Harvey, C. (1982). Unusual defensive behaviour in the Children's Python (*Liasis childreni*) Gray, 1842. *Herpetofauna* 13 (2): 26.

Sheargold, T. (1979). Notes on the reproduction of Children's pythons (*Liasis childreni* Gray, 1842). *Herpetofauna* 10: 2–4.

Smith, L. A. (1981). A revision of the *Liasis olivaceus* species-group (Serpentes: Boidae) in Western Australia. *Rec. West. Aust. Mus.* 9: 227–233.

Smith, L. A. (1985). A revision of the *Liasis childreni* species-group (Serpentes: Boidae). *Rec. West. Aust. Mus.* 12 (3): 257–276.

Chondropython

Murphy, J. B., Carpenter, C. C. & Gillingham, J. C. (1978). Caudal luring in the green tree python, *Chondropython viridis* (Reptilia, Serpentes, Boidae). *J. Herpet.* 12: 117–119.

Morelia

Banks, C. & Schwaner, T. D. (1984). Two cases of interspecific hybridisation among captive Australian boid snakes. *Zoo. Biol.* 3: 221–227.

Covacevich, J. (1975). Snakes in combat. *Vict. Nat.* 92: 252–253.

Gow, G. F. (1977). A new species of *Python* from Arnhem Land. *Aust. Zool.* 19: 133–139.

Gow, G. F. (1981). A new species of *Python* from central Australia. *Aust. J. Herp.* 1: 29–34.

Smith, L. A. (1981). A revision of the python genera *Aspidites* and *Python* (Serpentes: Boidae) in Western Australia. *Rec. West. Aust. Mus.* 9: 211–226.

Swanson, S. (1979). Some rock-dwelling reptiles of the Arnhem Land escarpment. *N. Territory Nat.* 1: 14–18.

Webber, P. (1978). A note on an aggregation of diamond pythons *Morelia s. spilotes* in the Grose Valley New South Wales. *Herpetofauna* 10 (1): 25–26.

Family Colubridae (Solid-toothed and Rear-fanged Snakes)

General

Ko Ko Gyi. (1970). A revision of colubrid snakes of the subfamily Homalopsinae. *Univ. Kans. Publs. Mus. Nat. Hist.* 20: 44–223.

Genera and Species

Cerberus

Gorman, G. C., Licht, P. & McCollum, F. (1981). Annual reproductive patterns in three species of marine snakes from the Central Philippines. *J. Herpet.* 15: 335–354.

Dendrelaphis

Swan, G. (1975). Notes on the incubation and hatching of eggs of the green tree snake (*Dendrelaphis punctulatus*). *Herpetofauna* 7: 18–20.

Enhydris

Griffiths, K. (1981). Macleay's water snake *Enhydris polylepis*. *Herpetofauna* 12: 31–32.

Stegonotus

McDowell, S. B. (1972). The species of *Stegonotus* (Serpentes: Colubridae) in Papua New Guinea. *Zool. Meded.* 47: 6–26.

Styporhynchus

Lyon, B. (1973). Observations on the common keelback snake, *Natrix mairii*, in Brisbane, south-eastern Queensland. *Herpetofauna* 6: 2–5.

Family Elapidae (Front-Fanged Land Snakes)

General

Covacevich, J. (1983). Dangerous snakes in Queensland. *Qd. Mus. Information Sheet.*

Gow, G. F. (1982). *Australia's Dangerous Snakes.* Angus & Robertson, Sydney.

Lillywhite, H. B. (1980). Behavioural thermoregulation in Australian elapid snakes. *Copeia* 1980: 452–458.

Longmore, R. (1986) (Ed). Atlas of elapid snakes of Australia. *Aust. Flora and Fauna Series No. 7.*

Mengden, G. A. (1983). The taxonomy of Australian elapid snakes: A review. *Rec. Aust. Mus.* 35: 195–222.

Mirtschin, P. & Davis, R. (1982). *Dangerous Snakes of Australia; an illustrated guide to Australia's most venomous snakes.* Revised edn, Rigby, Adelaide.

Pearn, J. (Ed.) (1981). *Animal Toxins and Man.* The Division of Health Education and Information (State Health Department), Brisbane.

Shine, R. (1977). Reproduction in Australian elapid snakes.

I. Testicular cycles and mating seasons. *Aust. J. Zool.* 25: 647–653.

Shine, R. (1977). Reproduction in Australian elapid snakes. II. Female reproductive cycles. *Aust. J. Zool.* 25: 655–666.

Shine, R. (1977). Habitats, diets, and sympatry in snakes: a study from Australia. *Can. J. Zool.* 55: 1118–1128.

Shine, R. (1978). Growth rates and sexual maturation in six species of Australian elapid snakes. *Herpetologica* 34: 73–79.

Shine, R. (1979). Activity patterns in Australian elapid snakes (Squamata: Serpentes: Elapidae). *Herpetologica* 35: 1–11.

Storr, G. M. (1979). *Dangerous Snakes of Western Australia.* 3rd edn, Western Australian Museum Press, Perth.

Genera and Species

Acanthophis

Carpenter, C. C., Murphy, J. B. & Carpenter, G. C. (1978). Tail luring in the death adder, *Acanthophis antarcticus* (Reptilia: Serpentes: Elapidae). *J. Herpet.* 12: 574–577.

Gow, G. (1981). Notes on the desert death adder, (*Acanthophis pyrrhus* Boulenger, 1898), with the first reproductive record. *N. Territory Nat.* 4: 21–22.

Hudson, P. (1979). On the birth and breeding of death adders in captivity. *Herpetofauna* 11: 11–13.

Shine, R. (1980). Ecology of the Australian death adder *Acanthophis antarcticus* (Elapidae): evidence for convergence with the Viperidae. *Herpetologica* 36: 281–289.

Storr, G. M. (1981). The genus *Acanthophis* (Serpentes: Elapidae) in Western Australia. *Rec. West. Aust. Mus.* 9: 203–210.

Austrelaps

Phillips, S. (1980). A consideration of the genus *Austrelaps* (Squamata: Serpentes: Elapidae). (Unpublished B.Sc. (Hons.) thesis) University of New England.

Shine, R. & Allen, S. (1980). Ritual combat in the Australian copperhead, *Austrelaps superbus* (Serpentes: Elapidae). *Vict. Nat.* 97: 188–190.

Cacophis

Shine, R. (1980). Comparative ecology of three Australian snake species of the genus *Cacophis* (Serpentes: Elapidae). *Copeia* 1980: 831–838.

Wells, R. (1980). Notes on Krefft's dwarf snake (*Cacophis krefftii*). *Herpetofauna* 11: 18–19.

Wells, R. (1980). Notes on *Cacophis squamulosus*. *Herpetofauna* 11: 26.

Cryptophis

Bridge, G. (1979). The small-eyed snake (*Cryptophis nigrescens*). *Vict. Herp. Soc. Newsletter* 13: 17–18.

Pollitt, C. C. (1981). Studies on the venom and blood of the eastern small-eyed snake, *Cryptophis nigrescens* (Günther). Pp. 44–54 in Banks, C. B. & Martin, A. A. (Eds) *Proceedings of the Melbourne Herpetological Symposium, 1980.* Zoological Board of Victoria, Melbourne.

Smith, L. A. (1978). The elapid snakes *Denisonia pallidiceps* and *Denisonia suta* in the Kimberleys of Western Australia. *West. Aust. Nat.* 14: 75–76.

Demansia

Covacevich, J. & Limpus, C. (1972). Observations on community egg-laying by the yellow-faced whip snake, *Demansia psammophis* (Schlegel, 1837) (Squamata: Elapidae). *Herpetologica* 28: 208–210.

Maddocks, M. (1975). A study of the yellow-faced whip snake *Demansia psammophis* in the field and in captivity. *Herpetofauna* 7 (2): 12–15.

Shine, R. (1980). Ecology of eastern Australian whipsnakes of the genus *Demansia*. *J. Herpet.* 14: 381–389.

Storr, G. M. (1978). Whip snakes (*Demansia*: Elapidae) of Western Australia. *Rec. West. Aust. Mus.* 6: 287–301.

Denisonia

Coventry, A. J. (1971). Identification of the black-headed snakes (*Denisonia*) within Victoria. *Vict. Nat.* 88: 304–306.

Shine, R. (1983). Food habits and reproductive biology of Australian elapid snakes of the genus *Denisonia*. *J. Herpet.* 17 (2): 171–175.

Smith, L. A. (1980). Taxonomy of *Denisonia punctata* and *Denisonia fasciata* (Serpentes: Elapidae). *Rec. West. Aust. Mus.* 8: 327–333.

Storr, G. M. (1980). A new *Brachyaspis* (Serpentes: Elapidae) from Western Australia. *Rec. West. Aust. Mus.* 8: 397–399.

Storr, G. M. (1984). Revision of *Denisonia suta* (Serpentes: Elapidae) and the description of a new species closely related to it. *Rec. West. Aust. Mus.* 11 (3): 249–257.

Drysdalia

Coventry, A. J. & Rawlinson, P. A. (1980). Taxonomic revison of the elapid snake genus *Drysdalia* Worrell, 1961. *Mem. Natl. Mus. Vict.* 41: 65–78.

Fleay, D. (1952). The crowned or coronated snake. *Vict. Nat.* 68: 146–150.

Shine, R. (1981). Venomous snakes in cold climates: ecology of the Australian genus *Drysdalia* (Serpentes: Elapidae). *Copeia* 1981: 14–25.

Storr, G. M. (1982). The genus *Notechis* (Serpentes: Elapidae) in Western Australia. *Rec. West. Aust. Mus.* 9 (4): 325–340.

Echiopsis

Shine, R. (1982). Ecology of the Australian elapid snake *Echiopsis curta*. *J. Herpet.* 16 (4): 388–393.

Storr, G. M. (1982). The genus *Notechis* (Serpentes: Elapidae) in Western Australia. *Rec. West. Aust. Mus.* 9 (4): 325–340.

Elapognathus

Storr, G. M. (1982). The genus *Notechis* (Serpentes: Elapidae) in Western Australia. *Rec. West. Aust. Mus.* 9 (4): 325–340.

Furina

Shine, R. (1981). Ecology of Australian elapid snakes of the genera *Furina* and *Glyphodon*. *J. Herpet.* 15: 219–224.

Storr, G. M. (1981). The genus *Furina* (Serpentes: Elapidae) in Western Australia. *Rec. West. Aust. Mus.* 9: 119–123.

Worrell, E. (1945). The orange-naped whipsnake. *Proc. R. Zool. Soc. N.S.W.* 1944–45: 32–33

Glyphodon

Shine, R. (1981). Ecology of Australian elapid snakes of the genera *Furina* and *Glyphodon*. *J. Herpet.* 15: 219–224.

Hemiaspis

Ormsby, A. I. (1950). The marsh snake. *Proc. R. Zool. Soc. N.S.W.* 1948: 29–31.

Rankin, P. R. (1972). Notes on the swamp snake (*Drepanodontis signata*) in captivity. *Herpetofauna* 5: 15–17.

Shine, R. (1987). Food habits and reproductive biology of Australian snakes of the genus *Hemiaspis* (Elapidae). *J. Herp.* 21 (1): 71–74.

Hoplocephalus

Adams, D. (1973). Broad-headed snake (*Hoplocephalus bungaroides*). *Herpetofauna* 5: 19–22.

Anstis, M. (1973). Notes on *Hoplocephalus bungaroides* (broad-headed snake) in captivity. *R. Zool. Soc. N.S.W. Bull. Herpet.* 1: 5–7.

Hayes, D. (1973). Observations on distribution of the broad-headed snake *Hoplocephalus bungaroides* (Boie). *Herpetofauna* 6: 27–28.

Hosmer, W. (1952). The broadheaded snake *Hoplocephalus bungaroides* (Boie) also known as the fierce snake, and night snake. *N. Qd. Nat.* 20: 14–16.

Shine, R. (1983) (1). Arboreality in snakes: Ecology of the Australian elapid genus *Hoplocephalus*. *Copeia* 1983: 198–205.

Wells, R. (1981). Remarks on the prey preferences of *Hoplocephalus bungaroides*. *Herpetofauna* 12: 25–28.

Neelaps

Storr, G. M. (1968). The genus *Vermicella* (Serpentes: Elapidae) in Western Australia and the Northern Territory. *J. R. Soc. West. Aust.* 50: 80–92.

Notechis

Bush, B. (1983). Notes on reproductive behaviour in the tiger snake *Notechis scutatus*. *West. Aust. Nat.* 15 (5): 112–113.

Morrison, J. J., Pearn, J. H. & Coulter, A. R. (1982). The mass of venom injected by two elapidae: the taipan (*Oxyuranus scutellatus*) and the Australian tiger snake (*Notechis scutatus*). *Toxicon* 20 (4): 739–745.

Schwaner, T. D. (1984). The identity of red-bellied black snakes on Kangaroo Island. *Trans. R. Soc. S. Aust.* 108 (2): 137.

Storr, G. M. (1982). The genus *Notechis* (Serpentes: Elapidae) in Western Australia. *Rec. West. Aust. Mus.* 9 (4): 325–340.

Webb, G. A. (1981). A note on climbing ability in tiger snakes (*Notechis scutatus*) and predation on arboreal nesting birds. *Vict. Nat.* 98: 159–160.

Oxyuranus

Broad, A. J., Sutherland, S. K., Tanner, C. & Covacevich, J. (1979). Electrophoretic, enzyme and preliminary toxicity studies of the venom of the small-scaled snake, *Parademansia microlepidota* (Serpentes: Elapidae), with additional data on its distribution. *Mem. Qd. Mus.* 19: 319–329.

Covacevich, J., McDowell, S. B., Tanner, C. & Mengden, G. A. (1981). The relationship of the taipan, *Oxyuranus scutellatus*, and the small-scaled snake, *Oxyuranus microlepidotus* (Serpentes: Elapidae). Pp. 160–168 in Banks, C. B. & Martin, A. A. (Eds). *Proceedings of the Melbourne Herpetological Symposium, 1980.* Zoological Board of Victoria, Melbourne.

Covacevich, J. & Wombey, J. (1976). Recognition of *Parademansia microlepidota* (McCoy) (Elapidae), a dangerous Australian snake. *Proc. R. Soc. Qd.* 87: 29–32.

Gow, G. F. (1980). History of the taipan *Oxyuranus scutellatus*—with two new distribution records. *N. Territory Nat.* 1: 15–19.

Mirtschin, P. (1981). South Australian records of the inland taipan (*Oxyuranus microlepidotus* McCoy, 1879). *Herpetofauna* 13: 20–23.

Morrison, J. J., Pearn, J. H. & Coulter, A. R. (1982). The mass of venom injected by two elapidae: the taipan (*Oxyuranus scutellatus*) and the Australian tiger snake (*Notechis scutatus*). *Toxicon* 20 (4): 739–745.

Shine, R. & Covacevich, J. (1983). Ecology of highly venomous snakes: The Australian genus *Oxyuranus* (Elapidae). *J. Herpet.* 17 (1): 60–69.

Pseudechis

Charles, N. (Unpublished manuscript.) Further notes on the captive breeding of the Collett's snake (*Pseudechis colletti*).

Charles, N., Watts, A. & Shine, R. (1983). Captive reproduction in an Australian elapid snake, *Pseudechis colletti*. *Herp. Review* (1): 16–18.

Charles, N., Whitaker, P. & Shine, R. (1980). Oviparity and captive breeding in the spotted black snake, *Pseudechis guttatus* (Serpentes: Elapidae) *Aust. Zool.* 20: 361–364.

Fitzgerald, M. and Mengden, G. A. (1987). Captive breeding in *Pseudechis butleri*. (Serpentes: Elapidae). *Amphibia-Reptilia* 8: 165–170.

Fitzgerald, M. & Pollitt, C. (1981). Oviparity and captive breeding in the mulga or king brown snake *Pseudechis australis* (Serpentes: Elapidae). *Aust. J. Herp.* 1: 57–60.

Mackay, R. D. (1955). A revision of the genus *Pseudechis*. *Proc. R. Zool. Soc. N.S.W.* 1953–54: 15–23.

Rankin, P. R. (1976). Mating of wild red bellied black snakes *Pseudechis porphyriacus*. Shaw. *Herpetofauna* 8 (1): 10–15.

Shine, R., Grigg, G. C., Shine, T. G. & Harlow, P. (1981). Mating and male combat in Australian blacksnakes, *Pseudechis porphyriacus*. *J. Herpet.* 15: 101–107.

Smith, L. A. (1982). Variation in *Pseudechis australis* (Serpentes: Elapidae) in Western Australia and description of a new species of *Pseudechis*. *Rec. West. Aust. Mus.* 10 (1): 35–45.

Pseudonaja

Banks, C. (1981). Notes on seasonal colour changes in a western brown snake. *Herpetofauna* 13: 29–30.

Gillam, M. W. (1979). The genus *Pseudonaja* (Serpentes: Elapidae) in the Northern Territory. *Territory Parks Wildl. Commn. Res. Bull.* 1: 1–28.

Miller, B. & Schwaner, T. D. (1983). The speckled brown snake *Pseudonaja guttata* Parker: An addition to the fauna of South Australia. *Trans. R. Soc. S. Aust.* 106 (2): 79–80.

Wells, R. (1980). Eggs and young of *Pseudonaja textilis textilis*.

Herpetofauna 12: 30–32.

Rhinoplocephalus

Christensen, P. (1972). New record of Mueller's snake, *Rhinoplocephalus bicolor*. *West. Aust. Nat.* 12 (4): 88–89.

Coventry, A. J. (1971). Identification of the black-headed snakes (*Denisonia*) within Victoria. *Vict. Nat.* 88: 304–306.

Fyfe, G. (1980). Breeding of the little whipsnakes (*Unechis flagellum*). *Vict. Herp. Soc. Newsletter* 20: 2.

Smith, L. A. (1980). Taxonomy of *Denisonia punctata* and *Denisonia fasciata* (Serpentes: Elapidae). *Rec. West. Aust. Mus.* 8: 327–333.

Storr, G. M. (1964). *Denisonia monachus*, a new elapid snake from Western Australia. *West. Aust. Nat.* 9: 89–90.

Storr, G. M. (1981). The *Denisonia gouldii* species-group (Serpentes: Elapidae) in Western Australia. *Rec. West. Aust. Mus.* 8: 501–515.

Simoselaps

Glauert, L. (1954). Herpetological miscellanea. III. A new burrowing snake from north-western Australia (*Rhynchoelaps approximans*, sp. nov.). *West. Aust. Nat.* 4: 85.

Mackay, R. (1949). The Australian coral snake. *Proc. R. Zool. Soc. N.S.W.* 1947–48: 36–37.

Storr, G. M. (1968). The genus *Vermicella* (Serpentes: Elapidae) in Western Australia and the Northern Territory. *J. R. Soc. West. Aust.* 50: 80–92.

Storr, G. M. (1979). Revisionary notes on the genus *Vermicella* (Serpentes: Elapidae). *Rec. West. Aust. Mus.* 8: 75–79.

Thompson, D. F. (1934). A new snake from north Queensland. *Proc. Zool. Soc. Lond.* 1934: 529–531.

Worrell, E. (1960). A new elapine snake from Western Australia. *West. Aust. Nat.* 7: 132–134.

Trophidechis

Beard, D. J. (1979). Rough-scaled snake, *Tropidechis carinatus*. *Herpetofauna* 10: 26–28.

Shine, R. & Charles, N. (1984). Ecology of the Australian rough-scaled snake, *Tropidechis carinatus*. *J. Herpet.* 16 (4): 383–387.

Trinca, J. C., Graydon, J. J., Covacevich, J. & Limpus, C. (1971). The rough-scaled snake (*Tropidechis carinatus*) a dangerously venomus Australian snake. *Med. J. Aust.* 1971: 801–809.

Vermicella

Bustard, H. R. (1969). Defensive display behaviour in the bandy-bandy *Vermicella annulata* (Serpentes: Elapidae). *Herpetologica* 25: 319–320.

Shine, R. (1980). Reproduction, feeding and growth in the Australian burrowing snake *Vermicella annulata*. *J. Herpet.* 14: 71–77.

Storr, G. M. (1968). The genus *Vermicella* (Serpentes: Elapidae) in Western Australia and the Northern Territory. *J. R. Soc. West. Aust.* 50: 80–92.

Family Typhlopidae (Blind Snakes)

Genus and Species

Ramphotyphlops

Gillam, M. W. (1979). Notes on the status of the 'blind' snake *Typhlina tovelli* (Loveridge). *Herpetofauna* 11: 2–4.

Gillam, M. W., Cawood, I. S. & Honner, G. J. (1978). New reptile records from Central Australia, Northern Territory. *Herpetofauna* 9: 18–25.

Hoser, R. T. (1980). Further records of aggregations of various species of Australian snakes. *Herpetofauna* 12: 16–22.

Kinghorn, J. R. (1929). Two new snakes from Australia. *Rec. Aust. Mus.* 17: 190–193.

Kinghorn, J. R. (1942). Herpetological notes. 4. *Rec. Aust. Mus.* 21: 118–121.

Loveridge, A. (1945). A new blind snake (*Typhlops tovelli*) from Darwin, Australia. *Proc. Biol. Soc. Wash.* 58: 111–112.

McDowell, S. B. (1974). A catalogue of the snakes of New Guinea and the Solomons, with special reference to those in the Bernice P. Bishop Museum. Part 1 Scolecophidia. *J. Herpet.* 8: 1–57.

Miller, J. D. & McDonald, K. R. (1977). A note on eggs and hatchlings of the blind snake *Typhlina nigrescens* Gray. *Vict. Nat.* 94 (4): 161–4.

Robb, J. (1966). The generic status of the Australasian Typhlopids (Reptilia: Squamata). *Ann. Mag. Nat. Hist.* 13 (9): 675–679.

Robb, J. (1972). A new species of the genus *Ramphotyphlops* (Serpentes: Typhlopidae) from Western Australia. *J. R. Soc. West. Aust.* 55: 39–40.

Shine, R. (1980). Reproduction, feeding and growth in the Australian burrowing snake *Vermicella annulata*. *J. Herpet.* 14: 71–77.

Storr, G. M. (1968). First Australian record of the Asian blind-snake *Typhlops braminus*. *J. Herpet.* 1: 98.

Storr, G. M. (1981). The genus *Ramphotyphlops* (Serpentes: Typhlopidae) in Western Australia. *Rec. West. Aust. Mus.* 9: 235–271.

Storr, G. M. (1983). A new *Ramphotyphlops* (Serpentes: Typhlopidae) from Western Australia. *Rec. West. Aust. Mus.* 10 (4): 315–317.

Storr, G. M. (1984). A new *Ramphotyphlops* (Serpentes: Typhlopidae) from Central Australia. *Rec. West. Aust. Mus.* 11 (3): 313–314.

Swanson, S. (1981). *Typhlina bramina*: an arboreal blind snake? *N. Territory Nat.* 4: 13.

Waite, E. R. (1918). Review of the Australian blind snakes. *Rec. S. Aust. Mus.* 1: 1–34.

Wells, R. (1979). New reptile records for the Northern Territory. *N. Territory Nat.* 1: 3–4.

Index

This index includes the common and scientific names of all reptiles covered in the book. Scientific names are indexed under genus, specific name and, where applicable, subspecific name. Bold numbers are the identifying numbers (not the page numbers) of photographs. Italic numbers are the page numbers of text references.

5   A   Sumba 120°E   TIMOR   B   *TIMOR*   130°E

Roti   *SEA*

Bathurst
Island

Cape Londonderry   *Joseph*
Bonaparte
Gulf

Bonaparte
Archipelago

4   *INDIAN*   KIMBERLEYS   *Lake*
Argyle

King Sound

Fitzroy   *River*

OCEAN

GREAT   SANDY
DESERT

Eighty   *Mile Beach*

Barrow Island   *Lake Mackay*   N

20°S   *Exmouth*   *Fortescue*   *River*
Gulf

North West Cape   HAMERSLEY   *Lake Disappointment*   M

Ashburton   PILBARA RANGE   GIBSON   DESERT

River

Tropic of Capricorn   WESTERN   AUSTRALIA

Lake McLeod

Gascoyne   *River*

Shark Bay   *River*

3   *Murchison*   GREAT   VICTORIA   DESERT

Lake
Barlee

Lake Moore   NULLARBOR

GOLDFIELDS

30°S   *GREAT*

Point Malcolm

Cape Naturaliste   *Blackwood River*

Hood Point

Cape Leeuwin

2   *INDIAN*

OCEAN

KILOMETRES			
0	200	400	600

1 centimetre on the map measures
180 kilometres on the ground

40°S

1   Simple Conic Projection

110°E   A   120°E   B   13